A CROWN FOR
ELIZABETH

ALSO BY MARY M. LUKE

Catherine, The Queen

A CROWN FOR ELIZABETH

Mary M. Luke

London

MICHAEL JOSEPH

First published in Great Britain by MICHAEL JOSEPH LTD
52 Bedford Square, London, W.C.1
1971

7181 0938 4

Set and printed in Great Britain
by Western Printing Services Ltd, Bristol
in Baskerville eleven on twelve point
and bound by Dorstel Press, Harlow

This book is for all the devoted
readers of *Catherine, The Queen* who asked,
'. . . And then what happened?'

Contents

Acknowledgments   9

Preface   13

A King and His Queens   19

A King and His Sisters   153

A Queen and Her Sister   299

A Queen   491

Addendum   494

Bibliography   495

Reference, Notes and Comments   497

Index   511

Acknowledgments

ONE of an author's many satisfactions upon completion of a work is the privilege of acknowledging the assistance of others. I am constantly gratified at the willingness of those who extend their time and resources in this respect.

I wish to extend my appreciation to the officials of the Public Record Office in London; to Miss Jane Southwell, of the National Portrait Gallery; to Miss Caroline Westmacott, librarian of the Courtauld Institute Galleries; and to Mrs M. Cornish of the Photographic Service of the British Museum. The latter found and expedited a reproduction of the sketch of the Tower of London which matched a similar rendition of Whitehall by the same artist owned by the Museum of Fine Arts in Boston, Massachusetts. They constitute the end-papers in this book. Officials of the Kunsthistorisches Museum in Vienna, particularly Dr Erwin M. Auer, the director, have been most helpful, as have officials in the Prado in Madrid, the Kupferstichkabinett in Basle, the Ashmolean Museum of the University of Oxford, the Courtauld Institute Galleries of the University of London, and the Library of St John's College, Oxford.

A notable collection of Tudor portraits in America is that of the Duke of Manchester whose California residence yielded the likenesses of John Cheke, William Paget, and Thomas Cromwell. I am grateful to His Grace for permission to use these portraits which originally constituted the Kimbolton Collection from the duke's ancestral home, Kimbolton Castle, where Catherine of Aragon died.

From Anne Boleyn's childhood home, Hever Castle in Kent, the Honourable Gavin Astor provided the rarely published portrait of the youthful Mary Tudor; Mr Astor was also extremely helpful in determining other portrait sources.

Those who have also been generous with their collections are the Viscount De L'isle, V.C., K.G., of Penshurst Place, Lord Brabourne and the Knatchbull Collection, the Earl of Warwick of Warwick Castle, the Earl of Bradford of Weston Park, the Marquis of Salisbury of Hatfield House, and the Duke of Bedford of Woburn Abbey.

I am indebted to Her Majesty, the Queen, for permission to publish selections from the Royal Collection.

Two other uncertainties, more conclusively resolved, are represented in the portraits of Katherine Ashley and Queen Katherine Parr. In correspondence of the period, Katherine Ashley is often referred to as Mrs *Astley*, and the owner of the portrait, Lady Marguerite Hastings of Norfolk, England, corroborates that this was, indeed, the *real* name of Elizabeth's beloved governess. Lady Hastings writes, 'It is such a pity that all through history the spelling has been wrong. Katherine Astley was a Champernowne, a Devonshire family, who married Sir John Astley, Kt., Keeper of the Jewel Office to Queen Elizabeth. . . . The picture is a "family portrait"—my husband was an Astley. . . .'

Regarding Queen Katherine Parr, I have often felt the frequently published dreadful image—so totally at variance with the known description of Henry VIII's sixth Queen—did not represent an authentic likeness. Through the kindness of Professor Lacey Baldwin Smith, the distinguished Elizabethan author, and Mr Charles L. Mee, Jr., Managing Editor of *Horizon* magazine, ownership of a rare portrait of Queen Katherine was traced to Major H. C. Parr of Aberdeenshire. Major Parr had, subsequently, disposed of the portrait through a well-known London auction firm. Happily, the purchaser was the National Portrait Gallery where, after being cleaned of the centuries' grime, the portrait was recently hung.

Two who have given me additional assistance in tracing portraits, sketches, and maps are Miss Hester W. Chapman, author of *The Last Tudor King* and Mr Michael Hanson of *Country Life* magazine, author of *2,000 Years of London*.

At the Tower of London, through the good offices of Colonel Sir Thomas Butler, the resident governor, I was privileged to visit the quarters where Princess Elizabeth and Lady Jane Grey were incarcerated, where Anne Boleyn awaited execution, and where Mary Tudor lodged prior to her coronation. Many things at the Tower have changed in four hundred and fifty years. The size of the small rooms in which the prisoners lived, their view of the river, the tiny walkway on the leads where Elizabeth often exercised, have not. I am grateful to Colonel Butler for his indulgence and for sharing his knowledgeable interest in the Tower's history.

I am grateful to the Wertheim Study of the New York Public Library for providing valuable and necessary research materials—and a convenient place in which to use them. My gratitude is also extended to the officers and directors of the Mercantile Library in New York City for allowing me to keep material while my manuscript was in work.

Three individuals who have contributed much deserve as great an appreciation as an author can offer. In London, Mr Raymond A. Donovan has provided valuable criticism and suggestions, as well as a completely typed manuscript. In Darien, Connecticut, Mrs Elisha Keeler, reference librarian of the Darien Library, rendered a dedicated assistance in obtaining necessary research materials from numerous sources and collections. In New York City, I have had the clever and enthusiastic guidance of a gifted editor, Patricia Brehaut Soliman. Every author should be so blessed.

Lastly, my daughter, Melinda, who lives with all the attendant demands of a working writer, deserves an accolade for her patience.

Preface

IN re-creating this story of the young Tudors, I have been spared the
hazard which so often confronts the historical writer: a dearth of
material which can lead to supposition and, inevitably, distortion or
untruth. Happily, the opposite has been true in this work. The life of
each young Tudor is fully documented; the major difficulty has been
the problem of selectivity—how best to tell the individual stories of
Mary, Edward, and Elizabeth Tudor, without being overwhelmed by
personalities, and the political and religious events which crowded upon
the years immediately following the death of Catherine of Aragon. It
seemed this could best be achieved by detailing their childhood, which
was spent amid the turbulent last years of the reign of their much-
married father Henry VIII and his unfortunate Queens. The events
of these years had great *personal* impact upon each young Tudor,
contributed much to their character development, and profoundly
influenced and directed their destiny.

For it was, unhappily, the fate of these royal children to be almost
continually at the mercy of those whose goals derived more from personal
ambition than unselfish consideration. From the moment of Henry VIII's
death in 1547, the religious and political life of the people of England
was in a state of upheaval for which the monarch who died, ironically
a 'good Catholic', had only himself to blame. The avarice of the
Catholic Church for power and material wealth had sown the seeds of
revolt among England's religious liberals. The indecision of the
various Popes attending Henry's divorce from his first Queen provided
the opportunity for the King to break the Roman bond, but it was not
until after his death that the true force of the Reformation, as we know
it, was unleashed. And the major results of this powerful movement
which—in the beginning at least was mainly political rather than
religious—were to fall on the shoulders of his young son and heir,
Edward, and his elder daughter, Mary. The former was too young and
sheltered to reign effectively. For the latter, the Reformation movement,
while a personal spiritual challenge, was a political catastrophe. It

[13]

became an unrelentingly destructive tragedy for Mary, one of the few of her era whose religious motives were always unremittingly honest, however misguided.

For Mary Tudor was too much a product of a world in the final throes of change. Stubborn and inflexible, lacking that touch of the true visionary, she could not compromise with the ideals instilled in her from birth. The result is the *real* tragedy of her life, a life which held all too many sorrows for one who had so little actual malice in her: the injustice of the name 'Bloody Mary' by which she is remembered in history. Mary's reign was bloody, but the guilt of bloodshed falls more fairly on those who advised or used her. Any real appraisal of Mary's story—the emotional deprivation of her adolescent years, the integrity and fortitude she displayed under pressure, the willing and brave heart she brought to the throne for which she had fought so courageously— will lead to a truer evaluation of this first Queen-Regnant of England who gave so much and received so little in return.

Solid in her place in the succession (and usually at a safe distance if she could manage it), Elizabeth, the third young Tudor, waited. Much of the fortitude, wisdom, wariness, and sheer gall she exhibited when the Crown finally came to her—as she always knew it would—derived from her observation of her younger brother and older sister as she saw them matched against the risks, demands, and obligations of the royal inheritance. For generations, historians have conjectured everything from a warped psychology to a deformed body as accounting for Elizabeth's preferred spinsterhood, whereas the simplest and most valid reason is often overlooked. Elizabeth chose to remain unwed rather than repeat her sister's mistake of marrying a foreigner. Should she marry an Englishman, there might be attempts to wrest the Crown from her: in this she had the example of the unfortunate Lady Jane Grey. Furthermore, the fate of her own mother and one stepmother, both of whom perished on the block, pointed to the perils of royalty allying themselves in wedlock. Elizabeth's greatest strength as a child, as an adolescent, and later as an authoritative Queen was first and foremost the preservation of self and of the royal prerogative. Better to be loved by thousands than just one, through whom she might lose all. Thus was the cult of '*Gloriana*' born.

The passage of time invariably offers a truer evaluation of people and events. Far removed from the emotional, one can view impartially the psychological and physical forces at work in the child that result in the adult. The extraordinary years 1536 to 1558 chronicle the picture of an England in a turmoil and violence remarkable for so comparatively brief a time. There were uprisings, persecutions, conflicts of Church and State, and intrigues at home and abroad. Through these events move the three young Tudors: all intelligent, attractive, courageous, and all, most assuredly, lonely. Each had a different mother and, as the Reformation gained ground in England, a different religious training. Each in turn, upon coming to the throne, was either supported or opposed by the powerful forces of Church and State. Each had to face the issue in a way compatible with age, training, and heritage. It follows naturally that each way was different.

Except one. And in this the young Tudors were united, and their story is the same. They were united in the pursuit of a dream, a goal for which each was willing to lie, to intrigue, and, if necessary, to die. This dream was none other than the attainment of the Monarchy itself: to be anointed with the Holy Oil, to be handed the Orb, to hold the Sceptre with the Cross, and to have placed upon their head the Crown of England by which a mortal was rendered Divine—and apart.

Here, then, is the story of three young and royal children in search of that glory which came with the Crown. They all found it and, for better or for worse, have left their mark on the history of their country, church, and people. They could do no less, for in addition to being royal, they were ambitious, devout, and unafraid. But first, last, and most of all, they were Tudors.

Ridgefield,
Connecticut   MARY M. LUKE

... while my father lives, I shall be only the Lady Mary, the most unhappy lady in Christendom. ...

Mary Tudor
Mary I

... no man that is in fault himself can punish another for the same offence. ...

Edward Tudor
Edward VI

This is the work of the Lord—and it is marvellous in our eyes! (Upon being informed she was to be Queen.)

Elizabeth Tudor
Elizabeth I

A King and His Queens

Chapter One

THE Princess of Wales. She remembered the pleasure she had experienced earlier in the year when her father, the King, had conferred upon her the title which made her heir to the throne of England. She had known even then of the abandoned hopes of both her parents that a son would be born to them. And so the King, still ruggedly handsome, still loving to her and respectful to her mother, the Queen, had made her Princess of Wales.

With the title went the responsibility for the government of the Welsh Marches. In August, 1525, the King had ordered 'to send at this tyme our dearest, best-beloved and only daughter, the Princess, accompanied and established with an honourable, said, discreet and expert Council to reside and remain in the Marches of Wales, and the parts thereabout. . . .'[1] The Marches of Wales, or that district comprising the borderland between England and Wales, was notorious for its rampant lawlessness. With no representative of the royal family among them, the clan chieftains exerted an undesirable power and influence. The Princess in residence with her Council was expected to remind them of where their loyalty lay and lend official sanction to district government.

She remembered the great preparations for the journey, the excitement at being so suddenly the centre of attention. A new household and court had been established for her and the servants to accompany her were dressed in her own colours of blue and green. Furniture, bedding, household utensils, and provisions had now been loaded into wagons and carts which carried her clothing and other personal belongings in large wooden and leather chests. To her great delight, she had many new dresses, cloaks, and caps to wear. Her mother, the Queen, had lived at Ludlow Castle on the Welsh border many years before. Remembering the ancient building with its incessant damp and draughts, she had insisted that warm undergarments be included for her daughter to wear beneath the stiff brocades, damasks, and velvets of the new wardrobe. The Queen also had appointed her dearest friend,

[21]

Margaret Pole, the Countess of Salisbury, as lady governess, with thirteen ladies and gentlemen to wait upon the Princess. The Council, a smaller version of her father's Privy Council, was headed by the Bishop of Exeter as President, with Lord Dudley as Chamberlain. John Russell and Thomas Audley were among the councillors. In the household, the Princess would have also the services of Dr Wotton as Dean of the Chapel and Mr John Featherstone as schoolmaster. Two other chaplains, an apothecary, a Herald and Pursuivant, a Cofferer, a Clerk of the Closet, and many others constituted the staff of 304, which, it was hoped, would firmly establish Tudor authority in the unruly border district.

She was trustingly confident of those in her household, sure of their desire to serve her and her parents. An unquestioning obedience to her father's policies and a firm loyalty to the House of Tudor were the two main requisites for those willing to represent the King at Ludlow. Now at the time of her departure, her father was involved again in the almost ceaseless negotiations to find her a husband. Already she had been betrothed to the Dauphin of France and later, when political expediency demanded a change, to the powerful Charles V, the Holy Roman Emperor, who was also her mother's nephew. Her Aunt Margaret, the Queen of Scotland, was eager, too, for the union of her son, James, with the Princess. The longest engagement had been the one to Charles, but again shifting political winds and the attraction of a larger dowry had caused him to wed a Portuguese princess instead. And now the activity had come full circle as a French marriage was sought once again.

She left her parents at King's Langley, one of the royal residences in Hertfordshire, on a bright September morning in 1525, sitting very straight in her litter as became a Princess, awaiting with her usual patience the moment when the long procession would begin. An early morning haze was lifting in a slight breeze that tossed leaves into the path of the horses. They stamped impatiently, eager to be off and away from the dogs barking excitedly at their hoofs. Lackeys ran everywhere with last-minute instructions, carrying parcels for the lords and ladies who were to accompany her. The gravelled path outside the huge red-brick building, its topmost standard ruffling in the breeze, was almost hidden, as those of her court, many in their most sumptuous dress, busied themselves in finding their proper places in the ever-lengthening caval-cade. From her place in a litter near the front, the Princess could not see the end of the long procession, swollen by families, sweethearts, and friends who had come to bid the party farewell. They stood now on the side-lines waving to husband, brother, or lover already in the saddle and impatient to be away. Listening to their gaiety and enthu-siasm, the girl was uncertain of her part in the spirited proceedings. At the final moment of leave-taking, not quite trusting her own emotions, she pretended not to see the tears in the Queen's eyes. The difficult moment passed and the royal blessing was given. The officers heading the procession signalled, and amid the repeated calling and waving of the spectators, the great procession rumbled to life and began its jolting, cumbersome journey to the west.

As she travelled through the shires of England towards distant Wales, through the vast forests where sunlight rarely penetrated, over heath and marsh, past small moated manor houses, over muddy lanes and on to the hard roads which remained from Roman times, cries of welcome greeted her. She remembered her mother and father's response to the greetings of their subjects, and now, gracious and cheerful, she returned the villagers' salutes and ordered alms to be dispensed. In large castles with their Great Halls and busy courtyards, their hidden minstrels' galleries, and inevitable small draughty sleeping chambers, the procession had brief respites while repairs to wagons were made and fresh supplies loaded on. She always acknowledged the greeting of the owner and, with great dignity, received his good wishes and welcome. One who witnessed her on the journey wrote to her father's chancellor, the great Cardinal Wolsey: 'My Lady Princess came hither on Saturday; surely, sir, of her age, as goodly a child as ever I have seen, and of as good gesture and countenance. Few persons of her age blend sweetness better with seriousness, or quickness with deferences; she is at the same time, joyous and decorous in manners.'[2]

Her name was Mary Tudor. She was the daughter of Catherine of Aragon and Henry VIII and, as Princess of Wales, heir to the Crown of England.[3]

She was nine years old.

Mary was to remain at Ludlow Castle, 'a fair manor standing in a goodly park . . .' for the next two years. Her mother, the beloved Catherine of Aragon, felt the separation keenly. Mother and daughter had always been unusually close. That the Princess was never far from the Queen's thoughts is shown in the following instructions sent to the Countess of Salisbury, upon whom Catherine depended to maintain a loving link with Mary:

. . . at seasons convenient to use moderate exercise, taking open air in gardens, sweet and wholesome places and walks (which may conduce unto her health, solace and comfort), as by the said Lady Governess shall be thought most convenient. And, likewise, to pass her time, most seasons at her virginals, or other musical instruments. . . . Likewise the cleanliness and well-wearing of her garments and apparel, both of her chamber and body, so that everything about her be pure, sweet, clean and wholesome, as to so great a princess doth appertain; all corruptions evil airs, and things noisesome and displeasant, to be eschewed.[4]

Even at nine, Mary Tudor enjoyed the power and perquisites compatible with her royal rank. Surprisingly, she was not lonely at Ludlow, for the countess and her ladies provided the close and enjoyable companionship her mother had known she would need. Several Welsh families joined her household and began the long association with Mary that was to extend over many years. She travelled much to show herself to her Welsh subjects and received their representatives at her small court. It was exciting for the child to visit the town of Ludlow, where handsome structures, newly built after the devastating Wars of the Roses, lined the streets. Ludlow Castle, at one end of the town, was not as forbidding to Mary as it was to some of her household. Built shortly after the Norman Conquest, it had been intended primarily as a fortress, and some of the aura of the military outpost still clung to its vast walls, overlooking the confluence of the Teme and Corve rivers. For Mary, it was vast and impersonal, but her own quarters had been made comfortable with the hangings and possessions she had brought from home. She was diligent in her studies and music lessons, but time was always found for her to be away from the schoolroom and her royal duties, to venture with some of the younger of her ladies down the steep bank to the river, a far distance below. In good weather, the banks of the Teme were laden with gentians and wild berries and the Princess and her companions would spend many a happy afternoon romping at the water's edge before returning with sunburnt arms and faces, their mouths stained with berry juice, to the ugly fortress above. Mary especially loved the ascent back up the steep hillside. The huge trees outside the castle walls cast sharp patterns on to their path; the calls of hundreds of birds harboured in their branches lent a raucous note to the happy cries of her weary companions.

From Ludlow, Mary often returned to court to the affectionate welcome of her parents, and growing now in stature and presence, she joined in the endless round of masques and court fêtes. The search to find her a suitable husband often required her presence in order that she might meet representatives of a foreign power, so that Henry could exhibit what Bishop Tunstal called '. . . the Princess in your hand, which is a pearl worth keeping.' Since Mary was heir to the throne—and a *woman*—finding the proper mate was a complicated and politically hazardous affair. In 1527, when Mary was eleven, a French alliance was again considered. Mary was brought from Ludlow to meet the French ambassadors and helped to entertain them by playing on the harpsichord. Later, she participated in a masque, causing one Venetian ambassador to write '. . . on her person were so many precious stones, that their splendour and radiance dazzled the sight. . . .' She enjoyed the company of both parents, especially her mother. She was a bit in awe of the King, but his boisterous good humour never failed to rouse her spirits.

A warm reminiscence of Mary dancing with the tall and jovial father she adored, still exists, evoking a poignant scene which must have often burned bittersweet in her memory:

> ... to see the sight that I did see,
>   I long full sore again.
>
> I saw a King and a Princess,
>   Dancing before my face,
> Most like a God and Goddess,
>   (I pray Christ save their Grace!)
>
> This King to see whom we have sung,
>   His virtue be right much,
> But this Princess, being so young,
>   There can be found none such.
>
> So *facund* fair she is to see,
>   Like to her is none of her age;
> Withouten grace it cannot be,
>   So young to be so sage.
>
> This King to see with his fair flower,
>   The mother standing by,
> It doth me good yet at this hour,
>   On them when that think I. . . .[5]

When Mary Tudor was born at Greenwich Palace at four o'clock in the morning on February 18, 1516, England had gone wild with joy. For seven years, through a sad procession of miscarriages and stillborn children, Catherine of Aragon had endeavoured to give her husband a son. Since she was six years older than the King, the matter of an heir for the Tudor throne had assumed a grave importance. The new baby might be only a girl, but she was nevertheless a healthy refutation of 'the Queen's reproach'. Henry, happy to have a living child at last, had joyously cried, 'We are both young. If it is a daughter this time, by the grace of God, sons will follow!' The people of England looked upon the handsome young couple with great affection and loyalty; they celebrated the birth of Mary Tudor with bonfires and gay abandon. Wine flowed generously from conduits, and whole oxen turned on spits in the streets. England had a living heir! Surely a son would follow. . . .

But Catherine's next—and last child—was stillborn. It had been the

[25]

sorely needed boy, and with the Queen now entering middle age, King and country faced the unpleasant fact that there would probably be no male heir. Mary, therefore, had been doubly cherished by both parents and watched over with anxious and loving eyes. Her babyhood was spent in the Queen's own apartments, and, later, a separate nursery was established for her at Ditton Park in Buckinghamshire and at Hanworth. Lady Margaret Bryan, a woman of extreme competence and impeccable character, was appointed governess to the small Princess.

Secure in the love of both parents and the admiration of a doting court, Mary had grown into a happy, healthy little girl. When Catherine and Henry were away on summer progresses or on such splendid journeys as to the Field of Cloth of Gold in France, they received daily reports on her health and welfare from those left in charge of the Princess.

Mary's education, supervised with great care by her mother, was formidable for one so young. Both Catherine and Henry had been extremely well educated, and their daughter, thought not brilliant, was diligent. At an early age, she studied French, Spanish, Italian and Greek. The great Spanish humanist, Juan Luis Vives, had been brought to court by the forward-thinking Catherine to tutor the young Princess, who applied herself industriously to mastering the Gospels, the Acts of the Apostles, and the Epistles, the works of Plato, Cicero, Plutarch, and the Maxims of Seneca. In addition, there were the more common-place arithmetic and astronomy and the constant challenge of rendering Latin into English. Vives had recommended that she have fellow pupils, 'for it is not good to be taught alone'; the young Princess, therefore, had companions to face the grim curriculum with her. One child quite near her age was Frances Brandon, the daughter of the King's sister, Mary Tudor, the 'Tudor rose'.[6]

Christmas was always a special delight to the young child. Despite its solemn religious observances, the court also celebrated the holiday and the following New Year's Day with festive balls, masques and feasting. Hundreds of candles blazed in the Great Hall and chambers whose ugly walls were hidden by hangings of cloth of gold and rich tapestries from the looms of Flanders. The flickering candle flames cast huge shadows on the ornately scrolled ceilings and lit up the dark recesses of the forbidding hammerbeams. Incense from Spain wafted through the crowded rooms as minstrels played behind screened galleries and the throng below roared at the antics of the King's Fool, or the Lord of Misrule. Gifts were always presented to the royal family at the New Year. Even as a child, Mary's gifts were impressive—a standing cup of gold from Cardinal Wolsey, a pomander of gold from her aunt, Mary Tudor. When she was four, the Duke of Norfolk sent her a pair of silver candle snuffers, but she much preferred the bronze-coloured smock sent by Lady Mountjoy and the purse of 'tysent satin' given by her nurse. Even those living around the royal residences did not forget the child. When Mary was two, she had been enchanted with gifts from two humble folk at the New Year—one a gift of Queen apples, the other a small rosemary bush with 'spangles of gold, from a poor woman of Greenwich'. There were tilts and jousts by day, music and masquing at night. Three boars were sacrificed for the holiday feast, and the boars' heads 'painted in sundry colours' were brought in 'crown'd with gay garlands and with rosemary, smok'd on the Christmas board'. From Christmas until Twelfth Day, the Lord of Misrule presided, and the 'many and goodly mummeries' continued with all manner of celebrations.

Mary's religious duties—the daily prayers, the fasting, the observances of Saints' Days, the mysteries of the Mass and Confession—early established a strong faith which came very naturally to a child who had inherited the religion of her mother. Catherine, a Spaniard born, was deeply devout, her faith as natural to her as the air she breathed. This firm religious conviction, the love of her parents, her position as the undisputed heir to the Crown of England, gave Mary early in her childhood a profound sense of security. Her life had always been comfortable, placid, and stable. There was little reason to think it would ever change.

And then, what Mary Tudor always referred to as 'the troubles' began. With no heir likely to be born of his marriage to Catherine of Aragon, Henry had set his heart upon the dark-eyed Anne Boleyn, as different in character, background, and appearance from his Queen as possible. Anne's sophistication and deft experience had been gained in early childhood at the dissolute court of France where she served as lady-in-waiting to Henry's younger sister, Mary, when she was briefly Queen of France. So completely did Anne captivate and enthral the King that his time, attention, and, ultimately, any personal interest in his wife and daughter all but ceased. Anne was twenty-four to the Queen's ailing forty-one. She sparkled with good health, energy and enthusiasm. Witty and sharp, Anne was as sleek as the greyhounds she often kept at her side. She accepted Henry's advances but firmly discouraged any suggestion that she become his mistress. She was not deeply in love with the King, but the prospect of wearing a crown tantalized the ambitious girl who dared not risk losing Henry by an easy surrender. In addition to keeping the royal ardour under manageable control, Anne Boleyn's major difficulty lay in persuading the King he must divorce his Queen.

Ultimately, she had her way. When Henry, cap in hand and with just the proper amount of deference, approached Catherine with the suggestion that she conveniently enter a convent, since he now felt—after twenty years of marriage—that perhaps their union was illegal,[7] he had been shocked and angered by the vehemence of the Queen's reaction. When she refused to cloister herself voluntarily, Henry petitioned the Pope for a divorce. The validity of his case was not without merit. Divorces had been granted by Rome in many instances where the need for an heir, political exigencies, or, indeed, the personal whim of a monarch could be satisfied. Other royalty, including Henry's own sister, Margaret, had been so convenienced by the Pope. Henry and his ministers argued that the succession of the Tudor line must be assured to avoid the civil war that would almost inevitably follow a disputed succession. A procession of dead children had cursed the twenty-year-old marriage, the Queen was past child-bearing age, and the King himself was getting no younger. Since the Pope had previously accommodated other monarchs, why not the King of England, too?

But Pope Clement, while anxious to assist the English King, also dreaded the English Queen's nephew Charles V, the powerful Holy Roman Emperor. Thus began the diplomatic tilting between Clement of Rome and the once-proud 'Defender of the Faith', Henry VIII of England. For six long years Clement delayed pronouncing sentence, while Anne Boleyn—virtuously and tantalizingly denying Henry the solace of her bed—urged the King on towards divorce. And during these years, as Mary left childhood for adolescence, she and Catherine were compelled to watch as the brazen daugher of Sir Thomas Boleyn, oblivious of the admonitions of others at court, held Henry Tudor in a thrall he was never to experience again.

When 'The King's Great Matter' became common knowledge, Henry's subjects rallied to Mary's mother. In agonizing letters to the Emperor and the Pope, Catherine reiterated that her marriage to Prince Arthur had *never* been consummated, that a Papal dispensation had sanctioned it, and that her daughter, Mary, *was* England's legitimate heir. She vowed that she would never voluntarily relinquish her position. 'Stiff and obdurate', she asked for counsellors and said she would fight any action to deprive her of the title, a deprivation that would render Mary illegitimate. In September, 1527, she made formal application to the Pope for a decision as to the validity of her marriage.

Opposition always brought out the worst in Henry, and the constant frustration of his efforts to effect some compromise with Catherine, with Anne, with the Pope, with the Emperor, and with the King of France—all consistent with his own desire to be free to wed and beget a male heir—finally brought his tolerance to an end. In great anger (and a sufficient display of pious righteousness), he ordered both Catherine and Mary from his court—and out of his life. The Queen was to go to The More, one of Cardinal Wolsey's old houses which she hated; the eleven-year-old Mary would live at Richmond. Catherine was forbidden to see her daugher again. Sadly she went into exile, protesting she would 'rather go to the Tower', maintaining that come what may, she was the rightful Queen. Her great courage, dignity, and integrity under stress impressed all who saw her. Mario Savagnana, an Italian visitor at court, wrote of her at this time: 'Her majesty is prudent and good and during these differences with the King, she has evinced constancy and resolution, never being disheartened or depressed . . . Her Majesty is not tall of stature, rather small . . . she is somewhat stout, and has always a smile on her countenance.'[8]

The smile hid the heartbreak which was to be Catherine's lot for the rest of her life. She saw neither husband nor daughter again, and she was obviously fearful for her life. She said, 'Since the King was not ashamed to do such monstrous things and, there being no one who could or dared contradict him, he might, one of these days, undertake some further outrage against her.'[9] Constant harassment by members of Henry's Council to force her to relinquish her title and 'enter religion' was a threat with which Catherine of Aragon lived daily. The eleven-year-old Mary shared the Queen's unhappiness. News of the indignities and insults directed at Catherine only strengthened her deep loyalty and love for her mother. For the King—the father of whom she had always been so proud—Mary felt an almost unbelieving bewilderment that the man she loved, respected, and trusted could be so cruel and unjust. For Anne Boleyn, who had caused it all, her hatred was fiercely bitter.

The Queen and her daughter had great support from the older nobility, most of whom hated Anne Boleyn, as well as from the common people. Those partisans of Catherine and Mary still at court regarded the King's actions with disgust and disbelief. Henry realized the precarious position of both mother and daughter had engendered great sympathy from the Catholic party. If the Queen's adherents chose to unite, their number might be formidable. But Catherine refused to sanction any uprising in her support. Henry was her husband and King; it would be unthinkable for a daughter of Isabella and Ferdinand of Spain to condone any revolt against the man with whom she had lived contentedly for so long and whom—in spite of everything—she still deeply loved.

And so, far removed from the happy security of her childhood, with a mother in exile and a father preoccupied with another woman, Mary Tudor spent her adolescence in months of neglect and loneliness, compounded by a yearning concern for her persecuted mother. It was, sadly, only the beginning of her long ordeal.

*

At this time Henry Tudor had barely begun the process of physical moral, and spiritual disintegration that so marked his later years. The second Tudor King had been crowned at nineteen—a tall, handsome youth, with the muscularly massive size of his grandfather, Edward IV, and the clear blue-eyed sensuality of his beautiful mother, Elizabeth of York. From her, too, came the love of music and learning that rendered Henry VIII one of the best-educated men of his time. His proficiency in languages and his knowledge of the arts and sciences made him adept in discussions with such distinguished scholars as Erasmus and Sir Thomas More. He was a gifted musician as well, superior in taste and appreciative of the music played at his court and in his Chapel. His athletic prowess was almost legendary, and participation in sports and in the rugged competitions of the tiltyard was a daily pleasure for the King, if a somewhat exhausting procedure for his opponents. The pleasures of the table and his consumption of mead were prodigious and had contributed to a widening of his already ample waistline and a deepening of his naturally florid complexion.

But the inner alteration in Henry was even more significant. The idealistic, almost naïve youth who had ascended the throne in 1509, with the shy and lovely Catherine of Aragon as his adoring Queen, had not survived in encounters with his Continental rivals, Francis I, the King of France, and Charles V, the Holy Roman Emperor. As they engaged in their endless rivalry, he had been either wooed or bullied as they saw fit, necessarily sustaining some lasting bruises in the process. The remarkable Thomas Wolsey, Henry's long-time chancellor, had used England to maintain the balance of power between Spain and France. Henry, now as ruthless, experienced, and opportunistic as either Charles or Francis, had become practised in the same technique, and, over the years, he had swung his allegiance to King or Emperor as expediency demanded. His relationship with the Emperor had been inevitably strained when he sought to divorce Charles's aunt.

At the Emperor's urging, Pope Clement refused to sentence until the case had been heard in Rome, and Henry was loud in his condemnation. Here was another example of the best interests of his realm being subjected to the will of the Holy Roman Emperor! As long as the situation persisted, England would be without a male heir, and civil war might well result should Henry die. The King's outraged pride, as well as genuine concern, urged him on. A stalemate of many months had occurred until Thomas Cromwell entered the picture. With the genius of the born administrator whose competence for discharging a distasteful task was equalled only by an unscrupulous ambition devoid of compassion, he set to work to resolve 'The King's Great Matter' once and for all. With the advent of the grimly able Cromwell, the high noon of the religious movement which would become known as the Reformation was approached. Cromwell's fortunes were inextricably tied up with the movement, not surprising for the opportunist whose father had been a blacksmith and whose uncle had been a cook to the Archbishop of Canterbury.

When Catherine's case was recalled to Rome and the King summoned to appear like a common criminal, Henry's rage boiled over. But Cromwell, the King's 'evil genius', who indisputably knew exactly where he was going, even if Henry did not, bolstered his will and spirit. In a bold move, the King separated the Catholic Church in England from the authority of the Pope and assumed the title, 'Supreme Head of the Church'. In this action and in the succeeding Parliaments, he effected the independence of the Church of England in his own realm. Parliament had been repressed in the time of Cardinal Wolsey's great power; indeed, at one point, Wolsey called no Parliament for eight years. Now, ironically Wolsey's rejected Parliament became Henry VIII's greatest instrument in asserting the unity and independence of the English Church and in establishing his own spiritual sovereignty. The 'Reformation Parliament' was to continue for seven years, and the vast changes it made in those years ensured not only an England different from any other Christian country on earth at that time, but preserved the importance and predominance of the Parliament itself.

From the assumption of his new title to the practical control of the Church was a matter of months. By May, 1532, after sufficient royal pressure had been exerted, the Convocation, with no Becket among them, trusting instead in Henry's 'most excellent wisdom, princely goodness and fervent zeal for the promotion of God, honour and Christian religion', surrendered completely, causing Henry's great and good friend, Sir Thomas More, now Chancellor of England to resign his office in silent reproach. Other important steps along the path of schism were directed by the nerveless Cromwell who possessed an exquisite sense of timing. Each action was a strong weapon aimed against the Papacy for exploiting his strength in case Clement should suddenly become co-operative.

In 1532 Parliament passed the Restraint of Appeals which made anyone appealing to Rome in any instance guilty of *præmunire* and subject to the penalties of treason against the monarch. All matters concerning 'matrimony, testaments and tithes' would be judged within the realm by the English bishops and archbishops. One indisputable result of this act, and undoubtedly one of the primary reasons for its being, was to deprive Queen Catherine of her right to appeal. Much to Henry's satisfaction, any legal manœuvres she might make would only be considered 'treasonous'. Vindication of himself and his actions was paramount with Henry; he was self-righteous to the point of indignation in his attitude towards the woman who was thwarting him.

[31]

The Restraint of Appeals Act only sustained his self-justification. The King was now forty-two and, despite his increased girth, still an impressive figure. An Italian visitor to the Tudor court has left a record of Henry at this time:

I saw the King twice and kissed his hand; he is glad to see foreigners and especially Italians; he embraced me joyously. He is tall of stature, very well-formed, and of very handsome presence, beyond measure affable, and I never saw a Prince better disposed than this one. He is also learned and accomplished and most generous and kind and, were it not that he now seeks to repudiate his wife, after having lived with her for twenty years, he would be no less than perfectly good, and equally prudent.

But this thing detracts greatly from his merits, as there is now living with him a young woman of noble birth, though many say of bad character, whose will is law to him, and he is expected to marry her should the divorce take place, which it is supposed will not be effected, as the peers of the realm, both spiritual and temporal, are opposed to it; nor during the Queen's life, will they have any other queen in the kingdom.[10]

By the middle of 1532, Henry's authority over the Church in his realm was almost absolute. The death of old Warham, the Archbishop of Canterbury, at the age of eighty-two—a most providential release for one labouring under a writ of *præmunire* for refusing to try the King's case in England—left the See of Canterbury to be filled at the King's pleasure. Warham's intransigence had been one of Anne and Henry's chief obstacles, and with his death, the ambitious Boleyn saw the Queenship almost in sight. A deeper involvement was needed to secure her marriage. For six long years Henry had sought physical possession of 'the Lady'; at last, Anne surrendered. In gratitude for her favours, the King created her Marchioness of Pembroke. In a splendid ceremony at Windsor on a Sunday before mass, attended by the foremost peers of the realm, he conferred upon Anne Boleyn precedence over every other woman of the same degree in England and allotted her a handsome pension. Shortly afterwards, arrayed in Catherine's jewels, revelling in her triumph, Anne accompanied Henry on a political visit to France to solicit Francis's aid in case Henry's defiance of the Papacy should provoke the Emperor to war. It was a visit fraught with diplomatic hazards for a King travelling openly with his now-acknowledged mistress, to visit a monarch whose wife was Catherine's niece.

As many had foreseen, possession of 'the Lady' somewhat sated Henry's interest which needed the constant challenge of the new, the forbidden, or the unobtainable. And the complications of his relation-

[32]

ship with her—diplomatic, personal, and social—were brought home to him daily. But Anne could be beguiling and Henry's heart was malleable. Anne could also be heartless and the King was intensely proud. Her constant taunt that the Pope, Catherine, Mary, the Emperor, and all their supporters had more influence in his own country than Henry, was a needling goad to the King. Finally, faced with the irrevocable fact that Anne was pregnant, 'the Lady' and the King had their own way again. In great secrecy, Henry married Anne Boleyn on January 25, 1533, at Whitehall Palace; Rome was not to know of the marriage until a way could be found to legalize it. After the furtive ceremony, they honeymooned at the King's new hunting lodge in St James's Fields, a 'safe distance in the fields' from the busy court.[11] Someone had to be found to deal with the situation, now more complex than ever. Henry chose the forty-three-year-old Thomas Cranmer, a former Cambridge University don, now the Archdeacon of Taunton. Cranmer possessed more than a tinge of the liberal, as his marriage to a niece of the reformer Osiander demonstrated. But whatever his spiritual rebellion, Cranmer was all Henry's man. The King recognized the prelate's loyalty and respect for the monarchy and Cranmer's disenchantment with the Papacy equalled Henry's own. Leaving his wife in Germany, he hastily returned to England, and application was made to Rome to confirm his appointment. Despite the warnings of Charles's ambassador that Cranmer was no friend of Rome, the Pope, unaware of the marriage, sent the necessary Bulls for Cranmer's consecration. The King was immensely relieved. Anne's child, his undoubted son and heir, must be born, even if not actually conceived, in honourable wedlock.

On March 30, 1533, secretly swearing he would consider no oath to the Pope as binding, but publicly swearing allegiance to Clement VII, Thomas Cranmer was consecrated Archbishop of Canterbury. On May 9, 1533, at Dunstable, he assembled a small court to hear the evidence against the King's marriage to Catherine of Aragon. Catherine, at nearby Ampthill, did not acknowledge the court's authority and, therefore, did not appear. Instead she signed a protest, stating that no tribunal other than the Pope's could judge the validity of her marriage. Secretly thankful—for he had not felt equal to a confrontation with his former Queen—Cranmer declared her contumacious. On his own authority, he pronounced her marriage to Henry null and void, a decision which was without precedent in any Christian country and which, when made known, erupted in a scandal unequalled in the other courts of Europe.

There was now no reason for concealing the King's new marriage, and by the end of May, Anne's condition was obvious. The announcement of the marriage was conveyed to Henry's subjects by priests at

Sunday services when they prayed for 'the King and Queen *Anne*'. In several incidents, the people showed their resentment of 'the Lady so hated by all the world' by abruptly leaving the churches. The clamour and indignation in the City forced the Lord Mayor of London by royal order to issue a proclamation forbidding any demeaning references to the new marriage.

When Mary Tudor was informed of her father's marriage, she maintained a wise silence. But in letters to her mother, she spoke of her shock and resentment, receiving sensible advice from the rejected Queen, who counselled that Mary 'go no further with learning and disputation in the matter. And wheresoever and in whatsoever company you shall come, obey the King's commandments. *Speak you few words and meddle nothing....*'[12] Though her heart ached for her daughter's distress at the King's high-handedness, Catherine realized Mary had nothing to gain by rebellion.

Her mother's understanding counsel helped Mary maintain her own self-control in the following weeks when Anne's coronation took place. From visitors, Mary learned that the people had regarded the new Queen coldly as the splendid procession passed from the Tower through Temple Bar to Whitehall. Anne had sat 'big in her litter', the undoubted son and heir securely in her womb, trying not to notice the silence that greeted her approach, the lack of genuine joyousness and thanksgiving which usually accompanied so magnificent a spectacle. The people sullen with the knowledge that their beloved Queen Catherine had been supplanted by the whore, Nan Bullen, showed no enthusiasm for the usurper, who was not only loose as far as her morals were concerned, but was also a known devotee of the Lutheran doctrines. Mary was not present at the coronation festivities; she was spared the sight of Anne Boleyn sitting in her mother's barge on the journey from the Tower to Whitehall. She was not required to attend the balls, tourneys, and jousts indulged in by an obedient court to celebrate Anne's triumph. But, as heiress-presumptive, she *was* required by tradition to be present at the birth of the heir-apparent. Remembering her mother's advice, the seventeen-year-old Mary, outwardly docile and compliant, awaited the summons that would precede the Queen's lying-in.

It arrived the first week in September, a scant nine months after the furtive wedding, on Sunday, September 7, at Greenwich Palace, between three and four in the morning. Anne Boleyn gave birth to her child. It was a girl. Henry had been sure his longed-for son was about to be born—court soothsayers and astrologers had confidently predicted a boy. The man who had begun the process by which the religious customs of his country would be irrevocably changed, and the pattern of his personal life altered forever in order to have a legitimate son and heir, did not take his disappointment lightly. His resentment was reflected in the attitude of his subjects who received the news with little enthusiasm. Eustace Chapuys, Charles's Spanish ambassador, wrote to the Emperor: 'The baptism ceremony was sad and unpleasant as the mother's coronation had been. Neither at court nor in the City have there been bonfires, illuminations, and rejoicings usual on such occasions.' What little merriment there was became more a celebration of Anne Boleyn's failure to produce a son. Once having observed tradition by being present at the birth, a relieved Mary was excused from further participation. Anne's hatred of Catherine of Aragon, who obstinately maintained she was still the lawful Queen, had now extended to Catherine's daughter. Both Catherine and Mary were the target of her threats, earning Chapuys's comment 'All seems like a dream. Her own party [Anne's] do not know whether to laugh or cry. . . .'

Those who hated 'the concubine' watched for signs of the King's dissaffection. Anne was well aware of the insecurity of her own position. Many were openly saying that if the old Queen had not been so inflexible, Henry would not have had to prove to himself and everyone else that he could marry Anne. Anne had hoped the French King would prove steadfast; the Emperor was no friend of hers. But Francis was still exhibiting qualms at openly defying Papal censure. And, above all, the people in the country, in the City, and at court hated her. Her own uncle, the Duke of Norfolk, told Chapuys 'that he had not been either the originator or promoter of this second marriage, but on the contrary, had always opposed it and had tried to dissuade the King therefrom.'[13] Chapuys wrote, 'If a tumult arose, I know not if the Lady . . . would escape with life and jewels.'

Anne was fearful of the shifting sands beneath her feet, and this, combined with the knowledge that Henry's eyes were straying again, made her difficult to live with. There was constant bickering, little peace or pleasure in his home; and while Anne still held some sway over him, her insolence in his court, the lack of serenity and family life he had enjoyed with Catherine in their happier years, often puzzled the man who was not in the habit of examining his own motives too deeply or of blaming himself for any situation that might prove less than he desired. Aware that Henry was daily less bewitched by his new wife, Chapuys wrote that when Anne insisted on a very elaborate and costly bed being brought from another wing of the palace for her lying-in, he could not forbear from saying that it was a good thing she had secured it before the birth, 'otherwise, she would not have it now; for she has been for some time past, very jealous of the King; and, with good cause, spoke about it in words that he did not like. He told her that she must wink at such things, and put up with them, *as her betters had done before her*. He could, at any time, cast her down as easily as he had raised her.'[14]

The christening of the unwanted girl whose birth had been such a disappointment to her father, and had so directly imperilled her mother, was three days after her birth on Wednesday, September 10, 1533, at Greenwich Palace. Wrapped in a mantle of purple velvet trimmed with ermine, she was christened Elizabeth.

Chapter Two

HENRY had begun a systematic persecution of Catherine designed to force her acceptance of his new title, 'Supreme Head of the Church'. Such compliance would lend at least a pretence of agreement on the Queen's part that her marriage had been illegal. Though Mary was forbidden to see her mother, the letters which reached her from the Queen and from loyal friends kept the girl in a tense and anxious state as she read of her father's efforts to subjugate his obstinate ex-Queen. Had Catherine acquiesced and adopted a religious life, there would have been little point in Mary's continued distaste for her father's remarriage. While she and Anne Boleyn would hardly have been intimate, Mary might have adopted a less diffident attitude when she was forced to be in the presence of the new Queen. As it was, the King's persistent harassment only bound Mary's loyalties more strongly to her mother; she clung to the hope that eventually they might be allowed to live together—outcasts from court perhaps—but at least together. But Catherine's undaunted conviction concerning her marriage only enraged the King and endangered the positions of both mother and daughter.

When Cranmer annulled the marriage, Catherine was ordered to relinquish her title. Henceforth, she would be called simply the 'Princess-Dowager'. When a deputation from the King arrived at Ampthill to inform her that by an Act of Parliament her title had been given to another, she scornfully replied 'that the Parliament had not married her, therefore, Parliament would not divorce her.' Contemptuously she struck at the hateful document which deprived her of the title she had borne with pride for twenty-three years. Pointedly she continued to sign her correspondence, 'Catherine *the Queen*'. Anyone who refused to address her as such was not permitted to remain in her household or be admitted to her presence if she could help it.

There was an important change in Mary Tudor's life also. From Richmond to Greenwich, to Hanworth, to Eltham, Catherine's daughter resided in the many royal residences much as she had done previously, but with a noticeable and poignant difference. There was no mother or father present. Anne would not have Mary around her, wrote Chapuys; 'The Lady has declared she would not have it, nor hear of her. . . .'[1] Each cruel indignity and fresh humiliation meted out by Henry to Catherine only further strengthened Mary's loyalty to the woman she so resembled in spirit and character. Following Catherine's advice, she wrote to her father occasionally, attempting to keep the relationship as normal and pleasant as possible. She often sent the King the present of a buck killed in one of the royal preserves and once, perhaps hoping a personal appeal would soften her resentment, Henry attempted a meeting with Mary in the fields outside Richmond Palace. For an awkward moment they stood, father and daughter, both trying to say the right thing, to make the most of their brief time together. It was not a success. Too much had happened for too long a time to allow the King to explain his position. It did not come easily to the bully in Henry to appeal for an understanding he felt his daughter owed him without question. The slight figure stood before him, no hint of reproach or resentment in her eyes or voice, but certainly no submission either. They talked of small things and inquired of each other's health; it was almost a relief when Anne Boleyn's servants appeared on the scene, sent with a message purposely to intrude, to forestall any possible reconciliation. Mumbling that he 'hoped to see her again soon', the King left. It was the last Mary saw of her father for several years.

Mary Tudor was seventeen when Henry married Anne Boleyn. She was small in stature like her mother, with the auburn hair of both parents and the beautifully clear complexion of the Queen. Her eyes were grey and candid, but extreme short-sightedness had caused a frown or furrow in her forehead, odd in one so young. It became more or less permanent as she withdrew into her books and perpetual religious works. Her voice was deep, almost mannish in tone, contrasting oddly with the petite figure, and it often startled a visitor hearing it for the first time. She had lovely long fingers which she adorned with many rings, for Mary had the Spanish love of jewels and colour; the rich fabrics of her clothing were as varied and extensive as she could afford. Inconsistent with her love of finery and jewels, her nature was simple but proud, her kindness and piety as deep and ardent as her mother's. She spent many hours each day in her chapel. Her generosity was well known in the villages surrounding the royal residences, and alms were dispensed daily at her door. She herself was always easily approached by travelling nuns or monks who passed her way, or by local villagers when they were in trouble. She went into the homes of many neighbouring families, playing easily with their children, often singing to the youngest the Spanish lullabies she had learned from her mother. When children were born to those who served her, Mary was invariably asked to be the godmother. She always presented a handsome gift of linen or plate to the child and a small purse to the nurse at the christening.

Apart from the upheaval her father's new marriage had caused and the heartbreaking separation from her mother, Mary was content with her life as it was—the pleasant moving between the royal residences, her religious duties, her needlework and studies, her comfortable house with its familiar and well-loved servants. The companionship of her ladies provided some outlet for her affections. Unassuming but proud with all the high idealism of one whose principles of right and wrong are strong and never easily swayed, she appeared, to those more demanding of material enjoyments, to lead an austere life. But Mary made it pleasant for those around her; they had been chosen mainly for their desire for a similar existence. She would tolerate no laziness, no inefficiency in her household, no moral laxness in her companions. Her standards were startlingly high for one so young. Her pride in her parents, in her own royal rank, her devotion to her God, her solicitousness for those less comfortably placed than herself—these were the important ingredients in Mary Tudor's life. She asked only to be left in peace and quiet to deserve and enjoy them.

She had kept a great many of her friends despite her stubbornness in 'The King's Great Matter', for many at court had known and loved the Princess Mary since her birth. The King's sister, Mary Tudor, wife of Charles Brandon, died shortly after Anne's coronation, and her daughter, Frances Brandon, often came to visit Mary. A year younger than Mary, Frances boasted of the suitors being considered for her hand. Sir Henry Grey, the Marquess of Dorset's son, was the most likely candidate, a not unattractive prospect for the heiress to the Suffolk fortune. Mary enjoyed her cousin's enthusiasm when the betrothal was finally announced, although she seemed less eager for one of her own. The subject of her marriage, always a matter of diplomatic importance was not likely to be resolved until the question of her legitimacy was settled.

And that was not likely to be soon. With the birth of the Princess Elizabeth, the King's Council sought to deal with the situation. They sent commission after commission to compel Catherine of Aragon to renounce her title, but to no avail. She wrote to Chapuys that the bishops had threatened her with the gibbet. Her reply had been a defiant query: Which one of them would be the hangman? Knowing that similar pressures would be exerted upon her daughter, she wrote to Mary, in a remarkable letter still extant, advising her to 'obey the King your father in everything, save only that you will not offend God and lose your soul.' Mary was to remain silent, to make no decisions as 'to any manner of living . . . until this troublesome time be past.'

The 'troublesome time', however, did not pass. In late 1533, Mary was living at Beaulieu, her house near Newhall Boreham in Essex. Shortly after Elizabeth's birth, Sir William Paulet of the King's Council appeared at Beaulieu carrying a letter, 'By the King's commandment, issued to the bearer of the Privy Council on the last Sunday at Greenwich.' The message, delivered to Sir John Hussey, the Princess's chamberlain, was short. Mary was to leave for Hertford, there to await the King's pleasure; Beaulieu was required for George Boleyn, Anne's brother. Her household was to be reduced and many of her servants replaced with those of the King's choice. Her own proud badge was to be stripped from her servants' livery and replaced with the King's device. And lastly, she was no longer to call herself the Princess of Wales. The title now belonged to Elizabeth, the daughter of Anne Boleyn.

Incredulous, Mary demanded to see the letter. It was, indeed, addressed to 'The Lady Mary, the King's daughter'. With trembling fingers, she held it even closer than usual to her eyes as she scanned its contents a second time, hoping perhaps her weak eyesight had played her tricks. Then, in great agitation, she turned and ran to her chamber. Still not believing what she had seen, she wrote to her father:

In most humble wise, I beseech your Grace of your daily blessing. Pleaseth the same to be advertised, that this morning my Chamberlain came and showed me that he had received a letter from Sir William Paulet, comptroller of your household; the effect whereof was, that I should, with all diligence, remove to the castle of Hertford. Whereupon I desired to see that letter, which he showed me, wherein was written that 'the Lady Mary, the King's daughter, should remove to the place aforesaid'—leaving out in the same the name of 'Princess'. Which, when I heard, I could not a little marvel, trusting verily that your Grace was not privy to the same letter, as concerning the leaving out of the name of princess, forasmuch as I doubt not that your Grace doth take me for your lawful daughter, born in true matrimony. Wherefore, if I were to say to the contrary, I should in my conscience run into the displeasure of God, which I hope assuredly that your Grace would not that I should do.

And, in all other things your Grace shall have me, always, as humble and obedient daughter and handmaid as ever was child to the father, which my duty bindeth me to, as knoweth our Lord, who have your Grace in His most holy tuition, with much honour and long life to His pleasure. From your manor of Beaulieu, October 2nd.

By your most humble daughter,

Mary, *Princess*.[2]—

With this letter to her father a separate one was sent to his Council so there should be no doubt concerning her own attitude as to her status. She told the Council:

My lords, as touching my removal . . . I will obey his Grace, as my duty is, or to any other place his Grace may appoint me; but I protest before you, and all others present, that my conscience will in no wise suffer me to take any other than myself for princess, or for the King's daughter, born in lawful matrimony; and that I will never wittingly or willingly say or do ought whereby any person might take occasion to think that I agree to the contrary. Nor say I this out of any ambition or proud mind, as God is my judge. If I should do otherwise, I should slander the deed or our mother, the holy church, and the Pope, who is the judge in this matter, *and none other*; and should also dishonour the King, my father, the Queen, my mother, and falsely confess myself a bastard, which God defend I should do, since the Pope hath not so declared it by his sentence. . . .[3]

Mary's attitude, as stubborn as her mother's, only further infuriated the King. The acquiescence of the former Princess of Wales, whose plight had stirred up what Henry and Anne regarded as a hornet's nest of sympathy from his subjects, must be obtained. Anne was almost uncontrollable when she learnt Mary had not accepted her loss of rank. Venting her anger upon the King, whose daughter was so perverse and wilful, she soon had her first revenge. In December, Mary was ordered—not to her own house at Hertford—but to Hatfield, where an establishment had been formed for the baby, Elizabeth. This was Anne's answer to Mary's rebellion. To make the former Princess of Wales reside in the home of her own child, who now bore the title, seemed a fit retaliation towards one who would not acknowledge her as Queen. Frantic, Mary wrote to Chapuys for advice. The ambassador who had recently informed the Emperor that, 'though the King is by nature kind and generously inclined, this Anne has so perverted him, that he does not seem the same man', was shocked by the force of the King's bullying of his former Queen and their daughter. He vigorously protested their treatment to the King, although privately, he thought it would do little good. He wrote to Charles: 'Sin, misfortune and obstinacy have closed the King's ears and something more than words will be necessary to move him'. His advice to Mary took the form of a written protest which she was to sign if forced to do anything against her will.

Mary, therefore, was somewhat prepared when the Duke of Norfolk, Anne Boleyn's uncle, arrived with Lord Morney, the Earl of Oxford, and Bishop Fox to order her removal to Hatfield. Remembering her mother's admonition to 'obey her father' and armed with Chapuys's protest, which she hurriedly signed in the privacy of her room, she told the Duke, 'Since such is my father's wish, it is not for me to disobey. , . .' Upon hearing she could not take all her servants with her, Mary was distraught. Turning aside from the shocked gazes of her unfortunate household, she begged a year's wages for those who would now be without a livelihood. The farewell between Mary and those who had served her—many since her childhood days at Ludlow—was a sad one. But the bitterest parting, one completely unexpected, was from the Countess of Salisbury. Margaret Pole had been Mary's mainstay, always ready to take the place of the absent Catherine and, since Henry's marriage to Anne, the only intimate companion on whom the girl could rely. They had an emotional farewell during which the Countess, in tears, offered to serve Mary at her own expense, but as Chapuys wrote, '. . . her offers were not accepted; nor will they ever be, for were the said Lady to remain by the Princess, they would no longer be able to execute their bad designs. . . .'[4] At the last, Margaret embraced Mary tightly and then, remembering her duty, softly spoke a few comforting words and was gone.

The journey to Hatfield was a nightmare. In the privacy of her litter, Mary wept for the loss of her own household and of one of her dearest friends, but even the release of tears did not lessen the ominous stirrings of fear as she tried to think what action she must take in the immediate future. There was nothing in Mary's past—she who had always been the proud Princess of Wales and heiress to the throne—to prepare her for whatever lay ahead. At one point during the journey, Dr Fox, the King's own almoner, rode up to her for a moment. Seeing her in tears, he hurriedly spoke a few words of comfort, saying she had answered Norfolk 'as virtuously as any woman could.' He advised her to remain firm. 'Or else,' he said, 'all the kingdom is in danger of ruin and perdition.' Then, not wishing anyone to notice his attention to Mary, he rode off quickly before she could reply.

When the Old Palace of Hatfield could be seen in the distance, Mary closed her eyes and prayed for courage and guidance. By the time the procession halted on the gravelled path before the courtyard, she had outwardly regained her composure and stepped disdainfully from her conveyance. The servants began unloading the wagons as the chamberlain of Elizabeth's household came forward to greet Mary. Norfolk escorted her across the courtyard and into the vast Great Hall and asked if she would like to pay her respects to the Princess. Mary turned and tartly replied she knew of no Princess in England other than herself. 'I will call the daughter of Madame Pembroke "sister" and nothing else!' she told the waiting Norfolk angrily. Anxious to leave after executing his distasteful commission, the duke asked if he could carry any word from her to the King. Distraught and near tears, she replied, 'Nothing

else, except that his daughter, the Princess of Wales, begs his blessing.'
Losing his temper, the duke shouted he could not carry such a message
to the King. 'Then leave it!' was Mary's brave reply as she ran from the
hall, her bravado gone, seeking her chamber, to weep again the tears
of frustration, anger, and fear.

She did not see the Princess Elizabeth that night.

Mary Tudor spent two years, passing from late adolescence into
young womanhood, in the household established for her half-sister.
In those years at Hatfield and later at Hunsdon, the corroding hatred
of Anne Boleyn became almost a physical presence with which she
lived daily. Lady Margaret Bryan (who had mothered Mary in her
early years) was appointed Lady Governess to the infant Elizabeth.
Perhaps it was hoped the presence of her former childhood nurse
would soften Mary's attitude to Anne and Elizabeth. Although nothing
served to lessen her aversion to Anne, Mary's own love for children
overcame what might have been a natural distaste for Anne's baby.
Daily she visited the nursery to see the tiny red-headed child whose
very existence had so undermined her own. Lady Bryan was obviously
devoted to her new charge, and she affectionately welcomed the lonely
Mary. Often they sat together in front of a blazing fire watching as
Elizabeth clutched at the cross hanging at Mary's waist or tangled
her fingers in Mary's hair, pulling her cap askew. Lady Bryan provided
almost the only friendly companionship in the household which was
governed by Lady Anne Shelton and Lady Alice Clere, a sister of Sir
Thomas Boleyn and widow of Sir Thomas Clere. Since Mary was aware
that everything was reported to Cromwell or the King, she kept her visits
brief so that Lady Bryan's position and safety would not be jeopardized.

She was very lonely. She missed the comfort of easy access to her
mother. The subsequent dismissal of the Countess of Salisbury left a
void in Mary's life which even the infrequent companionship of Lady
Bryan and the little Elizabeth could not fill. The sheer magnitude of
the rejection by her father was brought home to Mary most pointedly
one day when Henry came to visit the infant. At Hatfield, Mary had
been given, as Chapuys said, 'the worst room in the house', where she
was waited upon by a common chambermaid. Communication with
her mother was becoming increasingly difficult since any who might
serve as messengers between Mary and Catherine were instantly
removed from the household. She knew from Chapuys that bills were
pending in Parliament which would settle the succession legally on
Elizabeth and render her own birth illegitimate. However, she was
elated at the thought of just seeing her father again. It had been so

[43]

long! Mary prayed long and earnestly on her knees that some reconciliation might end their bitter estrangement.

The King had also resolved to deal personally with his older daughter since his emissaries were having little luck in obtaining her submission. But the visit was doomed to end in disappointment. As Chapuys said, 'When the Lady [Boleyn] considered the ... beauty, virtue and prudence of the Princess might assuage his wrath and cause him to treat her better and leave her title, she sent Cromwell, and then other messengers after the King to prevent him seeing or speaking with her.'[5] Cromwell, in accordance with Anne's instructions, waited upon Mary instead. He stressed the importance of her submitting to her father's will. Should she do so, she could return to court and enjoy all the comforts she had previously known. Her father had a new Queen and another child and was not likely to be understanding if she did not obey, Cromwell said.

But no threat could move Mary. Loneliness, the enforced solitude, and the daily, grinding humiliation of her altered position had not lessened the passionate defence of her injured mother. To admit that her parents' marriage was not sanctioned by God after a Papal dispensation had been issued was more than the sensitive girl could face. To agree that she was the product of an incestuous union, because of her mother's former marriage to her father's brother, to admit that she was not the Princess of Wales and, therefore, not the legal heir to the Crown, was to confirm that she had lived a false life for almost nineteen years. It was not in the slim frame of one who carried in her veins the blood of her grandmother, the great Isabella of Spain, to crumple at such pressure. She told Cromwell she had given her answer, 'it was labour wasted to press her, and they were deceived if they thought that bad treatment or rudeness, or even the chance of death, would make her change her determination.'[6] She begged again to visit the King and kiss his hand, but her request was rudely denied.

At Henry's departure, Mary took matters into her own hands. She climbed the innumerable steps of the tower turret to the rooftop of Hatfield and remained on the leads in the hope she might at least *see* the father she had not set eyes on for so long. At last Henry emerged into the courtyard. Some last glimmering of love or respect for the girl he had disdained must have remained in the King, for on seeing Mary kneeling on the leads, 'he bowed to her and put his hand to his hat. Then all present, who had not dared to raise their heads to look at her, rejoiced at what the King had done, and saluted her reverently, with signs of good-will and compassion.'[7]

It was not always easy to be impartial in Henry's new England.

*

That fateful assembly, the Reformation Parliament, was summoned early in 1534 to complete the separation of the English Church from Roman authority. To enact these laws and to repeal the old heresy laws so that violators could be suitably punished, the King was selective in calling to his Parliament—which was not then an elective body—only those members whom he knew would favour his cause. Many nobles of known Catholic partisanship avoided the court and hoped that a blessed anonymity would prove some measure of protection for them. Those who felt, in conscience, they must attend also realized what a small minority they constituted.

Even at the last, Henry apparently had second thoughts about carrying through the final act of severance. The French ambassador said the King would not have done anything hurriedly, but he constantly needed the prompting of both Anne and Cromwell who had urged each step along the path of schism. Henry's defiance of and separation from Rome was never a planned policy motivated by a spirit of religious idealism. It was a long drawn out process which occurred as he was hampered from time to time by forces *outside* England and supported and directed by forces *inside* the country. As each step was taken, retreat became even more impossible. Faced with potential excommunication, Henry had but two solaces. He would be Pope-King in his own realm, and remembering how he had used Wolsey as a buffer when attempting to divorce Catherine, he knew he could always hide behind Anne and Cromwell should his subjects react too violently to the changes.

In Rome on March 23, 1534, the marriage of Catherine of Aragon and Henry VIII was declared good and valid by Pope Clement. Excommunication would follow if the King persisted in his present marriage. Defiantly, Henry's pliable Parliament acted. Previously, the King had taken steps to diminish Roman authority. Now Parliament passed the final Act of Severance; there would be no turning back. In the future, to procure any Bulls or Briefs from the Pope would be considered treason. Henceforth, all licences and dispensations would be issued by the Archbishop of Canterbury under royal sanction. The payment of all monies to Rome was abolished on the grounds that England was not subject to any laws made by any authority outside the realm. That it was a threat made to induce the Pope to soften his sentence is obvious in that it was not to take effect for a year. The abbeys and monasteries would be visited by royal commission; all future visits by Roman authorities were prohibited. The Act for the Submission of the Clergy was reaffirmed, and with his supremacy now assured, an Act of Succession vested the Crown in the heirs of Henry and Anne Boleyn. An oath was to be taken by all the King's subjects making it an act of high treason to slander his marriage or to question the succession 'by writing, print, deed or act.'[8] The Princess Mary was declared illegitimate; the Princess Elizabeth was now the heiress-presumptive.

The acts of the Parliament of 1534, which rendered such awesome changes in the daily lives, spiritual teachings, and moral comforts of the people of England, produced little change in the resistance of the King's former Queen and daughter. Many swore the oath—some out of fear, some with enthusiasm, many in bewilderment. Those who could not suffered the penalty of treason: hanging, drawing and quartering, for England had now entered upon a period of torment which is, fortunately, unique in its history. The Terror which claimed Sir Thomas More and John Fisher the Bishop of Rochester, the holy Carthusian monks, and Elizabeth Barton, the hapless nun of Kent, as victims, could conceivably reach Catherine and Mary also. But even this knowledge failed to shake them. Charles V, Catherine's nephew, had violently protested their treatment, their exile, and the deprivation of their rank. Now, with a Bull of Excommunication hanging over his head, the King feared the Emperor might enforce the Papal decree with something stronger than bitter recrimination. Henry felt called upon to defend his action by replying to Charles that Catherine had 'in most ungodly, obstinate and inobedient wise wilfully resisted, set at nought, and contemned' the laws of the new Parliament. As for Mary, 'whom we do order and entertain as we think most expedient, and also as to us seemeth pertinent . . .' Henry was more guarded, only chiding Charles for implying that 'her own natural father' would not have her good interests at heart.

The King knew his treatment of Catherine and Mary had drawn angry denunciation from his own people. The possible loss of markets in Spain and Flanders, vital for English exports, was a potent threat. Should more stringent measures be taken, an uprising at home would be an open invitation for invasion from abroad, and the merchants, bitter at the loss of their trade, might act in concert with the nobles who hated Anne. Henry admitted the depth of Catherine's resistance, 'knowing as I do the heart and temper of the Queen', and he respected her courage, even when it infuriated him. That steely will might *never* acquiesce to his supremacy or to the loss of her title. But his daughter's continued refusal was, however, another matter entirely and daily moved the King to violent oaths of impatience. Mary was his daughter and owed a father obedience. Previously, Henry had been sure his shameful persecution of the Queen would be enough to break both their spirits. But despite the iniquities heaped upon them, their reaction was neither submission nor retaliation. Instead, they had exhibited a cool and dignified acceptance of what they realized they could not change or combat but only refute. It was baffling, bewildering—and enraging

[46]

—to the monarch whose will was rarely challenged and whose talent for self-righteous justification was boundless.

And Mary had continued to remain stubborn. When Elizabeth was six months old, Anne had gone to visit her child at Hunsdon. She sent a message to Mary saying that if Mary would 'honour her as Queen', a means of reconciliation with the King might be found and that she, the Queen, would 'intercede with him for her and she, Mary, would be better treated than ever.' Mary had replied she knew of no Queen in England except her mother and 'if Madame Boleyn would do her that favour, she would be much obliged.' Chapuys wrote to Charles, 'The Lady repeated her remonstrances and offers and, in the end, threatened her—but could not move the Princess.'[9] Mary could do little else. The whole fabric of her resistance, of her heroic loyalty to her mother, her belief in her own position, continued unabated. There was virtually nothing to distract her from her problem. Her daily routine was simple, for she now had no royal duties to perform, and entertainments or diversions for the household were meagre. With no rank, her position had deteriorated. Often sleepless at night and plagued with headaches by day, she suffered in silence as the nightmarish reality of her circumstances tore at her nerves. And when her exercise was further restricted, her health—never robust—declined still further.

Above all, she worried about her mother who had been ill. Her own melancholy and depression were intensified by the scraps of information that came to her about the Queen. Catherine of Aragon had been besieged by councillors of the King to forsake her title, and her servants had been removed, but she remained resolute as ever in her tower chamber at Buckden. She told the commissioners they would have to 'bind her with ropes' to dislodge her, the rightful Queen of England—a task which quailed the spirit of even the doughty Charles Brandon, the Duke of Suffolk. Possibly her mother's example helped Mary when, one morning in early March, Henry ordered his two daughters to The More. Almost numb in her despondency, rigid, and unyielding, Mary refused to go. It is possible she thought some physical protest, some noisy public scene—*anything*—might make the others of the household, who must be as heartily sick of her and her attitude as she was of them, leave her in solitude and blessed peace. But such was not her luck. Struggling mightily, her thin body shaking with sobs, the young face pinched with anger and shame as she sought to hide her tears, trying desperately to hold on to some semblance of her pride, the former Princess of Wales was lifted bodily by two common lackeys and thrust roughly into her litter. Chapuys was appalled at Mary's stubborn defiance. 'I should not have advised the Princess to have gone to this extreme, for fear of irritating her father. . . .' he wrote to Charles.[10] Then, taking his courage in his hands, he appeared before the King, protesting and asking more consideration for the Princess. Henry's reaction was unexpected. While stating he considered his treatment of Mary his own business, his eyes surprisingly filled with tears and he sighed, 'It is her Spanish blood . . .'

Chapuys feared that Mary's continued resistance would provoke the King's further wrath. Mary herself was also aware of the danger, and when, several months later, she was ordered to Eltham, in desperation she wrote to Chapuys 'three times in less than twenty-four hours to know what to do.' Chapuys's advice was sensible. 'I thought that, to prevent her father and his Lady from imagining she was worn out and conquered by ill-treatment, she should speak boldly, and with her accustomed modesty, but not go to the extremity of allowing herself to be taken by force, as on the former occasion.'[11]

The Act of Succession and its attendant Oath placed Mary in even greater peril. When the commissioners of the King arrived to exact the Oath from the anxious household, they had no trouble until they confronted the King's daughter. Stubbornly, Mary refused to swear. After the commissioners left, Lady Shelton did not spare Mary. She shouted at the unfortunate girl, 'If I were the King I would kick you out of the house. . . .' To terrorize Mary further, she said that the King himself had threatened he would 'make her lose her head for violating the laws of the realm.'[12] The message sounded so plausible and so like her father that Mary's anxiety and anguish almost overwhelmed her, resulting in an illness which kept her in bed for several days.

Angered by Mary's enduring rebellion, Anne Boleyn ordered those in charge of her daughter's household to 'give her [Mary] a boxing on the ears now and then for the cursed bastard she is.' Anne boasted, said Chapuys, 'that she will make the Princess one of her maids, which will not give her too much to eat; or will marry her to some varlet. . . .'[13] Lady Clere defended Mary, saying she was a 'good girl and deserved respect and kind treatment . . .,' but Lady Shelton had no such compassion. She taunted Mary, pointed out the foolishness of her defiance. She insisted the girl eat at the common table in the Great Hall rather than have her meals served in the blessed solitude of her own chamber.

As the weeks went on, clothing and other necessities were deliberately withheld, and at one point, Mary was compelled to send to the King for money, but, unyielding as always, ordered the courier not to accept any answer in which she was not entitled Princess. She kept apart from the household as much as possible, although she continued to look in upon the small Elizabeth almost daily. Attendance at mass in the church adjoining the house had been forbidden, but she found great spiritual release in the devotions she performed in the privacy of her chamber. There were few visitors. Those who dared to see her faced the interrogation of Henry or his ministers when they returned to London, and a few were actually lodged in the Tower for their presumption.

News of her mother became even more scarce. Catherine had left Buckden for nearby Kimbolton Castle, where, fearful of assassination by poison or outright murder, she kept entirely to one chamber where her maids cooked her food over the fire. The incredible situation which had reduced the daughter of Isabella and Ferdinand of Spain and a Queen of England for twenty-five years to such circumstances had not sapped her courage, however. Upon hearing of Mary's refusal to swear the Oath, she wrote approvingly to Chapuys, saying she thought her daughter 'did well to show her teeth to the King'.

Word of Mary's treatment reached the villagers, and they gathered outside the Palace hoping to see the girl. When they glimpsed her walking in a gallery in the Solar Room at Hatfield, they shouted their encouragement, calling 'Princess for all that!' and cheered her warmly. Such public demonstrations of affection and support, dreaded by the King and his councillors, called for more severe measures. Suspecting she might be in touch with outside sympathizers, they deprived her of writing materials, and her liberties were even further curtailed. With the consolation of her faith withheld, the difficulty of communicating with her mother, the lack of visitors or other diversions in the hostile household, Mary's temper became short and her disposition more introverted, as her frayed nerves approached the breaking point. Almost the saddest burden to bear was her utter abandonment. There was no one to confide in or turn to for comfort and encouragement—no mother, no father, no governess, no solicitous servant or sympathetic visitor. Only those in the accursed household in which she was virtually imprisoned knew the extent of her daily humiliations.

Another illness, more serious than before, beset her, and those in her household were fearful enough of her condition to send to the King for a physician. When he arrived, he must have treated Mary with some affection and respect, and the abused girl grasped at his presence as an outlet for her fears. Orders had been given that she was never to be left alone with any visitors. Although others were standing by, Mary summoned her courage and, as if trying to make conversation under difficult circumstances, mentioned 'it had been a long time since she had spoken Latin'. The busy physician, anxious to do his duty and be out of the tense household, replied absentmindedly that she might try. As he listened to Mary's words, precise and controlled—words the onlookers did not understand—it must have required a great effort not to show his horror. Mary had indeed not forgotten her Latin. Precisely, she detailed the nature of her life in her sister's residence, and she repeated that the King was threatening her with execution for her continued resistance. All the good man could do was to finish his examination hurriedly, mumbling that 'her Latin was not every good.' But the courageous doctor went at once to Chapuys who had heard similar ominous rumours at court. Chapuys wrote to the Emperor 'that God had not so blinded her as to confess for any kingdom on earth, that the King, her father, and the Queen, her mother, had so long lived in adultery, nor would she contravene the order of the Church and make herself a bastard.' He said Mary had accepted what fate might send her, and if Henry did order her death, she was sure she 'would go straight to Paradise and be quit of the tribulations of this world.' He ended by saying that 'her grief is about the troubles of the Queen her mother.'[14]

In August, 1535, the new Pope, Paul III, outraged by Henry's revolutionary upheaval of the Church's very foundations in England and horrified by the executions of the gallant Sir Thomas More and Bishop John Fisher, issued the Bull of Excommunication, *Eius qui immobillis*, which the dawdling Clement had so long withheld. Though it was not unexpected, Henry again needed the bolstering of both Anne and Cromwell. Thomas Cromwell had cultivated the confidence that came with the knowledge that he alone in all the realm possessed the brains and the stomach to perform whatever unpleasant action was necessary to do the King's will. He was now the Vicar-General and his competence was unquestioned. Anne's supremacy with Henry was another matter, for her influence had diminished. Henry could not help but regard her as the starting point from which all the troubles now besetting England had begun: the divorce from Catherine and the grumbling of his subjects who openly loathed 'the concubine', and held her responsible with the King for Catherine's exile. Now what seemed divine retribution had resulted in ruined harvests, incredibly bad weather, and a visitation of the plague.

Even though Parliament had made it an act of treason to say so, Henry knew his marriage was considered by many to be no marriage at all. It left the status of his two daughters open to question, especially abroad where husbands must be found for them. The deaths of More and Fisher, which had sickened his own people and shocked the monarchs and ecclesiastics of Europe—all led back to Anne, to his infatuation with her. It might have remained only an infatuation but for her insistence on wearing the Crown which had led him now to the end of his schismatic path. With the excommunication, Henry's disillusionment with Anne reached its height, and Cromwell could not fail to notice, nor to listen with the proper amount of sympathy, to the King's complaints. When Henry was Anne's undisputed champion, so was Cromwell, although he and the new Queen personally disliked each other intensely. Now that the King's love and support of Anne was diminishing, Cromwell could look ahead, realizing her status might well change. Since they had been companions in steering Henry on his rebellious course, some method must be found whereby, if Anne were to be sacrificed, Cromwell would survive.

Anne was certainly aware of her precarious position. She knew herself to be as vulnerable now as Catherine had been when she had reigned as Queen. Ironically, their positions were very similar. Henry displayed more than a passing interest in the many pretty faces around the court —interest that led to stormy scenes when Anne protested. She knew she must endeavour to keep the volatile man who was her husband content if she were to remain Queen. She courted the friendship of Francis, the King of France; but now Francis's marriage to Eleanor, a sister of Charles V, put him in an awkward position. Francis was willing that the King of England have his mistress, but when marriage to that mistress resulted in a political and religious revolution and, inevitably, excommunication. Francis could and did assume an aloof and disapproving attitude. Anne frankly told Palamedes Gontier, a secretary of the French Minister, Chabot de Brion, that Francis's distant attitude in regard to her 'had caused and engendered in the King, her spouse, many strange thoughts of which,' she said, 'there was a great need that a remedy should be thought of unless he [Francis] would that she should not be maddened and lost; for she found herself near to that, and more in pain and trouble than she had even been since her espousals.' And then, presuming upon the friendship she had formed with the French King in what seemed another lifetime when she had been a carefree companion to Henry's sister, Mary Tudor, at the French court, she asked Gontier to intercede for her. 'She could not speak so amply to me as she would, for fear of where she was and of the eyes that were watching her countenance, not only of the said Lord, her husband, but of the princes with him. . . .' Gontier wrote to de Brion in France, 'Assuring you, Monsieur, that the said Lady, as I well know, is not at her ease, presuming upon my poor judgment, that she has doubts and suspicions of this King, which I mentioned to you before I took this journey.'[15]

The 'doubts and suspicions' concerned the King's interest in Jane Seymour, a pale and unassuming woman 'of middle height . . . nobody thinks that she has much beauty,' wrote Chapuys to the Emperor. Jane Seymour's one redeeming feature in the eyes of Charles's ambassador was that 'she was formerly in the service of the good Queen [Catherine] and seems to bear great goodwill and respect to the Princess.' The King's interest in Mademoiselle Seymour, now one of Anne's ladies-in-waiting, was watched with venomous eyes. Anne Boleyn knew all too intimately every move in the delicate game that Jane and the King were playing. She was comforted with the realization that Jane lacked the ambition and initiative she herself had possessed

[51]

when she had sought the Queenship. There was another solace; she was again pregnant. If she could only have a son, she would be safe. No mere lady-in-waiting could replace the mother of the heir to the Tudor throne. Henry might stray, but if she had a boy, she would remain his Queen for as long as she might live.

The shocking events of 1535, both in the realm and in her own life, continued to tax the heart and soul of Mary Tudor. She suffered another and more severe illness which kept her, weak and feverish, in her chamber. Those in her household reacted almost in panic, for if she should die, they might conceivably be blamed. Henry might honestly desire his oldest, most troublesome daughter dead, but the whim and fancy of the King was known to be fickle, and if any under-handed poisoning of the Princess was discovered, it might go badly with the culprit. Catherine was certain she herself would follow in the path of the martyrs when the next Parliament met, and she was fearful and anxious for Mary. She wrote Chapuys, requesting him to obtain permission for her daughter to join her at Kimbolton, saying she would treat her 'with her own hands' and 'if God pleased to take her from this world, my heart will rest satisfied; otherwise, in great pain.' She begged Chapuys to tell Henry 'that there is no need of any other person but myself to nurse her; that I will put her in my own bed where I sleep, and will watch her when needful.'[16]

Chapuys took the letter to the King, but Henry was adamant. The King said 'he wished to do his best for his daughter's health, but he must be careful of his own honour and interests which would be jeopardized if Mary were conveyed abroad, or if she escaped, as she might easily do if she were with her mother; for he had some suspicion that the Emperor had designs to get her away.' Together, he said, they could comfort each other and their resistance would be strengthened. Moreover, they would offer 'unknown persons' too much opportunity to spirit them out of the kingdom. Chapuys, who had been told by Mary she would willingly 'cross the Channel in a sieve', presented his usual bland countenance to the King lest Henry suspect him of being one of the 'unknown persons'. But he did obtain a concession from Cromwell that Mary might go near enough to her mother so that Catherine's own physician, Miguel de la Sa, could attend her.

From de la Sa, Catherine heard in abundant and eloquent detail the rigours of Mary's two-year imprisonment. She herself had been far from well. Worry over Mary only added to her anguish and fear for her own safety. Chapuys had written warning her 'to take care to fasten securely the door of her chamber at night and to have the room searched before she retired.' She knew 'the Lady' had said she 'would never be satisfied until both the Queen and her daughter had been done to death.' The heads of More and Fisher lately impaled on London Bridge and the execution of her own confessor, Father Forrest, had appalled the ageing Queen. Men of stature and good conscience were dying rather than submit to Henry's will and Catherine suffered keenly at the fate of those who died upholding her cause.

The King, goaded like a bull by any defiance of his laws, was proving his case by terror. The whole environment of the England Catherine loved, of the adopted country in which she had reigned as an influential and beloved Queen for almost a quarter of a century was changing, and the persecutions and outrages committed in the name of Christ sickened and revolted her. The knowledge of her daughter's sufferings only served to deplete what little remaining strength Catherine possessed. Weakened and anxious, the woman who had proved such a majestic symbol of resistance to Henry Tudor did not linger. Mary had no more than begun to recover from her illness when the blow fell. The Queen died at Kimbolton Castle on Friday, January 7, 1536, at two o'clock in the afternoon. Except for her beloved Maria de Salinas and the few maids who had remained faithful for the past several heartbreaking years, she was completely alone. But she was remembered by the many thousands who lined the roads as her funeral procession passed. In fear, her people had sworn the awesome Oath, but now at the last they honoured the one they considered their rightful Queen. With wet eyes and caps respectfully doffed, they paid tribute to Catherine whose terrible courage in the face of royal oppression had never wavered.

The generation which had known Catherine of Aragon as Queen of England never forgot her; she was always remembered as a symbol of everything they morally respected and spiritually loved. At her death, this love and respect for her and for a social and religious order that was being dealt a deathblow, was transferred to her daughter, Mary Tudor. It was a bequest passed on in love, but a heritage that Mary, ironically of all the Tudors, was the least endowed to receive. For Mary, unfortunately, was now the product of a royal union which had foundered, and the unhappy events of her years of exile and seclusion had left their mark upon her. For Mary Tudor, with her youthful years poisoned by personal sorrow and reduced to intense frustration, it was to prove a heritage of misfortune, bitterness, and abject failure.

Chapter Three

THE death of Catherine of Aragon relieved Henry Tudor of the embarrassing presence of a Queen whose indomitable will was the equal of his own—one whose very existence had been a constant reproach for six years. Her persistent defiance had undermined the authority of the revolutionary laws which had led to the destruction of England's religious foundations. Reading her last sad letter in which she forgave him for the 'many miseries' he had inflicted upon her, Henry could even weep, and throughout England and abroad the mourning for Catherine of Aragon was heartfelt and impressive. The English ambassador at Venice, Edmund Harvel, wrote to Thomas Starkey, later the King's chaplain, 'the Queen Catherine's death had been divulged there, and was received with lamentations, for she was incredibly dear to all men for her good fame, which is in great glory among all the exterior nations. Great obloquy had her death occasioned; all dread lest the royal girl [Mary] should briefly follow her mother. I assure you men speaketh *tragice* of these matters, which are not to be touched by letters.'[1] *Tragice* indeed, and not to be referred to too openly if one valued one's life and property.

There were many who believed that the Queen had been poisoned and the same thought must have occurred to Catherine's daughter as she remained secluded in her chamber, shattered by her loss. A few pathetic possessions of her mother's—the most cherished a small gold cross and chain—were brought to Mary, but there was little left from the Queen's long exile. What little there was of any real value was confiscated by Cromwell.

When Catherine died, Anne sent Mary a note in which, as Chapuys said, she threw out 'the first bait to the Princess telling her . . . that if she will discontinue her obstinacy and obey her father like a good girl, she [Anne] will be the best friend in the world to her. . . .'[2] She acknowledged that should she return to court, Mary would not have to carry the royal train, but, instead, they would walk side by side Lady Shelton read the letter to the bereaved Princess, but Mary turned a deaf ear, saying such actions would 'conflict with her honour and conscience.' Now that her adored mother was gone, there was little in England for her. Previously Chapuys had hinted at escape, and though in her moments of desperation Mary had often hoped for refuge abroad, she could never bring herself to forsake Catherine while the Queen was alive. Now she prayed some means might be found to convey her to her mother's country, to the Emperor and some blessed peace of mind. 'On this subject,' wrote Chapuys, 'she had a long conversation with one of my men, begging me most urgently to think over the matter. Otherwise, she considered herself lost. . . .'[3]

On January 29, the day of Catherine's funeral, Mary was allowed to attend chapel to pray for her mother's soul. Afterwards, as she lay dry-eyed and miserable in her chamber, she received word from court from which she must have derived intense satisfaction. Queen Anne had miscarried. It had been a boy—Henry's long-awaited heir. When Mary had refused Anne's belated offer of friendship, Anne, goaded by the girl's obstinacy, had said to Lady Shelton '. . . if I have a son, as I hope shortly, I know what will happen to her. . . .' Anne was well aware that in the eyes of the King and his subjects, her one hope of redemption lay in presenting England with an heir. She who had joyfully cried at Catherine's death 'Now I am indeed a Queen!' at last felt the weight of the crown balanced so precariously upon her head.

Henry's anger at the miscarriage knew no bounds. He upbraided Anne for the 'loss of his boy' and stormed from her chambers, saying ominously 'she would have no more boys by him!' Henry's emotional instability when deprived of anything he deeply desired or desperately needed was a frightening reality with which the despairing Anne was all too familiar. Her failure to provide an heir, her husband's capriciousness, her unpopularity at home and abroad, were barriers that seemed insurmountable. She was no longer young and Henry's threat terrified her. The diadem on her brow which should have been her greatest protection was suddenly her greatest danger.

Ironically, the life of Catherine of Aragon had been Anne Boleyn's greatest security. Several months previously, Henry had discussed with Cromwell the possibility of divorcing Anne if she failed to give him a son. He had been told he 'could not divorce himself from Anne without tacitly acknowledging the validity of his first marriage and thus falling under the authority of the Pope.'[4] Neither could he revoke the legislative measures made since his marriage to Anne, many of which he sincerely believed were for the good of his realm. While Catherine was alive, any return to his former Queen had been unthinkable. Thus, with her death, his present Queen became poignantly vulnerable. Instead of Catherine and Anne as obstacles to a new marriage which might produce the needed heir, there was now only Anne.

*

The political atmosphere in England had also changed with the death of Catherine of Aragon. The threat of invasion by the Emperor was gone and Mary's position as the true heir to the throne strengthened. Charles V had returned from a victorious campaign, wresting Tunis from the notorious Turk, Barbarossa, thus freeing 20,000 Christian prisoners. In April, 1536, the King of France invaded Italy in his ceaseless quest for possession of Milan. Charles was furious at Francis's treachery and cried, 'If the King of France will not have peace, I shall be forced to stake all, and whichever of us wins will buy his victory dearly, for the Turk will be master of Europe if God do not intervene; for man cannot prevent it.'[5] Henry's Council realized the necessity of recouping England's lost prestige at the court of the Holy Roman Emperor, and of opening the way for a possible reconciliation with Charles. Henry himself felt the poetic justice of an alliance with the Emperor against Francis whom he declared had all but abandoned him in his fight with the Papacy.

Thus, when Chapuys went to Greenwich to plead for Mary after Catherine's death, he was received with gracious deference. Several weeks previously, in a secret conference at Austin Friars, Cromwell had told Chapuys that any agreement between Spain and England would bring about some reconciliation with Mary and a recognition of her legitimacy and a possible degree of compromise with the Pope,[6] views even one as confident as Cromwell would hardly have advanced had he not known the King's mind. Chapuys closely questioned the ministers on Henry's 'nouvelles amours'. Leaning in a window embrasure, Cromwell told Chapuys he felt sure the King would continue in his present marriage. As he spoke, with a furtive movement he hid a smirking smile behind a pudgy hand, a gesture Chapuys interpreted as Cromwell wished—knowing full well there was little hope of reconciliation with the Pope and Emperor if the King continued in the marriage to Anne. From that moment, Chapuys knew 'the concubine's' days were numbered.

The loss of his son had brought Henry to the end of his marriage, although how it was to be terminated legally, he did not know. As soon as he could rid himself of Anne, he would be free to wed elsewhere. He was getting no younger and the succession must be assured. Anne was in her thirties; she had lost the lovely freshness, the striking vivacity acquired at the French court, which had led people to say she 'was like a Frenchwoman born'. The spitfire temper had accelerated from the quarrels in their private chambers to public arguments. Several of Henry's ministers had not escaped Anne's overbearing criticism. When her uncle, the Duke of Norfolk, had tried to remonstrate with her on one occasion, she 'used terms which would not be used to a dog', and sent the furious Duke from the room, muttering she was a '*grande putaine*'. Many nobles had pointedly left Henry's court rather than risk Anne's shrewish temper and arrogance. Henry knew his marriage and the measures taken to legalize it had won him universal condemnation and disfavour, that many regarded it as mere concubinage. Could he bring the matter to an end, he was convinced he would have peace at home and abroad—and be at peace himself. He was in an intolerable position, and Cromwell was well aware it was his task to extricate the King—and that as soon as possible.

And, in addition to recouping political prestige and maintaining the succession, there was a more personal reason for another marriage. A few days prior to her miscarriage, Anne had surprised Henry and Jane Seymour in a surreptitious embrace. The unhappy Queen had long resented Henry's interest in the demure Jane Seymour. Jane's very obvious contrast to the domineering Anne was her compelling attraction for Henry, an attraction Anne soon found she was helpless to combat. When she recognized a bauble around Mistress Seymour's neck as having come from the King, she had boxed Jane soundly on the ears. To have found them embracing so soon after the loss of her son had sent Anne to bed in shock. She had shrieked that Henry's dallying with her lady-in-waiting had brought on the miscarriage. The flirtation was apparently well known outside court circles. When the miscarriage was over, the midwife attending Anne said knowingly, 'It was never merry [happy] in England when there were three Queens in it.'* Her companion's reply was, prophetically, 'there will be fewer shortly.'

With all signs pointing to a new Queen, Cromwell acted. Though they disliked each other personally, Cromwell and Anne had been willing partners in schism. But Cromwell's wise encouragement of Henry to mend his fences with the Emperor enraged Anne, and she threatened to 'see his head off'. Knowing her ascendancy over the King had come to its end, Cromwell had only to conceive the method by which Henry could be free. Ever the realist, the minister wanted no tinge from further association with someone regarded as a 'diablesse, a tigress, the author of all the mischief which was befalling the realm.'⁷ He, Cromwell, might be the victim of Anne's downfall as Cardinal Wolsey had been the victim of Catherine's. Henry told his minister he felt 'quite justified in taking another wife'. The King said 'he had been seduced into marriage with Anne by sorcery, and consequently that he considered it to be null, which was clearly seen by God's denying a son.'⁸ When Cromwell grasped the ominous significance of that single word

* Meaning the as-yet-unburied Catherine, Anne herself, and Jane Seymour.

'sorcery', he set to work to end the marriage which at one time he, along with Thomas Cranmer, had gone to considerable trouble to justify.

Despite the controversies involved in Henry's hoped-for alliance with the Emperor and a compromise with Rome, life at court went on as usual. But there were several noticeable differences. The Council was openly advocating improved relations with the Emperor, and Chapuys joyously reported that only great good would result for Mary. Henry's rift with his Queen had not ended; he pointedly left Anne alone for many weeks. He declined to remove Jane Seymour from court, and Anne was obliged to watch the courtiers who had once been her partisans scurrying to seek the favour of her own lady-in-waiting. With the continued coolness of the King, the disinclination of Cromwell or any of the Council to offer support, Anne became desperate. She resorted to flirtations which may have been harmless enough but were certainly reckless for one in her position. Ever vain, she tempted extravagant compliments especially from close friends such as William Brereton, Sir Henry Norris, and Sir Francis Weston. They held positions of trust in the King's Privy Chamber and were gay rakes in the court, where their good looks, charm, and lack of social pretensions had endeared them to Henry.

Mark Smeaton, a skilful musician, had been installed by Anne as a Groom of the Chamber; he had openly adored her for years—a fact known and humoured by many. Anne was rash enough in her abandonment to flirt with him and several others, encouraging an apparently jealous competition among them, however real or feigned. She gave Smeaton presents of money so he boasted horses and apparel extravagant for one in his position. She encouraged them all to speak of her in a way that could be interpreted as desire, elaborate flattery, or presumptuous intimacy; at one time or another, she even allowed Smeaton to make an avowal of his feelings for her. Court gossips were buzzing, and when one of Henry's councillors rebuked his sister for her 'light behaviour', the sister tartly admitted her offence but said it was nothing in the behaviour of the Queen.[9]

Cromwell's net was tightening. Lady Worcester, a Lady of the Bedchamber and a daughter of Sir Anthony Browne, Henry's Master of the Horse, was questioned and, terrified, admitted that the Queen had been imprudent and careless in her frivolous attempts to capture attention, compliments, and favours.[10] Any scandal of this nature inevitably reached the ears of Cromwell and, aware of his royal master's need, he was astute enough to instigate a quiet investigation, the outcome of which might relieve the King of the woman from whom he was virtually estranged and—more important to Cromwell—open the way for an alliance with the Emperor. As a result of his preliminary questioning, Smeaton was confined in the Tower.

On May Day, 1536, at a joust in Greenwich which Henry also attended, Anne, either deliberately or by accident, dropped a handkerchief from the balcony at the feet of Henry Norris, one of the participants. Norris picked it up and held it to his face for a moment, either kissing it or absentmindedly using it to wipe his sweating brow. He then returned it to the Queen on the point of his lance. Henry started up with an oath, and then, paling at what he considered a bold example of *lèse majesté*, stalked from the balcony, leaving the Queen and her attendants alone and in great agitation at his abrupt departure. It was the last Anne Boleyn was ever to see of her husband. Sufficient evidence had by then been racked from the hapless Smeaton in the Tower to condemn Anne and remove her from Henry's life once and for all. Upon Smeaton's testimony, Francis Weston, William Brereton, and Henry Norris were arrested and brought to the Tower. The arrest of George Boleyn, Lord Rochford, followed.

Anne herself was taken into custody on May 2, the day after the Greenwich joust, and brought by barge to the Tower of London in full daylight. Her uncle, the Duke of Norfolk, and two chamberlains attended her. She had barely seated herself when the Duke spitefully told her that 'her paramours had confessed their guilt' and angrily turned aside as she protested her innocence and asked after her father and brother. By the time she reached the Tower, she was almost hysterical, asking Sir William Kingston, the Constable, 'Wherefore am I here, Mr Kingston?'

Anne Boleyn spent the next two weeks in seclusion in the Tower. Two women were placed there by Cromwell with instructions never to leave her alone and to report her every word and action. They slept on a pallet at the foot of her bed, refusing to answer Anne's frantic inquiries for the safety of her family, attempting only to draw her into incriminating admissions. She would speak of Henry, fearfully at first and then, as if to prove the foolishness of her own words, laugh shrilly, saying of her imprisonment, 'But I think the King does it to prove me!' When she asked for religious counsel, Thomas Cranmer, the Archbishop of Canterbury, was sent to her. His first appointment upon leaving the comparative peace of Cambridge for the complexities of court life had been as chaplain to Anne Boleyn. They had shared a mutual partisanship for the Lutheran teachings, and Cranmer was, personally, much attached to Anne. He wrote to Henry that his mind was 'clean amazed' at the charges against the Queen, for 'I never had a better opinion in woman than I had of her . . .' he said. But later, after conversations with Cromwell, Cranmer too, could see the direction he must go. He again wrote to Henry:

And from what condition your Grace, of your only mere goodness, took

[59]

her, and set the crown upon her head, I repute him not your Grace's faithful servant and subject, nor true to the realm, that would not desire the offence to be without mercy punished, to the sample of all others. And as I loved her not a little, for the love I judged her to bear towards God and His holy gospel, so, if she proved culpable, there is not one that loveth God and His gospel that will ever favour her, but must hate her above all other; and the more they love the gospel, the more they will hate her, for then there never was creature in our time that so much slandered the gospel. And God hath sent her this punishment for that she feignedly hath professed the gospel in her mouth, and not in her heart and deed. . . .[11]

He ended his letter by saying that he lamented 'such faults as could be proved on the Queen as he had heard from their relation.'

There could be only one result. A monstrous farce of a trial ensued in which the Queen was accused of adultery with Brereton, Norris, Weston, and Smeaton. A further charge of incest with her own brother, George Boleyn, was added mainly on the shameful evidence of Lady Rochford, his wife. This evidence consisted of Lady Rochford's assertion that her husband had spent several hours alone with the Queen in her chamber, and on one occasion, as he took leave of her, he was seen to lean over Anne's bed to kiss her good-bye. Norris, Weston, and Brereton courageously maintained their innocence as well as the Queen's. Norris was accused of having had sexual relations with the Queen less than one month after Elizabeth's birth. Fragments of conversation surreptitiously overheard were revived and twisted to suit the charges. It was further stated that George Boleyn had ridiculed Henry, his attire, and manners and had hinted the King was impotent.

On May 16, in the Tower of London, half of England's fifty-six peers sat in judgment; all were Henry's picked men. Anne's uncle, the powerful Duke of Norfolk, and his son, the Earl of Surrey, both of whom hated Anne, were among them, as was Henry Percy the Duke of Northumberland.[12] Of all the prisoners, Smeaton alone was racked; Smeaton alone admitted the adultery. Anne and her brother scorned the evidence with dignity—evidence that could never be proved except on the slimmest circumstantial grounds. But it was mercilessly used by the King and his council. Chapuys, never any partisan of Anne's, wrote to the Emperor, 'The King has been heard to say that he believes upwards of a hundred gentlemen have had to do with her. You never saw a prince or husband show or wear his horns more patiently and lightly than this one does.'[13] The Lord Mayor of London's own reaction to the trial was blunt. He said, 'he could not observe anything in the proceedings against her, but that they were resolved to make an occasion to get rid of her.'

In her comfortable room with its panelled walls and great stone fireplace bearing the carved initials of other illustrious State prisoners, Anne Boleyn waited. The Thames could be seen from a small, narrow window—a frustrating symbol in its ceaseless grey flow of the freedom she had endangered and lost. A few paces from the room, beyond a stout door leading to the Tower cells, was the cold, empty fortress-like room where Sir Thomas More had spent his last days, not mourning his lost freedom but praying instead for physical strength to maintain his spiritual integrity.

A piteous letter addressed 'To the King from the Lady in the Tower' was sent by Anne, begging Henry to 'let me have a lawful trial, and let not my sworn enemies sit as my accusers and as my judges; yea, let me receive an open trial for my truth shall fear no open shame. . . .' The letter ended with poignant cry, 'If ever I have found favour in your sight, if ever the name of Anne Boleyn have been pleasing in your ears—then let me obtain this request. . . .'[14] But Henry had long turned a deaf ear to his Queen's plight. Mercy was promised the condemned men if they would admit their guilt. 'No one', said Sir Edward Baynton, 'will accuse her, but only Mark, of any actual thing.'[15] All seemed to realise the finality of their sentences and did not ask the King for mercy. In his prison chamber George Boleyn played a lute. At the very end of his imprisonment, he wrote the words of Wyatt's poem:

> Now cease, my lute, this is the last
> Labour that thou and I shall waste,
> For ended is that we begun;
> Now is the song both sung and past.
> My lute be still, for I have done.[16]

Brereton, Norris, and Weston were beheaded on Tower Hill where George Boleyn, the last to suffer, exhorted them to 'die courageously'. Mark Smeaton, because of his low birth, was hanged. When Anne eagerly asked whether Smeaton had cleared her name while on the scaffold and was told he had not done so, she cried, 'Has he not, then, cleared me from the public shame he hath done me? Alas! I fear his soul will suffer from the false witness he has borne. My brother and the rest are now, I doubt not, before the face of the Greater King, and I shall follow tomorrow.'[17]

Anne now abandoned all hope of pardon and seemed anxious for her ordeal to be over. 'This lady has much joy and pleasure in death,' Kingston said. During her last full day on earth, she made peace with her conscience. Casting aside the superficial interest in the New Learning, which had once so excited her, she remembered the spiritual comforts of her youth. She called for a confessor and received the

Sacraments. Remembering her harsh treatment of the King's daughter, Mary Tudor, she pleaded with Lady Kingston, the Constable's wife, to go to the Princess immediately after the execution. Lady Kingston was to kneel before Mary and ask forgiveness in Anne's name for the wrongs she had inflicted on her. The good woman, a former lady-in-waiting to Catherine of Aragon, was fond of Mary Tudor and solemnly promised to honour Anne's request.

Anne's thoughts then turned to her husband, the man and King who had waited six long years for her, promising an undying love for which he had torn apart the religious foundations of his realm. To a member of the King's Privy Chamber, she said, 'Commend me to His Majesty, and tell him he hath been ever constant in his career of advancing me. From a private gentlewoman he made me a marchioness; from a marchioness a Queen; and now he hath left me no higher degree of honour, he gives my innocency the crown of martyrdom.'[18] The bitter words of Anne Boleyn also reveal the bold courage with which she had determined to meet her death. She was led to the scaffold erected on Tower Green before the Church of St Peter-ad-Vincula, at noon on May 19, 1536, four months after Catherine of Aragon's death. She had dressed with care in a robe of black damask with a deep, white cape falling over it. A little pointed black velvet hood, edged with pearls, covered the long lustrous black hair. She eyed the spectators unflinchingly: Norfolk, Surrey, Suffolk—uncle, cousins, and friends. Even the Lord Mayor and Sheriff of London, Henry's illegitimate son, the Duke of Richmond,* and Cromwell were there. She spoke briefly to them: 'Good Christian people, I am come hither to die according to the law. ... I am come hither to accuse no man, nor to speak anything of that whereof I am accused, as I know full well that aught I could say in my defence doth not appertain unto you ... and that I could draw no hope of life from the same. ...'[19] Asking that the assemblage pray for her, with shaking hands she removed her hood and collar and handed to Mary Wyatt, a childhood friend, a small book of devotions, bound in gold and enamelled black. Anne Boleyn's last words, 'O Lord God, have pity on my soul, have pity on my soul,' were heard by an eyewitness near the scaffold. The executioner, a skilled swordsman especially brought over from Calais, struck the blow, and, in a moment, held the severed head high. The first woman to be so executed in England had no funeral service, no ceremony, and no honour. She who had triumphed over Catherine of Aragon in life had no triumph in death. The mangled head was stuffed, along with the bleeding corpse, into an old elm chest meant for the storing of arrows, and hastily buried in St Peter's Church.

* The Duke of Richmond, Henry's son by his liaison with Bessie Blount in 1519, was soon to follow Anne. He died of consumption two months later.

On the same day, Thomas Cranmer, who had once declared Anne's marriage as good and valid, now declared it was null and void and granted the King a dispensation to wed again. Henry promptly announced his betrothal to Jane Seymour.

The King's new Queen was the eldest of Sir John Seymour's eight children. The family seat, Wolf Hall, in Wiltshire, was a handsome manor estate of some 1,200 acres, part of which were known picturesquely as Sudden Park or Red Deer Park. Here guests walked from the magnificent thatched wooden Tithe Barn, where festivities celebrating the week-old marriage were held. The family was prominent in the neighbourhood; Sir John Seymour had won his knighthood under Henry VII. He had accompanied the younger Henry in his French campaigns and had attended the King and Catherine of Aragon at the celebrated Field of Cloth of Gold. Like the Boleyns, the Seymours were minor country gentry of no individual brilliance, who had enhanced their fortunes through a series of auspicious marriages. Similarly, as a child, Jane, along with Anne Boleyn, had been a companion to Henry's sister, Mary, when she was briefly wed to Louis XII of France. Her brother, Edward Seymour, served as a page in the same court. Upon her return to England, Jane had become lady-in-waiting to Catherine and then filled a similar post with Anne when Catherine was exiled. As Jane's favour with Henry deepened, Edward Seymour had been made Viscount Beauchamp, with numerous lucrative offices, lands, and pensions. The younger brother, Thomas Seymour, became a Gentleman of the Privy Chamber, with appropriate honours, much as George Boleyn had gained wealth and privileges when Anne became Queen.

However, similarities in birth and background and an eagerness to share in newly acquired wealth and honours, were all that Jane and the dead Anne had in common. Jane Seymour's appearance was almost the exact opposite of her predecessor. To be unwed in one's thirties indicated either a lamentable unattractiveness or a reluctance to assume the married state. Jane Seymour was not unattractive, although some might have found the small thin lips, compressed in matronly self-satisfied primness, a little smug and forbidding. In contrast to Anne's vivid colouring, Jane was pale-complexioned with rather narrow eyes, light and a very clear blue, set deep in her white face. The straight nose and pointed chin lent a sharpness to her features which was misleading, for her nature and character were soft and placid. Undemanding and unimaginative, Jane was happy in her virginity, at ease with her life which had presented so few complexities and little unpleasantness.

If she was no beauty, Henry Tudor seemed to care little; he had had enough of beauty. He now wanted peace, respectability, and the approval of his court, country, and the nations abroad.

Jane Seymour's reputation was unassailable, and this perhaps was what piqued the King's interest when he visited Wolf Hall in September, 1535, and first noticed her. Away from the busy court and the chambers of the unhappy Anne Boleyn, the small, quiet, fair-haired woman suddenly seemed very desirable. Ambition played little part in Jane's acceptance of the King's advances. More likely, her will—never strong because it had been rarely challenged—became almost at once sub-servient to the overpowering personality of Henry Tudor. Jane Seymour was also human enough to be fearful; one did not disdain a King's advances with impunity, and she could clearly see—for she was far from stupid—that Anne's days were numbered and her influence gone. Jane had been deeply sympathetic to the dead Catherine and was openly fond of the Princess Mary, a fact relished by Chapuys, who wrote to the Emperor, 'I will endeavour by all means to make her continue in this vein.'[20] If her lack of scruple in preparing for a wedding while her former Queen languished in the Tower awaiting execution leaves something to be desired in Jane's character, there were many willing to overlook the delicate situation, and they optimistically encouraged any small spark of ambition in Henry's new favourite. She was regarded by the Catholic and Imperial parties as a reliable cat's-paw with whom they hoped a rebel King might be brought back into the fold—one who would help halt further political and religious destruction and, in so doing, strengthen the claim of Mary Tudor as the true successor to the Crown.

For his part, Henry was well pleased with his new Queen. The tranquillity she brought to his days, her unquestioning acceptance of his actions or motives, was a happy change from the turbulent Anne. Her dependability, docility, and trust beguiled the King, encouraging in Henry a unique protectiveness. It is revealed in a letter sent to Jane while Anne was still in the Tower, in which he tells her of 'a ballad made lately of great derision against us, which if it go abroad and is seen by you, I pray you to pay no manner of regard to it. I am not at present informed who is the setter forth of this malignant writing; but if he is found out, he shall be straitly punished for it. . . .'[21] He and Anne would have roared with laughter over the slanderous ballad; Jane must be shielded. Since he wished a wife whose virtue was irre-proachable, there had been no assults on her honour, no improprieties in their relationship, other than the regrettable exigency of promoting his suit while one Queen was alive. He had had one wife labelled a whore; his new wife would come to the throne as unblemished as when he found her, even if somewhat tarnished in his subjects' eyes for her haste in marrying so soon after Anne's execution.

With his boundless capacity for self-pity and self-justification, Henry was aware of his subjects' opinion regarding his quick remarriage and, therefore, was the first to approve when Audley, now Chancellor of England, went to great lengths to justify the wedding. In Parliament, Audley stated, 'Ye will remember the great anxieties and perturbations which our invincible sovereign suffered on account of his first unlawful marriage; so all ought to bear in mind the perils and dangers he was under when he contracted his second marriage, and that the Lady Anne and her 'complices have since been found guilty of high treason, and had met their due reward for it. What man of middle life would not this deter from marrying a third time? Yet this, our most excellent prince, again condescendeth to contract matrimony, and hath, on the humble petition of the nobility, taken to himself a wife this time whose age and fine form give promise of issue.'[22]

Parliament also obligingly repealed the Act of Succession which had made Elizabeth heiress-presumptive, and she was not declared illegitimate as Mary had been before her. In an unprecedented action, Henry retained the right to dispose of the Crown of England as he saw fit, if Jane had no children. Otherwise, it was entailed upon her issue. Sir John Russell summed up the court's opinion of the marriage. 'She is as gentle a lady as ever I knew, and as fair a Queen as any in Christendom; the King has come out of hell into heaven for the gentleness in this and the cursedness and unhappiness in the other.'[23]

Jane Seymour's motto was 'Bound to Obey and Serve'. This she did with a passiveness that delighted the King whose whole matrimonial experience had been with an obstinate first wife and a demanding second one. 'The most virtuous and veriest gentlewoman that liveth'[24] suited Henry in every way, and court and country settled back with a prayer for divine blessing that a son might come to the man whose only surviving children now were two illegitimate daughters, one nearly twenty and one not quite three.

With Henry's marriage to Jane Seymour, there was a hopeful upsurge of confidence that the King would now relent in his harsh treatment of his eldest daughter. Jane had always been devoted to Mary, and she sent the girl a friendly message and a gift of money. Knowing how deeply his subjects resented the Princess Mary's exile, she urged Henry to bring Mary to court, to reinstate the girl in his affections. But Henry could not restore any honours to Mary if she refused to swear to the Act of Succession. He roughly told Jane her own children should be more important than his bastard daughter. The new Queen received the news in silence and, true to her motto, said no more on the subject. Should she have a son, the issue would soon be resolved once and for all.

Mary was still at Hunsdon, in the household of the baby Elizabeth, when her father remarried. With the lack of logic which had so characterized her mother, Mary reasoned that now that 'the Lady' was gone, so were 'the troubles', and the stress of her own position would be alleviated now that Henry had a new Queen. She had received Lady Kingston and heard Anne's penitent request for forgiveness. It was not in Mary to be malicious; gently she thanked Lady Kingston for her kindness, making no comment on Anne at all. It was through Lady Kingston that she obtained some writing materials, and encouraged by Jane Seymour's gestures of friendship, she wrote to Cromwell:

Master Secretary,

I would have been a suitor to you before this time, to have been a means for me to the King's Grace, my father, to have obtained his Grace's blessing and favour, but I perceived that nobody durst speak for me *as long as that woman lived* which is now gone (whom I pray God of His mercy to forgive). Wherefore, now she *is* gone, I am bolder to write to you, as one which taketh you for one of my chief friends. And therefore, I desire you for the love of God to be a suitor to me of the King's Grace, to have his blessing and licence [leave] to write unto his Grace, which shall be of great comfort to me, as God knoweth, who have you ever more in His holy keeping.

Moreover, I must desire you to accept mine evil writing, for I have not done so much for this two years or more, nor could have had the means to do it at this time, but my Lady Kingston's being here. At Hunsdon, 26th of May,

By your loving friend,

Mary,[25]

It was a beginning. The long process by which father and daughter were to be reunited was begun, but it was not to be made easy for the rebellious Mary. Cromwell obtained leave for her to write to the King, earning Mary's gratitude. She urged him to 'continue in his good offices till it may please his Grace to permit her to approach to his presence. . . .' With this note to Cromwell, she enclosed the first letter to her father in several years, a letter remarkable for its servile tone in which 'in as humble and lowly a manner as is possible', she asked her father for pity and forgiveness, promising to 'submit me in all things to your goodness and pleasure.' Mary asked her father to 'consider that I am but a woman and your child, who hath committed her soul only to God and her body to be so ordered in this world as it shall stand with your pleasure. . . .' Her regard for Jane Seymour was obvious in her mention of the 'comfortable tidings concerning the marriage which is between your Grace and the Queen' and she asked her father 'to be so good and gracious lord and father to me as to give me leave to wait upon the Queen. . . .'[26]

The letter indicates Mary had reached a point in her own mind where any action, other than the assumption of the Oath itself, was possible. Having in no way abandoned her own convictions or offered any slight to her conscience she ended her letter, calling upon Henry's sympathy and paternal pride. She told her father that to 'come into your presence . . . ever hath and shall be the greatest comfort that I can have within this world, having also a full hope in your Grace's natural pity, which you have always used as much or more, than any prince christened. . . .'

Mary's letters were received at a court busy with tiltings, masques, and festive junketings. Lamp-lit barges carried lavishly dressed courtiers and their ladies from one noble mansion to another. There were joyous water pageants on the Thames, and Chapuys wrote: 'I hear that on one occasion, returning by the river to Greenwich, the royal barge was actually filled with minstrels and musicians . . . playing on all sorts of instruments. . . .'[27] When Cromwell informed the King of Mary's penitent attitude, Henry professed himself pleased. But he had not waited two years for her submission to be reconciled now with a few servile words. He knew his people looked to Mary as a symbol of the 'old ways', as a rallying point around which any rebellious Papist factions at home, or enemies abroad, might choose to challenge his supremacy. Mary was now in the same difficult position as her mother had been. But Catherine, even when she knew many would have come to her aid, had refused to consent to actions which might result in civil war or any invasion in her defence. Mary might be used by these same radicals who had much to gain by such an insurrection. The King, therefore, was determined to use every means within his power, including force if necessary, to compel Mary to renounce her birthright. Such an admission on the part of his elder daughter would, in turn, render his enemies helpless. Henry resolved to let reconciliation wait.

During this time without any word from her father, Mary became distraught. Anxious days brought a recurrence of the severe headaches she had previously suffered and, to complicate her nervous condition further, there was a flare-up of a painful toothache. While she lay sleepless in her lonely chamber, her mind revolved confusedly around the problem—how best to extricate herself from the humiliating position without stigmatising her birth, refuting her mother's marriage, and offending God by taking an Oath that renounced all she felt to be just and true. She waited in dread suspense for word from court. There was little to intrude upon her days to relieve her anxiety. No callers, entertainment, or other diversions helped mitigate the stress. The

[67]

household staff pointedly left her alone, aware of the pressure being brought to bear on her.

After an agonising week, Mary wrote once more to Cromwell for his favour, saying 'that she took him for her chief friend next to God and the Queen'. But suspecting that neither Cromwell's nor Jane's influence was enough, she again wrote humbly to her father, asking for 'mercy and forgiveness for mine offences to your Majesty'. Mary reminded her father of the permission she had been given to write to him and said, 'yet shall my joy never return perfectly to me, nor my hope be satisfied, until such time as it may please your Grace sensibly to express your gracious forgiveness to me. . . .' Mary was explicit; she wanted word from him—some proof of her father's forgiveness. In the flickering candlelight she wrote hurriedly, the pen scratching across the page, telling the King that to 'penetrate an access to your presence' would 'of all worldly things be to me most joyous and comfortable.'[28]

The answer, however, was not quite what she expected. Cromwell devised a draft urging *unconditional submission* to the King's wishes, and he suggested she sign it immediately. Mary was frantic; she could sense the pressure of the demand and the enormity of what she was being asked to do. She signed the draft, after altering the phraseology and inserting 'Next to Almighty God' which removed a good deal of the sting. The draft was forwarded to Cromwell and with it a plea that 'Wherefore, I desire for the passion which Christ suffered for you and me, and as my very trust in you, that you will find such means through your great wisdom, *that I be not moved to agree to any further entry into the matter than I have done.* For I assure you by the faith that I owe to God, I have done the uttermost that my conscience will suffer me and I do neither desire nor intend to do less than I have done. But if I be put to any more (I am plain with you as with my great friend), my said conscience will in no way suffer me to consent thereto. . . .' And then Mary's gallant and heroic effort to maintain her integrity in the face of royal pressure collapsed as she ended fearfully '. . . I would not have troubled you so much at this time, but that the end of your letter caused me a little to fear that I shall have more business hereafter. . . .'[29]

Henry's patience exploded when he saw Mary's changes in the draft, and Cromwell, fearful now for himself as well as for Mary, devised a second copy. When he received nothing that would satisfy the King, he knew the time had come for stricter measures. A commission consisting of the Duke of Norfolk, the Earl of Sussex, and the Bishop of Chichester, arrived at Hunsdon unannounced, with a list of articles for Mary to sign. If she refused, legal action would be taken against her. There was no mistaking the intent. She was to sign; otherwise, imprisonment and possibly death would follow.

It was now some six months since Mary's mother had died and some five weeks since her father's remarriage. Dressed in her heavy black mourning, her face white, drawn, the eyes ringed by sleeplessness and discomfort, the furrow in her forehead deepened by anxiety, she faced the gentlemen of the court. Many she had known since birth. She had been bullied unmercifully for several years, and the accounts of the sufferings of those who had defied the King and his Council, the rackings, hangings, beheadings, and burnings, the suppression of many Holy Orders, were vivid in her mind. But even so, she met the Council's demands with as much courage and dignity as she could muster. She refused to acknowledge her mother's marriage as incestuous, her own birth illegitimate, or to admit that Henry was Supreme Head of the Church. She stood her ground even when the commissioners threateningly cried that she was 'an unnatural daughter'. 'If you were mine, or any man's daughter', Norfolk cried, 'I would beat you to death and knock your head against the wall till it was as soft as a baked apple!'[30] Four days in which to change her mind were all the bishops allowed. Then, as Lady Shelton took up the abuse of the now trembling Mary, they left.

Mary Tudor's submission to her father's will now became the principal aim of King, minister, and Council. Cromwell wasted little time in advising the girl of the reaction to her refusal, and in the same letter his renunciation of her is plain:

Madame,

I have received your letter whereby it appeareth you be in great discomfort and so desire that I should find the means to speak with you. How great soever your discomfort is, it can be no greater than mine who hath, upon [the receipt] of your letter spoken so much of your repentance, for your wilful obstinacy against the King's highness, and of your humble submission in all things, without exception or qualification, to obey his pleasure and laws, and knowing *how diversely and contrarily you proceeded at the late being of His Majesty's council with you*, I am as much ashamed of what I have said as afraid of what I have done, inasmuch as what the sequel thereof shall be God knoweth. . . .

Cromwell then proceeded to say that Mary's persistent refusal would only 'undo yourself and all who have wished you good. . . .' He said that contempt of Henry's laws was punishable by death, and if she continued, 'it were a great pity ye be not made an example in punishment . . .,' ending, 'Wherefore, Madam, to be plain with you, as God is my witness, I think you the most obstinate and obdurate woman, all things considered, that ever was. . . .'

With the letter had come what Cromwell called 'a certain book of articles.' To it, Mary was to subscribe her name, and once done, he,

Cromwell, 'would venture to speak for your reconciliation' with her father. The letter then continues:

But, if you will not speedily leave off all your sinister counsels, which have brought you to the point of utter undoing without remedy, I take my leave of you forever, and desire that you will never write or make means to me hereafter, for I shall never think otherwise of you than as the most ungrateful person to your dear and benign father. I advise you to nothing; but I beseech God never to help me if I know it not to be your bounden duty, by God's laws and man's laws. . . .[31]

At the receipt of what she could only view as the ultimatum in her long ordeal, Mary was terrified. She realised the finality of Cromwell's attitude; his patience, too, was gone. She could not blame him. He could hardly continue his efforts on her behalf without some tangible co-operation from her. To do so would only endanger his own position. There was no one—no King, Council, minister, or governess—to whom she could turn. Her mother was gone and in her place a new Queen who offered friendship and love, but only on her father's terms. Sick in body, distraught in mind, and utterly beaten in spirit, she wondered if she had the strength or the capacity for martyrdom. And as she considered such a possible fate, what few natural feelings of survival remained in her rose in rebellion: she was young, she had much to live for, and, incredibly, she still loved her father. She had not seen him for nearly five years, except at a distance. Her isolation in the hostile household of the child Elizabeth had led her into a degradation shameful for one of her high birth. Her whole spirit cried out for release and a return to her father's affection and some semblance of normal life. There was no mother now to be wounded by any submission; the only danger was to Mary herself, and then only if she persisted. Chapuys, to whom nothing was secret, counselled submission, realising the awful penalty if she did not. He was persuasive: if Henry had no son, she would be Queen when the King died. She was England's one hope—she *must* stay alive. He softened his advice by giving Mary a protest which she must sign acknowledging the pressure exerted on her, and he promised to use it to gain absolution from the Pope.

When she had prayed for guidance, her natural common sense asserted itself. She had done all she could. In good conscience, no one could ask more of her. She must try to see the issue with some degree of objectivity, even though her inborn sense of justice might be outraged. She wrote to Cromwell, 'because you have exhorted me to write to his Grace again, and I cannot devise what I should write more, but your own last copy, without adding or minishing, therefore, I do send you, by this bearer, my servant, the same word for word, and it is unsealed, because I cannot endure to write another copy, for the pain in my head and teeth hath troubled me so sore these two or three days . . . that I have very small rest day or night. . . .'[32] Wearily she took Cromwell's hated document and, without reading it, scrawled her name in the places he had marked.

The Lady Mary's Submission

The confession of me, the Lady Mary, made upon certain points and articles underwritten, in the which, as I do now plainly and with all mine heart confess and declare mine inward sentence, belief, and judgment, with a due conformity of obedience to the laws of the realm, so minding forever to persist and continue in this determination, without change, alteration, or variance, I do most humbly beseech the King's highness, my father, whom I have obstinately and *inobediently* offended in the denial of the name heretofore, to forgive mine offences therein, and to take me to his most gracious mercy.

First, I confess and acknowledge the King's Majesty to be my sovereign lord and King, in the Imperial Crown of this realm of England, and to submit myself to his highness, and to all and singular laws and statutes of this realm, as becometh a true and faithful subject to do, which I shall obey, keep, observe, advance, and maintain, according to my bounden duty, with all the power, force, and qualities that God hath imbued me during my life.

(signed)

Marye

Item: I do recognise, accept, take, reput, and acknowledge the King's highness to be Supreme Head in Earth, under Christ, of the Church of England, and do utterly refuse the Bishops of Rome's pretended authority, power, and jurisdiction within this realm heretofore usurped according to the laws and statutes made in that behalf, and of all the King's true subjects humbly received, admitted, obeyed, kept, and observed; and also do utterly renounce and forsake all manner of remedy, interest, and advantage which I may by any means claim by the Bishop of Rome's laws, process, jurisdiction, or sentence, at this present time or in any wise hereafter, by any manner, title, colour, mean, or case that is, shall, or can be devised for that purpose.

(signed)

Marye

[71]

Item: I do freely, frankly, and for the discharge of my duty towards God, the King's highness, and his laws, without other respect, recognise, and acknowledge that the marriage heretofore had between his Majesty and my mother, the late Princess-Dowager, was by God's law and man's law, incestuous and unlawful.[33]

(signed)

Marye

It was eleven o'clock at night in the mean little chamber at Hunsdon when Mary signed the dread articles. She was quite alone, as she had been for years. The King and Council had done their work well. The submission of the Lady Mary was complete and the way was open now for a return to court, to the King's affection, to an honourable life such as she had known before. But it would be different. Because when she signed away her birthright, her conscience, and her honour, in fear and in despair, Mary Tudor entered a life as foreign to her nature as it would have been to her mother. In effect, in signing the Articles of Submission, she saved her life but surrendered her soul. Life in England as she was to know it in the future would never be the same as it had been in her more peaceful past. And the Lady Mary, once more a Princess, would never be the same again either.

Chapter Four

WHILE Mary Tudor was undergoing her ordeal, another change was taking place at the manor of Hunsdon which concerned Anne Boleyn's child, Elizabeth. Henry had not seen his younger daughter since she had been brought to Greenwich shortly before Anne's death. While the King honeymooned with Jane Seymour and attended to the more important business of Mary's submission, the child Elizabeth and the household at Hunsdon had received little attention. Money was in short supply, and with small supervision from Council, King, or minister, those in command grew lax.

Elizabeth's governess, Lady Bryan, struggled as long as she could with what she privately considered outrageous conditions and, when even the servants became undisciplined, wrote to Cromwell for advice and support. She reminded him that she had served Princess Mary as a child in the same capacity as she was now serving Elizabeth. However, Elizabeth was no longer the heiress-presumptive, but merely the bastard child of an executed Queen. Lady Bryan was frank to say in her letter that since Elizabeth was 'put from that degree she was afore, and what degree she is at now, I know not but by hearsay; therefore, I know not how to order her, nor myself, nor none of hers that I have the rule of, that is, her women and her grooms. . . .' Her bewilderment was followed by a more prosaic appraisal of Elizabeth's material needs. The child's wardrobe had become depleted and, since she was growing fast, obviously required replacements. Lady Bryan requested:

. . . and that she may have some raiment, for she hath neither gown nor kirtle, nor petticoat, nor no manner of linen for smocks, nor kerchiefs, nor sleeves, nor rails [nightgowns], nor body stitchets [corsets], nor handkerchiefs, nor mufflers [mob caps], nor biggens [nightcaps]. All these her Grace must take, I have driven off as long as I can, that by my troth, I cannot drive it no longer! . . .

She beseeched Cromwell to take some action with Henry or the Council to find out 'what is the King's Grace's pleasure and yours; that I shall do in everything.' She then unburdened herself of her distaste for the conditions in the household, especially as they affected the young Elizabeth.

Mr Shelton, a relative of Anne Boleyn, had been a minor figure at Hunsdon, unnoticed until the death of the Queen when he attempted to assert some unwanted authority over Elizabeth's establishment, much to Lady Bryan's disgust. She complained to Cromwell that when he 'saith he is master of the household, what fashion that may be I cannot tell, for I have not seen it afore!' She asked Cromwell's help, a decision to 'see the house honourably ordered, as it hath ever been aforetime', saying dryly that if Shelton is to have charge, 'I fear it will be hardly enough performed.' Then her exasperation with the man whose arrogant meddling had caused so much dissension at Hunsdon exploded in indignation. From Lady Bryan's letter it can be seen that, given half a chance, Elizabeth was already asserting her independence in even so small a matter as choosing her own food from the table:

My lord, Mr Shelton, would have my Lady Elizabeth to dine and sup every day at the board of estate [the main common meal which all attended]. Alas! my lord, it is not meet for a child of her age, to keep such rule yet. I promise you, my lord, I dare not take it upon me to keep her Grace in health, and she keep that rule, for there she shall see divers meats and fruits and wine, which would be hard for me to refrain her Grace from it. Ye know, my lord, there is no place of correction there. And she is yet too young to correct greatly. I know well and she be there, I shall neither bring her up to the King's Grace's honour, nor hers, nor to her health nor my poor honesty. . . .

The good lady went on to plead with Cromwell that Elizabeth be allowed a 'mess of meat to her own lodging, with a good dish or two, that is meet for her to eat of . . . according as my Lady Mary's Grace had afore. . .' She explained Elizabeth 'hath great pain with her teeth, and they come very slowly forth, and causeth me to suffer her Grace to have her will more than I would have. . . .' From this letter, it is plain that Elizabeth had already found a warm place in Lady Bryan's affections. Conscientious in her desire that the child be well taken care of, gently disciplined, and still be a credit to her care, the kind woman could not resist putting in a good word for the innocent girl—a courageous, considerate and gracious gesture, in view of the recent execution of the mother and the continuing disinterest of the father: '. . . and so I trust the King's Grace shall have great comfort in her Grace. *For she is as toward a child and as gentle of conditions as ever I knew any in my life.* Jesu preserve her Grace!' [1]

Elizabeth Tudor, at three, was without doubt an endearing child. Her colouring was vivid; she had the olive skin and magnificent wide grey-black eyes of her mother and the glowing mop of red hair, reminiscent of Henry's sister, Mary Tudor, the 'Tudor rose'. The pointed oval face of Anne Boleyn was sweetly childish in Elizabeth. Like her mother, she had beautiful hands of which, even at three, she had heard praised enough to be vain. Her appetite and enjoyment of her food and the sweetmeats she begged daily from the servants were hearty in one so young, and consequently she was a well-formed, healthy, appealing little girl, whose whole forthright manner and uninhibited behaviour could beguile or irritate, according to her mood. While very much aware she was a Princess and her father a King, she had lived in a household free from much of the ritual and etiquette to which she would have been constantly exposed at court. At Hunsdon everyone adored Elizabeth, a fact she understood and encouraged.

Her charm was largely the magnetism of Henry coupled with the precocious awareness of her own compelling personality that had been so integral a part of Anne Boleyn. She was highly intelligent, loving, though far from meek, and wise enough even at her young age to be responsive to the mood of others. She could only vaguely remember her mother; Anne had seen little of her child during the last year of her life. But she could conjure up Henry at any time—a large man with a red beard, a loud voice, and a hearty laugh. His scowl could send delicious shivers down her small back, but she could rarely resist the opportunity, whenever it came her way, to see if she couldn't transform the scowl into a smile. She loved her governess with a guileless affection; instinctively she knew she could always depend upon Lady Bryan.

Her sister, Mary, was a different matter. Elizabeth was puzzled by her older sister. She had soon sensed that, for some reason, many of the others in the household disliked Mary. They talked about her behind her back, stopping short in their conversation when Elizabeth appeared. She knew Mary had done *something*—that the King and his gentlemen were very angry with her. Even in the nursery, she had heard the harsh words they had spoken to her sister the last time they had visited Hunsdon. Elizabeth would have liked to be friendly with Mary and depend on her as she did on Lady Bryan. But Mary was often shut up in her chamber, weeping and refusing to see anyone. Elizabeth had decided that although she liked Mary, she didn't feel very comfortable with her, for Mary was undependable. When she went to Mary's room, Elizabeth never knew whether she would be brusquely asked to leave, for Mary might be busily writing her never-ending letters or perhaps just lying on her bed with one of her headaches or toothaches. Elizabeth could appreciate the pain of a toothache and she would have liked to stay and comfort Mary, as Lady Bryan comforted her when *her* teeth hurt. But one did not approach Mary that easily. Elizabeth also knew that Mary's mother had just died, and Mary was old enough to have known and loved her mother well. Elizabeth decided that although her own mother had also died, she was glad she had not known her so well, for then she would have had to be sad, too.

And life, it seemed, if one knew what one was doing, didn't have to be sad. She now had a new stepmother, Queen Jane, Mary had told her, and soon they might all be returning to court. It was exciting to think of being the centre of attention again, of having new smocks to wear, and perhaps even a new cap with a small jewel in it! There would be picnics in the woods outside the City and perhaps a ride in the royal barge on the Thames to that glorious red-brick palace down at Greenwich where Lady Bryan and she might peep through the shrubbery and watch her father and the knights jousting in the tiltyard. Her father! *That* would be the best of all. She would see the King again, and this time—no doubt of it—she *would* make him smile.

Mary Tudor also had hoped the King would smile at *her* once more. She reasoned that, since she had obeyed her father, she would magically be restored to the King's affections and to her rightful place at court. Everything would be as it had been years before. She might even be escorted on her return by a procession of lords and bishops much as she remembered from the time before 'the troubles'. She was anxious to see her father and his new wife who was her friend—to be away forever from the environment at Hunsdon that had been so much a part of her misery during the past few years.

The reunion between Mary and her father, however, was accompanied by no blast of trumpets heralding the once-disgraced Princess back to a paternal embrace. Instead, some three weeks after her submission—weeks spent in anxious waiting—an apprehensive Mary was summoned quite casually to a small manor house at Hackney where, said Chapuys, 'the kindness of the King was inconceivable, regretting that he had been so long separated from her. He made good amends for it in the little time he was with her, continually talking with her with every sign of affection, and with ever so many fine promises. The Queen gave her a beautiful diamond, and the King about a thousand crowns in money for her pleasures, telling her to have no anxiety about money, for she should have as much as she could wish.'[2] Henry promised to restore her household to some semblance of rank and comfort, and in the next few weeks, the hated Sheltons left. The return of her favourites —Mary Brown, Margaret Baynton, and Susan Clarencieux—soon followed. Randall Dodd, a Welshman devoted to Mary, had gone to

Calais when deprived of his position in her household. To Mary's joy, he and Anthony Roke, who had served Queen Catherine before her exile, now appeared at Hunsdon. In addition, there were four gentle-women, a physician, four gentlemen, two chamberers, a chaplain, five yeomen, four grooms of the chamber, one footman, four grooms of the stable, a laundress, and a woodbearer.[3] An exultant Mary welcomed them happily; there was much rejoicing at Hunsdon as those long separated from their mistress were reunited.

Cromwell, who had become the Lord Privy Seal, was relieved that Mary had at long last restored herself in her father's favour when he had considered her (and possibly herself) all but lost. He sent Mary a horse, earning her grateful thanks. 'I have never a one to ride upon sometimes for my health, and besides that, my servant showeth me that he is such a one that I may of right accept not only the mind of the giver, but also the gift,'[4] she wrote to the minister. Life at Hunsdon was now miraculously changed; the joy in the household was infectious, engulfing the small Elizabeth and the kindly Lady Bryan in its warmth. Often, now, Mary found herself spontaneously hugging her young red-haired sister dressed in her bright new clothes. While riding her new horse, she would place the child square in the saddle with her and then, holding Elizabeth securely, canter slowly around the courtyard, as Elizabeth clutched the horse' mane, crying to the servants to come and watch her.

So the days passed. If at times, especially when she was not feeling well, Mary grew nostalgic, she tried to put any unhappy thoughts from her mind. But there were moments when the sunshine of summer was dispelled in a quick pall of rain. She and Lady Bryan would scurry to the quickly dampened chambers where the servants were busily lighting fires. Then suddenly the memory of experiencing a similar moment with her mother would overwhelm her with an almost unbearable clarity. She would try to dismiss it, but the sense of in-justice, of a deeply buried resentment and anger, lingered. Others in the household were aware of these melancholy moments and they tried to cheer her, withdrawing only when Mary asked to be alone. She would then shut herself firmly in her chamber. There she would remember and try to draw comfort from Chapuys' repeated admonition—that she had acted in the best possible way and taken the only course open. Her protest had gone to the Pope, and Chapuys was sure she would receive absolution. He had warned her again and again that she must 'not dissemble' with the King or his Council. If Henry had no son, she, the Princess Mary, was heir, and she 'would set many things right by her good sense'. Chapuys advised her to use to good advantages the opportunities resulting from her submission. So, she would resolutely write her father a long letter, full of her joy at receiving 'his gracious mercy and fatherly pity', telling the King she had been 'almost lost in mine own folly', but now he must consider her 'as your most humble and obedient child and subject'.[5]

And then, remembering her own neglect at the time of her mother's disgrace, she considered Elizabeth. The little girl was now as vulnerable as Mary once had been, although, thankfully, much too young to comprehend the situation or suffer rejection by a beloved parent. Elizabeth was proud of her father, mostly that he was a King; Mary could smile at the child's pride. But she also knew too well how swiftly the King's fancy could change. He had had little opportunity to know Elizabeth as well as he had known his first daughter in her earlier years; the child might be unnecessarily hurt. However, Mary knew her father's pride in his children could be touched. If she could help Elizabeth avoid the King's disdain, it would be only honourable to do so. Without any hesitation, Mary ended her letter to her father, saying,

My sister, Elizabeth, is in good health (thanks to our Lord) and such a child towards, as I doubt not, but your Highness shall have cause to rejoice of in time coming (as knoweth Almighty God), Who send your Grace, with the Queen my good mother, health, with the accomplishment of your desires. . . .[6]

If ever there was an example of Mary Tudor's selflessness, it is in these words that derive from her own bitter experience—words that seek to avoid for her younger sister the terrible penalty of a father's abandonment. In praising Elizabeth, Mary was also risking the King's displeasure for championing the child of his executed Queen. Her praise of Elizabeth, her appeal to Henry's interest, was a gesture of sympathy, courage, and graciousness. When one remembers that this thoughtfulness and consideration were being exercised for Anne Boleyn's daughter who had, indirectly, been the cause of her own suffering, Mary's compassion seems almost unbelievable.

In 1536, Henry VIII was forty-five years old. The 'very well-proportioned body of tall stature' had thickened; small broken veins showed in his face and neck. Earlier in the year, on a frosty morning in the tiltyard at Greenwich, he had fallen from his horse and remained unconscious for more than two hours. Reluctantly, he had accepted the fact that participation in the vigorous sports he so loved would have to be curtailed and, in a moment of surprising frankness, even told Chapuys he was beginning to 'feel old'. The chronic ulcer on the 'sorre legge' often tormented him, and this, combined with the restriction of his exercise, resulted in a petulance unusual in a man whose disposition was normally pleasant. He now had time to ponder more deeply the changes in his realm, his relationship with his subjects, his Council, and his children.

The year had wrought irrevocable changes in England and its prestige abroad. Two Queens had died, one by the shameful process of public beheading. Two daughters had been bastardized, and the Duke of Richmond, Henry's beloved seventeen-year-old illegitimate son by Bessie Blount, had also died. By consent of Parliament, Henry had the right to dispose of the Crown, but to whom could he bequeath it if Jane did not give him a son? The King knew his people almost unanimously favoured Mary, and he had tried, in several private talks with her, to discern her true feelings regarding her submission, a submission Henry suspected to be a mere outward compliance masking a strong inward dissension. Mary was Catherine of Aragon's daughter, after all, and while the King knew he had browbeaten her into a kind of obedience, the ideals and conviction of his former Queen were undoubtedly just as strong in her child. He was genuinely fond of the girl. Obtaining her submission, rather than ordering a wanton persecution, had been of prime political importance, and the King would have happily welcomed a frank discussion. But it was obvious the troubled years of her abandonment and her recent humiliating ordeal had made an undeniable difference in their relationship. Mary had been an idealistic, trusting child of fifteen when her mother's exile began; she was an embittered, prematurely aged, resentful young woman of twenty when she acceded to the royal will. Moreover, she was still the hope of the strong Catholic and Imperialistic Party and, bastardised or not, ever a potential source of anxiety to her father.

The King's troubles, which had started with the fall from his horse, were acute by the autumn of 1536. The plague had come to England that summer, sending many of the court fleeing from the diseased City and postponing any coronation for Jane. Francis and Charles were still grappling in Italy, leaving the King of England relatively free of foreign entanglements, although loudly proclaiming to the Continent his desire to be a benevolent mediator on their behalf. At home, his own domestic situation had deteriorated. The death of Catherine, the execution of Anne Boleyn, his early remarriage, and the doubtful status of their beloved Princess Mary had had a debilitating effect on the morale of the people of England. And the final issue which brought Englishmen to rebellion and open revolt was the wholesale suppression and ultimate destruction of the monasteries.

The religious houses of England from the smallest monastery housing a few monks to the great abbeys such as Fountains, Jervaulx, Kirkstead, and Bridlington which maintained hundreds, had for many years been an integral and influential part of English life. The great religious orders, such as the Carthusians and the Franciscans, provided opportunities for inspiration, learning, and study in the arts and were a haven and sanctuary for the sincere religious advocate. Qualifications for entry into these orders were demanding and the routine of the life austere. The character of each house was often a direct reflection of the Abbot, or other head, who governed it. Thus a few were grossly overstaffed, housing members of questionable character, where learning was absent and religious study a mere excuse for luxurious living. But the majority provided inspiring examples of selflessness, moral living, and service. They dispensed free meals to the poor and hospitality to the traveller (a necessity in a land where inns or lodging houses as such were few). They gave liberally of their funds for educating the young and for medical care of the aged, sick, and poor. Above all, they provided places where those with the desire might live and study in peace, worship God in privacy, and serve their fellow men.

The initial inspiration and guiding force behind the suppression and ultimate dissolution of the monasteries was the King's new Vicar-General and Lord Privy Seal, Thomas Cromwell, and was the means by which he hoped to fill England's empty treasury. The wealth of the Roman Church in England had always exceeded the Crown's. In 1536, by royal decree, an appraisal was to be made of each religious house by a personal visit of qualified commissioners. In the past, such visitations had been made by the Church at different intervals to judge the worth and the viability of their continued maintenance. Now, such supervision would be the responsibility of the Crown—a potent reminder to the clergy of its usurped authority.

The two instruments Cromwell used for his attack on the monasteries were the Oath of Supremacy and the Articles of Inquiry. Already many religious Orders had suffered, primarily because of their reluctance to regard the King as Supreme Head of the Church in England. The Observant Friars, a particular favourite of Queen Catherine, were suppressed; the leaders of the noble Carthusian Order had been hanged, drawn, and quartered in retribution for refusing to take the Oath. Many acceded in fear and bewilderment in the hope they might be left in peace. But others could not in conscience, and soon priests in their holy dress, hanging from the gibbet, became a common sight. Monks in chains, fettered and hobbled—the objects of derision to those who were pitiless, of pity and compassion to those who, even secretly, still professed loyalty to Rome—were left to wallow in their own filth and die of starvation.

Dr Richard Layton and Dr Thomas Legh were the commissioners who carried the Articles of Inquiry. By March, 1536, they had allegedly 'visited' some 2,000 houses which covered one-third of England, an impossible feat to accomplish thoroughly in seven months. Their haphazard inefficiency, their readiness to accept bribes, or to help themselves liberally to the churches' treasures, were accompanied by an insolent attitude to the houses' inmates; the brethren of one wrote after a 'visitation': 'He [Layton] handled the fathers very roughly.' On each such occasion, the Articles of Inquiry were read—articles sadly lacking in realism and objectivity, and that led many of the stunned inmates to believe (not without justification) that the desire for 'reform' was, really, a desire to impose a secular discipline which would destroy the monastic system itself.

The commissioners' report also dwelt with malice and prejudice on the alleged scandalous behaviour of monks and nuns. Undoubtedly a few of the institutions were mismanaged and often reflected the ill-educated, weak, and conscienceless majority of the inhabitants. But the all-inclusive condemnation of the majority of the religious houses by Legh and Layton was proven false when the monasteries were later permanently dissolved. The great and worthy monasteries of England were irreproachable institutions in which the religious lived lives of the highest character bearing out the statement of Cranmer's predecessor, the incorruptible Archbishop Warham, who declared 'there were few moral evils and certainly no widespread corruption.' After receiving the commissioners' reports, Parliament enacted bills that would lead ultimately to the destruction of many of the noblest Christian monuments in the world. But it did not happen easily. The bill which abolished 376 houses, threw 10,000 people on the land without shelter or living, and brought the Crown some £32,000 per year in revenues, was long debated in the House of Commons. Too long for Cromwell and the King. At last, Henry summoned the members and told them, in effect, he would 'have the Bill or he'd have their heads.' The nobles in Parliament were not as troubled. Scenting the rich monastery-owned lands which would become available, they were already petitioning Cromwell with requests for acres to be purchased or given them outright.

In addition to determining the worth of the monasteries, Henry also ventured, as Supreme Head of the Church, to give his people a form of religious definition worthy of the Defender of the Faith. In his Ten Articles, he upheld most of the dogma of the Catholic Faith: Baptism, Penance, and the Eucharist were necessary. Purgatory was abolished, although prayers for the dead were deemed commendable. Images were to be regarded as symbols, as 'representers of virtue and good example', but were not to be venerated. All the ceremonial ritual beloved of the people—the rich vestments, the holy water, the bells and lights—were to continue, again symbolically; they had no power to remit sin. Saints might be venerated, but were not to be used as intercessors. The doctrine of Transubstantiation was affirmed. While abolishing a few

[81]

religious holidays, especially those that induced idleness at harvest time, Henry's Ten Articles were not provocative. What outraged many of the clergy and the people, however, was that they had been issued by the King *instead* of the clergy.

The areas most affected by the suppression of the smaller religious houses were the remote northern provinces of Yorkshire and Lincolnshire. The people were troubled with the very real problems of enclosure of public lands, increased taxation, and the incessant interference and restriction by the Crown on liberties their ancestors had long enjoyed. The Northerners were apprehensive of the guidance the King received from Cranmer and Cromwell, and it was the latter's scheme for suppressing the smaller monasteries that provided a potent spark to the tinder box of resentment smouldering among them. Taxation, with commissioners poking their inquisitive noses into one's personal fortunes was one thing. Inquisition of the parish priest, abbot, or friar was odious but possibly necessary if abuses were to be kept to a minimum. Such inquisition, when applied to a monastery above reproach, however, bordered on persecution. When Cromwell's commissioners arrived to 'visit' a local religious house, to strip lead from roofs and dismantle bells, to loot the building of its valuable rood screen and ornaments, to note the value of the woods and fields surrounding the property, the temper of the Northerners flared. Rumours flew from village to village: that the King proposed to have all the gold in the country brought to the Tower of London; that smaller churches, stripped of their ornaments would be converted into one church 'for every seven or eight miles'; and that the buildings which were 'one of the beauties of the realm to the stranger passing through', where their ancestors lay in quiet, dim graveyards, were to be thoroughly despoiled.

On a cool October evening in the little village of Louth in Lincolnshire, the spark which was to end in the tragic Pilgrimage of Grace was kindled. The people gathered in the twilight on the village green and, with the great silver cross of the parish before them, marched through the streets in protest at the coming of John Heneage, one of Cromwell's examiners, to 'visit' the local church. They established a guard over the property, and when Heneage appeared the next morning, the people swarmed into the streets, protesting the injustice of the visit with loud voices and weapons. When Heneage attempted to read Cromwell's commission in the marketplace, a 'hideous clamour' broke out. The people bore down on the hapless man, tearing the book from his hand and threatening him with a sword at his breast; his companions were put into the stocks. Then, ironically swearing loyalty to the King, to the Commonwealth, and to the Holy Church which they revered, the good residents of Louth retired to their humble cottages unaware they had challenged Thomas Cromwell, the Vicar-General; Thomas Cranmer, the Archbishop of Canterbury; the King's Council, including some of the most powerful nobles in the realm; the Parliament and, in the end, the authority of Henry Tudor, King of England.

The Lincolnshire uprising spread quickly and, several days later, more than 40,000 men marched behind a banner proudly displaying the insignia of a Plough, a Horn, a Chalice and a Rose and the Five Wounds of Christ. A 'Pilgrimage of Grace', the insurgents called the movement. Articles demanding the restoration of the suppressed religious houses and of the churches' treasure, and the reinstatement of their festival days, were sent to the King by a people far removed from the intrigues and hypocrisy of the court. The people of the North—where action, not words, was the measure of the man—felt they had acted judiciously, and the movement subsided momentarily as they awaited the royal reaction.

It was not long in coming. Henry notified the good people of Lincolnshire that two armies had been mustered to 'invade their counties, to burn, spoil and destroy their goods, wives and children' unless they ceased all rebellious activity. The people heard their monarch's ringing denunciation: 'How presumptuous then are ye, the rude Commons of one shire, and that one of the most brute and beastly in the whole realm, and of least experience, to find fault with your Prince in the electing of his councillors and prelates. . . !' The King advised them 'withdraw yourselves to your own houses . . . cause the provokers of this mischief to be delivered to your lieutenant's hands or ours . . . and you yourselves submit to such condign punishment as we and our nobles shall think you worthy to suffer!'[7] In the light of the rebels' considered injustices, in their belief that a simple appeal to the King's goodness would bring an immediate remedy, the effect of Henry's proclamation must have been enlightening and disillusioning. Gibbets were erected in Louth, Horncastle, and Lincoln, and forty-six rebels were hanged to give emphasis to the King's decree.

But Henry's reponse did not quell the movement which now spread into Yorkshire, causing Henry and his Council to order further forces north to deal with the rebels. Jane Seymour, her traditionalist Catholic heart with the rebels, found the courage to fall on her knees to the King and beg him to 'restore the abbeys'. The Pilgrimage was a judgment on Henry's actions, she said. Roughly, the King told her to get up, tend to her own pursuits, and remember what had happened to her predecessor who had meddled in the country's affairs. Bound to obey and serve, Jane did as she was told.

The end was predictable. The leaders of the rebellion were executed in York and Hull where the Duke of Norfolk reported that one leader had been 'hung above the highest gate of the town, so trimmed in chaius that I think his bones will hang there this hundred years.' The noble seventy-year-old Lord Darcy, who had aided the rebels with arms, money, and advice, was taken to the Tower of London, where he protested any disloyalty to the King's person. 'An' I had seen my sovereign lord in the field,' he cried, 'and I had seen his Grace come against us, I would have lifted from my horse and taken my sword by point and yielded it into his Grace's hands.' While his feeling for the King was admirable, he had no such opinion of Cromwell. He told the King's Vicar-General to his face, 'Cromwell, it is thou that art the very original and chief causer of all this rebellion and mischief ... though thou wouldst procure all the noblemen's heads within the realm to be stricken off, yet shall there one head remain that shall strike off *thy* head!'[8]

Prophetic words and ones which must have seemed to Thomas Cromwell, now at the very height of his powers, the foolish ravings of an aged and fallen soldier. But—as time was to show—the very processes of destruction which had been initiated by the Vicar-General and approved by the King could be turned, even upon one as mighty as Thomas Cromwell.

The Pilgrimage of Grace, a civil insurrection in Henry's eyes, brought home to him the urgent need for an heir. By midsummer, Jane was pregnant, and the King could write that 'a humour has fallen into our legs', and because of the Queen's condition, 'it is thought we should not go further than sixty miles from her.' The rebellion and resulting executions had deeply distressed Jane Seymour. When Henry asked, 'how happeneth it you are not merrier?' Jane replied there were few at court she wished as companions and asked that the Lady Mary join her. Mary was duly summoned from Hunsdon and met the King and Queen at Richmond. It was the first time in several months that she had seen her father, and one courtier wrote of the meeting:

The King and the Queen were standing in the Chamber of Presence by the fire. This worthy lady, Mary, entered with all her train. So soon as she came within the chamber door, she made a low curtsey unto him; in the midst of the chamber she did so again, and when she came to him, she made them both a low curtsey, and falling on her knees, asked his blessing, who—after he had given her his blessing—took her up by the hand and kissed her, and the Queen also, both bidding her welcome. Then the King, turning him to the Lords there in presence, said, 'Some of you were desirous that I should put this jewel to death!'

'That had been a great pity,' quoth the Queen, 'to have lost your chiefest jewel of England. . . .'

'Nay! Edward! Edward!' quoth he, and clapped his hand on the Queen's belly. Then, upon these words, this good lady, not knowing that when her father flattered most, mischief was like to ensue, her colour going and coming, at last in a swoon fell down amongst them. With that, the King being greatly perplexed ... sought all means possible to recover her, and being come to herself, bid her be of good comfort, for nothing should go against her, and after a perfect recovery, took her by the hand, and walked up and down with her.[9]

As soon as Mary had regained her outward composure, Henry said she might have apartments at court where she would be near the Queen. 'She who did you so much harm and prevented me from seeing you for so long hath paid the penalty', the King gently told his anxious daughter.

The nation, court, Council, and King now awaited the birth of Jane Seymour's child. There were those greedy for the throne should she fail: the proud Norfolks; the kindred Douglasses and the Suffolk children; the arrogant Montagues and Poles with their Plantagenet blood. Henry's own niece, Frances Brandon, had married her Henry Grey and would soon give birth to a small girl—the ill-fated Lady Jane Grey.

The collective hopes of all who coveted the throne of England were blighted on October 12, 1537, the feast-day of St Wilfrid, when at two o'clock in the morning at Hampton Court Palace, after months of prayers to conceive and after three days and two nights of agonizing labour to deliver, Jane Seymour gave birth to a healthy child. A boy! Her long and painful labour was a dread concern to those who served her and had grown fond of the Queen. The news was abroad in London by daylight, and the City erupted in a frenzied reaction of joy and delight. Henry's overwhelming relief and thankfulness were mirrored by his subjects. By nightfall, bonfires blazed throughout the land with the joyous message that the House of Tudor at last had a living male heir.

All manner of celebration, brawling, and feasting in the streets—where, by royal decree, the wine flowed generously from conduits—gave ample evidence of the people's and sovereign's pleasure. The bells of St Paul's, pealing continuously, were soon joined by those of other City churches and a magnificent *Te Deum* was sung in the vast cathedral. Messengers rushed to carry the great tidings to all the cities in the realm, and envoys made ready to hurry abroad with impressive proclamations that a Tudor prince was born. 'The shooting of guns, all day and night, in the goodliest manner' from the Tower of London, proclaimed to the jubilant throngs gathered near the Palace to await the return of the King, the universal satisfaction that heralded the birth of Prince Edward. It all culminated in a splended christening held by torchlight on a cool autumn evening in the chapel at Hampton Court

Palace, where one may still see Jane Seymour's initials intertwined with those of her husband. Princess Mary, her plain honest face glowing with pleasure, proudly viewed the infant in the arms of Lady Exeter, as they stood under a canopy of gold supported by four noblemen. Edward Seymour, the Queen's brother, carried the small, red-haired Elizabeth, her grey-black eyes large with pride at being allowed to clutch the jewelled chrisom in her very own hands. She watched the three god-fathers—Thomas Cranmer, and then her mother's uncle, the Duke of Norfolk, and her own uncle, the Duke of Suffolk. Her grandfather, Thomas Boleyn, a towel round his neck, held a taper of virgin wax during the ceremony. She missed nothing of the scene: the massive silver font brought especially from Canterbury Cathedral, the heralding of the trumpets, the richly robed and befurred nobles standing nearby, the proud and imperial glance of her father, which bordered on a smile when he saw *her*. Her stepmother, she noticed, was lying on a pallet, holding the King's hand and looking weak and uncomfortable.

And then the lighting of the torches interrupted her reverie. The trumpets sounded and the Proclamation was read, 'God of His Almighty and Infinite Grace, give and grant good life and long to the right high, right excellent and noble prince, Prince Edward, Duke of Cornwall and Earl of Chester, most dearly entirely beloved son to our most dread and gracious lord, King Henry VIII. Largesse! Largesse! Largesse!'[10]

Another blast of trumpets and the young Prince was borne away to his mother's chamber, where a proud King held his infant son in his arms, tears of pure happiness coursing down his cheecks. Courtiers crowded into the room to offer their congratulations, and it was after midnight before the exhausted Queen was left alone. The next day she suffered a relapse and a high fever, finally receiving Extreme Unction. Though a brief rally sent hopes racing through the court, it was all in vain. On October 24, her duty to obey and serve finally complete in the delivery of a Prince, Jane Seymour died. Her son, Prince Edward, was less than two weeks old, and he was now as motherless as his sisters, Elizabeth and Mary.

Chapter Five

ONCE Jane was buried at Windsor, life at court resumed, though at a quieter pace. Henry returned to the Palace at Westminster and 'kept himself close a great while'. The King genuinely mourned his dead Queen, and Edward, for the moment, occupied the centre of his thoughts. The indispensable Lady Bryan was summoned with Elizabeth to Havering-atte-Bower in Essex where a household for the little Prince was established. Sir William Sidney was named chamberlain to 'have the keeping, oversight, care and cure of his Majesty's and the whole realm's most precious jewell, the Prince's Grace. . . .'[1] In addition to his wet-nurse, Sybilla Penn, there was his own personal physician, Dr George Owen, and numerous chamberlains, stewards, and other servants, including four rockers.

At Havering-atte-Bower, Lady Bryan received the King's instructions regarding the scrupulous sanitation required in and around the royal nursery, and lest there be any misunderstanding, Henry had set the orders out in his own hand. The Prince's food was to consist of 'all kinds of bread, meat, milk, eggs and butter . . .' and was to be 'elaborately tested and assayed' to avert the danger of poisoning. No one was to approach the royal cradle, no matter what his rank or degree, without authority from Henry himself. Everyone was to observe the strictest rules of hygiene: all beggars and sickly persons seeking alms or food were to be kept away from the palace gates under penalty of dire punishment. Every piece of the Prince's clothing was to be washed only by his own servants; every utensil used in the kitchens and every article from the chambers was to be scrubbed after use. Every hallway, chamber, reception room, inside court, and outside walk was to be swept daily, with pets confined to their kennels. Henry now had his heir, and there was to be no laxity about the Prince's safety. The threat of not only the King's wrath, but imprisonment or worse, emphasised Henry's determination to protect his son from accident, illness, or physical danger.

Periodically, all three young Tudors rejoined their father at Hampton

Court, Greenwich, or Richmond. During this time of Henry's bereavement, the King was as close to each of them as he was ever to be. He spent hours in the royal nursery where, on one occasion, he took Edward 'with much mirth and joy, dallying with the Prince in his arms a long space, and so holding him in a window to the sight and comfort of all the people.' Mary, who so adored children, loved the baby Edward and hardly needed the urging of her father to visit the Prince whenever the King himself was absent from court. Elizabeth was delighted with her small brother and begged to be allowed to visit too. She was too young to know the meaning of Parliament's action in illegitimatising her prior to the Prince's birth, but she sensed the change in status immediately. When told she was to be known simply as the 'Lady Elizabeth', she replied with a sting remarkable in a child of just four, '. . . and how hap it yesterday "Lady Princess" and today but "Lady Elizabeth"?'[2] Her early maturity was apparent even to those who saw her only occasionally. Thomas Wriothesley, later a chancellor of England, wrote: 'I went then to my Lady Elizabeth's Grace, and to the same made his Majesty's most hearty commendation, declaring that his Highness desired to hear of her health, and sent his blessing; she gave humble thanks, inquiring after his Majesty's welfare, and that with as great a gravity as she had been forty years old. . . .'[3]

But, for the moment, the centre of all attention was Prince Edward. Lord Chancellor Audley paid a visit to Havering-atte-Bower, later writing of Edward, 'I have never seen so goodly a child of his age, so merry, so pleasant, so good and loving countenance and so earnest . . . and it seemeth to me (thanks be to our Lord) His Grace increaseth well in the air that he is in. I cannot comprehend nor describe the goodly, towardly qualities that is in my lord Prince's Grace. He is sent of the Almighty God for all our comforts. My daily and continual prayer is, and shall be, for his good and prosperous preservation, and to make his Grace an old Prince. . . .'[4] Lady Lisle called him 'the goodliest babe that ever I set mine eyes upon . . . I think I should never weary of looking at him.' But visiting the royal nursery was expensive; it was traditional that gifts should be brought, and Lady Lisle apparently begrudged the cost, for she says it was 'the King's pleasure I should do so; howbeit it was costly unto me, for there is none cometh but they give great rewards. . . .'[5]

Following Jane's death, the King's older daughter, Mary Tudor, now in her middle twenties, had returned to a life at court where she had been genuinely welcomed by the many who had known and loved her since birth. But her happiest moments were those spent in her own household—at Hunsdon, Hatfield, or the more ponderous Hertford Castle. Her account books offer a fascinating glimpse of the only remaining peaceful years she was to know. They are a detailed record of her amusements, visitors, the customs of the royal household, and they even provide a record of Mary's illnesses. They disclose the method by which the kitchens were kept in fresh food and other necessities. Small sums, for instance, were given to 'a pore woman bringing apples to my Lady's Grace'. Eightpence went to Mistress Parry's servant for bringing 'qwynce payres', while seven shillings fetched 'partriches, larks, chese and phesants'. Similar small sums purchased 'a bottle of sack' or 'wine in a small vessel'. Strawberries were purchased at the gate 'at diverse times' for two shillings which also procured the cream for them; 'nutts and appels' costs a shilling. And someone with the quaint name of 'Typkin' brought 'cherys', receiving a shilling, the 'cherys' being made into a 'comfiture'.

The royal account books repeatedly emphasised that Mary's return to a normal life after her long restraint, whether in her own establishment or at court, was accompanied by all the pleasures, privileges, and responsibilities of one of her rank. The names of those who attended the household and its occupants abound: Mary Finch, who kept the accounts and was also custodian of the Princess's jewels, 'stood very high in her Mistress's favour' (despite the fact that the Princess often had to correct her additions). Randall Dodd, of whom Mary said that any favour extended to him 'is so thankfull to me that I accompte it done to myself' was the recipient of many of the Princess's indulgences. Philip Van Wilder, 'Philip the Luter', a musician of extreme competence, gave Mary music lessons. When his child was christened, the Princess made a gift to the nurse and presented his wife with a gold enamelled chain. 'Nicholas of the Stable', 'Parker's wife of the Buttery', or 'a Yeoman of the Guard for bringing a Leek on St David's Day'—all were remembered by the Princess with small monetary gifts.

The physicians who served her were special recipients of Mary's favour. A dentist 'sent by the King's Highness to draw her teeth' received fifteen angels of gold—roughly forty-five shillings. Dr William Butts, Henry's own personal physician, apparently aided Mary on one occasion during the 'the troubles', and, as soon as possible, twenty-two shillings and sixpence was sent to the good doctor 'by him lent to my Lady's Grace . When Dr George Owen, another royal physician attended Mary, he received not only his fee of ten pounds but also a 'doublet cloth of satin from the grateful patient.

Court life was expensive, and sums for 'partlets embroidering, for remaking of gowns, for capsis [caps] of silver and gilt' and for her 'kirtle of cloth of silver' were numerous. A goldsmith, one Farnando, received twenty-eight shillings for the 'fascion of a gyrdle' for Mary while William Lock received thirteen pounds for 'certen sylks'. Monies disbursed for 'mending the clockes' and for the repair and 'setting of the virginals' appear often. When Mary travelled to wherever the court might be assembled, she was expected to leave gratuities. At Hampton Court, Richmond, Windsor, and Greenwich, the gardeners, launderers, woodbearers, watermen and others were all recipients of her largesse. Even the 'workmen on the leads at Westminster'—the old Palace was apparently undergoing some repairs—were gratefully surprised by a small purse sent to them by the visiting Princess.

Amusements were simple but plentiful. Musicians or minstrels provided lighthearted gaiety as a background for the antics of Jane the Fool.* Each time Jane's head was shaved, it cost Mary fourpence. That the Princess was fond and thoughtful of Jane is indicated by the numerous items showing hose, shoes, damasks for smocks, even some embroidery needles, which were purchased for the female jester, or 'Fool'. Further amusements were provided by the attendance of travelling groups of gypsies who appeared at the household gates, asking to play before the Princess and receiving generous reward afterwards. Mary also loved to play cards, and frequent disbursements of twenty or thirty shillings 'given to my Lady's Grace in her purse for the cards' are noted in the records.

Visitors were many—and costly. An old servant, a Groom of the Buttery, Davy Candeland, came to visit and received seven shillings and sixpence as a gift from Mary when he departed. A servant of Cromwell's accepted several coins for 'bringing to my Lady's Grace, Swete Waters and fumes', and John Carey, a servant accompanying 'John Heneage bringing the King's New Year's Gyfte' received a generous token of the Princess's gratitude. People travelling to London or abroad brought Mary small presents or executed commissions for her, and the Princess had to be generous. Thus, Thomas Borough, who went to London 'at diverse times' on errands for Mary, could be sure of four or five shillings for his efforts. While there, he left twenty shillings 'at the prisen houses of London' in Mary's name. Those who travelled abroad brought her 'Eastern stuff', 'Spanish gloves', or 'Stuff from Spain, for which Mary was financially responsible.

Services were expensive too. Christopher Bradley received five shillings and eightpence for the keeping of 'My Lady's greyhounds from Mydsomer to the last day of this month [August].' Thomas Gente, in a burst of enthusiasm when promoted from the Buttery to the Stable, responded by presenting the household with 'two gynny-cokks scalded', and was adequately compensated. Sums were constantly given in alms to a

---

* Court Jesters were well maintained and highly regarded. Will Somers, Henry VIII's Fool, was devoted to the King. Keeping a female Fool was relatively rare, and there does not seem to have been much competition for the position, perhaps, as one historian has noted, 'because of the difficulty of meeting with one of the fairer sex who was silly enough to undertake the office. . . .'6

'pore man' or a 'pore woman called Mother Anne' for rendering small services, or simply because they were obviously in need. If anyone died in Mary's service, she was expected to bear the burial expense. Thus the 'item payed for the bureng of one Will'am ap Richard and his wife', apparently the victims of an accident, shows their interment cost the Princess thirteen shillings and sixpence. And, at the time of Jane Seymour's death, Mary remembered the 'Qwene's three chamberers, every one of them, one souyane [sovereign]', and smaller sums went to the Queen's page, footmen, and gardener. After Jane's burial, Mary paid thirteen shillings for Masses for the dead Queen at 'Hampton Co't and Windeso'.[7]

The Privy Purse Expense books of Mary's household show this older daughter of Henry VIII as one very aware of her position and its ensuing responsibility. She was generous to a fault and efficient in the management of her financial affairs (many of the listings and additions in the books are corrected in her own hand). The items are revealing, showing her interest in and consideration for her family, her household, and the people who served her. None of the expenditures is inconsistent with her rank or environment, but the King was not always dependable where her allowances were concerned. At one interval, while Mary was living at Hertford Castle, which demanded more servants and main-tenance than usual, she was forced to write to Cromwell that her forty pounds quarterly allotment was insufficient for that particular time and 'I would desire you, if your wisdom thought it most convenient, to be a suitor to the King's said Highness . . . somewhat to increase that sum. And thus, my lord, I am ashamed always to be a beggar to you, but that the occasion at this time is such that I cannot choose.'[8]

At Edward's residence, Lady Bryan was having similar financial difficulties. She complained of lack of funds properly to clothe the child. She told Cromwell that Edward's best coat was of tinsel only. 'He hath never a good jewel to set on his cap!' she said. And it 'was the best of my power with such things as here is to do it withal: which is but very bare . . . The Prince', she ended, 'is in good health and merry, and his Grace hath four teeth, three full out and the fourth appeareth.'[9]

The meagreness of the royal children's household funds did not result from any deliberate indifference on the part of Henry or his Council. The King had immense problems facing him, both at home and abroad, which required time and money. Charles and Francis had come to the end of their long and expensive war. Any joint or single offensive by them against the excommunicated King of England would have been pronounced a regrettable but desirable necessity by the Pope, as Henry was poignantly aware. The King knew the Pope had also attempted to pressure the King of Scotland, James V, Henry's nephew, to invade England. With the possibility of a pincer invasion from north, east, and south, Henry was concerned enough to build new defence measures on his coasts and repair old ones. He made personal 'laborious and painful journies towards the sea coast ... had set his navy in readiness at Portsmouth ... and in all things furnished for the wars.'[10] Local militias were mustered, including one in London where 15,000 men covered 'all the fields from Whitechapel to Mile-End, from Bethnal Green to Radcliffe and Stepney.' Archers, pikemen, musketeers, and artillery-men, in bright new uniforms, entered the City at Aldgate early in the morning and 'so passed through the streets ... until they came to Westminster'. Upon reaching the Palace, they found the King and all the nobility waiting 'to see how gladly every man prepared him, what desire every man had to do his prince service, it was a joyful sight to behold of every Englishman.'[11] The King stayed, reviewing his troops from nine o'clock in the morning until five o'clock in the after-noon.

In addition to the possibility of a foreign invasion, Henry had a more personal problem: he had no wife. For a man who liked feminine companionship, who had not been without a wife for thirty years, it was an unhappy situation. A country with a widower King should have an undeniable advantage in the marriage market, and wagers on who the King's next bride might be were numerous. Within months of Jane Seymour's death, English envoys were busy in foreign courts discussing candidates for marriage with Henry, provoking considerably less enthusiasm from the nominees than was flattering. When the King sought the younger daughter of the Duke of Guise as a bride, he grandly told the French representatives he would like to meet her and all others who might be considered. 'I trust no one but myself', he cried, 'the thing touches me too near! I wish to see them and know them sometime before deciding.'[12] Francis was enraged at the thought of parading ladies of the French nobility 'like hackneys' before the King of England. When Henry further said he would like to hear them sing and also see how they behaved, the French ambassador, with stinging cynicism suggested that perhaps the King would like to try them in other ways also?—at which Henry had the grace to flush.

As Francis continued to show little interest in providing a French wife, Henry sought the hand of the beautiful Christina of Denmark, the widowed Duchess of Milan and a niece of Charles V, whom it was said '... he would willingly take, even if she were delivered to him naked, without a penny. ...' Holbein painted the Duchess, a regally beautiful woman, to whom Sir Thomas Wriothesley spoke in praise of the King, telling her she would be 'matched with the most gentle gentleman that liveth; his nature so benign and pleasant, that I think till this day, no man hath heard any angry words pass his lips.' Wriothesley said she smiled, and he thought she would have laughed out 'had not her gravity forbidden it. . . .'* Charles had been anxious for peace with France saying, 'whichever of us conquered shall give full aid to the victor for war against the Infidel.'[13] Henry had offered to act as mediator between France and Spain in their search for peace, and Charles used Christina's beauty to prolong Henry's interest. But the Emperor 'knit one delay to the tail of another', and Henry marvelled 'at the frosty coldness and slack remissness' of Charles's agents. Everything became clear when Francis and Charles signed a peace treaty, meeting personally a month later at Aigues-Mortes, to cement their new alliance. Instead of Henry, it was the Pope who mediated to bring France and Spain together in peace. He promised to meet with the two monarchs personally to bless their reconciliation, causing Cromwell to say, 'I begin to perceive that there is scarce any good faith in this world!'

Faced with the material reality of a combined Catholic triumvirate of Scotland, France, and the Holy Roman Empire, Henry was now on the outside looking in. He had broken from the Papal fold and there was no return; no marital or political alliance could be effected between countries of differing religious policies.

At home, too, religious unrest had been furthered by the publication of the Bible in English which, since September, 1538, had laid open for reading in each parish church. A 'diversity of opinions' had arisen among Henry's subjects. Many who followed the New Learning and considered themselves free from the bonds of Rome went to the extremes of personally proclaiming the Word of God. These self-styled preachers delivered sermons in their backyards, in the City's alleys, in the public houses—wherever a rapt audience could be found to listen to one of their own kind daringly usurping privileges formerly exclusive to the Church. The clergy was disdainful of the 'strawberry preachers', as they were called, since, Latimer noted, 'like strawberries, they come once a year.'

There was never any doubt, however, of the King's position regarding religious matters. The actions of his subjects did not extend to Henry Tudor whose own conservative Catholicism manifested itself on Good Friday when he crept to the cross devoutly and served the priest at Mass that same day, 'his own person kneeling on his Grace's knees. . . .' The King was concerned that too liberal a reading of the Bible would only confuse the layman. In the Act of the Six Articles, the King insisted his people accept the traditional Catholic doctrine of Transubstantiation, celibacy for the clergy, the privilege of Confession and the Mass.

* The Duchess's gravity on this occasion was much at odds with her reputation for charm and wit. She had little enthusiasm for the English marriage and allegedly said 'they would lose their labours, for she wished not to fix her heart that way'. The remark, true or not, for which she gained immortality, was her more realistic comment that if she had two heads upon her shoulders, one would be at the disposal of His Majesty, the King of England.

Henry's conviction, his hope 'that the Scriptures would be read with meekness, with a will to accomplish the effect of them—not for the purpose of finding arguments to maintain extravagant opinions'[14] emphasise again that the King's battle with the Church was, first and foremost, opposition to its appropriation of secular authority, rather than any differing religious doctrine.

His orthodoxy, painful to Cranmer and Cromwell, which resulted in the 'Whip with the Six Strings' as the Act came to be called, caused the people great satisfaction. The French ambassador observed, 'The people show great joy at the King's declaration concerning the Sacrament, being much more inclined to the old religion than to the new opinions. . . .'[15] The enactment of the Act of the Six Articles was viewed by Henry's Council as a sign of Cromwell's waning influence. But the religious motives of Henry's chief minister were always malleable in the face of political expediency. When snubbed by both Catholic powers in his search for a bride for his King, Cromwell did not hesitate to turn to Germany and the Protestant princes, convincing Henry at the same time of the advantage such an alliance would provide should Charles and Francis combine against England. Though the King had, personally, little enthusiasm for the venture, in view of the meeting between Charles and Francis, he had little choice. Thus, when German envoys arrived at the Tudor court, presumably for theological conferences and to discuss the possibility between the Princess Mary and the young Duke of Cleves, it was hinted to the Lutherans that—should they provide a strong support in case of attack upon England by France or the Emperor—the King of England himself might be at their disposal.

The outcome was Henry's betrothal to the Flemish Anne, the thirty-four-year old daughter of the Duke of Cleves, a plain-faced woman of medium stature with soft, appealing brown eyes, her sallow skin slightly marred by the ravages of smallpox. Holbein's portrait of her is not unattractive, and the advance reports sent to the King stated 'everybody praises the lady's beauty, both of face and body.' She could read and write in her own language but none other; nor could she sing or play any instrument, 'for they take it here in Germany for a rebuke and an occasion of lightness, that great ladies should be learned, or have any knowledge of music . . .'[16] wrote Henry's ambassador, Nicholas Wotton. If these advance reports of Anne's capabilities caused Henry any doubt as to the desirability of his bride, his first sight of her at Rochester on New Year's Day, 1540, confirmed his worst suspicions, for he was so 'marvellously astonished and abashed' at what he saw he forgot to present her with the sable furs he had brought as an engagement present.

The King thundered his disappointment to all who would listen. He lamented 'the fate of princes to be in matters of marriage of far worse sort than the condition of poor men. Princes take as is brought them by others', he said, 'and poor men be commonly at their own choice!' He cried to Lord Russell, '. . . whom should men trust? I promise you I see no such thing in her as hath been showed unto me of her, and am ashamed that men have so praised her as they have done. I like her not!' he finished bluntly.[17] To Cromwell, who had directed, urged, and guided the Protestant alliance to result in the marriage of his King with a daughter of the House of Cleves, Anne's appearance and Henry's repulsion were a personal calamity. When he ventured to ask the King how he liked his proposed bride, Henry was curt: 'Nothing so well as she was spoken of,' he said and then, turning to his minister, asked, 'What is the remedy?' For once, Cromwell's facile tongue could offer no ready solution. 'I am not well handled!' wailed Henry. 'If it were not that she is come so far into my realm, and the great preparations that my states and people have made for her, and for fear of making a ruffle in the world, and of driving her brother into the hands of the Emperor and the French King, who are now together, I would not now marry her!'[18]

But the 'great preparations' went inexorably on amid the repeated whisperings of the court ladies about Anne's peculiarly Flemish clothing, her guttural voice, her lack of accomplishments and social graces and what the English called 'manners'. Henry, a continual 'study in pensiveness', tried all devices to escape. 'Is there then, none other remedy but I must needs against my will put my neck into the yoke?' he asked abjectly.[19]

The royal head was put into the yoke on the Feast of the Epiphany, January 6, 1540, apparelled in a 'cloth of gold, raised with great flowers of silver, and furred with black jennettes. His coat, crimson satin, slashed and embroidered, and clasped with great diamonds, and a rich collar about his neck.' Henry called to the anxious Cromwell, who was puffing about nervously, his rod of office in hand, his dismay apparent to all, and said, 'My Lord, if it were not to satisfy the world and my realm, I would not do what I must do this day for any earthly thing.'[20] If Anne of Cleves, who appeared at her wedding 'demure and sad' in her gown of rich cloth of gold, embroidered with flowers of oriental pearls, had any personal thoughts on the acceptability of the ageing monarch who was to be her husband, she had sense enough to keep them to herself—a talent which was reflected in her motto, *God Send Me Well to Keep*. And in the next few trying months, merely keeping her head, literally and figuratively, became Anne's chief aim in life.

The morning after the wedding, in answer to Cromwell's inquiry if he liked the Queen any better, Henry was mercilessly explicit. 'Surely my lord, as you know, I liked her not well before, but now I like her much worse, for by her belly and breasts she should be no maid.' He

proclaimed himself to have been so 'strake to the heart' by this experience, that she was 'nothing fair and have very ill smells about her,'[21]
that he had not the courage to try to prove anything further, and
therefore 'surely he would not have any more children for the comfort
of the realm.'

And thus matters stood. Henry referred to his bride as 'the Flanders
mare,' although he was obsequiously polite to her while in her presence.
When several of the court ladies told Anne they wished to see her with
child, Anne said she was not, at which Lady Edgecombe asked how it
was possible she knew. 'I know it well I am not', Anne replied stubbornly,
at which the ladies teased her for being still a maid. Anne pretended a
humorous naïveté, saying that 'each morning the King said "Farewell
darling"' and each night he was faithful in saying 'Goodnight Sweetheart' and asked wide-eyed, 'Is not this enough?' Lady Rutland, one of
Anne's ladies-in-waiting, replied tartly, 'There must be more than this,
Madame, if we are to see a Duke of York ... !' 'Nay', said Anne,
smiling to herself, 'I am contented I know no more....'[22]

The King's marriage accomplished, the attention of the court
centred on Mary's proposed betrothal to Philip, the Duke of Bavaria, a
relative of Anne of Cleves. Mary had little enthusiasm for the union and
told Thomas Wriothesley, 'Albeit the matter were towards her of great
importance, and besides, of such sort and nature, as, the King's
Majesty not offended, she would wish and desire never to enter that
kind of religion, but to continue still a maid during her life....'[23]
The Duke had 'declared to the King his resolution to take her to wife,
provided that his person be agreeable to the said lady.' When he arrived
for the wedding of Anne and Henry, he did his utmost to ingratiate
himself with Mary. But Mary could not accept a husband who was a
Lutheran, and some of her feeling extended to Anne. She felt awkward
with a stepmother only ten years older than herself, and both women,
so unlike in personality, background, and religion, with no common
language, observed at first the merest formalities. Just three days before
her father's marriage, Mary was ill, and Lady Kingston, who attended
her, was anxiously writing that 'she could neither sit nor stand, but was
fain to go to her bed again for faintness.' She begged the King to send
Dr Butts to Mary 'because he hath been with her in such cases in times
past.'

If her father's marriage to a Lutheran and her own proposed alliance
with a Bavarian noble sickened and distressed Mary, her seven-year-old
sister, Elizabeth, was enchanted at having another stepmother. She
begged Lady Bryan to obtain the King's permission for her to meet Anne
at once, causing Henry's only recorded allusion to the dead Anne
Boleyn. 'Tell her', he said, 'that she had a mother so different from this
woman, that she ought not to wish to see her.'[24] With the uninhibited

enthusiasm of youth, however, Elizabeth put her thoughts on paper in her own handwriting, Lady Bryan undoubtedly helping with the words:

Madame,

I am struggling between two contending wishes—one is my impatient desire to see your Majesty, the other that of rendering the obedience I owe to the commands of the King my father, which prevent me from leaving my house till he has given me full permission to do so. But I hope that I shall be able shortly to gratify both these desires.

In the meantime, I entreat your Majesty to permit me to show, by this billet, the zeal with which I devote my respect to you as my Queen and my entire obedience to you as to my mother. . . .[25]

Elizabeth's childish kindness must have cheered the neglected Anne of Cleves whose own Dutch attendants were dismissed shortly after her marriage, leaving her to the ridicule of the English ladies. Lonely and unsure of herself, the new Queen was also sufficiently intelligent to realise that her marriage, which was no marriage at all, could not continue indefinitely. Anne of Cleves was no dissembler, nor was she a hypocrite. With her blunt German manner, she found Henry as difficult as he found her unattractive, and though ostensibly they lived a normal married life, she soon ceased to tolerate silently his indifference and the half-veiled contempt of the court ladies. In his own words, Henry told Cromwell that his bride had 'waxed wilful and stubborn with with him.'

Well she might, for in addition to her neglect and the disdain of her ladies, she knew the King had noticed the radiance and charm of little Katherine Howard, another niece of the Duke of Norfolk and a cousin of Anne Boleyn. This rosy-cheeked youngster with the auburn hair and capricious, lighthearted personality and enormous zest for living, was the complete opposite of Anne of Cleves, and Cromwell, seeing the way the King's fancy was leading him, became distraught. He warned Anne ' of the expediency of doing her utmost to render herself more agreeable to the King'. But Henry remained uninterested and by May, 1540, again had his way.

After five months of marriage, the tender conscience of Henry Tudor rebelled at having a Lutheran for a wife, and there remained only the necessity of finding a plausible excuse for divorce. At one point in their relationship, Henry had piqued Anne into admitting 'if she had not been compelled to marry him, she might have fulfilled her engagement with another, to whom she had promised her hand.' Once an excuse was acquired, a petition was presented to Parliament for the dissolution of his marriage by reason of Anne's previous contract with the Duke of Lorraine which was sufficient to 'perplex and complicate' any second marriage. She had been 'espoused against her will', said Henry, and he himself 'lacked the power and the will to consummate the marriage'. He ended by vowing he 'was ready to answer any questions that might be put to him for he had no other object in view but the glory of God, the welfare of the realm, and the triumph of truth.'[26] In July the accommodating Cranmer—who would now dissolve the third of Henry's marriages in twice as many years—stated his 'doubts of the validity of the marriage between the King and Queen.' The compassionate clergy, assisted by Parliament and a relieved Anne, who consented to be known as the 'King's Good Sister', guaranteed the marriage being dissolved on July 13, 1540. The King ordered Anne to write to her brother that she wished to remain in England, where she would have precedence over all other ladies of the realm—a not unhappy prospect for Anne, who had dreaded being sent back to a dull Germany. He was generous to the woman who was willing to let him go so easily. Anne received an allowance of £4,000 a year, the manors of Bletchingly and Richmond for her personal use, silver and gold plate, expensive hangings, and the King's undying gratitude for her willing co-operation. With a stout *Ja*, Anne agreed to everything Henry and his ministers suggested. And in answer to one question at least, she was quite firm. Wishing to be sure Anne had no further redress against Henry once the marriage was annulled, Cromwell asked if she had any complaints against the King—had her husband neglected her? In this, Anne of Cleves was quick to reply: No, she said, she had no complaints whatever. The King had not neglected her; she had 'received quite as much of His Majesty's attention as she wished. . . .'[27]

Much of Mary Tudor's distress during 1540 was caused not only by her father's Protestant alliance and her own proposed engagement but by the appalling persecution of the religious orders and the outright plunder of the monasteries. Cromwell was pitiless in his search for the slightest pretext which would deliver monastic lands to the Crown, and what he could not obtain easily by virtue of surrender, he seized by attainder of the Abbot and confiscation of the property. When governing heads of the monasteries could not, in good conscience, swear the Oath of Supremacy, they found themselves in mortal danger. Thus, when the abbot of Woburn Abbey, in the privacy of his chamber, cursed perilous times in which they were living and praised Sir Thomas More and Bishop John Fisher for their noble deaths, he was condemned and hung, with two abbey monks, at the entrance gate.

Often the monetary worth alone governed the fate of a religious house.[28] One of the last to fall was the rich Abbey of Glastonbury where, tradition held, Joseph of Arimathea had originally erected a small church and planted his staff of thornwood. King Arthur and Queen Guinevere were buried at Glastonbury, the Isle of Avalon; Saint Patrick had died there. This 'perfect poem in stone' which had arisen from humble beginnings fifteen hundred years earlier, was the 'greatest, finest, richest and most splendid' of the abbeys of western England, which seemed sufficient reason for Cromwell's investigators to institute a surprise search. The result may be found in Cromwell's notebooks. 'Item, the Abbot of Glaston *to be tried at Glaston and also executed there*',[29] written in Cromwell's own hand, preceded the visit of his agents. And so it happened. Richard Whiting, the eighty-year-old Abbot, was tied to a hurdle and drawn to Tor Hill and hanged in sight of the magnificent Abbey which had been his life. His head was placed on the gate and the quarters of his body exhibited as a warning at Bath, Ilchester, and Bridgwater.

Canterbury was next. The rich shrine of Thomas à Becket was revered throughout Christendom, visited by 'pilgrims'—princes, peers, and commoners alike. Now Becket, dead in his grave for some four hundred years, was declared to have 'usurped the office of saint'. His bones were ripped from the tomb and burned and his shrine despoiled of its gold plating. The votive offerings were forfeited to the Crown, and Henry had several of the brilliant jewels, including the magnificent ruby, the 'Regal of France', made into finger rings.

The methodical, organised, and premeditated destruction continued by men ordered 'to pull down all the walls of the churches, steeples, cloisters, frateries, dorters, chapter houses. . . .' The exquisite 'Lady Shrines' at Worcester and Walsingham were desecreated, and their ancient carved statues of the Virgin publicly burned. Sculptures, paintings, delicately brilliant window glass of glowing colours—all were wantonly trampled upon, broken, and mutilated. Lavishly decorated copes and other priceless religious vestments became bedcoverings and hangings, while thickly embroidered altar pieces, the life work of a dedicated artist, were used for tablecloths. Handsomely illuminated books were ripped apart and scattered to the winds. Magnificent gold and silver crosses, chalices, and other holy objects were melted down; anything remaining was left to those who supervised the destruction 'and they did tread with their feet to break them all in pieces'.

Once the looting and plunder was complete, the buildings themselves awaited the final destruction. Choir-stalls, ancient carved wooden screens, stout roof timbers—all were piled in the naves of the churches and torches thrown into their midst, causing the dry wood to roar into a blazing mass. The climbing flames could be seen for miles—their glow

[99]

reflected in the bewildered stares of the parishioners or abject brethren who looked on. They clung to one another, shocked and unbelieving, as they watched the immolation of sacred monuments which had been the centre of their spiritual and communal life for as long as they could remember.

By 1540, the last monastery was gone. Buildings already several hundred years old and built to last centuries longer, were razed to the ground or left as gaunt warning skeletons:

> Level, level with the ground,
>   the towers do lie,
> which with their golden glittering tops,
>   pierced once to the sky!
> Where were gates, no gates are now;
>   the ways unknown
> where the press of peers did pass,
>   while her fame far was blown.
> Owls do shriek where the sweetest hymns
>   lately were sung;
> toads and serpents hold their dens,
>   where the palmers did throng.....[30]

It took five years for Cromwell, with the authority of the Crown behind him, to complete the dissolution of the monastic system. If any evil had existed in the system itself, it was more than compounded by the social and economic chaos which erupted from the Dissolution as thousands of monks and nuns were sent homeless into the world. They joined the bakers, millers, gardeners, stewards, carpenters, and others of non-religious affiliation who had depended on the monasteries for their sustenance and were now, with their families, thrown from their cottages and hovels. Destitute, they had little recourse except to roam from village to village, seeking work, often being whipped for vagabondage instead or hanged for thievery when they stole to feed their families and themselves.

To prevent any renaissance of the religious orders or the rebuilding of the abbeys, the land and few buildings left standing were parcelled out to Henry's nobles or those whom Cromwell thought it politically wise to satisfy. If the wealth were shared, there would be little complaint from even the more conservative councillors, the King and minister rightly reasoned. Among those subsequently enriched was Audley, the Speaker of the House. He received the best of the abbey lands, which gift it was thought would help 'clear the Speaker's voice and make him speak clear and well for his master'. Other nobles and some ecclesiastics such as Thomas Cranmer were happy recipients of priories, abbeys, and nunneries; the Duke of Norfolk as first noble of the realm received no less than thirteen religious houses and colleges and their properties. For their rich bounty, it was understood there would be little discontent, either political or religious, over the lands which the Crown chose to retain. Though Henry had originally declared the monasteries' wealth would be diverted for colleges, schools, and the creation of twenty-one new bishoprics, only six of the last were ever created.

If the sufferings of the religious and the heartbreak of her now proposed Protestant engagement were not enough to unnerve Mary Tudor, one final horror awaited which took her to the very edge of her sanity, faith, and hope. What it accomplished in terms of security for Henry's throne is questionable. What it accomplished in the sensitive, unflinchingly honest and loyal older daughter of the King was a further retreat into the shelter of her own world and the companionship of her people, with whom she felt safe. Mary did not feel equal to, nor did she desire, a deeper closeness with the Crown. Better to be apart and protected, she reasoned, than risk her new-found security.

The horror which Mary Tudor was now to experience did not happen quickly. The terror unleashed in England under the guise of religious reform did not, however, discriminate. Among those who found themselves the victims of careless words and even more careless actions were the sons of Margaret Pole, the Countess of Salisbury, Mary's beloved old ex-governess. Reginald Pole was a grandson of Lionel, the Duke of Clarence, and boasted blood in his veins as royal as Henry's. After strong words with the King over Henry's treatment of and divorce from Catherine of Aragon, he had left England for the Continent. From the safety of a Continental residence and now a Cardinal of the Catholic Church, Reginald Pole felt called upon to write a book, terrifyingly critical of the King, to whom he also had the poor taste to send it. The book, *De Unitate Ecclesia*, compared Henry with Nero and Domitian. The King did not merit the title, 'Defender of the Faith', wrote Pole, for he killed those who defended the faith and left others to deal with the infidel Turk. 'Who', asked Pole, referring to the martyred Thomas More and Bishop Fisher, 'does not acknowledge the hand of God beyond nature, that lengthened his life to your same that he might perish by your sword, and allowed him to be enrolled among the number of Cardinals that it might be known to the whole world that you had slain not merely an excellent bishop, against whom you had no just cause, but a Cardinal over whom you had no authority?'[31] The King, he charged, had no real thought of compassion for his people, his nobles, or his clergy but had harassed and 'plundered' them for twenty-seven years.

The Pole family were appalled when they learned what the Cardinal had done. Their private opinions differed little from his, but they were very aware of the jeopardy in which his words placed them. Another son, Henry Pole, Lord Montague, had openly deplored the plunder of the monasteries and the brutal treatment of the religious hierarchy, saying, 'Knaves rule about the King!' Another nobleman, Henry Courtenay, the Marquess of Exeter and Earl of Devon, descended from Edward IV and heir to the English Crown if Henry died without lawful issue, was suspected of mustering the western counties of Cornwall and Devon in support of his own claim to the throne. The two gentlemen with their royal blood—all too perilous to possess—were reckless and foolish. Their suspected treason, combined with a fear of invasion from Scotland, France, and Spain, did not endear his relatives to Henry Tudor. By the end of 1538, sufficient evidence led to the arrest of a younger, weaker brother, Sir Geoffrey Pole. After two months of strict confinement and interrogations, he admitted, under threat of torture, enough incriminating information concerning Cardinal Pole to confirm the disenchantment of the Pole family with the King. A Bill of Attainder was passed against both families. Courtenay, his wife Gertrude, and their small child, the twelve-year-old Edward, were imprisoned in the Tower on charges of '. . . machinating the death of the King and exciting his subjects to rebellion, and seeking to maintain the said Cardinal Pole in his intentions, the Marquess of Exeter did say to Geoffrey Pole, the following words: "I like well the proceedings of the Cardinal Pole; but I like not the proceedings of the realm, and I trust to see a change of this world."' Montague had professed to his brother, Geoffrey, to 'like well the doings of my brother, the Cardinal, and I would we were both over the sea, for this world will one day come to strifes. . . .'

Their rash, impatient words were enough to condemn them. On a bleak morning in December, Montague and Exeter ascended the barren rise from their prison to Tower Hill and were executed. For his services to the Crown, Sir Geoffrey Pole was released and, after one abortive attempt at suicide, 'lived like one terror-stricken all his days'. The Marchioness of Exeter and her son, the twelve-year-old Edward Courtenay, remained in the Tower with the mother of the Poles, the elderly Countess of Salisbury, to suffer a long and arduous imprisonment. Margaret Pole had been one of Catherine of Aragon's dearest friends; she had been a second mother to Mary Tudor. As a young man Henry had described her as 'saintly'. He held her in great esteem, even agreeing that one day Princess Mary and Reginald Pole might wed. He had restored the family estates confiscated by his father, and upon the Countess's retirement from court to the family seat at Warblington Castle, he had given her a generous pension. But now, at the zenith of

[102]

his political and religious supremacy, there was no mercy for this woman whose uncle had been Edward IV and whose children were reckless in their talk and ambition. The Countess was confined in the Tower 'where she made great moan that she wanteth necessary apparel to change and also to keep her warm. . . .' For eighteen months she suffered the hardships of cold, poor food, and repeated interrogation by Henry's commissioners. She parried their questions and stormed at them so vigorously that her questioners became exasperated. 'We assure your lordships', Wriothesley wrote to Henry's Council, 'we have dealed with a one as men have not dealed with tofore; we may rather call her a strong and constant man than a woman!'[32] But all her fierce contempt of her interrogators, all her staunch protestations of innocence and injustice, availed her nothing. Upon such flimsy evidence as the charge that she had corresponded with her sons and the display in Parliament by Cromwell of a silk tunic, the Countess was condemned to death for treason. The tunic was embroidered at the front with the arms of England, three garlands of pansies for Pole and marigolds for the Princess Mary. The Five Wounds of Christ with the name 'Jesus' written in the midst—the same popular symbol that had emblazoned the banners of the Pilgrimage of Grace—were mingled with the flowers. Cromwell maintained that the garment had been made in the hope of a marriage between Mary and Reginald Pole and 'betwixt them both should again arise the old doctrine of Christ.'

There was never any trial for Margaret Pole. In the spring of 1541, in great secrecy, she was half-dragged, half-pushed to the scaffold at Tower Green, where five years before, Anne Boleyn had suffered. Reaching the scaffold, she struggled and refused to ascend voluntarily. Hauled up and ordered to lay her head on the block, she stormily refused. The block was for traitors, she said; she was no traitor! Turning her head every way, she told the executioner, 'if he would have it, he must get it as he could.'[33] The brute who held the axe was pitiless. Clutched in a vicelike grip from which she once escaped, she was attacked as she stood upright by the angry executioner. He hacked away viciously at her neck, the blows striking her head, shoulders, and ears. It took seven strong blows before the butchery was complete and the sixty-nine-year-old Countess was dead. In Rome Cardinal Pole said, 'I am now the son of a martyr. This is the King's reward for her care of his daughter. . . . Let us be of good cheer! We now have one more patron in heaven.'

The beautiful chantry which Margaret Pole had prepared for her burial lies empty and can be seen today at Christchurch Priory in Hampshire. The body of this staunch and courageous woman, 'the last Plantagenet', who resisted the tyranny of Henry Tudor, lies ignominiously with its severed head in the Church of St Peter-ad-Vincula at the

Tower of London. Her last message and thought had been for her beloved former charge, Mary Tudor. If Mary suffered any reaction other than sickening horror at the death of her old governess, the events of the past few years had taught her the wisdom of silence. What passed in her mind and heart at the slaughter of one of her oldest and dearest friends can only be imagined.

Chapter Six

T HE dissolving of his sister's marriage outraged the Duke of Cleves, and he ended all negotiations for Mary's proposed union with Philip of Bavaria, much to her intense relief. Though bitter at Henry's actions, the Duke was mollified by the generous settlements Henry made and Anne's obvious satisfaction at the prospect of remaining in England. One ambassador wrote of the discarded Queen, 'she had gained the love of the people of England—has a more joyous countenance than ever. She wears a great variety of dresses and passes all her time in sports and recreation.' Free at last from a sombre life in Germany and an unwilling husband, she was almost beautiful.

The King's severance of all Lutheran ties caused Catholic hopes to rise, and Mary Tudor was thrust once more into the forefront of political and marital importance. The two most seriously discussed suitors for her hand were Charles, the Duke of Orleans, the younger son of the King of France, and, incredibly, her cousin Charles, the Holy Roman Emperor. Charles's beloved wife, Isabella, had died in childbirth leaving behind three children—Philip, Marie, and Juana. The Emperor was desolate and retired to a Hieronymite monastery for seven weeks of prayer and meditation upon his loss. While he was in seclusion, the French ambassador wrote to Francis of the bride proposed for his son:

She is of middle stature, and is in face like her father, especially about the mouth, but has a voice more man-like for a woman than he has for a man. To judge by portraits, her neck is like her mother's. With fresh complexion, she looks not past eighteen or twenty, although she is twenty-four. Her beauty is mediocre, and it may be said that she is one of the belles of the Court. She is active, and apparently not delicate, loving morning exercise and walking often two or three miles. She speaks and writes French well . . . she understands Latin and enjoys the books of the *lettres humaines*, which were her solace in sleepless nights at the time when she was molested. She delights in music and plays the spinet *singulièrement*. In conversation together with sweetness and benignity, she is prudent and reserved.[1]

Henry had no reason to hasten the French union since the Emperor might be ultimately available; many hours of dallying might be spent in negotiations. The King offered 300,000 crowns for Mary's dowry, but Francis had loftier notions of his son's worth, and his minister urged Henry to reconsider. The English representative, Paget, was a member of Henry's Privy Council and a shrewd bargainer. He demurred, observing that Orleans was the King's *second* son which, he said, caused 'the French admiral to heave twenty sighs, and cast up his eyes as many times, besides crossing himself . . . then sending forth one great sigh, he spoke his mind pathetically on the smallness of the Lady Mary's *dote*.'[2] Francis was less dramatic and more verbal; he lost his temper and castigated the English representative for Henry's miserliness until Paget said his poor heart 'frobbed'.[3]

When the Emperor's ambassador, Eustace Chapuys, the '*especial amigo*' of Catherine of Aragon and Mary Tudor's great friend, returned to England, rumours were rife that he had come to discuss her marriage to the Emperor. Henry continued the French negotiations, hoping to stimulate Charles's interest, while at the same time keeping Francis in reserve should the Emperor's grief remain chronic. In the end, as many had expected, he did nothing. His greatest strength was to remain neutral. Little would be gained for England if his daughter wed a foreign Catholic power, other than providing more substance to her legitimacy and a stronger claim to the throne—a claim directly endangering his son's position.

So the years in which Mary might have been a wife and a mother passed. Now in her middle twenties, she met her potential suitors as they came to England, or listened respectfully to the King and his councillors when they discussed her possible marriage. In her own words, however, she reveals how well she understood that it was all pretence and politically motivated. She was King Henry's daughter, she said, and regarding any marriage, 'there was nothing to be got but fine words and while my father lives, I shall be only the Lady Mary, the most unhappy lady in Christendom.'[4]

Contributing to her depressed spirits, her health was a constant trial to Mary and to those around her. She was still plagued with poor eyesight, aching teeth, and neuralgia—all of which undoubtedly contributed to the headaches which a scanty and painful menstruation each month did nothing to minimise. Highly strung, she attempted to hide her discomfort and acute sensitivity by assuming an aloof attitude, buttressed by an imperturbable reserve, that only those nearest Mary realised masked a deep insecurity.

There were compensations, however. She who supposedly had no claim to the throne conceivably had less responsibilities than one who did and must live at court constantly surrounded by place-seekers, intrigue, and gossip. Mary spent her days in various residences, often her own, at times in those of her brother or sister. On several occasions— perhaps to save expenses or to make other use of a royal dwelling— Henry ordered all three households combined. Thus, Mary witnessed the event so charmingly described to Cromwell by Lady Bryan, Edward's governess:

Pleaseth your Lordship to understand that, blessed be Jesus, my Lord Prince's Grace is in good health and merry, as would to God the King's Grace and your Lordship had seen Easter night, for his Grace was marvellously pleasantly disposed. The minstrels played, and his Grace danced and played so wantonly that he could not stand still, and was as full of pretty toys as ever I saw a child in my life. . . .[5]

Mary enjoyed the months she spent with young Edward, to whom she was devoted. She delighted in the beauty and intelligence of her three-year-old brother, and his presence helped to alleviate the melancholy that possessed her as she watched these years in which she might have been having children of her own pass by.

When Mary went visiting, she was often accompanied by the seven-year-old Elizabeth—still very much a child with her bright red hair combed decorously beneath its cap, the demure soberness of her manner contrasting with the eyes alive with an excitement that consumed everything and everyone at a glance. Mary was never as comfortable with Elizabeth as with other children, and the lack of ease with her younger sister often caused her to reproach herself. Elizabeth, however, with her passionate exuberance showed great affection for Mary who, in many ways, fulfilled the function of an aunt or surrogate mother. At Hunsdon, Hatfield, Oatlands, or Hertford, at her brother's residence at Tittenhanger, the two Tudor sisters, one a sober twenty-four, the other a 'royal imp' of seven—each so unlike the other—shared a life which was pleasant, comfortable, and placid in most respects. When they were apart, they exchanged small gifts: Mary sent Elizabeth some much-desired yellow satin for a kirtle, receiving in return a small gold chain. The child was often without coins in her purse, and Mary was always generous, sending her twenty or thirty shillings, or leaving her coins 'to play withal' when she departed after a visit. She was interested in Elizabeth's studies, for it was obvious the child had a quick and retentive mind, and while Elizabeth never equalled Mary or her father as a musician, she quickly learned the simple songs Mary taught her for the lute or viol. All children were taught needlework while very

[107]

young and Mary, who had inherited her mother's deftness, set the small fingers of Anne Boleyn's daughter to work, causing Elizabeth great satisfaction in presenting Edward, on his second birthday, with a simple shirt of cambric made entirely by herself.

Mary saw her father often at Greenwich, Windsor, Hampton Court, or the gaudy new Nonsuch Palace at Ewell where Henry had demolished the whole village of Cuddington to erect a building incongruous in the Surrey countryside with its minarets and balconies, its vast courtyards and painted towers. She had learned the value of prudence and constantly presented the face of a dutiful and loving daughter. It was not always easy. Henry had become 'very stout and marvellously excessive in drinking and eating, so that people with credit say he is often of a different opinion in the morning than after dinner.'[6] Henry's mood and impatience were also direct reflections of a general discomfort. The ulcer on his leg so irritated him that at times he became purple in the face with pain. He was cantankerous and changeable and did not spare those around him, and his irritability often extended to his children, as both Mary and Elizabeth had discovered. But Mary could exhibit a genuine sympathy, for she still loved her father, and whatever her private thoughts might have been regarding the dreadful toll persecution was taking of her relatives, friends, or the religious hierarchy, she kept them to herself. Such emphasis was placed on religious associations that even Mary herself did not entirely escape. Her household was always open to visiting prelates, monks, or nuns. When her father was informed that she had received presents from the Abbess of Barking and the Abbot of Stratford, and that she had entertained certain friars of Chelmsford, she was severely rebuked by Cromwell. 'I fear the worst has been made of the matter . . .' she wrote to the minister. But she was not going to endanger her hard-won position and knew there was only one answer. She ended the letter saying, 'I will promise you, with God's help, from henceforth to refrain from it so utterly, that of right none shall have cause to speak of it.'[7] She didn't mention what it cost her to issue the orders to have all the dispossessed, wandering, and homeless monastics turned away from her gate in the future.

Mary had other visitors, though, who were more welcome in her father's eyes. Either at her Newhall residence or at their own vast estate, Mary often saw her cousin, Frances Brandon, now the wife of Henry Grey, the Marquess of Dorset. Frances Brandon was the eldest daughter of Mary Tudor, Henry's sister, and Charles Brandon, the Duke of Suffolk. The Greys lived at Bradgate Old Manor, a 'fair park and lodge' in the Leicestershire hills, amid pollarded oaks, huge stands of elm bordering a stream upon which broods of swan proudly glided. Three hundred servants, their own tiltyard, and a private lake liberally stocked with fish kept them in reasonable comfort. Their oldest child,

Jane, had been born a few days before Edward and had been named after Henry's late Queen. Mary was always charmed by the diminutive Lady Jane Grey whose beautiful oval face and fair skin (which was just beginning to freckle) belonged more to her grandmother, the 'Tudor Rose', than the fleshily coarse but handsome features of Frances Brandon or her uncle, the King. The Marquess, with his high-nosed, dark-eyed piercing glance and his affable and cultured manner, welcomed his wife's cousin with great enthusiasm, for Henry Grey was very conscious of his place in the varied set of 'new men' who were rising about the King, replacing those of the diminishing older nobility. While Grey was considerably more noble than many of his associates— his grandfather had been a stepson of Edward IV—he had further secured his position and purse by marrying the King's eldest niece.

He and his wife had profited handsomely from the Dissolution when the King presented Frances Brandon with most of the property in and around London belonging to the Carthusian Order. In addition to Bradgate and other outlying possessions, the Greys also owned a fine London mansion, Dorset Place, not far from Whitehall Palace. Their motto *A Ma Puissance*, two unicorns ermined, armed, and crested, surrounded by a royal circlet of gold, was everywhere in the magnificent residence with its beautiful gardens and terraces stretching to the Thames. If the semi-royal manner in which they lived, so at odds with the frugal conditions which prevailed in her own household, presented a telling contrast to the King's older daughter, Mary was astute enough to keep silent. It probably mattered little to her that the King's niece lived better than the King's children. For Mary, pride of place was more a part of the spirit than the possession of manors, jewels, or chests of gold. The 'Spanish Tudor' did not begrudge others the material wealth she and her sister lacked. As with her mother, principle and infallible integrity meant more to Mary than material riches; for these she would continue to fight. The grandeur of great wealth and position, the pursuit of ambition to enrich oneself further—these were unknown to Henry's elder daughter who held justice, righteousness, and her God in much higher esteem.

The King's annulment of his marriage to Anne of Cleves preceded the fall of his great minister, Thomas Cromwell. Just as years previously when Cromwell's sponsor, the mighty Cardinal Wolsey, had fallen into disgrace during Henry's attempted divorce from Catherine of Aragon, so during the process of ending Anne's marriage, Thomas Cromwell became the victim of his own ambition. Early in his career, he had arbitrarily dismissed many pro-Catholic members of Henry's Council, increasing their desire for vengeance which had not abated with the minister's participation in the conviction of Exeter and Montague. The King's displeasure with the Lutherans was further directed at Cromwell, who had instigated the alliance. When the marriage failed, Cromwell's doom was sealed. Anxious now to show his own traditional Catholicism with none of the liberal Cromwell-Cranmer tendencies, the King reinstated Cromwell's greatest enemy, Gardiner, the Bishop of Winchester, and the Bishops of Durham and Bath—all previously dismissed by Cromwell—to his Council. The Catholics were jubilant. Cromwell's greatest project, the Dissolution of the Monasteries, was not complete, and any plunder that had come to them had been secured. Cromwell could serve the King no longer; indeed, he would be a hindrance. 'Cranmer and Cromwell do not know where they are', the French ambassador wrote.

The animosity of the nobles, the clergy, the Parliament, and the King finally resulted in matters coming to a head. Hinting that Cromwell had received a bribe from the Duke of Cleves to effect the marriage with Anne, that he had accepted numerous other bribes and pensions, and, 'being thus enriched he had held the nobles in disdain', that he had plotted to wed the Princess Mary and had worked at odds with the King in the settlement of religious affairs, Henry allowed himself to be persuaded of Cromwell's culpability. The King also wished to be exonerated of all tinge of association with his former minister.

To the intense satisfaction of the Council which had always resented the haughty overbearing arrogance of 'the blacksmith's son', his influence with the King, and, probably, his extreme competence, Cromwell's apprehension followed. On June 10, 1540, as a group of the Council was leaving a sitting of the House of Lords to proceed across Whitehall for the midday meal, a gusty wind whirled Cromwell's cap from his head. Custom decreed that should one gentleman's head become uncovered, all gentlemen present should immediately remove their own headgear. Cromwell looked about and saw the heads of all his companions covered. 'A high wind indeed must this be, to blow my cap off, and for you need hold yours on!' he shouted angrily into the wind. No one answered. During the meal he was left alone, but he could hardly have overlooked the furtive whisperings and gestures among the Council members. At three o'clock in the afternoon, while the Privy Council was meeting at Westminster, the Captain of the Guard arrived to arrest Cromwell. The minister protested violently, throwing his cap to the ground in disgust, crying he was no traitor, that such action 'was a fine reward for all his services!' A gloating Norfolk strode up and tore the ribbon of St George from Cromwell's neck. The seedy Fitzwilliam roughly stripped the badge of the Garter from his gown as the trembling man was taken to the Tower. Cranmer too trembled; he and Cromwell had been great friends. He wrote to Henry, professing to be 'sorrowful and amazed' that Cromwell should be declared a traitor, saying he had 'loved him as my friend, for so I took him to be. . . .' But later, ever pliable, Cranmer could say, '. . . if he be a traitor, I am sorry that ever I loved or trusted him; and I am very glad that his treason is discovered in time. . . .' He lamented, '. . . . whom shall the King trust thereafter ?'[8]

Among the witnesses against Thomas Cromwell was the notorious Richard Rich who had conspired with Cromwell to condemn Sir Thomas More with perjured testimony. During the Dissolution, Cromwell had allowed Rich to purchase the handsome Priory of St Bartholomew in the City for a nominal sum, but now no tie of loyalty to his former sponsor bound him. Among the weapons used in condemning Cromwell was the Act of Attainder which Parliament passed without giving the accused a hearing. Cromwell had insisted, against all previous custom, on this illegal procedure when the Countess of Salisbury had been charged and condemned without a hearing. At the time, Parliament had hesitated to use such an unprecedented measure, but the minister's influence prevailed. With exquisite irony, Thomas Cromwell now became the second victim of the despotic instrument he himself had furnished the Crown. But he could not believe that Henry would abandon him. He wrote to the King of the 'labours, pains and travails' he had taken so that Henry might 'live ever young and prosperous'. He had wanted to make Henry rich, he said, and when much of the bounty of the monasteries—ornaments of gold, platters, dishes, magnificent jewelled crosses, huge quantities of rich silks and velvets—were taken from the cellar of Cromwell's home and given over to the Crown, he did indeed enrich the royal treasury in addition to the previous plunder from the Church which had come to Henry's coffers. He ended his letter, 'written at the Tower this Wednesday the last of June with the heavy heart and trembling hand of your Highness's most heavy and most miserable prisoner and poor slave, Thomas Cromwell. Most gracious prince, I cry for mercy, mercy, mercy!'[9]

Within two weeks it was all over, and Thomas Cromwell, whose influence with his monarch, Parliament, and the Church had been supreme for eight years, suffered the same shameful fate as his more illustrious victims, Bishop Fisher, Sir Thomas More, and the Countess of Salisbury. He had sought power and wealth and had obtained both. He had wished to emulate his former employer, Cardinal Wolsey, but he lacked Wolsey's vision, grace, and style. He left little behind him but the angry denunciation of the nobles, the loathing of the clergy whom he had done his best to ruin, and the contempt of the poor, now deprived of their monastic alms or livelihood and forced into stark poverty. On a hot July morning at Tyburn, the fifty-year-old minister stood on the scaffold professing he died a true Catholic, not a heretic. The leader of a religious revolution, the plunderer of the monasteries, a statesman of almost unequalled competence, a superb administrator with the tactics of his idol, Machiavelli, did not have an easy death. While 1,000 soldiers stood guard to keep the jostling crowd of onlookers from approaching the scaffold, the 'cleverest head in England' was brutishly hacked away by the incompetent bungling of the executioner. He died unmourned. 'The foul churl is dead', said Norfolk's son, the Earl of Surrey, 'now he is stricken with his own staff.'[10]

It was a staff that was destined to strike many more.

With his fine disregard for a more subtle display of good taste, the King chose the day of Cromwell's execution to wed Katherine Howard. Neither Mary, Edward, nor Elizabeth Tudor attended the fifth marriage of their father at Oatlands. Mary found it wiser and less costly to her emotions to remain as much as possible in the background, although she came to Hampton Court in early August when Katherine Howard was publicly proclaimed Queen. In this marriage to his 'rose without a thorn', Henry Tudor felt he had found the ideal companion for his autumn years. The King was now a corpulent figure, older looking than fifty-one, with grey streaking the auburn hair and lines seaming the fleshy face. When his ulcerated leg bothered him, he was forced to hobble about, and if such a figure seemed an incongruous mate for the hazel-eyed girl of eighteen, it was of little importance in contrast to the last surges of passionate youth Katherine Howard inspired in Henry Tudor.

Katherine's proud Howard lineage showed in the same straight nose as her uncle's, the great Duke of Norfolk, and she had all the gaiety, vivaciousness, and charm of her dead cousin, Anne Boleyn. She had, however, little of the learning, taste, wit, or intelligence of either of them. In accordance with the custom of sending children to other residences of the nobility in order that they might learn the manners and graces necessary to their position, Katherine Howard had been parcelled out very young to the household of Agnes, the aged Dowager-Duchess of Norfolk. Katherine came from a penniless branch of the family. Her father, Edmund Howard, had distinguished himself at the Battle of Flodden which seems to have been the one redeeming moment in a mediocre life. Weak and inefficient, he early incurred the dislike of Henry and the rest of his family and was often so imprudent that he had to go into hiding to escape his creditors. His daughter Katherine spent a relatively obscure and loveless childhood—little better than a dependent waif—in the vast home of the Dowager-Duchess, accepting what largesse came her way from her step-grandmother, with little or no supervision, less education or religious training, and lacking the pretty clothes, attention, and care which were her birthright. If nothing else, however, Katherine Howard was a realist; her upbringing had left too many scars for a late-blooming sensitivity. While she was hardly in love with the King, she could respect what he represented, and Henry's ageing corpulence did not repel her. To come from the backrooms of ducal mansions to preen over the other court ladies at Whitehall was more intoxicating than anything Katherine had ever hoped for. Once the King 'did cast a fantasy to Katherine Howard' and her Norfolk relatives realised that another member of their staunch Catholic family might influence the King more than any minister or foreign power, they sought her advancement in every way. Better to forget that she could barely read or write, that she was more at home with the boisterous and high-living members of her relatives' family, that she had given her heart (and a bit more) to several of the gentlemen employed in various capacities in the Duchess's homes. She was eighteen, vibrant and glowing with a great sense of fun and a youthful radiance that Henry found irresistible. *No Other Will But His* became her motto, and the King was enchanted. He showered her with jewels, rich clothing, and more loving attention than she had ever known before in her neglected youth.

The new Queen had little in common with her oldest step-daughter, Mary Tudor. In addition to her fine Spanish heritage and her cultivated taste, Mary was also six years older than Katherine Howard. So the Queen sought to hide her uncertainty with Mary under an assumed arrogance. Mary was coolly polite to Katherine and absented herself from court as soon as possible. Katherine fared better with Anne Boleyn's daughter. Elizabeth was thrilled to be summoned to court, and because she was a blood relative, she was given a place of honour at the table. It was even more exciting when her own dear Anne of Cleves arrived to pay homage to the new Queen. Before leaving for her comfortable retirement at Richmond, Anne had declared to Henry that 'to have the young Princess for her daughter would have been a greater happiness to her than being Queen,'[11] and Elizabeth had formed a warm tie with the 'King's Good Sister'. Enjoying all the creature comforts of a luxurious life such as neither of the King's daughters could boast, and with no sullen husband to spoil it all, Anne of Cleves could be generous. She brought Katherine Howard a gift of two horses with rich velvet trappings of violet, earning an especially warm greeting from the Queen, who tactfully refused to let Anne kneel to her. All three sat and then dined together, the King openly caressing his new wife in the presence of his former while, to the vast amusement of the court, the seven-year-old Elizabeth watched it all.

*

The death of Cromwell and Henry's angry insistence on submission to his Act of the Six Articles emphasised anew the dissension prevalent in England as political parties—all evolving from separate religious policies—struggled for supremacy. The minority group which had decried the divorce from Catherine of Aragon and Henry's assaults upon the Church and which regarded Princess Mary as legitimate were the staunch Papists. The most powerful faction were the Henricians. These were the 'new men' around the King, and they were with Henry all the way—all pro-Catholic, but denying any allegiance to the Pope. The active Reformers, who would later be called Protestants, were looked upon more as heretics and troublemakers, and the King had had his share of these during the last few years. Another uprising in the rebellious North, still smarting from the tragic effects of the Pilgrimage of Grace—which had shaken the Tudor confidence more than Henry liked to admit—had convinced the King and Council of the necessity for Henry's presence in the troubled areas. Consequently, in the summer of 1541, the roads leading to Lincoln, York, Newcastle, and Hull, witnessed the first visit by a Tudor monarch to the 'brute shires' which had expressed so much dissatisfaction with the government. At Hull, the bones of one of the rebels, Robert Constable, were still dangling over the gate of the city when Henry passed through. In addition to confronting his rebellious subjects whom he hoped to conciliate by a display of royal benevolence combined with just the right amount of might, Henry also wished to meet his nephew, James V of Scotland, in order to counteract the strong influence of France, Scotland's traditional ally. In one of the last great displays of his long reign, the full court assembled to accompany Henry Tudor on his progress, while Archbishop Cranmer, Chancellor Audley, and Edward Seymour remained at home as deputies for the King. Henry had a thousand armed soldiers, a regal and lavishly dressed nobility, and a beautiful young Queen to help to dazzle his subjects.

Preceded by the drawn bows of eighty archers, the tremendous cavalcade swept through city after city of the North, whose citizens now saw their King for the first time. The firing of artillery pieces and the pealing of church bells were all but drowned by the rumblings of the wagons holding the 200 tents needed to house the visitors. More than 5,000 horses followed, carrying the magnificent tapestries, the finest jewelled plate, and other provisions necessary for the royal comfort. Mayors, noblemen, and common citizens bowed before Henry and Katherine, a wondrous sight for the young Queen to whom attention was still a heady novelty. Even more pleasing were the moments when bags of gold were presented to the monarch. It was a great political triumph, marred only by the fact that James did not venture on to English soil at York, thereby snubbing the royal uncle who had waited patiently for twelve days to meet him. James's marriage to the beautiful Mary of Guise not only emphasised the snub, but secured his French alliance even more strongly.

Arriving home in October, Henry found the four-year-old Edward ill of quartan fever. The Prince was so sheltered and supervised it was inconceivable to anyone that he should be ill. Mary Tudor had been dispatched to watch over her sick brother, but the dangerous fever had continued to the despair of the worried girl and the King's faithful and competent old Dr Butts. When Henry asked for news of his son, he was told the child was no worse, but neither was he getting any better. Rumours were prevalent that the child would die. He was 'so fat, unhealthy and overfed, he cannot live long', the French ambassador wrote. Within a few weeks, however, to Henry's and Mary's intense relief, the Prince was well enough to be moved to Ashridge, and in a matter of days the youngster was exhibiting a natural rebellion at the constant wariness and supervision which surrounded him. He wanted to get out of bed, to be able to play with his toys, and to be away from the incessant queries about how he felt—did he sleep well?—did he want a drink of water? His impatience extended to his food—he longed for solid meat instead of the soups and milk puddings allowed during his illness. When Dr Butts agreed the Prince might have his meat, he attacked the dish with relish while the physician, governess, sister, and chamber servants all stood by, smiling. When he had finished, Dr Butts inquired of the Prince—did he feel all right or did he wish to vomit? Edward's childish impatience finally burst its bonds and his reply was short; he'd had enough of feminine and medical surveillance. 'Go away, fool!' he cried to the doctor, striking the air with a small fist. Dr Butts was overjoyed at this sign of returning normality and cried, 'If I tarry till he call me knave, I shall say *Nunc Dimittis!*'[12]

Satisfied his son was well, Henry went hunting, returning finally to Hampton Court and circumstances which led to tragedy. He attended Mass and, at the end of his devotions, gave thanks not only for his son's recovery but for his happiness with Katherine Howard, saying aloud, 'I render thanks to Thee, O Lord, that after so many strange accidents that have befallen my marriages, Thou hast been pleased to give me a wife so entirely conformed to my inclinations as her I now have.'[13] He instructed his confessor, the Bishop of Lincoln, to make a public thanksgiving at Mass on the following All Saints' Day.

During Henry's progress to the North, the three appointed deputies —Cranmer, Audley, and Seymour—had come upon news of the Queen which placed her destruction within their power. The staunch Catholicism of the Howards was too conservative for the more reform-minded ministers. The old Duke of Norfolk had told them he would rather tilt with the devil than read Scripture. 'It was merry in England afore the new learning came up', he said, wishing that 'all things were as hath been in times past'. The ministers resented the Howard influence in the Council, on the King, and found Katherine, personally, too flighty in her manners. Since she had not as yet presented the King with an heir, she had been of little use to them or the realm and the evidence they possessed might now encompass her fall.

The following day, at the conclusion of the service, instead of the public announcement which the King had requested, Cranmer placed in Henry's hands a slip of paper which the archbishop asked him to read in strict privacy since 'he didn't have the heart to tell him by mouth.' His fine sensitivity aside, the prelate may also have lacked the courage to tell the man so obviously in love that his new wife had 'lived most corruptly and sensually'. To his credit, Henry's first reaction was one of honest disbelief at any of Katherine's suspected infidelities. Instead, he regarded the charges as political calumny of the lowest order directed at one 'whom he so tenderly loved . . . and had conceived such a constant opinion of her honesty, that he supposed it rather to be a forged matter than the truth.'[14] He summoned Russell, the new Lord Privy Seal, Fitzwilliam, the Lord Admiral, Sir Anthony Browne, and Sir Thomas Wriothesley and ordered them to conduct a quiet investigation to discover the perpetrators of such an attack on Katherine, saying that in so doing, 'no spark of scandal should arise against the Queen'. The charges, he said, were fraud; 'he could not believe it to be true. . . .'[15]

But, in the next few days, the whole sordid story came to light. Katherine's relations with Henry Manox, a music teacher in the household of the Duchess of Norfolk and, later, her more serious affair with Francis Dereham, a gentleman-pensioner also living in the Duchess's home, gave substance to the charges. Witnesses were found who had attended the midnight parties in the maidens' dormitory at which 'wine, strawberries, apples and other things to make good cheer' had preceded the seduction of the thirteen-year-old Katherine Howard by Dereham. Far from being shocked by the girl's behaviour—not unusual for the era—the former associates of the Queen had encouraged and aided the relationship which lasted several months. Later, they had not hesitated to use such knowledge of her conduct to presume upon Katherine's own innate kindesss—or weakness—and ask for appointments in her household. Katherine had not always given these places willingly. But the polite pressure of her former companions stopped just short of blackmail. With the knowledge of her past indiscretions always before her, Katherine had satisfied them as best she could, even to admitting Dereham to her service as her secretary. In addition, many of her relatives, aunts, cousins, sisters, and their husbands, had received appointments in the royal establishment. Her brothers, George and Charles, her Uncle William and cousin Henry were recipients of favours in the form of monastic lands, political perquisites, and expensive clothing, thus creating further envy, especially in the hearts of those whom the Queen could not accommodate. The reformers in the land and those who tended towards reform, such as Cranmer, regarded her Catholic conservatism as a hindrance, especially in view of the King's great attachment to her. When John Lascelles, a rabid reformer and a brother of one of the Duchess's women who had participated in the dormitory parties, was accosted by Henry's councillors, he was eager (though somewhat tardy) to tell his story, saying, 'he would rather die in the declaration of truth, since it so nearly touched the King, than live with the concealment of the same.'[16]

Within three days, depositions had been taken from the unfortunate Dereham, who admitted to carnal relations with the Queen, and Manox, who admitted to intimacy just short of adultery. Henry left Hampton Court on Sunday, November 5, 1541, to hear the results of the investigation in a session of the Council which lasted all night. Upon arrival at the London residence of Stephen Gardiner, the Bishop of Winchester, the King exhibited a tolerance only age and experience could bestow; he obviously expected to hear that his Queen had been unduly profaned and her suspected infidelities were, in reality, innocent, adolescent fancies. He sat now, ageing and hardened—yet oddly vulnerable—and his minsters, with many personal, political, and religious motives to satisfy, did not spare him. The King was incredulous and listened, with an expressionless face, as they related the 'abominable, base, carnal, voluptuous and vicious life' Katherine Howard had led prior to her marriage. Henry sought for control, saying 'his heart was pierced with pensiveness', and then the cold reality of his position swept over him at the deception of his 'rose without a thorn', and suddenly, his Council was faced with the image of their normally invincible monarch, 'strong in his courage', sitting at the Council table, his mouth working as tears welled in his eyes. All at once his composure was gone, and with shaking shoulders the huge man covered his lined and seamed face and wept uncontrollably, as the last possible hope he might have retained of Katherine's innocence vanished and the detestable charges pounded in his ears.

The revelation of Henry's ministers prompted a closer look into Katherine's activities since she had become Queen. Once knowledge of her previous indiscretions was out, those near the Queen knew themselves to be in mortal danger; their only defence lay in heaping as much slander on Katherine as they could, with a view to saving their own skins. Previous to her marriage, the Queen had held Thomas Culpeper, a distant relative, in great affection. Culpeper was a member of Henry's Privy Chamber and close enough to the King that he often slept in the same chamber as Henry. Culpeper's attraction for Katherine was noted

[117]

by one Margery Morton who told the Council she had been with the Queen at Hatfield 'when she saw Her Majesty look out the window to Mr Culpeper in such sort that she thought there was love between them.'[17]

During the recent triumphal progress to the North, Culpeper and Katherine had been incessantly thrown together and she contrived to meet him wherever the royal cavalcade halted. From Greenwich to York, many backstairs meetings had ensued with the shallow Lady Rochford, George Boleyn's widow, standing guard as the Queen and Culpeper met. Patiently the Council, led by the wily Thomas Wriothesley, built its case against Katherine which encompassed most of her Howard relatives, including the Dowager-Duchess of Norfolk. The old Duke himself scurried to the safety of Kenninghall, writing to Henry of the 'abominable deeds done by two of my nieces against your Highness, hath brought me into the great perplexity that ever poor wretch was in. . . .'[18] Norfolk feared Henry's retaliation, and, a 'poor wretch' indeed, he reminded Henry he was the one who had first uncovered the Duchess's misdemeanors and begged the King's indulgence for himself.

Henry did not see Katherine Howard again. The unfortunate girl—still not realising the ready target she was for her unscrupulous persecutors—was ordered to Syon House, a former Brigittine nunnery which Princess Mary hurriedly vacated on orders from the King. Henry alternated between grief and rage, leading Marillac, the French ambassador, to write that the King 'had taken such grief at being deceived that of late it was thought he had gone mad.'[19] He rode off alone at odd times in 'wild fashion' without informing anyone of his destination. Then between bouts of honest tears at his loss or angry tears of self-pity, he regretted his 'ill luck in meeting with such ill-conditioned wives' and threatened that 'the wicked woman had never such delight in her incontinency as she should have torture in her death.'[20] Even Eustace Chapuys, who probably knew Henry as well as any other envoy, wrote that the King 'wonderfully felt the case of his Queen.' Not only had Henry suffered a tragic blow to his male ego, but the buoyant illusion of youth which he had sustained throughout his eighteen months of marriage was now lost as well. Gone forever was the royal lover, dancer, and merrymaker. Gone forever was the joy in being the proud husband of a youthful beauty. There was nothing left for Henry Tudor now but the startling hurt of his betrayal and the spectre of old age.

Substantiating Lady Rochford's testimony, the Council unearthed a letter written by the Queen to Thomas Culpeper. With little regard for her royal position or the danger in which she was placing Culpeper or herself, Katherine thoughtlessly wrote on the occasion of an illness which prevented his attendance at court.

Master Culpeper,

I heartily recommend me unto you, praying you to send me word how that you do. I did hear that ye were sick and I never longed so much for anything as to see you. It maketh my heart to die when I do think that I cannot always be in your company. Come to me when my Lady Rochford be here, for then I shall be best at leisure to be at your commandment. . . . [21]

The letter, signed 'Yours as long as life endures', was all the Council needed to accuse the Queen of adultery *after* her marriage. Fearing any lingering tenderness on Henry's part for his beautiful wife, the councillors loudly and hurriedly proclaimed her indiscretions to all foreign ambassadors. A publicly cuckolded King would be less likely to forgive and forget. The French ambassador wrote that Culpeper had been close enough to Henry to share the intimacy of the King's own chamber and 'apparently wished to share the Queen's too'.

At Syon, the visits by Cranmer and the Council left little doubt at last in Katherine's mind of her situation. Alternating between depression and bouts of hysteria reminiscent of her cousin, Anne Boleyn, the terrified girl admitted her improprieties with Manox and Dereham but strongly denied any carnal relationship with Culpeper. In her confession addressed to Henry, Katherine admitted she had allowed Manox 'at sundry times to handle and touch the secret parts of my body which neither became me with honesty. . . .' She admitted that Francis Dereham 'by many persuasions procured me to his vicious purpose and obtained first to lie upon my bed with his doublet and hose and used me in such sort as a man doth his wife many and sundry times. . . .' But she insisted their relationship had ended a year before Henry's marriage to Anne of Cleves. And later, when Henry had first seen her, she said, 'I was so desirous to be taken unto your Grace's favour, and so blinded with the desire of worldly glory, that I could not, nor had grace, to consider how great a fault it was to conceal my former faults from your Majesty. . . .' [22]

Dereham and Culpeper came before the commissioners at the Guildhall on December 1, 1541. Admitting that he had been deeply in love with Katherine Howard and 'ill with grief' when she wed the King, Culpeper nevertheless insisted no guilty act had been committed despite their secret meetings. Outside of her own admission of her premarital indiscretions, there was never any proof that Katherine had committed adultery with Culpeper. Both denied the charge to the end. However, anyone who might 'maliciously wish, will or desire by words or writing, or by craft, imagine the King's death or harm' was guilty of treason in the eyes of the Tudor courts. Henry had certainly been harmed, and the intent or 'craft' of Culpeper, particularly, and of Dereham who had sought and secured a royal appointment from the Queen made their end predictable. On December 10, the two young men were drawn from the Tower to Tyburn. There, Culpeper was beheaded as befitted one of gentle birth. Then Dereham was 'hanged, membered, bowelled, headed, and quartered'. The Queen's family—cousins, brothers, sisters, and even the matriarch of them all, the gruff old Dowager-Duchess—remained incarcerated for misprision of treason. The King's commissioners repeatedly questioned the Duchess who found herself 'so enmeshed and tangled' in her evidence that the interrogators remarked, 'it will be hard for her to wind out again'. All were anxious to dissociate themselves from Katherine's folly, to save their lives and the confiscation of their estates.

After a miserable Christmas during which there was little merry-making, Henry opened Parliament and then withdrew from attendance as it went through the process of condemning his wife. By February 8, the Bill of Attainder against the Queen had been issued, and Katherine was informed of the sentence. She begged 'his Majesty not to impute her crime to her whole kindred and family', a remarkably solicitous gesture from one who had received so little support from her relatives since her arrest. On February 10, 1542, she went by barge to the Tower. Dressed in sombre black velvet, Katherine was much in control of herself until the fearful moment when she approached the landing stairs at Syon for her departure. It was a grey, overcast day and the river stretched before her, with darkness just descending. She knew what lay at the end of the journey. Her complete abandonment and loneliness, all combined with a natural repugnance at facing imprisonment and death, caused the Queen to suddenly draw back and cry out. She was quickly surrounded and led by force into the barge where she sat, trembling, as it swept downstream, shooting the torrent at London Bridge just as darkness fell. Mercifully it hid the impaled rotting heads of Dereham and Culpeper and the sightless eyes which could no longer see the woman they had loved and whose ambition had destroyed them all. During the journey, Katherine had regained composure, and with a dignity she had often lacked as a royal consort, she entered Traitor's Gate where Sir John Gage, the new Constable of the Tower, 'paid her as much honour as when she was reigning.'

On Sunday, the twelfth, when told she would suffer the extreme penalty on the morrow, Katherine Howard startled Gage by asking that the block be brought to her chamber so she might 'learn how to dispose her head upon it.' When it arrived, she knelt and rehearsed the wretched role she was destined to play. By seven the next morning, she was ready. The green in front of St Peter-ad-Vincula, which had seen the blood of her cousin, Anne Boleyn, spilled only six years previously, was covered with an early morning frost. Outside the grim walls, a weak sunlight was dispelling the thick clammy fog which hung over the river. Inside the Tower precincts it still remained, enveloping the scaffold and those standing nearby. With the exception of the Dukes of Norfolk and Suffolk, the entire Council, which had accomplished Katherine Howard's downfall, was in attendance, bantering with one another, stamping their feet and blowing on their fingers in the damp cold. She faced them, and in a rare moment of maturity and composure which contrasted deeply with the babbling of Lady Rochford who stood half crazed with fear nearby, she spoke to them. Katherine followed the custom of acknowledging a fault against the King. She grieved that 'Culpeper should have to die through me', saying, 'sin blinded me, and greed of grandeur, and since mine is the fault, mine also is the suffering. . . .' After pardoning the executioner and asking him to hurry, she uttered the words which left no doubt where her heart had been. 'I die a Queen', she whispered, just before the blow fell, 'but I would rather have died the wife of Culpeper. . . .' The axe descended, and Katherine Howard, the victim of family pride and her own shallow ambition, was dead. As the executioner cleaned the blade and Lady Rochford was pushed towards the block, the Queen's body and its severed head were taken to the church to be buried near Anne Boleyn, of whom it could also be said,

'The beauteous toy, so fiercely sought,
Had lost its charms by being caught. . . .'[23]

The Act of Attainder against Katherine Howard carried a clause which incurred the penalty of treason for any woman who ventured to wed the King if her previous life had been unchaste. 'Few if any ladies now at court', said the cynical Chapuys, 'would henceforth aspire to such an honour.'[24] Or, he might have added, been eligible. At first, the King plunged into a round of social activity designed to help him forget his dead Queen. He paid particular attention to the ex-wife of Thomas Wyatt who had been divorced for adultery. 'She is a pretty young creature, with wit enough to do as badly as the others if she were to try', continued Chapuys. But the ambassador knew Henry well enough to know his heart was not involved, saying, '. . . the King had never been merry since first hearing of the Queen's misconduct. . . .'[25]

And so, nearing the end of his life, half sick in body and poisoned at heart by his wife's deception, weary of the shallowness and emptiness of court life, Henry Tudor turned to his children and the governing of his realm to forget. He could not know in the midst of his sorrow that one other woman would occupy the throne, and she, of all those who had preceded her, would prove a capable, warm, and affectionate stepmother to the three young Tudors.

Chapter Seven

THE remaining years of Henry's life were spent in a London bursting from its medieval background and boundaries. Though he frequently journeyed to the river palaces of Windsor, Hampton Court, and Greenwich, to the royal manors of Oatlands, Oking, and Nonsuch, the life of the court and the governing of his realm centred in Cardinal Wolsey's old York Palace, newly renamed Whitehall.

The Palace of Whitehall was situated along the Thames just as, in a gleaming arc, the river curved eastwards. Its walls stretched from the Cross in the little village of Charing to the park which bordered on Henry's 'house in the fields', the Palace of St James. It was nearer to the City itself with its familiar landmarks of St Paul's, the twenty-arched London Bridge, and the Tower, than the venerable Palace of Westminster which was farther upstream, across the road from the ancient Abbey.

The King had lavishly enlarged and rebuilt Wolsey's erstwhile York Place into a mélange of rose-coloured brick, landscaped terraces and gardens, aviaries, and splendid state rooms. In his Waterside Gallery, which extended out over the Thames, Henry could see from London Bridge to Lambeth Palace on the opposite bank. Rearing their massive towers at two different entrances, the gates of Whitehall straddled the 'Streete', a narrow cobbled thoroughfare connecting the main route of traffic from the Cross at Charing to the Abbey. The artist Holbein lived in one of the towers which was constructed of small square white stones and flint boulders of two distinct colours, 'glazed and disposed in a tesselated manner'. The gate, with its connecting wall of rosy brick, overlooked a tennis court, tiltyard, and cockpit. Here the court gathered to watch the jousts, tiltings, and military exercises so dear to Henry's heart. Farther on, the 'Streete' passed to the other entrance, the King's Gate—four semicircular towers with cupolas, which overlooked a Bowling Green.[1] Nearby, between the Strand and the river, was the home of Henry's brother-in-law, Charles Brandon, the Duke of Suffolk. Stretching along the river's edge were the palatial mansions, gardens, and terraces of other nobles. These imposing estates of the wealthy, all enclosed by magnificent trees, had helped to preserve areas of lush greenery adjacent to the City itself.

At the end of many streets or lanes one could perpetually glimpse the shining Thames. From the river resounded the cries of the watermen carrying passengers to the Surrey side or along the length of the water-way where tame swans dodged the barges of the great nobles or the smaller boats of the humble. The booming of guns from the Tower mixed with the clatter of traffic on the wooden roadway of London Bridge where heads of criminals were exhibited on pikes at the Southwark end. Shops lined each side of the structure. Farther upstream, horses, men, and wagons were taken across the river by the Horse Ferry near the old Westminster Palace, and here, Cranmer, the Archbishop of Canterbury, often crossed from Lambeth Palace to attend services in the Abbey before proceeding down the 'Streete' to Whitehall. More modest homes, the City dwellings of lesser nobles who resided mainly in the country, clustered around Westminster. It was an easy walk down the the 'Street' to the Great Hall of Westminster Palace with its magnificent hammerbeam roof which had miraculously survived a disastrous fire in 1512, to the little church of St Margaret or to the Abbey, where the Commons held its Parliament in the Chapter House.

Nearby, in New Palace Yard, was the dreaded Star Chamber which still meted out punishment in the form of the pillory, imprisonment, branding, or worse. More welcome, especially to thirsty citizens and travellers, were the Inns, the 'Antelope' and the 'Blue Boar'. The 'Streete', today's Whitehall, stretched through Charing to the Strand and into the City of London with its steeply-winding thoroughfares still laid out in medieval pattern. All narrow, muddy, all cluttered with rubble, filth, and human excrement, the lanes and tiny streets were shunned by anyone who could afford to travel by the river. Many of the structures, while three and four stories high and a welcome distance from the smells below, were built of plaster and timber and presented a dangerous fire hazard. Windows which did not open contributed to the stench inside. The congestion was immense. Harried men and women, often with dirty sickly children, pursued their livelihood in trade, in service, or apprenticeship—for the City of London was wealthy, fashionable, and a great port and centre of commerce. Beggars and prostitutes assailed the citizens inside and outside the City walls. The disorder was compounded by the vendors' stalls where apprentices in blue caps sold rabbits, oysters, fresh loaves, sweets, and sundries. The shops of the more prosperous merchants gleamed with bolts of brilliant cloth from Flanders and goldsmiths' work from Italy; others were laden with precious leathers and wines from France, Italy, and the Mediter-ranean countries, or oil from Spain. The taverns which housed the traveller and fed guest and citizen alike were redolent of beef, mutton, and venison or savoury rabbit pies, which were washed down with a monthly brewed beer. Each was identified by a sign bearing a painted symbol for a population which was, with few exceptions, illiterate; they were the many social centres and meeting places for revolutionary and reactionary alike.

In contrast to the sordid and dingy surroundings, processions were a common and colourful sight. On a Whit Sunday, the citizens of London might watch the bishop of St Paul's in his scarlet vestment, preceded by priests holding aloft great silver or gold crosses and followed by a retinue of ecclesiastics carrying burning candles. Or they might cheer the pompous, violet-cloaked Lord Mayor and his aldermen clothed in scarlet as they departed to officiate at the Guildhall or the Temple. Grubby-faced children in tattered clothing were held high to see the hurried passage of a nobleman accompanied by some hundred horsemen in bright velvet uniforms rich with embroidery, as they clattered by, all bound on the King's business. These same citizens lined the pavements to watch the spectacle of a foreign embassy on its way to present credentials to the King. They gaped at the banners of Spain, Venice, or France held by standard bearers whose costumes produced as much comment as their drummers, trumpeters, or flutists playing what the Londoners considered outlandish music. Harlequin-clothed jesters, Morris dancers, minstrels, troubadours, and mummers brought up the rear, with more than a fair sprinkling of vagrants. These were the yeomen and their families evicted from their homes by the enclosure of agricultural lands and ecclesiastics cast from their monasteries. They had one thing in common. Both groups were dangerous, with the quiet desperation born of acute hunger, deprivation, and a burning sense of injustice.

If the City was thronged and busy during the day, it was also alive at night, but with another element. Cut-throats, pickpockets, vagabonds, and harlots—all professional and hardened criminals—some little more than children. They roamed the streets either singly or in groups, preying on anyone foolish enough to venture abroad in the dark alone. The citizen bound for the ladies of pleasure in Southwark, the merchant on his way to his favourite tavern, the lackey attending a cockfight or bear-baiting—all walked abroad at great risk. The foreign merchants and artisans especially were ready targets for the students from the nearby Inns of Court, for the Englishmen basically distrusted the foreigners in their midst. The guilds were jealous of the craftsmanship of the goldsmiths of Italy, the leather-workers of Spain, the weavers of Flanders, the painters of France. More than one street brawl, fire, or murder resulted from the students and guild apprentices. Many a hot-headed young Englishman found temporary shelter in the fields of

Finsbury or Moor Fields north of his home until tempers and passions had cooled; surveillance was spasmodic, for the sheriffs were overworked, underpaid, and too few in number to deal effectively with the crime spawned in the rabbit-warren complex that was the City of London.

This was the centre of Henry Tudor's world and here—from a respectable distance at Whitehall—he dealt with the manifold duties of a sovereign holding the physical and spiritual life of his subjects at his pleasure, while keeping a wary eye on his Continental rivals, Charles and Francis. But it was not enough to keep Henry occupied. At fifty-two, the King felt the loneliness and depression which comes with age, sickness, and boredom. There was no companion to share his bed, his table, or the beauty he had wrought at Whitehall or his great new palaces of Nonsuch and St James. Necessary abstinence from the tennis court, the tiltyard, and the hunt—and his compensating indulgence in food and wine—had contributed to his already considerable waistline. Henry had always been a big man; now he was immense. Prematurely aged and ill, his beard streaked with grey and somewhat sparse, the puffy eyelids narrowing the blue eyes above the sagging jowls, the King was no prize for any woman, though it is doubtful that such a fact, so obvious to others, occurred to him or would have hindered him if it had. A year after Katherine Howard's death, his restlessness had increased to the point where his need for another wife was serious.

Henry's selection for his sixth Queen was Lady Latimer, Katherine Parr—a petite, gracious, extremely fair woman of thirty-one with brilliant hazel eyes which radiated an enormous kindness and compassion that Henry, with the wisdom of age and experience, could at last appreciate. Of impeccable lineage, blameless reputation, and related to many noble families, Katherine Parr had been married, when little more than a child of twelve or thirteen to Edward, Lord Borough of Gainsborough, a man old enough to have adult children of his own. Shortly widowed, she married John Neville, Lord Latimer of Thornton Briggs, again a man much older than herself with a family of growing children. Neither marriage had produced offspring, though her fondness and talent for managing her stepchildren were well known. Henry viewed Katherine Parr's love for and ability with children as another important asset to her other considerable virtues. He had watched his older daughter, Mary, moving aimlessly from one residence to another, growing older and more withdrawn, her face bearing unmistakable traces of illness and sadness, her reticence to speak intimately with him rendering her almost a stranger. He had wondered what was to be done with her. He was aware of her reluctance to wed and ruefully reasoned he had hardly provided her with an inspiring example of wedlock. The treatment meted out to her potential suitors and his act illegitimatising her had not improved her desirability in foreign courts. Henry's conscience could plague him about Mary—although not too deeply or too often.

Edward and Elizabeth were of more immediate concern; Edward it would be who would provide a future Tudor heir. Elizabeth was comely and still young enough to be quite a prize in the matrimonial sweepstakes. He doubted that Elizabeth would ever have any aversion to marriage—surely not with her looks and heritage! Both his younger children were bright, intelligent, excelling in their studies, and apparently healthy. But they lacked the solace of a mother's loving care. Edward had his nurse 'Mother Jak' and Elizabeth her procession of governesses. Mary certainly had been thoughtful of both his other children. Still they needed a mother, and the King needed a wife whom he could love and respect. He had done his best to forget the radiance of Katherine Howard; the memory of her faithlessness was something which could still cause pain.

When Lord Latimer died, Henry remembered the appealing Lady Latimer and, in a burst of paternal anxiety and self-pity, paid serious court to the widow. Katherine Parr was terrified at the King's intentions and honest and direct enough to say frankly that 'it was better to be your mistress than your wife!' But the King wanted no mistress; mistresses were easily obtained. He now desired a wife, a mother for his children, a companion for his last years, and who better than the woman who had had experience in caring for two older men?

Katherine's reluctance to accept Henry was further strengthened by the fact that, free at last to follow the dictates of her heart, she had encouraged the attentions of Thomas Seymour, the dashing brother of Jane Seymour and one of Henry's intimate companions. To have such a young, virile, and gay suitor after eighteen years of being nurse-wife to ageing men delighted the elegant Katherine Parr. Her life, for all its physical comforts and social distinction, had been incredibly dull, and the widely travelled, experienced sophisticate who now paid her marked attention found his advances most welcome. Seymour had never been eager for marriage, but he was approaching the age when it would be wise to settle down, and, thrift not being one of his greater virtues, the wealth as well as the loveliness of Lady Latimer was a strong inducement to the married state. But once Seymour saw the direction the royal affection was taking, he was prudent enough not to endanger his position, and possibly his head, by competing with the King. He withdrew from court, either at Henry's request or by his own preference, serving at the English embassy in Flanders and later in France. He did not return until after Henry and Katherine had been wed for some time.

Chapuys had said of Henry, 'When the King takes a fancy for a person or a thing, he goes the whole way.' Once he had chosen and

Seymour had discreetly withdrawn, there was little for Katherine Parr to gain by refusing the King except his angry reprisal. They were married at the 'Queen's Privy Closet' in Hampton Court on July 13, 1543, almost thee years to the day since he had wed Katherine Howard. Instead of the surreptitious ceremonies in which he had married Anne Boleyn and Katherine Howard, Henry and Katherine Parr became man and wife in a simple rite in which she promised 'to be bonayr and buxome in bed and at board, till death us depart.' Stephen Gardiner, the Bishop of Winchester, officiated. Both Henry's daughters, Mary and Elizabeth; his niece, the Lady Margaret Douglas, daughter of his sister Margaret, the late Queen of Scotland; and many of his Council also attended. While the bridal party made merry, the spectator most likely genuinely happy with her father's choice was the King's eldest daughter, Mary. Katherine had been a great friend and champion of Mary Tudor. Both women were much alike—cultured, gifted, thoughtful, and well educated. They shared similar tastes—Katherine could speak as many languages as Mary and loved music and reading. Both were gentle and warm yet high-principled and self-disciplined.[2] Katherine was as superb a needlewoman as Mary's mother had been. Many months before her marriage and before Henry had made known his intentions, she had presumed upon her friendship with the King to help enlarge Mary's wardrobe, with an order for Italian gowns, hoods, and kirtles, noting on the bills sent to Henry, 'for your daughter'. On her wedding day, she did not forget the children, presenting suitable gifts to Edward and Elizabeth and a magnificent pair of gold bracelets adorned with rubies, diamonds, and emeralds to Mary. Wisely, an additional gift of money went to Mary, very welcome for her ever slim purse.

Katherine and Henry had no honeymoon owing to the shifting political situation which caused the King and Council to meet daily. The King of France, still dreaming of a dominion beyond the Alps and frustrated that his alliance with the Emperor had produced so little, declared war on the Empire. Henry was content to sit back and watch the direction the conflict might take while he organised a summer progress to introduce his new Queen to his subjects. Mary was overjoyed to be invited to accompany her father and Katherine to Woodstock, Grafton, and Dunstable. But the happy visiting with her new stepmother was interrupted by an illness which overtook her on the road. Her menstrual difficulty, which Mary had come to call her 'old guest', marred the girl's summer. She was removed to Grafton in the Queen's own litter and Dr Owens was sent to attend her. His remedy for Mary's frequent indispositions was invariably bloodletting. 'This is the real cause of her paleness and the general weakness of her frame', the Venetian ambassador was frank to say, for Mary was left more wan than ever after the debilitating treatment. For the girl who cherished her daily exercise enough to walk a mile or two each morning, who loved to course with her greyhounds in the great royal parks or open fields of some remote manor, the illnesses were a double privation. She went to Ashridge to be with Elizabeth and Edward, hoping the company of her small brother and sister would compensate for her disappointment in the ruined progress. Sharing a household every now and then was also less of a strain on Mary's purse. Katherine showed her awareness of Mary's need with a further gift of money which helped Mary to cope when her staff was suddenly stricken with an autumn illness. Ashridge was not large enough for the many who were sick; they were lodged in nearby villages or manor houses—all at Mary's expense. Even Jane the Fool was ill and cost Mary twenty-two shillings and sixpence 'in the tyme of hir seekness' with a further expenditure of five shillings for six ells of cloth to make a pair of sheets for the stricken girl.[3]

The effect of Henry's marriage was soon felt in other ways at Ashridge. Fate had deprived Katherine of children of her own, but her interest in those of her new husband was apparent. Besides her love for Mary and her affection for Elizabeth, she was concerned about the youngest Tudor, Henry's heir. Edward was now six, a 'marvellous sweet child, of very mild and generous conditions.' Everyone in his household adored the motherless little boy who had just begun the arduous routine of an education befitting a future king. Edward never possessed the depth of intellect of his sister Mary or Elizabeth's brilliant talent for assimilating whatever might prove useful. But an enviable capacity for learning was his by heritage. At six it was directed in a manner which resulted in a surface—if somewhat artificial—brilliance. The axiom 'to be a great gentleman, it is a notable reproach to be well-learned', which had made the young and talented Henry VIII such an exceptional figure in a semi-illiterate court, no longer applied as the end of his reign approached. Greek and Latin were taught orally to children before they could even write. Roger Ascham, Elizabeth's tutor, propounded a doubly startling philosophy. He contended that no child should be taught unwillingly; '. . . whatsoever the mind doth learn unwillingly, with fear, the same it doth quickly forget', said the wise old scholar.

Edward had been happy at Ashridge with Elizabeth or other children who were brought to play with him. One was a pretty six-year-old, Jane Dormer, the granddaughter of Sir William Sidney. Jane lived a short distance from Ashridge, and when Edward was lonely—as he often was when Elizabeth and Mary were absent—Jane came to spend the day, 'passing her time with him either in reading, playing, or dancing, and such like pastimes answerable to their spirits and innocency of years.' Edward became devoted to the little girl, calling her 'my Jane'. It was nice to have someone just one's own age and all to oneself; he became quite possessive in a lordly six-year-old way, and one day as they played at cards and Jane lost, he consoled her, saying, 'now Jane, your king is gone. I shall be good enough for you. . . .'[4] Years later, grown-up and married to the powerful Duke of Feria, Jane Dormer recalled with great fondness Edward's charm, kindness, and generosity, and his love especially for his older sister, Mary Tudor, who had almost fulfilled his need for a mother.

Henry had always thought—probably correctly—that the ladies of Edward's household, the rockers, nurses, maids, and governesses, were cosseting the child too much. Once married, Katherine yearned to have the blond, beautiful child with her. Therefore, just before Edward reached his seventh year, Lady Bryan was given another post, and those attached to Edward's household were rather peremptorily dismissed. Henry decided no past influences would be allowed to intrude into the brighter future now facing his only son. Amid tears all around, Edward and his sisters came to live at Hampton Court with Henry and a new and loving stepmother. The little boy felt the change keenly, remembering it years later as the time 'he was separated from the women. . . .' Once at Hampton, the matter of his education was undertaken with even greater emphasis. In addition to Dr Cox, the noted Dr John Cheke was appointed for the Prince's instruction in Latin and Greek. Edward's pastimes also became more varied than at Ashridge, with lessons in music, composition, singing, and—much to his pleasure—he was taught the rudiments of tilting, tennis, cards, chess, and more simple games. As an indulgence, he was even allowed to go hawking at times with some of the younger gentlemen of the court.

The middle Tudor child, Elizabeth, was ten years old at the time of her father's marriage to Katherine Parr. Physically, she had inherited the best from each of her parents. She had the build of the Tudors; the tall slimness and wiry agility which had so earmarked her father as a young Prince lent her own figure a lissom grace. The warm olive complexion of her mother, and Anne Boleyn's beautiful dark eyes, were framed by the bright red-gold hair of her father. Completely feminine, she loved dressing in as adult apparel as her governess would allow, and she cherished the simple jewellery and other adornments that Mary and a succession of stepmothers had given her. Outwardly she was an attractive, amiable, self-possessed, and intelligent young girl, poised at the brink of a future that would undoubtedly include a brilliant marriage and possibly a throne. By a new Act of Succession made shortly after his marriage to Katherine Parr, Henry placed Elizabeth in line for the throne after Edward and Mary or any male issue by his new Queen.

But the spirit and character of Elizabeth Tudor, had it been known to her father, brother, sister, or stepmother, would have startled, perplexed, and angered them. Even at ten, Elizabeth found ambition, pride, and resentment all struggling for predominance in a life which did not permit any rebellion at the fate which had made her the King's middle child. Rather, she was expected to exercise great self-discipline, piety, and thankfulness for the privilege of being the King's illegitimate daughter, and should dissatisfied feelings occur, she was to cast them aside. Compliance with the rigid rules of court etiquette and protocol was assumed.

In addition to this rather daring sense of defiance in the face of royal authority and custom, there was another emotion to which Elizabeth could not possibly have put a name, though she was very much aware of its existence. She yearned to be loved, appreciated, to mean something to somebody, and, above all, to be *someone*. In the even deeper recesses of her mind and soul, hastily and firmly smothered each time it ascended to her upper consciousness, was the knowledge of her mother's disgrace and execution, or the similar infidelities of her other Howard relative, the former Queen. She recognised the look which often came her way as 'Anne Boleyn's brat'—it was a look which at times could even come from the King himself. Because of his treatment of his former wives, including Mary's mother and even her own dear Anne of Cleves, Elizabeth regarded her father with a respect more strongly tinged with apprehension than love. She had learned to mask this feeling whenever he deigned to pay her any attention, which was not very often. She could accept with little bitterness that she was the least favoured of his children, for she had disappointed him by not being a boy and her mother had behaved in such a fashion he had cut off her head. Compensating for this knowledge perhaps, she had almost intuitively determined to excel in everything she undertook, hoping to win her father's approval and the respect of those around her. Like her mother before her, Elizabeth Tudor basked in compliments and praise, and there had been little enough of these in her life. Elizabeth had, however, managed to win many in her household, for she possessed all of Anne's personal magnetism, without the surface vivaciousness; she knew when to be quiet. This knowledge had become a small form of power, and she used it on all the governesses and minor servants in her household. Even at ten, she was an accomplished diplomat who dominated those around her with great skill, often without their conscious awareness of exactly how much she manœuvred them. Approaching early adolescence, she could not judge herself in contrast with other children, for she had few intimate friends her own age. She knew she was much cleverer than Mary whose very goodness and sincerity rendered her infinitely vulnerable. She knew Edward to be too malleable; even at six she had not been as submissive as her brother. What was the good of being a Prince and heir to the throne if you must continually follow the will of others?

[131]

Thus, with another new stepmother, all of Elizabeth's inner compulsions, dissensions, and desires—so different from her outward deference—warred within her. When summoned to court, she found many of these more fundamental feelings rising to the surface. A whole new life, full of opportunity, awaited her! In genuine gratitude, she wrote to Queen Katherine:

Madame:

The affection that you have testified in wishing that I should be suffered to be with you in the court and requesting this of the King, my father, with so much earnestness, is a proof of your goodness. So great a mark of your tenderness for me obliges me to examine myself a little, to see if I can find anything in me that can merit it; but I can find nothing but a great zeal and devotion to the service of your Majesty.

Knowing her father's disaffection for her, Elizabeth strengthened her defences with Katherine Parr in words that years later would seem ironical to both child and Queen:

I can assure you also that my conduct will be such that you shall never have cause to complain of having done me the honour of calling me to you; at least, I will make it my constant care that I do nothing but with a design to show always by obedience and respect. I await with much impatience the orders of the King, my father, for the accomplishment of the happiness for which I sigh, and I remain, with much submission,

Your Majesty's very dear,

ELIZABETH.[5]

Elizabeth arrived at court in high expectation of a life very different now that her father had a wife with whom he was happy and to whom she would find it easy to be a loving and dutiful daughter. It is, therefore, mysteriously tantalising, that despite all the child's good intentions, she soon afterwards so angered her father that she was ordered from the court. The gentle intervention of Katherine Parr who asked indulgence for the ten-year-old child availed nothing; Elizabeth had to go, and she was forbidden even to write to the King. Whatever the nature of Elizabeth's offence was, it has escaped the dedicated probing of historians for more than four hundred years. But by a process of elimination, it is possible to guess at what might be the truth without knowing the details.

The offences for which Elizabeth might have been so publicly punished are not the usual misdemeanours of a young girl: petty thievery, unwise sexual experimentation, or disrespect or insolence to a parent or others. It is certain that none of these was Elizabeth's provocation. She was too intelligent and too aware of her rank to steal, although at court there must have been many temptations for a child whose own household boasted few luxuries. She was too young and too supervised to be sexually compromised by a young groom, page, or other minor servant, and no jaded courtier would have dared entice the ten-year-old daughter of the King while that King was still alive. To be deliberately insolent to her father or stepmother or anyone of high rank would have been unheard of. Elizabeth's offence, then, had to be something she was not consciously aware would bring about the punishment it entailed; it was something she thought would bring a *different* reaction from Henry than actually occurred. And it was—to be sure—an accident, in that Elizabeth would never have knowingly incurred her father's wrath. It is also significant that in an era when the slightest and most trivial items are detailed with an almost ridiculous solemnity, the nature of her offence is not recorded anywhere. Whatever it was, it never went beyond Henry, Katherine, Mary, and Elizabeth. There can, then, be only one conclusion: her offence had something to do with her mother, her stepmothers, or with Henry's religious policies, on which Elizabeth may have been childishly opinionated. The last is doubtful, for Elizabeth's later malleability in the matter of religion was certainly formed in her youth. Her offence, therefore, probably arose from an innocent query, remark, or opinion on Anne Boleyn or her other relative, Katherine Howard. In a moment of unwonted and certainly unusual family harmony and buoyed by a security she did not realise was precarious, Elizabeth perhaps ventured to speak of her mother or Anne's cousin, and these were two subjects on which the King could bear no looking back.

The reaction was prompt and stunning, and the hapless child was packed off immediately in deep disgrace to St James's Palace. Elizabeth wept at the humiliation of her departure, her disappointment at leaving Katherine and the court, her anger at her own clumsiness and naïveté. But by the time she entered her barge, she could ignore the sympathetic looks of her retinue. Only the tight lips revealed her unhappiness. As the days passed and she took up her studies in the lonely solitude of St James's, Elizabeth reviewed her mistake and consciously absorbed its lesson. She realised the extent to which her lack of tact had rendered her terribly vulnerable in the face of a more powerful authority. If one wanted something, Elizabeth concluded, one must be more careful in its pursuit; above all one must never be too straightforward or forthright or one might easily lose all. It was a lesson Elizabeth Tudor never forgot.

Chapter Eight

THE last years of Henry VIII's life held one more joust with those battle-hardened contemporaries, Charles V of Spain and Francis I of France, with whom he'd spent a lifetime of political tilting amid shifting loyalties, outright deceit, and collusion. Now, while their war waged in Italy, both Francis and Charles wooed Henry separately, but with the wisdom acquired in a disillusioned past, the King had not committed himself. England and France were acknowledged enemies, however, and Henry leaned more towards the Emperor and Spain. Chapuys, ageing now and sick after his long years in England, longed to return home. He wrote, 'If the Emperor wishes to gain the King, he must send hither at once an able person, with full powers, to take charge of the negotiations.'[1]

But Henry was not to enter the struggle without sufficient gain for England. The King had long cherished an imperialist goal: the unification of Scotland and England into one Kingdom of Britain. The Scottish King, James V, the son of Henry's older sister, Margaret, did not share his vision. Instead, he had continued to rely on France. James was loyal to the 'old religion' and had sheltered many rebel refugees from the Pilgrimage of Grace, refusing to extradite them at Henry's demand. He had sanctioned many border raids and had snubbed his royal uncle on Henry's visit to the North in 1541, saying he must consult with the French King before any such meeting. By October, 1542, Henry's patience—somewhat remarkable in the face of James's continued provocation and arrogance—had vanished. He knew any future war against France must be fought only after he had dealt with Scotland; he could not fight a war on two fronts simultaneously. He sent 20,000 men headed by Thomas Howard, the Duke of Norfolk, across the Tweed. Anxious to regain Henry's favour which had been understandably strained during the Katherine Howard affair, Norfolk reduced farms, villages, towns, abbeys, and harvests to ashes before returning to Berwick where, due to lack of supplies, he left only a small force and returned to York. A month later the Scots retaliated with a raid into Cumberland. Sir Thomas Wharton, Warden of the Western Marches, rode out of Carlisle with some 300 men, gathering further recruits and horses as he went. When he reached the Leven, his forces numbered some 3,000. The Scots, however, assumed it was Norfolk's larger army and retreated towards their own border. But it was too late. In a wild rout, they rode for home as best they could, hampered by tents, cannon, ammunition, and other supplies. At Solway, they were met by the incoming tide. Many flung away their arms to facilitate their flight; others plunged into the water only to be swept away. The English caught up with the main portion of the army at Solway Moss and, reminiscent of Catherine of Aragon's stunning victory at Flodden Field some twenty-nine years previously, when James's father had been killed, ground Scottish pride into the dust. The defeat was ignominious; 1,200 Scots—earls, barons, lairds, nobles, and numerous pieces of ordnance were surrendered at the cost of seven English lives. Heartbroken by the disaster, James V died at Linlithgow a few days later 'from grief, regret and rage'. Four days previously, his beautiful French wife, Mary of Guise, had given birth to a baby daughter. As the end came, James turned his face to the wall and muttered, 'The devil go with it. It will end as it began. It came with a lass and it will pass with a lass.'[2]

Possibly, in his nearness to death, James Stuart could see that the 'coming of the lass'—his mother, Margaret Tudor—to Scotland, had been the initial tangible step in uniting Scotland and England. Realising he was leaving his country leaderless—with only a newborn girl as heir —he knew it would undoubtedly end with this same 'lass', his daughter. He was not far wrong. The fatherless little child was named Mary; one day she would be known as the Queen of Scots.

Henry's happiness with Katherine Parr was interrupted by the worsening political situation. The Scottish victory had stimulated the King's ambition. When the Scots, against all previous agreement, betrothed the infant Mary Stuart, whom the King 'looked upon as his own daughter', to a French prince, Henry was enraged. He wanted Mary for his own son Edward. He ordered the Earl of Hertford, Jane Seymour's older brother and one of the more capable members of Henry's Council, to enter Edinburgh, raze Holyroodhouse and 'sack Leith and burn and subvert it and all the rest, putting man, woman and child to fire and sword without exception . . . and extend the like extremities and destructions in all towns and villages . . . to spoil and turn upside down the Cardinal's town of St Andrews'. Hertford was to leave 'not one stick stand by another, sparing no creatures alive with the same'. And he was to pay particular attention to the agricultural areas, for 'now especially that it is seed time, from the which if they may be kept and not suffered to sow their grounds, they shall by the next year be brought to such a penury as they shall not be able to live nor abide the country.'[3] The tough Hertford, inured as he was to war and its sufferings, was appalled at the degree of Henry's revenge and dared suggest the fortification of Leith as a wiser measure than spreading such desolation. But his counsel was repelled, and he wrote that 'he could not sleep this night for thinking of the King's determination for Leith.'

With the Scots momentarily subdued and the Emperor set to invade France, the French stood 'like a deer upon the land'. Taking full advantage, Henry declared war. He cited his numerous grievances against Francis, mainly the French support of Scotland. The King wanted Boulogne, Montreuil, and Therouanne, his ancient 'rights' in France, he said, and also the arrears of his lapsed French pension. Francis showed sufficient concern to send word to Henry: 'We are both great Kings and well-stricken in years', he said and proposed a meeting 'for the sake of peace'.

But Henry turned a deaf ear to Francis's plea as well as to the discontent of his subjects with whom the war was unpopular. The English people were unmercifully taxed, and their lack of enthusiasm for Henry's venture was compounded when, at the King's command, the coin of the realm was debased by reducing the amount of silver and adding lesser alloys. To gain additional needed monies, Henry hurriedly sold Crown lands and incurred loans at high rates of interest. In great gulps, the war effort swallowed the fortune Cromwell had brought the royal treasury from the spoilation of the Church and other sources.

There had been no thought of Henry participating in the conflict personally. Obese as he was, half sick, and in almost constant pain from his leg, the King nevertheless longed for one last encounter on the field of battle. Even Katherine's wifely protestations were brushed aside, and there were few at court brave enough to hint to Henry that he might be more of a liability than an asset to the army. Charles was anxious to have Henry's active support, and one of the best ways to ensure the result was an appeal to the King's vanity.

The Imperial ambassador, Chapuys, clucked to Henry that the Channel crossing might be too much for him; the hardships of campaign were for younger, more agile men, he said. Bristling, Henry retaliated that his infirmities were no more than Francis's chronic illness or the Emperor's gout! The die was cast, and the three ageing weary old monarchs prepared to meet for the last time on the field of battle. Triumphantly, Charles sent an Imperial representative, the Duke of Najera, to England to advise the King on war matters, and in February 1544, a splendid reception was held at Whitehall for the Spanish grandee and his embassy. The visitors were awed by the magnificence of the

Palace and its gardens, replete with precious sculpture, its 'knott' gardens and pools. Pedro de Gante, Najera's secretary who attended the festivities, has left a stunning picture of Queen Katherine and Princess Mary at the reception for the Duke:

After the dancing had lasted several hours, the Queen returned to her chamber, first causing one of the noblemen who spoke Spanish to offer some presents to the Duke, who kissed her hand. He would likewise have kissed that of Princess Mary, but she offered her lips; and so he saluted her and all the other ladies.* The Queen is graceful and of cheerful countenance and is praised for her virtue. She wore an underskirt, showing a front of cloth of gold and a sleeved overdress of brocade lined with crimson satin . . . she wore hanging from the neck two crosses and a jewel of very magnificent diamonds and a number of splendid diamonds in her headdress.[4]

The ambassador said Mary's dress rivalled that of the Queen, consisting entirely of cloth of gold and purple velvet. He described her as 'pleasing in countenance and so popular in England as to be almost adored.' Among other of her virtues, he said, 'is that she knows how to conceal her acquirements, and surely this is no small proof of wisdom.'[5]

Once Hertford's reluctant butchery was accomplished in Scotland and the threat of a northern invasion allayed, Henry VIII sailed on his last voyage of conquest, 'undertaking a voyage royal, in his most royal person, into the realm of France against the French King.' Accompanied by those elderly war horses, Norfolk and Suffolk, the King left Dover for Calais on July 14, 1544, in a ship rigged with sails of cloth of gold. In his absence, Katherine Parr was made Queen-Regent of England and Ireland. One of her first actions was to compose a prayer imploring divine protection and aid for Henry and his realm. The Queen said England had been 'enforced to enter the war and battail', and she humbly beseeched God 'to turn the heart of our enemies to the desire of peace that no Christian blood be spilt. Or else grant, Oh Lord, that with small effusion of blood and little damage of innocents, we may to Thy glory obtain victory. . . .'

Though a Catholic by birth and upbringing, Katherine Parr had been influenced by the New Learning, which was, primarily, the interest of the reforming party in England. The accomplishments of her female associates—not only of Mary, but of little Lady Jane Grey and her sisters, and other noble children who had acquired an appetite for

* Foreigners were always surprised at the willingness of English women to be greeted by a kiss on the lips. Royalty did not indulge in this practice as frequently as others; in this instance, Mary was 'saluting' a representative of her mother's country, an envoy from the court of her cousin, the Emperor.

learning once disdained as unfeminine—set her to further study. A Master of Eton, Nicholas Udal, said, 'it was a common thing to see young virgins so nouzled and trained in the study of letters that they willingly set all other pastimes at nought for learning's sake....' Katherine convinced the staunchly Catholic Princess Mary to undertake a translation of Erasmus's Latin Paraphrases of the Gospel of St John, a work particularly venerated by the reformers, thus rendering the Scriptures more easily accessible to those who did not understand Latin or Greek. That Mary would accept a commitment so identified with the reforming movement is an example of her trust and love for Katherine Parr and her faith in the people of England to assimilate the word of God, whether in Latin, Greek, or English. She had about completed the manuscript when a return of her 'old guest' sent her to bed, and her chaplain, Dr Francis Mallet, finished the work for the printer. Katherine entreated the shy Mary to publish the Paraphrases under her own name, saying 'you will, in my opinion, do a real injury if you refuse to let it go down to posterity under the auspices of your own name....'[6]

The Queen sent a messenger noted for his 'skill in music' to entertain the stricken Princess. To Mary she wrote she soon hoped to 'salute [her] in person' and signed herself, 'most devotedly and lovingly yours ... Katherine the Queen'. Katherine's goodness was a balm to Mary. While recuperating, she sat for her portrait, paying John Hayes four pounds for 'drawing her likeness' on a wooden slab. At twenty-eight, Mary was 'small, fragile and of a singularly beautiful complexion, but of a very different tint from that of her father', said a contemporary, who, continued, '... when a girl, she was much celebrated for her beauty; but the troubles she underwent in her father's reign faded her charms prematurely, though she was very far from ugly. Her face was short, her forehead very large, her eyes dark and lustrous, and remarkably touching when she fixed them on anyone.'[7]

At Hampton Court, where he remained under Katherine's motherly eye, little Edward Tudor was at last exercising a royal determination to have his own way. It was, perhaps, a justified rebellion at the burden of his studies which included, as his tutor Dr Cox said, 'the eight parts of speech [which] he hath made his subject and servants, and can decline any manner of Latin noun and conjugate any Latin verb—unless it be *anomalum*....' The Prince had already mastered the rudiments of grammar, the tutor said, and 'hath made a forty or fifty pretty Latin verses ... and is now ready to enter into Cato'. Dr Cox had prescribed a good dose of Scripture for Edward also. 'Every day at Mass time, he readeth a portion of Solomon's Proverbs for the exercise of his reading ... and learneth how good it is to give ear unto discipline, to fear God, to keep God's commandments, to be aware of strange women....' Perhaps all these pious exhortations, so dull and unnecessary in the mind of a child of seven, resulted in a disobedience born of boredom and frustration and the exercise of Edward's own will in protest. Shortly afterwards, Dr Cox wrote that when the little Prince desisted too much, he had taken 'his Morris pike . . . and gave him such a wound that he wist not what to do.' He ended by saying 'labour and exercise shall chase away all of the boy's objections, for he is a vessel most apt to receive all goodness and learning, witty, sharp and pleasant.'[8]

Edward was not the only young Tudor feeling the weight of learning and the responsibility of a royal position. His sister, Elizabeth, now approaching twelve, was still in disgrace. Living apart from the court, she diligently pursued her studies of French, Italian, Spanish, Flemish, and Latin.* Geography, mathematics, and the principles of astronomy also formed part of her daily curriculum. She wrote poetry and practised her music and needlework in her leisure hours, although the routine of her education left little time for such feminine dalliance. The rigid discipline of these early years of study ingrained in Elizabeth a love of learning she retained all her life. A result of her competence was her remarkably clear and beautiful handwriting in an age when a crabbed scrawl was more the norm. The child took great pains and pride practising her letters methodically; daily she wrote her signature 'Elizabeth' in large flourishing script, with gracefully flowing lines beneath. From eleven years of age Elizabeth knew how her signature should look, and once she had decided, it was never changed during her lifetime.

But the disgrace that had banned her from court for almost a year still rankled. She had had no word from her father who had sailed to France as if she had ceased to exist. As the weeks of the French war continued and the dullness and solitude of St James's became more unbearable, she wrote to Katherine Parr:

Inimical fortune, envious of all good and ever revolving human affairs, has deprived me for a whole year of your most illustrious presence, and, not thus content, has yet again robbed me of the same good; which thing would be intolerable to me, did I not hope to enjoy it very soon. And in this my exile, I well know that the clemency of your Highness has had as much care and solicitude for my health as the King's Majesty himself. By which thing I am not only bound to serve you, but also to revere you with filial love, since I understand that your most illustrious Highness has not forgotten me every time you have written to the King's Majesty, which, indeed, it was my duty to have requested from you. For, heretofore, I have not dared to write to him.

* Years later, as Queen, Elizabeth was to tell a foreign ambassador she was not afraid of making important national decisions, but she was terrified of making a mistake in Latin.

Having thus shown her gratitude to the Queen for her care in exile, Elizabeth with an uncharacteristic directness, came to the point:

Wherefore, I now humbly pray your most excellent Highness, that, when you write to His Majesty, you will condescend to recommend me to him, praying ever for his sweet benediction, and similarly entreating our Lord God, to send him best success, and the obtaining of victory over his enemies, so that your Highness and I may, as soon as possible, rejoice together with him on his happy return. No less pray I God, that He would preserve your most illustrious Highness, to whose grace, humbly kissing your hands, I offer and recommend myself.

Your most obedient daughter, and most faithful servant,

ELIZABETH. [9]—

Katherine Parr had conducted her regency with diligence, goodwill, and competence. Nothing in the court, Council, or the lives of Henry's children escaped her notice. She wrote to the King often, chatty and informal little letters which state 'love and affection do compel me to desire your presence' and '. . . time therefore seemeth to me very long, with a great desire to know how your Highness hath done since your departing. . . .'[10] At the conclusion of one letter, she ventured, if only obliquely, to mention Elizabeth. 'My Lord Prince and the rest of your Majesty's children are all, thanks be to God, in very good health; and thus, with most humble commendations to your Majesty, I pray Almighty God have the same in His most blessed keeping. . . .'[11]

It was the first step. In subsequent letters, in which she spoke of the long days which 'maketh me that I cannot quietly pleasure in anything until I hear from your Majesty'. she continued to appeal to Henry's paternal feelings. Her intercessions and an outbreak of the plague caused Henry to extend a somewhat impersonal forgiveness to Elizabeth. He wrote boastingly to the Queen, anticipating an exhilarating victory in France:

At the closing up of these our letters this day, the castle before named, with the dyke, is at our commandments, and not like to be recovered by the Frenchmen again, as we trust; not doubting, with God's grace, but that the castle and town shall shortly follow the same trade, for as this day which is the eighth of September, we begin three batteries, and have three mines going, besides one which hath done his execution in shaking and tearing off one of their greatest bulwarks. No more to you at this time, sweetheart, but for lack of time and great occupation of business saving, we pray you, to give, in our name, our hearty blessings to all our children, and recommendations to our cousin Margret[12] and the rest of the ladies and gentlemen, and to our Council also.

Written with the hand of your loving husband,

Henry R.[13]—

Within several days of such 'shaking and tearing', Boulogne fell. Henry entered the town in great triumph, only to hear that Charles and Francis, weary of war and lacking any scruple whatsoever, had signed a treaty at Crépy. Henry was outraged, crying, 'Let the Emperor make peace for himself if he likes, but nothing must be done to prejudice my claims!' Though the Council deemed a 'public thanksgiving should be offered up to Almighty God in all the towns and villages throughout England for the taking of Boulogne', it was obvious even to the disillusioned Henry that he had been deserted by his ally in a war which had cost between £600,000 and £700,000 a year and had won for England only one French town. The King, whatever his faults, was a realist. He knew Francis would venture to regain his territory and realised the Scots would subsequently be more troublesome than ever. His country was saddled with debts, its coinage debased, its court, Council, and subjects split by a Pandora's box of religious conflicts he himself had never foreseen. He knew his health to be poor; he could not live forever. The financial and religious problems of his realm must be solved and marriages made for his three children, with an eye to the succession for which he had sundered his country's religious foundations. Once the Boulogne victory was assured, Henry was anxious to return home. There were many things he must do before the end came.

Awaiting the King's return, Mary, Edward, and the now-forgiven and repentant Elizabeth held a joyous reunion at Oking marred only by an outbreak of the plague. Issuing a proclamation which forbade any infected person to enter the area of the royal dwelling 'under the Queen's indignation and further punishment at her pleasure', Katherine set out in her businesslike manner, to keep herself and her stepchildren busy—and well. With an eye to her father's homecoming and to have some tangible proof of her industry, Elizabeth undertook a translation from the French of *The Mirror (or Glass) of the Sinful Soul*, a devotional treatise which she dedicated 'To Our Most Noble and Virtuous Queen, Katherine, Elizabeth, her humble daughter, wisheth perpetual felicity and everlasting joy.' The 'lyttel boke' written in English on vellum, contained one hundred and twenty-eight pages in Elizabeth's beautiful script. It was bound in canvas upon which the child had embroidered

[141]

Katherine Parr's initials. Purple heartsease and other flowers were meticulously executed in yellow with a tiny green leaf motif throughout; the edges of the book were held together with small gold braids. Every letter, stitch, and scroll was the work of Elizabeth Tudor. Proudly, she presented the volume to Katherine with a letter in which she said she had translated it '. . . out of the French rhyme into English prose, joining the sentences together, as well as the capacity of my simple wit and small learning could extend themselves. . . .' But that Elizabeth was still either childishly apprehensive of her accomplishment or overcome by a sudden tinge of unusual modesty is seen in her request '. . . But I hope that after to have been in your Grace's hands, there shall be nothing in it worthy of reprehension, and that in the meanwhile no other [but your Highness only] shall read it or see it, lest my faults be known of many. . . .'[14]

Henry VIII spent the remaining few years of his sovereignty ailing in body, disillusioned in spirit, and burdened in mind. Many familiar faces were disappearing from his court. Henry's good physician' Dr Butts died suddenly; Charles Brandon, the Duke of Suffolk, who had eloped with Henry's red-haired sister, Mary, almost thirty years previously, also died of heart failure, dropsy, and, undoubtedly, the debilitating effects of a boisterous life which had denied him few pleasures. The loss of Brandon, the nearest to the King in personality and character, was bitterly resented by Henry. Another old friend, the Spanish ambassador, Eustace Chapuys, met Mary walking with Katherine Parr in the palace garden at Whitehall as he arrived in a litter to say farewell to the King. After twenty years he was going home, he said. The kindly Queen bade him stay in the chair from which he could alight only with great difficulty and, after a few words, tactfully left him alone with Mary. The girl stepped forward, her mind ranging back through the unhappy years when his staunch support of her mother, and later of herself, had seemed the one tangibly solid bulwark in a world dominated by persecutors. Tears in her eyes, she bade Chapuys remember her to the Emperor. Then, remembering the strained relations between England and Spain arising from the Emperor's betrayal of her father in France, she told Chapuys his health would undoubtedly be better 'on the other side of the sea'. The ambassador later wrote that Mary advised him he 'could do as much on the other side as here, for the maintenance of the friendship of which I had been one of the chief promoters. For this reason, she was glad I was going. . . .'[15] Mary told the ambassador he had performed his duties well and had been greatly trusted by the King. And then, remembering she was keeping the Queen waiting, she finished her farewell, pressed the old gentleman's hand affectionately, and hurried on.

Mary's concern for England's relationship with Spain reflected that of the King and his Council. Should Spain and France or France and Scotland, Catholic powers all, unite against an England burgeoning with the vigour of the reforming party, the threat must be met with some kind of unity at home. And in latter months there had been only argument, tension, and strife between fellow Englishmen. On Christmas Eve, 1545, in a remarkable speech before Parliament, Henry Tudor addressed his subjects for the last time, demonstrating once again the magnetism which held them spellbound even when they disagreed with him. It was an occasion of great emotion. 'He spoke', said an onlooker, 'so sententiously, so kingly, so rather fatherly, that many of his listeners were in tears.'[16] The King himself was moved. He told Parliament '. . . no Prince more favoureth his subjects than I do you, nor no subjects or Commons more love and obey their Sovereign Lord as I perceive you do me. . . .' Having started amicably, Henry proceeded to the most important point of his address—his subjects' religious policies. He deplored the different interpretations of Scripture which had sown such seeds of turmoil in his realm. 'Charity and concord is not amongst you, but discord and dissension beareth rule in every place', he said. He placed the blame squarely upon the clergy, speaking accusingly, '. . . you, the fathers and preachers of spirituality . . . preach one against the other, teach one contrary to another, inveigh one against another, without charity or direction! . . .' He asked heatedly, 'How can poor souls live in concord when you preachers sow amongst them in your sermons debate and discord?' Henry said he had given his people a precious privilege in permitting the Bible to be read in their mother tongue; yet they were abusing this privilege in their misinterpretations. The laity also shared in his criticism; he told them they were not 'clean and unspotted of envy; for you rail at the bishops, speak slanderously of priests and rebuke and taunt the preachers'. The King commanded them to 'amend these crimes, or else I, whom God hath appointed will correct these enormities.' The proper belief was in his Act of the Six Articles, explained the King, and yet some of his subjects still sought to advance their own opinions. 'Some are called Papists, some Lutherans, and some Anabaptists . . .' said Henry. 'I am very sorry to know and hear how unreverently that precious jewel, the Word of God, is disputed, rhymed, sung, and jangled in every alehouse and tavern.' The King finished with obvious emotion, counselling his subjects to '. . . be in charity one with another, like brother and brother. Have respect to the pleasing of God, and then I doubt not that the love I spake of shall never be dissolved betwixt us. . . .'[17]

The struggle for theological supremacy over the minds and souls of

Henry's subjects extended to his Council. The Catholic element, headed by Stephen Gardiner, the Bishop of Winchester, challenged the opposing Council members who favoured reform by testing the King's affection for his long-time prelate, the Archbishop of Canterbury. They had long feared Thomas Cranmer because of his association with the reformers. Cranmer was disliked as much for his learning as for his enviable talent of expression, and they were supremely jealous of his influence upon the King and the partisanship shown him by the Queen. When the Council intimated that Cranmer was guilty of encouraging heretical beliefs and practices, Henry challenged the statement. If such evidence could be found, Cranmer might be imprisoned in the Tower, said the King. While the papers were being drawn up by Gardiner, the King secretly visited the Archbishop at Lambeth Palace. Cranmer, humbly grateful, was sure no injustice would be permitted. The King, while admiring the prelate's naïveté, was more realistic. He gave Cranmer a ring, saying, 'When they are committing you to the Tower, forthwith appeal from them to me and give them this ring.'[18] Then both King and Archbishop waited. Being duly summoned before the Council, Cranmer was rudely kept waiting in an ante-room among humbler petitioners before being admitted to their presence. When charged with heretical activities, he demanded to see his accusers. When no one stepped forward and he was instead ordered to the Tower, he silently produced the King's ring. The meeting broke up in great confusion with Lord Russell shouting, 'Did I not tell you, my lords, that nothing would come of this matter? I knew right well that the King would never permit my Lord of Canterbury to have such a blemish as to be imprisoned ... !'[19] Henry's defence of his Archbishop 'whom he loveth well' was continued when Cranmer's accusers were summoned to court and treated to a superb example of the royal wrath. The King's final gesture demonstrated his contempt for the investigators and contained a nice Henrician touch: he formed a commission to investigate the extent of alleged heretical activities in his realm. To head and direct the commission, he appointed Thomas Cranmer, the Archbishop of Canterbury.

Henry's disdain of his Council's action did not discourage the arrogant Gardiner. Where one lost with an Archbishop, one might succeed with a Queen. Katherine Parr's fascination with the New Learning had rendered her no favourite with Gardiner. Her sympathy for the reformers had deprived the Catholics on the Council of her support, and her influence on the King and his children—particularly the young and impressionable Edward—was deplored. Once more using religious bias as a stalking horse for political aspirations, Gardiner tried again. In his venture against the Queen, he was supported by the odious Wriothesley, now the Lord Chancellor, and assisted by the variable temper and chronic discomfort of the King himself. Incapacitated by the open sore on his leg and a body which had become so tremendously bulky he had to be propelled along by machinery, Henry found the days trying.

Katherine Parr spent many hours with him, dutifully applying hot compresses to the ugly ulcer on his leg. She spoke to Henry with the natural brightness of an intelligent woman aware of the necessity of taxing every ounce of her wit, strength, and eloquence to keep her husband entertained. They often discussed theological subjects and the prevalent religious conditions. On one occasion, when Henry's malady was more painful than usual, the Queen ventured an opinion as she had been wont to do many times in the past. Much to her surprise and chagrin, Henry abruptly changed the subject, testily saying, 'A good hearing it is when women become clerks; and a thing much to my comfort to come—in mine old days—to be taught by my wife!'[20] It was a moment of royal peevishness rare in Henry's domestic life with Katherine Parr and would have passed forgotten except for the Bishop of Winchester. Gardiner was witness to the King's irritation; he soothed Henry by stating that the heresy existing in high places was in reality treason in another guise. Henry's petulant reply was that such treason should be punished. Seeing the King was receptive, Gardiner insinuated that 'he could make powerful discoveries if he were not deterred by the Queen's powerful faction'—meaning the many friends and relatives Katherine had at court. He flattered the still irascible Henry whom he said 'excelled the princes of that and every other age, as well as all the professed Doctors of Divinity . . . insomuch that it was unseemly for any of his subjects to argue with him so malapertly as the Queen had just done.' It was a long chance and Gardiner, of whom some said, 'he had drawn his bow in order to bring down some of the head deer', obtained permission to draw a Bill of Articles against the Queen. When it was presented to Henry, he waspishly signed it. If treason existed in palace chambers, it should be ferreted out, he reasoned. If not, though it was a 'terrible jest', it might frighten the Queen sufficiently so she would cease to display her eloquence to win controversies when Henry was in no mood or condition to argue.

In a matter of days, the Council's investigators were busily questioning the Queen's ladies, searching their rooms and breaking open locked coffers for forbidden reading material or questionable documents— anything that might incriminate Katherine Parr. And then a fortuitous fate, in the unlikely person of the Lord Chancellor, intervened. The order for the Queen's arrest was accidentally dropped by Wriothesley at Whitehall, picked up by one of Katherine's attendants, and conveyed with all speed to Her Majesty. Unbelievingly, the Queen read the document; the effect was instantaneous. At the sight of the familiar signature, 'Henry R.,' hysteria promptly took possession of the terrified woman. Her shrieks continued for several hours, much to the discomfort of the King in the adjoining apartment. He finally sent for Dr Wendy, Katherine's physician, who told him 'the Queen was dangerously ill, and that it appeared that her sickness was caused by distress of the mind.'[21] Henry could appreciate such distress; it was impossible for him not to hear the lamentations from the next room.

His conscience bothered him just a little also—he remembered the kind and selfless ministrations of his Queen during periods of his own distress. He signalled to be helped to his feet. Propelled clumsily into Katherine's chambers, he found her 'heavy and melancholy', although the sight of her husband, standing shakily with the aid of mechanical contrivances, 'greatly revived and rejoiced her', said the shocked woman. She had missed him and feared she had displeased him, she continued, but he must remember she was 'but a woman accompanied with all the imperfections natural to the weakness of her sex. . . .'[22] Henry comforted his distraught wife, glad to see his Kate meek again and so relieved as to reveal to Dr Wendy that there were some who did not wish the Queen well, a fact the good physician hastened to impart to Katherine. The next day when the Queen dutifully presented herself in the King's apartments, she avoided being drawn into any argument or discussion and refused to comment on any matter of importance, saying to Henry, 'God hath appointed you as the Supreme Head of us all and of you, next unto God, will I ever learn.'

'Not so, by St Mary!' cried the King, who could be gracious when he had won, 'ye are become a doctor, Kate, to instruct us, and not to be instructed of us as often time we have seen. . . .'

But Henry's 'terrible jest' had taught Katherine a lesson. She told her husband that her 'meaning had been mistaken'—any difference of opinion between them had been only her method of helping him 'pass away the pain and weariness of your present infirmity. . . .'

'And is that so, sweetheart?' replied the King. 'Then we are perfect friends', he said joyously, kissing her with great tenderness.

The following day, happy again with a considerably more docile Queen, Henry sat in the garden overlooking the Thames when Wriothesley, puffing with importance, led forty of the Tower guard to arrest the Queen. As he appeared before them, Henry lost his temper, shouting 'Beast! Fool! Knave!' to the uncomprehending Lord Chancellor. Wriothesley gaped in amazement to see the woman he had hoped to escort to the Tower and subsequently to the block obviously once again in favour with a husband and monarch who now waved an impatient hand in his direction, ordering him to 'avaunt from my presence!' Katherine Parr could afford to be generous at her safe deliverance. She sought an excuse for the astonished Wriothesley, saying she 'deemed his fault was occasioned by mistake.' 'Ah!' replied the King, 'thou little knowest, Kate, how evil he deserveth this grace at thy hands. On my very word, sweetheart, he hath been to thee a very knave.'[23]

The result of this incident, which had become serio-comic owing to the royal caprice, proved disastrous for the Bishop of Winchester. Henry's association with Stephen Gardiner ranged back to the time of his divorce from Catherine of Aragon. Yet he never forgave the Bishop for his attempt on the Queen's life. He ordered Gardiner, whom he called a 'wilful heady man', removed from the Council and forbade him to come into the royal presence. To emphasise his profound distrust of the prelate, he removed from the list of executors of his will not only Gardiner but also Thirlby, the Bishop of Westminster, because 'he had been schooled by Gardiner'.

Henry had drawn his will in 1544 when he sought conquest in France. It was a remarkable document wherein, 'In the name of God and of the Glorious and Blessed Virgin, our Lady St Mary, and of all the Holy Company of Heaven . . .' the King endeavoured to guarantee for his only son a throne secure and strong. In the last year of his life, the monarchy had been challenged on two occasions. In the summer, a French invasion attempt, in which Francis—incredibly—had sent some 200 ships up the Solent, was badly defeated, leading the English commander John Dudley, Lord Lisle, to say, 'The poor [French] fishermen say that there was never journey so costly to France as this has been, for so short a voyage, nor more shame spoken of amongst themselves.'[24] The victory, due as much to a providential shift of wind as to any superior fighting prowess, buoyed up the King's spirits and his faith in his own invincibility. A more personal challenge to the throne had resulted in the imprisonment of Henry Howard, the Earl of Surrey, and of his father, the ageing premier noble of the realm, the Duke of Norfolk. Young Howard, a brilliant poet, 'the most foolish, proud boy that is in England', had nothing but scorn for the 'new men' in the Council, including the Seymours, Edward and Thomas, uncles of the young heir. He loudly threatened that 'when God called away the King, they would smart for it.' The Seymours regarded the staunchly Catholic Howards as their major political enemies on Henry's Council and, in a reckless play for power, as the King lay ill, succeeded in almost the complete destruction of the House of Howard. The overweening pride of Henry Howard caused him to commission a painting in which the arms of his own house were quartered with those of the royal house, the motto *Honi soi qui mal y pense* being replaced with the ominous words, 'Till then thus'. The swaggering Howard was tremendously popular with the citizens of London, with whom he lost no opportunity to say that when the King died, there was 'none so meet to govern the Prince' as his father. However, at this critical point in his life, the King did not intend to suffer a juvenile Pretender. Both father and son were imprisoned in the Tower of London. In a bitter trial at which he taunted one of the King's councillors that '. . . the kingdom has never been well since the King put mean creatures like thee in the government!'[25] Henry Howard was sentenced to a treasonous death. When the death sentence was read, there was much lamenting by the common people, which turned to cheering when the prisoner cried, 'I know the King wants to get rid of noble blood around him and to employ none but low people!'[26] The King remained unmoved, and on January 19, 1547, the heir to England's proudest Dukedom was beheaded on Tower Hill while his father remained in prison, waiting to tread in the footsteps of those he himself had helped to the block—Thomas More, Thomas Cromwell, the Countess of Salisbury, and his two nieces, Anne Boleyn and Katherine Howard.

The Howard affair brought into focus the need for a more ordered trusteeship when the King was gone. Henry again reviewed his will, remarking to Sir Anthony Denny there were 'some he meant to have in and some [who were] in, whom he meant to have out'. He changed the document indicating his awareness that he 'must drive the lions and panthers, with other proud beasts, out of the way, leaving no stumbling logs in the walks of his tender son.'[27] Wisely, so he thought, he named no Lord Protector, no guardian to rule *in loco parentis*, for in so doing, power, lands, monies, and political prestige would immediately be conveyed to the beneficiary at the expense of his legitimate heir, young Edward Tudor. Instead, Henry named a Council of sixteen trusted advisers, and in this he balanced the conservative forces consisting of Wriothesley, Anthony Browne, Paget, and Paulet, with the reforming element headed by Edward Seymour and Thomas Cranmer. He did not sign the will. In not signing, Henry held a giant sword of Damocles over those chosen to govern when he was gone. Their behaviour while he was alive was their best guarantee to gain upon his death.

During his last few months the King's life was full, with no acceptance of the fact that death might be imminent, though it was written in every fold of his face and in the decaying body. This remarkable body, so majestic in youth, so formidable in middle years, and so gross in old age, was to keep Henry wholly capable and in full possession of his faculties to the very end. His ulcerated legs, never given a chance to heal, caused him immense pain, further compounded when the doctors tried cauterising the sores.[28] He had endured a serious illness in the late spring but recovered sufficiently to have his children with him at Hampton Court during the summer. Perhaps some premonition of his own mortality, albeit reluctantly acknowledged, led him to distribute impressive quantities of jewellery to his family. Diamonds, pearls, rubies, a 'girdle of gold of Friars knots', some 'beads of crystals trimmed and gauded with gold', and a great pearl pendant with roses and pomegranates, obviously a piece belonging to her mother, went to Mary.[29] Similar but smaller pieces went to Elizabeth. For Edward, the heir, were reserved the most magnificent items of all—including, as he gratefully wrote to his father '. . . chains, rings, jewelled buttons, neck chains and breast pins, and necklaces, garments and many other things, in which things and gifts your fatherly affection towards me is conspicuous.' Showing a practicality even at nine, Edward reason, 'For if you did not love me, you would not give me these fine gifts of jewellery.'[30]

Shortly thereafter, the young Prince assumed his first royal responsibility, replacing a father whose health did not permit easy mobility. Claude d'Annebaut, the Lord Admiral of France and ambassador of Francis I, arrived in England to ratify the peace between the two countries. The King ordered Edward to meet d'Annebaut upon arrival. The boy was naturally eager to acquit himself with credit and wrote to Kathleen Parr to 'inform him whether the Admiral understood Latin well, for if he does, I would wish to learn further what I may say to him when I come to meet him.'

The last great display of grandeur at Henry VIII's court commenced with the visit of the French embassy. After their arrival at the Tower of London, d'Annebaut and his companions were summoned to Hampton Court. Young Edward Tudor, astride a massive charger, waited in the August sultriness at Hounslow Heath to escort them. The handsome and sensitive heir to the throne, accompanied by Edward Seymour, the Earl of Hertford, and other nobles, headed a cavalcade of 500 horsemen, 'attired in gorgeous but quaint array, having velvet coats with sleeves of cloth of gold.'[31] Edward conducted himself graciously, saluting and embracing the Admiral of France, and welcoming him with winning grace, in such courteous and honourable manner that the beholders greatly rejoiced and marvelled at his audacity and ready wit.'[32] With great pomp and an admirable recognition of his royal duty, the young Prince led the procession to Hampton Court, where for ten days magnificent entertainment and feasts were provided for the visitors by the ailing King.

By October, Henry was again stricken. Those in the court moved cautiously lest they endanger their places in the Council at the whim of a monarch whose age and general debility had rendered him no less imperious or fickle. In his last weeks on earth, the King exhibited an almost superhuman physical strength and courage. But the recent alleged treachery of the Howards and his own increasing feebleness ultimately caused Henry at last to consider his end might be near; just before the New Year he again reviewed his will.

And when the end came, it came with great speed. Shortly after the holiday, at which he had given an audience to the French ambassador and attended to other affairs of State, the King received Princess Mary. Possibly, at last, some inkling of his approaching end caused Henry to ask Mary to be 'as a mother' to her young brother 'for look, he is very little yet. . . .' When his Queen visited the sickroom, Henry became especially solicitous. Addressing her, he said he had ordered his Council to 'honour and treat you as if I were living still; and, if it should be your pleasure to marry again, I order that you shall have £7,000 at your service as long as you live and all your jewellery and ornaments.'[33] The Queen was so overcome she was gently led away, weeping. For his other children there was no word; possibly Henry thought there would be time later. Both Elizabeth and Edward knew their father was ill, but he had been sick before, and no more emphasis had been placed on this illness than on previous ones.

By the end of January, the more alert at court could see signs of further physical deterioration and anxiously wondered at the fate of the realm and of themselves when the seemingly indestructible Henry Tudor died. There was a Council to act in his place when he was gone, but the will appointing that Council was still unsigned.[34] Who would be brave enough to inform the King he should put his house in order? To even mention his possible death was treasonous, and Henry's petulant and ominous temper in the midst of his extreme physical discomfort was too well known for even the most daring to venture.

On the evening of January 27, 1547, as dusk hung over the Thames, the King lay breathing heavily in his great canopied bed at Westminster Palace. The room was dank with the wintry dampness and the smell of running, open sores, of decay and death. Outside, the guards stood alert but apprehensive of what was taking place within. Members of the Council waited nearby, and everywhere there was silence. The physicians, not of the stamp of old Dr Butts, were timid: who would inform the failing King—good Catholic that he was—that he should make his peace with God? At last, one more courageous than the others, Sir Anthony Denny, entered the chamber. Leaning over the bedside, he gently but firmly whispered to Henry that his life might be coming to an end. The sick man nodded weakly, saying he had 'abused his life' and then, almost in a stupor, said, 'Yet is the mercy of Christ able to pardon me all my sins, though they were greater than they be.' Sir Anthony asked if anyone should be summoned with whom the King might 'confer withal and open his mind unto?' Henry murmured weakly, 'Cranmer . . .' and then, apparently unable to convince himself that death was imminent, he said with almost a trace of jauntiness, 'But first, I will take a little sleep, and then, as I feel myself, I will advise upon the matter. . . .'[35]

The 'little sleep' was over in a matter of hours. Cranmer had been summoned from Croydon. No other person near or dear to the King was present. The Queen was at Greenwich, Mary at her country home, Elizabeth and Edward at Hunsdon. No one—least of all the King—could accept the fact that death was actually occurring. But when the Archbishop of Canterbury arrived at midnight, distraught and anxious, there was no longer any doubt. Henry was sightless and speechless, the huge body either disturbingly quiet or suddenly flailing at the bed-coverings as he gasped for breath. Apprehensive, yet fully conscious of his duty to his great protector and friend, Cranmer 'speaking comfortably to him, desired him to give him some token that he put his trust in God, through Jesus Christ. . . .'[36] To this hurried question, Henry could only clutch Cranmer's hand and press hard. Sometime between twelve and one o'clock in the morning, on January 28th, a man, a King, and an era died.

Henry VIII had done his best to ensure as safe a throne for his young son as was humanly possible. He had named no one to head the government which would rule during the Prince's minority; instead sixteen 'entirely beloved' and trusted councillors, whose decisions must be made by a majority, composed the Council of Regency. Presumably each member would act as a check on the ambitions of the other, should any venture to usurp the powers of the throne.

But fate recognises no royal prerogative—no one can rule from the grave. The breath had hardly left the corrupt body before forces were at work which would ultimately place one of his blood on the throne of England. The greatest Tudor of all—one who would lead the nation to Empire and glory and render a name to an era—was not destined, however, to be Edward Tudor.

A King and His Sisters

Chapter Nine

WHEN Henry died, his three children were in their separate households and the Queen, their stepmother, at the riverside Palace of Greenwich. Messengers had been busy during the last weeks of the King's illness, carrying letters from one royal dwelling to another. In this way, Henry's family sought to derive some comfort and assurance as they faced a future without the awesome presence of a father, husband, and sovereign lord.

The youngest Tudor, Edward, particularly had felt the disruption of the close family life Katherine Parr had endeavoured to provide in the midst of court ritual, invasion threats, and the King's sickness. The three years before Henry died had been the happiest of Edward's short life. Her pursued his studies under the Queen's supervision and enjoyed the association of his sisters when they, too, lived at court or visited for long periods. And there were always those magical moments when the huge man with the grey beard, which still showed tinges of red, was there to fondle him, to tell tales of his exciting exploits in France, or to question him on his studies. Often his father spoke to him in French or Latin, and Edward was expected to hold his own in these exchanges. If he failed, the King's anger—always terrifying to the sensitive boy—was directed at him or his tutors, Dr Richard Cox and Dr John Cheke.

Edward was as fond of his two teachers as they were of him; Cox called him a boy 'of such towardness in learning, godliness, gentleness, and all honest qualities . . .' that he was to be regarded 'as a singular gift sent of God, and an imp worthy of such a father.'[1] Cox was also the recipient of one of Edward's more humorous little notes. The boy had been instructed to write his absent tutor a letter. Not wishing to spend more time than necessary on such a dull task, he slyly wrote in Latin, neatly absolving his shortcoming with a classical quotation:

I sent to you a short letter, my dearest almoner, because I know short letters are to you as acceptable as long ones. For I am well aware that you have read in Cato's first book, twentieth verse, 'When a poor friend gives you a little present, accept it kindly, and remember to praise it amply.' Though my letter is short, it wanteth not good will.

I pray God to preserve you in safety and in health.

Edward[2]

Edward's other tutor, the thirty-one-year-old John Cheke, a Fellow of St John's Cambridge, had been brought to court on the advice of the late Dr Butts, Henry's valued personal physician. He, together with Dr Cox, the French teacher John Belmain, a Mr Randolph who taught German, and Sir Anthony Cooke who instructed in 'manners and deportment', were Edward's friends as well as his teachers. Under their tutelage, the boy's natural inclination for learning had been stimulated. In particular, John Cheke possessed a ranging, highly intellectual mind, and in an era when the stern schoolmaster was the norm, the warm and witty tutor showed a rare compassion for the small boy in his charge. He had insisted that Edward have classmates, and therefore eight or ten other children of similar age were assembled to form a Palace school, giving the Prince companions in sports and games, as well as the stimulus of competition in the classroom. Among them were the sons of Henry's courtiers; others were of lesser birth. Robert Dudley, the son of John Dudley, Viscount Lisle, was one; he was four years older than Edward and an especially good friend of Elizabeth. They had much in common and always managed to be together when Elizabeth visited the court.

Barnaby Fitzpatrick was Edward's closest friend and 'whipping boy'; the Prince loved him dearly. As the little Prince grew older, it was not considered politic to correct him physically. Barnaby, therefore, suffered the corporal punishment each time Edward misbehaved. It was said, 'it was not easy to affirm whether Fitzpatrick smarted more for the default of the Prince or, the Prince conceived more grief for the smart of Fitzpatrick.' In any event, Edward's affection for his 'whipping boy' was well known at court and was probably the greatest guarantee of the Prince's good behaviour.

Edward was equally an affectionate and rewarding child with his sisters and stepmother. Despite the boy's great love and respect for Katherine Parr, however, his most loving letters were reserved for his older sister and godmother, Mary Tudor. When she was ill, Edward wrote solicitously, 'I am glad that you have got well, for I have heard that you had been sick, and this I do from the brotherly love I owe you, and from my goodwill towards you. I wish you uninterrupted health both of body and mind. Farewell in Christ, dearest sister. . . .' He could also exhibit a somewhat Puritanical priggishness rare for his nine years but not unusual considering his rather cloistered existence. Or perhaps it was a minor brotherly jealousy that compelled him to write to the Queen of Mary's activities after she had regained her health and was participating in the festivities which accompanied the French ambassador's visit: 'Preserve, therefore, I pray you, my dear sister Mary, from all the wiles and enchantments of the evil one, and beseech her to attend no longer to foreign dances and merriments, which do not become a Christian princess. . . .'[3] To Mary, who loved all music, dancing, and minor forms of gambling—so at odds with her usual gravity—the advice must have seemed both amusing and touching.

Edward looked forward to Elizabeth's visits too, for then she joined him in the classroom. Once studies were over, they were free to mingle with other children or any visitors such as his cousin, Lady Jane Grey. Jane was Edward's age; he secretly thought her the cleverest girl he knew, though she was not as much fun as Elizabeth who didn't make such a point of her accomplishments. Often the older girls would take the two younger children into the royal park and play simple games with them, then retire to their embroidery frames where Mary—whose proficiency with the needle was well known—would instruct any other young ladies who might be present. In the evenings, Elizabeth would play the virginals and Mary would sing in her warm contralto while Edward and Jane listened respectfully and the King dozed near the fire, his sore leg resting snugly in Katherine Parr's lap.

Such comforting moments came to an end as the King's illness worsened and all dispersed to their own residences. Elizabeth was allowed to visit Edward for several days at Hunsdon. When she left for her own manor of Enfield Chase, the boy was depressed. Facing a lonely Christmas, far from a court and Queen preoccupied with a sick monarch, he wrote her sadly, 'Change of place did not vex me so much, dearest sister, as your going from me. Now, however, nothing can happen more agreeable to me than a letter from you, especially as you were the first to send one to me, and have challenged me to write. . . .' Both brother and sister had obviously and daringly discussed the future when their father might be gone, for Edward wrote somewhat forebodingly: 'But this is some comfort to my grief that I hope to visit you shortly, *if no accident intervene with either me or you*. . . .'[4] Ill health had again prevented Mary from seeing Edward, but she had sent a New Year's gift. Edward wrote her just after the holidays had passed: 'This one letter, my dearest sister, serves for two purposes, the one to return you thanks for your New Year's gift, the other to satisfy my desire of writing to you. Your New Year's gift was of that kind that I needs must set a very high value on it, on account of its great beauty, and very much prize it because of the love of the giver. My fondness for writing to you is so great, that although I hope to visit you shortly, yet as I have leisure, I can scarcely be satisfied with myself, unless I write to you, for I cannot but love ardently one by whom I find myself so much beloved. May the Lord Jesus keep you in safety.'[5]

Edward Tudor did, indeed, find himself 'much beloved' by many. It was easy for those who came in contact with this child of Henry and Jane Seymour to find their attention, sympathy, and affection engaged. He was a thin, pale-complexioned boy, very much a duplicate of his mother with her fair hair, pointed chin, and rather tight lips. As a small child, his beauty had been singular. As the chubbiness of babyhood disappeared and his young body took on a delicate slimness, he wore his silks, velvets, damasks, and brocades with such an assurance and easy grace that even the fact that one shoulder was a bit higher than the other did not matter. As much as he was his mother's child in appearance, he was every inch a Tudor in his awareness of the royal responsibility. His willingness to cultivate a natural intelligence into something resembling precocity, while still maintaining a loving disposition, charmed all who knew him.

Edward was not immediately informed of his father's death. By order of Edward Seymour, the Earl of Hertford and the Prince's uncle, not one word of the death left the Palace gates. First, physical possession of the heir must be obtained so that the succession might proceed smoothly. But there was another reason. Within moments of Henry's last breath, in a gallery outside the death chamber Hertford and Sir William Paget, the secretary of state, had whispered to each other of the King's will.

Henry had left the Crown to Edward and his heirs, then to Mary and her heirs, to be followed by Elizabeth and her heirs. In default of any issue by any of his children, the King had bypassed the granddaughter of his older sister, Margaret Tudor (the five-year-old Scottish Queen, Mary Stuart) and left the throne to the children of his younger sister, Mary Tudor and Charles Brandon—Frances Brandon, the Marchioness of Dorset and then her sister Eleanor. Though Henry had hoped his son's inheritance would be protected by a Council, with no *one* person in authority, such equality did not appeal to the ambitious Hertford, and he, with Paget, now tried to set the device aside. Hertford felt that the stringency of Henry's laws, combined with the mixed religious and political content of the Council itself, made the efficient functioning of such a body all but impossible. Before he left with his younger brother, Thomas Seymour, to bring their nephew to court, he told Paget that the Council must be convinced that 'some special man . . . should be preferred in name and place before others, to whom, as to the head of the rest, all strangers and others might have access, and who for his virtue, wisdom and experience in things were meet and able to be a special remembrance, and to keep a certain account of all our proceedings. . . .'[6] There was to be no doubt that the 'special man' was to be Edward Seymour, the Earl of Hertford.

The Prince was brought to Elizabeth's household at Enfield Chase the next day. The two met joyously and retired, still unaware of their father's death, for Hertford, who had accompanied Edward, was waiting word from Whitehall. Assurances were ultimately received from Paget that silence was being maintained, but secrecy could hardly be kept much longer. The will was required to be read in Parliament on the following Monday. Henry had handed his will to Edward Seymour not because of any unusual regard for him, but as a gesture of confidence that Edward's own uncle would prove deserving of trust. It had been locked away safely at Whitehall, with Seymour retaining the key. Paget now asked for the key so that the will might be read in Parliament. Hertford hesitated only a moment and, with instructions to Paget to read only the parts of the will which were deemed suitable, he gave the startled messenger the key, crying, 'Haste, post haste! Haste with all diligence! For thy life! For thy life!'

The next day, Sunday, the thirtieth, Edward and Elizabeth Tudor were brought into the Presence Chamber at Enfield and told of their father's death. Shocked by the abruptness of the disclosure, the two children, nine and fourteen, turned and clung to each other in tears, their sobs intensifying as they realised the enormity of the seemingly impossible fact that their fearsome, majestic, and dominating father was actually gone. Their grief was sincere. Though their relationship with their royal parent had at times been frustrating and anxious, they had loved him. One chronicler says, 'Never was sorrow more sweetly set forth, their faces seeming to beautify their sorrow. The most iron eyes . . . were drawn thereby into the society of their tears.'[7] As Edward sobbed, Elizabeth—aware of being the elder—protectively held his hand in hers until he had regained his composure.

On Monday, January 31, 1547, three days after it had occurred, the death of Henry VIII, 'their most puissant master', was announced to Parliament by Chancellor Wriothesley who 'was unspeakably sad and sorrowful . . . and being almost disabled by tears from uttering the words.' His listeners made 'great demonstrations of sorrow' and immediately dissolved Parliament for a period of mourning. The people, stunned by the news of the King's death, were informed of Edward's accession by the heralds' proclamation in the yard of Westminster Hall.

In the late afternoon, Edward Tudor arrived to claim his royal inheritance. Amid cries of 'Long live King Edward!' he entered the City at Aldgate where he was met by the lord mayor. His uncle, the Earl of Hertford, and Sir Anthony Browne rode beside him, a long cavalcade of the nobility stretching far behind. As they neared the City, many of the country gentry 'to their great joy and comfort' joined in escorting their Prince to the Tower. It was cold, a wintry day in which the thin sunlight—when it appeared—had been welcome. It had dappled the spots in the road where puddles had frozen, obliging the horses to pick their way more carefully, making the journey longer than had been intended. The icy air of the Thames was bracing, and as the Tower loomed in sight, the spirits of the child, saddened and apprehensive as they had been, rose exultantly. Suddenly, beside the wall of the Crossed Friars near Tower Hill, it seemed as though his subjects appeared *en masse*, many in tears of sorrow, pride, and joy. 'Long live King Edward!' they shouted, their enthusiasm increasing as they ran along the narrow thoroughfares, hoping to see the boy enter the Tower. Their noisy acclaim was drowned by the firing of the Tower guns, which momentarily took Edward by surprise. The first salvo startled his horse, and the Prince quickly sat more upright, gripping the reins firmly. As the firing continued, the people's ardour and affection became infectious, and Edward was too much a Tudor not to respond. The young Prince's smiles, beauty and grace only increased their admiration. 'His eyes', said an observer, 'seemed to have a starry liveliness and lustre' as they ranged the crowd, smiling at those near him and looking expectantly beyond to the Tower and the river, where bells and whistles sounded from the many small hastily decorated craft.

At the Tower Sir John Gage, the Constable, waited. To the delight of the onlookers, both Hertford and Anthony Browne tacitly reined in their horses as they approached the outer bastion, and Edward Tudor rode into the Tower of London alone, the welcoming cries of his subjects still ringing in his ears and floating over the forbidding walls that now enclosed him.

So far, Hertford had done well. He now had to gain the approval of the remaining councillors to whose care the young King had been confided, that he alone should be the 'special man' in authority. It did not come easily; Wriothesley in particular was opposed. But Paget had done his work well. After a heated night-long debate, the councillors —Archbishop Cranmer, Chancellor Wriothesley, Lord St John, Lord Russell the Privy Seal, Cuthbert Tunstall the Bishop of Durham, Knights Sir Anthony Browne, Sir Edward North, and Sir Anthony Denny, William Paget the Secretary of State, Lord Montague, Sir William Herbert—piously proclaimed 'being all assembled in the Tower of London, the last day of January, have reverently and diligently considered the great charge committed to us and calling to Almighty God for His aid and assistance, have resolved and agreed with one voice to stand to and maintain the last Will and Testament of our late master, and every part and article of the same, to the uttermost of our power, wits and cunnings.' The shameless hypocrisy of their statement is demonstrated in their next resolution in which 'upon mature consideration of the tenderness and proximity of blood between our Sovereign lord that now is and the Earl of Hertford, being his uncle, and of the great experience which he hath in all affairs of this realm', Edward Seymour was given the 'chief place among us and also the name and title of the Protector of all the realms and dominions of the King's majesty and governor of his most royal person.' They had hedged their compromise with the 'special and express condition that he shall not do any act but with the advice and consent of the rest of the executors, in such manner, order, and form as in the Will of our late Sovereign lord is appointed and prescribed.'[8] Despite their lofty statements, their actions were in direct opposition to Henry's more experienced evaluation that equal authority and responsibility would prevent any one member from taking control.

The councillors also felt bound to distribute honours and dignities commensurate with their new responsibilities. Hertford became the Duke of Somerset with lands worth £800 annually 'and £300 of the next Bishop's lands which should fall vacant'; he was also named Lord Treasurer and Earl Marshal of England, usurping the office of the Duke of Norfolk,[9] still languishing in the Tower. John Dudley, the Viscount Lisle, became the Earl of Warwick, and for his co-operation, Wriothesley was made the Earl of Southampton. The Protector's younger brother, Thomas Seymour, became Lord Seymour of Sudeley, with lands worth more than £500 and replaced Dudley as the Lord High Admiral of the Navy.

And so it was done. The aggressive and ambitious Hertford—now the powerful Protector and Duke of Somerset—had had his way, and the life of the new child-King of England was henceforth to be dominated by the presence of both Seymour uncles, to a much greater extent than it had ever been dominated by his own father.

The Seymour brothers had come into power in one way only: through the marriage of their gentle sister Jane to Henry VIII. Their positions had been secured and enriched by the birth of Edward Tudor, and as uncles of the heir, they had increased in a power and prestige, solidly buttressed with more than their share of royal and monastic lands, dignities, preferments, and titles. As a young man, Somerset, along with Anne Boleyn, had been in the bridal retinue of Mary Tudor, Henry's sister, in France. He had accompanied Henry and Catherine of Aragon to the Field of Cloth of Gold, later competently serving as Governor and Captain of the Island of Jersey and eventually as Chancellor and Chamberlain of North Wales. After his sister's marriage to the King, he had distinguished himself in the Scottish and French Wars. Following the Boulogne victory, he was appointed Lieutenant

[161]

Governor of the French city, replacing the unfortunate Earl of Surrey who had lost his head on Tower Hill just before Henry died.

Now, at forty-seven years of age, and at the height of his power, the new Protector was an imposing figure. A magnificent flowing beard lent an aloof distinction to his long features, made even more angular by an aquiline nose. His thick-lipped, well-formed mouth normally bore the set expression of one who does not deal easily in words. Somerset was a quiet man, with a deliberate and authoritative manner. His very restraint gave an impression of strength and maturity which was misleading, for beneath the beneficent appearance lay a highly dictatorial nature. Undoubtedly ruthless, he yet retained something of the visionary, at times displaying a quixotic impractical idealism frustrating to his more opportunistic colleagues. Courageous and daring on the battlefield, the very qualities which had made him an excellent soldier, however, were not compatible with the more subtle requisites of a politician and statesman.

The younger Seymour, Thomas, the new Lord Sudeley was similarly tall with a magnificent carriage and hazel eyes set boldly above a full and lush beard. There the resemblance ended, however. In comparison with the quiet, unobtrusive, and undemonstrative manner of his older brother, and in a court where arrogant, handsome, swaggering, boastful gallants were the rule—Thomas Seymour was exceptional. The new Lord Admiral was noted not only for his charm with the ladies—with whom his prowess was considerable—but also for his capacity for hard drinking, fighting, and enjoyment of good living and all it entailed. His ambition was well known and feared; his courage bordered on foolhardiness. In contrast to his brother's conservative manner, Thomas Seymour was something of a hot-headed rake with one outstanding talent in which he was admittedly the most adept at court: his talent for blasphemy was absolutely unrivalled, and his eloquent and colourful vocabulary was regarded with awe and repeated with savour. Thomas Seymour had served on several foreign embassies where he had moderately distinguished himself more by a display of charm than any unusual intelligence. Hard as nails, outstanding with the brilliance of the unprincipled, shallow and without his brother's capacity for industry and temperate living, Thomas Seymour was described 'as 'fierce in courage, courtly in fashion, in personage stately, in voice magnificent, but somewhat empty in matter.'[10] Of both brothers, jealous courtiers observed, 'their *new lustre* did dim the light of men honoured with ancient nobility.'

But now, as uncles of the reigning King, their 'new lustre' took on the patina of the permanent, and whatever their private reservations might have been, the Council had capitulated. Along with the rest of the country, they were now saddled with the brothers Seymour. And

[162]

the consequences of their rise were directly to affect each young Tudor, who could only watch powerless as forces momentarily stronger than themselves threatened to destroy them.

During the next three weeks Edward Tudor received more attention than at any time in his short life. If the young King found it bewildering, he gave no sign. That he found it satisfying was eminently apparent in his confident manner towards his Council and other courtiers as they thronged about him, anxious to shine for a moment in their new sovereign's youthful ambience. From his chair of State in the Tower, under a canopy of cloth of gold, Edward received the homage of each noble who came to kiss his hand and say, 'God save your Grace!' With a youthful maturity—touching to the more sensitive of those present— he acknowledged their fealty by raising his cap to them saying, 'We heartily thank you, my lords all, and hereafter in all ye shall have to do with us, in any suit or causes, ye shall be heartily welcome.'

The funeral of Edward's father was held on February 18 when the royal coffin, over which was cast a 'pall of rich cloth of gold, and upon it a goodly image like to the King's person in all points, wonderfully richly apparelled with velvet gold and precious stones of all sort ...' was placed upon a hearse drawn by eight black horses and taken to Windsor Castle for burial. Noblemen and knights in mourning escorted the hearse and the cortège which wound four miles behind. It was a fine sunny day, unusual for winter, and the funeral procession was viewed by many thousands. As the day darkened, the mourners kindled their torches to light the way. More than a thousand of these 'goodly lights' were held aloft along the route, and they flickered in the winter wind, lighting the golden pall, the waxen effigy of the King, and the arms of England and the House of Tudor emblazoned on the trappings of the horses drawing the hearse.

Neither Edward nor his sisters attended their father's funeral.[11] But the boy heard the details from those who did accompany Henry to his grave. He was told it had taken six stout yeomen of the guard, aided by a mechanical device, to lower Henry's huge casket into the vault of the Chapel floor, to lie beside Jane Seymour. The sorrowing officers of the household and the members of the Council had ringed the gaping vault, their staves and rods of office in their hands. As the coffin finally came to rest, Edward was told, the men 'broke their staves in shivers upon their heads, and cast them after the corpse into the pit with exceeding sorrow and heaviness, not without grievous sighs and tears. . . .' Edward's momentary puzzlement at seeing these same officers return to the Tower with the staves in their hands is reflected in his diary in which he wrote that 'they must have had others given to them' afterwards.

The coronation of Edward VI began the next day, nearly three weeks after the father's death. In addition to all the details of the dead King's funeral, time had been needed to make the tremendous preparation necessary for the crowning of a new monarch, and the investiture of the newly made peers had taken place earlier so they might participate in the celebrations according to their new rank.

At one o'clock in the afternoon of the next day, Saturday, February 19, 1547, in weather so icy the streets were strewn with gravel to prevent the horses from slipping, a brilliant procession issued from the Tower Gate. It had taken all morning to assemble the vast cavalcade of courtiers, clergymen, foreign emissaries, halberdiers and simple yeomen which would escort Edward to Westminster Abbey, and the confusion behind the Tower's forbidding walls had been overwhelming. Eventually, all was in readiness. In a doublet of white velvet, decorated with Venetian silver, diamonds, rubies, and love-knots of pearls, a white velvet cap and buskins of the same soft material on his legs, Edward finally rode out of the Tower Gate for Westminster. A small, slim, and beautiful child of nine, the last male Tudor sat astride the huge stallion which tossed its head impatiently and defiantly in the cold damp air of the Thames. Edward had waited long just inside the gate until the signal was given to proceed, and the excitement and chill air had touched his cheeks with colour. His horse, caparisoned in crimson satin, embroidered with pearls and gold, became even more skittish as they rode up Tower Hill. As a precaution, three knights rode on each side of the King; the Protector, the Duke of Somerset, rode just behind and to the left. The area from Gracechurch Street to the 'little conduit in Chepe' had been railed off for the spectators, and the streets were decked with rich hangings of cloth of gold, tapestries, and arras; buildings were 'garnished with streamers and banners as richly as they might be devised.' Priests and other clerics, with their crosses and censers, followed along the way to 'cense the King'. When Edward entered Mark Lane, a tremendous salvo of the Tower cannon boomed along the river, causing his horse to stamp nervously. At Cornhill, another conduit ran generously with sweet wine, to the delight of the assembled people. Choirs sang from mounted settings as Edward passed, and short 'fantazies' were played before him with small children symbolising Regality, Justice, Truth, and Mercy. Musicians played nearby, and as Edward approached, the richly dressed children recited,

> 'Hail noble Edward, our King and sovereign,
> Hail, the chief comfort of our commonalty,
> Hail, redolent rose, whose sweetness to refrain,
> Is unto us such great commodity.'[12]

To the deafening din of church bells, the tremendous procession advanced with the youthful monarch at its head. The people, aglow

with pride at the sight of the handsome boy—and sated with free wine
—roared as the colourful cavalcade approached. Many eyes were wet
with tears of affection and joy, and cries of 'God Save the King!' filled
the air. At each stop, Edward dutifully reined in his horse to receive
his subjects' acclaim. As time wore on, it became obvious that the whole
procedure was taking longer than expected. Each guild, minor official,
and neighbouring church wished to participate in some appropriate
ceremony. So it was three hours before the boy reached the Cross at
Chepe, which was 'very well painted and gilded'. Here ritual, allegory,
'fantazies', and mummery were abandoned; the Lord Mayor and his
aldermen, after a blessedly short address, handed the startled child a
large purse containing a thousand marks of gold. An observer noted,
'His Grace received it and gave them thanks.' But a minor embarrassment followed, for the unexpected purse was too heavy for the boy to
hold. Momentarily at a loss, he turned to the Protector and said, 'Why
do they give me this?' Somerset assured him it was a custom of the City
and signalled to the captain of the guard to take the heavy bundle.

And so the great retinue rumbled on into Chepe. At St Paul's a
radiant Edward gazed in delight as a 'Spanish rope dancer . . . descended
from a rope which was stretched from the spire of the Cathedral down
to the Deanery gate, and there made fast to an anchor, and without
using apparently either hands or legs, glided down on his breast like
an arrow from a bow, and when he reached the ground he came to the
King, and kissed his Majesty's foot, and after addressing a compliment
to him, departed and went up the rope again, and played a variety of
feats, to the delight of the King, who tarried with all his train a good
while to behold them.'[13]

It was nearly dark when an exhausted Edward reached the old Palace
of Westminster. Possibly his very exhaustion helped to allay any twinge
of sorrow as he passed the chamber in which his father had so recently
died. He was awakened very early the next morning, and again accompanied by his uncle, the Protector, he came by barge to the Whitehall
privy stairs at nine o'clock. Walking the short distance to Westminster
Hall, he was robed in a surcoat, train, and gown of crimson velvet,
embroidered with gold and trimmed with miniver and powdered ermine.
Surrounded by the Protector who carried the Crown, the Duke of
Suffolk[14] who carried the Orb, and the Marquess of Dorset who carried
the Sceptre, Edward Tudor walked slowly to Westminster Abbey.
Glancing at those nearest to him, he was pleased to see his uncle,
Thomas Seymour, and William Parr, Queen Katherine's brother. But
his most obvious delight was reserved for his schoolmates, the noblemen's
sons who stood nearby, nervously self-conscious as they waited to carry
part of the royal regalia as Edward walked to the Abbey.

In the vast spaces of Westminster Abbey a small white throne rested on a stage built in front of the altar for the coronation. Because of the youth of the King and his obvious fatigue, it had been decided to cut the ceremony from its usual eleven hours to seven. So, as soon as the youthful sovereign was seated in St Edward's Chair, the Archbishop of Canterbury, Thomas Cranmer, proclaimed him as the 'rightful and undoubted inheritor by the laws of God and man of the crown and royal dignity of this realm. . . .' Turning to the vast assemblage of noblemen and church dignitaries, he questioned, 'Will ye serve at this time and give your wills and assents to the same? . . .'

'Yea, Yea, Yea! God Save King Edward!'—the response poured through the great canyon of the Abbey, almost overwhelming Edward in its intensity. He was then led to the high altar where, at Cranmer's direction, he prostrated himself and the *Veni Creator Spiritus* was sung, the boy lying uncomfortably face downwards. Taken to a side chapel, he exchanged his vestments for a coat of crimson satin and a 'coif of gold on his head'. When he returned to the altar again, Cranmer anointed him, held the ancient crown of Edward the Confessor[15] over him, and then placed upon Edward's blond hair a smaller, more suitable diadem. As each crowning occurred, the sound of trumpets echoed in diminishing reverberations throughout the Abbey, and the choir burst into a mighty *Te Deum*. When the 'ring of gold was set upon the King's Grace's marrying finger', after he had recited his vows and the bracelets, spurs, Sceptre, and Orb had been handed to him, only then was he allowed to sit—a small, lonely figure almost dwarfed by the heavy Sceptre and Orb—on the special white throne. But still his ordeal was not over. Each peer came forward 'and kneeled down and kissed his Grace's right foot, and after held their hands between his Grace's hands, and kissed his Grace's left cheek and so did their homage . . . ending with a loud cry of 'God Save King Edward!' A High Mass was then sung, 'with good singing in the choir and organs playing' before Edward was taken to the four corners of the Abbey dias and formally presented to the nobility. Cranmer then spoke directly to the boy and the people within the Abbey, exhorting Edward of his duties, declaring the divine right of Kings made the new King one of 'God's anointed . . . for the better raising and guiding of his people'. He told the child he must reward virtue, revenge sin, justify the innocent, relieve the poor, procure peace, repress violence, and 'execute justice throughout your realm.' Only then, implied Cranmer, will the 'Lord pour out his blessings in abundance.' A frightening bargain for a young and very tired child to contemplate.

A reception lasting four hours was held in Westminster Hall, and again the boy-King was called upon the display grace, patience, interest —and stamina. Sitting between Somerset and Cranmer, he was undoubtedly stirred when Sir John Dymoke, following ancient tradition, entered the mighty Hall 'upon a courser richly trapped with cloth of gold' and three times repeated the challenge, 'If there be any manner of of man, of whatever estate, condition so ever he be, that will say and maintain that our Sovereign Lord Edward VI, this day here and present, is not the rightful and undoubtful heir to the Imperial Crown of this realm of England . . . I cast him my gage!' No one challenged the knight, and Edward, now being served wafers and hippocras and still wearing his ceremonial robes, was finally permitted to leave for one last royal duty of the day—a meeting with the French envoys. 'With ease and readiness' he spoke with them in Latin, impressing the visitors and another emissary, who remarked 'It should seem he were already a father, yet passeth he not the age of ten years. . . .'[16]

Later, jousts were held in the courtyard of Westminster Palace before the company returned to the Hall for a massive coronation feast where Edward was allowed 'a goodly void of spices, confections', and liberal sips of wine from a golden cup. At the conclusion, he knighted forty-one noblemen with the Order of the Bath before mercifully being allowed to return the short distance by barge to Whitehall. There, his fatigue dispelled by excitement and the liberal consumption of wine, he reviewed the tremendous events of the day. Neither his beloved Katherine Parr nor his dear sisters, Mary and Elizabeth—not even Anne of Cleves or the Protector's wife or his cousin Jane Grey—had been present to witness his glory. The difficulty of precedence among wife, ex-wife, and relatives had baffled the Council and Protector alike. Since no one lady could be summoned unless *all* were summoned, it was deemed wiser to have none.

Thus a newly crowned King retired into a huge bed, in an enormous Palace, confronted with a frightening array of responsibilities conveyed to him by Archbishop Cranmer. Though he was surrounded on all sides by protective figures, there was not one among them with whom he actually wished to be. He had hoped Barnaby Fitzpatrick would be there, but he had not seen him. There was no one to laugh with about the ropedancer; no one to talk to about his great triumph that day when he had tried so hard to please everyone. There was no one, really, to care.

Chapter Ten

WITH the death of her father, Mary Tudor's interest in life at at court lessened. She loved her young brother dearly, but she understood that the aura of the monarchy, with its attendant responsibilities and duties, was not conducive to intimacy. Between Edward and herself now stood the Protector and the Council. Each time brother and sister wished to see each other, permission must be asked and then debated by others. As the weeks passed, it became increasingly apparent the Protector and Council wished the boy to live in a masculine world, away from the influence of the Queen and his sisters, surrounded by advisers and restrained by his age and inexperience from exercising any opinion of his own.

There was little doubt that Edward missed such feminine companionship. His sisters, as well as the Queen, often wrote to the boy, maintaining some semblance of relationship to relieve his loneliness, as well as giving him 'a goodly exercise' of the Latin language in which he was always expected to reply. Shortly after his accession, in a burst of youthful exuberance and childlike affection, he wrote to his '*Sorori Mariae*' from '*E Turri Londinese*'—'So far as in me lies, I will be to you a dearest brother and overflowing with kindness!'[1]

The only recorded attempt on the Princess Mary's life provoked a warm response from the new King. The previous summer, a religious fanatic, urged by the imminency of Henry VIII's death and fearing the strongly Catholic Mary's popularity, had attempted to enter her home. Sir Edward Browne had apprehended the criminal, and when the matter came to the youthful King's attention, he wrote in gratitude to Sir Edward: 'It has been represented unto us that in the course of last summer you did, at your own imminent peril and at the peril of your life, protect the house wherein our dearest sister was residing at the time, from being entered in the night by a bloodthirsty and murderous villain, who might, perchance, have done an incredible damage to our said sister. . . .'[2] Mary treasured these instances of Edward's affection and support. These were the days when her peace was genuine. She was happy in the knowledge that her brother's accession had been accomplished, however much it contributed to a widening gulf between them. While the matter of her marriage was still tediously discussed within the Council, Mary was not anxious to alter her way of life. She was thirty-one years old and past any youthful expectancy or desire. She took a quiet pride in administering her various homes at Kenninghall, Beaulieu, and Copt Hall, and in seeing those old and valued companions whose friendships had been tried and proven strong. She derived great comfort from her religion. While viewing the growing influence of the reforming party with dread and dismay, she knew she was powerless to interfere.

About her were many who had come from Spain with Catherine of Aragon, and they held the Princess Mary in great affection. They were growing older—places and pensions must be found for them. Her compassion for those who had served her mother and remained faithful during all her own trials is shown in a letter written to one of them, Anne Stanhope, once a lady-in-waiting to Catherine of Aragon. From Beaulieu, Mary wrote to the woman, now the wife of the Protector, the most powerful man in England, mentioning an old servant, Richard Wood, stating he 'had sustained great loss, almost to his utter undoing, without any recompense hitherto, which forced me to trouble you with his suit before. . . .' Mary reminded her friend of the Protector's promise to help her, 'for I consider it impossible for him to remember such matters, having such a heap of business as he hath.' And then, somewhat embarrassed, she mentions another deserving member of her household: 'And thus, my good Nann, I trouble you with myself and all mine; thanking you with all my heart for your earnest gentleness towards me in all my suits hitherto, reckoning myself out of doubt of the continuance of the same. Wherefore, once again I must trouble you with my poor George Brickhouse, who was an officer of my mother's wardrobe and beds from the time of the King, my father's coronation, whose only desire is to be one of the knights at Windsor, if all the rooms be not filled.' Mary wrote that her servants were 'persons [who] have served me a very long time and have no kind of living certain. Praying you . . . that they may have pensions, as my other servants have, during their lives; for their years be so far passed, that I fear they shall not enjoy them long.'[3]

The serenity of Mary's days—those incredibly placid days upon which she was later to look back almost in disbelief—was broken by an event which caused her hot Spanish blood to rise. Katherine Parr and Mary had always been close companions. In the artificiality of a court environment a quiet bond of affection, friendship, and mutual respect had grown between them. The widowed Queen had lived away from her stepchildren in semi-retirement since Henry's death. In addition to her legacy from the late King, she had two fortunes from former husbands. She was, indeed, a very rich woman, and she had often remembered Mary with welcome sums when the girl's own resources were strained. Katherine had bitterly resented not being appointed to the regency, especially regarding the care of young Edward. As the Queen-Dowager, she had gone to live in her imposing manor house at Chelsea, a small replica of St James's Palace, with turrets above the long windows looking out over the beautiful gardens and orchards to the Thames. A little stone basin used as a fishpond by Edward and Elizabeth was a poignant reminder of the happier days when she and Mary had romped with the children at the river's edge, scooping up snails and plant life to put into the makeshift pond. Katherine missed her stepchildren. She also missed the ritual and pageantry, the small symbols of authority and power, which had been the fabric of her life for the past several years; she had been thrust into the background. Her considerable income, plate, and the portion of the royal jewels she had retained were comforting. But to a woman who had spent years in being *needed*, it was not enough. At thirty-five she was still a handsome and charming woman, and as she thought of the years ahead, she must have wondered—where can a woman look for happiness after she has been a Queen?

The answer was not long in coming—to the distress of Mary and all those who loved the gentle Katherine Parr and wished her well. In the months after the Protector's assumption of power, a power which increased daily, there had been much dissension and overt grumbling in the Council, though no one dared any outright opposition. In particular, the young brother, Thomas, Lord Seymour of Sudeley, felt the gnawing discomfort of a consuming envy. Though it is doubtful he had any precisely detailed plan of retaliation—for such careful calculation was not his nature—it was soon apparent that Thomas was dissatisfied with a brother enjoying the perquisites of power while he had been palmed off with a mere Admiralty. Aware of his brother's discontent, the Protector had done what he could to placate him: he presented Thomas with an imposing residence, Bath House, in the Strand, which belonged formerly to Bishop Barlow. The estate was noted for its magnificent trees, parks, gravelled walks, and gardens.* An orchard abutted on the Strand, leaving a clear view from the house to the broad river beyond. Renaming the area Seymour Place, the younger brother cast about for a suitable marriage. Thomas had never regretted his unmarried state; he thrived on the freedom of a bachelor's life. But now he needed a wife to grace his new mansion and give his establishment some tinge of respectability and permanence.

* The gardens covered the area of the present Arundel Street, Norfolk Street, and Surrey Street.

As an uncle of the King, Seymour needed the royal permission to marry. He knew his relationship with his nephew to be on firm ground, for Edward much preferred his gay, flamboyant uncle to the Protector who rarely seemed to have much time for him. But instead of appealing to Edward directly, Seymour asked an intermediary, Thomas Fowler, a member of the King's Privy Chamber, to solicit Edward's opinion. Subsequently, when Fowler 'marvelled that my Lord Admiral marrieth not' as the boy was undressing for bed, Edward absentmindedly agreed. Fowler, then guilefully presumed to wonder whom Edward, in his noble wisdom, would wish the Admiral to marry. Playing the game—for such he thought it—Edward innocently replied, 'My Lady Anne of Cleves. . . .' Then, thinking further, he stopped short and added, 'Nay! Nay! I would he married my sister Mary to turn her opinions. . . .' Both Seymours were ardent reformers. A rapid succession of sweeping religious changes had been tentatively introduced in the Council with the Protector loudly proclaiming his goal of 'getting rid of the bishops'. And already Mary's firm Catholicism was being pointed out to Edward as a singular example of the 'old religion' not giving way to the New Learning.

But Thomas Seymour aimed higher than a homely ex-Queen or a Princess whose very goodness and compassion bordered on sanctity—or dullness. He had always been amused and charmed by Henry's second daughter, the red-haired Elizabeth. He had known her from her babyhood, and beneath the decorous and proper façade she assumed whenever they met, Seymour sensed a fiery nature that might well astonish the person lucky enough to kindle it. He could remember the old King's passion for Elizabeth's mother, Anne Boleyn—indeed, he himself could remember the quicksilver charm of that dark-eyed beauty. Elizabeth was young, but girls were considered of marriageable age at fourteen, and the Princess on the verge of womanhood was—he sought the right word—almost ageless. In his eyes, she was much more a woman than her older sister Mary who could be distressingly firm about her religion. Elizabeth, he suspected, would be much more malleable.

Therefore, it was only a matter of a few weeks after Henry's death, as the Protector's influence mounted, that the hot resentment of Thomas Seymour caused him to approach the Princess Elizabeth and offer his hand in marriage. He wrote begging 'pardon for the liberty I am taking in revealing my feelings to you so soon. . . .' He implored her to believe that it was her 'beauty and other excellent qualities, both of mind and person which have made me so bold and have so bewitched me, that I am no longer master of myself. . . .' He wrote effusively, asking for only 'two lines from you to know whether I am to be the most happy or the most miserable of men. . . .' Ending the letter, he proudly signed it, 'Thomas, Admiral'.[4]

Elizabeth received Seymour's proposal in Katherine Parr's riverside palace at Chelsea where she had been sent by the Council to live. 'The weeks be shorter at Chelsea than any other place!' Katherine said happily after her stepdaughter arrived. Elizabeth brought her own household staff of 120 including the woman who served as her governess, Mistress Katherine Ashley, whose husband was a minor relative of Anne Boleyn's. By the terms of her father's will, Elizabeth was third in the succession, with a yearly income of £3,000 and a marriage portion of £10,000. If she married without the consent of her brother or the Council, she forfeited everything. She knew her father had once intimated that Seymour might ultimately be a suitable husband for her, but there was now no father to give the union such royal sanction. Elizabeth had always liked Seymour; indeed, it was difficult not to like anyone so brazenly good-looking and witty as the Lord High Admiral. Even so, she knew what her answer must be. In a reply to which she had obviously given a great deal of thought, the fourteen-year-old Elizabeth exhibited a commendable mixture of eloquence and diplomacy. Addressing him as 'My Lord Admiral', she thanked him for his letter which she called 'most obliging' and then gently chided him:

... I confess to you that your letter, charming as it is has greatly surprised me, since, aside from the fact that I have neither the age nor the inclination to think of marriage, I should never have expected to find myself asked to a wedding at a time when I can only weep for the death of my father. Too great, my lord, is the obligation which I owe to him to mourn his death for less than two years; and how shall I persuade myself to tread the path that leads to wifehood, until I have enjoyed for a few years the state of maidenhood, or until I have attained the years of discretion?

Therefore, my Lord Admiral, permit me to say frankly that since there is no one in the world who holds your great merit in higher esteem than I do, nor finds greater pleasure in your society while I may regard you as a disinterested friend—I shall continue to preserve the satisfaction of looking upon you as such, apart from that closer intimacy of marriage, which often causes the possession of personal merits to be forgotten. Let your lordship be persuaded that if I refuse the good fortune of being your wife, I shall never cease to interest myself in all which may add greater glory to yourself, and that I shall make it my greatest pleasure to remain,

Your servitor and good friend,

ELIZABETH.[5]—

[172]

Rebuffed by Elizabeth, Seymour now turned his attention to Katherine Parr. The Queen-Dowager had never forgotten the handsome Seymour who had paid her ardent court before her marriage to Henry. Now, when he approached her again—a mere four days after receiving Elizabeth's letter—she was at once responsive, though very aware that many at court thought him unsuitable. When the two had met shortly after the King's death, Lady Paget had asked Katherine what she thought of the dashing Admiral's looks. The royal widow had coloured prettily and said she liked his looks very much. 'All the ill I wish you, Madam', replied the sympathetic Lady Paget, 'is that he should become your husband. . . .' Katherine remarked she 'could wish that it had been her fate to have him for a husband', and then, remembering her rank, she added, 'but God hath so placed me that any lowering of my condition would be a reproach to me.'

However, the sensitive and isolated Katherine proved no match for the Admiral. He laid earnest siege to the woman he had once lost; possession of a Queen-Dowager would indeed help compensate for his brother's expanding power and influence—and who knew what such a marriage might accomplish in elevating a mere Admiral to greater prestige? Within a few days, Katherine wrote to him, 'I would not have you think that this, mine honest goodwill towards you to proceed of any sudden notion of passion; for as truly as God is God, my mind was fully bent, the other time I was at liberty, to marry you before any man I know.' Katherine pleaded with Thomas Seymour to obtain the consent of young Edward, as well as the more influential members of the Council, but her sensible advice was disregarded. First Seymour intended to gain the person of the Queen-Dowager herself. He took to visiting her at Chelsea, surreptitiously at first, and the lonely woman —stimulated by his ardour—quickly lost that firm common sense which had so characterised her in other, less emotional, matters. Soon she was writing that 'ye must take some pain to come early in the morning . . . I pray you let me have knowledge overnight at what hour ye will come, that your portress may wait at the gate to the fields for you. . . .'[6] From 'waiting at the gate' for her lover to final capitulation was almost foreordained by the very measure of Thomas Seymour's ambition, passion, and charm. Within five weeks of Henry's death and less than two weeks after Edward's coronation, Katherine Parr and Thomas Seymour were secretly wed.[7]

Once the marriage was achieved, Edward was enchanted. Since proposing Anne of Cleves or the Princess Mary as prospective brides for his uncle, he had been led step by step, by the impetuous Admiral, into favouring the marriage with the Queen-Dowager. As well as the satisfaction of being privy to a great secret, he dearly loved Katherine, and his Uncle Thomas was infinitely more compatible than the austere

Protector who, besieged with the country's religious and monetary problems and executing final plans for a Scottish campaign, paid even less personal attention to his royal nephew than before. Fearful of the Somerset's wrath once the marriage was revealed, the newlyweds prevailed upon Edward for his royal support. The generous child wrote the Queen-Dowager consoling her anxiety, saying, 'Wherefore, ye shall not need to fear any grief to come, or to suspect lack of aid in need. . . . But even as without cause you merely require help . . . . so may I merely return the same request unto you, to provide that he [the Admiral] may live with you also without grief. And I will so provide for you both that hereafter, if any grief befall, I shall be sufficient succour in your godly or praiseable endeavours. Fare ye well, with much increase of honour and virtue in Christ. From St James, the fifth and twenty day of June. . . .'[8]

Still keeping the marriage secret, Seymour had written to the Princess Mary 'of a suit unto the Queen's Grace'. Innocent of the extent to which she was being asked to sanction a union which had, in fact, already taken place, the Princess replied to Seymour's request in a letter which poignantly echoes her feelings for her dead father, as well as leaving little doubt that she wanted no part in the affair:

My Lord,

After my hearty commendations, these shall be to declare that according to your accustomed gentleness, I have received six warrants from you by your servant this bearer, for the which I do give you my hearty thanks, by whom also I have received your letter wherein (as methinketh) I perceive strange news, concerning a suit you have in hand to the Queen for marriage, for the sooner obtaining whereof, you seem to think that my letters might do you pleasure.

My lord, in this case I trust your wishes doth consider that if it were for my nearest kinsman and dearest friend on live [alive], of all other creatures in the world, it standeth least with my poor honour to be a meddler in this matter, considering whose wife her Grace was of late, and besides that if she be minded to grant your suit, my letters shall do you but small pleasure. On the other side, if the remembrance of the King's Majesty my father (whose soul God pardon) will not suffer her to grant your suit, I am nothing able to persuade her to forget the loss of him, *who is as yet very ripe in mine own remembrance.*

Wherefore, I shall most earnestly require you (the premises considered) to think none unkindness in me, though I refuse to be a meddler in any ways in this matter, assuring you, that (wooing matters set apart, wherein I being a maid am nothing cunning) if otherwise it shall lie

[174]

in my little power to do you pleasure, I shall be glad to do it as you to require it. . . .

From Wanstead, this Saturday at night, being the 4th of June,

your assured frend to my power Mar ye] [9]

When the marriage was finally made public at the end of June, it stunned Mary, appalled the court and country, and outraged the Protector and his Council. Edward wrote, with some satisfaction, in a small notebook:* 'The Lord Seymour of Sudeley married the Queen, whose name was Katherine, with which marriage the Lord Protector was much offended.' Mary's first thought—once her shock and anger had worn off—was of Elizabeth. The child, now at the impressionable age of fourteen, must leave the home of Katherine and Thomas Seymour. Offended at the indecorous remarriage of her stepmother, she wrote to her young sister, offering her a home and urging haste in departing.

At Chelsea, Elizabeth faced an important decision. She had matured noticeably in the few months since her father's death. She was taller than Mary, with a figure which was well developed for her years. She wore her brilliant red hair parted in the middle and drawn in two gently swelling curves over her ears to the nape of her slim neck. Her caps of muslin, brocade, or damask were set prettily on the shining hair, revealing a high widened brow. The reddish lashes of her father bordered the grey-black eyes which held a piercing, alert, and oddly adult look contrasting sharply with the innocent appeal of her childish mouth. Elizabeth's bearing was straight and dignified; her thin shoulders carried the simple gowns she wore in the privacy of her home, or the more heavily ornate and jewelled ones of social occasions, in unself-conscious distinction. Only on the long tapering fingers did her vanity show; she adorned them with the rings which her father, Mary, and the Queen had given her, choosing them with great care. There was also the image of the changeling about Elizabeth: today she was a child—tomorrow she might be a woman.

The loss of her father had deepened Elizabeth's own natural wariness and reserve. That such a seemingly impregnable human being should

* Though later writers refer to this simple paper book of sixty-eight pages as *The King's Journal*, Edward referred to it as *A Chronicle*. It is obviously a record of occurrences he considered important, a repository in which he would record various events as time and his inclination allowed, often long after the episode itself had occurred. It was written entirely in longhand by the boy and may be seen in the British Museum.

prove mortal after all only accentuated her silent conviction that, since life was so transitory, it should hold all the experiences, benefits, and rewards possible. The fact that she was only third in the succession did not alter her belief that she must be as prudent, as diligent in her studies, and as careful of her virtue as if she were the heir. She knew the furore the Queen's marriage to the Admiral had caused. She was only too aware that living in the same household she might be touched by some tinge of censure. But Elizabeth had an admirable objectivity for one so young, and her understanding of the human elements involved in the highly emotional situation, is obvious in her reply to Mary's request that she leave Chelsea. Elizabeth was sincerely devoted to Katherine Parr. Her feelings for the Admiral, who she had always known as a bold man and an engaging semi-relative, must certainly have been piqued by his passionate marriage proposal. To any adolescent, however intelligent or ambitious, to leave such an exciting situation for the simple security of Mary's household, could hardly have been attractive. In her letter Elizabeth obviously tried to placate Mary, while still retaining her own independence. In her shrewd evaluation and solution of the predicament may be seen an admirably balanced mixture of pious indignation and confident feminine logic:

Princess and very dear sister:

You are very right in saying, in your most acceptable letters, which you have done me the honour of writing to me, that, our interests being common, the just grief we feel in seeing the ashes, or rather the scarcely cold body of the King, our father, so shamefully dishonoured by the Queen, our stepmother, ought to be common to us also. I cannot express to you, my dear princess, how much affliction I suffered when I was first informed of this marriage, and no other comfort can I find than that of the necessity of submitting ourselves to the decrees of Heaven; since neither you nor I, dearest sister, are in such condition as to offer any obstacle thereto, without running heavy risk of making our own lot much worse than it is; at least so I think. We have to deal with too powerful a party, who have got all authority into their hands, while we, deprived of power, cut a very poor figure at court. I think, then, that the best course we can take is that of dissimulation, that the mortification may fall upon those who commit the fault . . . let us console ourselves by making the best of what we cannot remedy. If our silence do us no honour, at least it will not draw down upon us such disasters as our lamentations might induce. . . .

Elizabeth reiterated that she understood her older sister's indignation, but 'the position in which I stand obliges me to take other measures;

[176]

The Princess
Elizabeth about
age thirteen
and a half,
by an unknown
Flemish artist
*From the Royal
Collection at
Windsor Castle
By kind per-
mission of
Her Majesty,
Queen
Elizabeth II*

Mary Tudor
by Antonio Moro
*From the col-
lection at Hever
Castle, Kent
Reproduced
with the kind
permission of
the Honourable
Gavin Astor*

Henry VIII, after Holbein
National Portrait Gallery, London

Catherine of Aragon, mother of
Mary Tudor, by Sittow
Detroit Institute of Arts

Anne Boleyn, mother of Elizabeth
Tudor, by Holbein
*Reproduced with the kind permission
of the Earl of Bradford*

Jane Seymour, mother of Edward
Tudor, by Holbein
Kunsthistorisches Museum, Vienna

Queen Katherine Howard
by Holbein
Toledo, Ohio Museum of Art

Anne of Cleves by Holbein
*Reproduced with the kind permission
of the President and Fellows of
St. John's College, Oxford*

Thomas Cromwell, after Holbein
*Reproduced with the kind permission
of the Duke of Manchester*

Margaret Plantagenet Pole, the
Countess of Salisbury, Governess to
Mary Tudor. Artist unknown
National Portrait Gallery, London

Katherine Parr
by William Scrots
(Stretes)
*National
Portrait Gallery,
London*

Thomas
Seymour,
Lord Sudeley
Artist unknown
*From the
Knatchbull
Collection,
Courtesy of
Lord Brabourne*

Edward Tudor
at age four by
Hans Holbein
*Kupferstich-
kabinett, Basel*

The Protector,
Edward
Seymour, the
Duke of Somerset
Artist unknown
*National
Portrait Gallery,
London*

Lady Jane Grey
Artist unknown
*National
Portrait Gallery,
London*

Edward Tudor
at six years of age
Artist unknown
*National
Portrait Gallery,
London*

Edward Tudor at ten years of age
From the painting at Windsor Castle
By gracious permission of Her Majesty, Queen Elizabeth II

John Dudley,
the Duke of
Northumberland
*National
Portrait Gallery,
London
Reproduced
with kind per-
mission of
Viscount De
L'Isle, V.C., K.G.,
from his collec-
tion at Penshurst
Place, Kent*

John Cheke,
Tutor to
Edward VI
Artist unknown
*Courtesy of the
Duke of
Manchester*

William Paget,
Lord Privy Seal
under Mary I
Artist unknown
*Courtesy of the
Duke of
Manchester*

the Queen having shown me so great affection, and done me so many kind offices, that I must use much tact in manœuvring with her, for fear of appearing ungrateful for her benefits. . . .'[10]

Thus Elizabeth challenged her fate. Instead of docilely submitting to Mary's sensible invitation to share a home with her, the girl—attractive and intelligent—cast her lot with the momentarily disgraced Queen and Admiral. It was one of the few mistakes Elizabeth Tudor was ever to make and—once extricated from the scandalous situation that cost her dearly—an error of judgment she was never to make again.

In the months following his marriage, Thomas Seymour proceeded to gratify his vanity and lust for a power to equal his brother's. Possession of Katherine, a handsome mansion near the court, and an impressive manor house in the country at Chelsea had only momentarily checked his envy. The arrogant Lord High Admiral needed a few more props for his insatiable ego. Elizabeth Tudor was destined to fill the first need; the second unsuspecting victim was to be the hapless Lady Jane Grey.

Lady Jane Grey was not ten years old, a small, serious creature, with features and colouring closely resembling her cousin Elizabeth. She did not, however, possess the vanity that caused Elizabeth to shun the sunlight. Jane's skin was becomingly freckled and her light blonde hair sun-streaked in the summer, testifying to many solitary walks through the pleached alleys and ornate flower gardens of Bradgate, her country home. She was a retiring, self-contained child, with considerable gravity for one so young. Her life in the home of her parents, Frances Brandon and Henry Grey, the Marquess and Marchioness of Dorset, had provided little occasion for merriment.

From birth, this niece of Henry VIII had been treated as a Princess, with all the responsibilities attached to one of that rank. She was taught Greek, Latin, French, Spanish, and Italian, repeating the phrases her tutors gave her before she could even read or write. She practised her music diligently, becoming proficient on the lute and harp. Luckily Lady Jane possessed the receptive mind of the Tudors. She relished her studies for the challenge they represented and in the very pursuit of the intellect, she had found a welcome haven from the tense and anxious life which was hers at Bradgate. With an acceptance devoid of bitterness, she once told Roger Ascham, Elizabeth's tutor, of her life with her parents. Ascham had come upon her unexpectedly—a small solitary figure in the library at Bradgate—reading the *Phaedo* of Plato, while the rest of the family was hunting in the valley close by. Lady Jane had little use for the bloody sports so beloved of her mother, or the gambling and the boisterous games in which the Dorsets indulged. Instead, she preferred the gentler pursuits of reading, or writing small poems and stories which she was careful to hide. Her very difference in the rather games-loving atmosphere of the Dorset home—whether at Bradgate or in London—only accentuated all the things her parents seemed to dislike in their pretty and studious daughter. Their retaliation took the form of a physical harassment to which Jane had grown accustomed until young John Aylmer, her tutor, arrived from Cambridge to further her studies. He treated her with such kindness and respect for her accomplishments that the classroom became a refuge for the abused child. When Roger Ascham asked her why she was not with her parents but studying so diligently instead, he was astonished at her reply.

'I will tell you', she said, 'and tell you a truth which perchance you will marvel at. One of the greatest benefits that ever God gave me is that He sent me, with sharp, severe parents, so gentle a schoolmaster. When I am in the presence of either father or mother, whether I sit, stand or go, eat, drink, be merry or sad, be sewing, playing, dancing, or doing anything else, I must do it as if it were in such weight, measure and number, even as perfectly as God made the earth, or else I am so sharply taunted, so cruelly threatened, yea, presented sometimes with pinches, nips and blows and other things, (which I will not name for the honour I bear them), so without measure so misordered, *that I think myself in Hell*—till the time comes when I must go to Mr Aylmer, who teacheth me so gently, so pleasantly, and with such pure allurements to learn, that I think all the time of nothing whilst I am with him . . . and when I am called from him, I fall to weeping, because whatever I do else but learning is full of great trouble, fear, and wholesome misliking unto me. . . .'[11]

This eagerness to escape her family's abuse was the catalyst that had produced in Lady Jane Grey a formidable capacity for learning. In fleeing to the classroom, she found solace not only in the classics but also in her formal religious studies. The tenets of the New Learning appealed primarily to the young, though the reactionary older generation still clung solidly and stubbornly to the Catholicism of their youth. Not for Jane the mystical comforts of the 'old religion'. She had studied the writings of the most advanced reformers, which appealed more to the intellect than to the emotions, and embraced their teachings wholeheartedly.

The chances of Lady Jane Grey ever ascending the throne were remote—all three of Henry's children would have to die or be set aside by political or religious factions before she could succeed. But the ambition of Thomas Seymour, which had multiplied since his marriage to the Queen-Dowager, led him to devise a further possibility. He knew Lady Jane's parents were great friends of his brother, the Lord

Protector, and that a marriage between Somerset's handsome young son and the girl had been discussed. Only a catch greater than a duke's son would foil the Protector's plans, and Thomas Seymour lost no time in the weeks before the marriage announcement in devising a scheme whereby Jane might indeed occupy the throne of England. He sent an intermediary, William Harrington, a friend as conscienceless as the Admiral himself, to approach Jane's father, the Marquess of Dorset, and insinuate that 'it were a goodly thing to happen if my Lady Jane, his daughter, were in the keeping of the Lord Admiral'. Harrington also quoted Seymour as saying that 'Lady Jane was the handsomest lady in England . . . and he would see her placed in marriage much to his [her father's] comfort.'

The opportunistic Dorset bit at once. 'And with whom will he match her?' he asked. Harrington replied, 'I doubt not but you shall see he will marry her to the King, and fear you not, he will bring it to pass. . . .'[12] With Harrington's words, the possibility of Jane's marriage with the Protector's son faded. From being fourth in the succession it appeared there was another way! The little girl who had been so badgered and humiliated might, indeed, be Queen of England—and all in the lifetime of her parents who would be the first to enjoy all the perquisites such a union might produce.

The obsessive ambition of Dorset, upon which Seymour had relied, forecast the result. To the unbelieving and ill-concealed delight of Jane herself (and with the payment of several hundred pounds to Seymour as her new guardian), the girl was free to go. In the summer of 1547, shortly after her marriage, Katherine Parr welcomed another child to Chelsea. It was the beginning of a magical summer for Jane. From the cold remoteness of her country home, she was suddenly there near a broad river by which she might even be at the court itself in very little time. Elizabeth was overjoyed to have a female companion approaching her own age and welcomed her little relative warmly. They were companions in the classroom as well as in the home. After their studies were completed, their music lessons practised, and their religious devotions over for the day, Elizabeth would show Jane how to scour in the reeds at the river's edge for small creatures to put in the make-believe fishpond. They would beg the Queen's boatman to take them for a short sail on the Thames and later, inevitably, lose each other in the maze of the manor-house gardens while an impatient gardener puffed irritably as he extricated them.

But best of all for Jane were the moments spent in the gentle company of the Queen, radiant in her new happiness, as they read in turn from the Bible or as she played her lute accompanying Elizabeth at the virginals, while Katherine listened and smiled appreciatively. Lady Jane blossomed at Chelsea. The Admiral was kind to the child—there was about him a warm wittiness and an easy charm Jane had never encountered before. As the weeks passed in the pleasant household, where even the servants treated her with respect, her parents' rough taunts seemed like a bad dream. That summer gave Lady Jane Grey, old beyond her years in learning and severely deprived of any emotional comfort, her first and only taste of carefree security. In the short nightmare life that was to be hers, the memory of the year spent with her new family at Chelsea and Seymour Place would be her only consolation.

Chapter Eleven

WITHIN two months of Henry VIII's death, his dissolute and disease-ridden contemporary, Francis I of France, followed him to the grave. The heir, the twenty-nine-year-old Henri II, ascended the throne at a period when relations between England and France were again strained. Two particular issues accounted for French animosity; one was a city and the other a small child.

Henri II bitterly resented the English occupation of Boulogne. He lacked the years of wisdom and experience that had enabled his father to accept the city's loss realistically. One hotheaded attempt to recapture Boulogne had failed, and when the English reciprocated by fortifying the harbour, Henri was outraged. He turned to Scotland—as his father had before him—as a means of retaliation. Not only was Scotland a traditional ally, but the four-year-old Mary, Queen of Scots, was half French, being descended from the Guise, one of the country's most influential families.

The Lord Protector, meanwhile, had pursued Henry VIII's design for the ultimate union of the two countries through the marriage of the little Queen of Scots to the ten-year-old Edward. But diplomacy, or even simple tact, was not one of the Duke of Somerset's stronger virtues. He had revived the claim of an English sovereignty over Scotland—a sovereignty Henry himself had never demanded, hoping instead to effect the same end by Edward's marriage to the Scottish heiress. Somerset's aggressiveness imperilled the marital negotiations and further incited the already hostile French, who warned that their young King 'would not suffer it to be written in the books and chronicles that the Scots, who had ever been faithful friends to France, and whom his ancestors had ever defended, should in his reign be lost. . . .'

Border skirmishes became bloodier, and Somerset, casting aside the advice of more temperate heads, prepared to invade. Even the Council could not dissuade him. Paget was in despair and wrote pleadingly to Somerset, 'Alas, Sir, take pity of the King [Edward], and of the conservation and state of the realm. Put no more so many irons in the fire at once as you have had within this twelve-month—war with Scotland, with France, though it be not so termed. When the whole Council should join in a matter and your Grace . . . wrest them by reason of your authority to bow to it . . . alas, Sir, how shall this year do well?'[1] Gardiner, the Bishop of Winchester, was more blunt. 'I would for a time let the Scots be Scots', he wrote to the Protector, urging Somerset to wait until Edward was older and might then settle the Scottish question himself. 'In the meantime, prepare him money for it, and set the realm in an order that it hath need of', was Gardiner's sage advice.

But Somerset was lusting for battle—and glory. In July, 1547, when the French fleet ominously appeared off St Andrews, English ships might have settled the problem then and there. Instead, in late August, with some 14,000 men, 4,000 horses, and 15 cannons, he hurried northward. Petitioning the Almighty to 'especially have an eye to this small Isle of Britain . . . that the Scottishmen and we might hereafter live in one love and amity, knit into one nation by the most happy and godly marriage of the King's Majesty, our Sovereign Lord, and the young Scottish Queen . . .'[2] he crossed the Border. Three days later, at the Battle of Pinkie Cleugh, some seven miles east of Edinburgh, the Almighty answered the Protector's prayer, and in a murderous slaughter reminiscent of Flodden and Solway, the Scots were decimated by the English forces and their hired mercenaries. Triumphantly, Somerset returned to England, certain he had settled the Scottish question in spite of the disapproving Council and ministers. It was not within the Protector's temperament to grasp that while he had won a great battle, he had forfeited once and for all any chance of a marriage between young Edward and Mary. 'The marriage may be weel enough, but I dinna' like the manner of the wooing . . .' was the dry comment of the Earl of Huntley when taken prisoner. Many in Scotland had favoured the match as a great advantage for their country; after Pinkie Cleugh, however, their support vanished in the aftermath of ruined harvest, smoking villages, and a battlefield littered with dead and mutilated corpses.

At home the problem of a single religion for the country continued to perplex the Protector. The hybrid religion of Henry VIII which was essentially Catholic in observance, excepting loyalty to the Pope, held little appeal for Somerset. For years he had leaned more towards the New Learning, and with his authority complete and his popularity with the people at its height after the Scottish campaign, he sanctioned a general 'purification' of the Church. The use of holy water and candles, the presence of images and holy paintings—even stained glass—were viewed with suspicion. Certain of governmental protection, the zealous workers in the reforming government, who were beginning to be called Protestants, went to work. They encouraged the destruction of the venerable saints' images, the whitewashing of ancient wall paintings by which generations had learned the Gospel and the Commandments. Stained-glass windows were smashed and many smaller churches pulled down to provide building materials.* A spoliation reminiscent of the dissolution of the monasteris commenced throughout the land, earning a rebuke from Gardiner who begged the Protector 'not to trouble the realm with novelties in religion so long as the King is a child. . . .' When processions were abolished and fasting declared a 'politic ordinance of men', so that the Archbishop of Canterbury, Thomas Cranmer, 'did eat meat opening in Lent, in the Great Hall of Lambeth Palace, the like of which was never seen since England was a Christian country', it bore all semblance of a nine-day wonder. Gardiner did not give up easily. He pointed out that the late King had settled the religious question before his death. 'Now I see my late sovereign slandered, religions assaulted, the realm troubled, and peaceable men disquieted!'[3] cried Gardiner.

Against this background of violence and religious dispute, the envy of Thomas Seymour for his brother's power had left him little peace. He had taken full advantage of the Protector's absence in Scotland, not only by harbouring the 'two strings to his bow'—Elizabeth Tudor and Lady Jane Grey—in his home but also by seeking to strengthen his influence with his nephew, the King. Edward must be won over to any scheme he might devise to accomplish Somerset's downfall. And Seymour was clever enough to realise the easiest way was by ingratiating himself firmly in the young boy's affection.

It was almost embarrassingly easy. Edward's days were filled with the exacting demands of royalty, with the rigid and impersonal etiquette which many less sensitive than he had found stifling. He was rarely left alone and yet lived in lonely isolation, surrounded by nobles who constantly waited upon him, exercising their hereditary rights and privileges. If the young King wished to wash his face, he must suffer some pompous fellow as the Bearer of the Towel—or the Basin—to help him. His Yeomen of the Wardrobe or the Bedchamber, his Gentlemen-Ushers and Groom of the Privy Chamber, were always near at hand. It took several of these stalwarts to undress the King at night and get him dressed again in the morning. Each task was accomplished in silence, in 'a reverent, discreet and sober manner', and—Edward might have added—in absolute boredom. But he suffered their well-meant ministrations with a sweet patience, if, at times, an inward rebellion.

* Two churches in the Strand had contributed to the building of the Protector's splendid new mansion, Somerset House, on the banks of the Thames. Only public outcry prohibited him from razing the small St Margaret's, adjacent to the Abbey, for the same purpose.

His days were spent in the company of his special friend, the tall, spare John Cheke, his tutor. In the intimacy of the classroom, Cheke provided a warm and welcome atmosphere for the young orphaned King, whose cloistered existence rendered him so vulnerable to the competitive pressure of his older classmates or the more sophisticated requests of adults seeking favours. Edward was gradually introduced to the study of Plutarch, of geometry and Italian, unconsciously absorbing Cheke's own enthusiasm for these subjects. Cheke arranged for Edward to study geography and history in Latin which the boy had already mastered. He read the Bible in English, particularly Proverbs, Ecclesiastes, and the Gospels, of which he could recite whole passages. There was little reading for pure enjoyment or relaxation. Each study was an exercise in instruction to feed the intellect not gratify the spirit. On days when Cheke was absent and Edward might have read for the sake of pleasure, Roger Ascham came to instruct him in handwriting exercises, determined to make the King as skilled as his sister Elizabeth.

There were few diversions. Edward was diligent in his religious ob- servances, attending Mass daily, and shortly after his coronation, he performed all the required ceremonies needing the royal presence at Greenwich on Palm Sunday, Passion Week, and at Easter. On Maundy Thursday, as tradition demanded, he washed the feet of ten old men, giving each tenpence in a purse and the gown from his back to one. Since the small robe was of little use to the man, it was later redeemed for an additional twenty shillings. This practicality extended to Edward himself whose sensible approach to contemporary matters often startled his companions. Riding from one royal residence to another, he viewed the ruins of a great monastery, the raw waste troubling him. Turning, he asked a companion what had happened to the building. 'A religious house, dissolved and demolished by order of the King, your Grace's father, for abuses . . .' was the answer. The spirit of his frugal grandfather, Henry VII, and his own inborn resourcefulness and logic, was expressed in the boy's surprising reply. 'Could not the King, my father, punish the offenders and suffer so goodly buildings to stand? And put better men that might have inhabited and governed them?' he asked. There is no record of the answer King Edward received.

He chafed a bit, as any child will, under adult restrictions; since he was a King, it often seemed the restraints were doubly severe. He could not help but hear the great oaths of his uncle, Thomas Seymour. Delightedly, he repeated them to his classmates as they played tennis or wrestled— sports at which he was invariably defeated because of his slightness— and in the rip-roaring, rolling phrases of each swearing syllable he found he could entirely surpass his friends, who joyously encouraged the King in his newly acquired talent. When Cheke eventually overheard Edward's vivid performance the truth was out; the whipping boy received a severe caning, and the next time, Edward was told, the punishment would be meted out to *him*, even if he was King!

As the reigning monarch, he had hoped to have some minor authority, but always the Protector made the decisions without even the face-saving gesture of consulting the boy. He studied hard, and yet even such small duties as signing dispatches had been executed by Somerset until the foreign ambassadors insisted on the royal signature which was Edward's natural right and privilege. Now he proudly and carefully wrote 'Edward' at the bottom of the documents which were brought to him daily. In official audiences, the ambassadors correctly addressed the young King first. But invariably, the Protector would answer before the child could even open his mouth to observe the social amenities. Somerset's own insensitivity, the pressure of work, and the war campaign, had left him little time to consider a child's pride, and Edward was continually left with the impression that he was a regrettable necessity to the continuance of the Protectorship. The result had been a natural disillusionment in the boy-King who remembered the many responsibilities that were his by birth and inheritance. He would have been much less a Tudor had he not yearned for the day when he could conduct his realm as he saw fit, when he could speak for himself and do just as he wished.

And then there was the matter of money. The Protector, whose own exchequer and estates were multiplying with what he considered a satisfying rapidity, allowed Edward little or no pocket money. The King rarely had coins to give in alms to petitioners, nothing for those visitors who brought him small gifts, for minstrels who might play for him, or just for the delightfully secure feeling of having a few coins to jingle in the pocket of his small doublet. The lack of funds had been a source of acute embarrassment to the generous boy, and Thomas Seymour, seeing his distress, consoled Edward by saying, he was 'hardly treated by Somerset' and should have more money and more liberty. He offered to give the child little sums—an offer which Edward eagerly accepted, and in the next few weeks he had the heady experience of dispensing largesse to his tutors, to a guard at St James's who had made him a present of a book, to a trumpeter who had played on the Thames outside his Greenwich Palace window, and to 'certain tumblers' who had entertained him on the lawn. 'If His Highness lacks any money, send to me for it—*and nobody else!*' Seymour ordered William Fowler of the King's Bedchamber, adding that Fowler himself 'should have anything he lacked' for payment.

Exploiting the advantage the Protector's absence offered, Seymour saw his nephew often, sympathising with his plight and further contributing to Edward's already deep sense of inadequacy: 'Your Grace is too bashful in your own matters. Why do ye not speak to bear rule as other Kings do?' Edward's pride might be momentarily touched, and he would reply curtly 'It needeth not; I am well enough.' But then, in several days, his purse would again be empty, and it was easy to say to Fowler, 'I should like some money now.' When Fowler asked how much, Edward was vague and the intermediary wrote to Seymour, 'His Grace would name no sum, but as it pleased your Lordship to send him, for he determines to give it away, but to whom he will not tell me as yet. . . .'[4]

By the end of the summer, Edward was indebted to the Lord Admiral for several hundred pounds. At each meeting with the young King, Seymour maintained, 'Ye must take it upon yourself to rule!' He said Edward was 'as able as other Kings'. And then, irritating the sore point, he ended, 'Ye are but a beggarly King now . . . ye have not enough to play or to give your servants!' Stung to the quick, Edward would heatedly answer that his cofferer had money—an empty reply, since he was well aware his uncle knew the money was for domestic purposes and not for small boy to spend.

With the Protector's victorious return under a 'halo of splendour', the Admiral's envy and resentment erupted. Thomas Seymour had neglected his duties in the Admiralty during his brother's absence, and his attentions to Edward, as well as Elizabeth and Lady Jane Grey, had not been overlooked by the Council members. They were repeated in anxious detail to the Protector who severely reprimanded his younger brother. Further compounding the distressing situation was the reaction of Anne Stanhope, the Duchess of Somerset, wife of the Protector. She denied Katherine Parr the respect due a former Queen, refusing to carry her train, even jostling the startled woman when Katherine exercised her right of precedence in the Royal Chapel. Urged on by his spiteful wife, the Protector withheld many of the jewels Henry had given Katherine as a personal gift. The Protector now haughtily announced they were actually Crown property and refused to surrender them, causing Thomas Seymour to observe bitterly, 'My brother is wondrous hot in helping every man to his right save me . . . !' Katherine shared his anger and was further outraged when the Protector leased her favourite manor of Fausterne, part of her jointure estates, against her wishes. From Chelsea she wrote furiously to her husband in London that 'my Lord, your brother, hath this afternoon a little made me warm —it was fortunate we were so much distant for I suppose else I should have bitten him!' Her contempt for the Duchess of Somerset is evident in her next remark, 'What cause have they to fear having such a wife? It is requisite for them continually to pray for a short dispatch of that Hell!'[5]

The feud between the indignant Queen-Dowager and the Protector's arrogant wife, and between their husbands, continued to 'raise much dust at court'. Inevitably, Thomas turned to his nephew as a means of regaining Katherine's jewels. He approached Edward, asking him to write 'a thing to the Lords of the Council for me.' When Edward asked what it was, Seymour was soothing, 'It is none ill thing', assuring the child it was for 'the Queen's Majesty'. The King was devoted to his stepmother but surprisingly did not exhibit the interest or sympathy Seymour had expected. With an almost adult firmness, he said bluntly, 'If it is good, the Lords will allow it. If it is ill, I will not write it.' Seymour was angered at the response. 'The Lords will take it in better part if *you* will write it . . .' he said, glowering at the boy. But Edward was not to be budged. Instead he moved towards the room in which Cheke, his tutor, was waiting, saying to the Admiral, 'Leave me alone. . . .' Later he confessed the whole matter to Cheke, who brightened his spirit considerably by saying, 'Ye were best not to write'.

For the moment, Seymour was foiled in his attempt to intimidate Edward. The reprimand he had received from his brother had fanned an angry antagonism which deepened when Katherine's jewels remained in the Protector's possession and access to the King was deliberately made difficult. Seymour's natural cunning, overwhelming ambition, and explosive temperament finally led him to actively plot Somerset's downfall. If he could limit the tenure of the Protector's office so that it depended upon Edward's pleasure, rather than upon his minority, he could possibly clip his brother's wings. Angrily he denounced Somerset's greed to anyone who would listen. '. . . There can neither bishopric, deanery, nor prebend fall void, but one or the other of them [the Council] will have a piece of it. But it will all come in again when the King cometh to his years . . .' the foolhardy Admiral cried, and then, with a great oath he piously proclaimed, 'I would not be in their coats for five marks when he [the King] shall hear of these matters . . . !'[6]

With no further word from his nephew, he again contacted the ubiquitous Fowler, who dutifully told Edward at his first opportunity he 'ought to thank the Lord Admiral for the gentleness he hath shown to you and for his money.' Edward already felt guilty about not showing his uncle sufficient gratitude. His warm nature thus appealed to, he dutifully wrote, 'My Lord, I recommend me to you and the Queen . . .' and then, remembering his ever empty purse—and preferring not to think of their last scene together—he finished, 'I pray you to send me as much money as ye think good. . . .' Encouraged at the resumption of the relationship, Seymour approached Cheke, whom he had hoped to bribe, asking that Edward sign a paper on which he had written, 'My Lords, I pray you to favour my Lord Admiral, mine uncle's suit.' Realising the paper's implication, Cheke bravely withstood Seymour's insistence. The frustrated Admiral swore loudly at Cheke and was still raging when he left. The tutor went directly to Edward and told him what had happened. 'The Lord Admiral shall have no bill signed nor written by me', the King solemnly promised Cheke.

[187]

But Seymour would not leave Edward alone and, through his intermediary Fowler, again approached the King. 'Would your Grace write anything to the Lord Admiral ... ?' Fowler asked the boy. 'Nothing ...,' Edward replied, remembering the promise to his tutor. Then, mindful of his uncle's generosity, of their old friendship, and thinking the impasse between them would lengthen if he remained stubborn, he compromised. He came to Fowler rather shamefacedly and said there was a note in his dining-room, 'under the carpet by the window. ...' Fowler found the message, written on torn and dirty paper, indicating Edward had not wanted to ask Cheke for proper writing materials. Innocent enough and hardly suitable for the Admiral's purpose, it merely asked Seymour to 'recommend me unto you and the Queen, thanking you always for your remembrance. ...' That was as far as Edward Tudor was willing to go. Some native wariness—and an unusual sense of guilt which had accompanied his writing of the note—was somewhat alleviated with the arrival of forty pounds from Thomas Seymour; it enabled the boy to send adequate Christmas gifts to his sisters and teachers and to dispense plentiful coins to his servants and court visitors during the holiday season.

Certain now that he could count on Edward, Seymour solicited the support of those on the Council who might hold grudges against his brother or who might be bought. For this he needed money, and in the person of the master of the Bristol Mint, Sir Thomas Sherington, who so falsified the account books and then clipped and sheared coins that he amassed some £4,000, Seymour found an unscrupulous aide. While the Admiral had shamefully neglected his legitimate duties, he had used the office to good advantage. He had willingly bargained with 'Thomessin', a renowned Channel pirate, giving him and his cut-throats illicit protection in return for a share of the plunder hidden—with Seymour's knowledge—on the Scilly Isles.[7] With this money he set about recruiting for an armed rebellion, stocking the ammunition in Holt Castle which would be his bulwark for defence should his brother's downfall have to be accomplished by force rather than deceit.

And then—as winter closed in on the manor house at Chelsea and Katherine joyfully told her husband of her first pregnancy—the pirates' loot, the questionable support of King and Council, even Seymour's hatred for his brother, were forgotten, Removed momentarily from the intrigues of court, Thomas Seymour relaxed in the feminine atmosphere of Chelsea with his adoring Queen-Dowager and his grateful and docile ward, Lady Jane Grey. There was also Anne Boleyn's daughter, who had always fascinated him as much as her mother had fascinated the old King. Only now there was every indication that Elizabeth was similarly bewitched, and in the exciting pursuit he saw ahead of him, Seymour anticipated a challenge too great to ignore and a prize tantalisingly ready for plucking. With all his magnificent competence with women, it never occurred to him that an inexperienced and untouched fourteen-and-a-half-year-old girl would be the innocent means by which his own destiny would ultimately be determined.

In the ten months she had been at Chelsea, Elizabeth had been relatively content. Her own retinue of some 120 servants provided for her comfort, and her governess, Katherine Ashley, was not so strict as to be a nuisance. With an admirable and simple sense of values, the governess had won an easy confidence and a great degree of affection from Elizabeth. Round-faced and plump, with streaks of grey in her hair, Ashley was never far from the Princess, who found in her a pliability and good nature comforting to be with and easy to outwit, if necessary.

Not that there were many opportunities for Elizabeth Tudor to misbehave or otherwise tax her governess's patience. Life at the pleasant manor house on the Thames was leisurely and unvarying; elegance, the more demanding social routine and its accompanying rituals, were reserved for Seymour Place in the City. Each day Elizabeth pursued her studies with William Grindal, and upon his death, Roger Ascham came to the Queen-Dowager's establishment. He said he wished 'her Grace to come to that end in perfectness' which her wit and 'painfulness in her study . . .' merited. Accordingly, he and Elizabeth read from Cicero, Livy, the orations of Isocrates, the tragedies of Sophocles, and then delved into the New Testament in Greek. Ascham's philosophy of teaching resembled that of Richard Cox, Edward's first tutor. Ascham said, 'Blunt edges be dull and endure much pain to little profit; the free edge is soon turned, if it be not handled thereafter. If you pour much drink at once into a goblet, the most part will dash out and run over; if ye pour it softly, you may fill it even to the top; and so her Grace, I doubt not, by little and little may be increased in learning, that at length greater cannot be required. . . .'[8]

Other than Roger Ascham and the gentlemen who served in her household, there was no one of the opposite sex around Elizabeth with whom she might have formed any kind of relationship. Her brother was always at a distance, surrounded by a court at which neither she nor Mary was welcome and where she could not venture without permission from the Protector or Council. Nor were there any young men near her own age suitable for her company at Chelsea or at Seymour Place or at the country residence of Hanworth. While the Council debated a marriage for her, she was, ironically, prevented from indulging in even the minor social pleasures which would normally have been hers under other more favourable conditions. With the

Admiral's frequent absences and Katherine's indisposition because of her pregnancy, Elizabeth was left with the Lady Jane Grey, Ashley, and her ladies-in-waiting. Jane was too young to understand Elizabeth's dissatisfaction with the dreariness of an overly restricted life. And Elizabeth instinctively hid her feelings during the occasions when ennui almost overcame her. The less her maidens or Ashley knew of it, the better. And the unvarying routine of her day simply made things worse. First, she was awakened by Ashley and hurried through her toilet, assisted by her ladies. After breakfast and a brief service in the Chapel, she and Jane studied with Mr Ascham until it was time to assemble in the Great Hall for the large dinner served at several sittings to the entire household. In the afternoon, she might write letters, embroider, practice the flute, the lute, or the virginals, prepare her lessons, or walk in the gardens with Jane or the Queen-Dowager. She rarely left the immediate vicinity of the Seymour household; Anne of Cleves was too far away at Richmond to visit easily and Katherine Parr liked having Elizabeth near her. At Hanworth it was even worse, unless luck brought Mary close by, and then they might spend a satisfying day together. Seymour Place in London was the best of all, for the pleasures of the City were to be seen (if not experienced), and Thomas himself was often there, to wag a reproving finger at her if she over-indulged in sweets at the table, to joke with her when she played a wrong note in her music, or simply to lift her spirits with an approving comment on her dress or hair—or just to note the simple fact that she was growing up! And, from the look of interest in his eyes, apparently growing up very becomingly.

Elizabeth had been acutely aware of Thomas Seymour since his proposal. The words of his letter noting her beauty that 'bewitched' him, of his wish to 'open his heart' to her, and his promise 'to adore her 'til death'—the remembrance of the passionate words had lightened her loneliness and contributed to fantasies which even the presence of his pregnant wife did not diminish. When Thomas himself appeared —tall, vivid with life, and full of a charming nonsense that bordered on insolence—she would colour prettily, feeling clumsy, ill at ease, and suddenly apprehensive. Her self-consciousness communicated itself to Thomas, whose talents with the opposite sex had made him alive to just the right moment when a beauty might be approached. Elizabeth's very air of uncertainty, combined with the subtly controlled eagerness, might have caused another more conscientious man to consider her vulnerability and ease her through a difficult period of transition with grace and consideration. But delicacy of motive, or of action, was not one of Seymour's virtues. Elizabeth's youth and susceptibility—not to mention her proximity—proved too strong a temptation for the Admiral to resist.

Therefore, in the early spring mornings at Chelsea, as Katherine Parr lay uneasily in her bed with morning sickness, Elizabeth was awakened not by Ashley or one of her ladies but by the Lord Admiral himself. The very proximity in which they had lived for several months had only fostered the as yet unacknowledged feeling existing between them. Thomas would use his own key to unlock her chamber door, open the bedcurtains some time before she was awake, and the strong handsome face with its cynical little smile would be the first thing Elizabeth beheld as she opened her eyes in the still silent household. She would obey her natural impulse and burrow further under the covers while he roared with laughter and, letting the hangings drop, left the room. Her own curiosity aroused, the next morning Elizabeth would feign sleep when he silently came into her room. But he always saw through her and, pretending punishment, would act as if he were about to kiss her in her bed while she hurried again to get under the covers.

One morning Ashley appeared in the doorway, her button mouth pursed in disapproval. 'For shame!' she scolded, amid the giggling and scuffling antics on the bed, and huffily ordered Seymour from the room. The Admiral pretended great terror and returned to his wife with mock subservience. Something in his manner, however, prompted the not normally astute Ashley to be more watchful and, from that morning on, to arrive earlier in the Princess's bedroom. But still the Admiral continued to appear, noisily inquiring if Elizabeth were up and if not, why not? If she were dressed, he would hide his disappointment and, contenting himself with striking her familiarly on the buttocks, the tomfoolery would begin again, with Elizabeth running to hide behind Ashley or the bedcurtains as Thomas, with a remarkable oath proceeded on through to the maidens' chambers. Ashley was anxious at such goings-on and threatened to go to the Queen. Invariably, Thomas wore his nightgown and slippers, and in such dishabille, his presence in the maidens' quarters carried more than a titillating aura of the forbidden. Ashley bore it as long as she could and finally she 'did tell my Lord it was an unseemly sight to see a man so little dressed in a maiden's chamber, with which he was angry, but left it.'

The morning visits interrupted for a time when the household was removed to the Queen-Dowager's manor at Hanworth, but soon the obvious pursuit of Elizabeth resumed and was carried on under the very eyes and with the apparent co-operation of the guileless Katherine herself. One morning, as if to mock Ashley's fears, Thomas brought the Queen-Dowager herself with him on his early morning visit and both of them 'tickled my Lady Elizabeth in her bed'. Still using his wife as an innocent foil, he followed Elizabeth into the garden one day where they entered into a game in which the girl was the captive and, while she was being held by the Queen-Dowager, the Admiral calmly—and slowly—cut her gown of black cloth into a hundred pieces, amid much laughter and joking. When Ashley 'chid the Lady Elizabeth . . .' the girl answered she 'could not strive with them' and said Katherine had been too strong. But she did not meet Ashley's eyes as she said it.

Elizabeth was a willing participant in the early morning romps; Seymour's impetuous and daring behaviour, so infuriating to Ashley and so tantalizing to her maidens, lent considerable spice to the days and was a challenge to which the girl felt equal. She was sublimely indifferent to any danger, but Mrs Ashley realised the improprieties implicit in the situation which, if allowed to continue, also reflected unfavourably on *her* proper supervision of the Princess. She again warned the Admiral about his behaviour, but the unpredictable Seymour took all the starch out of her anger and only further confused the simple woman by replying angrily, 'By God's precious soul! I will tell my Lord Protector how I am slandered—and I will not leave off, for I mean no evil!'[9]

However 'well-intentioned' the Admiral thought he was, Elizabeth's lack of initiative in responding to his advances other than the provocative early morning play urged him to attempt a more definite reaction from her. He told the Queen he had 'looked in at the gallery-window and saw my Lady Elizabeth with her arms about a man's neck.' Katherine took the matter up with a distressed Ashley who hurried to deal with Elizabeth. The girl was appalled at the charge and furious that no one realised it for what it was: another of Thomas Seymour's jokes and one in which she realised there was a definite hint for her. Weeping, she denied the charge and told Ashley heatedly to 'ask all her women if there was any man who came to her, excepting Grindal [the school-master]. . . .'[10]

Ashley's indignation also reflected Katherine Parr's belated awareness that Elizabeth might be a temptation to her susceptible husband. In sending the reproof through her governess instead of confronting the girl herself, the Queen-Dowager exhibited an aloof censure which Elizabeth was quick to recognise. Katherine had not, however, voiced her suspicions to her husband. He was at home more frequently now; the spring thaw had made the roads to London muddy and difficult, he said. And he seemed to be wherever the Princess Elizabeth could be found. Always he watched her with an oddly expectant and calculating look; the very air between them was vibrant with a compelling promise which never seemed to materialise. Elizabeth could sense his desire and the hidden passion behind it yet it did not displease her. Instead of fear or shock, there was a heady sense of power accompanying her own feeling for Thomas. But it was tempered by the knowledge that the remarkable situation, involving a married man, an orphaned Princess, and a royal and pregnant stepmother and wife, could go no further. It must remain a game—a dangerous game, perhaps, though an enjoyable one.

The tensions engendered by this duel of wills—their cat and mouse wariness of each other—reacted upon the others of the household. The very atmosphere became clandestine and furtive. Both Ashley and Thomas Parry, Elizabeth's cofferer, reasoned with the girl who stubbornly insisted she was doing no wrong. But she was also bluntly frank. She told Parry 'that she feared the Admiral loved her but too well, and that the Queen was jealous of both.' Elizabeth was later to prove most adept in dissimulation, but she could also be artlessly candid when she chose—especially when she had done nothing seriously wrong.

The presence of a predatory man, a suspicious wife, and a singularly attractive and nubile girl under one roof soon came to a predictable end. Tiring of the waiting game which only seemed to exhilarate Elizabeth, Thomas accosted her when she was alone. The lure of the young and untouched beauty proved too much for him, and he embraced her tightly. The skirmishing had just begun when Katherine herself walked into the room, and the scene that followed put an end to Elizabeth's stay in the Queen-Dowager's household. Though nothing more had happened than the pursuit of a flirtatious girl by a jaded and unscrupulous rake, the result was far-reaching in its effect on Elizabeth's temperament, health, reputation, and future. Katherine Parr at last acknowledged the seriousness of the situation, and for the second time in four years, Elizabeth Tudor was sent away in disgrace. Though she had not begun the attempted seduction, neither had she been completely innocent or reluctant to encourage it. Her senses had been aroused, her imagination stimulated, and her wits challenged; in many ways, it had been very satisfying. But she was realistic. Katheine Parr had a long talk with the girl prior to her departure. The magnitude of Elizabeth's actions offered no excuse, and she wisely kept silent. That she did feel some pangs of conscience, however, can be seen in the letter Elizabeth wrote Katherine from her residence at Cheshunt:

Although I could not be plentiful in giving thanks for the manifold kindness received at your Highness' hand at my departure, yet I am something to be borne withal, for truly I was replete with sorrow to depart from your Highness, especially leaving you undoubtful of health; and albeit I answered little, I weighed it more deeper, when you said you would warn me of all evils that you should hear of me; and if your Grace had not a good opinion of me, you would not have offered friendship to me that way.

But what may I more say than Thank God for providing such friends to me! Desiring God to enrich me with their long life, and me grace

[193]

to be in heart no less thankful to receive it than I now am glad in writing to show it. And although I have plenty of matter, here I will stay, for I know you are not quiet to read.

From Cheshunt, this present Saturday,

Your Highness' humble daughter,

Elizabeth[11]

Katherine had obviously chosen to view the whole episode as the momentary aberration of a foolhardy husband and an imprudent child. The affection between Katherine and Elizabeth was still deep and is evident in the promise the Queen made to warn the Princess 'of all evils' or gossip which might have ensued from the girl's rapid departure from Chelsea as well as the loose tongues of the royal servants. It spoke well of both the Queen and her stepdaughter that the distance which must be put between them—and between Elizabeth and the Lord Admiral— did not diminish the basic love and respect they held for each other. It was only the beginning of a final disenchantment for Katherine with her husband. For Elizabeth, there was still a long way to go.

A somewhat chastened Thomas Seymour returned to court determined somehow to accomplish the removal of his brother from the Protectorate. Riding to the opening of Parliament, he grumbled to his companions that the responsibility should be shared and the authority and power distributed between both uncles of the King. 'If I be thus used', he said petulantly, 'they speak of a Black Parliament . . . by God's precious soul, I will make the blackest Parliament that ever was in England!' When Lord Clinton replied, 'If you speak such words, you shall lose my Lord [the Protector] and undo yourself!' the distraught Seymour protested, 'I would you should know, by God's precious soul, I may better live without him than he without me . . . !'[12]

Word of his brother's resentment and treacherous activities, the suspicious relations with his nephew, and the vague gossip emanating from Chelsea concerning the Princess Elizabeth resulted in Somerset's hauling Seymour before the Council where he arrogantly denied everything. He was simply a victim of gossip, he stated coolly. Insolently, he dared them to send him to the Tower. Instead, the Protector, whose lenience with his younger brother was well known, released him with a warning and soothed him with additional grants of land. Such an effort at reconciliation enraged Somerset's wife. Furiously the Duchess warned: 'I tell you that if your brother does not die, he will be your death!'

Thomas had acted with assurance. Not only had he relied upon his brother's affection and support, but his position as uncle to the reigning monarch and husband of an ex-Queen of whom the young King was fond, gave him an undeniable security. He could not know, as Katherine moved to the magnificent Sudeley Castle in the rolling Gloucestershire countryside to await the birth of her child, that a once-solicitous fate was about to remove his greatest protection.

On August 30, 1548, Katherine gave birth to her child, Mary Seymour.[13] She had spent a peaceful month with Lady Jane Grey and Lady Tyrwhitt as companions, the unhappy memories of Chelsea fading as autumn brought her lying-in nearer. She wrote letters to her husband Thomas, telling of the stirring of the child in her womb, 'I gave the little knave your blessing, who like an honest man stirred apace after and before.' She wrote to Elizabeth letters the girl said were 'most joyful to me in absence', and she rejoiced in the good wishes of a reconciled Mary Tudor who, from distant Norfolk, wrote she 'trusted to her good success of your Grace's great belly; and in the meantime, shall desire much to hear of your health, which I pray Almighty God to continue and increase.'[14] The lying-in chamber had been fitted with costly tapestries illustrating the history of the Nymph Daphne, and the bed had a new scarlet tester and curtains of crimson taffeta. A small room nearby, with a lovely oriel window overlooking the peaceful and hazy countryside, and hung with 'counterpoints of imagery to please the babe', was to be the nursery.

Though disappointed that the 'little knave' should have been a girl instead, Katherine had had a safe delivery, and it was not until some six days later that she became delirious. The Queen had complained to Lady Tyrwhitt of not feeling well and said 'she did fear such things in herself, that she was sure she could not live.' Lady Tyrwhitt remonstrated with the sick woman while Seymour stood anxiously nearby. But Katherine would not be deterred. 'My Lady Tyrwhitt, I am not well handled,' she said tremulously, 'for those that be about me care not for me, but stand laughing at my grief, and the more good I will to them, the less good they will to me.' Seymour laughed indulgently at his wife's words and leaned down to her, taking her hand in his. 'Why, sweetheart, I would you no hurt', he said gently. Katherine interrupted firmly. 'No, my Lord, I think so', she said into his ear, but overheard by Lady Tyrwhitt, 'But my Lord, *you have given me many shrewd taunts!*' Distressed, Thomas indicated he 'would lie down on the bed by her, to look if he could pacify her unquietness with gentle communication.' As he spoke softly to her, she turned 'roundly and sharply' and said to him, 'My Lord, I would have given a thousand marks to have had my full talk with Huick [the attending physician] the first day I was delivered, but I durst not for fear of displeasing you.' Hearing the

Queen's sad words, Lady Tyrwhitt turned aside sorrowfully, 'perceiving her trouble to be so great, that my heart would serve me to hear no more.'[15]

For the remainder of the hour Seymour endeavoured to comfort the distraught and feverish woman. But it was futile. On September 5, two days before Elizabeth's fifteenth birthday, the gracious and sweet-tempered Katherine Parr died. None of the three stepchildren to whom she had given a mother's devoted care were allowed to attend the splendid funeral held in the chapel of Sudeley Church,[16] which stood surrounded by stately old trees on a slight hill adjoining the castle gardens. Lady Jane Grey was the chief mourner. The unhappiness of the child who had lost her benefactor, and had only a reluctant return to an unhappy home to anticipate, was deep and genuine. It was reflected in the painful shock the Queen-Dowager's death gave to Mary, Elizabeth, and Edward Tudor. In their lives which had held all too little trust and emotional security, Katherine Parr had been a gentle companion, a joyous friend, and a kindly and loving stepmother. They were not to know her like again.

The death of Katherine Parr altered the fortunes of her husband and her stepchildren, as well as the future of the twelve-year-old Lady Jane Grey who tearfully returned to the 'nips and bobs' of her parents at Bradgate. Once the shock of her loss had worn off, Thomas Seymour petitioned for Jane's return to his household, earning an inane reply from her father. Playing for time to see how the Admiral's destiny fared without a royal wife, the Marquis of Dorset wrote:

Considering the state of my daughter and her tender years wherein she shall hardly rule herself as yet without a guide, lest she should, for lack of a bridle, take too much the head and conceive such opinion of herself that all such good behaviour as she heretofore learned by the Queen's and your most wholesome instruction, should either altogether be quenched in her, or at the least much diminished, I shall . . . require your Lordship to commit her to the governance of her mother, by whom, for the fear and duty she owes her, she shall be most easily ruled and framed toward virtue. . . .[17]

However, within three weeks of such pious words and the exchange of an additional several hundred pounds, as well as the promise to further a marriage with Edward, the Dorsets again relinquished Lady Jane to Seymour's care. At Michaelmas, he personally came to Bradgate to escort the child who so enhanced his own status to Seymour Place in London. Jane later wrote to him in gratitude for his 'goodness from time to time' and noted that he 'had become towards me a loving and kind father.'

Jane's respite did not last long, for time was running out for Thomas Seymour. Bent on his brother's downfall, he still disdained his Admiralty duties, spent the Mint funds freely and the proceeds from the pirates' sea-plunder to provision Holt Castle further, and endeavoured to recruit enough country yeomen to 'keep ten thousand men in the field for a month.' He attempted to re-establish a relationship with Edward and Elizabeth Tudor, but Edward—whose disenchantment with his Seymour uncles was plain in his description of Katherine Parr's brother William as 'mine *honest* uncle'—maintained a barely hidden resentment towards both the Protector and the Admiral. Their meddling, the lack of honest consideration for him as the reigning monarch, and the deception they employed against each other had caused a deep distrust and an absence of any honest good will towards either of them. And underneath all his hostile small-boy feelings lay the disquieting fear that he was the only male who stood between his uncles and the power and wealth of the Crown. Edward knew his history well enough to know that Princes and boy-Kings had perished before. The less he saw of the Admiral the better; the Protector he had to put up with for the time being.

With Elizabeth, Seymour had better luck. Though still uncertain that she would accept him in marriage, he did not feel his attentions would be unwelcome, and the red-haired daughter of the great Henry suited him far better than anyone else. As her husband, his position would be greatly strengthened; together they might force the Protector to share the power of his office. At Christmas, he offered his London house for Elizabeth's use, as she had no lodging of her own, and intimated he would soon visit her in the country as 'Ashridge was not far out of his way. . . .'

Elizabeth guessed the Admiral's intentions. Gossip and speculation in her own household foretold Thomas's early emotional recovery from the loss of his wife. When news of Katherine Parr's death was brought to Elizabeth by an officer of Seymour's household who mentioned that 'his Lord was a heavy man, for the loss of the Queen, his wife', the kindly Ashley bade Elizabeth write a letter of condolence. She was surprised at the girl's tart reply. 'I will not do it, *for he needs it not . . .*' said Elizabeth firmly. 'Then if your Grace will not, then will *I!*' mumbled a surprised Ashley, bristling at what she considered an arrant display of bad manners.

In the weeks that followed, Elizabeth's awareness of Thomas Seymour was further emphasised by the subtle pressures exerted upon her by

[197]

those who should have been more exactingly conscious of their responsibilities to a royal child lacking parents or an intelligent adult guardian to guide her. Her ladies-in-waiting teased her about the handsome Seymour at every opportunity, and Lady Tyrwhitt gossiped to Ashley that 'it was the opinion of many that the Lord Admiral kept the late Queen's maidens together to wait on the Lady Elizabeth, whom he intendeth to marry shortly.' Later, upon a return from the City, when Elizabeth asked her governess 'What news she had from London?' The woman archly replied, 'They say your Grace shall have my Lord Admiral, and that he will shortly come to woo you. . . .' Elizabeth had smiled and replied, '. . . It was but London news', to which Ashley reminded her of Seymour's proposal before he wed Katherine Parr. Elizabeth absorbed it all, giggling at times with her companions or contrarily, as one of them dwelt at length on the charms of Thomas Seymour, turning on her curtly and threatening 'that she would have her thrust out of her presence if she did not desist.' It was all part of the same game she had played at Chelsea, only now the winning of it seemed possible—and pleasant.

Seymour was heedless of the danger inherent in his pursuit of Elizabeth, and any attempt to warm him was rebuffed. Lord Robert Tyrwhitt told the Admiral he would not wish to be in his place if he wed Elizabeth for 'if they [the Council] catch hold of him, they will shut him up.' When Wriothesley, the ex-Lord Chancellor, was approached for support, he vehemently protested, 'For God's sake, my Lord, take heed of what you do!' When Thomas said he would 'have things better ordered', Wriothesley replied, 'My Lord, beware how you attempt any violence. It were better that you had never been born, yea, that you had been burned quick alive, than that you should attempt it!'[18]

Undaunted, Seymour continued his fatal course, scarcely bothering to hide his intentions. When Russell, the Lord Privy Seal, also tried to warn Seymour of his dangerous ambition, of the 'certain rumours bruited of you' in respect to Elizabeth, he asked the Admiral pointedly, 'And what money, my Lord, shall ye have . . . ?' Seymour knew Elizabeth's income and replied, 'three thousand pounds', to which Russell hotly stated there would be no such sum if she married without the Council's consent. He told the Admiral firmly, the other monies, goods, and plate would not be enough to 'maintain your charges and estates.' Seymour had continued to staff both Seymour Place and Sudeley Castle with full retainers in the hope of a prospective bride. He angrily retorted that Elizabeth 'must have the three thousand pounds a year also!' When Russell strongly denied the fact, Seymour taunted, 'By God, none of you all dare say nay to it!' Russell, ruffled and disquieted said, 'By God, I *will* say nay to it, for it is clean against the King's will!'[19]

Rumours of the Admiral's intentions and the continued household gossip kept the situation very much alive for Elizabeth. When her cofferer, Thomas Parry, said he had 'heard of a marriage between them', Elizabeth blushed to the roots of her hair and showed such 'countenance of gladness . . . I took occasion to ask her whether, if the Council would like it, she would marry with him?' Elizabeth still would not commit herself, saying only that 'when that time comes to pass, I will do as God shall put in my mind.'[20]

But she never had the chance. The strain of his furtive activities, the frustration of his relationship with Elizabeth, and his estrangement from Edward, the uncertainty of his future which seemed to indicate the best might be behind him—all contributed to a deterioration of Thomas Seymour's own cunning and perspective. When he realised the Protector knew his purpose and had 'penetrated his daring design to raise troops for the purpose of dethroning the royal sovereign and seizing the Crown' as Elizabeth's husband, he became distraught. On the night of January 16, 1549, he slipped into the Palace, intent upon gaining the person of the King. With a total lack of caution, he had resolved in his distress that if he could at least *see* Edward, he might regain the King's confidence. It was well after midnight when Seymour approached the outer chamber and, in one of fate's more magnificent coincidences, found the guards had left it for a moment and he was alone at the entrance. It led to an inner hallway where the door to the royal bed-chamber was closed. For some reason, Edward had become restless during the evening and, perceiving that the halberdiers had left the outer entrance unguarded for a moment, had put his small spaniel dog, which usually slept in the same room with him, outside the chamber door, which he then securely bolted. The Admiral, however, had acquired a key, and as he attempted to unlock the door, the little pet— 'the most faithful guardian of the King's majesty'—barked threateningly at the disturbance. Infuriated, Seymour lost all control and shot the dog, killing it immediately. The noise caused the Palace to come alive: from all directions raced the guards, servants, and Gentlemen of the Privy-Chamber each of whom now realised they had left the little King of England completely alone at a most unpropitious moment. Seymour seemed dazed by all the resulting commotion and could only mumble he had meant no harm and just wished to see that 'His Majesty was safely guarded.' The next day he was in the Tower of London.

A list of thirty-five charges was drawn up against the Lord High Admiral. In addition to gaining control of the Princess Elizabeth and Lady Jane Grey, Seymour was accused of conspiring to overthrow the Protectorate through fraud, illicitly storing arms, and raising a small army. When the charges were read to him, his 'resolute answer was, that for a reply they should not look for it from him.' But others were more co-operative—Sherington of the Mint, Fowler of Edward's Privy-Chamber, and even Lady Jane's father, the Marquess of Dorset, were questioned by the Council. Each told and retold the part they had played in the conspiracy. Seymour loudly demanded an open trial; he was well aware his own image had captured the public imagination, and he counted on his brother's lenience and distaste for persecuting one of his own blood.* He refused to sign any of the articles drawn against him, saying, 'I am sure I can have no hurt if they do me right. They cannot kill me, except they do me wrong. And if they do, I shall die but once. And if they take my life from me, I have a master that will at once revenge it.'[21]

However, the 'master' was but a twelve-year-old boy very aware of the limits of his own authority; the real power lay with the Protector. Could Somerset have done so easily, he would have given his brother an open trial, but it is doubtful if such a trial would have altered the outcome. There was little question that the charges, as admitted by Seymour's accomplices, were treasonous. An open trial would only inflame the public and perhaps influence the older brother to an unwise leniency. The Council—particularly in the person of John Dudley, the Earl of Warwick, and Somerset's own wife, the implacable Duchess —was adamant that Seymour be punished. Conscious of Somerset's previous indulgences where his brother was concerned, the Council 'perceiving that the case was so heavy and lamentable to the Lord Protector ... said they would proceed without further troubling or molesting either his Highness or the Lord Protector', and, therefore, Somerset 'for natural pity's sake' was excused from attendance when the case was presented to Parliament.

Once all the evidence was collected and since there was to be no trial, official sanction to sentence was required. On February 24, five weeks after his apprehension, Thomas Seymour was informed that the Protector, citing the 'sorrowful case' and his 'bounden duty to the King's Majesty and the Crown of England' was leaving the decision to Edward—one of the few decisions the child had been allowed to make since his accession. If it was difficult, he gave no sign. He mentioned the 'great things objected and laid to my Lord Admiral, mine uncle—and they tend to treason. . . .' He required the Council to see 'justice to be done.' Two weeks later the Council united to present the document for Seymour's execution. In the Presence Chamber, Edward waited in his chair of State, the Protector standing beside him as the death penalty for uncle and brother was read. At the conclusion, there was a long silence. Then the King spoke, words he had obviously rehearsed. 'I have

* Elizabeth told her sister Mary in later years that she had heard the Protector say that if his brother 'had been suffered to speak with him, he would never have been executed'.

well perceived your proceedings therein, and give you my hearty thanks for your pains and travail, and the great care you have for my surety. I will and command you that you proceed as you request—without further molestation of myself, or of the Lord Protector. I pray you, my Lords, do so.'[22] The strain was telling on the child, however. As he signed the warrant, the small hand was shaking.

And so it was done. The authority and power of the Crown of England had been challenged—indirectly through the Protectorate, to be sure—but challenged all the same. Inviolate and remorseless, the penalty for such treason was foreordained by the very measure of Thomas Seymour's ambitious foolhardiness. For all his unscrupulousness, however, the Lord Admiral was no coward. 'His own fierce courage hastened his death, because equally balanced between doubt and disdain, he was desirous rather to die at once, than to linger long upon courtesy and in fear.'[23] He was brought to the scaffold on March 20, 1549, where 'he died without flinching; not, it would seem, at the first blow.' Even here, however, the lack of discretion that so characterised Thomas Seymour was evident. Before he died, he bade one of his servants to 'remember his charge'. The careless words being overheard, the servant was questioned. In the sole of the dead man's shoe, two letters were found 'written with great ingenuity. He had made his ink so craftily and with such workmanship as the like has not been seen. He made his pen of the aglet of a point that he plucked from his hose.' The letters were for Mary and Elizabeth Tudor and urged them to further conspiracy against the Protector. Even in death, the arrogant Seymour could not relinquish a corrosive and foolish jealousy. It had cost him his life and now endangered that of another as vain and ambitious.

Chapter Twelve

IN the two months preceding the execution of Thomas Seymour, as the Council gathered sufficient evidence for an attainder, a similar investigation had begun at the Palace of Hatfield, its avowed purpose being to assess the extent of Elizabeth's implication in the conspiracy. Accordingly, those nearest to her—Katherine Ashley, her husband, and the cofferer Thomas Parry—were taken into custody to await the Council's examination. Elizabeth begged to see Edward or the Protector on their behalf, but was told she could see no one until she had confessed her guilt. She was to be held under restraint until she admitted her involvement with Seymour and, to lend emphasis to its edict, the Council sent a commissioner in the person of Sir Robert Tyrwhitt to Hatfield to question Elizabeth. His special charge was to gain the girl's confidence and, having done so, to lure her into admitting her alliance with Seymour, both personal and political. Deprived as she was of any friends or advisers at Hatfield, both the Council and Tyrwhitt felt the task would be relatively uncomplicated. The presence of a stern representative of the King, Protector, and Council would easily intimidate any fifteen-year-old girl. They had no doubt of her guilt or complicity; only the formality of a confession was needed. Tyrwhitt approached his task with great assurance. In less than a few days, however, he concluded both he and the Council might have been prematurely optimistic.

Distraught and wary as she had been at Seymour's arrest and imprisonment, Elizabeth had not realised the full implication of her own danger until she saw her servants unceremoniously taken into custody. Parry's reaction, particularly, had unnerved her. As the officers were dealing with the Ashleys, the distressed cofferer ran to his chamber, crying to his wife, 'I would I had never been born! I am undone!' His wife had tried to calm him, but 'pale and sorrowful, he cast away his chain from his neck and his rings from his fingers' so that his captors could not steal them. Tyrwhitt took full advantage of the scene, frightening enough in its ugliness, to terrify a young girl whose own mother had been executed by royal command. As he later wrote to the Protector, he advised Elizabeth to 'confide her honour and the peril that might ensue, for she was but a subject; and I further declared what a woman Mistress Ashley was . . . saying, that if she would open all things herself, that all the evil and shame should be ascribed to them [the Ashleys], and her youth considered both with the King's Majesty, your Grace and the whole Council.' It was a tidy offer, smacking of condescension and bribery and must have appeared quite efficient in its simplicity: lay all the blame at the Ashleys' door, and she herself because she was young and had been in their care, would gain an official pardon. The Council would have the necessary information to incriminate Seymour further, and the Ashleys would be the official scapegoats. But Elizabeth did not grasp the olive branch offered by Tyrwhitt. Instead, as he informed the Protector, she was 'marvellously abashed and did weep tenderly a long time. . . .' It puzzled Tyrwhitt and was his first intimation of Elizabeth's loyalty to those she loved and of the artifice she could use when cornered. It was to prove an enlightening experience all around.

In the following days, the game of wits between the girl and her gaoler became more sharply defined, with Tyrwhitt's cool cajolery wearing somewhat thin as he sought, with little success, to bait the wary Elizabeth. He had asked that she 'open all things to him'; Elizabeth was adamant in stating she had nothing to confess. During one period of interrogation, Lady Browne arrived from court and Elizabeth hastened to question her sharply, asking if the Ashleys 'had confessed anything or not.' Being told they had remained silent, she sent for Tyrwhitt and, with a cautious air, according to his report, said she had 'forgotten certain things . . . which she would open unto me and all other things which she could call to her remembrance that she had done. . . .' Eagerly, Tyrwhitt listened. The 'certain things', however, were disappointing. Elizabeth told how she had petitioned Seymour for a favour for one of her chaplains. She had also allowed her cofferer, Parry, to write a letter to the Admiral when his London lodgings were offered for her use. She also said, with wide-eyed breathlessness, that Parry had written to the Ashleys from London stating the Admiral might visit her on his way to Sudeley. The statements were trifles, hardly important or even provocative, and the irritated Tyrwhitt did not hide his disappointment when he wrote to the Protector, 'But in no way she will not confess any practice by Mistress Ashley or the cofferer concerning my Lord Admiral; and yet I do see it in her face that she is guilty and do perceive as yet she will abide more storms ere she accuse Mistress Ashley. . . .'[1] Sir Robert still did not comprehend Elizabeth's talent for dissimultation or recognise that in this particular instance, she might be telling the truth.

[203]

The Council continued to press him more urgently for evidence. Reluctant to admit failure, Tyrwhitt somewhat pompously wrote to the Protector that he had 'deliberated with my Lady's Grace in many matters . . . but all I have got yet is by gentle persuasion, whereby I do begin to grow with her in credit . . . This is a good beginning; I trust more will follow.' Elizabeth continued to be agreeable to such 'gentle persuasion', but still revealed nothing. When she again inquired if the Ashleys had disclosed anything and was told they had not, Sir Robert noted, 'she doth not a little rejoice'. And then somewhat apologetically, he told the Protector, 'I do assure your Grace she hath a very good wit and nothing is gotten of her but by great policy.'

Tyrwhitt then tried another tack. While waiting further instructions from the Council, he investigated the household at Hatfield, particularly Thomas Parry's accounts which, as he wrote the Protector, 'we find very uncertain and his books so indiscreetly made, that it doth well appear that he had little understanding to execute his office.' Hoping to ingratiate himself with Elizabeth and to lesson her loyalty to her servants, he took this example of Parry's incompetence to the girl, informing her she could not afford such negligence, stating that a 'meaner [lesser] officer will serve . . . and save £100 a year.' Elizabeth exhibited all the proper interest but made no further comment other than requesting Tyrwhitt to beg of the Protector that 'if any make suit to you to be her cofferer, that your Grace will stay until she speaks with you. . . .' Hoping further to gain her confidence, Tyrwhitt showed her a letter which he alleged to be from the Protector, implying he endangered himself greatly by revealing the supposedly confidential words. It was not a success. As he wrote to Somerset: 'I have showed my Lady your letter, with a great protestation that I would not for £100 to be known of it . . . notwithstanding, I cannot frame her to all points, as I would wish it to be.'[2] Elizabeth merely expressed her gracious thanks to Tyrwhitt for his confidence, and coolly withdrew. Her continued reluctance to 'confess more than she hath already done, frustrated the old gentleman, who did not relish the situation or the picture he was presenting to the Council. His patience was wearing thin, and he allowed himself the luxury of a personal opinion: 'I do verily believe that there hath been some secret promise between my Lady, Mistress Ashley, and the cofferer, never to confess to death, and if it be so, it will never be gotten out of her, unless by the King's Majesty, or else by your Grace.'[3]

A meeting between the young King and his sister, however, was the last thing the Council wanted. It was enough that the Protector's own brother was in the Tower awaiting sentence, without stirring up another hornet's nest in the royal residence. Tiring of the game Elizabeth was apparently willing to play for as long as necessary, the Council decided that an affront to her good name might produce the evidence they sought. They informed her, through Tyrwhitt, that it was common knowledge that she was about to bear Seymour's child, a foolhardy accusation. Elizabeth was realistic enough to be aware of how very vulnerable she was, and this insult to her honour at a time of such extreme helplessness caused a definite reaction—but not exactly the one the Protector or Council had in mind. Determined to settle the matter once and for all, on January 28, 1549, two weeks after Seymour's imprisonment, Elizabeth wrote to Somerset:

My Lord,

Your great gentleness and good will towards me, as well in this thing as in other things, I do understand, for which, even as I ought, so do I give you most humble thanks; and whereas your Lordship willeth and counselleth me as an earnest friend, to declare what I know in this matter, and also to write what I have declared to Master Tyrwhitt, I shall most willingly do. . . .

Elizabeth again enumerated the instances which she had declared to Sir Robert of her contact with Seymour; and she took full advantage of the situation by mentioning the imprisoned Ashleys and bolstering their defence. She continued:

And as concerning Kate Ashley, she never advised me unto it [a marriage with Seymour], but said always. . . . that she would never have me marry, neither in England nor out of England, without the consent of the King's Majesty, your Grace's and the Council's. . . . and I also told Master Tyrwhitt that to the effect of the matter, I never consented unto any such thing, without the Council's consent thereunto. And as for Kate Ashley or the cofferer, they never told me that they would practise it [the furtherance of the marriage]. These be the things which I both declared to Master Tyrwhitt, and also whereof my conscience beareth me witness, which I would not for all earthly things offend in any thing, for I know that I have a soul to save, as well as other folks have, wherefore I will above all things have respect unto this same. If there be any more things which I can remember, I will either write it myself, or cause Master Tyrwhitt to write it.

Having thus unburdened herself in defence of her servants, Elizabeth then took up her own:

Master Tyrwhitt and others have told me that there goeth rumours abroad which be greatly both against my honour and honesty (which above all other things I esteem) which be these: that I am in the Tower

[205]

and with child by my Lord Admiral. My Lord, *these are shameful slanders*, for the which, besides the great desire I have to see the King's Majesty, I shall most heartily desire your Lordship that I may come to court after your first determination; *that I may show myself there as I am.*

Written in haste, from Hatfield this 28th of January, 1549,

And there it was. If a determined Council wished to resort to unscrupulous methods for its own ends, Elizabeth was willing to co-operate. The letter—a masterpiece of logic and defiance—is an impressive example of the not quite sixteen-year-old Elizabeth Tudor's shrewdness. In words not meant to conciliate but merely explain, she defended her servants and made a subtle bid for the Protector's sympathy. She acknowledged the enormous risk involved in marrying without the consent of the Council whereby she would lose her place in the succession, and she reiterated that Ashley was firm on this point also. But it is in her final paragraph that Elizabeth shows herself to be a true child of Henry VIII. With her father's fine gifts of eloquence and self-expression, she disdainfully throws the accusation in the face of a suspicious Council and reproves the mighty Protector with the words, 'My Lord, these are shameful slanders . . . !' and challenges him to let her 'come to the court . . . that I may show myself there as I am.' But if, when the letter was read, there was any doubt in the minds of Protector or Council as to where the victory lay in the sad little comedy, there was none at all in the mind of Elizabeth. Instead, it only served to disclose the deadly purpose of the treacherous Council, and it jolted Elizabeth into a truer understanding of her precarious situation.

Foiled for the moment, the Council admitted defeat and looked to the Ashleys and Parry for further information. Imprisonment and constant interrogation had not stiffened Thomas Parry's spine. As the days in his Tower cell lengthened, as the cold sapped his strength and his fingers grew numb with chilblains, offers of the Council's lenience for his co-operation became more attractive. He, himself, he reasoned, had done no wrong—the greater wrong was in withholding what he did know, and until he disclosed the information, the Protector would continue to keep him imprisoned. Inevitably—perhaps helped by a few blows from the Tower guards and in fear of greater torment—Parry broke. His long confession enumerated the many instances of the Admiral's interest in Elizabeth, the visits to Ashridge, the favours he had done for her and of his quest for information as to the extent of the Princess's lands and other holdings. Apparently Elizabeth's own curiosity had been piqued by Seymour's questions about her inheritance. Parry said in his deposition, 'she asked me what I thought he meant thereby; and I said I could not tell, unless he go about to have you also, for he wished your lands and would have them that way.' Seymour had suggested that Parry advise Elizabeth to petition the Protector for an exchange of her lands in Gloucestershire for some of Seymour's in Wales. For the grant of a London house as well as other favours, he advised her to 'entertain' the Protector's wife, the formidable Duchess of Somerset 'for these purposes'. To this Elizabeth had been derisive, saying scornfully, 'I dare say he did not so, nor would so', to which Parry had replied that such was Seymour's intention. Elizabeth had been angry and possibly not a little disillusioned that she, a royal Princess, should petition or entertain anyone for favours. Hotly, she told Parry, 'I will not do so—and so tell him!' and muttered to herself, 'In faith, I will not come there, nor begin to flatter now. . . .'[5]

Parry also disclosed that Elizabeth had insisted Mrs Ashley be told of Seymour's queries, and liking a good gossip, the cofferer had repeated the Admiral's conversation. Unwilling to concede that Parry might know something regarding Elizabeth that she, herself, did not know, Ashley had replied, with pursed lips, that 'she knew the situation well enough'; she further told Parry that had Henry lived, Elizabeth would have been given to Thomas Seymour, and that she 'would wish her his wife of all men living'. Not only was the governness an incurable romantic, but also she relished the thought of the frustration and irritation such a union—if it could be accomplished—would provoke in the Protector and his wife. Ashley's pride in her management of Elizabeth had been sorely bruised when the Duchess had 'found great faults with her for my Lady Elizabeth's going in a night in a barge upon the Thames, and for other light parts. . . .' The laxity of strict surveillance and such giddy privileges as midnight boating parties did not coincide with the Duchess's notions of child discipline, and she told Ashley, in a blistering interview, 'she was not worthy to have the governance of a King's daughter, and many other things. . . .' All of which merely increased the governess's support of Thomas Seymour, and she repeated fervently of Elizabeth, 'I would wish her to none before him.' She said the Admiral loved the girl 'but too well' and then, her restraint gone and with an air of great confidence, she told Parry of Katherine Parr finding Elizabeth in Seymour's arms. Having revealed the titillating facts, Ashley's conscience seemed to overcome her and 'she seemed to repent that she had gone so far with me and prayed me, in any way, that I would not disclose these matters—and I said I would not . . . for her Grace should be dishonoured forever, and she likewise undone.' Sending her good wishes to the Admiral, 'she required me to great secrecy', Parry noted as he calmed the governess's fears by saying he would 'rather be pulled with horses' than ever disclose her statements.[6]

Encouraged, Tyrwhitt wrote to the Council that Elizabeth was still firm and he doubted 'that she will no more cough out matter than she doth.' But with the craven Parry's disclosures at hand, he suggested that if Mrs Ashley could be made to 'open any of these things', and if Elizabeth could 'see some part of it, then I would have good hope to make her cough out the whole.' Ashley was duly confronted with Parry's confession and, with the royal cat out of the bag, gave a similar account. Both depositions were forwarded to Tyrwhitt at Hatfield, and he lost no time in confronting Elizabeth with the signed documents, commenting that since her servants had confessed, there was little to be gained by her own continued stubbornness. Elizabeth held the papers tightly and, 'at the reading of Mistress Ashley's letter, she was much abashed and half breathless before she could read it to an end.' Flushing at the vulgar familiarities which were divulged—the early morning romps at Chelsea with an Admiral in his nightshirt and she in her bed, of the last distressing moment when Seymour had tried to kiss her and the Queen had come upon them—of her own subsequent dismissal in disgrace from the household, Elizabeth fought for control—and for time. Studiously and slowly, she read each word and then minutely examined the signatures at the end which Tyrwhitt said, she 'knew both—with half a sight, so that she fully thinketh they have both confessed all they knew.' Though she said nothing, her anxiety showed in her face. Tyrwhitt took advantage of the silence to say, not unkindly, that Ashley had been staunch in her refusal to utter anything 'until she and Parry were brought face to face', and when Parry had stated in her presence that everything he had said was true, Ashley had flung at him contemptuously, 'False wretch!' and had reminded him he had promised he 'would never confess it to death!'

By now, Elizabeth had regained her composure. There was still nothing in the confessions to prove that she herself had conspired to wed the Admiral or promote his treasonous activities. Faced with the evidence of her servant's betrayal, she handed the documents back to Tyrwhitt with the stinging words, 'that it was a great matter for him to promise such a promise—and then break it.' But she also knew something more must be done if her name was to be cleared. There had been no word from Mary or Edward since her restraint at Hatfield, and she knew all too well the gossip rampant among the people. Her servants had told enough to cast a slur upon her reputation, and she was realistic enough to care about public opinion and to recognise that only she could set things right. And so, the day after the receipt of the incriminating documents, a docile and suddenly co-operative Elizabeth handed Sir Robert a letter for the Protector which contained certain articles, a detailed 'confession' of her relationship with Thomas Seymour. She told Somerset in the letter, 'I will declare them most willingly, for I would not (as I trust you have not) so evil an opinion of me that I would conceal anything I know. . . .' At the end of her remarks, she assured the Protector, 'that if there be any more which I have not told you (which I think there be not), I will send you word of them as they come to my mind. . . .'

Tyrwhitt was delighted with Elizabeth's apparent capitaulation— until he read the 'confession'. It told the Council nothing it did not already know: the instances of Ashley's arch hinting of a marriage between Elizabeth and the Admiral, the favours Seymour had rendered the Princess, and of his interest in her lands and inheritances. Elizabeth allowed herself a touch of humour in telling of the occasion when Parry had teased her about marrying the Admiral should the Council give its consent. Elizabeth had asked him, 'Who bade him say so?' Parry had replied that 'nobody bade him say so, but he gathered by his [Seymour's] asking of these questions before, that he meant some such thing. . . .' Elizabeth had smiled and told Parry, 'it was but *his* foolish gathering. . . .'[7]

The disappointed Tyrwhitt forwarded the 'confession' to the Council with the comment that it 'is not so full of matter as I would it were . . . but in no way will she confess that our Mistress Ashley, or Parry, willed her to any practice with my Lord Admiral, either by message or writing.' A glimmering of impatience can be seen in the comment from a frustrated Sir Robert: 'They all sing one song', he wrote, 'and so I think they would not do unless they had set the note before. . . .'[8]

Stronger measures were obviously needed at Hatfield, and they arrived in the person of Sir Robert's wife. Lady Tyrwhitt brought a letter from the 'good lords of the Council' to Elizabeth in which they stated that since 'Katherine Ashley . . . hath shown herself far unmeet to occupy any such place longer about your Grace . . . we thereby thought convenient to send unto you the Lady Tyrwhitt, to remain about you in lieu of the said Ashley, and to commit unto her the same charge about your person that Ashley had.' Lady Tyrwhitt was a daughter of Katherine Parr's first husband, the aged Lord Borough, and had lived in the royal household at Chelsea and had, indeed, over-heard Katherine's last words on her deathbed. She had been severely rebuked by the Council for not divulging the Seymour intimacies earlier and was to be given another chance to redeem herself by replacing Ashley. She was ordered to Hatfield to deal with the obstinate Princess to whom it was commanded 'that you will accept her service thankfully, and also hear and follow her good advice from time to time, and especially in such matters as we have at this time appointed her to move unto you. . . .'[9]

Elizabeth was taken by surprise at Lady Tyrwhitt's arrival and was considerably less than gracious at their first meeting. The young girl, whose pride was offended by the replacement, said heatedly 'that she had not so demeaned herself that the Council should now need to put any more mistresses unto her.' The sting of the Council's reprimand had not improved Lady Tyrwhitt's disposition either. She did not relish an enforced seclusion at Hatfield with only a disgraced Princess and a crusty old husband for company. She coolly replied that if Elizabeth had allowed such as Ashley to be her mistress, 'she need not be ashamed to have any *honest* woman to be in that place.' Defeated for the moment and frustrated by her own ineptitude, Elizabeth 'took the matter heavily.' Storming from the room, she shut herself up in her chamber where, according to the disconcerted Tyrwhitt, she wept through the night and 'lowered all the next day', refusing to speak to anyone.

During the following week, as Lady Tyrwhitt prevailed on Elizabeth to reveal her association with Seymour, the girl's usually smooth brow seemed cast in a perpetual frown, and the mouth was set and hard in her young face. The strain was beginning to tell. It had been a month since Seymour's imprisonment and her own detention at Hatfield, and nothing had been resolved. The Tyrwhitts spared her nothing in telling of Seymour's danger and its probable conclusion; the thought of the virile, witty, and charming man on the scaffold tore repeatedly at her heart and conscience. The cat-and-mouse game the Council played with her, and the constant vigilance needed to maintain her own security, had taxed her young strength. 'She beginneth now a little to droop . . .' Tyrwhitt wrote joyously to the Protector, 'by reason she heareth that my Lord Admiral's houses be dispersed. And my wife telleth me that now she cannot hear him discommended, but she is ready to make answer therein; and so she hath not been accustomed to do, unless Mrs Ashley were touched, whereunto she was very ready to make answer vehemently. . . .' Only now did Elizabeth concede that Seymour might lose not only his estates but his head as well and, finally realising the futility of defending a man beyond saving, she took refuge in utter silence. She sorely missed Ashley, and the appointment of Lady Tyrwhitt still rankled. 'She fully hopes to recover her old mistress again', wrote Sir Robert, 'the love she yet beareth her is to be wondered at.' When Elizabeth complained that the 'world would note her to be a great offender, having so hastily a governor appointed her', he replied to the troubled girl that, her age considered and the danger she faced, it was better to have a governess than 'to make delay to be without one one hour.' It made little impression on Elizabeth. 'She cannot digest such advice in no way', said the tired Tyrwhitt who was confronted not only with a petulant Princess but also a cross and impatient wife, 'but if I should say my fantasy, it were more meet she should have two [governesses] than one . . . !'[10]

After two days of repeated questioning by the Tyrwhitts and two sleepless nights in which the spectre of Seymour's fate and a gnawing anxiety for her own future dominated each miserable moment, Elizabeth insisted upon writing to the Protector again. Tyrwhitt attempted to advise her of what to say, but she 'would in no wise follow, but write her own fantasy', he said despairingly. Elizabeth had accepted the fact that she was helpless to act for Seymour; what mattered now was her own reputation and freedom. Underlying her skilful letter to the Protector was a dogged determination to force official support of her position:

My Lord,

Having received your Lordship's letters, I perceive in them your good will towards me, because you declare to me plainly your mind in this thing, and again that you would not wish that I should do anything that should not seem good unto the Council. . . .

And whereas, I do understand that you do take in evil part the letters that I did write unto your Lordship, I am very sorry that you should take them so, for my mind was to declare unto you plainly . . . because . . . you desired me to be plain with you in all things.

And, as concerning that point that you write, that I seem to stand in my own wit. . . . I did assure me of myself no more than I trust the truth shall try; and to say that which I know of myself, I did not think should have displeased the Council or your Grace.

Having thus defended her right to express her opinions, which the Protector had apparently questioned, Elizabeth then discussed the implication inherent in the presence of Lady Tyrwhitt—whom she still refused to mention by name:

And, surely, the cause why that I was sorry that there should be any such about me, was because that I thought the people will say that I deserved, through my lewd demeanour, *to have such a one*, and not that I mislike anything that your Lordship or the Council shall think good, for I know that you and the Council are charged with me, or that I take upon me to rule myself, for I know that they are most deceived that trusteth most in themselves, wherefore I trust you shall never find

[211]

that fault in me, *to the which thing I do not see that your Grace has made any direct answer at this time*—and seeing they make so evil reports already shall be but an increasing of these evil tongues.

The Protector had told Elizabeth that if she 'would bring forth any one who were accusing her, the Council would see it redressed', but had evaded taking any initial action himself. Elizabeth, however, was not to be baited, and she adroitly refused to involve herself in her own defence, saying, 'which thing . . . I would be loath to do, because it is mine own cause . . . and so get the evil will of the people, which thing I would be loath to have.' Elizabeth was not deterred by modesty from speaking on her own behalf. She knew intuitively how futile such a procedure would be. Like her father before her, she desired always to appear above reproach in the public eye. She, therefore, should not have to defend herself! This was the responsibility of the Protector and Council, and she minced no words in challenging them:

But it might seem good to your Lordship, and the rest of the Council, to send forth a Proclamation into the counties that they refrain their tongues, declaring how the tales be but lies—it should make the people think that both you and the Council have great regard that no such rumours should be spread of any of the King's Majesty's sisters. . . . Howbeit I am ashamed to ask it any more, *because I see you are not so well minded thereunto.*

And then, lest the Protector and Council believe she was being deceived by their promises of co-operation so directly in contrast to their actions, she ended the letter in a tone bordering on impudence:

And, as concerning that you say I give folks occasion to think, in refusing the good to uphold the evil, I am not of so simple understanding nor I would that your Grace should have so evil an opinion of me, that I have so little respect of my own honesty, *that I would maintain it if I had sufficient promise of the same* . . . and so your Grace shall prove me when it comes to the point.[11]

Somerset for once was silenced. Faced with the unrelenting obstinacy of a fifteen-and-a-half-year-old girl who staunchly defended her reputation in the very teeth of the Council's suspicious ill will, the Protector issued the desired proclamation. Any evil remarks concerning the King's sister were to be punishable by fine or imprisonment, but behind the threatened penalty lay the more important fact that the Princess would not receive an official, albeit reluctant, protection and support.

But there was still Seymour's ordeal through which she must live.

Within two weeks, the Admiral was sentenced to die on the scaffold. The announcement produced no word from Elizabeth Tudor which might incriminate her, but its effect could be seen in her lacklustre attitude towards the Tyrwhitts, who at last grudgingly admitted their defeat. Never once did her gaolers see the Princess falter. If Elizabeth permitted herself the solace of tears at Seymour's fate, it was in the privacy of her chamber behind locked doors. She was well aware some fortuitous Destiny—and her own compelling young wisdom and natural cunning—had saved her from a similar end.

Now she must hoard her physical strength, her emotional reserves, and, with an assumed cynicism, live through the agony of Thomas Seymour's execution. Then she must recoup her reputation, her freedom, and her place at court. Necessary to all three of these endeavours was Ashley—never had Elizabeth missed her governess and confidante more. There was no one in the household to whom she could unburden her grief or from whom she might seek advice, although she realised she had quite independently and remarkably extricated herself from a dangerous position. However, there was still enough of the child in Elizabeth to yearn for the comforting presence of her beloved old nurse. Somerset's action in issuing the proclamation gave Elizabeth courage to speak on behalf of Ashley who—good and simple soul that she was— might languish in the Tower throughout the following cold winter months if no one came to her aid. In her darker moments, Elizabeth recognised that both Ashley and Parry might later suffer a fate as severe as Seymour's. Therefore, on March 7, shortly before the Admiral's execution, Elizabeth wrote to the Protector from Hatfield:

My Lord,

I have a request to make unto your Grace which fear made me omit till this time because I saw that my request for the rumours which were spread abroad of me took so little place, which thing when I considered it, I thought I should little profit in any other suit.

Howbeit, now I understand that there is a Proclamation for them (for the which I give your Grace and the rest of the Council most humble thanks) I am the bolder to speak for another thing. . . . which is Katherine Ashley, that it should please your Grace and the rest of the Council to be good unto her. Which thing I do, not to favour her in any evil (for that I would be sorry to do) but for these considerations that follow:

First, because that she hath been with me a long time, and many years, and hath taken great labour and pain in bring me up in learning and honesty; and, therefore, I ought of very duty speak for her; for Saint Gregory sayeth, 'that we are more bound to them that bringeth us up well than to our parents, for our parents do that which is natural for them that bringeth us into this world, but our bringers-up are a cause to make us live well in it.'

The second is, because I think that whatsoever she hath done in my Lord Admiral's matter, as concerning the marrying of me, she did it because knowing him to be one of the Council, she thought he would not go about any such thing without he had the Council's consent thereunto. . . .

The third cause is, because that it shall, and doth make men think, that I am not clear of the deed myself; *but that it is pardoned to me because of my youth*, because she I loved so well is in such a place.

Thus hope, prevailing more with me than fear, hath won the battle, and I have at this time gone forth with it; which I pray God to be taken no otherwise than it is meant.

Written in haste from Hatfield, this seventh day of March. Also, if I may be so bold, not offending, I beseech your Grace and the rest of the Council to be good to Master Ashley, her husband, which, because he is my kinsman, I would be glad he should do well.[12]

Your assured friend to my little power,

ELIZABETH[13]

There was no immediate response from the Protector or Council, busy with the final details of the execution. Aware that her slightest action, her most innocent word, might still entrap her, Elizabeth maintained an imperturbable silence, her eyes veiled, her manner distant. The bitter experience through which she had passed now threatened both her health and disposition.

Her profound unhappiness was not helped as she remembered those warm and carefree days at Chelsea with Katherine, Thomas, and Jane Grey; her conscience would not be quieted, and inevitably her sense of self-esteem suffered accordingly. A flirtation begun so innocently (if unwisely, considering the circumstances) had ended in disaster for those she loved and grave danger to herself. She—a Princess of the blood royal, a sister of the reigning monarch—had so far forgotten herself as to encourage the attentions of a man who was not only the husband of a beloved stepmother but also the brother of the woman who had supplanted her own mother, Anne Boleyn. Elizabeth knew the cloud under which her mother had died—she realised now that she herself had presented a similar picture of licence, frivolity, and coarseness, which even an official proclamation could not wholly erase. Her shame and humiliation became a torment, and in the weeks prior to the execution, the girl painfully mustered her remaining strength for the coming ordeal. Any dreams she had entertained of a life with Thomas

Seymour had ended long before he ascended the scaffold. In those wretched weeks, as she walked alone as if in a nightmare, a degrading sense of self-abasement mingled with her sorrow and remorse. When she was informed of Seymour's death, many intently watched her reaction. If they had hoped for tears or an abandoned passionate outcry, they were disappointed. Aware now as she had never been before of the stakes at hand, the daughter of Anne Boleyn and Henry VIII knew something was expected of her, and she did not disappoint her listeners. She shrugged her shoulders and spoke tersely. 'This day died a man of much wit—and very little judgment', she said. It was all her gaolers received from Elizabeth Tudor on the day the Admiral's head fell.

Thomas Seymour would have relished the remark. And understood.

In the weeks following the execution, Elizabeth's mute misery gave way to a despondent lassitude, and she became grievously ill. She was confined to her bed at Hatfield, as the worried Tyrwhitts wrote to the Protector of her condition. Though her illness was described as 'the rheums' (rheumatism), throughout the rest of the year the Princess preferred to remain apart from the household in her own chamber. She slept badly at night and had little interest in food, which further aggravated a chronic anaemia. Compounding her physical distress was a shortness of breath and an erratic behaviour pattern: fits of temper vented on the hapless servants or the Tyrwhitts, to be quickly replaced by a lethargy in which she seemed not to notice them or anything else. Her studies had been discontinued, and the days were passed in deep depression. The melancholia was abated only by alternate fits of despondent weeping—all of which revealed the general breakdown of a nervous system revolting against the prolonged tension and strain placed upon it. The Protector, anxious as her illness continued and thinking to hurry her recovery, sent her long-delayed letters patent, securing her estates and income. He also sent his physician, along with his personal good wishes for her recovery, earning the girl's grateful reply for 'sending unto me not only your comfortable letters, but also physicians, as Dr Bill, whose diligence and pains have been a great part of my recovery. . . .'

As the months passed and Elizabeth remained in her chamber frail and weak, there was time to think, and in the process, she left adolescence behind. The effect on the young girl was tremendous. In her darkened room, her books forgotten, oblivious to the concern of those outside her door, she reviewed the past months and, with a chilling finality, realised she was lucky to be alive. She knew she had outwitted a group of experienced statesmen and a powerful Protector. One false step might have cast her into prison or put her on the scaffold with poor Thomas.

For the first time, Elizabeth recognised the inherent danger which lay perpetually waiting to strike at those eligible to succeed to the throne. Not only had she endangered her life, but also she had almost thrown away her slender right to wear the Crown of England. She had been as foolishly feminine as her mother before her. She could vaguely remember the shadowy outline of the dark and laughing woman who, one day, had walked out of a room and out of her life forever. Before that, there had been Mary's own mother, the Spanish Queen Catherine, who had fought the royal power and paid for her presumptuousness with exile, callous persecution, and divorce. Katherine Howard had behaved badly and lost her head and, as Henry's wife, Katherine Parr had been similarly endangered. None of her stepmothers, except for poor dear old Anne of Cleves, had fared very well—each had paid a heavy price for the privilege of wearing the Crown. Again, Elizabeth burned with shame as she remembered the audacious behaviour to which she had been a willing partner, and now, in retrospect, the risk she had taken seemed meaningless, even absurd. *What a fool she had been!* Was any man—King, councillor, great lord, or even a Prince of the Church worth the risk of losing her tenuous opportunity to wear the Crown? Slim it might be, nevertheless, there was a chance. Her brother was young and she loved him; he might reign for a long time, but she herself was only four years older. Mary, who already appeared older than her years, might be in her grave by the time the next monarch was proclaimed. A frightened, shocked, and emotionally depleted Elizabeth Tudor, languishing in a state of severe physical weakness, soon found her answer. Towards the end of 1549 when—shaky and tight-lipped—she emerged from the sickroom, it was obvious to all that the volatile and capricious child of Chelsea was gone. In her place was a self-contained young woman, hardened by adversity and her own unsparing self-appraisal, a woman of firm purpose and an unshakeable will to survive—and to win.

Chapter Thirteen

THE great popularity which had attended the Protector's return from a victorious Scottish campaign was diminished by his cold-blooded abandonment of Seymour to the scaffold; many said he had 'sealed his doom the day on which he signed the warrant for the execution of his brother.' Somerset maintained 'that the persuasions were made to him . . . that he was brought in belief that he could not live safely if the Admiral lived, and that made him give his consent to his death.'[1] The criticism was further compounded by the political, religious, and social problems of the realm. Somerset's untimely insistence and heavy-handed urgency in accomplishing further reform in the Church, in needed improvement in the country's economic condition, and in the lot of the common people generally, provoked those who did not share his social conscience. The nobles particularly disapproved of his concern for the masses; those same masses disliked and were unprepared to accept the proposed changes in their religious beliefs. Somerset was also handicapped by his lack of political astuteness; while praying 'that it would please God to accomplish a marriage between King Edward and the young Queen of Scotland, and the happy union of their realm', he was informed that little Mary Stuart had been spirited away to France and betrothed to the Dauphin. Meanwhile Henri II, urged on by his spiteful, English-hating wife, Catherine de Medici, planned the recapture of Boulogne. Scotland was again in foment; the cruel decimation at Pinkie Cleugh and Mary's French betrothal only broadened the already wide gulf between Scotland and England, whose reigning sovereigns were children, their destinies so much at the mercy of others.

Politics did not concern the more lowly of King Edward's subjects, however. Instead, the more pressing problem of survival—how to get shelter from the elements and find food to keep body and soul together— was the preoccupation of the homeless thousands who flocked to the larger cities seeking employment. The government labelled them vagrants: the dispossessed wanderers evicted from the ecclesiastical lands of the dissolved monasteries or private lands which, from ancient times, had been farmed for their meagre living. The nobles or the families of Henry VIII's 'new men' had acquired most of these lands; they followed the example of the smaller independent landowner who had also driven his tenant farmers away and enclosed his holdings with hedges for the more profitable business of raising sheep for the burgeoning wool trade. The two unfortunate elements from the monasteries and the farms were thus thrown completely on the land. Any possessions they owned were soon sold, and when no work or assistance could be found, they set out to survive as best they could, often by violent means. Bands of desperate, half-naked men and women constituted a threat to travel and commerce. They were whipped, imprisoned, and persecuted whenever they were caught; their wretched plight was deliberately overlooked by those who might have helped. Latimer preached before the court and spared them nothing. 'In times past, men were full of compassion', he stormed from the pulpit, 'but now there is no pity! In London, their brother shall die in the street for cold, he shall lie sick at the door . . . and then perish for hunger. Charity is waxen cold . . . for almost no man helpeth to maintain them!' [2] Latimer said the people's misery was 'entirely due to the new order of things', and he placed the blame squarely where it belonged, accusing his listeners who now owned the fine abbey lands, 'I fully certify you as extortioners, violent oppressors . . . through whose covetousness villages decay and fall down and the King's liege people, for lack of sustenance are famished . . . you unnatural lords, you have for your possessions yearly too much!' [3] When Somerset issued a proclamation urging that land enclosure be halted, the people took measures into their own hands and 'plucked down men's hedges' the hated symbol of their oppression. But their defiance only earned Somerset, 'the Good Duke', the animosity of his fellow nobles and councillors whose vast properties were rebel targets.

The people were also outraged by the new religious reforms urged by Somerset, by the liberal members of the Council, and by Cranmer, the Archbishop of Canterbury. 'Innovations!' Bishop Gardiner termed them, prior to his incarceration in the Fleet Prison for refusing to sanction the proposed doctrinal changes. Gardiner did not take his gaoling silently; he protested bitterly to the Protector at the infringement of his right to criticise religious reforms which '. . . it pleaseth him [Cranmer] to call truth in religion, not established by any law in the realm.' Gardiner was firm on this point, 'A law it is not yet, and before a law made, I have not seen such an imprisonment as I sustain. . . .' Even Henry VIII had 'suffered every man to say his mind' without imprisonment until the matter was established by law, Gardiner stressed. 'I take it to be true,' the prelate wrote to Cranmer, 'that if the wall of authority . . . be once broken, and new water let in at a little gap, the vehement novelty will flow further than your Grace would admit.'[4]

But the Protector, Council, and Archbishop had their way. Soon Henry's Six Articles, 'good and useful as they had been in the past times', were repealed. Holy Day rituals—the Creeping to the Cross on Good Friday, the use of ashes on Ash Wednesday, and the carrying of palms on Palm Sunday were forbidden. On November 4, 1548, Cranmer celebrated Mass at the opening of Parliament for the last time. It was this Parliament which passed the 'Act for the Uniformity of Service and Administration of the Sacraments throughout the Realm.' In effect, the act abolished the Mass in favour of the ceremony set forth in Thomas Cranmer's *Book of Common Prayer*[5] which was distributed to all congregations on Whit Sunday, June 9, 1549. Again Gardiner spoke out from the Tower. He wrote to the Protector, 'If he could have written with the blood of his heart, he would have done it, to have stayed this thing till it had been more maturely digested.'

Gardiner's concern was not only for the doctrine itself, but for the unprepared state of the people being asked to accept such radical changes. But he had no influential support; there was little cohesion among the remaining English Catholics who might have opposed the drastic reforming measures. Too many of the old faith, such as Montague, Exeter, and Mary's old governess Margaret Pole, were gone. The titular head of the Catholic party, the great Duke of Norfolk, still languished in the Tower, happy his ageing head was still on his shoulders. Wriothesley had been removed as Chancellor, to be replaced by the infamous Richard Rich, who had perjured his way to power and wealth, with the head of Sir Thomas More as one part of the payment.

Among the least prepared for the new orthodoxy were the simple priests whose whole religious life had been concerned with a doctrine they did not question and a ritual that was second nature. Now the doctrine was changed and the ritual replaced by a service calling for more personal participation, especially in the new practice of sermonising. Previously sermons had been limited to Festival or Lenten Days; few priests were considered competent enough to prepare a sermon each Sunday. Earlier Cranmer had issued a *Book of Homilies* which gave the unlearned country priest assistance by providing material for the spiritual needs of his congregation. Even so, the new service had not been an unqualified success. In the country, counterparts of the golden-tongued Latimer and Ridley of London, who could hold a congregation spellbound, were sadly lacking. 'Our curate is naught', said one disgusted parishioner, 'an ass-head, a dodipot, a lack-Latin and can-do-nothing! Shall I pay him tithe that doth us no good, nor none will do?'[6] In the cities particularly, the lack of reverence for ecclesiastics had become so widespread that an order went forth chastising those who used 'such insolency and evil demeanour towards priests, as revelling, tossing of them, taking violently their caps and tippets to them.'

There were many who opposed the religious reform on the grounds that such changes should wait until Edward was older and more able to judge for himself. Gardiner advised eager reformers to 'draw the plat diligently, to hew the stones, dig the sand, and chop the chalk in the unseasonable time of building, and when the King's Majesty cometh to full age, to present their labours to him; and in the meantime, not to disturb the state of the realm. . . .'[7] Bishop Hooper was more succinct: 'As long as the King is in his tender years, the Council should do nothing in the matters of religion!' Their objections were reflected in the varying degrees of disenchantment of young Edward's subjects with the new doctrine. For a quarter of a century, their basic beliefs had been repeatedly challenged and changed—first at the whim of an unpredictable King, now by order of the Protector, his Council, and the Archbishop of Canterbury. Such changes were not difficult for the more sophisticated, the more learned and opportunistic of the cities, where enthusiasm for the new was more prevalent. But in Parliament, those representatives of the country towns and villages, many of them remote indeed, were aware of the disquiet permeating the small congregations as further changes in the familiar service were made. Many had never recovered materially, spiritually, or psychologically from the loss of an adjoining monastery or abbey. Now the beloved ritual of the Mass itself was suppressed and the people forced to worship in a desecrated church, with broken crucifixes, defaced images, and whitewashed walls, as an often incompetent priest read from a book with which both were unfamiliar.

The advent of *The Book of Common Prayer* was noted by Edward in his *Chronicle*, 'A Parliament was called where an uniform order of prayer was instituted, before made by a number of bishops and learned men gathered together in Windsor. . . .' To charges that the change in doctrine was too severe, Cranmer replied, 'It seemeth . . . it is a new service, and indeed it is none other but the old: the self-same words in English which were in Latin, *saving a few things taken out*.' For Edward, the work of his godfather, Thomas Cranmer, was a natural deliverance from what he considered slavish superstition and idolatry, to a more wholesome and widespread worshipping of God. All his twelve years had been spent in an atmosphere of religious turmoil. Beginning with his tutors, Cox and Cheke, he had absorbed the pleasures and gratifications of the New Learning. In the past two years, since his father's death, he had been led by the Protector and Cranmer to relinquish Henry's hybrid Catholicism, but the process had been so subtle, appealing as it did to the boy's natural instinct for reason, justice, and truth, that it had been almost painless. His conscience, too, was involved: he

[220]

had been told repeatedly that the spiritual salvation of his subjects was his special charge. Never an assertive or venturesome child, Edward accepted the books he was given to read, the answers he received from his tutors and chaplains, and the opinions of friends and relatives of the court. Few near him were devotees of the old faith, or even of the Catholic beliefs of Henry VIII; the Council had seen to that. So Edward welcomed the change in religious doctrine in the summer of 1549 as a necessary and 'godly' tool by which his people might be saved from the misery of a false faith leading to spiritual doom.

With the inauguration of *The Book of Common Prayer* and the suppression of the Mass, anyone participating in the old ritual did so furtively, recognising the danger of flouting a new law of the realm. But in at least one royal household, the Act of Uniformity had no meaning. While Elizabeth, ill and still in disgrace at Hatfield, received the announcement from her chaplain with little interest or protest, her sister Mary Tudor was more definite—and accordingly more vulnerable. When *The Book of Common Prayer* was presented to her chaplain, she ordered its refusal, saying, 'Although the Council had forgotten the King, her father, and their oaths to observe his will, yet for herself she would observe his laws as he left them.' For Mary there was no turning away from a responsibility which was hers until her brother was old enough to govern. Neither was there any change in her household, her chapel—or her heart.

Mary had spent the two years following her father's death in her various residences in as deep a seclusion as she could achieve. Of all her houses she loved Beaulieu in Essex best. In the reign of Edward III, it had been exchanged by the monks of Waltham Abbey, the owners, for three other more suitable properties. Beaulieu was a fine mansion somewhat like a miniature cathedral with three soaring towers, one of which housed the chapel where her grandfather, Henry VII, had installed a beautiful stained-glass window made expressly for him at Dort in Flanders.* Beaulieu had belonged briefly to the grandfather of Anne Boleyn, but even that unfortunate association could not diminish its appeal to Mary. Her father, too, had loved the comfortable and spacious old house and had given it its name. His protrait hung in the Great Hall; Mary could remember the young Holbein who had painted portraits of both her mother and father. Beaulieu's furnishings were in keeping with the mansion itself and reflected the tastes of the former

---

* It can now be seen at St Margaret's Church adjoining Westminster Abbey and features Mary's mother, Catherine of Aragon, in one panel.

royal owner: there were exquisite hangings of velvet and carpets from Turkey, brocades from Florence, and beautifully inlaid Italian bedsteads and chairs, and hanging in magnificent splendour in the private chambers were the incredibly detailed and handsomely multicoloured tapestries from the looms of the Low Countries. Beaulieu had extensive gardens in which Mary took great pride, and much of the produce—particularly the cherries and grapes—was often sent to the other royal dwellings.

Here, and to some extent in her other residences, Mary found great comfort in the pattern of her days. Ever loyal to the memory of her father and to the stalwart courage of her mother, she had endangered the anonymity she so prized, venturing to court only to see her brother. The visits were made as much for the purpose of counteracting the heretical influence to which she knew the boy was exposed as for the pleasure of his company. She was proud of Edward and she loved him, and often his obvious loneliness, his very vulnerability, saddened the young woman who felt a twinge of guilt as she compared their existences. Always apart from the hothouse atmosphere of court intrigue, *she* at least had the peaceful solitude of her own home with her beloved and devoted companions, as well as the sustenance of an unquestioning faith. In her own view, her brother had none of these things. Instead, he was revered, esteemed, and paraded as a small figurehead of majestic royalty, informed by the Protector and Council of his awesome responsibilities and how he might dispense them, and told how he might worship by his godfather Cranmer and the Protestant preachers who so delighted him. Surrounded as he was by children who parroted the opinion of their elders, Mary realised there was no way for Edward to grow spiritually or emotionally as he was growing in body, stature, and presence.

Mary did what she could to counter such influence, knowing almost intuitively the little good it did in relation to the risk she incurred, but her conscience was such she could do nothing else. Often these episodes between brother and sister ended unhappily, emphasising anew the ever widening gulf between Mary and the small boy she loved.

On one occasion, shortly after the official suppression of the Mass, she visited Edward who, 'carrying her that respect and reverence, as if she had been his mother, made little effort to hide his delight in seeing her.' His former playmate, little Jane Dormer, noted years later in her memoirs that 'he took especial content in her [Mary's] company', and when discussing the new doctrine, Mary 'in her discretion advised him in some things that concerned himself, and in other things that touched herself; in all showing great affection and sisterly care of him.' Mary's desire to set Edward on the path of unquestioning faith only succeeded in further confusing the poor boy so badgered by other opinions that he 'burst forth in tears, grieving matters could not be according to her will and desire . . . he besought her to have patience until he had more years, and then he would remedy all.' Jane Dormer's memories of those religiously tumultuous years of Edward's boyhood demonstrate the vulnerability of the child who was King of England, especially at the impressionable age when he had been asked to sanction what he had been told was a purer and more desirable religion for his people. Yet, to please the others, he must refute the orthodoxy of Mary, who was dear to him. Tears were his refuge, and then, ashamed at what he considered behaviour unworthy of a King, he would 'call for some jewel to present her' and 'complaining that they gave him no better . . .' dry his tears as Mary stood by distressed.

The visits were necessarily brief, for distances were long, and after sundown no cavalcade, not even a royal one, wished to be on the roads made perilous by the vagrants. When Mary was ready to leave, Edward 'seemed to part from her with sorrow . . .' and a long bout of melancholia for the remainder of the day bespoke the small royal conscience warring within as it struggled anew with another example of the conflict which seemed to beset his days. When his distress was noted by his tutors, 'order was taken that these visits should be very rare, alleging that they made the King sad. . . .'8 And so Mary's natural desire to shield and advise her brother, and his love and expressed wish to help and understand her only restricted their opportunities to be together.

Mary's concern for the spiritual salvation not only of Edward but also of his subjects, led her to write to the Protector of the 'naughty liberty and presumption' which she prophesied would divide the realm if the 'executors go not about to bring them to that stay that our late master left them.' She was critical of Protector and Council, stating their actions would win them only the obloquy and derision of other nations. Somerset's only reply was 'these words written or spoken by you soundeth not well, so can I not persuade myself that they have proceeded from the sincere mind of so virtuous and wise a lady, but rather by the setting on and procurement of some uncharitable and malicious persons, of which sort there are too many in these days, the more pity. . . .'9 Her deep awareness of her lack of influence to combat those who would erode her father's dictums was compounded by her regret at the substantial wedge driven into her relationship with Edward. Her frustration was emphasised by worry over her young sister, Elizabeth, whose own recent recklessness was known at Beaulieu. The inevitable symptoms of emotional tension—headaches, neuralgia, and nervousness—became acute, and Mary was ill a good part of 1549, forced to give up the exercise she loved, lacking the blessed serenity she so cherished. She realised the jeopardy in which her insistence on religious observances placed her; she realised with chilling dread that to preserve her own household and religious freedom from official harassment she must be wary and decisive —two qualities altogether foreign to her temperament.

In the midst of her illness, Mary's worst fears were realised. Word of her defiant attitude to the suppression of the Mass reached the court. She had written to her cousin, the Emperor, informing him of her predicament, and he had sent his ambassador, Van der Delft, the successor of Chapuys, to intervene with Somerset. The Protector was sympathetic to Mary, telling the ambassador '. . . she shall do as she thinks best till the King comes of age and, meanwhile, she shall find me her good servant. . . .' Somerset was prepared to overlook Mary's religious nonconformity, but he was overridden by others on the Council, particularly John Dudley, the Earl of Warwick. Realising the Council would have its way and, possibly to find a scapegoat to satisfy them and spare Mary, Somerset ordered that her chaplain, Dr Hopton, her chief household officer, Sir Francis Inglefield, and her comptroller, one Rochester, appear before the Council for interrogation regarding the form of worship of her household.

Mary recognised the implication of the request. The bitter experience with her father had demonstrated that one did not flout governmental authority lightly. From Kenninghall in Norfolk, she replied that she could not spare Rochester. Courageously and bluntly, she said that if the Council 'had anything to be declared to me *except matters of religion,* ye will either write your minds or send some trusty person with whom I shall be contented to talk.' A commission was duly dispatched intent upon gaining her compliance. Continued disregard of what was now an established law could not be encouraged by allowing a Princess, a sister of the reigning monarch, any immunity withheld from a disgruntled populace.

Upon their arrival, Mary faced her inquisitors with little show of fear. She told them 'her house was her flock', and she would support her servants' desire to worship as she herself did. She said she was a King's sister and not subject to the Council's rule, and she reminded them, grimly, she was also the cousin of a Catholic Emperor who insisted on her religious freedom. Here she uncomfortably impressed the councillors who were, even then, obsequiously soliciting the Emperor's friendship and support as they saw their concern for Boulogne imperilling their relations with France. They left, taking no further action. But two weeks later, in a letter leaving little doubt that the Princess's prompt compliance was expected, her servants were again summoned. The uncompromising tone of the letter shocked Mary, particularly because, as she noted in her reply to the Protector, 'of the extreme words of peril to ensue towards them in case they do not come. . . .' Nevertheless, Mary realised that continued opposition might only endanger her officers further. She bowed as gracefully as possible to the Protector's request, even as she reproved him for what she considered an unwarranted insolence. Though her 'poor sick priest' and comptroller would 'be put to hazard by the wet and cold painful travail' of the journey, they would appear before the Council, Mary said. And then, so there would be no doubt of her own feelings, she ended her letter:

But for my part, I assure you all, that since the King, my father, your late master and very good lord, died, I never took you for other than my friends. But in this it appeareth contrary . . . I would not have troubled with writing. . . . not doubting but you do consider that none of you all would have been contented to have been thus used at your inferior's hands—I mean, to have had your officer, or any of your servants, sent for by force (as ye make it) *knowing no just cause why.* Wherefore, I do not a little marvel, that ye had not this remembrance towards me, who always willed and wished you as well to do as myself. . . .[10]

Mary's letter was written eighteen days after the *Book of Common Prayer* was distributed to England's churches and is indicative of the haste with which the government met any opposition to the new service. And there was more opposition than either the Protector or Council had expected. Only old Paget, blessed at times with an omniscient common sense and a tart tongue, could remonstrate with Somerset over the Protector's concern for the poor of the realm, and the image he hoped to secure by improving their conditions. Referring to the revolts in the West Country, Paget allowed himself the luxury of sarcasm, 'I told your Grace the truth and was not believed; well, now your Grace seeth it— and what is the cause? Your own leniency, your softness, your opinion to be good to the poor, the opinion of such as saith to your Grace, "Oh, sir! there was never man had the hearts of the poor as you have!" . . . It is a pity that so much gentleness should be an occasion of so great an evil as is now chanced in England by these rebels.'

Paget had also advised Somerset against the hurried changes in orthodoxy, saying, 'To alter the state of a realm would ask ten years' deliberation.' Now, with discord becoming rampant, again Paget could say truthfully, 'The use of the old religion is forbidden by a law—the use of the new is not yet printed in the stomachs of eleven or twelve parts of the realm.' He reminded Somerset of the pact they had made. 'Remember what you promised me in the gallery at Westminster before the breath was out of the body of the King that dead is? Remember what you promised immediately after, *devising with me concerning the place which you now occupy* . . . and that was to follow mine advice in all your proceedings, more than any other man's!'[11] He finished despairingly, hoping to stay Somerset's hand, 'Your Grace may say, "I shall lose the hearts of the people"—of the good people you shall not, and of the evil, it maketh no matter.' He urged an immediate reprisal against any uprisings and then said, 'Take pity upon the poor men's children, and of the conservation and stay of the realm, and put no more so many irons in the fire at once!'

The revolts in the West Country spread, uncomfortably reminding the Protector and Council of the Pilgrimage of Grace. Everywhere people spurned the royal edict and Act of Parliament which had made the *Book of Common Prayer* a law of the land. Papal supremacy was no longer the issue it had been during Henry's reign; England was spiritually independent, and for most people that was well and good. But the suppression of many of the rituals of the old faith was another matter. 'We will have the Mass in Latin as it was before and celebrated by a priest!' people cried. 'We will have our old service of Matins, Mass, Evensong and processions as it was before ... !' The Cornishmen, particularly, were blunt. 'We will *not* receive the new service ... it is like a Christmas game!'[12]

When the disturbances spread to Wiltshire, Sussex, Hampshire, and then northwards through the Midlands to Yorkshire, a stunned Council declared martial law throughout the realm. Everyone proclaimed his loyalty to the King, who was 'much grieved and in great perplexity' over the reaction of his people. Edward's distress was genuine and obvious to all. In twelve-year-old fashion, he wrote in his *Chronicle*, 'In England rose great stirs, like to increase much if it had not been well foreseen. . . .' Though such 'great stirs' had not been anticipated, the King was undoubtedly soothed with the optimistic assurance that the trouble would be settled quickly.

Throughout the summer and early autumn of 1549 the nobles battled the King's subjects. Lord Russell was sent to deal with the West Country where 'he behaved more like a wild beast than a human being.' Sir William Herbert went into Wales and Lord Grey into the Midlands. They were accompanied by German and Italian mercenaries, for not enough Englishmen could be found to fight their brothers. Soon reports 'of the most horrible butcheries . . . that ever did happen in this world' were filtering back to the court—of priests hanged from their own church beams, of mayors and other officials of small county towns strung up several on one gallows, of the pitched battles and assaults as the people met the ruthless imported *Lanzknechts*. In July, John Dudley, the formidable and ambitious Earl of Warwick, quelled the most notable—and nearly successful—Norfolk rebellion of the Kett brothers in which 3,500 insurgents were cut down by royal forces. The brothers were hung in chains—one from a wall of Norwich Castle, the other from the steeple of Wymondham Church. Because of the proximity of the rising to Mary's residence, she was accused of aiding the malcontents

[226]

and 'her proceedings in matters of religion being openly known, had given no small courage to the rebels.' She angrily denied the charge. It is doubtful if the possibility of actively participating in their fight for religious justice ever occurred to Mary Tudor. She was too much her mother's daughter, too loyal to the young brother she loved, to sanction officially any movement against him. Had she done so, many of the powerful Catholic families who preferred quiet during the risings might have joined and supported her and thus provided a very different conclusion to the unrest.

By the end of August it was all over. Ten thousand Englishmen had died at the hands of the royal forces and mercenaries, a fact which Paget said 'killeth my heart to hear. . . .' The leaders returned to court to confront Somerset with the magnitude of internal strife, of the deep-seated antagonism of a rebellious populace. The Protector had remained in London to safeguard his authority and, ostensibly, the person of the King; in so doing, he miscalculated badly. No one questioned his personal courage, but the exploits of the Earl of Warwick and his victory over the Norfolk revolutionaries made him the hero of the day.

Since the death of Henry VIII, the darkly handsome Dudley, 'avid for glory', as the French ambassador described him, had awaited his opportunity. The King of France had attempted the capture of Boulogne, and Dudley now capitalised on Somerset's inability to defend it because of the domestic insurrections. The exchequer was empty, and loans had to be negotiated at ruinous rates of interest. The realm was divided as never before by the economic, social, and religious changes the Protector had insisted on; the public was incensed by the confiscation of Church lands intended for public purposes but appropriated by the nobles instead. Scotland was lost, Boulogne imperilled, and the Emperor's friendship jeopardised. The Protector had grasped at an authority not intended in the King's will and had broken his promise to do nothing without the Council's consent. Matters had not been helped by Somerset's inflexibility, by his contemptuous and arrogant treatment of his fellow advisers. Overworked and harassed, confronted by the failure of many projects, Somerset spared no one his famous rages. Paget tried to reason with the Protector, mentioning one courtier—the target of Somerset's anger—saying the man had 'come to my chamber weeping. . . . of your handling of him, seemed almost out of wits and out of heart. Your Grace had put him clean out of countenance.' Paget entreated Somerset to change his ways and listen with patience to those who happened to differ from him '. . . and not to give way to choleric fashions.' He reminded him that no one, not even King or Cardinal, formerly spoke to the Council as Somerset now did and warned him 'however high his position in the realm might be, it would not long be tolerated.'[13]

[227]

But the Seymour lack of judgment which had so characterised his executed brother sealed the Protector's doom—and aided Warwick in his conspiracy. Somerset sensed the Council's disaffection, its lack of support, its silence when he thundered at them, its aloofness as he belatedly assumed a false jocularity. Suddenly he was afraid. He resorted —as his brother had before him—to inept and absurd measures to regain his vanishing control. When he heard that some of the Council had dined at one another's houses without him, he became suspiciously agitated. He was confident of his popularity with the people; he must try to outwit his fellow councillors before they could muster support. Taking Cranmer, the indispensable Paget, and young William Cecil, his secretary, he commanded Edward's removal to Hampton Court. On October 5, he ordered an inflammatory proclamation distributed to the people of London and the adjacent shires, alleging that 'certain lords, gentlemen and chief masters, which would depose the Lord Protector and so endanger the King's royal person . . .' were challenging his authority. He urged the people 'to repair with all haste . . . to his Majesty's Manor of Hampton Court, in most defensible array, with harness and weapons, to defend his most royal person. . . .' At Hampton Court, the Protector ordered further strengthening of the guards, the battlements and towers, and 500 suits of armour were delivered from the armoury for the officials and servants. Previously, the Council had decided to confront Somerset with the fact that 'he had not been contented with the place of Councillor whereunto he was called' and had sought 'by all ways and means he could devise to rule . . . but contrary to his said promise, he began to do things of most weight and importance . . . without calling any of the Council thereto.' Somerset was to be told 'that the Council could suffer no longer, unless we would in effect consent to him in his naughty doings.'[14]

There had been no thought of violence, merely restraint of Somerset's powers, and the councillors, booted and spurred and 'ready to have mounted upon their horses', were dumbfounded by the Protector's antagonistic actions. He further threatened—'having some intelligence of their Lordship's intent—if they came to Hampton Court, 'to have destroyed them.' They all repaired to the Earl of Warwick's mansion in Ely Place, Holborn, where they assessed their own strength, devised their strategy, and, in subsequent meetings with the Sheriff of London and the Constable of the Tower, laid their plans. Neither side actually wanted a confrontation, but bluffing could continue for only so long.

When the news of the lords' actions reached the Protector, the effect was disastrous. His appeal for loyalty and support had drawn no great throng to Hampton Court; the common people had little leadership. Arrayed against him was the might of the Council, its retainers, and the forces of the Tower and the City. Somerset had nothing but the palace guards and officials, his archbishop, Thomas Cranmer, whom he could see wavering, and old Paget whose expression was distressingly ominous. He had no one but his nephew, the son of his sister, Jane. But that nephew was *still* the King. Hurrying to Edward's apartments, he roused the sleeping boy, telling him of the treachery brewing in London and of the few hundreds who had gathered outside the palace. The boy was quickly dressed and, white-faced and shivering, urged with little ceremony through the draughty hallways where tall sentries stood silently. Passing through the arched gateway surmounted by the great clock his father had commissioned, he came to the gates of the Base Court. Here huge torches burned, illuminating the faces of the people milling on the opposite side of the moat. They crossed the bridge, the smell of stagnant water assailing the boy's nostrils in the cold night air. The mumble of conversation grew louder as they approached. There was a pause, and then a loud cheer rang out as the people recognised their King.

Edward waited, uncertain of his role, until the Protector's hand on his shoulder signalled it was time to speak. He had been told what to say, and now he shouted it into the night with all his strength, 'Good people—I pray you be good to us—and to our uncle!' The answer came back at once—loud, long cheering and whistles, which encouraged Somerset to step forward. Taking Edward's hand, he held it high as he proclaimed, 'I shall not fall alone. If I am destroyed, the King will be destroyed. Kingdom, commonwealth—all will be destroyed together!' He let Edward's hand drop as the crowd quieted further, listening intently to every word. The boy's face was strained as he peered up in the flickering torchlight at the tall figure of the Protector who now pointed ominously at him as he continued, 'It is not *I* that they shoot at—*this* is the mark that they shoot at. . . .' Edward felt an unfamiliar cold stirring in his stomach, and he tried bravely not to show the tears of fright in his eyes as his uncle ended, '. . . if I die, this is he shall die before me. . . .'[15]

His threat ended, he took the boy's hand, striding so quickly to where the horses were waiting that Edward had difficulty in keeping pace. The stamping beasts were skittish in the night air, unnerved by the throng and the protective guard of soldiers. Edward mounted, unaware of where they were heading, a lumpish fear almost clogging his throat as he settled his feet in the stirrups. The crowd pressed around him, avid for a closer look at the boy-King. Their faces were not menacing, their manner only curious, and Edward felt their concern. Suddenly he drew a small prized dagger, which his father had given him, from his doublet and, calling to the people, shouted, 'Will ye help me against those who would kill me?' The horse spun round as Edward brandished the dagger in the pale fog beginning to rise off the moat. The people were moved. 'Sir, we will all die for you! God save your Grace! . . .' As the procession sped away into the darkness, the King could hear his subjects' expressions of love and support called after him until he was out of sight.

Edward never forgot the wild ride to Windsor Castle. He was already ill with a cold, and the icy autumn air so penetrated his small frame that he arrived at the austere stronghold chilled to the bone, his racking cough aggravated by fatigue and fear. Despite his discomfort, there had been time to think and wonder during the long ride. He remembered his other uncle who had intrigued against him and killed his little dog; perhaps he had even meant to kill his own nephew. Now another uncle, sworn to protect him and his realm until he attained his majority, had so earned the enmity of the Council that he himself must ride for his life to a castle he hated, endangering his own health and well-being. Edward did not believe his own people would hurt him; everywhere he had always met with loving reverence. Who would want to kill him? And why? Why were people rising all over England so that foreigners must kill his own subjects who refused to obey the dicates of his uncle and Council? If the boy had ever entertained doubts as to his uncle's competence, the terrorising midnight ride to Windsor Castle—the effects of which left him shaken and ill for several days—helped to resolve them and only increased his own fear for the safety of his Crown and person. He did not doubt Somerset's basic affection for him; what he could only accept now was that it might not be *enough*.

But, for the moment at least, Somerset was still in command. The next day he asked Edward to write to the Council, 'lamenting our present state—being in such imminent danger.' Through Edward, Somerset tried to placate the councillors. 'Each man hath his faults, he his and you yours', Edward wrote at his uncle's dictation, 'and if we shall hereafter as rigorously weigh yours as we hear that you intend with cruelty to purge his, which of you shall be able to stand before us?' Even if his uncle had erred, the letter continued, 'lieth it in us to remit it, for he is our uncle, whom you know we dearly love, and therefore, the more to be considered at your hand.'[16]

Edward signed the document when Somerset finished dictating; there was little else he could do. In his heart, he was still troubled and fearful; there were so few to protect them at Windsor against the forces of the City and the Tower! His concern showed in an unusual petulance as he waited, coughing and feverish throughout the next day, for word from London. Cranmer, Paget, and the Protector were constantly in session, and there was no one else who might have comforted the boy or listened to his anxieties. Once, as Cranmer bustled through his chambers, Edward asked him bluntly what they might be doing. To which his godfather replied brusquely, 'Sir, it is sufficient that we are here. . . .' Edward's resentment and impatience exploded when he replied, 'Methinks I am in prison!'

In London, the Earl of Warwick took firm command of those Council members who wavered when Edward's letter recommending mercy for his uncle arrived. A reply was sent to Cranmer and Paget at Windsor reminding them of their own position as Council members and declaring the lords' 'resolution of removing Somerset from the office of Protector.' Faced with such an ultimatum, and, fidelity to a lost cause never appetizing to either of them, they asked to mediate with the Council. 'Life is sweet, my Lords, and they say you seek his blood and his death', wrote Paget, 'which if you do, and you may have him otherwise conformable to reason, and by extremity drive him to seek extremity again, the blood of him and others that shall die on both sides innocently shall be by God justly required at your hands!' Paget's wavering loyalty became more firm as he continued '. . . incline your hearts to kindness and humanity, remembering that he hath never been cruel to any of you. . . . and why should you be cruelly minded to him ?'[17] As the discussions continued,[18] it then became merely a matter of determining the conditions under which Somerset would resign. Promised his freedom and retention of his property after he had gone through the formality of an official arrest and, in view of his remarks at the moat at Hampton Court, requested expressly not to frighten his small nephew or turn him against the Lords of the Council, Somerset had little choice but to yield.

He would relinquish his office and his estates, but he hoped the Council would be lenient. Referring to his dead brother, he begged that the 'realm be [not] made in one year a double tragedy and a lamentable spoil, and a scorning stock of the world.' He received Sir Philip Hoby who brought the Council's terms. Hoby attempted to comfort Somerset by saying, 'My Lord, be not you afraid.' Pointing to his neck, he continued, 'I will lose this if you have any hurt. There is no such thing meant. . . .' He then stated that the Council merely wanted a 'reordering' of the Protectorship. The emotional Paget— torn both ways—was overcome. Thanking God, he burst into tears of relief, saying to Somerset, 'Oh, my Lord—ye see now what my Lords be!'[19]

There was genuine relief all around, throughout countryside and City, as well as Council and court. No one felt the lifted weight of fear and uncertainty more happily than Edward. His cold was better, and his spirits were raised by a delegation of Council members, headed by Warwick, who came to greet their sovereign and explain their position before Somerset was removed. Kneeling before Edward, they lined up so that each might kiss his hand. The boy's happiness was obvious to all; he was safe and he was still the King. In merry exultation, he asked the kneeling Lords, 'How do your Lordships?' and as they thronged about him, he smiled graciously, 'You shall be welcome whenever you

[231]

come!' For the first time for months—since his other uncle's execution, in fact—Edward Tudor felt strong and self-confident. His uncle had made the right decision, one on which the boy felt he could count. The Crown was still his.

The next day Edward returned to Hampton Court 'where they [the Council],' he wrote in his *Chronicle*, 'appointed by my consent six Lords . . . to be attendant on me, and four knights. . . .' Four days later, he returned to Westminster, riding in state through the City streets, dressed in new robes of cloth of gold and silk, his horse resplendent in new trappings. Everywhere the young monarch was acclaimed. He arrived at Westminster Palace, exuberant and optimistic, his peace of mind restored. There, in an audience including both Thomas Cranmer and the Earl of Warwick, he was met by a distraught Duchess of Somerset. Unknown to Edward, Somerset had been taken to the Tower, and a list of twelve charges had been drawn up against him. The tearful Duchess flung herself at the startled boy's feet, crying that if Edward 'did not pardon him, the Council will kill him!' Edward's only exclamation was 'Jesu!' No one had told him of his uncle's imprisonment; he had thought Somerset apprehended only temporarily. He told his aunt that he had been informed Somerset was ill, and turning to Cranmer, asked, 'Godfather, what hath become of my uncle, the duke?' Cranmer replied haltingly that Somerset was in the Tower. 'What evil hath he done . . . that he should be arrested?' the boy asked indignantly. Continued imprisonment had not been the Council's promise at the time of Somerset's surrender, he knew. Cranmer spoke of the 'great harm' the Protector had caused, adding that 'we feared he might kill you. . . .' an obvious manœuvre to frighten Edward into abandoning Somerset. Edward scoffed, 'The duke never did me any harm!' and then, with naïve reasoning, he said if the duke had gone so willingly to the Tower, 'it is a sign he be not guilty.' Suddenly he again felt bereft of his newly regained security. Somerset was, after all, one of his own blood. 'I would see my uncle', he said imperiously as the duchess, with floods of tears, cried, 'His life is in your hands!'

A meeting of the full Council was called. No one had thought Edward would interfere, but the young sovereign's sense of justice was affronted at his first confrontation with judicial treachery. He was convincingly determined as he rose in support of the Lord Protector. Anxious for no further emphasis of the matter, Warwick—in command of everything except the official title—spoke soothingly to his fellow councillors, 'My Lords, we must return good for evil. . . .' he said and, wishing particularly to ingratiate himself with Edward, he finished, '. . . as it is the King's will that the Duke be pardoned, and it is the first matter he hath asked of us, we ought to accede to His Grace's wish.'[20]

The moment was different from what Warwick had expected; he had thought Somerset a lost man. Now he must bow to the royal edict, for Edward must be made to depend upon *him* once the Protector was stripped of his powers. His own moment had not as yet come. Though Somerset was momentarily safe, the Earl had little doubt that in the end his own power and authority would rule. It would only take a little more time.

Chapter Fourteen

THE year 1549 which had begun with the execution of Thomas Seymour and ended with the imprisonment of his brother, the Protector, culminated in a turning point in the life of each young Tudor. Recovering from her breakdown, a weakened and pale Elizabeth Tudor dutifully adhered to the new religious service, thereby accentuating Mary's opposition. Anxious to redeem her reputation, Elizabeth affected a severe and colourless mode of dress, a prim and sedate manner, unrelieved by humour or levity of any kind. She resumed her studies, a process more painful than she had anticipated. The toll her illness had taken, not only in bodily distress, but also in enthusiasm for her beloved studies, is apparent in the dispirited letter she wrote Edward apologising for not sending him a New Year's gift.

I am able, most noble King, to offer many excuses that I have not followed my old custom, in preparing some fresh little present at this season for your Highness. For, in the first place, every description of learning, which in me was ever small, has been either so wasted by the long duration of my sickness, or so far cut off by my being unused to study, or so hindered by the infirm state of my health, that my old custom of bringing something or other out of my scanty literary storehouse—a custom always very easily performed by me, when very well approved by you—has been now altogether taken from me. . . . But from this concern about selecting something excellent, which I might with propriety offer you, my Lord Protector relieved me, by whose counsel it has been arranged that this custom of sending New Year's gifts should be abolished; and the wisdom of his policy, I shall willingly follow. . . .[1]

In the next few months, Elizabeth applied herself to learning—and forgetting. She was so diligent in her religious devotions and the study of languages, particularly, that the noted reformer, John Hooper, said, 'Not only did she know true religion, but had become so strong in Latin and Greek that she was capable of defending it with the most judicious arguments and dextrous ability, so that she was victorious over almost all adversaries she encountered.' The kindly Roger Ascham, her tutor, who regarded the classroom as a 'sanctuary against fear', so delighted in Elizabeth's brilliance that he was extravagant in her praise.

'Numberless honourable ladies of the present time surpass the daughters of Sir Thomas More in every kind of learning', he wrote to a friend, 'but amongst them all, my illustrious mistress, my Lady Elizabeth, shines like a star. . . .' In addition to Latin and Greek, Elizabeth spoke French and Italian, 'like English' Ascham continued, '. . . she read with me almost the whole of Cicero, and a great party of Livy . . . after which she read select orations of Isocrates and the tragedies of Sophocles. . . . For her religious instruction, she drew first from the fountains of Scripture, and afterwards, from St Cyprian, the *Commonplaces* of Melanchthon, and similar works, which convey pure doctrine in elegant language.'[2]

Once Ashley and Parry were restored to her household, Elizabeth prudently resigned herself to accepting Lady Tyrwhitt's continued presence as evidence of further penance. She judiciously accepted a small volume of morning and evening prayers and *Divers Hymns and Meditations* as a peace offering. The volume admonished Elizabeth to 'Think upon the needy once a day', 'Help to pacify displeasure', 'Kill anger with patience', and 'Make much of modesty'. In the last, with her extreme simplicity of dress, devoid of any jewels or other ornaments, Elizabeth was especially successful; Edward called her 'my sweet sister, Temperance.'

Mary, meanwhile, had spent the remaining part of the year apart from the court, yearning for an elusive anonymity, aware the truce between herself and the Council was only tenuous. She had appealed to her brother for sufferance, reminding him of the Emperor's intercession on her behalf and Somerset's disinclination to pursue the restriction of her Mass. Indicative of his love for Mary, and 'knowing your good nature and affection for us', Edward had compromised and allowed her to celebrate the Mass which, he stipulated, must be held in her private chambers and attended only by those of her household. He noted Mary's continued refusal to accept the new service as 'a certain grudge of conscience. . . .' He intimated it might be 'for want of good information and conference with some godly and well-learned man.' Edward suggested that Mary might receive some instruction in the 'new religion'; there was little doubt that he expected her conformity some time in the future.

The presence of any 'godly and well-learned man', however, was the last thing Mary wanted, and she sought to divert attention by absence from court. During November she pleaded an illness, 'It being the fall of the leaf, at which time I have seldom escaped the same disease these many years', she wrote apologetically to a councillor, excusing herself from the forthcoming holiday festivities where, she realised, it would be impossible to worship in her traditional manner. Though the illness was legitimate, Edward was told merely, 'that the Lady Mary had refused to come to him.' There were always those around the boy who used any excuses to discredit the King's older, more independent-minded sister.

Meanwhile, after pleading guilty to all charges and throwing himself on the mercy of the court, the Duke of Somerset had been released from the Tower. By an Act of Parliament, he was deprived of all offices and of land valued at £2,000. He was readmitted to the Council under conditions that he attend no meetings unless summoned, that he have no private access to the King, and that he venture no farther than four miles from wherever the Council was sitting. Realising he was lucky to be alive, Somerset assented to the Earl of Warwick's assumption of authority with remarkable docility. The Protector's release had been an occasion of great joy among the common people with whom he was enormously popular; they had few illusions about Warwick. Their opinion was echoed when, referring to the charges lodged against Somerset, Mary Tudor said scathingly, 'they [the Council] are all equally guilty, having given him [Somerset] their advice and consent!'

If the King's subjects and the King's older sister regarded him with fear and bitterness, Warwick fared better with the monarch himself. The twelve-year-old boy, whose loneliness had been constant, relished the companionship of the handsome and affable fifty-year-old Warwick, who paid him more attention than Edward had ever received from his own father or the Protector. Warwick had five sons; he was quick and expert in assessing the boy's desires and satisfying them. He astutely recognised the growing King's need to take an active part in the governing of his realm. Such indulgence would be remembered when the King came of age—and rewarded accordingly. Warwick was shrewd in assessing Edward's sense of inadequacy and recognised the necessity for the boy to expand his consciousness, as well as his person, beyond the confines of the schoolroom and the chapel, which had so far constituted the larger part of his world.

Warwick's perception was the result of a varied background and career. The son of Edward Dudley, who had suffered a not-altogether-justified execution for extortion during the previous reign, he had risen in the royal service as a soldier and diplomat and been enriched with honours and lands. As Lord Lisle, he had been part of that small group of nobles who had accompanied the nine-year-old Mary Tudor to Ludlow Castle. Later he served under Henry during the French War and had been second-in-command to the Protector at Pinkie Cleugh. He had relinquished his post of Lord High Admiral to Thomas Seymour when he himself became the Earl of Warwick on the eve of Edward's coronation. While outwardly co-operative, he had bitterly resented Somerset's assumption of the Protectorship. Both men were opportunistic and ambitious, very much *arrivistes* and startlingly similar in their goals, with one exception: the method by which their ultimate success might be achieved. For all his faults, Somerset was not an inveterate plotter, his strengths and weaknesses being only too obvious. Warwick, on the other hand, was a gifted conspirator, a devious and shrewd manipulator with the determination and patience necessary to successful cabal. Possibly the greatest hindrance to a truer understanding between the Protector and his late brother—especially after Thomas Seymour's arrest—had been due to Warwick's sly cunning. He emphasised the Admiral's ill will towards the Protector. Written messages had been mysteriously lost, verbal ones misquoted, and adroit insinuations from Warwick had often succeeded in a misunderstanding between the brothers as unfortunate as it was needless. No one knew Warwick's thoughts—his taciturn nature was enhanced by a strong, handsome face and a tall, commandingly virile presence. Outwardly demonstrating great strength, he was one of the most decorative of the nobles of Edward's court, while inwardly a ruthless and conscienceless lusting for power and the destruction of his opponent urged him forward to his goal which was nothing less than complete command of the realm and the King.

In his new responsibility he had disdained any formal title, but his authority was unchallenged. To their shock and dismay, he relegated several of the Council to minor official duties. Others—especially the Protector's former aide Paget and his secretary William Cecil—were elevated in title and authority, it being tacitly understood that the 'new blood' on the Council would provide unquestioned allegiance to the man who had advanced them.

In order to divert Edward from the distressing events of the past several months, Warwick ordered an elaborate summer progress which, throughout the summer and autumn of 1549, moved the court to Windsor, Hampton Court, Greenwich, and the royal residences at Guildford, Oatlands, and Richmond. Barnaby Fitzpatrick returned from France and, with John Cheke, became a Gentleman of the Privy Chamber. Edward relished the closeness of his dearest friends. Warwick urged the King's close involvement in all his royal duties, and he directed the boy's progress in the classroom. The King studied Aristotle and translated Cicero's *Philosophy* into Greek. Though not as proficient as Elizabeth in languages, Edward complimented his beloved tutor by translating Cheke's favourite authors, Demosthenes and Isocrates, into Italian and French. He was equally diligent in his religious devotions, zealously embracing the ideology of Cranmer and

[237]

Latimer, enthusiastically conversing with the foreign reformers who, at Warwick's invitation, moved freely throughout the court. One of them wrote to a contemporary, 'Believe me, my much esteemed friend, you have never seen in the world for these thousand years, so much erudition united with piety and sweetness of disposition. Should he live, and grow up with these virtues, he will be a terror to all the sovereigns of the earth. He receives with his own hand a copy of every sermon that he hears, and most diligently requires an account of them after dinner from those who study with him. Many of the boys and youths who are his companions in study are well and faithfully instructed in the fear of God and in good learning.'[3]

In addition to perfecting his mind with his studies and replenishing his soul with his religious devotions—all so that he might eventually become 'more fatherly' to his subjects—there was also time for the King's merriment and relaxation. Warwick, a noted athlete, ordered that Edward spend more time in the company of the younger courtiers and that he participate in games of tennis, bowls, and archery. Exercise in the open air lent a healthy glow to the boy's once pale cheeks. The rather listless manner, born of many hours in the classroom and chapel, disappeared as Edward engaged in the shouting, wagering, sweating, and aggressive competition that occupied the younger element of his court. The skills of fighting and the tactics of war were displayed for the King in an entertainment at Greenwich when 'A castle or fort was built up of turf, which was besieged, stormed and defended, to show his Majesty some passages in the art of war, wherein he took great delight.' The *Chronicle* reflects Edward's enjoyment: '. . . six gentlemen did challenge all comers at barriers, jousts and tourneys and also that they would keep a fortress with thirty of them against a hundred!'[4] he wrote wonderingly. As a guest of Lord Clinton, the Admiral of the Fleet, he went to Deptford, 'where before supper I saw certain (people) stand upon the end of a boat without holding of anything and ran one at another till one was cast into the water!'[5]

As he attended royal functions and social events previously prohibited either by his youth or by the Protector, the young King's activities became more varied and pleasant. At Greenwich, he enjoyed the pomp of visiting the great ship his father had commissioned, the *Henry Grace De Dieu*, and later, when the French ambassador M. de Chenault arrived with many of the French court, 'the King sent his galley, called the *Subtle*, royally fitted up with plate, tapestry, and all things proper for the occasion. . . . with an honourable banquet on board, and so conducted them to Durham Place, the mansion appointed for the lodging.'[6] The visitors were overwhelmed by the lavishness of the reception and the great display of gold plate. Their Catholic hearts might have been dismayed had they known that such 'church stuff as mitres, golden missals and primers . . . and relics' had been melted down for the service.[7] The French were later subjected to several of the more distasteful sports in which the Tudor court indulged—Edward notes in his *Chronicle* the bear-baiting and bull-baiting provided as entertainment for the embassy at Durham House. The following day, the visitors were invited to hunt in Hyde Park, and later Edward escorted them 'on the Thames, and saw the bear hunted in the river, and also wild-fire cast out of boats and many pretty conceits.'[8]

In the midst of the festivities, two prominent weddings were also recorded by the King. The first took place at Sheen 'where was a marriage made between Ambrose Dudley, the Lord Lisle, the Earl of Warwick's son and the Lady Anne, daughter to the Duke of Somerset. . . .' Edward presented the bride with a ring worth forty pounds for her wedding, and if he entertained any thoughts on the marriage of the deposed Protector's daughter to the son of the man who had accomplished Somerset's downfall, he did not reveal them. Another less tactful observer merely noted, 'after the solemnity of this marriage, there appeared outwardly to the world, great love and friendship between the Duke and the Earl, but by reason of carry-tales and flatterers, the love continued not long. . . .'[9] The following day, the third Warwick son, Robert Dudley,[10] wed pretty Amy Robsart in a ceremony which, at the time, had no political implications. Edward wrote of the post-nuptial entertainment: 'there were certain gentlemen that did strive who should first take away a goose's head, which was hanged alive on two cross-posts.'[11]

The King enjoyed exercising his prerogative. One was the knighting of those the Council wished to favour for their services, and the boy's enthusiasm for this ceremony was well known. A particularly endearing example of one of Edward's more lighthearted moments is related in the annals of the Throckmorton family. Nicholas Throckmorton was a handsome young courtier only a few years older than the King and, as a cousin of the boy's beloved stepmother, the late Katherine Parr, was well known to him. After distinguishing himself in the Scottish campaign, Throckmorton arrived at court bearing a letter in which, for his services to the Crown, Edward was asked to provide some commission which would enable the young man to live in the royal household. The King did more than requested. He liked Throckmorton immensely. 'He would jest with me merrily', said the visitor, 'and when wearied much with lords and others more, alone with me into some place would go.' Upon reading the letter, Edward replied happily that not only would he have Throckmorton live in the royal household, but he would also knight his friend! Throckmorton was certain the King was joking; knighthoods were conferred only with the Council's consent. However, taking his cue from the boy, he decided to treat the matter as a joke.

He turned from the young sovereign and quickly ran, in mock horror, from the room. Entering into the spirit of the game and shouting joyously, Edward clutched his sword and took off in pursuit through the Palace hallways, calling loudly and wildly waving his sword as the guards looked on in stunned disbelief. They watched as the King searched for Throckmorton who had hidden behind a large piece of furniture. Edward soon discovered him, and putting down his sword, he dragged the young man from his hiding place. With more shouting and uproarious laughter from both, the King quickly grasped the heavy sword and, as Throckmorton said later, 'bestowed the accolade of honour upon him then and there.'[12] The frolic continued with exaggerated courtesy and clowning as sovereign and newly dubbed knight returned to the royal chamber. Throckmorton was later ordered before the Star Chamber to explain his sudden knighthood, escaping with a fine because of the royal indulgence. It did not help him to escape the wrath of his father, the Warwickshire Squire of Coughton Court, who was now confronted with a younger son holding a knighthood while his elder son and heir had none.

As Edward grew older, the royal responsibilities became more demanding, especially of his temperament and emotions. The hunt for those the government labelled heretics was never ending. One was Joan Bocher, a pretty girl of Kent, who had been taken into custody for 'holding that Christ was not incarnate of the Virgin Mary. . . .' She steadfastly refused to recant, and after she had spent a miserable year in prison, the Council demanded the death penalty. Edward, however, hesitated to sign the warrant for her execution. He recoiled from sending the woman to the stake, arguing with John Cheke that heretics' lives should be spared, for in their ignorance they were spiritually more vulnerable than the believer. When 'the Council could not move him to put-to his hand' to the warrant, they sent Thomas Cranmer to deal with the reluctant King. Even in the face of Cranmer's convincing argument that heretics were a scourge and a bad example to the populace, Edward temporised. 'What, my Lord, will ye have me send her quick to the Devil in her error?' asked the King resentfully. Cranmer later confessed that 'he had never so much to do in all his life as to cause the King to put-to his hand' on the execution order. When Edward finally did so, with an almost tearful anger, he cried, 'he would lay all the charge thereof upon Cranmer before God!' But the Archbishop, who should have been loath to take life, had his warrant. Edward wrote in his *Chronicle*, 'Joan Bocher, otherwise Joan of Kent, was burnt for holding that Christ was not incarnate of the Virgin Mary, being condemned the year before, but kept in hope of conversion; and the thirteenth of April, the Bishop of London and the Bishop of Ely were to persuade her. But she withstood them, and reviled the preacher

that preached at her death, telling him, he lied like a knave. . . .'
Edward's *Chronicle* entries are too often misleading; many are blunt in
the extreme, especially in instances where he was sensitively affected.
They produce an erroneous conception of the young monarch which is
unfortunate, for the boy obviously intended his *Chronicle* to be merely
a calendar of incidents and dates, rather than an intimate repository
of his thoughts and feelings.

In addition to the King's concern for the spiritual salvation of his
subjects, the refusal of his elder sister, Mary Tudor, to embrace the new
doctrine was a cause of concern for both himself and the Council.
Warwick, particularly, was adamant that Mary should conform. Her
continued opposition and the temporary immunity extended her in the
past, presented an unfortunate example to a populace otherwise
expected to obey. Mary remembered Warwick from those long-ago
happy days at Ludlow when, as Sir John Dudley, he had been the
Chamberlain of her household. She told the Spanish ambassador that
Warwick was 'the most unstable man in England'. It is doubtful if
Warwick knew the daughter of Henry VIII and Catherine of Aragon as
well, and when, with her indomitable courage, Mary continued openly
to celebrate the Mass in her household, she was eventually summoned to
appear before the King. She appealed to her brother, telling him her
health was such that she could not make the journey and begging him
to wait 'till you were grown to more perfect years . . . in matters touching
the soul.' But Warwick gave Edward no peace about his sister's Mass.
If a King could not extract obedience from his sister, how could he
expect to govern a realm effectively? The barb hit home, for Edward
was enjoying a hitherto unknown and heady authority. Therefore,
Mary was again warned to 'be conformable and obedient to the
observation of his Majesty's laws, to give orders that the Mass should
be no more used in her house, and that she should embrace and cause
to be celebrated in her said house, the Communion and other Divine
services set forth by his Majesty.'[13]

Faced with such an impasse, Mary reluctantly journeyed to Windsor.
She was fearful of her reception and made little effort to hide her bitterness. Mary could accept philosophically any loss of comfort or material
luxuries. Loss of honour, of rank, or an assault on her conscience, however, caused an agonising insecurity which further tore at her frail
health and disposition. The meeting with the King and Council was a
failure, for brother and sister were compelled to confront each other in
the midst of an assemblage in which one must accuse and the other
defend. The warm family rapport that Katherine Parr had stimulated
was not forgotten, but months had passed in which one uncle had been
executed and another imprisoned for treason. One sister lay ill and
disgraced, while the eldest of the family exhibited only stubborn refusal

[241]

to consent to measures Edward had been convinced were necessary for the spiritual welfare of the English people. They faced each other—the twelve-year-old boy, his beauty and dignity contrasting sharply with the appearance of the thirty-three-year-old woman who stood defensively before him. The voluminous folds of her clothing could not hide the outline of the sparse flesh which covered her tiny frame, and the apprehension she felt was obvious in the dark and lustrous eyes. But she held herself straight, her fingers clasped tightly together. With no dissimulation—nor the least indication of tact or diplomacy—she spoke resentfully. Mary mentioned the promise given to the Emperor 'nearly a year before, by virtue of which I and my household were given entire freedom to have the Mass celebrated.' She mentioned the Protector's earlier decision to 'wink at her services', an unfortunate allusion under the current circumstances. She staunchly defended her position, telling the King and Council that, while she was the King's good subject, she intended to live and die in the faith in which she had been born. Mary was never comfortable in the limelight, and after her difficult opening, she turned to Edward. He, too, had been born in that faith she said, and she was equally firm in stating she considered the laws being made by others during his minority no just laws at all. And then, as she realised the inevitable challenge this presented the Council which had sat silently listening, her courage broke.

The King was merely a child, for all his beauty, dignity, and authority. The real power, she knew, lay with those twenty-five faces regarding her with cold scorn. 'Do you not know me?' she flung at them. 'How it is you make so small account of me? I am the daughter of Henry the Eighth and the sister of Edward the Sixth! It was a great pity that my brother's kingdom should fall into your hands!'[14] Suddenly, she began to weep bitterly, and at the sight of his sister's distress, Edward, too, burst into tears and cried to her, 'I think no harm of you . . . !' All at once the Council came to life, and with expressions of sympathy, the meeting ended with the King being taken to his own quarters. Mary was permitted to withdraw with the lame remark from a minister that 'The King had no other thought but to inquire and know all things'. Weak with relief that no further restriction was immediate, Mary hastened to leave. She was not deceived, however, and could not forbear saying bitterly to her brother's Council, 'His Majesty has been hardened against me. . . . God knows who were his advisers in this!' If there was a touch of irony in her remark, the ministers did not dwell on it.

The ordeal of the meeting left Mary in panic, and she resorted, as had her mother before her, to her powerful Spanish relative, writing to the Emperor that he must consider 'my present supplication more than any other made by me to your Majesty in this, my latest and most dire extremity.'

It was early winter at Beaulieu and visitors were rare, for the harsh weather made the roads hazardous, and there was little except her unhappy situation to occupy Mary's mind. The previous summer she had thought of escape. In treadmill fashion her thoughts revolved on her present predicament. Escape had seemed the only solution; she had so few real supporters outside her household. She told Charles's ambassador 'if there is peril in going and peril in staying, I must choose the lesser of two evils!'

To Mary, the worst imaginable evil was to live a faith abhorrent to her upbringing, her conscience, and her peace of mind. Yet she knew her own frailty and wondered if she had not only the physical capacity but also the emotional fortitude to forsake the land of her birth, to leave brother, sister, and her few friends, for the unknown hazards of permanent exile. She was first in the succession. This, too, she would forsake if she left England; the Crown would then belong to Anne Boleyn's daughter. Charles did not encourage Mary's flight with any great enthusiasm, for he, too, was aware of the importance of the Spanish Tudor remaining in England. She was the one strong tie with Spain and, should the throne ever come to her, the one hope of overthrowing the work of the reformers and reinstating the old religion in her country.

But honest compassion and courtesy—mingled with a reluctant awareness of family obligations—demanded some show of support. Ships were sent to lie off Maldon, five miles from the Essex shore, and three more waited off Harwich, should Mary choose to leave. During the hot summer nights, tortured by indecision, the beleaguered young woman had paced the confines of her stifling chamber, aware that escape was possible—but would it be successful and safe? What would await her in a foreign country and—here her mind almost refused to consider the alternative—what would await her if the plot failed? There was no one she could talk to; not even the closest of her ladies was to be trusted, the ambassador had stressed. Irresolute, Mary waited that moment too long. With their commercial ventures completed, the continued presence of the foreign ships offshore excited comment. When news reached the Council, as Edward noted in his *Chronicle*: 'Sir John Gates was sent into Essex to stop the going away of the Lady Mary. . . .' Shaken at the turn of events as she realised she had lost her one chance of escape, Mary spent the following months in dread of continued intimidation by the Council. There was little they could take from her—her material possessions were insignificant indeed in comparison with many of her relatives. Her health was a constant concern made worse by worry and insecurity. The one honest necessity of which the Council might yet deprive her was the freedom and means to worship as she pleased, and this, she knew, could result in a fight to the death.

Accordingly, in the next few months during her lonely winter at Beaulieu, she mustered her strength for the coming ordeal.

The beginning of the second attack on Mary Tudor coincided with
Warwick's determination to cast his lot with the reforming movement.
Previously an enigma whose religious convictions were known only to
himself, Warwick had correctly surmised that the reforming movement
would provide more glory for the house of Dudley than the more
reactionary old faith. Everywhere he was hailed by the reformers as 'a
most holy and fearless instrument of the Word of God'. Together, he
and Henry Grey, Lord Dorset, the father of Lady Jane Grey, were
considered 'the most shining lights of the Church of England', however
shoddy the background of their luminosity in the City and court. The
newly formed political administration and the removal of the ancient
shackles of a demanding Catholic faith had provided the reformers with
an unparalleled opportunity for social, political, and religious abuse.
Licentiousness, greed, immorality, corruption—all became the order
of the day.

As endowments for scholarships were suppressed and the universities
themselves labelled 'stables of asses, stews and schools of the Devil',
their libraries were plundered, the contents thrown to the winds, burned
in darkened courtyards or carted off to grace a noble's mansion. The
School of Arts at Oxford was confiscated for more utilitarian purposes,
and laundresses dried their clothing in its courtyards. Holy buildings
fared worse. The venerable St Paul's became the 'stock exchange of the
day, where merchants . . . met for business, and the lounge where the
young gallants gambled, fought and killed each other.' The more profane
did not hesitate to chop missals into pieces and snatch bread from the
altar and trample it underfoot in a parody of the Mass. Others rode
horses through the aisles or used the space between monuments for
stabling, the filth of the animals creating an unbearable stench. As
hospitals, schools, and almshouses were plundered for building materials
and the ruins left to rot, the starving poor and needy retaliated with
brutal lawlessness. Death was preferable to a life of misery, famine, and
degradation in which they were counted little better than stinking,
savage nuisances. Again Latimer thundered to the court and Council,
telling them they would 'cough in Hell' if they did not make some
restitution to the miserable poor. '. . . Because ye have no eyes, ye shall
hear it with your ears!' he cried wrathfully, 'Ye have deceived the King
and the universities to enrich yourselves!'

Edward could not help but be impressed with his preachers's eloquence. Seated in the window embrasure of his chamber, the sun

touching his thin cheeks, surrounded by books, papers, and the copious notes he made from sermons, the boy read the advice of the noted reformer, Martin Bucer, who noted the 'miseries . . . brought on the German States by their sins and want of religious discipline. . . .' Aware of recent rebelliousness of his own subjects and his minister's scathing criticisms, the King, after much thought, tried to give his people guide lines to enable them to recognise the cause of the evils and abuses that had provoked the insurrection. First, Edward recognised the responsibility of the clergy to the people. 'For as the good husbandman maketh the ground good and plentiful, so doth the true preacher with doctrine and example print and graft in the people's mind the Word of God, that they at length become plentiful', he wrote laboriously. Noting the economic misery confronting his subjects, he continued, 'The husbandmen and farmers take their ground at a small rent, and dwell not on it, but let it to poor men for treble the rent they took it for.' The greed of the farmer, the artisan, the merchant, and particularly of the nobles, the malpractices of the lawyers and judges, who invariably sentenced according to rank and status, were all censured by the King. 'Hellhounds they be!' he wrote vehemently.

The King's 'own remedy' was set forth in the youthful penmanship which, although it never quite equalled his sisters', was firm. His comments testify to hours of diligence in assimilating the true extent of conditions caused by the Council and his nobles. His proposed solution combines a mixture of earnest common sense, an almost adult understanding of the troubles besetting his realm, which he compared to 'sores which must be cured with these medicines or plasters', and a naïve willingness to assume that his remedy would right all wrongs.

The first step, in Edward's opinion, was a 'good education' and the 'devising of good laws' which must be executed 'without respect of persons'. Noble rank or wealth should shield no one from a just sentence, and here, said Edward' 'the example of the ruler' was paramount—'for no man that is in fault himself can punish another for the same offence'. Illicit profiteering must be prevented by statutes, said the King, and if vagabonds and 'idle persons' must, of necessity, be punished, it would be wiser in the future to see that 'youth . . . be brought up in some husbandry, some in working, 'graving, gilding, joining, printing, making of clothes, even from their tenderest age. . . .' Royal though he might be, Edward himself had been 'brought up in husbandry' and his *Discourse About the Reformation of Many Abuses* is evidence of his personal concern and his honest desire to alleviate his people's misery. He concluded the *Discourse* by stating that the adoption of his remedies would ease the situation, and asked that his nobles return to their counties and see the statutes fully and duly executed to 'help advance the profit of the commonwealth.'[15]

If the aims of the King and Council differed in some instances, they were one in their endeavour to force Mary Tudor's compliance with the Act of Uniformity. Edward's position, however, was more difficult than his nobles'. He dearly loved his older sister, but the constant emphasis of his responsibilities, the appeals to his conscience, and his relentless religious indoctrination, had been effective. Edward possessed neither the vision of his father, who could always compromise when necessary, nor Elizabeth's respect for the inevitable that made her bend when she knew she must. In this he and Mary were much alike; it accounted now for their virtual estrangement. The boy's natural piety, formerly so simple and innocent, had altered with his councillors' emphasis on his infallibility, and he had taken on the tinge of the bigot; he fearfully viewed his sister living a faith which could only place her soul in danger of eternal hellfire. 'The King's conscience will receive a stain if he allow her to live in error. . . .' one nobleman told Jean de Scheyve, the Emperor's ambassador. De Scheyve had already discerned the close-minded zeal in Edward, whose support of the New Learning, so scorned by traditional Catholics, had become obsessive. 'The King takes increasing pleasure in disputing and upholding the said doctrine, and there is no hope therefore that I may obtain anything from him', he reported to Charles. 'He would more likely pride himself on overthrowing my arguments!'[16]

Edward also prided himself on his Council's thoroughness, its attention to his income, expenditures, and land holdings. Soon after Mary left for her country home, the Council requested her to exchange certain lands situated in Norfolk for less desirable ones owned by the King. Mary replied that 'she had always been willing and ready to serve the King, her brother, and would not fail to gratify and oblige him now.' But her concern showed in her honest answer that 'she hoped the King would not seek to diminish her slender substance.' De Scheyve was less tactful and wrote to the Emperor's sister, the Queen of Hungary, 'it seems, Madam, that the Lords wish to try her in every way.'[17]

As the harassment intensified, letters couched in harsher terms were delivered to the Lady Mary who nevertheless insisted she would maintain her religious freedom in the 'ceremonies performed in the manner in my late father's time'. She again reminded the Council of the promise given the Emperor, a promise Charles had insisted upon, she said scornfully, 'because you change governors and councillors so often that he feared any fresh change might lead to a re-opening of the question later on!' Now, she said, reminding them of her recent visit to court, 'none has any recollection when I lately visited the King of any promise being given!' Mary was angrily disdainful as she wrote, 'God knows the contrary to be the truth and you in your own consciences (I say to those who were then present) know the opposite!' Mary stressed that her faith and religion were the same held by 'all Christendom . . . under the late King, my father, until you altered them with your laws'. Her disdain of their methods shows as she finished '. . . to the King's Majesty, my brother . . . I confess me to be his humble sister and subject, but to you, my Lords, I owe nothing beyond amity and good will, which you will find in me as I meet with the same in you'.

Though she had little confidence, she said she hoped that Edward would not be turned against her. 'It seems not suitable that he should be robbed of freedom . . . by laws passed during his minority', she wrote firmly, her concern for her brother evident. And this was to be her 'final answer to any letters you might write to me on the matters of religion'. She had been suffering ill health and an 'attack of catarrh in my head', she pleaded, and 'were you to know the pain I suffer in bending down my head to write . . . for love and charity you would not wish to give me occasion to do it'. She concluded the letter, saying, 'My health is more unstable than that of any creature and I have all the greater need to rejoice in the testimony of a pure conscience. . . .'[18] The measure of Mary's angry conviction is apparent in her remark to de Scheyve who suggested that the tone of her letter might be too firm. Mary replied that she 'was in the habit of writing roughly to the Council . . . and she thought if she now adopted a milder tone, especially on so important a subject as this, they might persuade themselves that they were winning her over and become more petulant and audacious.'[19]

The reply did not come from the Council. Surprisingly, it came from the King himself, and it did not alleviate Mary's anxiety to read Edward's accusing words. The promise should be considered as an 'indulgence we displayed towards you . . . to incline you to obey. . . .' said Edward, and her continued disobedience could be viewed only as 'license to break our laws and set them aside'. How, asked the King, would *she* feel if someone in her household openly persisted in disregarding orders? At the close, the King wrote in his own hand. 'Sister, consider that an exception has been made in your favour for this long time past, to incline you to obey and not to harden you in this resistance, whereas the example of our loyal subjects who hold their souls as dear as you hold yours, might have suffered to move you.' To the woman whose tears had so moved him, Edward finished, 'Truly sister, I will not say more and worse things, because my duty would compel me to use harsher and angrier words. *But this I will say with certain intention:* that I will see my laws strictly obeyed, and those who break them shall be watched and denounced, even as some are ready to trouble my subjects by their obstinate resistance.'[20]

The letter, in Edward's childish scrawl, almost broke Mary's courage, and she recognised that now, in addition to Warwick and the Council, she must contend with His Majesty himself. She replied to Edward sadly, 'I have received your letters. . . . the content whereof do more trouble me than any bodily sickness, though it were even to the death; and the rather that for your Highness doth charge me to be both a breaker of laws and also an encourager of others to do the like. I most humbly beseech your Majesty to think that I never intended towards you otherwise than my duty compelleth me unto; that is, to wish your Highness, all honour and prosperity, for the which I do and daily shall pray.'[21]

In the early winter of 1551, the Earl of Warwick summoned Mary Tudor to court once more—an ordeal she viewed with dread, and delayed as long as possible. On March 18, 1551, after several days and nights spent in prayer for the success of her journey, 'with fifty knights and gentlemen in velvet coats afore her, and after her, four score gentlemen and ladies', Mary rode to London to see Edward, dreading what change she might find in the attitude of the young boy to whom she was do devoted. Word of her arrival had spread throughout the City, and the people left the busy streets and lanes and, for six miles from Wanstead to Fleet Street and on into the Strand, crowded the thoroughfares to see the King's elder sister. It was a brutally cold day, and neither Mary nor the court had expected any welcoming demonstration. But loyalty to the family of their former King, and a moment's respite from their miserable lives—a moment to enjoy colour, pageantry, and majesty—sent them scurrying to the roadsides for a glimpse of the Lady Mary. They saw a small, regal woman, looking older than her thirty-five years, who held her head high, casting them pleasant, aloof glances which did not linger but held a trace of melancholy kindness. There were shouts of affection from the onlookers that brought a becoming colour to Mary's pale cheeks, and smiles appeared on the faces of those accompanying her. Many of the bystanders whispered of the sombre shades in which the former Princess was dressed, and pointed to the large ornate golden cross and the black rosary beads hanging conspicuously from her girdle. In mute support of their Princess, everyone in her numerous retinue wore similar crosses and carried 'beads of black'. The challenging symbols met with disdainful mockery by some in the crowd, but even they were intimidated by the wholehearted roar of approval that thundered all along Mary's route to her lodging.

After resting overnight at her house in St John's, Clerkenwell, Mary rode to Westminster the following morning. The tacit displeasure of King and Council was apparent in the lack of ceremony at her reception where only old Wingfield, the comptroller, waited. Mary followed him apprehensively into the Presence Chamber. Edward's greeting was warm, but it failed to put Mary at ease. She found it difficult to return his youthful enthusiasm, aware of the tenuous truce existing between them. Edward felt the awkwardness too; neither of them had the gift of small talk which came so easily to their sister Elizabeth. Both Edward and Mary were relieved to be summoned to 'a goodly banquet', where for the next two hours at least no further conversational efforts need be made.

But inevitably the issue had to be dealt with. Walking to the Council Chamber, the trembling Mary prayed for strength. Once seated, and as if anxious to have the distressing moment behind him, Edward lost no time in stating, 'how long I suffered her Mass *against my will** in the hope of her reconciliation; but how (now being no hope which I perceived by her letters) except I saw some short amendment, I could not bear it.'[22]

Mary was ready with her replies—on the ride to Westminster she had carefully considered what she would say. She answered that 'her soul was God's and her faith she would not change, nor dissemble her opinion with contrary words'. Edward replied that her faith was her own; no restraint was being placed on her personal beliefs but only on her outward practice, and added, 'I will you ... as a subject to obey.' Mary reverted staunchly to her premise that laws made during a minority were not just laws, and facing Edward squarely, she entreated that 'riper age and experience will teach your Majesty more yet'. With as little contact with the King as had been allowed her, she did not realise that Edward, too, had grown in conviction as well as stature, and—his vanity stung—he replied quickly and sharply, 'You also may have somewhat to learn. None are too old for that!' Mary revealed that it would be very difficult for her to forsake her religion in which the King, my father, bred me and left me at his death'. Her reference to Henry led the Council to accuse her of disregarding her father's will. Such presumption enraged Mary, and she turned on them bitterly, 'I have carefully read the will, and am bound but on the point of my marriage. Your Lordships have said no Masses for the King, my father's soul as he commanded. . . .' She was not allowed to finish, for the incongruity of a former Princess being hauled before the Council to plead for a ritual commanded by their late King, was nothing to which the ministers wished Edward exposed. Instead, Warwick interrupted in a tone which he hoped might lighten the moment. 'How now, my Lady', he said teasingly, 'it seems your Grace is trying to show us in a hateful light to the King ... ?'

* These words were later crossed out by the King in his *Chronicle*, apparently after some deeper thought. When Mary first complained to Edward of the threatening letters from the Council, before Edward himself found it necessary to write her, the boy replied, 'I knew not of them. . . .' Both incidents reveal the Council often acted independently of the King, using Edward to persecute Mary only after their own methods had failed, to her great personal distress and certainly contributing to Edward's own puzzled bewilderment and similar anxiety for his sister.

Mary disregarded Warwick. Instead, she turned directly to her brother, whose face was beginning to show an anxious and shameful distress, and said, 'I would have hoped that because of the great and boundless good with which God has endowed your Majesty, and also because I am your Majesty's near kindred and unworthy sister, that your Majesty would have allowed me to continue in the old religion.' Mary pleaded with Edward, 'There are but two things—soul and body. My soul I offer to God and my body to your Majesty's service. I would rather it pleased your Majesty to take away my life than the old religion, in which I desire to live and die.'

Edward's voice trembled as he replied, and his hands clutched at his doublet, leaving small patches of sweat, 'I desire no such sacrifice. . . .' he said, glancing hastily at Warwick and the Council to see if the answer sufficed. Before anyone could reply, Mary begged the boy, 'to give no credit to any person who might desire to make him believe evil of me, my religion, or anything else' and then asked for permission to depart. With obvious relief, Edward consented, and shaking with nervous exhaustion, the equally relieved woman hastily returned to St John's. She was comforted later by a solicitous message from Edward who told her she was at liberty to stay at the Palace or return to her country home. Unable to believe her good fortune, the frightened Mary gave orders for her immediate departure.

On the eve of Mary's anxious journey to meet her brother and his Council, Elizabeth Tudor also came to London, at the invitation of Warwick and the Council, an invitation the banished girl contemplated with great expectation. Reconciliation between the King and his other sister was now considered possible and desirable. In the previous weeks, Edward had asked for her portrait, earning Elizabeth's delighted reply. With the presentation of the picture, she wrote, 'For the face, I grant I might well blush to offer, but the mind I shall never be ashamed to present. For though from the face of the picture the colours may fade by time, may give by weather, may be spotted by chance; yet the other nor time with her swift wings shall overtake, nor the misty clouds with their lowerings may darken, nor chance with her slippery foot may overthrow. . . .'[23]

Accordingly, shortly before Mary's entry into the City, Elizabeth proudly 'rode on horseback through London, to visit St James's Palace, attended by a great company of lords, knights and gentlemen, and about two hundred ladies.'[24] The sisters did not meet; Elizabeth remained in seclusion while Mary was undergoing her ordeal. The wily Warwick, from whom the Catholic faction had hoped for more support, saw their expectations doomed to final failure in his warm reception of Elizabeth. After Mary's interrogation, the younger girl was summoned to see her brother, and '... she came from St James's through the park to the court. The way from the park-gate to the court was spread with very fine sand. She was attended by a very honourable confluence of noble and worshipful persons of both sexes, and was received with much ceremony at the court gate'. The contrast the sisters presented to the people—one devoted and strongly loyal to the old faith, the other indisputably an advocate of her brother's religious policy—was pointed, deliberate, and planned. But it was also evident that Warwick had overestimated any widespread aversion to Mary and to what she represented. Her welcome had been warm and real.

A similar demonstration of affection awaited the seventeen-year-old Elizabeth. In contrast to her more distant sister, she had responded enthusiastically with smiles and gracious gestures to the insatiable curiosity of the welcoming throng, and there was little doubt the once disgraced Princess and her cavalcade enjoyed the favour of the crowd. Elizabeth's triumph can be seen in the effusive letter she wrote Edward upon her return to Hatfield:

No more frequent or plainer proofs can be given of your love to me, Oh most serene and illustrious King, than those of late, when I enjoyed the treat of your most delightful society. This when I call to mind (and I daily do so) I seem, as it were, still enjoying the courtesy of your conversations. And farther, when those your countless favours to me come into my mind, with which you received me on my arrival, and with which you dismissed me on my departure, I cannot easily express how my mind is drawn divers ways, and I feel a double anxiety. For while perceiving, from the greatness of your boons, your fraternal affection most greatly inclined to me, I conceive no little joy and delight therefrom; so, on the other hand, weighing in a just and fair balance the multitude of your services towards me, I am grieved, because I am convinced I can never repay their real value. . . .

Secure once more in the brotherly affection—and conscious of Warwick's approval—Elizabeth said she had intended a 'small work', presumably of poetry or an essay, to be sent to Edward in gratitude. What was becoming an inordinately tortuous mode of expression on her part is evident in the following passages when she excuses her lack of effort. Referring to the absent 'small work', she says:

But, since it could not, (as I supposed it would) be brought to a close by me, on account of the shortness of the time, which I see flows from me even faster than water, I now hope that this letter, however rude, will plead my cause when absent, before your Majesty, and at the same time, evince, in some degree, my disposition towards you; for that this can be done fully and amply enough by me in these dumb words, I reckon to be quite impossible, especially as (your Majesty is well aware) it is peculiar to my disposition, not only to express in words as much as I think, but also not to say more than I think. Of which the latter fault (I mean, the saying more) as few detest, so many practice, on most occasions, but especially in the courts of princes and kings, who must especially beware that they do not seem to have more flatterers in their private chambers, than birds of prey outside their palaces. . . .[25]

The visit of Edward's sisters to London had accomplished two purposes of which Warwick, Mary, and Elizabeth were not long to remain ignorant. The older, Catholic sister, revered by the traditionalists, and the younger Elizabeth, now the darling of the Protestants, were from then on placed in circumstances which made them open rivals for the affection and support of the King. As each returned to her respective household, the memory of their differing receptions lingered. If Mary viewed the meeting with her brother with anguish and her reception by the Council bitterly, for Elizabeth there was now the prospect of further royal indulgence, a delightful awareness that for her it was only a beginning.

Chapter Fifteen

MARY'S plea to her cousin, the Holy Roman Emperor, not to abandon her in her 'dire extremity' soon resulted in welcome support. Shortly after her departure from court, the English government denied the Mass to the Spanish ambassador resident in London. A furious Emperor had retaliated, forbidding the use of the 'new religion' ritual of Communion to the English representative at the Flemish court, Sir Thomas Chamberlain. 'I will suffer none to use any doctrine or service. . . . that is not allowed of the Church!' cried Charles. Angrily he confronted Dr Wotton, the English envoy, telling him the English were 'so far out of the way . . . they did infect his own realm'. When Wotton demurred, Charles continued vehemently, '. . . you say you have chosen a good way; the world takes it for a naughty way'. Remembering his cousin, he said, 'Ought it not to suffice you that ye spill your own souls, but ye have a mind to force others to lose theirs, too? My cousin, the Princess, is evil-handed among you. . . .' When Wotton said that Mary lived in her own house, surrounded by her own companions, and that he had heard nothing to the contrary, Charles exploded wrathfully, 'Yes, by St Mary! There *is* to the contrary . . . and I will not suffer it! Is it not enough that my aunt, her mother, was evil entreated by the King that dead is, but my cousin must be worse ordered by Councillors now? I had rather she died a thousand deaths than she should forsake her faith. The King is too young to skill of such matters. . . .' Should his ambassador in England be restrained from celebrating the Mass, Charles warned that he 'should tomorrow depart . . .' and if Princess Mary 'might not have her Masses still . . . he would provide for her remedy. . . .'[1] Charles's tolerance had obviously been strained to the utmost, and the stormy interview ended with Wotton's distinct impression that the 'remedy' might not be merely a Spanish bluff. The spectre of war might yet indeed prove a potent 'remedy' for the Emperor's English cousin.

To Mary herself, Charles sent a comforting letter advising her to submit to demands that she alone hear the Mass in her house. And if faced with an ultimatum to relinquish the Mass, she must do so but must also refuse to conform to the 'new religion' or to 'commit such enormity as communicating in both kinds. . . .' To Mary, whose temperament made such dissimulation impossible, the advice that *she* might observe the ritual and deprive others in her household was depressing. And to relinquish the beloved ceremony itself would be admitting a defeat she could only view as monstrous.

Charles, however, was in a position to make himself felt in England since, for the moment, the Emperor was enjoying unparalleled power. By a series of fortunate marriages, he had consolidated his vast empire. His brother, Ferdinand, was powerful in Germany, and his sister, Mary, was Queen of Hungary. His young son, Philip, had been sent to the Flemish court, and his grandchildren were marrying into the courts of Europe. His seventy-three-year-old mother, the mad Juana, a sister of Catherine of Aragon, still languished in her cell in the battlemented Palace of Tordesillas. She would linger for four more years and then die a tormented death in the same year as her son, the Emperor, would lay down his sword and prepare for death himself.

But in 1551, Charles's political star was in the ascendant. His extraordinary ability, sound judgment, and cool tenacity had been tested when the Protestant leaders in Germany had bound themselves together in the Smalcaldic League. Because of his external wars with France, the Turk and the Barbary pirates, Charles had never waged war against the coalition, and the moral conflict engendered by the Reformation in England had only clouded further relationships with that country. While Pope Paul III cried out for retribution against the heretical England, he was also jealous of the extent to which the Imperial Eagle's shadow hovered over so much of Europe. Wishing an ally for his own Papal armies and as a buttress to his own invincibility when the inevitable showdown should occur, he so wooed Henri II and French interests that Charles had been heard dryly to remark that if the Pope's body were ever opened, three fleurs-de-lis would be found upon his heart.

Charles had ultimately vanquished the leaders of the Smalcaldic League at the Battle of Muhlenberg and entered Augsburg in great triumph, a weary, ageing warrior, ailing in a body tortured with gout and conscious that since his old opponents Henry VIII and Francis I were dead, his remaining years would be challenged by more youthful and aggressive adversaries.

Charles had hoped the Council of Trent might foster some method of pacifying the differing religious factions inside his Empire. When he annexed two Italian principalities which had been given by Pope Paul III to his natural son, Peter Louis Farnese, the Pope, in retribution, withdrew the Council from Trent to Bologna, where it was hoped

Italian influence might predominate. Defensively, the Protestants objected; the Catholic countries fought among themselves. Within the Council chambers, the Spanish and Italian bishops battled while the Pope manœuvred everyone so his authority might not be subject to the Emperor. Jealousy and distrust were evident on all sides, and the tenor of the Council was revealed when one prelate, the Bishop of Capua, in blazing anger, 'did lay his hand on the beard of his brother prelate . . . and did tear away many of the hairs thereof.'[2]

The Protestants refused to acknowledge the Council of Trent's authority if it sat in Italy. Playing for time, in which he hoped passions might cool, Charles attempted to appease everyone by a temporary reprieve before the Council would be summoned again, to debate a firm foundation upon which a single faith, acceptable to all, might flourish. This was the famous *Interim*. It solved nothing, only delaying any final action, but at the time of Mary Tudor's continued persecution, it provided her with a potent and aggressive support in the form of her cousin, now master of most of Europe. It was patently obvious to all, especially the English Council, that the Emperor's 'remedy' for his cousin might find England, riddled with dissension as it was, a vulnerable target. For once, time was Mary's ally.

Frustrating though it might be, Warwick realised he was powerless to challenge Charles. The earl was too politically sophisticated to bear the burden of refusal himself; some scapegoat must be found to mollify the Emperor. And the resolution of the situation came from the least expected source: the young King himself.

When the Emperor's challenging message had been received, Warwick suggested the clergy be consulted since the issue involved was 'a point of conscience'. When Cranmer, Ridley, and their associates were informed that war with Spain might result over Mary's restriction and 'the realm . . . like to be utterly undone, if either the Emperor would take no nay or the King would give him no yea . . . ,' they acquiesced, after a night's deliberation, saying that 'although to give license to sin was sin, yet if all haste possible was observed, to suffer and wink at it [Mary's observance of Mass] for a time might be borne'.[3]

In line with Warwick's wish to include Edward in all decision making, the boy was invariably briefed by William Cecil before each Council meeting. In this instance, he was not. Ralph Starkey, a courtier who witnessed the meeting between King and Council, wrote an account which borders on humour, pathos, and naïveté:

A God's name! The King was now come into the Council chamber, sent for and set in such haste as though his realm had been already upon the sacking. Down is the Treasurer [Paulet] upon his knees, and then might the King guess the matter was bad, for when it had either profit or pleasure to the King, the Treasurer was not put to the pain. Down go the rest. Was not this beginning able to bid a King beware of sleights and to tell him there was some practice in hand?...⁴

Edward was informed of the Emperor's ultimatum—'a message of war if I would not suffer the Princess to use her Mass', as he later wrote in his *Chronicle*. Having no knowledge of the Council's desire to temporise until the political winds had shifted, he was astonished and angrily asked the ministers, 'How are these perils grown?' When it was explained one must beware of Charles's antagonism and, for the moment, allow Mary some leniency, the boy retorted heatedly 'to license his sister to use idolatry in his realm, he neither could do it as Councillors' advises, neither would agree to it at any King's or Kaiser's entreaty!'

The Council sat stunned; they had expected no opposition. When Cranmer attempted to justify the bishops' decision by referring to Biblical parallels, Edward turned on his godfather sharply and said that 'as examples when they are good, and had God's word to allow them. ... so are evil examples set out ... but utterly to warn us ... !' He then, in turn, parroted numerous instances in Scripture in support of this view-point, and the joust between King, Archbishop, and Council began in earnest. Edward, however, continued adamant. 'I shall require you to fear God with me ... and to condemn any peril, than to set light God's will, thereby to please an Emperor!' he cried. The Council was quiet, each member struggling with his own reaction to a childish obstinacy which refused to consider the political implications involved in the royal stubbornness.

At last they were confronted with the offspring of the efforts of the former Protector, the Archbishop of Canterbury, and the new Earl of Warwick. Here was a boy obsessed by a new religious creed which had been dinned into him night and day, a child whose conscience was an inviolate possession, a royal personage who had been repeatedly told of his divine right to govern. Here was the young King of whom the Spanish ambassador had said, 'He is naturally of a gentle nature, but is being corrupted by false doctrines and practices.' And, the ambassador might have added, whose religious convictions were unhampered by any thoughts of prudence, of diplomatic or political expediency so strong in his Council. For Edward there was no recanting or turning back. 'If the Emperor speak but in sport to see whether I be knit to my religion or not, I should stain it and shame myself in abandoning it. If the Emperor mean good earnest, God I hope meaneth but to taste us in sport, and will give us stomach to serve Him where we ought, and to gratify the Emperor where we may.'

He had one final word for the councillors, the clerics, and his godfather. 'I know,' he said, 'God is able to defend me against as many Emperors as ever the world had, if they came at once with as many men as they had in all their whole times!' When Edward concluded that the Emperor did not frighten or deter him, that the Council should not try to persuade him to deny his conscience, that 'he would choose the surer side', meaning his God, the Council knew themselves beaten. Referring to Charles, Edward continued, '. . . if he will not learn, let his harms teach us not to fall into God's hands, Who hath made the days of a King a long span—their lives are as nothing before Him.' Misguided as he might be in his refusal to compromise, and reckless in his faith that divine right was on his side, Edward Tudor confronting an assemblage of adult peers and churchmen with his own idealism and conviction which, in turn, so emphasised their hypocrisy, moves the heart. It tantalises the imagination to consider the councillors' emotions as they realised they now had no retort strong enough to move the boy.

To one last warning that he personally might suffer some danger, Edward said, 'I must do as God giveth me in commandment, and then I shall not want to lay for myself in reason, nor want an aid able to overturn the force of the whole world, in case it come wholly against me' and added he would rather die than agree to any procedure which he knew to be against the truth. When a councillor hurriedly pointed out that it was God's prerogative to take a life and that Edward had responsibility for the safety of the realm, the boy said, 'I will shed my tears for both. . . .' And then the strain of the moment having reached breaking point, he was no longer a mighty King and a Vicar of Christ on earth but merely a child as he burst into tears and sobbed, 'Let me alone. . . .'[5]

Faced with the Emperor's ultimatum and Edward's determination, Warwick made one last attempt to coerce Mary into observing the Act of Uniformity. Her Comptroller, Sir Robert Rochester, and two other household officers, one Mr Waldegrave and Sir Francis Inglefield, were summoned to the Council and ordered to prohibit Mary's chaplains from observing the Mass. Though they bravely protested and made many excuses 'to avoid the report of this matter unto her Grace . . .' they were forced, on pain of imprisonment, to comply. With troubled hearts, the three made their way to Copt Hall in Essex where Mary was spending the summer. She had received similar messages from the Council, and when the gentlemen attempted to present their commission, she told them bluntly she knew their message and 'they need not rehearse it'. When they insisted they must obey the Council and read their orders, she 'consented to hear their message, but was marvellously offended . . . and forbade them to declare the same to her chaplains and household'. If they did, Mary continued, 'they must no longer consider her as their mistress; moreover, she would leave the house directly.'

The three officers parted from her in distress, their reluctance to perform the distasteful task offset by their relief that it was finally over, and they excused themselves from proceeding further 'fearing that the troubling ... might bring on an attack of her old disease'. Instead, they returned to London to face the wrath of the Council who sharply rebuked them for not dealing with the chaplains and again commanded them to return to Copt Hall separately and execute their orders. Rochester found the courage to answer by saying, he 'had had enough of the first commission. They might send him to prison if they liked, but as to face his mistress on any such errands, he would *not!*'[6]

The disgraced officers were temporarily lodged in the Fleet and Tower, and a further commission, composed of Lord Chancellor Richard Rich[7] and the royal Secretary, Sir William Petre, visited Mary a few days later. With them they brought Sir Anthony Wingfield, Edward's own Comptroller, to replace the deposed Rochester. Mary received them on the morning of August 29, following two weeks of uneasy waiting. She had written to Edward, appealing for his intercession, explaining her distress that 'any of my servants should move or attempt me in matters touching my soul. . . .' and courageously emphasising that the faith in which she had been brought up must remain the same, for 'my conscience doth not only bind me, which by no means will suffer me to think one thing and do another. . . .' Edward's cool reply only stressed the gulf existing between them. He, too, had a conscience, wrote her royal brother from Windsor, and out of concern for her he was, therefore, sending his Chancellor and two councillors with a message 'touching the order of your house' to which Mary was commanded to 'give them firm credit in those things they shall say to you from us'.

Mary had no alternative other than to receive her visitors, for, with the knowledge that her brother had seemingly abandoned her, there was now no authority in England to whom she could turn for help. During her relatively peaceful summer at Copt Hall, she had tried to suppress the nagging doubt that such calm could not last, and she wondered—how must she react when the ultimatum became final? Her anxiety was revealed in the tightly pressed lips and the forehead perpetually creased by a nervous frown. She attempted to hide her misgivings by concealing her hands which, under stress, she would clasp and unclasp in the folds of her long gown, from which a large gold cross hung conspicuously from the girdle. Nothing, however, could hide the scorn in her eyes as she waited in silence for her visitors to read their order. She knew them all well; they had been about her father's court for years. Memory of her father gave her courage to speak, and as the Chancellor handed her Edward's message, from which dangled the Great Seal, she fell to her knees and said, 'For the honour of the King's hand . . . she would kiss the letters, but not for the matter it contained in them.' Arising, she opened the dispatch, saying ruefully, 'I would take it to proceed not from his Majesty, but from you of the Council. . . .' She then stood apart from the group and quietly read the letter carefully. 'Ah! Good Mr Cecil took much pains here!' they heard her say almost humourously. As she returned to the visitors, Rich launched into a lengthy explanation, earning Mary's suggestion that he hurry: 'For', she said, 'I am not well at ease . . . and I will make you short answer, notwithstanding that I have already declared and written to His Majesty plainly, with my own hand.'[8]

For the next half hour the commissioners sought to convince the King's sister. When they attempted to show her the names of all who had subscribed to the restriction of the Mass, she waved them aside contemptuously saying, 'I do not care for a rehearsal of their names. . . . I know you be all of one sort therein.' Again she repeated her conviction that any religious changes should wait until Edward 'shall come to such years that he may be able to judge these things himself'. The ministers, however, did not wish to dwell upon the royal competence. Instead they reverted to the restriction of her chaplains' celebration of the Mass and demanded that no service other than 'that set forth by the laws of the realm' should be said in her house. For this, Mary was ready, and she retorted that she would always obey her brother in every commandment saving this one thing and rather than do that 'she would lay her head on a block and suffer death.' Her voice was tremulous as she finished, 'If my chaplains do say no Mass, I can hear none. . . . I know it shall be against their wills, as it shall be against mine.' Then anger overtook Mary as she referred again to her priests. 'They know what they have to do. The pain of your laws is but imprisonment . . . and if they will refuse . . . for fear of that imprisonment, they may do therein as they will —but none of your new service shall be used in my house!'

Somewhat nonplussed by the vehemence of the tiny woman's answers, Rich shifted his tactics and mentioned the Emperor's promise that she might have the Mass without restriction. So far Mary had withstood their entreaties with an iron will, but at the mention of the discredited promise, she could no longer contain her emotions. Near tears, she repeated that seven of the Council knew of the promise and the Emperor, 'whom I believe better than all of you' had written to her of his support. 'Though you little esteem the Emperor', she said bitingly, 'yet should you show more favour to me for my father's sake—for he made the more part of you all—almost out of nothing!'

As the commissioners made ready to depart, they stated they would leave Sir Anthony Wingfield as a replacement for the imprisoned Rochester. Mary would have none of it. 'I will appoint my own officers; I have years sufficient for that purpose!' she cried; 'if any such man is left here, I will go out of the gates for we two will not dwell in one house!' Then, tiring of the procedure and denouncing their 'fair words' which hid the deeds 'which be always ill towards me', Mary held out a ring to the amazed Lord Chancellor Rich and in a shaking voice said, 'I most humbly command myself to His Majesty. I will die his true subject and sister and obey his commandments in all things, except in these matters of religion touching the Mass and the new service.' After handing the ring to Rich, she adjusted the folds of her skirt and turned away, speaking almost as if to herself, '. . . but this shall never be told to the King's Majesty'.

From a window she watched silently as, after some discussion, her chaplains gave the required promise to the King's emissaries. Mary had regained her composure, but as she saw her priests bullied into submission, her pride and temper made her again summon the Chancellor and his companions to the window embrasure. When they offered to come inside to her chamber, she waved them aside and delivered her message. She had won one small victory, and she was feminine enough to wish her persecutors to be aware of it. She had not accepted the new Comptroller. She asked that Rich request the Council to consider the return of Rochester, and that very soon. 'For, since his departing, I take the account myself of my expenses and learn how many loaves of bread he made of a bushel of wheat', said Mary. She was tired of it all. 'I know my father and my mother never brought me up with baking and brewing and, to be plain with you, I am weary of my office. Therefore, if my Lords will send my officer home, they shall do me pleasure. Otherwise, if they will send him to prison, I beshrew him if he go not to it merrily, and with a good will.' She waited a moment to be certain they were catching every word as she spoke out to them and, taking the casement window latch in hand, finished, 'And I pray God to send you well to do in your souls and your bodies too—for some of you have but weak bodies!'[9] And with that, as the Lord Chancellor, Comptroller, and royal Secretary gaped in amazement, Mary Tudor shut the window with a resounding bang.

Through the remainder of the year, the disgraced Mary remained isolated at Copt Hall. At Hatfield, Elizabeth diligently pursued her studies, her newly acquired sobriety a suitably grave accompaniment to her plain, almost ugly attire. They did not see their royal brother before he left on a summer progress which successfully endeared him to his subjects, as much by his physical beauty as by his gracious manner. 'He is of good disposition, and fills the country with the best expectations, because he is handsome, graceful, of proper size, shows an inclination to generosity and begins to wish to understand what is going on', wrote Barbaro, the Venetian ambassador. 'In the exercise of the mind and the study of languages, he appears to excel his companions. He is fourteen years of age.'[10]

With such a prize, the Council had continued to hope for a betrothal of Edward to Mary Stuart, the little Queen of Scots. Therefore, 'for the nourishing of amity between his realm and France', an exchange of honours between Henri II and Edward was instigated when William Parr, the Earl of Northampton, a brother of Katherine Parr, visited France to invest the King with the Order of the Garter. Hopefully, he would also induce Henri to 'send the Queen of Scotland to England for the consummation of the marriage'. Suspecting there might be considerable opposition to the marriage after Pinkie Cleugh, Northampton carried a second commission—the proposal of Edward for the hand of the six-year-old Elizabeth, Henri's eldest daughter.

While awaiting the French reply, Edward turned homewards from his progress, 'riding through Greenwich Park unto Blackheath with my Lord Derby, my Lord of Warwick, my Lord Admiral Clinton and Sir William Herbert, the trumpeters playing and all the guard in their doublets, and those with bows and arrows and halberds, two and two together and the King's Grace in their midst. . . .' Later, Edward wrote in his *Chronicle* that, on the same night, he supped at Deptford in a ship where 'I was banqueted by the Lord Clinton at Deptford where I saw the *Primrose* and the *Mary Willoughby* landed.'

Arriving at Hampton Court Palace, Edward prepared for the French envoys' visit, and on July 14 the distinguished Marechal de St Andre and a brilliant retinue from the French Court arrived to discuss the alliance and the terms of the dowry of Princess Elizabeth, the daughter of Henri II and Catherine de Medici. Two days later, the investiture of King Edward into the Order of St Michael was accomplished in impressive ceremonies in which Edward was arrayed in the Order's 'coat of silver with small fringe of gold, and over this the mantle, hood, tippet and collar', to be followed by the order's chain of scallop-shells which hung about his neck. An emotional interlude followed in which the French and English nobles embraced one another tearfully and, as Edward confessed in his *Chronicle*, 'after the Communion was celebrated, each of them kissed my cheek. . . .' There were several days of festivity— of tournaments, shooting, and hunting with the hounds, of fireworks and banquets in the evenings after the ministers had negotiated during the day. Edward played his lute for the visitors, and they dutifully watched as he practised riding in the tiltyard. Here Edward was obviously showing great improvement, and when one ambassador complimented him, he sighed and said, 'It is but a small beginning . . . as time passes, I hope to do better.'

St Andre and his companions also noted the extreme pressure on the boy-King who must excel in everything while showing great charm, graciousness, and ease at all times. They noted many instances when he appeared to be under strain. Wily and hardened as they were in the political mainstream which was their calling, they were undeniably impressed by the young King of whom one wrote he was 'as an angel in human form—a more beautiful face and figure, it was impossible to imagine, set off by the brilliance of a mass of diamonds, rubies, pearls, emeralds and sapphires.' When M. de Theligney du Bois-Daulphin was designated to remain in England as the new resident French ambassador, the visitors also savoured a bit of Edward's wit. Du Bois-Daulphin was a very tall and uniquely stout French gentleman, and at the final banquet two weeks later, gesturing to the portly envoy, Edward whispered to the departing M. le Marechal, 'You will bring me to shame through this ambassador for, not finding in this country the delicate food he is used to in France, he will waste away, which will be a constant reproach to me. . . .'[11] and he joined St Andre in the great burst of laughter that followed. When the embassy made its departure, gifts were dispensed all around. Edward gave St Andre a diamond ring, 'for your Lordship's pains—and also for my memory', said the boy. An unwonted and unusual attachment had formed between Edward and the distinguished old Frenchman during the short visit. The memory did not fade; years later St Andre would speak of the young King of England amid tears of affection and regret.

By Edward's side at all the royal functions moved the two foremost gentlemen of the court, the Earl of Warwick and the Duke of Somerset, now fully restored to his place in the Council. Outwardly, Warwick seemed satisfied with his responsibility in the management of the King and the realm. Inwardly, however, he had never ceased to resent the presence of Somerset. And, within the court, the continued appearance of the former Protector at Council meetings—meetings he had once ruled with a heavy hand—was viewed with amused scepticism by all. Wagers were made that the apparent 'great love and friendship. between the two men, a relationship cemented by the marriage of their children, would not last. Somerset's continued championing of Bishop Gardiner and Mary Tudor, and his criticism of Warwick's monetary procedures, had been a constant thorn in the earl's side. While Somerset favoured reform in religion, he decried the too hasty and unplanned measures the Council had taken. Many troops had been disbanded, no new warships built, and fortifications had been allowed to decay owing to lack of funds. His concern for the social conditions and welfare of the common people had earned him their undisputed loyalty—and Warwick's scorn. The people as such meant little to Warwick, and to a man, they detested him.

The earl's religious convictions usually took the prevailing form demanded by monarch or church; for the moment he was as rigidly Protestant as Edward, over whom he had established a firm control. Warwick often appeared in Edward's bedchamber after everyone else had retired and would brief the boy on matters to be discussed the following day, leaving a tired child to contemplate his responsibilities when sleep came with difficulty. He indulged Edward in his delight in pageantry, often parading the boy through the City, dressed in the silks, damasks, brocades, and jewels he so loved. He impressed upon Edward the value of the French alliance in view of the Emperor's attitude and a possible Spanish reprisal.

Two months after the departure of the French embassy, Warwick was at the height of his power, and on October 11, in the Great Hall of Hampton Court Palace, another significant investiture took place when the Earl of Warwick and those particular adherents to his cause received honours from the King's hand. William Cecil and John Cheke were knighted. Jane Grey's father, the Earl of Dorset, became the Duke of Suffolk. Old Paulet, the Lord Treasurer, was made the Marquis of Winchester and Sir William Herbert became the Earl of Pembroke. But the most glittering prize was reserved for Somerset's opponent. From plain John Dudley, son of a disgraced and executed civil servant of the previous reign, one who had climbed successively to a viscounty and an earldom, the Earl of Warwick now assumed the noble and ancient title of the Percy family, becoming the Duke of Northumberland.[12] As one of the four dukes in England (and one of these, the aged Norfolk, still languished in the Tower) Northumberland was in a position of power and authority actively to encompass his great rival's downfall.

He was unwittingly assisted in this by one of Somerset's own retainers, Richard Whalley. When Whalley attempted to sound out members of the Lower House of Lords (where there was considerable dissension over Warwick's elevation to a dukedom) on Somerset's regaining the Protectorship at the next Parliament, he was lodged in the Fleet Prison for several days until his conversations were adjudged 'foolish prattle' and he was dismissed. The matter might have died right there; it probably coincided with the *beginning* of a plot against Somerset. When rumours of another rebellion were heard and seditious bills were cast about the streets of London 'exciting the people against the Council', it was easy to infer that Somerset was behind it. Northumberland summoned Whalley to him and much impressed him by 'showing the inward grief of his heart with not a few tears' over Somerset's alleged subversive activities.

'What meaneth my Lord in this wise to discredit himself and why will he not see his own decay therein?' he questioned the uncomfortable

Whalley. 'Thinks he to rule and direct the whole Council as he will, considering how his late governance was misliked?' A few days previously Somerset and Northumberland had tangled in an argument over the continued imprisonment of Bishop Gardiner. Somerset wanted the cleric out of the Tower and was so vigorous in his defence that, as Northumberland said, 'He taketh and aspireth to have the self and same overdue an authority ... as his Grace had ... being Protector.' With his recent imprisonment in mind, Whalley abandoned Somerset, joined the Northumberland camp and repeated the conversation to William Cecil, now the Secretary of State, who reported it to the Council.

Fate then intervened to aid Northumberland's intrigues. One of Somerset's servants, ill of the sweating sickness at his London residence, Somerset House, caused the duke to remain at Syon House at Isleworth. During the time of the duke's enforced absence from Council meetings, the hand of Northumberland worked swiftly to bring his rival to bay.

The plot to destroy the Duke of Somerset is not easy to discern. It is a tragedy marked by Northumberland's eagerness to gamble on Somerset's vulnerability and the former Protector's own lack of suspicion concerning the extent of his opponent's malice. An account of Somerset's treasonous activities was supposedly divulged to the new Duke of Northumberland in the garden of his home four days before his elevation by Sir Thomas Palmer who, on his own admission, had led a 'profligate and abandoned life'. Somerset was planning to 'raise the North', Palmer said, naming as his confederates, Lord Grey, who was to incite the people, Sir Ralph Vane, who supposedly had 2,000 men ready to assault the royal guards, and Sir Thomas Arundel who was to secure the Tower, while Sir Miles Partridge would 'raise London and possess the Great Seal with the aid of the City apprentices'. The elderly Paget was to hold a banquet in his home for Northumberland and all the Council, at which they would be assassinated, said the informer. Incredibly, Palmer was neither detained nor examined by the Council, nor were any of Somerset's alleged accomplices accosted. Northumberland still was not positive the evidence was sufficiently damaging.

The elevation of Warwick and his adherents within the Council alarmed Somerset who sent for Mr Secretary Cecil, asking the meaning behind the Council changes and noting his concern that his enforced absence had created an aura of danger for his welfare. 'I suspect some ill ...' he confided to Cecil, certain the man's long tenure in his service would cause him to reveal any possible peril. The cool answer he received failed to reassure him. If your Grace be not guilty, you may be of good courage', said William Cecil, 'If you are, I have nothing to say but to lament you.'[13]

Somerset bitterly resented his abandonment by Cecil. The encounter with the man his patronage had raised to power and influence only emphasised the great danger which was swiftly enveloping him. He sent a bitter 'letter of defiance' to Cecil, from whom he could rightfully have expected more support, and then, attempting to put the anxious questions from his mind, continued to sit at the Council table and pursue his official duties. There was no question of his leaving the realm which, at that particular moment, he might have done easily. In view of his former conduct, when he fled with Edward to Hampton Court at the first sign of the Council's uneasiness with his Protectorship, his behaviour is telling. He obviously felt the rumours would die, and since he had done nothing that could be construed as treasonous, the best possible procedure would be to follow a normal routine and lull any suspicions.

It was, therefore, a great shock when, On October 16, five days after Warwick's investiture, Somerset was arrested at Hampton Court and formally accused of high treason. He was taken to the Tower, and his family followed him a few hours later. Though nothing had been proved against Somerset, Northumberland wasted no time in defaming him, and on the very next day letters were sent to all 'parishes, Emperors, Kings, ambassadors, noblemen and chief men, of the late conspiracy', which Somerset had allegedly masterminded.

By the middle of November, depositions had been taken from witnesses within both the Somerset and Northumberland camps. Somewhere in between these two factions, a few innocent people were bound to be tarnished with suspicion or hurt by the accusations against 'the good Duke'. One of these was Edward Tudor. He had been kept in complete ignorance of Somerset's suspicious activities until two days before his uncle's arrest, and when Northumberland gave the boy his own version of the plot, Edward was incredulous. Since the frightening experience at Hampton Court, his relationship with Somerset had been pleasant and unstrained. The Protector no longer had any power to curtail the royal privileges, therefore the boy could enjoy his uncle's company on the rare occasions when they were together. With no father for guidance or companionship, Edward's relationship with men such as John Cheke, Northumberland, and Somerset compensated for this lack. He and the former Protector were not close; Somerset was not as easy with children as Northumberland, or as intimate and comfortable as Cheke was with the King. Nevertheless, Edward found it hard to believe that the uncle who had moved with quiet competence and little provocation throughout the court, who had been conscientious in his attendance at the Council table, could actively plot Northumberland's downfall. He was bewildered by the sudden turn of events and shocked at the implication of the charges—and the penalty that might result.

Bit by bit, Northumberland hammered home to Edward the great peril under which the Council members had lived. He spoke of Somerset's dislike of the French alliance and his desire to impede the progress of the 'new religion', of a return to the hated Six Articles and possibly even the Pope himself! Similarly, Somerset was known as one of the Lady Mary's staunchest supporters, and his duchess was one of her best friends—could Edward not understand the threat this presented to the French alliance in view of the Emperor's attitude? Edward was always uncomfortable when reminded of Mary's religious practices and the threat of Spanish intervention on her behalf. But still the boy remained unconvinced, and when the Council presented documents asking for the supreme penalty, he refused to sign them.[14] Edward's apparent reluctance—or fear—was too much for Northumberland. For the first time he lost his temper with the King and, in a bullying tone, shouted at the boy, banging his fist as he reviewed the charges against Somerset. Repeatedly he stressed the duke's inward violence—had he not placed Edward in great danger when fleeing from Hampton Court to Windsor Castle? For emphasis, he took care that only those who would condemn Somerset were around Edward. The ambassadors at court during this period often found the King 'pensive' and 'grieving'; to a man, they were positive the boy's mind was being poisoned against his uncle. It took six weeks to accomplish, but inevitably the fourteen-year-old monarch was no match for the monumental aggressiveness of Northumberland. By the end of November, all was ready.

It was, perhaps, at Edward's own insistence that Somerset was granted an open trial. It was within the prerogative of Northumberland and the Council to deny it, and, conscious of the duke's great popularity with the common people, they would have preferred a quiet sentencing. The trial was set for December 1, and on the day before, a proclamation was issued 'that every household should keep within doors, and that in each house one man at least should be ready with his arms, to be called out, if order was disturbed.'[15] On the morning of the trial, however, the area in front of Westminster Hall was packed with people who had defied the proclamation, anxious to support 'the good Duke, by their presence if nothing else. Inside the Hall, Somerset faced his interrogators. Paulet, now the Marquis of Winchester, sat as High Steward of England under his cloth of estate. Behind him were the twenty-six lords. By nine o'clock the trial was under way, and as he searched every face and listened to the indictments as they reverberated throughout the vast length of the Hall, Somerset became angry and bitter. He declared he had 'never minded to raise the North', and the idea of raising the City of London and assaulting the royal guards 'was too extravagant to enter into the head of any man whose intellect was not deranged', he exclaimed.[16] It would have been a 'mad matter', cried the duke, for him to 'enterprise with his one hundred men against nine hundred'.

[266]

What emerges from the remaining depositions of witnesses and prisoners[17] read at the trial is that the former Protector was brought to trial and sentenced because of an *intent* rather than an actual illegal act. Upon his own admission (and in this, perhaps, lies the most convincing statement of his innocence) is Somerset's confirmation that, in a moment of frustration, anger, and despondency over the Council's policies, he *had* thought of assassinating Northumberland and certain councillors. Later, he said, he 'determined after the contrary' and merely thought of '*apprehending*' the differing faction within the Council and replacing it with his own supporters. He agreed he had spoken to Lord Arundel of the matter and then 'was sorry he had gone so far'. Arundel confirmed Somerset's statement that their later intention towards the Council had not 'meant any hurt to their bodies, but we *would* have called them to answer and to reform things'. That such was the only provable piece of evidence against the Duke of Somerset is seen in the fact that, with the exception of Sir Thomas Palmer whom Somerset called a 'worthless villain', no other witnesses were summoned. Lord Grey was neither called nor examined; Lord Paget, in whose house, allegedly, the assassination was to have taken place was neither examined nor arrested at first; later he was lodged in the Tower for questioning, but never tried. Arundel was never even brought to trial. Only the lesser accomplices were charges and punished. That the *apprehension* of certain ministers and a desire to 'change and reform things' was Somerset's only crime is shown in the failure of the prosecution ever to prove otherwise. A few bitter remarks and a desire for some change of the Council's policies, however, hardly constituted treason. Therefore the charge was abandoned, but after six hours of deliberation, the duke was found guilty of violating the Act of Unlawful Assembly,[18] a weak charge to be sure, but as such violation was a felony and carried the death penalty, equally capable of removing Somerset from the scene as a charge of treason. His fellow peer, the Marquis of Winchester, pronounced the death sentence as Somerset, paling and staggering at the verdict, sank to his knees. Northumberland rose and said, 'Oh, Duke of Somerset, you see yourself a man in peril of life and sentenced to die. Once before I saved you in a like danger, nor will I desist to serve you now, though you may not believe me. Appeal to the mercy of the King's Majesty, which I doubt not he will extend to you. For myself, gladly I pardon all things which you have designed against me, and I will do my best that your life may be spared.'[19]

As Somerset left the Hall under heavy guard, the axe of the Tower was not, as custom demanded, carried before him since he had been acquitted of treason. The waiting throng, mistakenly assuming Somerset had been pardoned, went wild and 'when they saw the Axe of the Tower put down, made such a shriek and casting up of caps, that it was heard into the Long Acre beyond Charing Cross . . .' said a witness. The premature shout caused those awaiting the verdict to ring the church bells and to light bonfires (which signalled the lighting of similar fires all the way to Bath) indicating that Somerset was innocent. 'God save him!'—'God save the Good Duke!' the people shouted with joyous enthusiasm and relief. One can hope it cheered the doomed man, still in shock at the severity of the sentence.

There was great indignation throughout the realm when the verdict was made known. On the Continent, a genuine puzzlement echoed the Queen of Hungary's remark. 'The thing' she said, 'is very strange.' The King's anxiety for his uncle, and the clamour of the people for the release of their favourite, only emphasised to Northumberland the necessity of annihilating his great rival. When Edward remained hesitant, Northumberland boldly told the boy that Somerset had confessed to the murder plot, though no official evidence exists to support his statement. [20] He added that Somerset had even pleaded for his life at the sentencing when, in truth, the condemned man had pleaded for his *wife* and children. When Edward continued to vacillate, Northumberland overcame his reluctance by insinuating Edward did not have the spiritual and physical welfare of his realm at heart. Dutifully Edward drew up an outline to examine 'the matter for the Duke of Somerset's confederates to be considered as appertaineth to our surety and quietness of our realm, that by their punishment, example may be shown to others'. Later, after it had passed to Cecil, it was partially erased and an interpolation substituted which reads, '. . . by their punishment and *execution according to the laws*'. At last the weary boy gave in, and to Northumberland's intense relief, he signed the hated documents. When, several days later, a reprieve was asked for one of Somerset's confederates, Edward had the satisfaction of reproving the Council, saying in a hardened tone, 'How is this, my Lords? There was no one to beg mercy for my uncle—yet for this man you all come! My command is that the law's behest be carried out!' [21]

On January 22, 1552, at nine o'clock in the morning of a bitterly cold day, 'splendidly attired as he used to be when about to attend upon the King', Edward Seymour, the Duke of Somerset, appeared on the scaffold on Tower Hill. A thousand men-at-arms ringed the execution site, pressing against the mob which had descended from all parts of the City and the surrounding countryside. They shouted invective at the soldiers and cheered Somerset when he appeared. Beckoning for silence, the duke had barely begun to speak to them when 'there was a rumbling as if it had been guns shooting, and great horses coming'. While the crowd shouted at the source of confusion—the arrival of a contingent of soldiers headed by Sir Anthony Browne—others ran in fear to their houses nearby, and the press of the jostling throng caused many to fall into the Tower moat. 'A pardon! A pardon!' screamed those nearest the scaffold, as they surged forward to take Somerset from the platform. But Somerset knew there was no reprieve. 'The good Duke all this while stayed', said a witness, 'and with his cap in his hand, waved the people to come together saying these words to their calls for pardon. "There is no such thing, good people, there is no such thing; it is the ordinance of God thus for to die, wherewith we must be content. I beseech you do not grieve for my fortunes, keep yourselves quiet and still, and make no disturbance or attempt to save me, for I do not desire a longer life. I pray you now let us pray together for the King's Majesty, to whose Grace I have always been a faithful, true and most loving subject."' And with a great moan, the populace replied, 'Yea, yea, yea,' while others muttered resentfully, 'It is found now too true.'[22]

After a 'brief confession unto God' made to Dr Cox, Edward's old tutor and now the Dean of Chichester, Somerset knelt in the straw and suffered his collar to be turned around his neck. He covered his face with his handkerchief, and one witness noticed 'before his eyes were covered there began to appear a red colour in the midst of his cheeks'. Awaiting the stroke, he was commanded again to rise and adjust his doublet, which hindered the executioner's aim. Doing so, he again knelt in the straw and crying, 'Jesus, save me. Lord Jesus save me. . . . !' at the third repetition, the executioner brought the sword down on the defenceless man's neck while the people 'made great moan and lamentation', crowding around the scaffold and dipping their handkerchiefs or pieces torn from their clothing in his blood to preserve as relics.

And so died the ambitious Edward Seymour, Duke of Somerset, the second uncle of the King to be beheaded. Whatever his faults—and they were many—such a death was hardly justified for one who had sought to serve the King and realm with some degree of integrity, if not wisdom. He was sentenced entirely upon the testimony of unscrupulous and untrustworthy witnesses; not a shred of evidence exists to demonstrate his guilt in working actively for Northumberland's assassination. His intention—and one which he soon discarded as unworkable—seems to have been merely to wrest from Northumberland the power he himself had once enjoyed. And this he was foolish—or trusting—enough to reveal to one or two associates. 'All this smoke could not be without some fire' said one historian, 'which whosoever kindled first, there is no doubt but that the Earl Dudley blew the coals and made it seem greater than it was.'[23] Once he was marked and his adherents—particularly William Cecil whom he trusted to the last—deserted him, there was no hope for Somerset. He was alone at the end. He had sought no help from Mary Tudor, aware of her uncompromising position with the King and Council. Mary, realising her own inadequacy, had not wished to endanger either herself or Somerset's family by any support of the duke.

When the doomed man asked Elizabeth, now wholly in favour with both her brother and his Council, to exert her influence on his behalf, the girl had replied that 'being so young a woman, she had no power to do anything in his behalf', and that 'the King was surrounded by those who took good care to prevent her from approaching too near the court and she had no more opportunity of access to His Majesty. . . .' than Somerset himself.

Even Edward, whose mind had been poisoned against his uncle, could do little but accept what Northumberland and the Council chose to tell him. The duke ordered an almost feverish display of Christmas merry-making to distract the monarch and his court 'for the especial purpose of recreating and refreshing the mind of the young King, who seemed to take the trouble of his uncle somewhat heavily.'[24] On the day of the execution, January 22, 1552, the King wrote briefly in his *Chronicle*, 'The Duke of Somerset had his head cut off upon Tower Hill between eight and nine o'clock in the morning.' It was all Edward Tudor would say of the tragic event. To the Spanish ambassador, de Scheyve, however, on the day of Somerset's execution, he confided sadly, 'I would not have believed that he would have been a traitor.'

Chapter Sixteen

THOUGH Northumberland bore the onus of guilt for the execution of 'the Good Duke', the last year of Edward's life was clouded by the death of his second uncle, and he was not spared some public condemnation. Mistress Elizabeth Huggons, a servant in the Duchess of Somerset's household, was heard to exclaim, 'The King is an unnatural nephew—I wish I had the jerking of him!' At the encouragement of her companions, she became even more daring, telling them of a rumour in the household that Northumberland might wed his younger son to a lady of the royal line. 'Have at the Crown—with your leave!' Mistress Huggons finished bitterly, with a rude gesture. When her remark was repeated, she was hauled before the Council and committed to the Tower for a lengthy imprisonment to contemplate the extent of her 'unseemly sayings, neither meet to be spoken, nor counselled of any hearer'.

Edward, apparently, had mixed feelings. At first he 'gave no token of any ill-tempered passion, as taking it not agreeable to majesty openly to declare himself'. But as time went on, 'he would often sigh and let fall tears. Sometimes, he was of the opinion that he [Somerset] had done nothing that deserved death, or, if he had, that it was very small, and proceeded rather from his wife than from himself.' Northumberland and the Council could see the King's distress. 'Albeit, his lords did much to help dispel any dampy thoughts which the remembrance of his uncle might raise, by applying him with great variety of exercises and disports. . . .'[1] In order to circumvent any unhealthy musing about the tragedy on Edward's part, Northumberland gratified the boy's wish that his majority might be obtained when he was sixteen—two years earlier than Henry VIII's will had ordered. He sought to keep Edward busy, so any doubt or feelings of guilt might be pushed into the background. 'His Majesty,' said the Emperor's ambassador de Scheyve, 'is an intelligent lad, of quick, ready and well-developed mind, remarkable for his age. The Duke of Northumberland—whom he seems to love and fear—is beginning to grant him a great deal of freedom in order to

[271]

dispel the hostility felt for himself and to cause the King to forget the Duke of Somerset as quickly as possible.'[2] That the tragedy did remain in the boy's mind, however, is shown in a remark Edward made to Northumberland while shooting in the butts with the earl and some younger companions. Edward scored particularly well and Northumberland cried, 'Well aimed, my liege!' Edward's reply—either in derision or earnestness—was terse: 'But you aimed better when you shot off my good Uncle Somerset's head.'[3]

Northumberland's domination had caused Edward to chafe a bit in the past. With the prize of his own independent rule less than two years off, Edward, naturally industrious, relished his new duties and applied himself to them with youthful vigour. John Cheke protested to Northumberland about the demands the extra tasks made upon the boy's time. At Hampton Court, Windsor Castle, at the rambling old waterfront palace at Greenwich, or in his Whitehall or Westminster residences, the King's business followed him with merciless demands. As Edward grew older, the Council insisted that he sign all principal acts dealing with policy. This, in turn, necessitated more frequent attendance at routine Council meetings to familiarise himself with their affairs. The additional reading and signing of documents strained the boy's energy further, and he complained of headaches and tired eyes, causing Cheke to insist again that the work be done by others. But the Council ministers were adamant that the King attend to each item personally.

Other portions of Edward's precious time were allotted to visiting preachers, both foreign and English, and he continued to take copious notes from their sermons for later discussion. And there were the foreign ambassadors with whom he must be gracious, considerate, yet firm—and always alert. When their visits ended, he must deal with those who were concerned with the starvation, filth, and disease ravaging his subjects, and the lack of hospitals, proper housing, and adequate employment. He must ponder an even lower debasement of the coinage, remembering the debts his country owed on loans from Antwerp. For solace, he might turn to his godfather Cranmer's Prayer Book but this, too, might give him a moment of discomfort, for he would then remember the peril of his sister Mary's soul, for she still continued in her heathenish worship in the detested Popish ritual of the Mass.

But there were lighter moments when he could write to his dear friend Barnaby Fitzpatrick, now on official business for the King in France, and when he could dress in one of his beautiful court garments adorned with jewels and embellished with rich embroidery, in the violet colour he so loved that all his courtiers avoided wearing it out of respect for his preference. One such occasion was the reception and entertainment for Mary of Lorraine, the Queen-Dowager of Scotland. Returning home from France, her ship was driven by a storm to a landing at Portsmouth. She begged Edward's word of a safe conduct to her northern realm, and accordingly the whole court assembled for a stately welcome at the Palace of Westminster where, on November 4, a lavish banquet, supplied with 'beefs, muttons, veals, swans and other kinds of poultry meats, with fuel, bread, wine, beer and wax', was held. The guests included not only all high-ranking officials of the court, but also the King's cousins, Lady Margaret Douglas and Lady Jane Grey. Edward and the beautiful Mary—she was still only thirty-five—dined together, and, later, the King personally escorted his royal guest throughout the Palace to the handsome gardens that ran, terraced, down to the river's edge.

Here they conversed pleasantly until Edward mentioned his recent rejection as suitor for her daughter, Mary Stuart, the ten-year-old Queen of Scots. The Queen-Dowager, who later said that of all the things she had seen in England, 'I am best pleased with its King', did not mince her words but told the boy the opportunity had been lost, 'that the barbarities committed by the Duke of Somerset and others . . . in devastating her realm with fire and sword, had not only made the idea of English rule hateful to Scottish men, but had compelled her to seek aid from France and had also enforced them to send their young Queen there for refuge'. That the Scottish Queen-Dowager regretted the matter resulting in her daughter's betrothal to the Dauphin and Edward's to the French Princess Elizabeth is evident in her remark to her own nobles that 'she found more wisdom and solid judgment in the young King of England than she would have looked for in any three princes of full age that were then in Europe'.[4] At her departure and as a mark of esteem, Edward presented Mary with two magnificent horses and a valuable diamond ring which had belonged to his beloved step-mother, Katherine Parr.

During all the festivities attending Mary of Lorraine's visit, at the ceremonies to which the Suffolks and other lesser family members had hurriedly scrambled to be present, the most conspicuous absentees were the King's two sisters, Mary and Elizabeth Tudor. Both had been relieved at not being summoned. Mary dreaded attendance at court where she was deprived of her manner of worship. For Elizabeth, who had suffered a recurrence of the anaemia that was to plague her all her life, any summons to the City, where Thomas Seymour's brother was awaiting a similar execution, would only stir too many painful memories and reawaken old lingering suspicions. She had not spent two and a half years in retirement, often unwell and affecting a meekness she was finding it difficult to maintain, to lose it all by a resurgence of the hated gossip. Elizabeth was now nineteen, and her self-discipline, while admirable, did not come easily. Dr Aylmer, Jane Grey's tutor, said of Elizabeth, 'The King, her father, left her rich clothes and jewels, and I know it to be true that in seven years after his death, she never, in all that time, looked upon that rich attire and precious jewels . . . and I am sure that her maidenly apparel . . . made the noblemen's wives and daughters ashamed to be dressed and painted like peacocks . . .'.⁵

At Hatfield, where she had spent her years of seclusion, Elizabeth dominated the household which again included her two beloved servants, Katherine Ashley and Thomas Parry. For all his incompetence with the household accounts, Parry was still her cofferer, but now his mistress herself audited the books. They are revealing. Elizabeth liked comfort; her cellar was stocked not only with beer but with Rhenish and Gascoigne wines, and the food served at her table was varied and ample. Her servants were well clothed and paid, while her own clothing expenses were minimal. She spent little on books, lost nothing at cards or wagers as her sister did, and in further comparison with Mary, the alms dispensed at her gate were meagre indeed. Her gardens were productive, but instead of sending the bounty to court or other noble residences as gifts, she ordered the product to be sold. At the bottom of each page of her account book, the final figures were added, and she signed 'Elizabeth' in a firm flowing script. At the year's end, she was doubtless not surprised to find that her thrift had been rewarded and that she retained a surplus of £1,500.

Elizabeth's still somewhat delicate health, combined with Northumberland's reluctance to have her at court where her presence might strengthen the affection Edward felt for 'his sweet sister, Temperance', had resulted in brother and sister—who were often less than a few miles apart—not having seen each other since Elizabeth's hurried visit at the time of Mary's interrogation. But when she wished to be heard at court, Elizabeth did not hesitate either to speak for herself or through William Cecil,⁶ now the Secretary of State, for her long period of dependence on and attachment to Cecil had commenced. Whenever business concerning her estates, income, expenditures, her favours or preferments for retired or pensioned servants, had to be determined, she instructed Parry, 'Write my commendations in your letter to Mr Cecil. Tell him that I am well assumed though I send not daily to him, that he doth not, for all that, daily forget me; say, indeed, I assure myself thereof.' The unerring ability to appraise a man's worth—so characteristic of her father—was also one of Elizabeth's inherited strengths. And in William Cecil she knew she had found one trustworthy voice at court. They were much alike; both possessed a tough resilience and an awesome ability to scent danger or other hazards long before they materialised. It was a trait which attracted them to each other, cemented their relationship in later trials, and endured for nearly half a century longer.

Elizabeth also ventured to assert her own independence, always within the prescribed framework of court etiquette, of religious, political, and social protocol. When Somerset died, Durham House in the Strand, which had often served as her lodging place, was given to Northumberland. Elizabeth did not hesitate to express her displeasure; *she* had prior claim to Durham House! She wrote a scathing letter to the Lord Chancellor saying 'she was determined to come and see the King at Candlemas, and requested that she might have . . . St James's Palace for her use *pro tempore*, because she could not have her own things so soon ready at the Strand [Durham] House'. Northumberland refused, in a coolly amused manner, intimating Elizabeth was making a fuss as a bid for the King's attention. 'Herein, I trust His Highness will defend me unto Her Grace, who indeed I would not offend willingly . . .' he said, adding, 'I am sure Her Grace would not have done no less, though she had *kept* Durham House!'[7]

Whatever his amusement at Elizabeth's haughtiness, the girl was growing up, and what to do with the middle Tudor offspring presented a pressing problem for Northumberland. He did not feel she would remain quiescent for long. Marriage was the answer, but finding the proper husband was not easy. The candidates were suitably noble and invariably wealthy and always, in view of Elizabeth's professed Protestantism, followers of the 'new religion'. But the unsettled affairs in England, the King's own betrothal, and the reluctance to promise a member of the English blood royal to a foreigner, combined to keep Elizabeth single. Which was exactly the way she hoped things would continue.

Despite her drab clothing and lack of feminine adornment, the nine-teen-year-old Elizabeth Tudor was, indisputably, a handsome young woman. The soft nubile innocence of childhood had gone, replaced by a self-assured awareness of her own compelling personality and attractive well-proportioned figure. The rounded face had lengthened to a set, pointed chin; this, combined with the high-bridged nose of her father gave her an air of resolution and determination. The bright red hair, or as much of it as she allowed to peep from beneath her modest caps, enhanced the light, almost imperceptible brows and lashes of the penetrating grey-black eyes. The child had given way to the adult, and the very obvious strength of the young Elizabeth was clear to everyone. The Council and Northumberland handled her more gingerly than Mary, whose motives were recognisable and reactions predictable. Elizabeth, on the other hand, remained an enigma. The Council had found she could speak compellingly for herself, refusing to be manipulated, and in challenging her, they were likely to come off the poorer from the encounter. Therefore, for the most part, they were happy to leave her alone, permitting her, as she said, 'to enjoy her own right in quietness'.

In one respect, however, the Council had been very successful. For varying reasons, they intended to keep Edward and his sisters apart, and Mary's religious obstinacy and Elizabeth's disgrace—combined with Edward's own demanding responsibilities—had played into their hands. There had been little contact. For Mary, the estrangement over the Mass was bitter, for she loved Edward and considered him a tool in the hands of hardened, grasping manipulative councillors—men her father had raised to power, who had shockingly disregarded his wishes in the matter of religion and the governance of the realm. Elizabeth was not as subjective as Mary. Though she knew the wedge between her and her brother was calculated, she was less emotionally involved than Mary. She had seen Edward only once since those few glorious months with Katherine Parr when they had all been together as a family at Chelsea. Letters were a way of salving her conscience; health was always a safe topic for discussion. Elizabeth attributed her negligence in writing to her ill health, her 'evil head' she called it as she strove to make amends to her brother for their separation:

. . . for such is the power of true and unfeigned love, that it binds together those separated even by the longest distances; I, then, who, from your tender infancy, have even been your fondest sister—how can I do other than follow you with heart, thought, and even dumb words, I mean, with my letters? Thus, though absent from you in the one part of myself, namely, in body; yet, I may prove to your Majesty that I ever am and have been present to you in that other part—the mind. And, since it is in mind that true love consists, which, like a god, (as it were), is not necessarily confined by the restraints of space, I hope, nay, I am sure, that by no interval of space or time, can I be excluded from your good-will to me. . . .[8]

In April, 1552, the King fell ill. Despite his deceptive frailness, Edward had always enjoyed good health, and he wrote, almost proudly, in his *Chronicle*, 'I fell sick of the measles and small-pox', and stated that 'the Parliament brake up and, because I was sick and not able to go well abroad, I signed a Bill containing the names of the Acts I would have pass, which Bill was read in the House'.[9] Elizabeth rushed to console her brother and wrote emotionally,

What cause I had of sorrow, when I heard first of your Majesty's sickness, all men might guess, but none but myself could feel, which to declare were or might seem a point of flattery; and therefore, I omit to write it. But, as the sorrow could not be little, because the occasions were many, so is the joy great to hear of your good escape out of the perilous diseases. And, that I am fully satisfied and well assured of the same by your Grace's own hand, I must need give you my most humble thanks, assuring your Majesty, that a precious jewel at another time, could not so well have contented, as your letter in this case hath comforted me. . . .[10]

And so letters remained their contact, and Elizabeth was grateful for the seclusion which gave her an opportunity to redeem her reputation. The Seymour affair had rendered her intensely cautious. She had learned a powerful lesson: the heart must not be trusted, especially where the Crown was involved. Even her own servants—and she recognised the extent of their devotion—had betrayed her trust. She considered her retirement at Hatfield—apart from the brother who was only four years younger than herself—a blessing. It provided an opportunity for her to recoup her prestige, and that was best achieved away from the intrigues of court and the presence of the King. Her own security depended on the fact that she must be responsible for and accountable to herself only.

Edward's illness appeared slight, for in a matter of weeks he was writing to Barnaby Fitzpatrick that 'now we have shaken that quite away'. By May he was at Greenwich, watching his guard at archery practice, running at the ring with his younger knights and reviewing a muster of his men-at-arms in Greenwich Park. To dispel any fears of his subjects, he rode among the people who had shown great concern upon hearing of his illness. He had barely recovered and resumed his normal activities when John Cheke, away in London, fell victim to the sweating sickness. Edward was disturbed over his tutor's illness and daily sent messengers to the City to assess Cheke's condition. After several such visits, they returned with a long letter from Cheke containing much loving advice for Edward, which ended 'out of my death bed'. Reading the dying man's letter, Edward found it difficult to conceal his emotions. Cheke had fulfilled the role of father, brother, uncle, and friend. Silently, the King retired to the royal chapel. The next day, when one courtier commiserated with Edward over the possible loss of such a benefactor, the boy seemed more at ease, and astonished his listener by saying, 'No, he will not die at this time, for this morning, I begged his life from God in my prayers and feel assured they have been heard'.[11] Obviously in Edward's mind, one who was so assured of a divine right to rule also possessed the privilege of divine intercession. In any event, a few days later the welcoming news from Whitehall was that John Cheke had, indeed, made a surprising recovery, confounding the doctors and everyone else—except the King.

Edward's own recovery from what was normally a debilitating combination of diseases was deceptive. Though the effects of his illness appeared insignificant, his heavy responsibility—so unusual for one of his youth—made it difficult to co-ordinate his obligations with the prolonged periods of rest and leisure necessary for a complete recuperation. In June, a demanding summer progress was organised, and for the next four months the court accompanied its young King on a tour which delighted Edward, even as it exhausted him. Edward had previously seen nothing of the more distant parts of his realm. Northumberland had wisely concluded that his own unpopularity would add nothing to the progress, and Edward therefore relished the companionship of the now recovered John Cheke and other young courtiers. By the time the royal cavalcade reached Petworth, it was pared from 400 to 150 because of the difficulty in feeding so many horses. From Cowdray, the boy who had so recently been relieved of an invalid's diet, jubilantly wrote to Barnaby Fitzpatrick, 'we were marvellously, yea, rather excessively banqueted!' and later he told of the progress, 'We have been occupied in killing of wild beasts, in pleasant journeys, in good fare, in viewing of fair counties . . .'.

Within two months, the procession had reached Portsmouth, and here the more astute noted the King was beginning to tire. The feasts, the speeches, the long rides through varying weather, and the constant awareness of the royal demeanour were taking their toll. But Edward was as relentless of his own energies as he was in demanding the best from his companions. At Portsmouth, he not only observed the somewhat ancient and outmoded dockyards and fortifications but stayed long enough to draw up plans for their modernisation or replacement, which, as he exultantly wrote to Barnaby, preceded his arrival in Southampton, where he noted, 'the citizens had bestowed for our coming great cost in painting, repairing and ramparting of their walls'. Edward was impressed with his great southern city. 'The town is handsome,' he wrote, 'and for the bigness of it, as fair houses as be in London.' There were many elderly citizens in the crowd which welcomed the golden-haired boy as he rode in the great procession through their freshly gravelled and ornately bedecked streets on his splendid stallion, who could remember another, taller, royal youth who had visited them many years ago. They were content now to dismiss his sins —his many marriages, his sensuality, his extravagances, the execution of two of his Queens and the casting aside of their 'good Queen Catherine'. They remembered now only their magnificent Henry, and they cheered his son and the loud, rumbling column of horses, litters, and wagons; the soldiers, archers, and exuberant nobles in their imposing array. Edward, absorbing a measure of their feeling, endeavoured to respond even more enthusiastically to the cap waving, the joyous cries, and the tears of pride he observed on all sides of the brillant procession which he headed. Later, when visited by an elderly bishop who had known his father, the boy was so eager to talk to the man, he hurried to a window, calling to the old gentleman as he was escorted across the busy courtyard. He inquired after the prelate's health and, as the bishop said of the visit, 'exhibited a very fatherly and earnest manner' towards him.

Through the denseness of the New Forest, on to Christchurch, the progress continued to the magnificent cathedral city of Salisbury. There the exhausted boy was at last allowed to rest—for four days. In view of his obvious fatigue, the projected journey was shortened and a few days of diversion arranged. During a hunting expedition, Edward became detached from his companions, and suddenly a novel experience occurred. He was completely alone, on his own, in a remote, unfamiliar area. Riding along, unperturbed and enjoying the bizarre sensation of complete solitude, the King met a child near the village of Bower Chalk. She stared in awe at the boy—so handsome and wearing clothes the like of which she had never seen before! He nodded to her with grave courtesy and rode on—just as his companions, red-faced from their embarrassment and exertions in finding their missing monarch, galloped up to rejoin him. The little girl never forgot the experience. As 'Old Good Wife Dew', as she was known in her parish, she lived to the venerable age of one hundred and three and, in 1649, was still telling of the day she had met the handsome young Tudor King—lost on Falston Lane—who remained so vivid in her memory she could still recall the event ninety-seven years later.[12]

By September Edward was home, depleted in strength and energy, appearing weak and tired to those who worried over him. Immediately the problems and responsibilities awaiting his return overwhelmed him. He was distressed by the long quarrel between John Knox and Thomas Cranmer over minor details of interpretation of the rituals in the new Prayer Book. He was concerned too for the great ships of England being outfitted for voyages of exploration to the New World. But his subjects' welfare held his prior attention, and here at last he could do something. When a sermon was preached by Bishop Ridley, exhorting the King 'to be merciful to the poor, above all, that such as were in authority should travail to comfort and relieve such as were in sickness, sorrow, or any other adversity', it was no new theme. The misery of the people was an old story, well known and much lamented; little, however, had actually been done by Northumberland, who lacked the social conscience of the Protector. But Edward was older now and some wellspring of concern caused him to summon the bishop to discuss the situation with him in private. 'My Lord,' said Edward, 'you willed such as are in authority to devise some good order for their relief; wherein I think you mean me, for I am in the highest place, and therefore am the first that must make answer to God for my negligence . . .'.[13] The boy told Ridley he did not know how to proceed and, mentioning the bishop's 'approved wisdom and learning', earnestly desired that Ridley tell him what he must do. 'I pray you, therefore, to say your mind,' he told the astonished old prelate. Ridley, once he had recovered from the surprise of having the ear of the sovereign all to himself, proceeded to advise Edward that the pressing needs were suitable asylum for the sick, a school for education of the poor, and some building which might serve as a place of correction for vagabonds, who, till then, further jammed the prisons already crowded with debtors, thieves, and petty criminals. Immediately, the boy dispatched a letter, which Ridley delivered personally, to the Lord Mayor of London. Within weeks, three institutions were founded. From the magnificent old monastery of the Grey Friars evolved Christ's Church School for teaching the City's poor children. St Thomas's Hospital ministered to the relief of the sick and diseased, and for the correction of vagabonds, Edward offered the old Bridewell Palace. If the Council was startled at this independent action on the part of the King, it said nothing; the end of Edward's minority was not too far off and few wished to earn his displeasure.

All the King's projects combined with the tedium of daily Council meetings demanded that much more of the boy sovereign. It alarmed John Cheke who told Northumberland of his concern, but little was done to relieve the boy. Edward continued to exhibit attention and diligence, but he was fast approaching the limits of his endurance. At last even Northumberland could see the cause of Cheke's alarm. Edward had lost weight, his colour had become more waxen pale, and his manner grave and listless. As he walked about the court, many remarked he appeared 'as an old man', and his somewhat elevated shoulder blade became even more noticeable, almost as though there was a physical weight pressing on the opposite side. Yet he did not give up easily. Only when a cough slowed up his speech, interfered with his thinking, and wracked his body with sharp, jabbing pains did he take to his bed.

Up until that time, the King had been thorough in committing the military, political, religious, and social events of each day to his *Chronicle*—even though it had long ceased to be an outlet for his private reflections. By the end of November, it was harder to write, and the handwriting of which he had been so proud noticeably deteriorated. Perhaps then some inner awareness of his own fate caused him to write in it, '*Laus Deo Finis*' and lay the book wearily aside with what might have been a sensation of relief. He was through with compulsions and duties, with the prodding of his own stern conscience, and with moral obligations. There was now, suddenly, only the startling awareness that he was tired, empty, and sick and—more than anything else—frighteningly mortal after all.

Neither Mary nor Elizabeth was informed of their brother's deterioration. Mary had come to court just before Edward's progress commenced, spending several days at her residence in St. John's, Clerkenwell, 'from whence she rode with a goodly company of ladies and gentlemen, on June 11th, to Tower Wharf.' From there she went by barge to Greenwich Palace. With her brother and his court away, she could wander in peace through the old gardens where memories of her mother and father faced her at every turn; both of them had dearly loved Greenwich, and she, like Henry himself, had been born there. It had been one of the first places her father had sent her mother when she defied him and refused to submit docilely to a divorce after twenty-five years of marriage.

Mary was fast approaching the age of Catherine of Aragon had been at that unhappy time, and as she passed through the chamber her mother had occupied—it had been much changed by a succession of Queens—she could feel some part of Catherine's agony. Here her mother must often have sat at her desk, penning her innumerable letters to her nephew Charles or to the Pope, asking for help, for solace, for *any* intervention that might stave off the disaster she could see engulfing her. Mary could sit at the same desk and look out at the magnificent Palace lawns, green and smooth in the summer sun, to the river beyond. At least the view had not altered, even if the chamber and she herself had changed completely. With eyes suddenly smarting, she would try to thrust the unhappy memory from her and swell more realistically upon the handsome young brother who was, at this very moment, strengthening the Tudor influence by journeying through the countryside. Her sister, Elizabeth, had, thankfully, become more dependable and at last was showing every sign of having gained some common sense from the sorry part she had played in the Seymour débâcle. Things could be much worse. True, the 'new religion' was gaining in influence everywhere in the cities. From experience, Mary knew that simple villagers and country people, far from the cities, cared little for it and embraced the doctrine, as prescribed by Cranmer and the Council, only out of fear. She herself still heard the Mass, but she no longer invited visitors or others from the outside to share it with her. In this way, she presented no 'bad example' to the King's subjects.

Subtle pressures had continued to be exerted against her. Only recently, Bishop Ridley—the same who had been so delighted at the King's help in relieving the poor—visited her. He had been greeted courteously by Sir Thomas Wharton and brought to Mary who welcomed him with obvious pleasure, telling the old prelate she remembered him from the time he had been chaplain to her father. She could even recall some of his sermons, she said. She then invited the bishop to luncheon, an invitation he accepted with evident pleasure. Upon leaving later, he told her the reason for his call. 'Madam, I came not only to do my duty to see your Grace, but also to offer myself to preach before you on Sunday next, if it will please you to hear me,' he said. Mary's face froze in disappointment at the bishop's blunder. But she answered evenly, 'Well, I pray you make the answer to this matter yourself—for you know the answer well enough. But if there be no remedy but I must make you answer, this shall be your answer—the door to the parish church adjoining shall be open for you if you come, and you may preach if you list. But neither I nor any of mine shall hear you!'

The bishop demurred. 'But Madam, I trust you will not refuse God's word?' Mary refused to be baited. Keeping her temper in check, she replied, 'I cannot tell what ye call God's word. That is not God's word now, that was God's word in my father's day.'

Mary's answer, slightly tinged with irony, did not escape the bishop. He said, 'God's word is all one in all times, but hath been better understood and practised in some ages than in others,' and he mentioned some books she might like to read.

At last she lost her Spanish temper. 'You durst for your ears have avouched that for God's word in my father's day that you now do!' she explained. 'And as for your new books, I thank God I never read any of them; I never did, nor ever will do!' The woman's pent-up feelings against the new religious laws led her to ask the bishop if he were now one of the Council, for he acted much 'as the Council goeth nowadays.'

Ridley replied he was not one of the Council and then, realising further discussion was useless, prepared to leave. Mary composed herself and said, 'My Lord, for your gentleness to come and see me, I thank you. But for your offering to preach before me, I thank you never a whit.' And with that she bowed lightly, turned on her heel, and left the bishop alone.

Ridley did not take his curt dismissal lightly, and while he was having a cup of wine with Sir Thomas Wharton before his departure, his anger burst its bonds, as he suddenly cried that he had been wrong in accepting the drink, 'For I have drunk in that place where God's word offered hath been refused—whereas, if I had remembered my duty, I ought to have departed immediately and to have shaken off the dust of my shoes for a testimony against this house!' His diatribe continued so vividly all the way to his litter that, as Wharton later said, 'some of the hearers confessed their hair to stand upright on their heads!'[14]

The incident had only further convinced Mary that *the old days had been the best*. Then everyone had followed the same dictates of heart and conscience, and much of the misery now enveloping the country had been unknown. Now all was different, but there was little she could do about it. All she asked was that others follow their own consciences—as long as they allowed her the same privilege.

Religious differences never affected her relationship with old friends like her cousin, Frances Brandon Grey, now the Duchess of Suffolk.[15] Though completely opposite in character, they had been close since childhood. Mary's affection for Frances Brandon and her daughter, Lady Jane Grey, had continued undiminished, even though Jane had embraced the 'new religion' with all the zeal and fervour of her deprived childhood. Mary had accepted the fact that, like so many others of the court, the Suffolk's spiritual conscience was merely an expediency of the moment. Frances Brandon Suffolk had inherited much of the Carthusian property in London as well as the Priory of Sheen, at the time of the Dissolution. Their mansion at Dorset Place had formerly belonged to the Church, and now, with their elevation, the vast Suffolk properties in Southwark were also theirs. By subscribing to the 'new religion' they now had almost royal possessions and income, and while Mary had no illusions about their motives, she recognised that Jane Grey was as fervent and sincere in her own beliefs as she was in her Catholicism. Still, they had continued as friends, and Mary met Jane and her parents with delight on her visit to London. Her pleasure in their union is reflected in a notation in her account books. 'Given to my cousin Frances, beads of black and white mounted in gold.' To 'my cousin, Jane Grey,' a girl now fifteen years old and growing in grace and beauty, she gave 'a necklace of gold, set with pearls and small rubies.' It is doubtful if presenting such valuable items from her own slim hoard of jewels to those who had so many seemed odd to Mary; they were her family and the gifts were a mark of her affection and esteem. But Jane, plagued now for several years with the 'nips and bobs' of her ruthlessly ambitious parents, who had driven her into an almost fanatical preoccupation with the 'new religion,' was not as tolerant as Mary.

Since her return from those enchanted months at Chelsea, Jane's home life had been a nightmare. The Suffolks had failed in an attempt to marry her to Edward, although as long as he lived there was always that opportunity. Since Thomas Seymour's death, there had been no home of sufficient stature—such as Queen Katherine Parr's—where Jane might be placed to learn the 'graces and manners' so necessary to her position. Therefore, her parents were left with her, and they made their displeasure painfully clear. Desperately Jane had turned to her books and religious study. Her correspondence with the noted reformers of the day, such as Bullinger and ab Ulmis, replaced in some measure the warmth, approval, and sense of personal worth her family denied her. 'Were I to extol you as truth requires,' she wrote to one Protestant divine, 'I should need either the oratorical powers of Demosthenes or the eloquence of Cicero . . . but I am too young and ignorant for either. . . . In this earthly prison you pass your days as if you were dead, whereas you live, and this not only to Christ in the first place, but also to others without number.'[16]

Jane Grey had few friends, and not caring for the gamey entertainments of her parents, she lived in an isolated world except for her tutors and the family retainers. Introverted and shy, her devotion to religion containing more than a tinge of bigotry, Jane was uncomfortable with her equally staunch Catholic cousin, Mary Tudor. When the Suffolks later arrived en masse to visit Mary at Beaulieu, the King's older sister strained every farthing from her cofferer and all the resources of her home to entertain them. She presented Jane with a rich gown of 'tinsel, cloth of gold and velvet, laid on with parchment of lace-of-gold.' Never was Mary's love of elegant fabric more evident than in the gift she gave her young cousin whose natural beauty she considered dulled by drab clothing. Jane viewed the gown in amazement; it was different from anything she had ever owned. She asked Mary's lady-in-waiting, who had brought the gift, what she must do with it? 'Marry!' replied the exasperated woman, 'wear it to be sure!' Jane's face crinkled in disdain. 'Nay,' she said tonelessly, 'that were a shame—to follow the Lady Mary, who leaveth God's word, and leave my Lady Elizabeth, who followeth God's word? Nay!'[17] When the remark reached Mary—as it was sure to do—it gave her pause.

By Christmas and Twelfth Night, the King's illness had stabilised. He seemed no worse, but neither was he better. The cough persisted, resulting in sleepless nights. As he lost even more weight, his frailness was starkly evident. His remarkable patience and good nature were dulled; his energy declined as his responsibilities enlarged. As if to stimulate Edward's waning enthusiasm, during the holiday at Greenwich, special pagents and revels were planned with drummers in Turkish costumes preceding the Master of the Revels, whose theme that year of 1552 was startlingly modern. He and the other courtiers would 'come out of the great waste of space, where there is neither fire, air nor earth'. These sixteenth-century spacemen would appear in a spaceship decorated in blue and white from which would descend the entertainers, tumblers, fools, and jugglers. There would be a splendid climax, a torchlight procession, featuring participants costumed as cats, monkeys, satyrs, monsters, and musicians—presumably the occupants of the planets Mars and Venus, which figured prominently in the performance.

Edward appeared pleased with the festivities, though his participation, unlike on previous occasions, was more passive. Shortly afterwards, feeling momentarily stronger and optimistic about his health, he imprudently indulged in a game of tennis, became overheated and suddenly chilled. The next day 'all the medicines and diet that could be prescribed were unavailing to abate his grief, which, so far from abating, daily increased by dangerous degrees.'[18]

At Whitehall, the King took to his bed, worrying his ministers and those in the bedchamber, one of whom said, 'It was not only the violence of the cough that did infest him, but therewith a weakness and faintness of spirit which showed plainly that his vital parts were strongly and strangely assaulted.'[19] Apart from the royal physicians, Dr Thomas Wendy and Dr George Owen, the only outside consultant called at this point in the King's illness, was Giralomo Cardano, a distinguished Italian doctor, whose reputation in medicine was equalled by his facility as an astrologer. Northumberland summoned Cardano to court and brought him directly to the King.

Edward's interest was momentarily aroused as he talked with the doctor about the concourse of the planets and the cause of comets; the lore of space had always fascinated the boy. During their talk, Cardano observed the King '. . . in whom no doubt there was great hope and expectation amongst all good and learned men, both for the ingenious forwardness and amiable sweetness which in his condition appeared. Where a kingly majesty required gravity, there you should have seen him a sage and an old man, and yet gentle and pleasant.'[20] Edward honoured the old doctor by playing upon his lute and then, tired, dismissed his visitor. Later they had one last conversation on government and more practical affairs than the stars, and Cardano was impressed with Edward, who, he said, 'took trouble over public affairs, was liberal of mind and in these respects, emulated his father . . . in his humanity, he was a picture of our mortal state . . . this boy of so much wit and promise was nearing a comprehension of the sum of things . . . and there was the mark in his face of death that was come too soon. . . .' That the doctor had an almost mystical insight is obvious from his final summary of Edward, whom he called 'a boy of wondrous hope, who, if he had lived, would have done much for the betterment of his kingdom.' He could hardly state—if he valued his life—what he saw in the royal horoscope or reflected in the King's face and body.

Instead, he told Northumberland that Edward would live till the age of fifty-five, pocketed the King's gift of four hundred gold crowns, and left England. Later, hearing of the boy's death, he would say, 'It would have been better, I think, for this boy not to have been born, or if he had been born, not to have survived—for he had graces.'[21]

But Edward needed more than grace to survive. In February, with the opening of Parliament facing him, he invited his sisters for a visit. Elizabeth, scenting danger, pleaded ill health. But Mary journeyed happily from Hunsdon, eager to see her brother after their last several unhappy meetings. At Westminster, her reception was remarkably different from her previous visit. Already rumours and whispers of the King's debility were circulating within the City and abroad. Some spoke of a wasting disease, some of a slow-working poison being administered by spies within the King's chambers. Others, remembering his two executed uncles, called it divine retribution.

Now, those at the court, re-examining their past behaviour towards Mary, hastened to adjust their attitude. Should the King die, the one from whom most of them had found it prudent to remain aloof, if not completely estranged, would be their Queen! Therefore, when Mary rode through Fleet Street to Westminster, accompanied by her own courtiers, she was startled to find herself greeted by 'a great number of lords, knights, and all the great ladies' who waited to accompany her the remaining distance to Westminster. The Duke and Duchess of Suffolk, Lady Jane's parents, met their cousin at the entrance. Katherine Parr's brother, the Marquess of Northampton, and even the Duke of Northumberland and his Duchess awaited her within the gates. Lined up behind them were all the nobility—Winchester, Bedford, Shrewsbury, even the Lord Chancellor himself. It was Mary's first intimation of the true extent of Edward's ill health. Why else would Northumberland and those members of the Council who had scarcely recognized her existence, except to harass her, come to welcome her?

Her worst suspicions were confirmed as she was ushered into the King's presence, and she could hardly conceal her alarm at his changed appearance. Edward lay in his bed, feverish, a congestion of the lungs making his breathing difficult. The visit was short. Mary would have dearly loved a private talk with her brother, but many had crowded into the stifling chamber for the interview and the physicians stood watchfully by the bed. Edward attempted to make the conversation pleasant—an inquiry for her health and well-being, a short discussion of her journey—and then she was dismissed. Mary remained at her residence for two days, hoping to be allowed to see him again. When no summons came, she returned, deeply disturbed, to Hunsdon. There, messengers brought her the welcome news that Edward was, indeed, better—he had even insisted on opening the Parliament. Though it might have been wiser to have stayed in bed, the boy had mustered enough strength to don his ceremonial robe with its crimson velvet train ten yards long and make what was to be his last public appearance in London. Out of consideration for the ailing boy, Parliament had transferred from the old Palace of Westminster to Whitehall so the King would not have to make the short journey down 'the Streete.'

For two days he appeared in Parliament before his strength gave out, and with it went the sweetness of disposition that had so character-ised Edward Tudor's short life. While attending the meetings of Council and Commons, the King had sought to deal with those projects dearest to his heart—his schools, hospitals, and other charitable institutions, the religion of his subjects, and, to Northumberland's distress, the currency of the realm. Possibly Edward realised this would be his last opportunity to give official sanction to these projects. His temper, usually so controlled and placid, was aggravated by his physical discomfort and the weakness of his spirit. However, when some of his ministers disagreed with him, he mustered some measure of strength and exclaimed irritably, 'You pluck out my feathers as if I were but a tame falcon—the day will come when I shall pluck out yours!' The Council sat stunned at the boy's outburst. For several, there was an uncomfortable remembrance of his late father who had told them on similar occasions that either he would have his way—or he would have their heads.

Late in the afternoon of April 11, as green was deepening the budding trees in the royal gardens and a late spring's warmth promised solace to the stricken boy who had endured a long winter of depression, lassitude, and extreme physical discomfort, Edward Tudor left London for the last time. A booming salvo of guns from the Tower and similar salutes from several ships being outfitted for a hazardous voyage to The Newfoundland greeted the royal barge on its way to Placentia, the favourite Palace of the Tudors, at Greenwich. Here Edward attempted to fulfill as many of his responsibilities as possible. The change of air and season undoubtedly benefited him, but his long illness had so depleted him that there were still days when he could not leave his bed. On one occasion he rose to receive the new French ambassador, Antoine de Noailles, who was to play such an eventful part in a future which, mercifully, Edward was unable to see. De Noailles's visit was very short. He was told the audience was 'merely to receive me and take leave of my predecessor, the Lords of his Council having previously entreated us not to make him [Edward] read the letters, nor yet to enter further into discussion with him than was absolutely necessary, but to wait till a further improvement in his strength allowed him to receive us again.'[22]

When Mary heard of the interview, she assumed her brother was better. He had sent her a magnificent table diamond, as if to make up for their disappointingly brief visit, and, encouraged that he was recovering, she wrote to him, 'My duty most humbly presented to your Majesty, it may please the same to be advertised, that as hearing of your Highness's late rheum and cough was as much grief as ever was any worldly thing, even so the hope which I have conceived since I received your Majesty's last token by my servant hath not been a little to my comfort, praying Almighty God, according to my most bounden duty, to give your Majesty perfect health and strength, with little continuance in prosperity to reign. . . .'[23]

The futility of Mary's hope was apparent as the summer weeks wore on. Edward rallied periodically for a day or two, but the expectations of those who loved him were always blighted by a more severe relapse. His cough persisted and his stomach became bloated. A high fever aggravated his breathing, and the small, wasted frame was tormented with bedsores. His doctor told the Spanish ambassador that Edward had developed a 'suppurating tumour on his lung' which caused him to eject 'a greenish-yellow and black' mucus from his mouth. Often it was tinged with blood. Powerful stimulants were administered to the boy each time it seemed he might relapse into a merciful unconsciousness, so his suffering was realised and continuous. Each day it became even more obvious the young Tudor King would not live much longer.

At the thought of Edward's death, John Dudley, the Duke of Northumberland, was horror-striken. The King had been his powerful support. Without Edward's advocacy—and protection—the duke's domination of the Council might be lost forever. Already, as the boy lay dying, Northumberland had seen the restlessness of the nobles, as they wondered what the King's death would mean to them. And who would succeed Edward? Only the Popish Mary Tudor, who would probably undo all the great religious reform he and Somerset had accomplished, who would reclaim the numerous church properties from the nobles, and who might further wreck the aspirations of the aristocracy by a foreign marriage. Her younger sister would be no better; both of them would have to take a foreign husband who would tolerate little interference from a Council—or a duke. Worse still, Elizabeth was even more difficult to handle than her sister. She was cleverer and bolder, and her professed Protestantism had made her— along with Lady Jane Grey—the darling of the reforming party.

So Northumberland prepared his plan. If Mary and Elizabeth could be set aside, the niece of Henry VIII, Frances Brandon Grey, the Duchess of Suffolk, was next in line for the Crown. Northumberland had little reason to like or trust the blowsy duchess. She might be the daughter of Henry's sister, Mary, the lovely 'Tudor Rose,' but she had inherited woefully little of the beauty, grace, or intelligence of that red-haired charmer who had briefly married a King of France and then, a widow three months later, risked her brother's wrath to wed her true love, Charles Brandon. Frances Suffolk would not tolerate even a duke's interference should she attain the throne. But her daughter, Jane Grey, who was youthfully idealistic and pliable, might be the channel through which Northumberland could retain some remnant of the authority he had so carefully amassed before and after the Protector's death.

Sir Richard Morrison, an ambassador to the Spanish court, once noted that Northumberland 'had such a head that he seldom went about anything but he had three or four purposes beforehand.'[24] It is doubtful, however if the duke's plans regarding the succession were patterned with such thoughtful deliberation; there had not been time. Facing ruin, he reacted as a cornered animal, attempting one tactic, then another, to escape the fate he saw waiting for him at Edward's death. His first step was to ally himself with the country's most powerful nobles, and in this he had the willing co-operation of Henry Grey, the Duke of Suffolk. In May, 1553, as Edward languished in tortured semi-isolation, London was startled by three simultaneous weddings involving the same family. The Lady Jane Grey was given in marriage to Lord Guildford Dudley, Northumberland's fourth son. Her sister, Katherine Grey, married a son of the Earl of Pembroke, and the youngest sister, the dwarfish Mary Grey, wed Lord Grey of Wilton.

Edward could not attend the ceremonies. He would have been distressed at the visible unhappiness of his cousin Jane, born in the same month as he, of whom he had always been so fond. Jane not only disliked the vulgar, conceited nineteen-year-old boy of whom it was said, 'of all of Dudley's brood, he had nothing of his father in him,' but she disliked and feared his parents as well. They were very much like her own mother and father—loud, domineering, and selfish. When Suffolk informed Jane she was to wed Northumberland's son, the girl was appalled. She replied with an unusual spirit that she did not like Guildford Dudley and had no wish to marry. Waving her objections aside, her father sneered that she had little choice. Desperately, Jane reminded her parent that she had been 'plighted elsewhere,' referring to a betrothal to one of Somerset's sons, made while the Protector was riding the crest of popularity and power. Suffolk told his daughter that Edward had ordained the marriage, and, coming menacingly close to the petite little figure with the fair hair and frightened eyes, he asked 'whether she intended to disobey her King as well as her father?' At this point her mother, the formidable duchess, arrived, drawn into the room by her daughter's cries of protest. A few harsh blows, loud curses, and angry threats, punctuated with pinches that left Jane's freckled arms bruised and sore, and the defenceless girl, now weeping openly, was subdued, a victom of her parents' ambition and Northumberland's lust for power.

If Edward wondered at the reason for the wholesale maritial disposition of all the Suffolk daughters, he gave no sign. He could not attend the ceremonies at Durham House where Jane, 'with a headdress of green velvet, set around with precious stones' which capped the hair hanging loosely around her shoulders, was led to the altar 'between two sweet boys, with bride-laces and rosemary tied about their silken sleeves.' There, her bridegroom, 'splendidly apparelled,' awaited her. The whole Northumberland clan was assembled in remarkably flamboyant costumes which had been taken from the Master of the Royal Wardrobe, another of Northumberland's sons, Sir Andrew Dudley. A rather macabre irony lay in the sequestering of this borrowed finery; the magnificent velvets, brocades, pieces of cloth of gold and silver were all from the confiscated estate of the executed Duke of Somerset.

Jane had been promised she might return to her parents directly after the ceremony. Instead, her now mother-in-law told the bride, 'there was no hope of the King's life,' and she therefore should not leave her house. When Jane inquired why and reminded the duchess of her promise, Northumberland's wife told her, as Jane later wrote, 'that when it pleased God to call King Edward to His mercy, I ought to hold myself in readiness, as I might be required to go to the Tower, since his Majesty had made me heir to his dominions.'[25] This was Lady Jane Grey's first intimation of the gravity of Edward's illness. Aghast at the implications, she became agitated, crying such action was only meant to 'deprive her of going home,' But Guildford Dudley's mother was firm. It was Jane's duty to remain near her husband, she said, and for five days the new bride remained at Durham House before being allowed to return to her parents who were then at the manor house at Chelsea. The return to that blissfully innocent place where she had spent a happy summer with her cousins, Mary, Edward, and Elizabeth Tudor, was too much for Jane. She suffered an attack from what some thought was poison but, in fact, was nothing more than the collapse of a fragile nervous system which had been exploited and condemned to more than it could bear.

The allegation that Jane would be 'heir to his dominions' must now be made a fact with the King, instead of just a hopeful presumption on the part of Suffolk and Northumberland. A few days after Jane's wedding, Northumberland appealed to Edward's conscience to put his affairs in order so the safety of the realm might continue should the King not recover. It was frankness an older and less stricken monarch might have deemed treasonous, but Edward was beyond caring. He did not expect to get well. *He* knew there was no remedy except death. When Northumberland exhibited concern about the succession, Edward was therefore solemn—but emphatic. Had not his father, with great wisdom and forethought, settled that issue at his death six years ago? The Princess Mary and her heirs would succeed him. If Mary should die and leave no heirs, then his 'sweet sister, Temperance' and her heirs would reign.

At this corroboration of his worst fears, the duel between Northumberland and the stricken King began in earnest. The duke needed more time in which to convince the boy the succession must be altered, yet both Dr Wendy and Dr Owen were certain Edward would live only a few days more. Without warning, Northumberland dismissed the devoted physicians and summoned two other consultants. One was his own doctor, a reputable Oxford professor. The other, a woman, was indisputably a fraud. She promised Northumberland to save Edward's life providing the King 'was altogether entrusted to her care.' Despite protests from all the physicians, the bargain was made, and the woman, whose name had escaped history, began her treatment. Innumerable medicines and stimulants, forcibly poured into the wasting body, resulted in Edward's arms becoming bloated and 'burthened his person much more than before.' His normally pale skin assumed a darker, unnatural colour, and the blond hair began to fall out, covering the pillow already wet with sweat. The ulcerating bedsores contributed to the sickening odour of the gangrene affecting the tips of his fingers and toes. No longer was it possible to carry him to the window where a grieving, anxious people might see the slight, pain-wracked form, or receive a weak wave in response to their cries of concern. No longer did Edward care that outside his windows, the ships of the Merchant Adventurers were being 'towed down the Thames by boats manned with stout mariners, apparelled in watchet or sky-blue cloth. . . .' In honour of the sick King, the ships' ordnance was discharged opposite the Palace 'so that the Kentish hills resounded, the valleys and the waters gave an echo. . . .' But Edward was slowly weakening. And, mercifully, the people outside did not know the incredible fact that the life of the King of England was now the exclusive responsibility of a quack.

It was then that Northumberland visited the boy daily, speaking to him of the succession and appealing to Edward's conscience—that stalwart conscience which had ruled his life, shaped his actions, and —to some extent, through his faithful attention to his responsibilities— brought him to his deathbed. The duke laboured the question of Mary and Elizabeth's legitimacy, which had been questioned for years, emphasising they were only half-blood to the King. To leave a disputed succession to two women, each of whom professed a different religious faith and who must marry out of the realm, would only undo all the magnificent work Edward and his father before him had accomplished. Northumberland called upon all the saints to witness that he did not consider "so much mine own interest in the business, as the benefit of the whole realm,' but for himself, he felt it better to put both sisters aside, let the Crown pass to the niece of Henry VIII, Frances Brandon Grey, the Duchess of Suffolk. The Duke was convincing and Edward could see the merit of his logic. While the duchess had no male heirs, her daughter, recently wed to Guildford Dudley might indeed have sons so that one of Tudor blood—somewhat diluted to be sure—would continue to occupy the throne. Edward's weakened and tormented condition proved no hindrance to Northumberland's aim. After days of argument the boy consented and, with trembling fingers, made draft after draft of a remarkable paper called *My Devise for the Succession*, which rests today in the archives of the Inner Temple. It is a testament to Northumberland's persuasiveness, to the King's physical weakness, and a conscientious awareness of his country's welfare which caused him to deny his father's will and forfeit his sisters' right to rule.

The *Devise* is crossed out, interlined, blotted, smeared, and uncertain in its physical execution, but ultimately clear in its meaning. The Crown was left to Jane Grey Dudley and her 'heirs male,' then to her sisters, both of whom had recently wed boys of Northumberland's choosing, sons of nobles on whose support he could rely.

Next, the Council had to be dealt with, and in this the determined Northumberland encountered the expected opposition. Cranmer, particularly, was aghast. During the King's illness, the archbishop had tried repeatedly to see Edward, 'but I could not be suffered, and so I failed of my purpose,' he said sadly. 'If I might have communed with the King alone, and at good leisure, my trust was, that I should have altered him from his purpose; but they [the duke's faction] being present, my labour was in vain.' When finally brought into the King's presence to subscribe to the document, Cranmer said the *Devise* 'seemed very strange to me,' at which point Edward turned on him sharply and said that he trusted that Cranmer alone 'would not be more repugnant to his will than the rest. . . .' Cranmer saw further resistance would be futile. Such words from his dearly loved godson 'surely grieved my heart very sore. And so I granted him to subscribe his will. . . .'[26]

Another courageous dissenter, Sir Edward Montague, the King's lord chief justice, was indignant—and fearful. He told Northumberland that Edward's *Devise* was in direct opposition to the Act of Succession and to sign it would be treason. Only Henry VIII had dared bequeath the Crown at will, and he had had sense enough to have the sanction of Parliament. Edward had not consulted Parliament, and to overlook Henry's stipulated heirs—Mary and Elizabeth—was foolhardy and dangerous. 'In God's name, my Lords,' pleaded Montague, 'think twice what you do—it will be treason to us all who have a hand in it!'

Northumberland was enraged. He recognised the weaknesses inherent in the *coup* he was building; it was not as strongly and efficiently bulwarked as he would have liked, but there was not enough time left. Edward was sinking rapidly. The strain had told on the duke, and when he confronted the elderly Montague, his patience exploded and '. . . being in a great rage and fury, for anger; and, amongst his ragious [outrageous] talk, called Sir Edward Montague traitor, and further said that he would fight in his shirt with any man in that quarrel!'[27]

When Montague appealed to Edward himself, the King showed little tolerance. The sick boy's anger was pitiful to see, and Montague's fear was real. He argued that to sign the document would be treasonous. He pleaded with Edward, 'I have served your Majesty and your Majesty's most noble father for nineteen years. I am a weak old man and without comfort . . .' he cried, bursting into tears, and then added, somewhat irrelevantly, 'I have seventeen children. . . .' Ultimately, he agreed to sign if Edward would grant him a general pardon for doing so. Montague's reaction was typical of the ministers' fears, though few had the old lawyer's courage. They were skirting dangerous grounds, and as Edward's condition worsened, as the emotional climate in the Palace and at the Council became further fraught with tension and bad tempers, many hastily decamped. Among the first to leave was William Cecil, who suddenly became inexplicably ill. He resigned his post and with little ceremony departed for his country home.

By the middle of June, Northumberland felt he had succeeded. The councillors had promised to support Lady Jane Grey as future Queen 'to the uttermost of their power and never at any time to swerve from it.' All that was left now was to organise the physical strength to support such a claim. The duke had done all he could. Now he could only wait.

Two who must be kept unaware of what was happening at Greenwich were Mary and Elizabeth. Northumberland sent frequent reports of the King's illness to the sisters, though none were as alarming as the boy's actual condition. Mary was gratified, if somewhat startled, to receive the reinstatement of her Seal, signifying her right to be called Princess, which had been taken from her by Cromwell years ago. Giacomo Sorranzo, the Venetian ambassador, said Mary never doubted the throne would come to her should Edward die. Northumberland had told her he would risk his life for her service, 'and thus he convinced her completely.' With a nature that recognized little dissembling or hypocrisy, she did not comprehend the duke's ulterior motive—to build favour with the King's older sister, while lulling any suspicions of the boy's true condition. 'He thus convinced her completely . . .' said Sorranzo, '. . . and thought he could gain possession of her whenever he pleased.'[28]

Elizabeth was not so gullible. Rumours reached Hatfield—perhaps from her good friend, Cecil—that her brother was dying. In an uncharacteristic move from one who so rarely took the initiative, Elizabeth gave orders that she would visit her brother, and she took care to see that her contemplated visit was well publicised. After two days on the road to Greenwich, she was intercepted by a detachment of royal guards and ordered, *at the King's command*, to return to her home. The action confirmed her worst suspicions. The order did not come from the King, she was certain. Apparently there were other more important reasons why she could not see her brother. That evening, she wrote Edward of her attempt to visit him:

Like as a shipman in a stormy weather plucks down the sails tarrying for better wind, so did I, most noble king, in my unfortunate chance on Thursday, pluck down the high sails of my joy and comfort, and do trust one day that, as troublesome waves have repulsed me backward, so a gentle wind will bring me forward to my haven. Two occasions moved me much and grieved me greatly, the one for that I doubted your Majesty's health—the other, because for all my long tarrying, I went without that I came for. . . .[29]

Elizabeth then said, 'of my grief I am not eased' and asked her brother's forgiveness for undertaking the journey, saying 'For if your Grace's advice that I should return . . . had not been, I would not have made the half of my way, the end of my journey. . . .' As she handed the letter to the waiting messenger, she wondered if it would be given to her brother, if he were still well enough to read it, or—worse still— if he were already dead. Her throat tightened at the thought of the lonely young boy, ill and with no member of his family nearby. Certainly there would have been no reason to refuse her arrival at Greenwich if Edward were reasonably well. She had discovered all she wished to know.

Elizabeth's letter never reached Edward. By the time it was delivered

[294]

to Northumberland and hastily set aside, the end was near. How long the King would linger, even the duke could not guess, but in view of the altered succession, physical possession of the two heiresses-presumptive was vital. Soon messengers were speeding along the hot dusty roads leading to Hatfield and Hunsdon, bearing summons to Greenwich. Alarmed, Mary made preparations at once, but Elizabeth, with her magnificent instinct and the memory of her recent refusal, decided it was probably already too late. She promptly took to the sickbed herself, telling her doctor to send her apologies—she was too ill to travel.

Even Elizabeth's cautious heart might have softened had she been able to see the outpouring of concern and love for Edward in London and at Greenwich. In the City, people assembled in small groups, whispering their fears and suspicions. Many had guessed at the signifi-cance of the cannon hauled to the ramparts of the Tower of London and the unusual number of soldiers assembled at the City gates. Ambassadors were not fooled by the sudden gathering of many ships on the Thames, ships ostensibly bound for the Barbary and Spice Islands. The King was dying—poisoned some said—and his sisters were on their way to London, unaware that imprisonment and possibly a similar fate awaited them.

At Greenwich, there had been a long vigil outside the Palace. It had been a hot, ominous day—the heavy stillness in the air which often precedes a thunderstorm—yet many hesitated to disperse to their homes. It was July 6, 1553, and many remembered it was the seven-teenth anniversary of the death of Sir Thomas More, sent to the scaffold by Henry VIII because, in all good conscience, More could not agree that the King's marriage to Catherine of Aragon was invalid. There were those who spoke of omens and portents; Henry had wanted a son, and now, on the anniversary of a major adversary's execution, that son lay at death's door. Perhaps he was already dead. Several days previously, Edward had been carried to the window, and, though too weak to acknowledge the people's anxious cries, he had at least been revealed as still alive. If they waited long enough, perhaps he might come out again. But inside the bedchamber, there was little thought of moving the King. The quack had done her worst and been dismissed. She departed, never heard from again.*

Edward's agonised body now only sought release from the revolting possets and potions which had been forced into it daily in hope of some cure. Frightened, Northumberland had recalled Dr Owen and Dr Wendy, and now they, with Sir Henry Sidney and Sir Thomas Wroth, kept the vigil in a royal bedchamber which reeked of death

* After Edward's death, it was surmised she had been murdered in order to forestall any true appraisal of her participation in the boy's care.

and decay. An old servant, Christopher Salmon, stood in one corner, despair and sadness stamped on his face. Salmon had been barber to the boy's father, Henry VIII, and his tie with Edward had been one of great affection and kindness. Wiping away his tears, he was startled to hear a voice issuing from the wasted form on the bed—it was little more than a whisper. The group moved nearer. Edward's eyes were still closed, but he was speaking—the first time in hours that he had shown any sign of life. 'Lord God deliver me out of this miserable and wretched life, and take me among Thy chosen. Howbeit, not my will, but Thy will be done! Lord, I commit my spirit to Thee. Oh Lord, Thou knowest how happy it were for me to be with Thee...' his voice trailed off and then he turned, looking at his friends assembled by his bed. Miraculously, there was a smile, a faint trace of the sunny smile, reminiscent of the sweet lad they had all known and loved since his birth. 'Are ye so nigh?' Edward spoke softly as they came closer so they might not miss a word. 'I thought ye had been farther off. ...' The rest of his words were drowned by a tremendous thunderclap, and suddenly rain hammered at the windows, opened to relieve the fetid air of the room. Dr Owen asked Edward what he had been saying, and the boy replied, 'I was praying to God.' When the windows had been closed against the gathering fury of the storm, the group knelt by the bedside. Wroth took the thin, shrunken form in his arms. Again the little smile miraculously appeared on the boy's parched lips as he sought to speak. There were tears in Dr Owen's eyes as he knelt to ease Edward; he had brought the boy into the world almost seventeen years ago. 'I am faint. ...' Edward gasped, clutching with maimed fingers at Owen's hand. 'Oh Lord, have mercy upon me and take my spirit ...'[30] he whispered before his grasp weakened. It was then they all knew the King was dead. The spirit of the boy who had had too many graces to survive was gone. At last, mercifully, the agony of the last male Tudor was finished.

Outside the windows of Edward's chamber, the day drew to a close in a violent storm that cast giant hailstones on much of England, flooding the lower areas of London, and moving to leave a wide swarth of ruined gardens, orchards, and uprooted trees in a ravaged country-side. Near the village of Hoddesdon in Hertfordshire, Mary Tudor and her companions sought shelter from the rain and hazards of muddy roads. Though Northumberland's orders had been that no news of the King's death should leave the Palace, the young man whom Edward had jauntily knighted, Sir Nicholas Throckmorton,[31] ably repaid his benefactor by sending an urgent message carried by a goldsmith to the trusting Mary: *turn back—do not come to London.* As Mary listened to the message, she realized her brother was gone, his short life extinguished in a distant room with none of his kin around him. With eyes blinded by tears, she turned to her steward and issued an order. There was little now that she could do for Edward. There was instead the challenge of fighting for the throne of her parents—if fight she must. They would go—and by the most obscure route possible— she told the steward in her deep voice which was suddenly authoritative, to Kenninghall in Norfolk. There she would arrange her strategy and muster her forces. She must think, plan, and execute in a manner worthy of her mother and her father, for she was now—by the Grace of God—Queen of England.

A Queen and Her Sister

Chapter Seventeen

NEWS of the seriousness of Edward's prolonged illness had caused the Emperor to send three ambassadors to England, ostensibly to inquire about the King's health. In reality, they were to assess all possibilities pertaining to Mary's accession but in no way to imperil relations between England and Spain. If Mary's succession was doubtful, Charles would be of no help, for his resources had been drained by his war with France. He needed Northumberland's goodwill; he could not fight both countries.

The distinguished visitors, de Marnix, Sieur de Thoulouse; de Montmorency, Sieur de Courriers; and Simon Renard, a shrewd and gifted pupil of the noted de Granvelle, arrived on July 6, the very day that Edward died. No word had left Greenwich of the King's death. When the Imperial ambassadors asked leave to present their credentials, they were merely told Edward was too ill to receive them. Their suspicions were increased, however, by the undue activity at the Tower, at the City gates, and on the Thames. It was emphasised by the furtive whisperings of the people that the King was already dead, probably poisoned by Northumberland,[1] who hoped now to bring the boy's bastard sister to London like a common criminal before any support could be mustered for her. If Edward's death could be kept secret long enough to secure Mary's person, then Jane Grey would be proclaimed Queen, the Council's anxiety relieved, and the success of the *coup d'état* assured.

Northumberland's son, Sir Robert Dudley, and 300 soldiers had raced from London to intercept Mary, but with Throckmorton's warning ringing in her ears, the stunned woman had turned back. She sent a message to Charles's ambassadors that she was hoping to reach Kenninghall and, reducing her train to two trusted women and six strong gentlemen of the household, went with the speed of the fugitive towards her furthermost manor. The party's one thought was to put the greatest distance between the heiress-presumptive and the net cast from London to enmesh her.

On the first evening after her brother's death, Mary sought refuge at Sawston Hall in Cambridgeshire, the valley manor house of a loyal Catholic friend, John Huddlestone. Before daybreak, after a few hours sleep, her party was again on the road, and this time Mary took the further precaution of adopting the disguise of a servant-woman, riding docilely behind a retainer of Huddlestone's. Climbing the Gog Magog Hills, they were horrified upon looking back to see Sawston Hall in flames, a terrifying warning that her pursuers were not far behind. Realizing what her shelter had cost John Huddlestone, Mary was nevertheless undaunted. 'Let it blaze!' she spoke grimly to her companions, 'I will build Master Huddlestone a better Sawston. . . .'*

Edward had died on a Thursday. By Saturday evening, after a day and a night of wild riding, Mary Tudor had reached the comparative safety of Kenninghall. To her great joy, the exhausted woman was joined by several of the Catholic aristocracy which had sought a safe country obscurity during the 'religious troubles' of her father's and brother's reigns. She was delighted to see familiar and approving faces —her friend, the Earl of Bath, Sir John Mordaunt, Sir Henry Beding-field, and Sir Henry Jerningham.[2] With many of the local gentry they had hurried to Kenninghall when the disturbing but still unconfirmed rumour reached them that the King was dead. As the news became more widespread, the people rallied to the rightful heir, and along the country lanes and roads, the squires and their tenants, the country merchants and simple farmers, strong country boys and their kin, swarmed to Kenninghall, to camp in the fields outside the manor house awaiting word from its royal occupant whether she would fight for her Crown or not.

Inside there was no such question. What chiefly puzzled Mary was why she had not been informed of Edward's death and proclaimed accordingly. A cautious approach was needed until more definite knowledge could be obtained. Heartsick as she was with her brother's death, Mary knew she must win the support of the Council. Accordingly, on the morning of Sunday, July 9, a lone rider left Kenninghall with a letter addressed to the lords of the Council in which Mary informed them she was aware of Edward's death, that 'the Crown and governance of this realm of England, with the title of France, and all things thereto belonging' had long ago been provided for by her father's will. No good subject, she said, could be ignorant of those provisions, and therefore 'we have, of ourselves caused, and as God shall aid and strengthen us, shall cause our right and title in this behalf to be published and proclaimed accordingly.' Mary wished little doubt left of her feelings in the matter. 'And albeit this so weighty a matter

* Queen Mary kept her word. Later in the year, a larger and more comfortable Sawston Hall was built at her command, and at her expense. It still stands.

seemeth strange, that our said brother, dying upon Thursday at night last past, we hitherto had no knowledge from you thereof. . . .' But, said Mary, their lack of consideration for her would not be held against them. Instead, 'we shall and may conceive great hope and trust, with much assurance in your loyalty and service and, therefore, for the time, intercept and take things not to the worst—and that ye will, like noblemen, work the best.' She emphasised she was not 'ignorant of your consultations to undo the provisions made for our preferment . . . to what end, God and you know. . . .' As Queen, she would overlook their lack of support and would 'fully pardon the same, and that freely, to eschew bloodshed and vengence against all those that can or will intend the same. . . .' Should they neglect now to acknowledge her true claim to the throne, she would be forced 'to use the service of other of our true subjects and friends. . . .'[3]

In London, Northumberland worked feverishly, with the knowledge that time was not his ally. He had summoned the Lord Mayor of London and six aldermen and informed them of the King's death. In the Tower, carts full of 'ordnance, great guns and small, bows, bills, spears, Morris-pikes, arrows, gunpowder, victuals money, tents, and a great number of men' revealed a campaign in the making. Though they had been spurred by the success of their venture so far, the councillors were still uneasy, and the cool confidence in Mary's letter did not allay their anxiety. However, they replied in a stinging rebuke, informing Mary that since an Act of Parliament had rendered her 'illegitimate and unheritable to the Crown Imperial', her brother had designated the Lady Jane Grey as heir. Therefore, Mary 'must not vex our sovereign Lady, Queen Jane, her subjects, from their true faith and allegiance . . . wherein you may be otherwise grievous unto us and yourself. . . .' The tone of the letter, probably dictated by Northumberland, did not accurately reflect the ministers' feelings, but all were too fearful of the bullying duke and his strong supporters to make any opposition.

As if to quell any fears and precipitate the moment when all must acknowledge another as Queen, Lady Jane Grey, still unaware of Edward's death, was brought from Chelsea to Northumberland's home, Syon House. She was met by a group of nobles and their ladies, all of whom, to her bewilderment, knelt before her. Mystified, Jane could only stare at them, her recent illness reflected in her pale face and apathetic manner. Nearby, her parents, her in-laws and their families were also kneeling. Sick with a dread she could not name, Jane listened as Northumberland read a well-prepared speech. Her cousin Edward was dead, he said grimly—that 'virtuous and praiseworthy life' was ended. In the midst of the pang she felt for the loss of the boy so near her in blood and age, she missed the next few words and then, incredulous, heard that the Lady Mary and the Lady Elizabeth had been previously declared illegitimate and anyone who should acknowledge them as heirs 'should be had for traitors'. Northumberland's final sentence answered her unspoken question: 'His Majesty hath named Your Grace as the heir to the Crown of England. . . .'

Jane was speechless. The enormity of the implications of Edward's death shocked the not quite sixteen-year-old-girl who was so completely unprepared by temperament, intent, or desire to wear the crown. Covering her face with shaking fingers, 'weeping piteously and dolefully lamenting, not only mine own insufficiency, but the death of the King, I swooned indeed, and lay as dead. . . .' she later wrote. When able to speak, she said the first thing that came into her mind, and it was, undoubtedly, straight from the heart. 'The Crown is not my right, and pleaseth me not. The Lady Mary is the rightful heir.'

It took courage to face her parents, her in-laws, Northumberland, and the assembled Council, and deny the Crown. They had all decided her fate without recourse to or concern for her, and the girl's spirit quailed equally at the thought of the awesome responsibility of the throne and at the prospect of the punishment her refusal might bring. But none of those who knelt before her could now resort to 'nips and bobs' at her small person. Neither could they strike a Queen. Furious as her objections made them, they checked their anger and instead began an assault on her conscience. As the rightful and lawful monarch, Edward had designated her his heir, they reiterated. Mary Tudor would only incite civil war, and her religion was an effrontery to the people of England. Steeped as Jane was in the reformed movement, it was probably this last which persuaded the frightened girl. Praying to God 'that if to succeed to the throne was indeed my duty and my right, that He would aid me to govern the realm to His glory.'[4] Jane submitted.

The following day—as Mary was reading the Council's rebuke in the remoteness of her Norfolk home—Queen Jane was taken by barge to the Tower of London, past the questioning stares of the silent throngs lining the banks. A deafening salute from the artillery inside the fortress greeted her arrival. She landed at three o'clock in the afternoon and stepped ashore, her diminutive figure made taller by three-inch clogs on her feet, so she might be seen as she walked in a magnificent procession from the landing site to the Great Hall of the Tower. By her side, with cap in hand and showing just the proper amount of deference, walked her husband, Guildford Dudley. Puffing with importance as she carried the new Queen's long train, was her mother, the red-faced Frances Brandon, the Duchess of Suffolk. There were few cheers along the way, for, as one Italian merchant who witnessed the procession wrote, 'She is now called Queen, but it is not popular, for the hearts of the people are with Mary, the Spanish Queen's daughter. . . .' Soon the procession was safely inside the Tower and Heralds-at-Arms galloped to St Paul's Cross in Cheapside to proclaim the new sovereign. The gates closed behind Jane Grey. Save for a few brief moments later at the Guildhall, she was never again to leave it.

Upon reading the Council's letter that Queen Jane had been proclaimed in London, Mary Tudor thrust aside the feeling of hot resentment for the girl, a relative of whom she had always been so fond and whose mother had been one of her closest friends. Common sense told her Jane had not voluntarily sought the Crown; Northumberland, obviously, had masterminded the *coup* to apparent success. Within hours, Mary left Kenninghall for the more distant safety of the massive Framlingham Castle, and within moments of her arrival, her standard floated from the ramparts of the vast battlements of the Suffolk home of the Howards. Seventeen-year-old Thomas Howard, a grandson of the imprisoned Duke of Norfolk, arrived with many Suffolk yeomen, who bore bitter remembrance of Northumberland's cruelty during Kett's rebellion. From all Suffolk, others came—the simple country people, the knights, the sheriffs, the merchants, the tenant farmers, and the merely adventurous—all made their way to the huge fortress-like castle on its great mound near the Orr River. There they made camp in the shadow of the ancient walls, encircled by three moats in which clumps of golden iris grew. Nearby an ancient Saxon church mouldered. Framlingham had long been a place of peace and tranquillity; suddenly it became a scene of frenzied clamour and urgent activity as the throng rushing to Mary Tudor's support grew daily. By nightfall of the eleventh of July, five days after Edward's death, there were, incredibly, some 13,000 supporters, ready to volunteer life and limb for their rightful Queen.

Inside the castle, wisely chosen not only for its location but also for its impregnability, Mary had formed a small Privy Council. Daily, she was encouraged as others of the 'old nobility' rallied to her cause, many of whom had supported her mother twenty years ago. Out of Cheshire came Lord Derby, reported marching south with some 20,000 men. Rumour had it that 10,000 of the militia of Oxfordshire, Buckinghamshire, Berkshire, and Middlesex under Sir Edward Hastings were marching on London to seize 'the Palace of Westminster and all it contained in behalf of the Queen's right and title'. Devonshire had declared for Mary, and the Earl of Oxford and Lord Sussex were on their way to her. Heartened as she was by the news, she doubted she was a match for any army Northumberland might lead against her.

She sent a desperate appeal to Simon Renard, the Imperial ambassador in London, that 'she saw destruction hanging over her unless she received help'. Renard regarded Mary's chances as very slight and told the Emperor he thought her actions 'would only lead to her inevitable destruction'. Northumberland had appealed to France for 6,000 troops! How could one lone woman without an army withstand the might of the Duke of Northumberland, the Council, and the enmity of the French King? Mary's appeal, therefore, went unanswered as Renard and the Emperor Charles V waited to see which way the tide would go.

For Mary there were no such doubts. Fear perhaps, certainly great anxiety. But for one whose grandmother had been the mighty Isabella of Spain, whose paternal grandfather had wrested the Crown from a Plantagenet at Bosworth Field and become the first Tudor King, there was no question regarding her right to the Crown—and, if necessary, her willingness to die in justifying her claim. Accordingly, and with the thoroughness which always characterised her actions in emergencies, Mary ordered that church plate and monies from Norwich be requisitioned to pay for supplies. Bakers were summoned to Framlingham to help to feed those encamped in the fields outside. From nearby Orford, she ordered 300 quarters of malt to be brewed for the thirsty mob. In the neighbouring forest, trees had been felled by stocky yeomen and thrown as blockades along the main roads and lanes surrounding the castle. If there was to be a siege, there would be no quarter given her; she would ask none of her enemies.

And then fate turned the tide. Six ships sent by Northumberland to intercept any attempt by Mary to flee were driven into the Yarmouth Roads by a storm. With a boldness typical of Mary's supporters, Sir Henry Jerningham was rowed out to meet the ships, informing the crew members they were 'rebels to their lawful Queen Mary' and asking where their captains' loyalty lay. The mariners replied, 'Ye shall have them or else they shall go to the bottom!' Wisely, the outnumbered captains submitted, relinquishing their ships, men, ammunition, and other ordnance, which provided Mary with essential war *matériel*. A few days later, 'all ships in the harbour of Harwich declared for the Queen, having deposed Sir Richard Broke and other captains from their command'. The mutiny was contagious. John Hughes, a comptroller of customs at Yarmouth, and John Grice, captain of the notable *Greyhound*, 'submitted themselves to the Queen's mercy and were sworn in her service'. Each defection brought fresh stores of food, able-bodied men, and ammunition to Framlingham Castle, its royal visitor, and those waiting outside.

By the sixteenth, almost 30,000 had gathered in the precincts. With a guard of 500, Mary ventured from the castle to review the troops stretching around its walls—a good-natured, jostling, rough-speaking throng. At the sight of the small plain woman in her sombre black dress with the great gold cross hanging from her waist, a shout of 'Long live our good Queen Mary!' arose, and in further salute, a salvo was fired as caps were tossed in the air. It was the first time Mary had heard the cheer—'Long live our good Queen!'—and as they continued their shouting, intermingled with curses and threats to Northumberland, her horse became frightened. Blinded by the tears suddenly welling, Mary found she could not control the beast. Instead, she dismounted and, with her ladies and part of the guard, walked the entire encampment. At the end, as she arrived back to the castle entrance, she felt uplifted and stronger than ever. All those loyal faces, those rough hands eager to reach out to her, those loving, strong and cheerful voices! Reassured, Mary summoned her Council and the decision was made. That evening a proclamation of defiance to Northumberland left Framlingham Castle. To the north, south, east, and west of England went the stirring words, 'Know ye, all the good subjects of this realm, that your most noble prince, your Sovereign Lord and King, Edward VI, is upon Thursday last being the sixth of July departed this world to God's mercy. And that now the most excellent princess, his sister Mary, by the Grace of God is Queen of England and Ireland, and very owner of the crown, government and title of England and Ireland and all things thereunto belonging to God's glory, the honour of the realm of England, and all your comforts. *And her Highness is not fled this realm, nor intendeth to do, as is most untruly surmised.*'[5]

The last was Mary's answer to one of the many rumours which had flooded the country upon Jane's proclamation. It left no doubt the Duke of Northumberland was a traitor, a fugitive from England's rightful Queen. For the capture of the scheming duke, Mary offered a reward—£1,000 in land to any noble, £500 to any gentleman, or £100 to any yeoman fortunate enough to capture Northumberland alive.[6] A defiant gauntlet had been flung; the fight between the rightful Queen and the usurper's forces had begun.

Before retiring for her first night's fitful slumber as sovereign, Jane had signed her proclamation, 'Jane, the Quene', and received the keys of the Tower after the fortress had been locked for the evening. Within its walls were not only the new Queen but the Council as well. By Northumberland's order, no one was to leave the Tower until Mary was a prisoner. The next morning, Winchester, the lord treasurer, brought Jane the royal jewels and the Crown, which he desired to fit upon her head, saying another would be made for her husband. As she viewed the glittering circlet, Jane protested fearfully. The crown was

[307]

'not a plaything for boys and girls', she said 'and had never been demanded by me nor by anyone in my name'. Guildford Dudley was not so reluctant; his family had given him every assurance he would be King Guildford as his wife was Queen Jane. But for Jane to have her husband proclaimed King of England was unthinkable. She would make him a duke, she said, but only Parliament could make him King. Previously, Jane's marriage had been only in name—a marriage of convenience to suit the ambitious Northumberland. That morning his wife, the duchess, arrived at the Tower resolving that not only should her son share the title, but he must now share the royal bed also. Hearing that Jane had refused her husband the crown sparked a furious scene. The duchess lost her temper and hurled epithets at Jane while a sulking Guildford burst into tears as he was forcibly pulled from the room by his enraged mother. After consulting the Earls of Arundel and Pembroke, a shaken Jane was prevailed upon to ask Guildford to stay with her. 'And thus', she wrote later, 'I was *compelled* to act as a woman who is obliged to live on good terms with her husband. Nevertheless, I was not only deluded by the Duke and Council, but *maltreated* by my husband and his mother.'[7]

In addition to her role as Queen, Jane had now to act the part of a patient, submissive wife, and it proved too much for the sensitive girl. She suffered a relapse of her illness and, depressed and frightened, remained in her chamber for the next few days.

By July 13, plans for a campaign into East Anglia to rout out the rebel Mary Tudor were complete. Jane's father, the Duke of Suffolk, would head the forces, leaving Northumberland behind to hold the Council in line. The new Queen, realising how defenceless she would be against the Dudley clan with no father present, anxiously prevailed upon Henry Grey and, 'with weeping tears, made request to the whole Council that her father might tarry at home in her company. . . .' Not only was Jane terrified of being left at the mercy of her in-laws; she was also afraid of her own mother. The Council could hardly overlook the first request their new Queen had made. That left Northumberland as the 'best man of war in the realm', the only one with enough 'experience, knowledge and wisdom' to lead the enterprise. Apprehensively, he agreed. He had little choice. Reluctantly, the duke told the Council, 'I and mine will go, not doubting of your fidelity to the Queen's Majesty, whom I leave in your custody.' After a disturbed night's rest, during which he pondered the depth of his ministers' loyalty, he gathered the Council together. He told them he was leaving 'upon the only trust and faithfulness of your honours, whereof we think ourselves most assured we do hazard our lives. . . .' He reminded them of the oath of allegiance 'made freely by you to this virtuous lady, the Queen's Highness [Jane], *who by your and our enticement is rather of force placed wherein than by her own seeking and request.'* He asked that his ministers 'abandon all malice, envy and private affections in these troublesome times', and did not refrain from voicing his suspicions. 'If ye mean deceit . . . God will revenge the same . . . I can say no more', he told them. As the Council protested, one councillor asked, 'My Lord, if ye mistrust any of us in this matter, your Grace is far deceived. For which of us can wipe his hands clean thereof?'[8]

At Durham Place the carts had been laden with ammunition, the artillery and field pieces brought into place. As Northumberland took his final leave of the Council, the Earl of Arundel approached him, regretting that he could not accompany Northumberland, saying, 'he prayed God to be with him and bear him company'. The two embraced, Arundel even taking the duke's body-servant, Thomas Lovell, by the hand, saying, 'Farewell, gentle Thomas, with all my heart. . . .' Early the next morning on the fourteenth, eight days after Edward's death, Northumberland, accompanied by Sir John Gates and Sir Thomas Palmer, with 3,000 foot-soldiers, and 1,000 horse, left the City by way of Shoreditch. Dawn was just brightening the roads over which a mist from the river lingered. The people were abroad early and watched in sullen silence as Northumberland and his troops passed; they could guess his destination. That the duke was sensitive to their lack of enthusiasm is evidenced by his comment to Sir John Gates, 'The people press to see us', he said bitterly, 'but not one sayeth "God speed"!'[9]

It was on this day that the tide began to turn for Mary at Framlingham.

Northumberland's campaign to capture Mary Tudor and bring her prisoner to London was doomed from the beginning. Once the aggressive personality which could dominate a whole Council was absent, each minister—a virtual prisoner in the Tower with its newly proclaimed Queen—weighed the chances of Northumberland's success, for the outcome would vitally affect them all. Should the duke's efforts result in Mary's destruction, their positions would be assured. Should he fail, they would certainly lose their church lands, their new titles, and be lucky indeed to escape with their heads. As additional counties yielded to Mary, 'many a nobleman's own servants refused to serve their lords against the Queen'.

When news of Mary's proclamation, her defiance of Northumberland, and the price she had put on his head became known, 'each man then began to pluck in his horns'. Their uneasiness was reflected in Arundel's wry comment, 'I like not the air.' The next day, a placard on the pump at Queenhithe announced 'that the Princess Mary had been proclaimed

[309]

in every town and city in England, London alone excepted'. All over the City, the people were becoming bolder, excitedly lighting bonfires which blazed far into the night, shouting, 'Queen Mary! Queen Mary'. When the defection of the six ships of the fleet to Mary's cause was revealed, the councillors' anxiety bore its predictable fruit. Telling Jane's father, the Duke of Suffolk, they must arrange for foreign mercenaries with Noailles, the French ambassador, a small nucleus left the Tower and assembled at Baynard's Castle.[10] These included the influential Pembroke, Lord Arundel, Winchester, Shrewsbury, and Bedford. Five days previously, Arundel had regretted he could not accompany Northumberland; now he could only remember his unjust imprisonment at the duke's orders after the Protector's downfall. He voiced his companions' unspoken thoughts: 'Now we may speak freely of our sentiments.' He reminded them of Northumberland's 'monstrous treatment' of Somerset, of his disregard of Henry's will which had designated the Princess Mary as heir, a succession the people desired and which might result in civil war if ignored. He professed amazement 'to think how the Duke had brought such great and noble persons [the councillors] to so mean a servitude, to be made the tool of his wicked designs', which had ended in Jane Grey occupying the throne with 'the cause of religion' justifying the usurpation. 'What madness it is', shouted Arundel, 'for men to throw themselves into certain destruction, to avoid an uncertain danger. I heartily wish there had been no such transgression; but since there has, the best remedy for a past error is a timely repentance....'[11] The French King had offered no help, Arundel noted, though Northumberland had promised such aid, and the wary Emperor was merely biding his time to see how successful the *coup* might prove. 'My Lords, and most worshipful brethren', continued Arundel, 'I implore your prudence and equity ... !' He said the Crown must be restored to its rightful sovereign, Princess Mary.

The Earl of Pembroke, whose daughter was married to Northumberland's son and upon whom, next to Suffolk, Northumberland had most relied, rose up and shouted emotionally, 'If the arguments of my Lord Arundel do not persuade you, this sword will make Mary queen else I will die in her quarrel!' His sword unsheathed, the blade flashed high in the air. The die was cast; Northumberland was abandoned. The Castle chamber rang with the councillors' shouts as they made plans for Mary's reinstatement, and the vengeful Arundel left immediately with Paget to arrest Northumberland. Should the duke refuse to obey, Arundel was commanded to say, 'the Council will persecute him and his, to their utter confusion'. With the Lord Mayor and Lord Warden of London, the nobles left Baynard's Castle and, between five and six o'clock in the afternoon of July 19, made their way to the Cross at Cheapside. They were accompanied by four trumpeters and two heralds, and as the people saw the small procession they congregated expectantly about the Cross.

After a fanfare of trumpets, Pembroke began to read the proclamation. He had proceeded no further than Mary's name when suddenly the throng milling about him exploded. As one witness wrote, 'Great was the triumph here at London. For my time, I never saw the like. The number of caps that were thrown up at the Proclamation were not to be told. . . . I saw myself money was thrown out at windows for joy. The bonfires were without number and what with shouting and crying of the people and ringing of the bells, there could no one hear almost what another said, besides banqueting and singing in the streets for joy!'[12] 'God save the Queen!' and 'God save Queen Mary!' the people shouted with voices already hoarse from emotion. Their enthusiasm was infectious, and with tears in his eyes, Pembroke himself flung his jewelled cap into the air and, opening his purse, scattered coins into the sea of faces and clutching hands, as he shouted, 'God save the Queen!' Moving into St Paul's, they joined in a mighty *Te Deum*. Emerging into a twilight reddened with bonfires, they found the City in an ecstasy of joy as people spontaneously embraced one another, already a little drunk on the liberal portions of wine and ale. Flocking to the hurriedly erected trestle tables where a banquet of fat capons and rabbits roasted over the fires, they danced, sang, and called to one another. Each time 'God save Queen Mary!' was shouted, the cheering became louder. And over all, the clanging of the bells continued.

The tumult could be heard in the Tower, where Jane had promised to stand as godmother at the christening of a Tower official's child. But an illness had prevented her, and Lady Throckmorton had gone instead. Jane awaited her companion's return, sitting in the Chair of State, under the royal canopy, when her father, the Duke of Suffolk, rushed in. White-faced and agitated, he pulled his daughter by the hand and, with a rare gentleness, said, 'Come down from that, my child, that is no place for you. . . .' Through the windows, Jane could hear the cries of 'God save Queen Mary!' and her father shook his head sadly, the tears coursing down his cheeks, unaware of the exultant relief on his daughter's face. Suddenly others rushed in, quickly stripping the chamber of its royal regalia and other emblems of majesty. 'May I please now leave? May I please go home?' Jane asked her father, touching his arm beseechingly. Suffolk could not answer. He was busily gathering his retainers together, for he had one last task to perform. Telling his men to leave their weapons behind, he hurriedly left the Tower and walked with them to Tower Hill. There he threw his cap into the air and, in a voice choked with tears and fear, shouted 'God save Queen Mary!' before returning to the fortress. There he found that both his and Northumberland's wife had fled to their country homes for safety—

that his daughter and her husband had now been declared prisoners of the State. Jane Grey's nine-day reign was over.

Northumberland had proceeded as far as Bury St Edmunds with troops whose 'feet marched forward, but their minds moved backwards.' Desertions were numerous as men slipped behind hedgerows into ditches and forest glades. The duke had requested reinforcements from the Council, but he was fearful of the consequences of his absence —fears confirmed when, 'having writ sharply to the Council on that behalf as well as lack of men and ammunition, but a slender answer he had. . . .' Disheartened, he returned from Bury to Cambridge 'with more sad thoughts than valiant soldiers about him'. On July 20, Arundel and Paget arrived to arrest the man to whom they had sworn fealty only six days previously. They were not unexpected, for the news of Mary's proclamation had sped joyfully throughout the countryside. There were several precious hours in which Northumberland might have escaped, but he made no attempt. Perhaps fear for his family, particularly Guildford who was still in the Tower, prevented him. Instead, he followed the example of his partner in deceit, Suffolk, when he strode with trumpeters and a herald to the foot of the cross in Cambridge Market Place. After tearing down the proclamation of Queen Jane, he threw up his cap full of gold coins and cried 'God save Queen Mary! Long live the Queen!' That he was still stunned at the Council's treachery, at the overtaking swiftness of the events that had effected his ruin, was obvious. One witness noted, 'he was more believing the grief in his eyes, when they let down tears, than the joy professed in his hands' when he tossed the cap full of coins to the crowd.

His tardy acknowledgment of Mary's success did not save him. When Arundel arrived to arrest him, Northumberland went on his knees to his erstwhile friend, asking that the Council 'be good to him for the love of God. . . .' He had done nothing without the consent of all its members, he reminded Arundel. 'I beseech you, my Lord of Arundel, use mercy towards me, knowing the case as it is', he pleaded. In the duke's eyes, all were as guilty as he but in his extremity he had forgotten that the perquisites of power leave little room for mercy or compassion. 'My lord', said Arundel coldly, 'you should have sought for mercy sooner. I must do according to my commandment. . . .'[13]

On the morning of July 25, less than two weeks after his uneralded departure, Northumberland was brought back to London, a pathetic figure, the jaunty cap and scarlet cloak gone, showing only weariness and despair. The citizens had been awaiting his arrival, and 'armed men were posted all along the streets, to prevent the people, greatly

[312]

excited as they were, from falling upon the Duke'. As they reached Bishopsgate, the abuse began, and the hapless man was pelted with stones, mud, or any gutter filth the crowd could lay hands on. They ran alongside the procession, jeering and calling 'Traitor! Heretic!' so that the soldiers were forced to fend them off with sharp Morris-pikes. Near the Tower, the press of the crowd further threatened the haggard man, his three sons and brother who rode behind him. They were hustled inside with little ceremony and, as the mighty gates closed behind them, the eldest son, the Earl of Warwick, gave vent to his emotions, slumping in the saddle as he covered his face with shaking fingers and wept the bitter tears of defeat.

On August 3, 1553, Queen Mary arrived in her capital city of London. Behind her were two incredible weeks in which a capricious fate that had dealt her so many humiliations in the past at last bestowed the accolade of honour, dignity, and justice. The French ambassador echoed the opinion of many when he wrote, 'I have seen the most sudden alteration of men that could be imagined, and believe that God alone has led to this work, raising up a greater affection ... than has ever before been seen among subjects, not only offering their persons for the service of their Queen, but also bringing her what little money, plate or rings they had, and when they had done her such service, as is evident from the success that favoured her in a few days, she could not get them to receive pay or any other benefit.'[14]

There had been a general exodus of the penitent to Framlingham, each assuring Mary that in his heart he had *always* acknowledged her Queen. She had received the Councillors' capitulation in a letter worthy of their treacherous betrayal in which, calling themselves her 'true and humble subjects', they beseeched her to pardon and remit our former infirmities and most gracious to accept our meanings, which have ever been to your Highness truly....' The author, William Cecil, had arrived personally with an *apologia* of his own in which he begged the Queen to regard him with 'some difference from others that have more plainly offended'. Mary had been generously forgiving; she had no lusting for vengeance for its own sake. Several of those in Northumberland's service joined her at Framlingham; others received their pardons by courier or by petition.

At Beaulieu, Mary proudly received dignitaries from London who knelt and presented her a crimson velvet purse containing £500 in gold sovereigns, another visible token of her triumph. Each acknowledgement of her Queenship was a sign from a merciful Saviour that justice was at last triumphant. Satisfying, too, was the knowledge that her victory was her own. No Council, no City officials, no Emperor* had lifted a finger in her dire need. No one had helped her except the ordinary people of England—the yeomen, squires, merchants, the small county officials, and tradesmen. They—her own simple subjects—had provided the strength that supported the declarations of those few nobles who had previously sought a country anonymity far from the searing effects of a religious revolution.

Her journey to London, which took several days, provided the Queen with the opportunity to review her triumph, to think and plan for a future in which she might, in turn, repay those people. And to Mary this meant, in essence, a return to the old ways for which she was sure they longed as intensely as she. Perhaps not as it had been in her mother's time, but certainly as her father had ordained in his will. The despicable reforms launched by Somerset and Northumberland would be repealed. She had promised the Suffolk supporters she would make no change in the 'new religion' they preferred, even though she knew it was not the preference of the entire realm. She would punish no free thinker; rather she would hope he might be led back to God by the true way as it had been practised in England by everyone before her brother's reign was corrupted by such as those who were now in the Tower. Her first duty, however, was to arrange the funeral for Edward, whose poor wasted body had lain awaiting decent burial for almost a month. Apparently, there had been no time during Northumberland's power struggle to pay that one last honour to the late King.

At Hatfield, that mellow, red-brick Palace with its tremendous Great Hall and solarium overlooking a garden where bees from an apiary droned incessantly in the July heat and comfort could only be found in the shade of the great oaks nearby, Elizabeth waited. After being forbidden—allegedly at her brother's command—to visit him at Greenwich, she had wisely stayed at Hatfield, until further news of his condition was received. It came on July 4. The King was ill and wished to see her, the letter read, but the absence of the royal signature gave her pause. This was no message from Edward himself, merely a summons. She held the paper tightly, her mind refusing to accept the thought which leaped full blown into her consciousness. *If the King were so ill he could not even write his signature, then he might already be dead.* Elizabeth's throat constricted at the thought of the young boy, almost grown to manhood and about to be King in deed as well as name. Had he faced

* Indeed, Simon Renard, the Imperial ambassador, even regarded the Council's capitulation as a further ruse to lure Mary to London and had, therefore, remained actively uncommitted to her cause until he knew she had succeeded.

a lonely isolated death or had he been murdered? If her brother was indeed dead, as she suspected, there was little need of her presence in London. If he were still alive, he might die before she could reach him. Then she would be at the mercy of Northumberland and the Council. Mary, too, must be far from London. Had she received a similar message? For the first time in months, Elizabeth devoutly wished for the presence of her older sister. If anything happened to Edward, Mary was Queen. Together they might advise and console each other, but apart? Apart they were each a likely prey for any vulture ready to swoop upon them once Edward's life was extinguished.

Elizabeth dried the tears which came at the thought of Edward; tears would solve nothing. She must think, plan, arrange. She knew intuitively her brother had not sent the message. From there, her intuition extended no further and logic took over. *When in doubt, do nothing*. Someone had once told her that—again, hadn't it been her good friend, William Cecil? She knew beyond doubt there was little she could now do for Edward, even if some small spark of life lingered.

Suddenly her mind was made up. She called Ashley and told the astonished governess she did not feel well; she would take to her bed immediately. Ashley was to tell the royal messenger that while she, Elizabeth, deplored her brother's illness, she was too ill to leave Hatfield. And with that she walked off in the direction of her chamber.

Within days, her suspicions were confirmed. While still in her bed, she received court officials who informed her of her brother's death and of his appointment of Lady Jane Grey as his heir. Both she and Mary had been set aside in the succession, but the Council was prepared to be magnanimous. For her compliance, the new government was ready to offer her, Elizabeth, a large sum of money and considerable lands; all she must do was withdraw her own rights in the succession and promise to offer no resistance to Queen Jane's accession.

The commissioners need not have worried. Resistance was the last thing in Elizabeth's mind, but even she was shocked at their cold presumption. Resentment flooded her being upon hearing the outrageous words, *Queen Jane*. That meek and mild little creature upon the throne of England! Elizabeth was now only twenty, but in awareness of intrigue, knowledge of betrayal, and caution she was older by decades. Even so, the blatant hypocrisy of the Council's offer took her breath away, and she was thankful for the guise of her illness as she lay in bed and gave way to tears at the news of her brother's death. As she wept, her mind revolved around the offer, seeking a way out. She was still stunned at the news of Jane's seemingly secure accession to the throne. What was she to do? Indignation and anger, a passionate declaration, would only play directly into the Council's hands. She remembered another piece of William Cecil's advice, 'to conform as much as might be necessary for her safety, and to avoid entanglements or engagements of every description'.[15] *God bless Cecil*, she thought, her mind made up. Drying her tears, she told the commissioners in a tremulous voice that they had no reason 'to make any agreement' with her. In a stronger voice she concluded, 'My sister is the only one with whom you need any agreement, for as long as she is alive, I have no claim or title to the throne to assign.' The sheer logic of Elizabeth's statement took the visitors by surprise; they did not see her deeper reasoning which not only relinquished any participation in their conspiracy but also protected her from Mary's reprisal in the event her older sister should fight for her Crown—and succeed. And again, though seething at the injustice of the blatant usurpation and genuinely saddened at Edward's death, Elizabeth's decision to remain silent and detached proved the wisest move.

Daily, news of what was going on in London was brought to her. Wounded as she was and as deeply outraged, the girl realised time must again be her ally. She made no further statements, put no thoughts on paper.[16] During all the nine days of Jane Grey's ill-fated reign, not one word emanated from Hatfield. Her constant thought was—could Mary cope with such a disastrous situation; would she even *dare?* Elizabeth's impatience and bitterness warred with a natural wariness which ultimately left her shaken and thoroughly depleted. For several days after the commissioners left Hatfield, her illness was genuine, for anxiety gave her no peace during the day and little rest at night. And in just under three weeks, she knew her gamble to have been wise. Somehow, somewhere, *something* good had happened. On July 28, three weeks after her brother's death, the word came to Hatfield. Her sister was on her way to London to claim her inheritance—and she wanted Elizabeth at her side! Miraculously, all signs of illness disappeared, and the household, which had lived through days of tense and fearful waiting, erupted in a joyous relief. The very next day Elizabeth set out on the London road with her servants and was later met by an escort of some 2,000 horsemen armed with spears, bows, and guns. She arrived at Somerset House in London, the home of the ill-fated Protector, and there she awaited word from Mary. Soon the summons came—the Queen wished to meet her at Wanstead so they might enter the capital together.

Elizabeth rode through Cheapside, out of the City gate, and on August 3, met the immense royal retinue. Someone brought Elizabeth forward, and after a separation of several years, the Tudor sisters were at last reunited. Elizabeth knelt in homage, and Mary, overcome at the meeting, joyously raised her up and embraced her. Then spontaneously she turned and kissed each one of Elizabeth's ladies. With much affection, she insisted her sister accompany her, and so, at seven o'clock in the evening, the citizens of London, already exhausted by the events of the past several days and weary from hours of waiting, were rewarded as the two daughters of Henry VIII entered the City through Aldgate, receiving a heartrending, inspiring welcome on their way to the Tower. First came the Queen, in a 'gown of purple velvet, French fashion . . . her kirtle all thick set with goldsmith's work and a great pearl . . . with a rich baldrick and great pearls on her head.' For such an occasion, the greatest in her life, Mary had indulged her love of glowing colour, rich fabric, and jewels. Even her horse was caparisoned in gold-embroidered trappings which swept to the ground. Behind her rode Lord Arundel and 'velvet coats' numbering over 740. Following were her household ladies and gentlemen, and behind them came the men of Northamptonshire, Buckinghamshire, and Oxfordshire, some 10,000 in all.

At their first sight of the Queen, a tremendous roar of greeting arose from those swarming at Aldgate. Her subjects saw Mary Tudor at her best—richly dressed, her eyes alight with joy, a rare smile transforming her plain features. An inner radiance transmitted itself to her people, and they shouted repeatedly, pummeling one another in sheer happiness. Mary was thin to the point of emaciation, but no one doubted the strength manifest in the face, prematurely lined with anxiety and suffering. When the Lord Mayor kissed the Sceptre and handed it to her at Aldgate, the crowd became silent for a moment, weeping as they remembered her mother and father, their valiant beloved Catherine and their mighty Henry. Mary accepted the magnificent Sceptre and, smiling graciously to the Mayor and the people, rode on.

Then another thunderous ovation rose from the throng, for here was Elizabeth Tudor, showing an obvious appreciation of their welcome. It had been years since many of them had seen the second Tudor heiress, and their patience was well rewarded. Elizabeth sat her horse proudly; she was regally dressed, her religious inhibitions forgotten in the importance of the event. Suddenly she was freed from the self-restraint of the past few years; her white face glowed with pride and exultation, and her grey-black eyes burned with excitement. Her figure was shapely and young with splendidly straight shoulders, and at each call she raised her hands with their lovely long, tapering fingers and responded to all the tumultuous acclaim. The crowd became delirious. They could not move to follow the sisters, for the whole way to the Tower was packed, but instead vented their enthusiasm with great burst of cheering until the two women were out of sight.

A deafening salvo from the turret guns welcomed Mary upon her arrival at the Tower. As the first contingent of the procession entered the gates, there on Tower Green, near the place of execution, knelt several people. Three she knew well; the other's identity she guessed.

There on his knees was Thomas Howard, the Duke of Norfolk, the old war horse her father had imprisoned and whose own life had been saved when the King died. There too was Stephen Gardiner, the Bishop of Winchester, whom the Council had kept imprisoned for several years And there was Anne Stanhope, the Duchess of Somerset, her 'good Nann', wife of the executed Protector. Near them knelt a graceful, handsome young man, Edward Courtenay, imprisoned as a twelve-year-old child when his father, the Marquis of Exeter, had suffered death at the time of Mary's governess's execution. The young boy had grown to manhood within the Tower precincts. The Queen did not hesitate. She dismounted rapidly, walked swiftly to the group, and, embracing each one separately and with tears of release choking her deep voice, said emotionally to all, 'These are my prisoners!'

And so, their first evening in their capital of London, the daughters of Catherine of Aragon and Anne Boleyn slept in the Tower, aware that the City and realm was once again under Tudor domination. What would happen in the future was in the hands of the Almighty—and in their own personal destiny.

Five days later the long-delayed funeral of Edward VI took place—a 'very shabby one, badly attended, with no lights burning and no invitations sent to officials', the French ambassador, de Noailles, wrote to his King indignantly. The body of the first English King to be buried according to the rites of the Church of England lay in repose in Westminster Abbey[17] while his godfather, Archbishop Cranmer, 'with many tears ...' in his last official function, read from the *Book of Common Prayer*. In the Royal Chapel at the Tower of London, the Queen listened to a solemn Requiem Mass for the soul of her dead brother. In Mary's eyes, the Mass for Edward was right and proper. He had been born and baptised a Catholic and, had others in power not disregarded his father's will, would have remained one.

Mary's decision to compromise on Edward's funeral service is indicative of a desire to begin her reign with the minimum possible controversy and in the same spirit of tolerance that had won her such a stunning, bloodless victory. Her supporters marvelled at the lack of angry reprisal from one whose throne had been usurped and who had been declared unworthy of the Queenship and a bastard by her opponents. There had been twenty-seven major offenders in the Northumberland conspiracy, including the Council. Had she determined upon active revenge, she would have had to imprison each one, depriving the government of any knowledgeable minister. Weeping, they had all insisted that however much they had accepted Northumberland's domination, their loyalty had always been hers. She reduced the list of offenders to eleven, including Northumberland, his sons and brother, the Duke of Suffolk, Sir Thomas Palmer, and Sir John Gates. Her cousin, Frances Brandon Grey, the Duchess of Suffolk, had flung herself at Mary's feet, begging mercy for her husband 'who was very ill and would die if shut up in the Tower'. In a quixotic gesture of compassion, Mary gave Suffolk his freedom.

There was not one word from the duchess, however, regarding mercy for her daughter, Jane Grey, who still remained a prisoner in the home of the lieutenant of the Tower. Perhaps the duchess knew Mary bore Jane no active hatred; perhaps she did not wish to imperil her husband's release by petitioning for her daughter's since Jane was no longer of any use to them. Their plan of placing her on the throne had brought disaster to them all; better the girl remain where she was. Jane had written Mary a dignified, eloquent, and loving confession. She had bared her heart, telling Mary she had not sought the throne voluntarily and beseeched Mary for 'hope of your infinite clemency, it being known that the error imputed to me hath not been altogether caused by myself. For whereas I might take upon me that of which I was not worthy, yet no one can ever say either that I sought it . . . or that I was pleased with it.'[18]

Mary could guess the sordid details. Through bitter experience, she was only too aware of the product of human nature when consumed by ambition. While others at court clamoured for Jane's blood, especially the Spanish ambassador, Simon Renard, even he was forced to agree that the Queen 'could not be induced to consent that she [Jane] should die'. Part of Mary's willingness to spare Jane was her knowledge that the girl had been an unwilling tool; part was an inviolate conscience which 'could not find it in her heart . . . to put her unfortunate kinswoman to death'. Mary reminded Renard that her cousin, the Emperor Charles, had cautioned her against the 'lust for revenge which probably burns in her supporters'. Prudence in reprisal was best, said the wily old Emperor, and Mary, whose heart was malleable, could only agree. In the meantime, Jane was allowed the companionship of her ladies and the liberty to walk daily in the garden and on the little hill within the Tower precincts.

By the middle of August, Mary had reduced the list of offenders who must suffer the extreme penalty to three: John Dudley, the Duke of Northumberland, and his confederates, Sir John Gates and Sir Thomas Palmer. All the rest of 'Dudley's brood', who would have shown Mary little mercy had she been defeated, were reprieved. She had even contemplated a full and general pardon for the major offenders, but the urging of the Emperor led her to sign their death warrants. Mercy for some was right and justifiable, said Charles, but to leave the major rebels free to inspire others to further sedition would be hazardous and bring Mary nothing but the contempt of the masses. The Council, too, was pitiless towards its former head.

Thus on August 18, less than two months after Edward's death, the Duke of Northumberland was brought to trial in Westminster Hall which had been newly refurbished for the occasion. The vast edifice had been the scene of the trial of his former great opponent, the Duke of Somerset. In triumphant vindication, Thomas Howard, the formerly imprisoned Duke of Norfolk, now sat as High Steward in the very place where Northumberland had sat to judge Somerset. Those lords who had previously bowed to the imperious Northumberland will, who had advocated his actions and assisted him in their completion, sat as the jury. Northumberland, who had had several weeks in prison to contemplate his fate, 'paid great reverence' to the peers and, protesting his faith and obedience to the Queen's Majesty, whom he confessed greviously to have offended, said he meant not to 'speak anything in defence of himself'. Instead, he asked the court, 'whether a man doing any act by authority of the Prince and Council, and by warrant of the Great Seal of England ... may be charged with treason for anything he might do by warrant thereof?' His second question, conceived with equal care, asked whether 'any such persons as were equally culpable in that crime ... might be his judges or pass upon his trial?'[19] an obvious reference to his former confederates who now sat, staring at him stonily, safe in their reprieves from the Queen.

But despite Northumberland's claims to royal and Parliamentary authority for his actions, the judges and peers chose to interpret otherwise. No king could alter a law already sanctioned by Parliament, they said. Therefore, Edward's *Devise* and its accompanying Seal were valueless. The Great Seal of Queen Jane was the seal of a usurper 'and therefore could be of no warrant for him . . .' they decreed. As for his former confederates now acting as his judges, the councillors said, 'so long as no Attainder were of record against them, they were, nevertheless, persons able in law to pass on any trial. . . .'[20]

Northumberland knew his defence had been weak. His acceptance of the fate which had brought him to such an ignoble end should be dignified, however. He asked the judges to grant four requests. He begged he might have 'that death which noblemen have had in times past, and not the other,'* He asked clemency for his family, saying he had induced them into conspiracy, which was true, certainly in Guildford's case. The duke then requested 'some learned men for the in-

* Noblemen were usually beheaded. Those of lesser birth were hung until not quite dead, then cut down, the living heart torn from their breasts, then disembowelled, their bodies quartered and usually exhibited as a warning to the populace.

structing and quieting of my conscience' and a further interview with two councillors to whom he might declare for the Queen's knowledge 'matters as be expedient for her and the Commonwealth. . . .'[21] Facing death, as in life, John Dudley was nothing if not thorough.

On the day appointed for his execution, Northumberland asked to hear Mass and receive the Sacrament. While contemplating death, the man who had been described as a 'terror and thunderbolt' towards the Papists had second thoughts. He appeared with his fellow prisoners in St Peter's-ad-Vincula for the service, 'which was said both with elevation over the head, the Pax giving, blessing and crossing on the crown, breathing, turning about and all the other rights and accidents of old time appertaining'. When ready to receive the Sacrament, Northumberland turned to the congregation and said, 'My masters, I let you all to understand that I do most faithfully believe this is the very right and true way, out of the which true religion you and I have been seduced these sixteen years past, by the false and erroneous preaching of the new preachers—the which is the only cause of the great plagues and vengeance which hath lit upon the holy realm of England, and now likewise worthily fallen upon me and others here present for our unfaithfulness.'[22] His accomplices, each weeping profusely, confessed the same. Northumberland's recantation confirms the statement once made by Sir Anthony Browne that the duke had told him 'he certainly thought best of the old religion, but seeing a new one begun, run dog, run devil, he would go forward'. But now his affirmation bore nothing of the political, and a general renunciation of the religious practices he had adopted for temporal gain followed when he and his companions determined to die in the faith of their childhood.

On Tuesday, August 22, shortly after ten o'clock, Northumberland, Gates, and Palmer appeared on the scaffold on Tower Hill. As they were on their way out of the Tower, Jane Grey saw the man responsible for her imprisonment pass beneath her window. She made no sign of farewell or sorrow. The previous evening she had dined, with several in attendance, in 'Partridge's House', the home of the lieutenant of the Tower.[23] During the meal, the conversation had turned on the duke's recantation. Jane was aghast that anyone could renounce his faith. Being told 'Perchance he thereby hoped to have had his pardon', Jane was scornful. 'Pardon!' she cried, 'woe worth him! He hath brought me and our stock in most miserable calamity and misery by his exceeding ambition . . . who was judge that he should hope for pardon, whose life was odious to all men? I pray God I, nor no friend of mine, die so. Should I, who am young . . . forsake my Father for the love of life? Nay . . . God forbid!'[24]

On the short walk to Tower Hill, before being released to the Sheriff of London, the condemned men were reviled by those waiting to witness the execution. One distraught woman rushed to Northumberland and, thrusting in his face a handkerchief encrusted with the dried blood of Edward Seymour, the fallen Protector, shouted, 'Behold the blood of that worthy man, that good uncle of that excellent King, which now revenges itself upon thee!' Pushing her aside, the guards hurried the prisoners along. The duke's arrival on the scaffold was greeted with derisive jeers and curses from the mob of over 10,000, swarming from all directions towards the execution site. Gowned in grey damask, Northumberland seemed unperturbed and, leaning on the eastern rail, spoke in the face of the hatred welling up from those around him. He mentioned his conversion, saying, 'I trust my lord, the Bishop here, will bear me witness hereof', and repeated 'almost in every point as he had said in the Chapel', before giving his gown in fee to the executioner. As he knelt, he said gently to the man who stood nearby with the axe, a lame fellow, clad in the white apron of a butcher, 'I forgive thee . . . do thy part without fear.'

Suddenly the bandage slipped from his eyes, and he was forced to stand once more to have it retied. Kneeling again, he laid his head on the block, saying resignedly, 'this must be. . . .' At one stroke the head was severed, and the crowd pressed forward to dip their bits of cloth in the blood seeping through the scaffold planks. Sir John Gates followed, telling the crowd he 'had been out of the way a very long time and, therefore, we are worthily punished. . . .' It remained for Sir Thomas Palmer to provide a touch of the comic. Pathetic in his eagerness to forestall the moment when he must suffer the bloody end of his companions which he had just witnessed, he bounded to the scaffold, bade the crowd a cheery 'good morning', and began a long oration. 'You must understand', wrote one witness, 'that Sir Thomas Palmer had much longer talk on the scaffold. . . .' The crowd began to grow restive, and unable to wait any longer, Palmer summoned a wry smile and, turning to the executioner who stood patiently waiting, said, 'Come on good fellow—art thou he that must do the deed? I forgive thee with all my heart.' Kneeling down, he said, 'I will see how meet the block is for my neck. I pray thee strike me not yet, for I have a few prayers to say and that done, strike in God's name. Good leave have thou!'[25]

In a moment it was all over. From their place near the scaffold, the sons of the dead Protector, the Duke of Somerset, watched the executions. On the previous day they had been informed that Northumberland and his confederates had confessed to contriving the false evidence that had been provided for the condemnation and death of their father.

Chapter Eighteen

ELIZABETH and Mary Tudor spent the next several weeks in the
Tower, awaiting the coronation which would render Mary the
first Queen to rule England in four hundred years. Though the
accession had been gained, the privileges of royalty, as remembered
from the days of their father's reign, were lacking in the present dangerous circumstances where a female sovereign dwelt a few hundred
yards from her usurper. Many who had been deeply involved in the
coup—in this case the councillors—were the very ones who must now
advise the new Queen, and already a jealous bickering had commenced
among them. Though Mary had miraculously gained a victory, no one
predicted a further miracle to ensure its success, and the precautions
taken within the Tower were formidable. Both Tudor sisters were
keenly aware of the strong forces surrounding them—forces which
inhibited their freedom of movement, their communication with the
world outside the Tower walls, and any initiative or enterprise on their
own part. Visitors were compelled to seek the Council's permission for an
audience, a fact which did not spare her ministers the sting of Mary's
words when she learned that even Renard, the Spanish ambassador,
did not have free access to her. When the Council pleaded such
restrictions were all in the cause of safety, Mary was contemptuous. She
knew them all too well. Even with the gift of her pardon in their pockets,
they still sought to dominate at the expense of her own independence.

Both Mary and Elizabeth had their own quarters and were attended
by members of their respective households. They saw each other briefly
each day and walked in the Tower garden together. After their years
of separation they had almost to become acquainted again. For both
it was to prove a disturbing experience.

Mary's observance of Elizabeth could hardly help but be that of an
older woman—she was thirty-seven to Elizabeth's twenty—quite old
enough to be the girl's mother. Her regard for her sister was coupled
with the indulgence of a Queen destined to wear a crown and over-
whelmingly secure in the belief of her right to do so. She would soon be

[323]

in a position to act as a guide and companion to her younger sister. She would see that Elizabeth was comfortably and honourably maintained, as befitted one of her rank, and later a suitable husband would be found for the girl. She would have the pleasure of a sister at her side in all the forthcoming months when the pressure of the Crown might weigh heavily indeed. Although Mary was not brilliant in her assessment of what the future might hold, she was realistic. She recognised the social, economic, and religious issues facing her realm, even if the more subtle nuances of these challenges escaped her. In her simplicity, she had little doubt that she could resolve any and all such problems. By birth and heritage she was endowed to do so. God had given her the victory and the throne; He would give her good counsel and strength to do what she must. She knew it would not be easy, but with the aid of the Emperor and the few she might salvage from a treacherous Council, she would cope with her country's plight. In her naïve assumption that she was sufficiently secure emotionally to right all wrongs, while maintaining an easy, albeit firm grasp on her government and people, Mary made her first mistake. And in the appraisal of her sister, she made her second.

For Elizabeth, too, the days following the triumphant arrival at the Tower were excitingly different. Instead of a quiet country life remote from the involvements of the court, she now lived in a London fortress, in the very shadow of the throne. Her days were ordered, regulated, and bore an inescapable, if somewhat novel, aura of surveillance. There was little for her to do. She still had no duties, only the small pleasures of feminine relaxation—needlework, reading, and playing at cards with her ladies—filled each day. But she enjoyed the added dimension her position as heir to the throne provided. Happily she acknowledged all evidences of the new respect and approval greeting her appearance— the deeper bows, the courteous, almost reverent regard. She was grateful for proofs of Mary's thoughtfulness but, to her surprise and concern, found it almost impossible to reciprocate, though her heart, as well as her own common sense, urged her to do so. She could be, and was, her agreeable self with Ashley and those of her ladies who were closest to her. Yet she found it difficult to be anything other than superficially responsive to her only sister. Elizabeth possessed enough critical capacity to wonder at her lack of rapport with Mary, for it disappointed as much as it puzzled the girl. Often when alone, gazing from her chamber towards the Thames, while the cries of the boatmen floated up to her window, she would lean her head against the casement window and try to understand. Each day as she had walked with Mary in the Tower garden, she had averted her eyes from that dread spot in front of the Church. Here, she knew, her own mother had died. And up there on Tower Hill, only a short distance away, poor Thomas Seymour had suffered a difficult death.

Her mother had sought the Crown and had trusted in its aura to protect her. Thomas, too, had sought power from the Crown, and she herself had barely escaped with her life because of her association with him. It seemed almost as if the Crown itself were a barrier prohibiting any impulsive demonstration of genuine feeling. It hampered and diminished any spark of a spontaneous outpouring of love or affection and curtailed any confidences or tenderness. Tenderness was wonderful —Elizabeth had received enough of Ashley's devotion to know the comfort it could bring. But tenderness directed towards the Crown entailed its own hazards, she reasoned. And this awareness often stilled her tongue as it closed her mind when Mary sought to reawaken the affection she had received from the small red-headed child who had begged, years ago, to be put in the saddle with her older sister so they might canter around a castle courtyard together.

In the days that followed, as they awaited the coronation, the intro- spection which was so deep a part of Elizabeth—and foreign to her sister—caused her to seek a demeanour she might assume with some degree of safety. Her future, both immediate and distant, would depend upon her behaviour during the present; there must be some level at which she could live with ease—spiritually, emotionally, and physically. Even so, she was hardly ready for the immediate issue which presented itself with the funeral of her late brother Edward.

Elizabeth had been summoned to attend the funeral Mass to be celebrated within the Tower. After a period of reflection, she politely declined. She did not think it proper, she pleaded, to attend services which were not those of her brother's faith. As much as Mary was a product of the Renaissance, Elizabeth was a product of the Reformation, and both were equally staunch in their beliefs. The years of religious revolution, which had placed the power of the almost extinct feudal barons in the hands of the 'new rich' who had filled their treasuries with the plunder of church and monastery, were the years in which Elizabeth had matured. While the more drastic of the Protestant 'innovations' left her uncommitted, the more reactionary tenets of the Catholic faith —especially the controversial Mass—filled her with foreboding. Not for Elizabeth the mystic submission of Mary in her incense-filled, candle-lit oratory. Mary's devoutness sprang from the heart and soul; Elizabeth's derived from an intellectual expediency and a pragmatism upon which she would later call many times for survival. Mary would put her trust in God to endure and to cope. Elizabeth would put her trust in Elizabeth.

She had been firm, therefore, in refusing to attend the Mass for Edward. Much as she regretted endangering the tenuous relationship between herself and her sister, she knew it was *too soon* to commit herself. A natural caution urged discretion. If nothing else, her refusal would produce some indication of how she must act in the future. Immediately,

[325]

her speculation was rewarded. If the results were less than she expected, they at least effectively gauged the wisdom of her blunt dissent.

Elizabeth's refusal had angered and disappointed Mary. It was difficult for the Queen to believe that one of her kin would refuse to participate in the obsequies for a beloved brother, to deny her, the older sister, the same moral support and loving comfort she herself had so recently shown Elizabeth and which she viewed as her right. Alienated as she had been from all but the most superficial aspects of the Protestant movement, Mary constantly underestimated the Reformation's impact on a younger generation. And, with her anger at her sister, rose all the antagonism and inborn resentment that had flourished during the years of her mother's exile and death, and her own misery, degradation, and humiliation at the hands of Elizabeth's mother. Though Mary had announced during the first days of her accession that she would interfere with none of the religious beliefs of her subjects and hoped all 'might live together in a quiet sort and Christian charity', she regarded the defiance of one so near to her as ill-considered and disturbing.

Mary could not recognise it immediately, yet the small rift with her sister was symptomatic of a larger division within the Council where basic religious disputes were augmented by the suspicious jealousy and ambition of the individual ministers. In an attempt to make some reparation for past injustices, Mary had restored the Duke of Norfolk to the Council, and her faithful household officers, Rochester, Waldegrave, and Inglefield, were promoted to positions of trust and importance. She had named Stephen Gardiner, whom the Council had kept imprisoned for years, Lord Chancellor, To Gardiner's credit, he used his new authority lightly at first, but his competence, conservatism, blunt honesty, and ill-concealed disdain for the Council did not endear him to its members. While he did not advocate any reconciliation with Rome, he favoured a Henrician brand of Catholicism and a reinstatement of the Act of the Six Articles. He wished for a return of the stolen ecclesiastical properties to the Church, which shocked even the devout and staunch Catholic councillors, much as it angered the Protestant members. Many of them, including the able Paget, now Secretary of State, could not abide Gardiner, and Paget particularly lost no opportunity of undermining the Chancellor's influence with the Queen. William Cecil, his pardon obtained, had thought it prudent to retire to a safe seclusion at Wimbledon. As Renard said, 'the Lords were all quarrelling among themselves and accusing one another and the Queen could not learn the truth on any point. . . .' But Gardiner well understood the Council's mood and knew those upon whom Mary could depend. There were not many. He recognised the Protestant element's approval of Elizabeth, and he realised *that* subtle intelligence could hardly remain unaware of such support in a court where everything was soon known and exaggerated. So immediately, the question of religion had blighted Mary's hopes for Elizabeth. Instead of being devoted sisters, or at least agreeable companions, they were prisoners of their parents' actions, their own upbringing, and at the mercy of their advisers. There were many who, with hopes of their own to pursue, did not wish either sister well and encouraged the rupture religious differences had produced.

In addition to her wrangling Council, Mary also faced the more immediate challenge of the French and Spanish ambassadors, M. Antoine de Noailles and Simon Renard. De Noailles had encouraged Northumberland under whose administration Boulogne had been surrendered and the garrison forces of Calais reduced. The Dauphin was betrothed to Mary's young cousin, Mary, Queen of Scots, and with Scotland so firmly allied to France, it was possible to conceive the English crown might yet be worn by a French Queen if the Tudors were overthrown. But, at Mary's accession, much to the Spanish ambassador's delight, the 'French frauds were turned into smoke'. Though he had done nothing to assist her during Jane Grey's nine-day reign, once Mary had triumphed, Simon Renard had hurried to her side with congratulations and advice. The Emperor, too, made a swift effort to compensate for his lack of active support during her ordeal. Regarding religion, which he understood would be her biggest obstacle, Charles was explicit. 'We advise her to take very great care, at the outset, not to be led by her zeal to be too hasty in reforming matters that may not seem to be proceeding in the right manner, but to show herself accommodating',[1] he informed Renard. The Emperor cautioned Mary to remember she owed her crown to the Protestants as well as the Catholics, and to be guided by her country's Parliament, to hear Mass in her chamber with those whom she wished around her, but to 'abstain personally from any action contrary to religion. . . .'

It was a wise warning and paralleled Mary's own inclination to be lenient with those she felt had been led from the true faith. But the impact of the Mass at Edward's funeral and its early celebration by eager priests, anxious to reinstate the ritual in several London churches, had angered many citizens. Within ten days of Mary's arrival in the City, the undercurrent of religious tension was brought to a head when Gilbert Bourne, the Queen's chaplain, narrowly escaped a dagger thrown at his heart as he preached the Sunday sermon at Paul's Cross. The occasion signalled an eruption of prejudice and violence, a proliferation of seditious pamphlets and placards left in the streets. The tumult in the City, encouraged as it was by the fanatical reformers as they urged the people to fight for religious supremacy, was startling on the heels of the wave of joyous enthusiasm that had greeted Mary's victory. The Queen rose to the challenge, attempting to deal with it firmly and, at the same time, with understanding. Five days after the incident at Paul's Cross, she issued her Proclamation Concerning Religion:

First, her Majesty, being now in possession of her Imperial crown and estate pertaining to it, cannot forsake that faith that the whole world knows her to have followed and practised since her birth; she desires, rather by God's Grace, to preserve it to the day of her death; and she desires greatly that her subjects may come to embrace the same faith quietly and with charity, whereby she shall receive great happiness. She makes known to her beloved subjects that out of her goodness and clemency, *she does not desire to compel anyone to do so for the present, or until by common consent, a new determination shall be come to;* but she forbids all and sundry of her loving subjects, of every age and condition, under the penalty of the law, to stir up tumult or sedition among her people, on the pretext of upholding certain laws of the kingdom made according to the fantasies of men; but rather, commands them to live quietly until fresh ordinances be made, because Her Majesty desires, and strictly orders and commands, that all shall live in peace and Christian charity. Words of recent introduction bandied as insults, such as 'papist', 'heretic' and so forth, shall be dropped. . . .[2]

Mary's tolerance went further. In London alone, there were over 15,000 French, Flemish, and German Protestants—15,000 potential threats to the Queen's authority. Facing a coronation, the Queen and Council did not desire the presence of hot-headed agitators who might provoke further riots. Mary and her Lord Chancellor Gardiner, therefore, firmly encouraged those sincerely devoted to the Protestant Faith —foreign or English—to leave England. She wished no bloodshed, said the Queen, and those committed to their belief should practise it elsewhere. The Flemish weavers, who had camped in the glorious ruins of Glastonbury, were among the first to depart. The French Protestants were subsequently startled at the ease with which their passports were secured, and they and their Dutch counterparts left for Denmark. The more fervid Protestant English bishops were warned to moderate their activities. When this failed, those who further disregarded Mary's Proclamation were imprisoned in the Tower, the Marshalsea, and the Fleet. Others, notably the bishops of Winchester, Wells, Chichester, and Exeter, left England for the Continent.

While trying for a peaceful settlement in which all 'might live harmoniously or leave the realm', Mary saw the whole issue of religious provocation further disturbed by one who seemed the least likely, one whose past history had been marked by toleration, vacillation, and compromise—Thomas Cranmer, the Archbishop of Canterbury. During the previous months, Cranmer had remained comparatively unnoticed, shunning Northumberland's intrigues. He was sadly aware that Edward's death had deprived him, the leading prelate of the realm, of his most powerful support and protection. During the years of Henry VIII's reign, Cranmer had been pliant, bowing to the royal edicts in religious and matrimonial matters with an ease that made Henry his greatest champion. During Edward's boyhood, Cranmer had encouraged the reforming movement, and his undoubted sincere devotion to the cause had contributed much to a success which had flowered in the *Book of Common Prayer*. At Mary's accession, Cranmer realised that however much the Queen spoke of tolerance in the beginning, the movement he had promoted was directly imperilled. At the revival of the hated Mass at Mary's ceremonies for his godson's funeral, he had learned that instrument of the devil, the organ, had again been played in St Paul's, and the services were once more being given in the detested Latin. Cranmer was infuriated. In the windows of the simple households of the City, he had seen the long-hidden figures of saints reappear and had watched the many citizens flocking to participate in the ceremonies of the old faith.

When rumours reached him that he was allegedly preparing to relinquish the tenets for which he had laboured so long and again accept the Mass, some long-dead spirit of rebellion arose in the Archbishop. He offered to dispute before the public, stating that the Mass 'had no apostolic or primitive authority' and—in an outburst that stunned those accustomed to his more placid nature, so adept in the arts of compromise—Cranmer wrote a stirring declaration in which he defiantly proclaimed his true intent and belief. Referring to the 'great abuses of the Latin Mass', which Henry VIII had reformed and which Edward had discontinued, Cranmer deplored the efforts to restore the hated practice, crying, 'If her Grace will give me leave, I shall be ready to prove, against all that will say the contrary, that all which is contained in the Holy Communion . . . is conformable to that order which our Saviour Christ did both serve . . . whereas the Mass in many things, not only hath no foundation in Christ, His apostles, nor the primitive church, but is manifestly contrary to the same and containeth many horrible abuses. . . .'[3] Cranmer challenged the Queen to dispute his contention that 'the faith that had been in the Church these fifteen hundred years' was the same as practised in the time of Christ. 'So shall they never be able to prove theirs!' he finished his declaration.

Such a challenge to Mary's own proclamation could not be overlooked. On September 14, Thomas Cranmer was arrested and, after a long debate in the Star Chamber, committed to the Tower for seditious actions. Friends came to the Queen to plead for the Archbishop, but Mary turned a deaf ear. It was Thomas Cranmer who, in the teeth of a Papal injunction declaring otherwise, had pronounced her mother's twenty-five-year-old marriage to Henry VIII invalid—illegitimatising their only child, Mary, the rightful heir. It was Cranmer too who had urged Edward on his heretical path. Even so, Mary had been willing to allow him an honourable retirement or to hope he might leave England forever. His friends had urged the Archbishop to follow his many associates to the Continent. Instead, Cranmer had replied, 'It would be in no way fitting for him to go away, considering the post in which he was; and to show that he was not afraid to own all the changes that were by his means made in religion in the last reign.'[4] But Cranmer had proved himself no friend of Mary or her mother in the time of their 'troubles' or even later, and when he thundered forth his challenge, he sealed his own doom.

Mary was angered and distressed by the Archbishop's action. Immediately, Simon Renard, the Spanish ambassador, took advantage of the Queen's indignation to emphasise that she could no longer tolerate the religious laxness in those nearest her—and he pointed specifically to her own sister. He insinuated that Elizabeth's refusal to attend the Queen's service for Edward had undoubtedly encouraged many others in their Protestant stubbornness. He pointed out that not only was her younger sister a heretic, she was also a focal point for the Protestants who 'through ambition or persuasion might devise dangerous matters and execute her devices by means that would be difficult to avoid.' And he reiterated that if 'any harm happened to the Queen and the Lady Elizabeth were raised to the throne, the kingdom would become entirely heretical and Catholics would be persecuted'. Mary had endeavoured to sway Elizabeth. Her plea that her sister accept *some* instructions in the old faith of their father had produced no change in Elizabeth's attitude. As the French ambassador, de Noailles, had written, 'Elizabeth will not hear the Mass, nor accompany her sister to chapel, whatever remonstrance either the Queen or the Lords on her side have been able to make . . . it is feared that she is counselled in her obstinacy by some of the magnates who are disposed to stir up fresh troubles.'[5] For de Noailles, who favoured Elizabeth because of her refusal as much as Renard comdemned her for the same reason, the situation was ripe with promise. Neither of the ambassadors was disappointed. Elizabeth sent Mary word she might consider embracing the old religion, but she must be given time to think; she also excused her lax behaviour in part to ill health. For several days Mary did nothing, but Renard continued to hammer home that Elizabeth must no longer provide a rallying point for the rebels who were causing such seditious eruptions throughout the City. She must either conform or be made to leave the court.

To Mary's credit, she left Elizabeth a way out. The Queen could remember the pressure brought to bear upon her by her brother's Council and later by Edward himself. She had no desire to exert such coercion upon her own sister. Mary never doubted that Elizabeth's conscience was as inviolate as her own had been in the perilous time when she had been pressured to change the religion of her childhood. She herself had been happy to leave the court behind in favour of an obscure and relatively safe retirement. She had also been meticulous in not allowing herself to be used by any Catholic faction. If Elizabeth's devotion to her creed was as devout as Mary knew her own to be, perhaps her sister would prefer a similar retirement. So Elizabeth was given her choice.

Elizabeth spent the days following Mary's ultimatum in anxious contemplation. To leave the court so soon after years of semi-exile, her only visits at the summons of father, brother, or councillor—to forsake living within the shadow of the throne—was the last thing in the world she wanted. She wanted to be near the Queen; only at court could one observe its actions and plan accordingly. She enjoyed being the sovereign's sister, and the glorious spectacle of the coronation was not far off. The thought of relinquishing such excitement for long, humdrum days in a country manor was intolerable. In great distress, she begged an audience with her sister; Mary had been chary of personal communication in the weeks following Edward's funeral. For two days the girl awaited a summons and then, with little notice, was suddenly asked to the Presence Chamber.

Accompanied by a lady-in-waiting, Elizabeth advanced slowly to where Mary was sitting. Within a few paces, she stopped, and both ladies-in-waiting withdrew to a discreet distance. No one had spoken; there was no greeting. Mary arose, and for a moment the sisters gazed at each other. The direct, steady, piercing light in the Queen's eyes, which had caused more than one recalcitrant councillor suddenly to capitulate, now focused on her sister.

Elizabeth had entered with some degree of certainty, her poise apparent in the straight shoulders and firm, uplifted chin. But the Queen's cool appraisal, the silent waiting, caused a lessening of confidence and a curious unexplainable stirring of fear deep within her. Elizabeth was taller than Mary. Nevertheless, in the presence of this woman so soon to wear the Crown, even her formidable courage quailed. Without realising what she was doing, she felt her knees give way as she sank to the floor, surprised at the tears welling in her eyes, and cried out 'that she no longer possessed the Queen's affection, and she felt sure that it was for some other reason than religion, since in that she was excusable because she had been educated in it, and she had never even heard the doctrines of the old faith.'[6] She finished with just a touch of belligerence, and when Mary remained silent, Elizabeth realised she must go further. Between sobs, her mind was actively working, and she appreciated now, as she had not before the confrontation, that an impasse had been reached. There must be some show of co-operation, of non-provocation. Somewhat resignedly, she begged the Queen to allow her some books 'controverting that religion which she had always been taught, so that she might see if the reading would enable her to overcome her scruples'. As a further inclination of her desire to placate, she asked Mary for 'some learned man to instruct her as to the truth'. When she had finished her plea, which even in her distress she was amazed to find had cost little assault on her conscience, she waited. If Mary believed her, she was safe. And, for the moment, that the Queen believe and regard her with loving affection again was a supreme necessity.

Mary considered the kneeling figure at her feet, and a natural sympathy almost overwhelemed her. She remembered her own bitter confrontations with power in the cause of her conscience and her God. If Elizabeth were willing, she might yet save this sister whose soul she saw imperilled by a religious training their own father would have denounced as blasphemous. She helped the girl to her feet and embraced her warmly, 'rejoicing to find so much devotion in her sister', and promising that the books and a priest would be sent to the girl's chambers at once. Everyone was relieved—none more so than Elizabeth. The crisis had been met and passed.

In the next few days, the Queen sent Elizabeth several impressive gifts—a brooch with a magnificent table diamond and four rubies, two volumes bound in gold and set with rubies and diamonds, and a white coral rosary, mounted in gold—lavish reminders of royalty the luxury-starved Elizabeth regarded with gratifying pleasure. She accepted Mary's gifts and the religious counsellor, and the books on Catholic doctrine were prominently displayed in her chamber. On September 8, Mary invited Elizabeth to attend the Mass of the Nativity of Our Lady. Perhaps her sister's repugnance of the detested Mass would disappear once she was exposed to the ritual. Elizabeth hastily excused herself because of a bad stomach-ache. Renard had warned Mary that Elizabeth's professed interest might be only pretence and emphasised that the girl must do more than pay mere lip service to the royal edict. Mary, therefore, insisted Elizabeth appear; she would hear of no excuse.

At the appointed time Elizabeth dutifully appeared and again 'tried to excuse herself, saying she was ill. . . .' The Queen said nothing, merely indicating they would proceed to the church. Taking advantage of Mary's apparent mildness, Elizabeth 'complained loudly all the way to the church that her stomach ached, wearing a suffering air. . . .' Her bad grace, coming so soon upon an apparently complacent acquiescence, infuriated Mary. The Queen, too, had had time to review Elizabeth's supposed capitulation. It had been almost too easy. For one as devoted as Mary was to her own faith, whose nature could bear little dissembling, it was monstrous of anyone to use conscience as a tool of momentary convenience.

After the service, the disillusioned Queen was firm with Elizabeth and told the girl plainly that 'she did not trust her'. Sternly, Mary said to Elizabeth, 'if she went to Mass in order to dissimulate, out of fear or hypocrisy', her actions were false and meaningless. Forgetting her stomach-ache, Elizabeth obediently bowed her head and whispered enigmatically that 'she did as she did because her conscience prompted and moved her to it; that she went of her own free will'. Whether she referred to her own desire to appease the Queen, or to her behaviour as a result of a bad stomach-ache, she did not explain. But as she spoke to Mary, those in attendance upon both sisters noticed that Elizabeth was trembling violently.[7]

Second only to the immediacy of the coronation itself was the necessity of finding a husband for Mary Tudor. It was unthinkable that the Queen should remain unwed; she would need the advice and support of a consort, and if a beneficent Providence continued to favour her, there might even be a male heir to inherit her hard-won crown. When Giovanni Commendone, the Pope's Chamberlain, came to Mary at her accession to bring the Papal blessing—as well as to assess the possibilities of England's reconciliation with Rome—they talked of her marriage. Though Mary had earlier stated her wish to remain unwed, she said she now considered marriage a duty of State and conscience. Commendone informed her that her cousin, Reginald Pole, the son of the martyred Countess of Salisbury, Mary's beloved governess, had been appointed *Legate a Latere* by the Pope and, as such, was anxious to return to his homeland. Years before it had been the dearest wish of Mary's mother and the countess that their children should wed. Pole had not yet been ordained a priest, and his deacon's orders could easily be dispensed with if Mary regarded him as a suitable husband.

Anxious as he was to return home, however, Pole had no desire for the married state. He was too old for marriage, he said and, with the licence of a near relationship, was frank to tell Mary she was also. Better that she work for the reconciliation of England with the Holy See, the return of the ecclesiastical lands to the Church, he said, and let the succession take care of itself.

In addition to the Pope, there was only one other person Mary trusted—her cousin, the Emperor. Days after her accession, Renard was delighted to write to Charles:

. . . she was determined to follow your advice, and choose whomsoever you might recommend; for after God, she desired to obey none but your Majesty whom she regarded as a father. She felt confident you would remember that she was thirty-seven years of age, and would not urge her to come to a decision before having seen the person and heard him speak, for as she was marrying against her private inclination, she trusted your Majesty would give her a suitable husband. . . .[8]

Mary's dependence on Charles is understandable; there was literally no one else at court upon whom she could rely. Neither was there any-one else in England of sufficient rank with whom she could contemplate marriage, except Edward Courtenay, whom she had so recently released from a long imprisonment. As the son of the executed Marquis of Exeter, whose maternal grandfather had been Edward IV, Courtenay's Plantagenet blood rendered him eminently suitable for royal marriage. But, warned Renard, Courtenay might be used by factions opposed to Mary to further his own cause. Indeed, Courtenay had provided more than a normal source of worry to the Queen. Upon his release from the Tower, Mary had conferred the earldom of Devon upon him. The heady air of freedom had proved too much for the handsome, weak boy who had been denied all comfort, ease, and pleasure for fifteen years. Immediately, he had embarked upon a debauchery which shocked even his hardened and sophisticated contemporaries. Mary sought to explain or forgive her cousin's actions, even as she viewed them with distaste.

But Courtenay's profligate nature only emphasised the soundness of Renard's advice. Despite her Council's obvious wish for an English match and her Chancellor's urging of Courtenay, Mary remained unconvinced. Her own reluctance was strengthened not only by personal distaste but also by a genuine distrust of her Council and other advisers. There had been little indicative of any *real* support from any of them in her past. They had forsaken the religious preference of her father and marred her brother's reign as they robbed the Church, their plunder a comforting sop for any guilty consciences. She would put her trust in the Emperor and wed outside England.

The conversations with the Pope's Chamberlain, the Council, and the Spanish ambassador were only the beginning of the intricate process of acquiring a husband for the new Queen of England. In the midst of the execution of Northumberland and his confederates, of establishing her authority within the Council, of dealing with Elizabeth's professed conversion, it became increasingly clear there would be no respite from the pressure for some decision regarding her marriage. And as this pressure intensified, Mary also faced the very personal challenge of a marriage in which not only her own future well-being but the welfare of her subjects and the fate of the throne were inextricably interwoven.

From childhood, Mary Tudor had been bartered in the matrimonial market, and only in the years since her father's death, had the subject lain dormant. In those years in which her shameful bastardisation had depreciated her marital value, she had left girlhood behind, passing through an unhappy and miserable young womanhood, as impoverished emotionally as she was handicapped by physical privation. Now, approaching thirty-seven, she was being asked to accept the incredible: to think of acquiring a husband, a companion, a *lover*, and, possibly, a child. Those tormenting years had seen the repression of Mary's natural longing for husband and family. Now, suddenly, on the heels of her almost miraculous accession, the whole question was revived with a stunning urgency. And in this immediacy, the stunted almost dead yearnings of a young girl struggled to revive in the Queen. In their reawakening, there were many around Mary who formed a small tableau of encouragement, each anxiously urging a candidate for her hand. And as the days wore on and the question of her marriage assumed national importance, the small, stifled promptings within Mary, who had never dared dream of husband or child, rose again to the surface. This time it was possible—it might all come true.

Though the Council debated the candidates—the King of Denmark, the Infante of Portugal, the Prince of Piedmont, and the Emperor's own brother, Ferdinand, the King of the Romans—there was never any question in Mary's mind. She would do as the Emperor advised. Renard wrote to Charles that not only was there a scarcity of eligible English candidates, but he knew Mary to be 'great-hearted, proud and magnanimous' who believed if she wed in England and had children, 'they would not be so much thought of as if her husband were a foreign prince'. With infinite skill, the ambassador played upon Mary's nostalgia for Spain, her mother's country, the realm of her cousin and the only sincere champion in the constant fight against the Infidel Turk.

Early in their discussion, Renard broached the name of the Emperor's son, the twenty-seven-year-old widower, Philip, 'so as to put the idea of such a marriage into her head; for if she takes to it, she will be better able to convert her councillors to it than anybody else in the world.'[9] Mary had even considered the Emperor himself; they had once been promised when Charles was a young man and she a mere child. At the mention of his son, Mary said she understood that Philip was engaged to the Princess of Portugal and also ventured that he was very young, some twelve years younger than herself, and would probably 'wish to live in Spain and administer his other countries and provinces. . . .'

Renard extolled Philip's virtues, even as he pointed out the Prince's engagement had not proceeded so far that it could not be terminated. True, Philip was only twenty-seven, but he possessed 'great sense, judgment, experience and moderation . . . and. . . . he was an old married man with a son . . . six or seven years old'. Renard could sense the impact his suggestion had on Mary, and his intuition was confirmed when the Queen declared, with an innocence which must have impressed even the sophisticated ambassador, that she had never contemplated a marriage until God had brought her such a momentous victory. Indeed, she confessed, she knew nothing of love. She was but a simple maiden, she said and then, with an astonishing frankness as she coloured prettily, confided that she knew little of voluptuous thoughts or passion. But Mary was intrigued; Renard could see her interest—an interest he fanned in the following weeks while she waited word from the Emperor.

Even as the thought of marriage preoccupied her imagination, Mary also had to prepare for her coronation and the opening of her first Parliament. The emotional climate in the City was fickle. Rumours of her intended Spanish marriage had met with ill-concealed antagonism from the people, 'who were unwilling to suffer the rule of a foreigner'. Inflammatory handbills were distributed urging the citizens to riot; one was even discovered in the Queen's chamber. De Noailles, the French ambassador, met secretly with the Council and others of the court and was frank to say that a Spanish match would end any friendship between England and France. He cautioned that England would become a mere colony of Spain, taking on that country's wars and responsibilities. English law might become subverted to Spain, the Parliament suppressed, and the dreaded Inquisition established.

In addition to her disputed marriage, Mary's position as Head of the Church of England was another stumbling block, for the Queen would have none of the hated title. Too much of her own youthful misery and her mother's broken heart were represented in the supremacy so flagrantly assumed by Henry VIII; the validity of her mother's marriage rested upon the Pope as Supreme Head. All these issues were endlessly debated in a divided Council. One faction, headed by Gardiner, favoured an English match, preferably with Courtenay. Others—their support secured by foreign bribes—hoped either for a French or Spanish alliance. All the councillors were adamant that Parliament should repeal the act that had illegitimatised Mary before her coronation, and they reminded the Queen that she inherited the Crown under her father's will only if the Council agreed on her choice of a husband. Mary could see the purpose behind their objection, but in a matter so intimate as her marriage, she would accept no political interference. She wished the coronation to take place so that she might confront Parliament with the authority of a crowned sovereign instead of a vulnerable woman whose destiny lay in their hands. In an unusual gesture of conciliation which startled the Council by its suddenness, she called them together on September 28, and told them she had appointed October 1 for her coronation. Before there could be any protest, Mary

Edward Tudor
at fourteen and a
half years of age
*From the
painting at
Windsor Castle
By gracious
permission of
Her Majesty,
Queen
Elizabeth II*

Charles V, Holy
Roman Emperor,
by Titian
*Prado Museum,
Madrid*

Katherine Astley
(Elizabeth's be-
loved governess
'Ashley')
Artist unknown
*Courtesy of
Marguerite,
Lady Hastings*

Sir Thomas
Wyatt
Artist unknown
*National
Portrait Gallery,
London*

Thomas Parry
*From the Royal
Collection at
Windsor Castle
By kind permis-
sion of Her
Majesty, Queen
Elizabeth II*

The Old Palace at Hatfield   *Courtauld Institute of Art
Reproduced with kind permission of the Marquess of Salisbury*

Princess Elizabeth   Artist unknown
National Portrait Gallery, London

Mary Tudor
Artist unknown
*Ashmolean
Museum, Oxford*

Philip II by
Titian
*Prado Museum,
Madrid*

Queen Mary I by Antonio Moro
Prado Museum, Madrid

King Philip and Queen Mary, 1558, by Antonio Moro
From the Woburn Abbey Collection by kind permission of His Grace,
the Duke of Bedford

Elizabeth I at her accession   *Courtauld Institute of Art*
Reproduced with kind permission of Lord Brooke, the Earl of Warwick

Cardinal
Reginald Pole
Artist unknown
*National Por-
trait Gallery,
London*

Philip II of
Spain by Coëllo
*Kunsthistorisches
Museum, Vienna*

Thomas
Cranmer,
Archbishop of
Canterbury, by
G. Flicke, 1546
*National
Portrait Gallery,
London*

continued. Unsparingly and unflinchingly, in words with a steely conviction reminiscent of her mother's, she reminded them of her early life as a cherished royal Princess, of her unhappiness and sufferings during her persecution, of her neglect and intimidation in the years of her brother's minority. She then emphasised the almost miraculous success of her accession, a success against such formidable odds that even her own Council and the Spanish representatives in England had counted her lost. Only divine intercession had led her to the throne, said Mary in her strong deep voice, and now her duty lay to God and to her subjects. She faced each one deliberately and, as she looked into their eyes, affirmed that she needed *their* loyalty, support, and affection. And then, amazingly for one not normally demonstrative, she went down on her knees before her startled ministers and cried, 'My Lords, on my knees, I implore you', and opened her arms in a sweeping gesture of submission.

The meeting ended with acknowledgments of undisputed defence of the Queen; many of the more sensitive of her councillors burst into tears at the impact of Mary's plea and emotionally pledged their support and aid. The Spanish ambassador, Simon Renard, witnessed the scene, and he gave Mary her due. 'No one knew how to answer, amazed as they all were by this humble and lowly discourse, so unlike ever heard before in England!...'[10]

In addition to the more political aspects of her coronation, the problem of crowning a sovereign *Regina* threw into stark relief the precarious position of England's monarchy. There were no male heirs. Should Mary die childless, Elizabeth would reign. If Elizabeth had no son, all the remaining heirs—Jane, Katherine, and Mary Grey, even the Scottish branch of the family in the person of the little Queen of Scots —were female. The innumerable consultations of court officials had, eventually, resulted in the manifesto that Mary, despite her sex, was to be crowned 'in all particulars like unto a King of England'. Unlike her predecessors, though, Mary was burdened with an empty treasury; de Noailles candidly wrote to the French King 'she is so poor that her want of money is apparent, even to the dishes put upon her table'. Mary met the problem with characteristic common sense. Instead of borrowing abroad at exorbitant interest rates, she appealed to her citizens of London for a loan of £20,000. Anticipation of crowning a penniless sovereign—and a female one at that—only lent a further air of expectancy to the great occasion.

The spectacle of which Mary Tudor had never dared even dream commenced on the eve of her coronation when, at two o'clock in the afternoon, she left the Tower to follow the route of all English sovereigns through the City of London. The warm autumnal weather bordered almost on the sultry. The rare sunshine lent an extra brilliance to the

[337]

sumptuous display of majesty. Mary was accompanied by seventy ladies of her court and household, each clad in crimson velvet; the Queen alone wore blue, its deep rich colour enhanced by the luxuriant ermine trim. Mary was not a large woman, but there was an unmistakably regal aura about her as she sat in her canopy-covered chariot, its six horses 'betrapped in crimson velvet'. Despite the heaviness of the exquisite caul of gold network about her hair, her proud bearing was shown to good advantage. Set with so many precious stones 'that the value thereof was inestimable', the circlet enclosing the caul had been made for a larger head, and, in order that it did not slip, one observer noted the Queen 'was fain to bear up her head with her hand'. But even this slight inconvenience did not dull the joy in Mary's face or in the faces of those faithful ladies who surrounded her. Susan Clarencieux, Mary Finch, Frances Baynham, all dearly loved by the Queen, bore similarly radiant expressions at this overdue acknowledgment of their mistress's heritage. Close to Mary in the procession was Frances Roper Basset, the daughter of Margaret More Roper, Sir Thomas More's 'beloved Meg'. They had shared the years of Mary's trials even as they now shared her triumph. Again the conduits flowed with sweet wine and the people, trying not to lose sight of the Queen, swarmed through the tapestry-bedecked streets, where shops were hung with streamers, bunting, and banners.

Following Mary came the chariot carrying Elizabeth, her pale features flushed with excitement as the long slim fingers clutched the folds of her white and silver tissue dress. The same colours covered the six horses drawing the chariot; it also carried Anne of Cleves, ageing and heavily jewelled, but buoyed now by a surge of pleasant expectancy as she revelled in a remembered splendour when the Crown had weighed too heavily upon her own head. Despite her subjects' concern over a foreign marriage, everywhere a tremendous outpouring of love and affection for Mary Tudor was evident—a tribute almost overwhelming in the face of her people's remembrance of the Queen's unhappy past and Henry's ill-treatment of her mother. But here now, riding joyously to accept the Crown, was Catherine of Aragon's daughter reaching every now and then to adjust the gold circlet on her head—a physical embodiment of justice triumphant.

The traditional route through Fenchurch, Gracechurch, and Cornhill Streets, was slow, for at each stop small pageants were enacted. In Cheapside a welcome purse of gold coins was presented by the aldermen, and in a moment poignant with remembrance of her brother who had once been so dazzled by the Spanish rope-dancer, Mary tarried at St Paul's to watch the antics of Peter the Dutchman as he performed on the gleaming weathercock of the old edifice. The procession had taken several hours to reach the Cathedral and the steeple was to have been illuminated, but as the sunshine dimmed, the wind from the river proved too strong for the torches. Proceeding towards Whitehall, many of the onlookers lit tapers in the dusk, tapers 'made of most sweet perfumes'. Their fragrances wafted towards the Queen as she passed through the splendid gates to where she would spend the night before taking the coronation oath the following day.

On October 1, 1553, Stephen Gardiner, the Bishop of Winchester, officiated at the coronation of Mary I in place of the imprisoned Thomas Cranmer.* The excellent weather had held, and under a canopy held by the Barons of the Cinque Ports, among cheering spectators, Mary walked on a blue cloth 'being railed on either side' from Whitehall Palace to the Abbey. Perhaps in deference to her financial plight, she wore the same blue velvet and the ill-fitting circlet of gold as, accompanied by the aged Bishop of Durham and the Earl of Shrewsbury, two notable remnants of her father's reign, she entered the richly decorated Abbey which had been strewn with fresh rushes and hung with exquisite tapestries. Behind Mary came Elizabeth, obviously basking in the approval that greeted the procession at every turn.

The past twenty-four hours had been a tremendous experience for both Tudor sisters. For years they had been shunted off in remote manors, the targets of their father's temper, the Council's scorn, and their brother's conscience. Now, suddenly and unbelievably, they were the recipients of not only curiosity on the part of the people but also of a sentiment bordering on adoration. Mary could remember the pageantry of court ritual and the exaltation of a people's affection from the days when she had thrived in the happy security of two united parents; for Elizabeth, there was no such comforting memory. Thus, for the first time, the younger sister could feel the fervour welling from the crowds on either side of the railings lining the blue-cloth way, and it beat against her with an almost physical impact. In the Abbey—one of the few times she had actually been inside—the overwhelming vastness and her proximity to the solemn ceremony caused Elizabeth to summon every effort of self-restraint, to effect the demeanour befitting a sister of the sovereign.

Gardiner led Mary in turn to the four corners of the dais, solemnly proclaiming at each, 'Here present is Mary, rightful and undoubted inheritrix, by the laws of God and man, to the crown and royal dignity of this realm of England, France and Ireland. . . . Will you serve her at this time and give your wills and assent to the same consecration, unction and coronation?'[11]

* During Mary's coronation ceremonies, the Tower cells of Cranmer, as well as of Ridley and Latimer, were left unguarded and all might have left London for the Continent—and safety—with ease. Many of the court and Council had hoped they would avail themselves of the opportunity but, underestimating the serious danger of their positions, they elected to remain.

As the ringing response 'Yea! Yea! Yea!' echoed through the Abbey, Elizabeth felt her throat constrict and her eyes blur with tears. As she watched the ancient ritual by which a sovereign was rendered divine and apart, the magnificent meaning of the ceremony burned indelibly into her brain. After the Litany, as Mary was led away to don new garments, she passed near her sister and smiled comfortingly. Elizabeth attempted an encouraging response. In common with those other women close to the Queen, she knew the demand the moment was making upon the shy Mary. As the Queen returned to the chancel and the ceremony proceeded with the singing of a mighty *Te Deum*, Elizabeth felt her absorption surrender to another feeling which, try as she might, would not be stifled. There—so near—was her older sister donning the bracelets of gold, accepting the emblems of royalty, the Sceptres, the Orb, the Spurs, and being garbed in the robes of authority and majesty. As the Crown Imperial was placed upon Mary's auburn hair, a small kindling resentment penetrated Elizabeth's consciousness. She felt the small circlet on her own hair tighten. Suddenly, her head throbbed, and she sought to still the feeling of impatience and envy which threatened to envelop her as Mary received the homage of each lord and bishop who promised 'to become your liegeman for life and limb of all earthly worship and faith'.

At last, nearly five hours later, robed in purple velvet furred with miniver and powdered ermine, the Crown Imperial still on her head, Mary proceeded under a canopy from the Abbey, and Elizabeth quickly took her place behind the Queen. As the procession moved through the great stone portals, a tremendous 'God save Queen Mary!' rose spontaneously from the waiting throng. Again Elizabeth stirred with an almost sensuous gratification; how blissfully satisfying to wear the crown! Nearby de Noailles, the French ambassador lingered. Approaching Elizabeth, he made the proper obeisance and commented on the impressiveness of the ceremony. Elizabeth sought a fitting reply, disappointed that she could only utter ineptly that the coronet she wore had proved heavy during the long ritual and had given her a headache. De Noailles looked at the Queen's sister for a moment, his eyes compelling her own glance to remain firm as he lowered his voice and whispered: 'Have patience—it is only the preliminary to one that will sit more lightly. . . .'[12] Startled at the ambassador's presumption, Elizabeth remained silent.

At the celebratory banquet at Westminster Hall that followed the solemn ceremony—interrupted only by the arrival of the Queen's champion, Sir Edward Dymoke, astride his great horse, who rode into the Hall and challenged 'any manner of man' who did not acknowledge Mary I of England—de Noailles' remark lingered in Elizabeth's mind. Even in the face of the boisterous court, amid the chattering nonsense of old Anne of Cleves relishing her moment as 'chaperone' to the Tudor sisters, in the gratifying homage paid to both the new Queen and herself, Elizabeth found her response required an effort. At one point, as the royal party left the festivities and entered the barge for Whitehall, Mary turned, impulsively embracing her sister, a triumphant happiness still visible on her plain features. Elizabeth tried to reciprocate with some degree of warmth. Apparently it was only she who found the crown heavy. But then, Mary's radiance was the brightness of victory— not second place.

The first Parliament of Mary I, its 430 members constituting what one historian has called 'the fairest election which had taken place for many years',[13] opened on October 5, four days after her coronation. Momentous challenges awaited. Uppermost in everyone's mind was the subject of the Queen's marriage. De Noailles had not been idle. Tirelessly, the French ambassador used every means at hand to turn Mary's Council, her courtiers, and her people against a foreign marriage. Neither did Renard, the Spanish ambassador, spare Mary the dangers inherent in her selection of a husband. 'Because the English hate and abhor strangers', he said, they would distrust *any* foreign Prince 'who may wish to alter the laws, customs and administrations of the land'. The Council, too, said Renard, 'will fear that a stranger may desire to introduce foreigners into that body and thus acquire authority'.[14] He was blunt in telling Mary her enemies were fourfold: the 'heretics and schismatics' of her realm; those who had been close to and supported the Duke of Northumberland, namely the Dudley family and the family of Lady Jane Grey; the King of France; and, startlingly, the Lady Elizabeth, 'who will not cease to trouble the Kingdom's peace and threaten your position. . . .'[15]

Renard remained adamant that Elizabeth, as first in the succession, would inevitably become a pivot for discontent. Together with Edward Courtenay, they might be used by factions opposed to Mary. But if Mary indeed would wed no Englishman (and on this the Queen had remained firm) 'distrusting them as she does', said Renard, then she should choose her cousin Philip, son of the Emperor. Then there would be no such meddling in her government, for Philip was 'a prince able and ready to give sufficient guarantees and to bind himself by treaty to abide by his word. . . .' Instead of a stranger from a foreign royal house who might prove too acquisitive and interfering for England's welfare, Mary would have at her side a relative from her mother's land, a ready helpmate, a beloved companion on whom she might rely for succour and comfort. She would have a *husband* upon whom she could depend for advice and aid in meeting the challenge implicit in the crown so recently placed on her head. It would have taken a soul more independent, more enterprising, and more imaginative than that of Mary Tudor to withstand such persuasive logic.

But still the Queen vacillated and argued, almost in an effort to convince herself. Indecisive and hesitant, her soul—that virginal, slumbering soul which could face an army or Council with invincible courage—quailed before the reality of a husband. Coupled with her timidity was her own unsparing appraisal of the image she must ultimately present to that husband, a stranger from another land—the image of a woman past that first youthful flush of beauty, aged beyond her actual years. How might a man receive such a bride?

Mary had some support on her Council—William Paget, the Earls of Arundel and Shrewsbury, Mr Secretary Petre, Tunstall, the Bishop of Durham, and the Dukes of Norfolk and Rochester—but the remainder, headed by the craggy old Gardiner, the Lord Chancellor himself, were vocal in their dislike of a foreign marriage. Gardiner, particularly, emphasised that 'Courtenay was the only possible marriage for her. . . .' He and Courtenay had spent years of imprisonment in the Tower and despite the young man's wanton indulgence and the arrogance that led one observer to say, 'he could not save himself from the charms of liberty', Gardiner was fond of the youth.

Against this background of internal dissension and her subjects' disapproval of a foreign match, obstacles which might have intimidated the most courageous of men, Mary opened her first Parliament, 'riding from Whitehall in her Parliament robes . . . and had a solemn Mass of the Holy Ghost sung in Westminster Church. . . .' In addition to the nobility, it was attended by all the heavily robed councillors, now piously observing the ritual of the woman who had long been the chief target of their persecution. The full extent of her ministers' acquiescence in other matters, however, was brought home decisively to Mary within the next few days when Parliament dealt with the subject of her legitimacy. A bill requiring the marriage of Henry VIII and Catherine of Aragon to be adjudged good and valid was passed and so restored Mary's good name, even as it confirmed Elizabeth's illegitimacy. And, with the further repeal of all the religious laws passed during Edward's minority, the nation at last returned to the Catholic fold. It was, to be sure, the Catholicism of Henry VIII entailing a complete abrogation of Papal authority, but requiring a celibate clergy and restoring the disputed Mass. Mary had a price to pay for Parliament's concurrence. Despite her known desire to have all appropriated ecclesiastical lands returned to the Church, the lords 'immediately showed her that whatever might be her own hopes or wishes, their minds on that point were irrevocably fixed'. Mary did not pursue the matter. She had obtained the two things nearest her heart: her good name and official recognition of her faith.

In a subsequent session, the tremendous question of the Queen's marriage arose. Daily she had listened to Gardiner argue against a foreign husband. Later the Chancellor would be followed by other of her advisers, and she would hear the arguments of William Paget or another sympathetic councillor who would stress the advantages of a Spanish match. They would point to the forthcoming union of the Dauphin and the Queen of Scots, a formidable combination of France and Scotland against Mary, a single woman, head of a single nation, ominously noting 'what a menace to her liberties' such a union would be.

But in the end, the Queen realised the decision must be her own. In conversations with Simon Renard, she begged for more time and for more information about Philip. If only she could see and hear this man who had been proposed as her husband! How could she choose a man she must love with all her being, to whom she must give all her loyalty, unless she could meet him? The sheer implausibility of Mary's requests must have strained every ounce of Renard's patience—should a Prince of Spain journey to England to face a possible rejection? Dealing with the fluctuations of a woman's timid moods was a necessary if somewhat tiresome part of his ambassadorial duties, however, and Renard persisted. Caught between spasms of doubt and yearning, Mary repeatedly asked him all he knew about Philip's habits, his disposition, and his temperament. At one point she clutched the startled ambassador's hand in a strong grip and asked him frankly whether he 'spoke as a subject whose duty is to praise his sovereign—or do you speak as a man?' Renard's reply was all Mary wished to hear. 'Your Majesty may take my life', he answered confidently, 'if you find him other than I have told you!'

The ambassador realised something more was needed to help the irresolute Queen make up her mind. He requested Philip's aunt, Mary of Hungary, to send the Titian portrait of Philip to England so Mary might see the Emperor's heir for herself. Several weeks after the opening of Parliament, the portrait arrived and was hurriedly brought to the Palace. With it came a letter to Renard instructing him to inform Mary that 'it will serve to tell her what he is like, if she will put it in a proper light and look at it from a distance, as all Titian's paintings have to be looked at. . . .' Philip's aunt obviously admired the portrait too, for she concluded, 'So you will present the portrait to her under one condition: that I am to have it again as it is only a dead thing, when she has the living model in her presence.'[16]

The Queen, tremulous and anxious, was brought into the chamber. Breathlessly she looked at the ornately framed portrait, hardly hearing the ambassador say that, since the painting had been executed, Philip had 'filled out and grown more beard. . . .' She saw a young man, slim yet manly, whose wide forehead implied intelligence and restraint, whose whole demeanour attempted a soberness at odds with his youth. The blue eyes were kind. In their glance and in the shape of the head was a resemblance to the Emperor himself. While each feature in itself was undistinguished, the composite portrait of Philip II of Spain was elegant, handsome, and agreeable, and Mary was struck with the forceful attractiveness of the Prince. Her second impressions was one of disbelief—that this neat, fine figure of a man might be hers. She whispered her thanks to the ambassador and left the room, the picture burned indelibly upon her consciousness.

During the next day Mary told Renard she had 'wept over two hours that very day, praying God to inspire her in her decision. . . .' The Queen, Renard wrote to Charles, said 'she could not do otherwise than follow your Majesty's good and trusted advice', and it is indicative of her edginess that even in this instance she burst into tears. Gardiner and her two trusted household officers, Waldegrave and Inglefield, had previously approached her and stressed the danger of the Spanish marriage. The long discussion with men for whom she had affection and respect had shaken her and contributed to a recurrence of her misgivings. Her dilemma: to remain unwed; to marry the only possible Englishman, the foolish Courtenay; or to wed the Spanish Prince. Such decision had frayed Mary's ever sensitive nerves. She had wrestled with this problem alone, aware indeed that if she remained unwed, she would have to face *all* problems alone. The thought of the dissolute Courtenay as her husband repelled her. But Philip? Everything about him was absolutely right, except his age and her people's distrust of a foreigner. If Mary dwelt at length upon the latter—and it is characteristic that she would—in this instance she let her heart rule her head, putting her own will before the will of the people. At last she sent for Renard, and at the end of October, a final poignant scene took place which the ambassador described to the Emperor:

On Sunday evening, the 29th, the Queen sent for me, and I went to her. In the room where she spoke to me was the Holy Sacrament, and she told me that since I had presented your Majesty's letters to her, she had not slept, but had continually wept and prayed God to inspire her with an answer to the question of marriage. . . . As the Holy Sacrament had been in her room, she had invoked it as her protector, guide and counsellor, and still prayed with all her heart that it would come to her help. She then knelt and said *Veni Creator Spiritus*. There was no one else in the room except Mrs Clarencieux and myself, and we did the same. . . . When the Queen got up . . . she felt herself inspired by God, who had performed so many miracles in her favour, to give me her promise to marry His Highness there, before the Holy Sacrament, and her mind, once made up, would never change, but she would love him perfectly and never give him cause to be jealous. She had pretended to be ill for the last two days, but her illness was really the travail that this decision had cost her.[17]

Mary's pretended illness had been to prevent, during her final uncertainty, any confrontation with the Chancellor and a deputation from the House of Commons. Once her mind was made up, however, she summoned them to her so quickly that in haste, the Speaker could not find his prepared address. They came into the Presence Chamber. At one end stood the Queen, her nervousness concealed, she hoped, behind a rigid, almost austere manner. There Gardiner, Paget, Arundel, and others of her Council waited as Mr Speaker apologised for losing his address but launched anyway into a fine oration emphasising the succession, the need for an heir, and the hope that Mary of England would wed within her realm. A foreign husband would involve the nation in his own country's wars, foreigners would sit in high places in the government, and any heirs might be spirited away to foreign courts—the speaker became so entranced with his own wordiness he did not notice the Queen's growing impatience. Eventually she gave up standing and sat down, her hands clenched together in her lap. When the monologue was finally over and before Gardiner, as Chancellor, could make a reply, Mary interrupted and, in her deep voice which she attempted to keep even, she said, 'For your desire to see us married we thank you; your desire to dictate to us the consort whom we shall choose, we consider somewhat superfluous. The English Parliament', said the Queen, her voice rising, 'has not been wont to use such language to their sovereigns, and where private persons in such cases follow their private tastes, sovereigns may reasonably challenge an equal liberty!'

The deputation had not expected such a forceful reply from the offended Queen, and they shuffled nervously, glancing at one another, as Mary continued stormily. 'If you, our Commons, force upon us a husband whom we dislike, it may occasion the inconvenience of our death. If we marry where we do not love, we shall be in our grave in three months and the heir of whom you speak will not have been brought into being. . . .' Mary said she had heard much mention of the 'incommodities which may attend our marriage'. Scathingly, she told them, 'We have not heard from you of the commodities thereof—one which is of some weight with us. . . . that of our private inclination!' Wearying of the scene, she told her ministers she had not forgotten her coronation oath and would 'marry as God shall direct our choice, to His honour and to our country's good.'[18]

Turning to leave, she heard Paget jibe at Gardiner, with whom he was at constant odds, that the Queen in her speech 'had usurped the Chancellor's office!' The levity in Paget's voice further irritated Mary, and in a rare fit of petulance, she turned on Gardiner, 'I have you to thank, my Lord, for this business!' Gardiner stoutly maintained his innocence. It had been the wish of the Commons to petition the Queen, he said, although it was true to some extent that he favoured young Courtenay as her husband, for he had come to know the young man well during their imprisonment. 'And is your having known him in the Tower', replied the Queen dryly, 'a reason that you should think him a fitting husband for me?' an answer which so stung the doughty old Chancellor that he burst into tears. Her patience at an end, the Queen turned abruptly, facing those remaining in the chamber. Obviously fighting for control, Mary said in a tight voice, 'I will never marry him—that I promise you—and I am a woman of my word. What I say, I do!' As she finished, she quickly departed, leaving the Chancellor to his tears and the Commons to their own private thoughts. There were to be no more submissions for Mary Tudor.

Chapter Nineteen

THE Parliament which had reinstated Mary's good name had, by annulling the marriage of Anne Boleyn and Henry VIII, bastardised Elizabeth. From 'motives of delicacy', however, the Queen had thoughtfully decreed that no such actual pronouncement be made. The matter of the succession now rested with the Queen, and Elizabeth's claim depended upon Mary naming her as inheritrix, a fact which did not escape the younger sister, even as it was not overlooked by those others of royal blood—the families of Jane Grey, Edward Courtenay, and Mary, Queen of Scots.

That Mary did not mean to name any successor, however, was obvious in her desire for an early marriage to Philip from which she hoped to have a child of her own, an heir raised in the religion of its parents. While there were many—remembering her mother's sad history of stillborn children—who laughed at the idea of the thirty-seven-year-old Mary Tudor producing a living child, it was not entirely impossible. With the Queen's recent good fortune, Providence might yet bestow another half-Spanish Tudor to reign in England. Such an heir would not only ensure a solid succession but provide also a firm buttress to the restoration of the Catholic religion.

Five weeks after Mary's poignant scene with Renard, the Council had capitulated to her wishes, and an agreement was signed for the marriage of Philip of Spain to Mary of England. Had the minute details of Mary's wedding agreement then been made known to her subjects, much of the subsequent torment of her reign might have been avoided. Lacking modern means of communication, however, the people relied more on the rumours that sped from town to village to hamlet, rumours that grew in the telling as they did in distortion. It was impossible for Mary's people to know immediately the hard bargain the Council had wrung from the Emperor, and when the details were finally made public, it was too late. The fears of those who spoke threateningly of their distaste and hatred of 'the coming of the Spaniard' might have been calmed had they realised how little Spain had actually gained. By the terms of the wedding agreement, Philip attained little beyond a dubious prestige from the union, which was, in essence, a hard-nosed snub at the proposed betrothal of Mary, Queen of Scots, Henry VIII's grandniece, to the Dauphin of France.

Despite the people's cry that 'foreigners would sit in high places' and shape England's foreign policy, neither Philip nor any other Spaniard could, as the marriage agreement stipulated, hold office on the Council, in the royal household, the Army or the Navy. Neither could they hold any political office or have access to England's wealth, a rather hollow restriction considering the country's empty exchequer. While Philip would be known as the King of England, it was valid only as long as Mary was alive, and though he bore the title of majesty, he had no authority to direct that England become involved in Spain's wars. Mary was to receive £60,000 as her marriage jointure. Any child of the union would inherit not only the English Crown, but the Crowns of Burgundy and the Low Countries as well. In the event of the death of Don Carlos, Philip's older son by a former marriage, Mary's child would also inherit the kingdom of Spain, Sicily, and Philip's other dominions. Yet, in the case of Mary's death, Philip would automatically lose his title and would be required to relinquish any claim upon his child. Upon all these points, the Council had been adamant. If they must suffer a foreign King, he was to be as powerless as possible, and it is significant of the Emperor's deep desire to see the wedding accomplished that the English Council won in every instance.

Other than the person of the Queen, all Philip was to have was a depleted treasury, tremendous national debt, the empty title of King of England, and the enmity of almost the entire nation. For the Emperor and for Philip it seemed worthwhile. With Philip taking Mary Tudor to wife, they would combat France, the traditional enemy of Spain and the French King's ambitions for Mary, Queen of Scots's claim to the English throne.

But Mary's subjects, lacking accurate information about the marriage treaty, reacted in the fashion predictable of a nation insular in its heritage. Throughout the length and breadth of England, the rumours flew—the Spaniards were coming, and once on English soil, there would be bloodshed, rape, the establishment of the Inquisition and the forcible imprisonment of the Queen herself, while foreigners took over the government and the realm.* No lone woman, especially the naïve and vulnerable Mary Tudor, would be a match for the shrewd Emperor, his son, and Simon Renard, their ambassador. The deviousness of the

---

* The extent of the fear which, in some areas bordered on hysteria, is shown in the action of the mayor of Plymouth who sent a message to the French ambassador, de Noailles, asking that the town—a possible landing-site for the Spanish fleet—be put under French protection with resident French troops.[1]

Spaniards would only result in the English nation becoming a virtual colony of Spain.

In all their fears, the people were ready prey for the professional agitators, either political or religious, who threatened that once on English soil Philip and his followers would also seize the Tower, murder the Queen, strip the nobles of their church lands, wealth, and power, and restore the country to the authority of the Pope. The subtle intriguings, particularly of de Noailles, effectively undermined Mary's hopes and plans. In meetings with the members of the Protestant faction, the French ambassador stressed the danger facing England should the Spanish marriage take place—dangers the Council had done its best to avert by a tough and advantageous treaty. From Thames-side wharves and taverns to the more elegant river mansions, through the southern counties, on to Devonshire and Cornwall, Protestants as well as those Catholics genuinely interested in England's future discussed the great issue, and all agreed that 'foreigners would not rule in their country'.

Amid the emotional turbulence greeting the announcement of the Queen's proposed marriage, Elizabeth remained at court. Daily her position became more difficult. A formally professed Protestant, child of a King, however illegitimate her birth might be, Elizabeth was younger, healthier, more attractive, and certainly more capable of bearing children than her ageing sister. Immediately, her name had been linked with that of young, profligate Edward Courtenay. Why should Elizabeth not wed this Plantagenet, descendant of Edward IV, and solve the foreign difficulty? Elizabeth had never been without friends in England; for years the Protestants had looked to her as their standard-bearer. Now they regarded her marriage to Courtenay as the only possible solution to the repugnant combination of Mary and Philip that not only affronted their national pride but directly endangered their religious doctrine as well.

Elizabeth was intensely aware of her predicament. Events had happened so quickly—scarcely four months had elapsed since the Queen's almost miraculous accession—that each day brought a fresh assessment of her own position, its relative safety and strength. She knew her claim to the throne rested on Mary's good will and on the Queen's failure to provide an heir. She knew the religious dissent of the reformers was of incalculable value, even as it posed an equally disastrous threat: it all depended upon where the power lay at the moment. As 'the darling of the Protestants', Elizabeth was now more conspicuously in the public eye, not only as the sovereign's sister, but also as the hope of a young, pulsating, and revolutionary movement which hoped to accomplish the ruin of the Queen and her hated husband-to-be.

There were those eager to flame any antagonism between the sisters. Renard, the Spanish ambassador, repeatedly urged Mary to send

Elizabeth to the Tower. There it would be difficult for her to serve as anything other than a figurehead of those Protestants who might demonstrate on Philip's arrival, to the embarrassment and possible physical injury of the Spanish Prince. Others around the Queen accused Elizabeth of co-operating with those small rebellious groups rumoured to be rising in the West Country. The warmth which the joy of her coronation had engendered in Mary for Elizabeth had waned with the knowledge that Protestant leaders had singled her out for confidential visits. Mary remembered Elizabeth's half-hearted attempt at conversion and told Renard that 'it would burden her conscience too heavily to allow Elizabeth to succeed, for she only went to Mass out of hypocrisy, she had not a single servant or Maid-of-Honour who was not a heretic, she talked every day with heretics and lent an ear to all their evil designs. . . .'[2] The Queen's own choice of a successor was her cousin, Lady Margaret Douglas, the Countess of Lennox, a grandniece of Henry VIII. The royal preference became pointed when the countess was given precedence over Elizabeth at court festivities. Previously, Mary had insisted on having Elizabeth at her side, often holding her sister warmly by the hand as they walked in procession. Now, because the poison of distrust and suspicion deliberately administered to the Queen had corroded their relationship, Elizabeth was compelled to walk behind the countess, and Mary's attitude to her younger sister had noticeably cooled. Immediately those in the Queen's entourage reacted similarly so that, except for the attention of some of the young courtiers, Elizabeth was virtually ostracised.

Two succeeding events did not diminish the girl's worry about her position. On St Andrew's Day, November 20, as she walked in a court procession to chapel, a malcontent glared in her direction, pointed, and shouted 'Treason!' The cry was so unexpected, the singling out so stunning, that Elizabeth felt an alien and searing surge of fear engulf her. She stumbled—aware that her awkwardness most likely appeared as glaring guilt to those who turned to witness her reaction. But the fear did not subside. Confused and obviously distressed throughout the service, Elizabeth returned to her chambers and told Mary's lady-in-waiting Mrs Clarencieux 'that she was amazed that the Queen had not retired after such a warning' and that she herself had trembled 'for fear some outrage might be attempted against her person'. Elizabeth knew the people's discontent with her sister's proposed marriage; she had seen the seditious pamphlets strewn in the streets—some had even been left in court chambers. On the very day after Mary's wedding announcement, a dead dog, with cropped ears, its head shaven to resemble a priest, with a halter around the neck and a label reading 'All priests should be hanged!' had been thrown into the Queen's chamber.

In the perplexing situation in which Elizabeth found herself—a situation in which she and Courtenay 'were proper instruments for the purpose of exciting a popular uprising'—Elizabeth acted predictably. Distance was best put between her and the throne. Much as she longed to remain in the brilliant court setting which compensated for so many years of provincial dullness, her own prudence asserted itself. Though Elizabeth had wisely remained actively uncommitted to any specific cause, she knew the visits of the French and Venetian ambassadors and the representatives of the Protestant movement had compromised her. They would not hesitate to use her as a threat to Mary and to the marriage which many regarded as a national tragedy. The emotional strain of the forthcoming marriage and Renard's repeated warnings might only aggravate the Queen further. However well-meaning those who looked to Elizabeth as a national hope might be, their preference might only precipitate her doom. She could be forcibly banished, imprisoned in the Tower, or at least made to suffer an unwelcome confinement far from court. Elizabeth, therefore, requested permission to leave for her country dwelling at Ashridge in Hertfordshire.

Simon Renard had spared the Queen nothing in stressing that Elizabeth's actions could be considered nothing less than treachery. Though he advised her immediate removal to the Tower, the Queen could not bring herself to imprison her sister. Beaten for the moment, the shrewd ambassador then suggested Elizabeth be allowed to depart for a place where she might be kept under close surveillance. In the relaxed atmosphere of a country manor, she might even be foolish enough to commit some indiscretion that would convince the Queen of her guilt once and for all. After some thought, Mary advised that Renard, as well as Councillors Arundel and Paget, should speak with Elizabeth and 'make the Princess understand that they were aware of the bad counsels which she was following. . . .' After that, Elizabeth was free to go.

Therefore, as the court prepared for its first festive Christmas with a newly crowned sovereign, and as Mary dreamed of Philip's imminent arrival, Elizabeth appeared before her sister to say good-bye. She had received the Council members and listened to their admonitions, attempting to combat their suspicions by saying her change in religion had been made by 'conscience and affection' and she would 'prove this by taking good churchmen with her and would send away any of her servants who were suspected and, in short, do all in her power to win the Queen's approval'. Now, as she advanced hurriedly to where her sister stood, she remembered these words. Quickly she knelt at Mary's feet, awaiting the Queen's command to rise.

Mary, on her part, felt the tension in the slim young girl at her feet. The Queen had been told by Renard to 'dissemble with the Princess', to give an impression of obvious reconciliation, thus earning the girl's trust and gratitude. Elizabeth might then depart—convinced she had succeeded in deceiving the Queen and her advisers—to play out in the comparative safety of her Hertfordshire retreat, any little treasonous plot her confederates may have been hatching. Mary bade Elizabeth rise and the two confronted each other, Elizabeth's height giving her the advantage over Mary's smallness. The Queen noted again the girl's wiry and supple figure, the gleam of her red hair beneath her simple cap, and her mind reverted to the miserable years in Elizabeth's house at Hatfield when she had carried a small child to the warming fire after a courtyard canter in the cold air. During those years—persecuted and bastardised herself—she had wandered from manor to manor, the happier moments being those few short weeks when she might have her young sister by her side. Was this the fate awaiting Elizabeth? She remembered their memorable summer at Chelsea with Henry, Katherine Parr, and Edward—feeding the fish in the make-believe pond, the music and merriment, the unconstrained joy of a family together. So many memories, so many conflicts, so many decisions!

The deeper complexity of an involved emotional nature was not Mary Tudor's by inheritance. Everyone at court had soon realised that the Queen was no 'dissembler' but a plain-speaking, courageously honest, and compassionate human being. Now as she viewed her silent, waiting sister—that sister whose mother had created so many sorrows for another Queen and wrought so much havoc in the nation—her own implicit goodness and love won out. She smiled warmly at Elizabeth and, taking her by the hand, bade her Godspeed and good health, trying not to notice the look of faint reproach in Elizabeth's gaze.

The girl attempted some conversation, saying that she recognised Mary's anxiety on her behalf; the Queen's councillors had made her position very clear. As she spoke of the ministers' warnings, her words came very fast, and she breathlessly begged Mary for an assurance of trust and confidence. She had not listened to any French or heretical advice, she said. Mary must believe her. Saying 'she was grateful for not having been condemned unheard', Elizabeth asked Mary outright —what of the future? How could the Queen be sure her sister's good name was not being used by dissenting factions to the girl's ultimate peril? Elizabeth's obvious fear of a future misunderstanding between them was the final stroke in banishing any remaining suspicion on the part of the Queen. With genuine satisfaction, Mary listened to Elizabeth pledge her loyalty and ask that the Queen 'never give credit to the calumnies that might hereafter be circulated against her, without allowing her an opportunity of justifying herself'. As she spoke, Elizabeth's voice was shaking, either from emotion or relief, that the Queen was hearing her out. Mary put her hand on her sister's shoulder and soothingly replied that she believed Elizabeth; the girl must not worry.

[352]

Previously, it had been agreed between Mary and Renard that this admonition—no matter what Elizabeth's attitude—would be given by the Queen in order to win the girl's trust and perhaps lead her over-confidently to reveal any treasonous activities. Now, surprisingly, Mary realised she meant every word she said. Surely this young woman who a moment ago had knelt so humbly and now spoke so openly would never connive against her sovereign! Assured, Mary turned, taking from her lady-in-waiting the gifts prepared for Elizabeth's departure. A luxurious hood of sable for the long winter journey and a gift of pearls, her sister's favourite jewels, were presented—to Elizabeth's surprised delight. And the Queen's next action, one that had not been agreed upon with any adviser, came directly from her heart. Hesitating only a moment, she suddenly removed a rich jewel from her finger and, taking Elizabeth's hand, slipped it upon a long finger. Then, patting it gently, she told the startled girl it was her token of trust. If Elizabeth was ever in danger and needed her sister's support, the ring would be their silent messenger. Almost weak with relief and overjoyed at the results of her reception, Elizabeth kissed the ring and then spontaneously grasped Mary's hands and kissed them also. Before the emotional moment had passed, both sisters embraced fondly, Elizabeth repeatedly murmuring her gratitude and joy to the Queen.

The next day Elizabeth left the court early to reach Ashridge by nightfall. She was tremendously gratified at the sight of 500 young guardsmen who had formed a voluntary escort for the momentarily disgraced Princess and her household. Elizabeth settled back in her litter in comfortable anticipation of her journey. Ashridge would be a most welcome haven from the near-disastrous element of intrigue that had surrounded her for the past three months!

After her departure, Renard wrote to the Emperor that 'Elizabeth was deeply engaged in plots against Her Majesty's Government, and that she only wished to escape from observation by withdrawing herself into the country, in order to have the better opportunity of carrying on her intrigues with the disaffected....'[3] Unknown to the relieved Elizabeth, the escort marching so bravely with her included several menials bribed by court officials to act as spies. They were there to report immediately any unseemly activity, note any and all visitors, and detect any treasonable correspondence or other designs on the part of the Lady Elizabeth that might be detrimental to her sister, the Queen of England.

Once Elizabeth had left court, Mary gave herself up to dreams of her marriage to Philip. Since her accession, she had dealt with problems the solution of which would have tried the patience and ingenuity of a King. She had executed those who had conspired against her throne, reaffirmed her legitimacy by Parliamentary action, and restored the ritual of the Mass. She had encouraged the rebuilding of some of the partially destroyed abbeys and monasteries, and word had gone out to the former nuns and monks, many of whom had left England, to return. She had dealt with the remaining conspirators—Lady Jane Grey, Guildford Dudley, and his brothers Ambrose and Henry. Along with the imprisoned Archbishop Cranmer, they had walked in a sad procession to trial at the Guildhall where, after a twenty-minute debate, the jury had found them guilty. Lady Jane Grey, her husband, and Thomas Cranmer were sentenced to death; a pardon was extended to Ambrose and Henry Dudley. It was a foregone conclusion, however, that Mary Tudor would not execute her luckless cousin, whom she knew had been a pawn in the hands of her obsessively ambitious father and his confederates. Indeed, Jane was lodged as comfortably as possible in the Tower and given full freedom to walk in the small garden near 'The Lieutenants' Lodgings'. It was merely a matter of time before she would be officially released. Once Mary was wed and, hopefully, the mother of an heir, the throne would be safe. But until that time, Lady Jane Grey must wait for an answer to her poignant question, 'Please may I go home?'

The challenge which had been nearest to her, other than the preservation of the Crown itself, was her relationship with Elizabeth. Now that too had been resolved, and happily for all concerned. Therefore, once the Christmas festivities were over, Mary surrendered to the luxury of anticipation and planning and to the almost unknown pleasure of simple daydreaming. In a life that had known all too little of such unexpected delights, her happiness revealed itself in eager excitement, a kindling of a touchingly joyous enthusiasm, and it lent the Queen a last fleeting beauty that led one ambassador to say that 'were not her age on the decline, she might be called handsome'. The same observer wrote of Mary's routine. 'She is of very spare diet and never eats until one or two o'clock in the afternoon . . . she rises at daybreak, when, after saying her prayers and hearing Mass in private, she transacts business incessantly until after midnight, when she retires to rest. . . .'4 He said that Mary gave audience 'not only to all the members of her Privy Council, and to hear from them every detail of public business, but also to all other persons who ask it of her'.

As she dwelt on the future which would include a husband and perhaps even a child, Mary often came to the room in which Philip's picture still hung. De Noailles wrote to the French King, 'she seemed to be possessed with him'. Mary would stand before the portrait, peering upwards with her short-sighted eyes, anxiously attempting to imagine this handsome figure not only as her husband and companion but also, she was sure, as a tower of strength upon whom she could rely when the problems of her realm seemed insurmountable. Mary was a realist; she knew her limitations in dealing with the sophisticated intriguers who divided the Council and with the manipulations of men like de Noailles. No longer would she be alone. She could give herself wholly to the joy of a complete surrender, not only in body, but also in the more elusive sense of will. If, at times, small stirrings of doubt crept into her thoughts and she wondered at the futility of a union with a man almost twelve years her junior, of the possibility of a woman nearing forty years of age bearing a living child, Mary suppressed such misgivings hurriedly. She had suffered much in her life, but when the moment came, she had risked all and fought courageously. Now—and so her simple reasoning went—the Creator would reward her and her people. The country would return to the religion of its fathers, its Queen would wed and bear them an heir, and prosperity would ensue.

And so the days passed in happy expectation which became even more pointed on January 2, 1554, with the arrival of the Emperor's envoys, 'for the knitting up of the marriage of the Queen to the King of Spain'. A great volley of artillery from the Tower welcomed the Count of Egmont, the Sieur de Courriers Jean de Montmorency, and Sieur de Nigry, Chancellor of the Order of the Golden Fleece, upon their arrival at the wharf. The Spanish entourage was met by Sir Anthony Browne, 'most gorgeously apparelled', and Edward Courtenay, the Earl of Devon. Courtenay led the embassy from the wharf through Cheapside, along the route of sovereigns, to Durham House. Usually the busy thoroughfare was filled with noisy, cheering multitudes. Today the people of the City of London stood silent and 'nothing rejoicing, held down their heads sorrowfully'. Their mute disdain of the Queen's proposed marriage was mirrored the following day when, riding to the court, the Spaniards were scornfully pelted with snowballs by several groups of boys, 'so hateful was the sight of their coming in to them'.

The arrival of the envoys and the formal announcement twelve days later by Chancellor Gardiner that the Queen's Majesty, 'partly for the wealth and enriching of the realm, and partly for friendship and other weighty considerations', had determined to match herself with Philip of Spain only increased London's pronounced anti-Spanish feeling. Everywhere voices of professional agitators mingled with those concerned primarily for their religious creed or political policy. And in growing numbers the common man revealed anxiety for his country's welfare so that 'almost each man was abashed, looking daily for worse matters to grow shortly after'. Now, for the first time, the full details of the marriage treaty were made known. But it was too late. With the arrival of the Spanish embassy and the knowledge that Philip would soon follow, it was only a matter of time before the ill-feeling would burst all restraint.

Mary met the envoys at a brilliant reception at Hampton Court Palace, and here they formally requested her hand for the Prince of Spain. The Queen's reply was all an Englishman might have wished to hear. 'It became not a female to speak in public on so delicate a subject as her own marriage', said Mary. For that, the envoys must confer with her ministers. Aware of her countrymen's anxiety, she spoke directly to the Spaniards, holding out her coronation ring to their gaze, saying, 'they must remember her realm was her first husband, and no consideration should make her violate the faith she pledged to her people at her coronation'. Even the Queen's staunch promise to consider her duties to her country before those to her husband did not convince her subjects, however, and as one chronicler wrote, once the ceremonies were over, and the outcome made public, 'the danger was so near . . . that it was high time for those messengers to depart without leave-taking, and bequeath themselves to the speed of the river-stream, and by water, pass with all possible haste to Gravesend' and to Spain. Before their departure, Simon Renard wrote of an incident that reveals Mary's longing for her future marriage. The Queen was sitting, lost in thought, when Lord William Howard entered into her presence and whispered something to her in English. 'Then', wrote Renard, 'turning to us he asked if we knew what he had said? She bade him not tell, but he paid no attention to her. He told us he had said he hoped soon to see *somebody* sitting there, pointing to the chair next to her Majesty. The Queen blushed, and asked him how he could say so? He answered that he knew very well she liked it, whereat Her Majesty laughed and the court laughed. . . .'[5] But once the formalities of the marriage treaty were concluded, it was impossible to ignore the noisy disapproval of the Queen's subjects. Her own ladies reflected the turmoil outside the Palace walls and often wept with concern for their mistress.

It was only a small way from dissent to open rebellion. Behind the polite court functions, de Noailles had worked tirelessly to combat the union. One of his main instruments was Edward Courtenay, the young man everyone hoped the Queen would wed and who now sulked because of his rejection. Courtenay listened to them all—the treasonous words of de Noailles and those councillors who dreaded the Spanish marriage. With his immense ego and superb naïveté, the product of his long imprisonment, he agreed with all, especially those who urged that the dreadful wrong could only be righted by his marriage to the Queen. If that could not be accomplished, Mary might be deposed, the Spanish marriage averted, and Courtenay might then wed Elizabeth, assuring both an English monarchy and the continuation of the Protestant faith.

While Courtenay hesitated, others had not been so indecisive and, by the middle of January, a full-blown plot had been organised for an uprising to take place on Palm Sunday, March 18, 1554, with Courtenay and his supporters as the leaders. Four insurgents would pledge the success of the plot. In the West Country, Sir Peter Carew, a hot-blooded young noble, would raise Devonshire and Cornwall. Sir James Croft would bring in the men of the Welsh Border and in the southern counties, Sir Thomas Wyatt* would lead the marchers to London. The choice of rebel to guarantee the Midlands was surprising, and the selection had far-reaching effects, for it was none other than the Duke of Suffolk, father of Lady Jane Grey. After the previous conspiracy, Mary had given Henry Grey his freedom, restored his property, and refunded his £20,000 fine. But now, his pardon from the Queen forgotten, Suffolk waited only the word to take part in the rebellion to dethrone his benefactress.

The success of the venture depended mainly on Edward Courtenay. Very probably it might have succeeded if Courtenay had kept his word and actively supported his fellow conspirators. Instead he moved through the court, a graceful and handsome sycophant, much impressed with himself and his nearness to the Queen, revelling in the practised flattery of the French embassy, spending hours in deliberation over such matters as his court costumes, all to the despair of de Noailles and his accomplices who were looking to the empty-headed young man to serve as a focal point for rebellion. De Noailles knew that all over the country, castles were being stocked with gunpowder, ammunition, and food, while relays of horses and men were being sent to strategic points. In London provisions were under way for the capture of the Mint, the Tower, and the Queen herself. The insurgents, wrote de Noailles to the French King, 'would surprise Elizabeth and carry her away, to marry her to Courtenay and then conduct them to Devonshire and Cornwall'.

As de Noailles watched Courtenay and admitted he was 'so timorous that he would suffer himself to be taken before he would act', faint rumours of what was happening throughout the realm reached the Lord Chancellor, Stephen Gardiner. He summoned Courtenay to his presence and sternly 'reproached him for offending against the Queen's goodness'. Relying on their old intimacy born in imprisonment, he questioned and cross-questioned Courtenay so minutely and entangled him so subtly that, before the young man realised it, he had revealed many of the details of the plot.

Gardiner hoped that by the prompt arrest of the various leaders, the conspiracy would dissolve. Sir Peter Carew was politely summoned to London but, wary of capture and swearing his loyalty to Mary, equally

* Sir Thomas Wyatt was the son of the noted poet, Sir Thomas Wyatt, who was an outstanding figure at the court of Henry VIII and one of the earlier swains of Anne Boleyn.

politely declined. He then vanished. Sir James Croft left the court for the comparative safety of his country castle. When Henry Grey was summoned, he told the Queen's officer sent to bring him to Gardiner, 'Marry! I was just coming to her Grace—ye may see I am booted and spurred!' Saying he would have his breakfast first, he left the unsuspecting officer but, instead of dining, collected as much money as possible, mounted his horse, and rode to the Midlands to warn his brothers, Lord John and Lord Thomas Grey that the conspiracy had been revealed.

There remained only Thomas Wyatt. The handsome twenty-two-year-old Kentishman was no coward. He scorned the desertion of his co-conspirators and understood that the success of the plot now rested with him and his supporters. Haste, plus the element of surprise must win for them what well-laid plans might have accomplished had they only been followed. Accordingly, on the morning of January 25, seven weeks ahead of the time, and four days after Gardiner's talk with Courtenay, the church bells of Kent rang in alarm. Proclamations were tacked to church doors and hung on Market Crosses, announcing that the Spaniards were coming to conquer England. Indeed, the Queen had received the first embassy only weeks before and additional numbers were now landing at Dover! Once in possession of the country and its monarch, there would be no Englishman, now free, who would not be subject to the foreign tyrant—to perhaps end his days in Spanish mines or galleys! Immediately the national prejudice against the foreigners brought yeomen, peasants, and squires of the southern county rallying to Wyatt's cause. Three days later Thomas Wyatt and his followers raised their standard at Rochester, seizing several vessels belonging to the Queen—vessels that yielded important artillery and ammunition. Heady with their preliminary success, they made plans to march on London, convinced they would meet with many supporters along the way, as well as in the City itself.

During the first troublesome days of the rebellion, Mary had been kept ignorant of the real extent of the danger; only Gardiner dared mention its possibility. Philip would soon arrive—Mary could think of nothing but her marriage—and her days were spent in happy wedding preparations. When Gardiner finally intimated there was an actual rising, Mary still did not comprehend its seriousness. 'Let the Prince come', she said confidently, 'and all will be well. . . .' Then, aware any demonstration might prove embarrassing to her future husband, she asked for a temporary guard of 8,000 men for herself and Philip (normally the Palace guard comprised a mere 200). Surprisingly, the Council demurred. The Queen could rely on the musters of the City and the retainers of the councillors themselves, they said. In their reaction—and in Gardiner's repeated honest warnings—Mary at last

[358]

recognised the gravity of the Kentish rebellion. Divided as always, the Council would not vote its Queen an extra guard—too many of the councillors agreed in theory with what Thomas Wyatt was attempting to accomplish in fact. If the rebels could bring it off, there would be many on the Council who would support them. Therefore, their sovereign was to be kept powerless and virtually defenceless by a motley group of ministers who would wait to see how well Mary Tudor's luck held on this occasion.

The ministers underestimated the Queen. Mary was enraged. Never was she more acutely aware of how few she could really trust. And then her subjects wondered why she turned to the Emperor, to Philip, and to their ambassador! She had no troops, little money, and less ministerial support. Yet she alone would be held responsible if Wyatt's conspiracy succeeded. In her dilemma, the Queen turned to the City corporation, and the councillors were startled to learn the good sheriffs and aldermen of London had voted her 500 men as a guard. Mary quickly put them to good use. She designated two others she knew she could trust—the old Duke of Norfolk and Sir Henry Jerningham—to head her forces. They departed immediately for Gravesend. A herald was despatched to Rochester where, in the Queen's name, he made known that Mary I offered a free pardon to all who would abandon their treasonous activities. The attitude of Wyatt's troops is apparent in their comment that 'they had done nothing wherefore they should need any pardon—and that quarrel which they took—well, they would die and live in it!'[6]

At Strood, Norfolk was momentarily encouraged with the arrival of the 500 guard and eight pieces of ordnance given Mary by the City officials. But his enthusiasm was short-lived, for their captain, Alexander Brett, surveying Wyatt's troops in the field, had an ill-timed change of heart. Drawing out his sword, he bemoaned that 'we go about to fight against our native countrymen of England and our friends in a quarrel unrightful and partly wicked . . . considering the great manifold miseries which are like to fall upon us if we shall be under the rule of the proud Spaniard . . . !' Crying that foreigners would 'as slaves and villeins, spoil us of our goods and lands, ravish our wives before our faces and deflower our daughters in our presence', Brett advanced to Wyatt's forces, saying, 'I think no English heart ought to say, much less by fighting to withstand them. . . . We will spend our blood in the quarrel of this worthy captain, Master Wyatt and other gentlemen here assembled.' The Londoners followed their captain, shouting, 'A Wyatt! A Wyatt!' and, in the mêlée that followed, Norfolk and his troops, 'being abashed', fled. Wyatt rode across the field to greet the deserters, saying heartily, 'So many as will come and tarry with us shall be welcome; and so many as will depart, good leave have they.' The eight

[359]

pieces of ordnance were left on the field for the insurgents. The Norfolk contingent and those Londonders on either side who chose not to fight, returned to the City—their rout leading one chronicler to say, 'You should have seen some of the guard come home, their coats turned, all ruined, without arrows or strings in their bows, or swords, in very strange ways, which discomfiture, like as it was a heartsore and very displeasing to the Queen and Council, even as it was almost no less joyous to the Londoners and part of all others.'[7]

The débâcle at Strood convinced Mary of the genuine threat from her southern county—a threat that could deprive her of the Crown, if not her life. Incessantly, Simon Renard debated with the Queen. She had been deserted by many Londoners, her Council gave her little support, he said scathingly, and there were few she could really trust. And who were the instigators of this crime against the Crown? Relentlessly, Renard pursued his quarry: Courtenay who had informed on the conspirators, and the Queen's sister, Elizabeth, whom she had graciously allowed to leave the court. And for her kindness, the younger sister had repaid Mary with treachery, the ambassador said bitterly. Only several days previously, a note being delivered to Elizabeth by the young Earl of Bedford had been confiscated by spies at Ashridge. It was sent instead to the Council and the Queen. In the note, Wyatt advised Elizabeth to move for safety's sake to the more formidable haven of Donnington Castle in Berkshire, some thirty miles farther west of the about-to-be-besieged capital. The receipt of the letter had caused an uproar in the Council chamber. Later, alone, Renard again warned Mary that Elizabeth was as guilty as Wyatt himself. She was merely awaiting the success of the rebellion; then she would flee with Courtenay into the West Country, and with greater forces, the two would march on London and seize the throne.

Shaken by the Wyatt letter but still unconvinced of her sister's actual complicity, Mary bowed to Renard's insistence that Elizabeth return to London. She could do little else. At court, Elizabeth could be kept under closer surveillance and prevented from communicating with the rebels. If the girl were innocent, she would at least be safe. If she were guilty, it would be almost impossible for her to do any real harm.

Therefore, as Wyatt moved triumphantly towards Greenwich, Mary wrote to Elizabeth, none of the fearful suspicion showing in her letter:

Right dearly and entirely beloved sister; we greet you well.

And, whereas, certain ill-disposed persons, minding more the satisfaction of their malicious minds than their duty of allegiance towards us, have, of late, spread divers untrue rumours; and by that means, and other devilish practices, do travail to induce our good and loving subjects

to an unnatural rebellion against God and us, and the common tranquillity of our Realm: we, tendering the surety of your person, which
might chance to come to some peril if any sudden tumult should arise,
either where you now be, or about Donnington (whither we understand
you are bound shortly to remove), do therefore think it expedient you
should put yourself in good readiness, with all convenient speed, to
make your repair hither to us, which we pray you will not fail to do,
assuring you that you will be most heartily welcome to us. Of your
mind herein, we pray you return answer by this messenger. And thus
we pray God to have you in His Holy keeping.

Given under our signet, at our Manor of St James, the 26th day of
January, the first of our Reign.

Your loving sister,

Mary the Queen[8]

Mary signed the letter, a trace of sadness on her plain, worried features.
She had done all she could for Elizabeth. Now it was up to Anne
Boleyn's daughter to do her part.

At Ashridge[9] Elizabeth had spent more than a month in the peaceful
solitude that pervaded the former sanctuary of the Bonhommes. She
had been ill on the journey from London, a possible reaction from the
strain of the past several months, but in the serenity lingering in the halls
and chambers of the ancient monastery, her spirits revived. The fine
old building of Totternhoe stone, part of which dated from the thirteenth
century, was surrounded by great stands of oak, beech, and sycamore;
the air was bracing and clean after the smells of London. From her
chamber window—it was too cold to be outside—Elizabeth often
watched the red deer standing in the sunlight that filtered through the
leafless trees of the adjoining woods. At times, the bravest would approach
the great tithe barn with its stores of grain, their natural fear dispelled
by their hunger. The tranquillity of the monks' garden could be
enjoyed only on the warmer days. Then Elizabeth and her ladies would
take their exercise along the still-frozen paths where the girl might
wonder whether she would be at Ashridge when the flowered beauty of
spring returned.

Once she had settled into Ashridge, Elizabeth sent for copes, chalices,
chasubles, crosses, and pattens for her chapel. No one would have the
opportunity to accuse her of not complying with at least the outward
semblance of religious assent! If Mary were going to wed the Spanish

[361]

Philip, there would be no alternative to her compliance with the court religion. Consequently, the picture Elizabeth soon presented at her remote retreat was of a loving and submissive subject.

The illusion had soon been shattered for both the sisters. The letter from the rebel, Thomas Wyatt, to Elizabeth at Ashridge, advising flight to Donnington Castle had not been accepted. Elizabeth understood immediately the danger in which it placed her. The knowledge that the letter was now in the Council's hands appalled the girl. She knew the effect it would have upon the Queen and her ministers, a mere several weeks after her inglorious departure. Did Wyatt not realise the peril in which he placed her? Even should he succeed, men such as the unsteady Courtenay and the treacherous Henry Grey were hardly likely to place *her* on the throne! Grey's recourse would once more be to his daughter, the imprisoned Lady Jane.

The agitation caused by Wyatt's letter kept Elizabeth nervous and wary for days as she tried to assess what direction she must take—for she might be called upon to act quickly. If she moved to Donnington, which she would have liked if only for the safety of its stout walls, it would appear she was in league with Wyatt. If she stayed at Ashridge, which was only a manor house, she was at the mercy of marauding loyalists, county rebels, or Wyatt himself if he chose to carry her off bodily. But Henry Grey, encamped in the neighbourhood, was her first worry. Elizabeth gave orders to increase the guard and fortify Ashridge, a move immediately misinterpreted by the Council as further evidence of her complicity with Wyatt for whom, they said, she was prepared to withstand any harassment until he came for her.

Underlying all the chaotic thoughts which streamed through her mind was the insistent question: how successful was Wyatt's rebellion? His letter to her must have been rashly confident. She hoped he would not write again, for, as much as she wished for the intelligence, she dreaded the risk even more. She had not answered the letter, but with the receipt of Mary's gracious invitation to return to court, she was aware she could not ignore her sister and must make some reply to what was, in effect, a royal summons.

She sat with the Queen's letter in her hand, reading and rereading the words, and again the dread and doubt gnawed at the thin veil of security her several weeks at Ashridge had provided. What would happen if she returned to court? Once there, the merciless Renard would bend all his energies to jeopardise her position. There she would again be at the mercy of well-meaning Protestant friends, of the Queen's suspicions, and those of the Council who felt that Elizabeth offered some alternative to the foreign marriage which they so despised. If the rebels *were* successful, she would then be at the mercy of the victorious Wyatt and the stupid Courtenay as well as de Noailles. The French ambassador would welcome any chance to dethrone Mary so the way to the English throne would be more clear for the Queen of Scots. But then, Elizabeth knew, *she* would be his next target.

Surprisingly, she did not shy from the possibility of Wyatt's triumph. She knew that between the strong Wyatt and a weak Courtenay there might be a chance of success, and she knew that she herself would share in any glory that came with a rebellion accomplished. Not only glory but the Crown itself, even if Courtenay had to be accepted as part of the bargain. But it was a success she must not endanger by any unwise or impulsive action.

Putting the Queen's letter away, Elizabeth assessed her chances. As she reviewed all the possibilities, one strong feeling kept recurring. Again it was the feeling that everything was being decided *too soon*. Again her best ally must be time—time in which to let events take their course before she was forced to show her hand. The confiscation of the Wyatt letter had left her badly shaken and ill at ease. It would not be too difficult to appear genuinely ill. Her mind was soon made up. She sent a message to Mary expressing her horror of the seditious uprisings and said she was 'too ill at present to travel' and asked that Mary send her own physician to Ashridge to attend her. When no reply came, Elizabeth directed her household officers to emphasise her indisposition to Mary, which they did, stating the Queen's sister was too ill to travel and 'considering this dangerous world, the perilous attempts and naughty endeavours of the rebels which we daily hear of against the Queen's Highness', possibly it was safer to remain at Ashridge. In any case, Elizabeth was not returning to court and 'prayed for her Majesty's forbearance. . . .'[10]

London was a city divided. Neighbours were pitted one against the other in support of either the Queen or the rebels. Daily reports of the coming of the Spaniards and of Wyatt's continuing victories kept emotions churning. The Queen was aware of the fear in the City; it had invaded even her own chambers where her ladies showed their apprehension in distracted silence in which they tried to keep busy. In this atmosphere of foreboding, Mary had sought to preserve a semblance of normality, but worry and indecision had given her little rest, and her face plainly showed the strain. Her disappointment and disillusion at Elizabeth's letter was not helped by the scornful remark of Simon Renard who said that the reply was proof of Elizabeth's treachery and recommended that the girl be forcibly brought to London and committed to the Tower. And fatal to the Queen's stubborn support of her younger sister was a translation into French of a letter Elizabeth had written to the Queen, which was found in the mail packet destined for the attention of Henri II, King of France.[11]

Before Mary could deal with Elizabeth, matters were taken out of her hands by pressing news of the rebel uprising. Wyatt's progress northward had been reported to the Queen and Council by spies in the field. The Council, divided by bickering, had done nothing for the protection of the City or its Queen. Renard was contemptuous of the councillors, writing to the Emperor that they were 'so strange' in their manner that he was not even sure they were not the real instigators of the rebellion. 'I know the Queen is so easy, so kind, and so little experienced in the affairs of the world and the state, such a novice in everything, and those about her so avaricious, that if anyone chose to traffic with them and purchase with presents and promises, they might be turned as he chose. . . .' Renard was under little illusion of their concern for the Queen. 'To tell you confidentially what I think of her', he wrote, 'I am of the opinion that if God does not take care of her, she will find herself deceived and abused, either by the practices of the French, or by private conspiracies of those of the country, with poison or otherwise. . . .' But the Queen's greatest threat, said Renard, was from one even closer than her Council or her people. 'The Lady Elizabeth', he ended, 'is much to be feared—for she is a spirit of incantation. . . . For all this, together with the bad and unpleasant news from her side of the Council, will make her [the Queen] take a plunge some morning. . . .'[12]

When the spies' reports indicated that Wyatt was finding few obstacles in his path, Mary tried once more to compromise. She offered to speak with him personally, that they might settle their differences peaceably. She also offered to treat with the troops by sending Sir Thomas Cornwallis and Sir Edward Hastings to Dartford to ask the insurgents' understanding.

Wyatt's reply, bordering on insolence, came from Blackheath. It would be better, he said, for the Queen and her Council to trust *him* than allow his forces to place their trust where they might be deceived. For a guarantee of his co-operation and trust, he asked that the Queen, the Tower, the Crown Jewels, and four of the Council be surrendered as 'hostages'. Mary was appalled. That such treason should be endured because she, the rightful sovereign, had exercised her own prerogative in her choice of a husband! Her patience gone, the Queen ordered the mayor and aldermen and as many of her citizens as possible to put on armour 'so that the streets were very full of harnessed men in every part'. With the arrival of Wyatt in Greenwich, further measures were taken. Lord Clinton and Lord William Howard mustered their forces, but Mary was not sure she could trust them to the end; they, too, might turn against her.

On Candlemas Day, a proclamation to her people was made in

Cheapside, Leadenhall Street, and at St Magnus's corner, with heralds and the Queen's trumpeters blowing for attention, that the citizens might hear it declared that 'the traitor Wyatt seduced simple people against the Queen. Wherefore, she willed all her loving subjects to endeavour themselves to withstand him.' Mary said other rebel leaders had been dispersed, and she did pardon 'the whole camp except Wyatt. . . . and that whosoever could take Wyatt should have a hundred pounds a year to them and to their heirs for ever!'[13]

Soon the drums were beating, commanding that musters be made in the fields of St James and in Finsbury. When news arrived that Wyatt was approaching Southwark across the river, orders were immediately given to 'each man to shut in their shops and windows and being ready in harness to stand every one at his door, what chance soever might happen. Aged men were astonished, many women wept for fear, children and maids ran into their houses, shutting the doors for fear. Much noise and tumult was everywhere, so terrible and fearful at the first was Wyatt and his armies coming, to the most part of the citizens, who were seldom or never wont before to hear or have any such invasion to their City.'[14]

Though many of the diplomatic element in London had fled before Wyatt's oncoming forces, Simon Renard had elected to stay with the Queen. In despair, he defied the Council that advised Mary to find sanctuary in the Tower. She might also find the Tower a prison, said Renard; he urged the Queen to stay within the Palace from which, if forced, she might flee. Neither would Renard sanction her leaving for Windsor Castle. There, she might admittedly withstand siege, but what would happen to the throne while she was away from her capital? The Tower, the Mint, and the Crown jewels, those emblems of royalty, might be lost by their rightful owner. Wisely Renard advised Mary to stay in London and meet this more impending threat to her Crown. 'If she did not wish to lose, not to move in extremity' was the ambassador's advice—all of which only buttressed Mary's own strong emotional conviction that she must remain with her people in a time of such danger. The Queen did not yet feel she was 'in extremity'; there was still a chance those loyal subjects who had cheered her so recently—was it only five months ago?—would rally to her standard. After further consultations with Renard, she made her decision. As Wyatt and his forces entered the Southwark fields, Mary decided on a gesture that would have cheered the stalwart soul of her mother, the redoubtable Catherine of Aragon, and of her grandmother, the formidable Isabella of Spain. She would see her people, the Queen told Renard and the Council; she would speak to them and convince them of the righteousness of her cause, of the just and good reasons why her proposed marriage should *not* be a cause for insurrection and possible bloodshed.

[365]

The Guildhall, the home of the powerful trade associations in the heart of her capital City of London, was the scene of what was perhaps Mary Tudor's greatest triumph. At about three o'clock in the afternoon of February 1, several days after the receipt of Elizabeth's letter, Mary rode from Westminster to the Guildhall 'with many lords, knights and ladies, and bishops and heralds-of-arms, and trumpeters blowing. . . .' All her entourage, except the ladies, were in armour. There was no way of knowing the immediate threat of the army encamped just over London Bridge in the heart of Southwark. At the steps leading to the Lord Mayor's court, Mary walked firmly, her courage and determination clear to all. There must be no doubt of her resolve if she was to convince her subjects, stubborn and implacable as they could be, of the probity of her actions.

Accompanied by her Chancellor, her Council, and several of her ladies, she stood on a small dais and spoke in her deep man's voice, always startling in contrast to her petiteness. Her words left little doubt of how Mary of England felt: 'I am come to you in mine own person', the Queen commended, 'to tell you that which already you see and know. That is, how traitorously and rebelliously a number of Kentishmen have assembled themselves against us and you. Their pretence . . . was for a marriage determined for us; to the which, and to all articles thereof, ye have been made privy'. Mary paused for a moment to let her words sink in and then told of the efforts she had made in the offer of pardons and conferences, all to no avail. 'It then appeared unto our said Council', continued the Queen' 'that the matter of the marriage seemed to be but a Spanish cloak to cover their pretended purpose against our religion; for that they arrogantly and traitorously demanded to have the governance of our person, the keeping of the Tower and the placing of our Councillors'. Her anger at Wyatt's impertinence showed in her rising tones. 'Now, loving subjects, what I am ye right well know. I am your Queen, to whom at my coronation, when I was wedded to the realm and laws of the same . . . you promised your allegiance and obedience unto me. And that I am the right and true inheritor of the Crown of this realm of England, I take all Christendom to witness. My father, as ye all know, possessed the same regal state, which now rightly is descended unto me; and to him always ye showed yourselves most faithful and loving subjects, and therefore I doubt not but ye will show yourselves likewise unto me, and that ye will not suffer a vile traitor to have the order and governance of our person, and to occupy our estate, especially being so vile a traitor as Wyatt is. . . .'

Murmuring swept through the crowd as Mary paused for breath; she could sense the impact her words had made on the listeners. She continued, 'As I say to you on the word of a prince, I cannot tell how naturally the mother loveth the child, for I was never the mother of

[366]

any, but certainly if a prince and governor may naturally and earnestly love her subjects as the mother doth love the child, then assure yourselves that I, being your lady and mistress, do as earnestly and tenderly love and favour you. And I, thus loving you, cannot but think that ye as heartily and faithfully love me; and then I doubt not but that we shall give these rebels a short and speedy overthrow. . . .'

Mary then dealt with the contentious subject of her marriage. 'As concerning the marriage, ye shall understand that I enterprised not the doing thereof without advice, and that by advice of all our Privy Council, who so considered and weighed the great commodities that might ensue thereof, that they not only thought it very honourable, but also expedient, both for the wealth of the realm, and also of you our subjects. And as touching myself, I assure you, I am not so bent to my will, neither so precise nor affectionate, that either for mine own pleasure I would choose where I lust, or that I am so desirous, as needs I would have one. For God, I thank Him, to Whom be the praise therefore, I have hitherto lived a virgin, and doubt nothing but with God's Grace I am able so to live still. But if, as my progenitors have done before me, it may please God that I might leave some fruit of my body behind me, to be your governor, I trust you would not only rejoice thereat, but also I know it would be to your great comfort. And certainly, if I either did think or know that this marriage were to the hurt of any of you my commons, or to the impeachment of any part or parcel of the royal state of this realm of England, *I would never consent thereunto, neither would I ever marry while I lived!* And on the word of a Queen, I promise you, that if it shall not probably appear to all the nobility and commons, in the high court of Parliament, that this marriage shall be for the high benefit and commodity of the whole realm, then will I abstain from marriage while I live. . . .'

Having bared her heart and issued a firm promise to her people, Mary then remembered the immediate danger to them all. With an encouraging smile and an uplifted voice, she cried, 'And now, good subjects, pluck up your hearts, and like true men, stand fast against these rebels, both our enemies and yours, and fear them not, for—I assure you—*I* fear them nothing at all! . . .'[15] And then, saying she was leaving Lord Howard and others to assist the mayor in the safeguarding of the City 'from spoil and sack, which is the only aim of the rebellious crew', Mary signified her entreaty was ended.

Immediately, the taut silence within the Guildhall was broken. A deafening roar split the air as people, amid tears and shouts, surged as near as possible to the small woman who had finally sat down in her chair, exhausted by the impassioned effort of her speech. 'God save Queen Mary! God save the Queen!'—the cries resounded within the venerable walls, and many—their fears and doubts cast aside—cried,

'God save the Prince of Spain!' a cheering acknowledgment to the Queen that her plea to her people had not been in vain. As she left the Hall, caps were flung into the air and shouts of loving encouragement re-echoed and followed her from all sides. Mounting her horse, she rode across Cheapside to the water-stairs of the Three Cranes in the Vintry. There, more of her people waited on the banks, still shouting and calling as the royal barge pulled away for Westminster. And then, suddenly, it turned and headed in the direction of London Bridge. Imbued with her victory and elated at her people's staunch defence of her position, Mary could not resist commanding her oarsmen to take her as near as possible to London Bridge and the Southwark banks. In the gesture was a royal challenge; the next move was up to Thomas Wyatt.

Chapter Twenty

WHILE Elizabeth delayed leaving Ashridge—a decision that seemed to emphasise her treasonous guilt to the Council and Queen—Thomas Wyatt arrived in Southwark across the Thames. The noise of his followers as they made camp, and the sight of his flags moving through the trees, added to the immediate pandemonium which struck Londoners with the knowledge that only the river separated the capital from the potential violence on the opposite shore. The City gates were closed and bolted. The drawbridge at the southern end of London Bridge was cut loose and orders given for the 'braking of all bridges' within fifteen miles of London. In great consternation, the mayor and sheriffs ordered the City to prepare for combat. One observer noted, 'then should ye have seen taking in wares of the stalls in most hasty manner! There was running up and down in every place . . . !'[1] In Westminster Hall, lawyers pleaded their cases in robes under which they wore armour. In the Palace chapel, Dr Weston preached, a coat of mail under his surplice.

Across the river, Wyatt sought to placate the Southwark citizens. Two thousand of his forces were encamped in the immediate neighbourhood, and he told the people 'that no soldier would take anything but that he should pay for it'. He himself came 'only to resist the coming in of the Spanish King', he said. Denied any looting by order of their commander, the troops contented themselves with plundering the Bishop of Winchester's house, where 'they made havoc of the Bishop's goods, not only of his victuals, whereof there was plenty, but whatsoever else, not leaving so much as one lock of a door, but the same was taken off and carried away, nor a book in his gallery or library uncut, or rent into pieces, so that one might have gone up to the knees in leaves of books, cut out and thrown underfoot.'[2] Once their petty vindictiveness was finished, a great trench was dug and ordnance placed at the Southwark end of London Bridge, another at St George's, and 'another going into Bermondsey Street. . . .'

Back in the City, a banner of defiance was raised atop the Tower of

[369]

London as citizens were again ordered to their homes and 'boats being brought to London side over the water, were commanded there to stay. . . .' When Sir Nicholas Poynings, the assistant of the Tower, asked the Queen's permission to open fire 'and so beat down the houses upon their heads', Mary's reply was quick. 'No', said the Queen, 'that were a pity, for many poor men and households are likely to be undone there and killed. I trust, God willing', she finished, 'that they shall be fought tomorrow'. Mary wished the onus of the offensive to rest with Wyatt; she herself would not order the opening salvo.

Instead of a barrage from the other side, however, silence fell across the Thames. And so it remained for three days—days of tension as Londoners waited for the ordeal to begin. Instead of grasping the offensive, Wyatt dallied in the hope that his supporters in the City, of which he had many, would declare for him. But nothing happened. Those who wished to assist him were disorganised and fearful in the face of the strength the Queen had mustered after her valiant speech at the Guildhall. When news of Mary's proclamation reached Wyatt—word that there was now a price of £100 on his head for anyone who might bring him in alive—the Kentishman removed his velvet cap with its trim of lace and, carefully and in 'fair-written' letters, defiantly pencilled 'Thomas Wyatt' on the front, so no one would mistake his identity.

Such bravado might have been somewhat diminished could he have seen the formidable preparations being made in the City. He had missed his chance of assault by surprise. Now London Bridge and all nearby bridges were cut, the next move was obviously up to him. However, Wyatt's confidence did not desert him. Once inside the tightly secured City, he had little doubt but that his many friends would follow the example of the 500 of the Queen's guard who had deserted to his cause at Strood.

He was undoubtedly right, but Mary's stirring plea for understanding and support had won many to her defence, and his lack of precise action during those fateful three days effectively undermined his chances. Puzzled and disappointed that no assistance was offered him, Thomas Wyatt at last made his decision. He would retreat further down river and surprise the capital by attack from the rear. His troops were given their wages, and he urged them to pay any debts they had incurred at Southwark. As he departed, the inhabitants said that 'there was never men behaved themselves so honestly as his company did there for the time of their abode. . . .' Still not comprehending the real danger of his position, at four in the afternoon of Shrove Tuesday, Wyatt left for Kingston where he hoped to cross the Thames. On his march, he accosted a traveller, Christopher Dorrell, returning to London, and he gave the man a message for its citizens. He told Dorrell that 'when liberty and freedom was offered them, they would not receive it, neither would they admit me to enter within their gates. . . .' Some hint of the discouragement the Kentish captain was feeling is evident in his words as he reproached those people who had not come to his aid, saying bitterly that he 'would have frankly spent my blood in that cause and quarrel, but now well appeareth their unthankfulness to us, their friends, which meaneth them so much good and, therefore, they are less to be moaned after when the miserable tyranny of strangers shall oppress them. . . .'[3]

With the news that Wyatt had left Southwark, there was an increase in the precautions taken in London as 'bills, Morris pikes, spears, bows, arrows, gunstones, powder, shovels, spade baskets, and other munition were loaded in St Paul's Church'. At five o'clock in the early misty morning air 'a trumpeter went along warning all horse and men-of-arms to be at St James's Fields' by six o'clock for muster. Preparations for defence went on throughout the day, and when an alarm reached the City 'that Wyatt had made a detour from the east of the metropolis on the Surrey bank of the Thames, which he had crossed at Kingston Bridge, and would be at Hyde Park Corner in two hours . . . ,'[4] barricades were hastily thrown up on the major roads. At Whitehall, 'the sudden news was so fearful that the Queen and all the court were wonderfully affrighted. Drums went through London at three o'clock in the afternoon, warning all soldiers to arm themselves and repair to Charing Cross. The Queen was at once determined to come to the Tower forthwith, but shortly after she sent word she would tarry there to see the uttermost.'[5]

Mary was still determined to stay. Even when Lord Chancellor Gardiner and members of the Council went down on their knees and implored her to seek sanctuary in the Tower, she had gallantly refused, saying 'she would set no example of cowardice! If Pembroke and Clinton proved true to their posts, she would not desert hers. . . .'[6] Renard was equally adamant Mary remain in the capital. He told the Queen if she left the City for Windsor, the people would lose heart and Mary might lose the Crown. For—if the people turned to Wyatt—Courtenay and Elizabeth would be swept to power on the tide of anti-Catholic feeling.

Mary's confidence was not echoed by her companions. 'The Queen's ladies', wrote one courtier, 'made the great lamentation . . . they wept and wrung their hands and from their exclamations may be judged the state of the interior at Whitehall. "Alack! Alack!" they said, "some great mischief is toward. We shall all be destroyed this night!"' When soldiers finally arrived to guard the Queen's own chamber, her companions only complained more bitterly: 'What a sight is this—to see the Queen's bedchamber full of armed men! The like was never seen or heard before!'[7]

At nine o'clock on the morning of Ash Wednesday, February 7, the struggle for the person of the Queen and the control of her capital began as Wyatt and his forces reached the Knight's Bridge. Behind them were seventeen hours of misery which would have disheartened anyone less dedicated than Thomas Wyatt. The weather was appalling. His troops had sloshed through miry roads in pelting rain. At Kingston, several of them had swum the icy Thames to reach the barges and other supplies needed to mend the broken bridge. Throughout the night they had worked, drenched, hungry, and half frozen. Then the long march to London, pulling their clumsy artillery which often sank axle-deep in the muddy roads. Several dozen of the rebels, fearful and disheartened, vanished into the security of the darkness and struck out for their homes in Kent. There had been further desertions along the way, climaxed by a long delay at Brentford when a wheel on a heavy piece of ordnance came loose. Wyatt ordered it repaired on the spot, refusing the pleas of his men to abandon it and press on to London where they might find warmth and food. Had valuable time not been lost on the broken wheel—which seemed to symbolise the disaster of all his plans—Wyatt's venture might yet have proved successful.

But by the time his exhausted dirt-stained troops, now a mere 300, arrived at the Knight's Bridge, the outer bulwark of the royal defence was in place at St James's Palace. Here Lord Clinton's forces were arrayed outside in the courtyard, watching for the first sight of the rebels as they marched from Hyde Park Corner to the crest of the hill opposite the Palace gateway. The Earl of Pembroke's main forces were at Charing Cross with smaller groups concentrated near the gates of Whitehall and Westminster Palace. The Queen had elected to stay at Westminster and Whitehall.* Once Mary placed her trust in Clinton and Pembroke, she retired to her Chapel. 'The Queen', said an archbishop, 'while the field was fighting, was fervently occupied in praying. . . .' When her prayers were finished, she went to the gallery of the Holbein Gateway 'to see the uttermost'.

Wyatt's own plan was to pass from Hyde Park Corner through distant Holborn to Ludgate in the City. There he had been promised admittance. He was prevented by the presence of the Queen's troops, for Pembroke's forces, filtering out from Charing Cross, rendered this route impossible. Immediately the clash began.

* Though historians are often confused as to where the Queen actually was during the conflict, it is possible she was, at one time or another, at both the royal Palaces. They were connected by a series of galleries, enclosed courtyards, and subterranean passages. By 1554, the Palace of Westminster (where today's Houses of Parliament stand) was quite old and used mainly for State functions. Whitehall Palace, the old York Place of Cardinal Wolsey, was comparatively new and comfortable. It was there the sovereign and court actually resided.

Sheer numbers alone guaranteed a royal victory unless divine inter-cession favoured Wyatt over the Queen. Undaunted, Wyatt fought on, trying to reach Ludgate, positive he would find further support once he could enter the City gates.* As the cannon at St James's roared out, many of the rebel ranks were decimated and others were taken prisoner. In the wild mêlée at Charing Cross, Wyatt came face to face with Edward Courtenay, astride his horse and fighting now with the Queen's forces. The unexpected confrontation with the man he had once promised to support proved too much for the earl, and he fled in the direction of Whitehall, crying 'All is lost! All is lost!' Lord Cornwallis watched his departure, calling after him scornfully, 'Fie, my Lord, this is the action of a gentleman?' But Courtenay was already out of earshot, on his way to Mary and the safety of the Palace gates. The fact that Wyatt's forces were enormously outnumbered did not reassure the coward Courtenay.

With Courtenay's arrival and his wild-eyed crying of 'All is lost!'—panic again broke out in the Gateway gallery. 'Then should ye have seen running and crying of ladies and gentlewomen, shutting of doors and such a shrieking and noise as it was wonderful to hear. . . .' a courtier wrote later. Only Mary remained calm, the high colour in her normally sallow cheeks revealing her inner excitement. To Courtenay's exclama-tion she said bitingly, 'It is *your* fond opinion, that durst not come near to see the trial!' She told those who were rushing in great agitation around her that 'she herself would enter the field to try the truth of her quarrel, and to die with them that would serve her, rather than to yield one iota unto such a traitor as Wyatt was. . . .'[8] Where was Pembroke? she asked. Being told he was still 'on the field', she replied, 'Well then fall to prayer and I warrant you we shall hear better news anon. For my lord will not deceive me, I know well.' Then musing almost to herself as she remembered previous deceptions from such as Pembroke, she said, 'If he would, God will not, in Whom my chief trust is—He will not deceive me.'[9]

Several of the rebels had approached the Gateway where Mary watched, and the gates had been hurriedly shut. Encouraged by the Queen's calm faith, her gentlemen-at-arms requested her permission to open the gates and deal with the 'hurly-burly' occurring there. Mary agreed only requesting they be ordered not to 'go forth of her sight, for her only trust is in you for the defence of her person this day'.

At Charing Cross, in a downpour of rain, the battle was waged with

* Readers should remember the City referred to encompassed (and still does) the area from the Tower along Fleet Street to Temple Bar. Here was the greatest concen-tration of population from which Wyatt assumed he would find aid. The area outside Temple Bar along today's Strand to Whitehall and Pall Mall to St James's Palace, had nothing but the royal Palaces, their walls and parks, and Westminster Abbey. All the rest of present-day London was open fields and narrow dirt roads.

gunshot, arrows, swords, and fists. It was difficult to discern the enemy, for the main troops here were those that had deserted at Strood, and their uniform was the same as the City forces. Only their muddy legs —remnant of their nightmare march—distinguished them from their fellow Londoners, and the citizens' cry 'Down with the daggle-tails!' echoed throughout the noisy scene. As the clamour mounted, prisoners on the leads at the Tower could hear the sounds of the skirmish and the cries of the wounded.

Wyatt himself had successfully passed through the mob and now made his way down Fleet Street to Ludgate where, he was still confident, the gates would be opened to him. But a change of guard had occurred, and Lord William Howard was in command. When Wyatt knocked for admittance, identifying himself to his supposed confederate, the answer sounded the death knell of his hopes. 'Avaunt, traitor!' called Howard, 'Avaunt! You enter not here . . .' In despair, Wyatt turned away, with the words 'I have kept touch . . .'. The heart-broken captain sat in his coat of mail on a bench at the nearby Belle Sauvage Inn and watched distractedly as his followers dispersed to their homes, hoping a quick change of clothing would preserve their anonymity. After a brief rest, he attempted to rejoin his troops at Charing Cross, meeting instead with a handful of the royal forces. He was advised to yield. 'You see this day is gone against you and in resisting, ye can get no good, but be the death of all these your soldiers, to your great peril of soul,' he was told. 'Perchance ye may find the Queen merciful and the rather if ye stint so great a bloodshed as is like here to be.'[10] Wyatt knew his enterprise was doomed. If he must yield, he would surrender to a gentleman, he said, as he gave himself up to Sir Maurice Berkeley who was nearby. With surprising thoughtfulness, Berkeley insisted that Wyatt ride with him on his horse, otherwise he might be injured by the mob as they rode to the Tower. And so, his high aspirations blighted—done to death by the desertion of his former confederates, as much as by ill luck and poor judgment—the prisoner passed through the portals of his final dwelling. As Sir John Bridges watched the bedraggled group accompanying Wyatt enter the Bulwark Gate, he confronted the rebel, telling Wyatt if it were not for the law 'which must justly pass upon thee, I would strike thee through with my dagger!' Thomas Wyatt, 'holding his arms under his side and looking grievously, with a grim look upon the said lieutenant, replied "It is no matter now . . .".'[11]

The following day, after a great and solemn *Te Deum* had been sung at St Paul's and as the church bells rang throughout London for the joyous liberation from fear, Mary Tudor faced the unpleasant issue of royal reprisal. It was an ugly situation, one the Queen had done her best to avert by offers of compromise or promises of pardon. Her overtures had been rejected, resulting in an armed conflict. God and her own quick wits had granted her another victory, though not as bloodless as the movement which had resulted in her accession. Her triumph was due mainly to her own staunch courage, the same as she had shown when Northumberland had challenged her. At that time, she had given her pardon freely to those who had aided and abetted the Duke, and only three had been executed, leading Renard who had hoped for a harsher reaction from Mary to say she was 'easily influenced, inexpert in worldly matters and a novice all round!' Then she had insisted upon clemency tempered with understanding for many, but now the Queen realised such indulgence was a luxury royalty could ill afford. Further toleration would be regarded as timidity, doubt, or weakness—an invitation to potential defiance and aggression from other malcontents. She could not suffer a third challenge to her throne. Her trust had been abused, and now, outraged and humiliated, embittered with the knowledge that one as close to her as Henry Grey, the Duke of Suffolk, had again threatened her authority, Mary realised there was no place for mercy. Citizens who had previously fought *for* her had chosen to fight *against* her because of her choice of a husband. If her marriage to Philip was to become a reality, she must rid her country of such dissenters. Punishments swift and terrible, such as her father had meted out to those who had challenged his authority, must be exacted. She was Henry Tudor's daughter, and if her people thought her weak because of her sex, they would find now a man's stout courage in a woman's body. They would know that a Queen might be graciously forgiving but— once disappointed and deceived—as severe and relentless as any King.

The following day the trials began. The watch was increased at the City gates, and those who ventured abroad still wore armour; most stayed inside their homes. Retribution was swift as wholesale executions took place. The condemned were so numerous that gibbets were erected in St Paul's Churchyard, in Smithfield, on London Bridge, in Fleet Street, and at Charing Cross as well as in Southwark. There were several near the Palace itself, so that 'the Queen could not go to the City without beholding the ugly sights of dangling corpses at every turn of the street'.[12] When these were found insufficient for the number condemned, prisoners were hung in front of their own shops or swung from their own doorways—an agonising sight for the families that must remain inside. The Tower gates opened to admit for the last time those of more illustrious and traitorous blood. The Duke of Suffolk, accompanied by his brothers, was captured passing through London on his way to the fortress 'pale as a ghost and shivering'. No preferential treatment was shown them. They were doomed and realised that now, unlike before, there would be no reprieve.

[375]

If at any time the fate of Suffolk, her cousin by marriage, caused Mary any uneasiness, Renard and the Council were there to allay such qualms. The Spanish ambassador prevailed on Mary to make a clean sweep of not only such as Suffolk, but also his daughter, the unfortunate Lady Jane Grey, and her husband Guildford Dudley. He reminded her that the Emperor would never allow Philip to enter England while such threats to his life and Mary's throne existed. The problem of Philip's safety loomed larger in Mary's consciousness with the events of the past several days. And the councillors—those merciless, opportunistic scoundrels 'who had been most instrumental at the death of Edward VI, in thrusting royalty upon poor Lady Jane, and proclaiming Mary illegitimate, were now the sorest forcers of men. Yea [they] became earnest councillors for that innocent lady's death.'[13] They urged the Queen to exact the ultimate penalty for the follies which had engulfed Suffolk and which they knew still touched them closely.

For Suffolk, as well as Wyatt and the hundreds of other conspirators, it was the end. Triumphantly, Renard wrote to the Emperor, 'the Queen's blood is up at last'. Regarding Jane, however, Mary still had misgivings. Jane had not sought the throne, the Queen insisted. She knew her cousin had been a pawn and spoke of extending mercy rather than punishment. Renard was appalled. Vehemently, he maintained that as long as Jane Grey was alive, she would be a source of discontent, the pivot of future plots which might prove disastrous to the Queen's cause. Not only should Jane and Guildford die, said Renard, but Mary's sister Elizabeth and the treacherous Courtenay must also suffer! The ambassador was firm. Should Mary desist now from meting out proper punishment, from ridding her realm of such danger, there would be no Spanish marriage—and no future heir to inherit her Crown. The factious elements would be encouraged by the Queen's dissembling, and there would be continued defiance with much bloodshed. And who would succeed but the heretics who had become so powerful during her brother's reign! If Mary were indeed to be a Queen in fact as well as in title, she must use every means of safeguarding her inheritance, emphasised Renard. And such means meant the death of an innocent sixteen-year-old girl.

Mary knew she had no choice. There was no way to combat the clamour of her ministers, the court, and Renard for the blood of one as blameless as Lady Jane Grey. Even Stephen Gardiner was adamant. He said that as the Queen had before 'extended her mercy' to those who had threatened her, 'she would now be merciful to the body of the Commonwealth and conservation thereof'. And that could not be, said the Lord Chancellor, 'unless the rotten and hurtful members thereof were cut off and consumed'.[14]

Therefore, on the day after Wyatt's capture, following a day of argument and debate in which the royal conscience fought for Jane's life, Mary reluctantly signed the already existing warrant for Jane's immediate execution. When Renard heard that Mary later authorised a reprieve of three days, he hurried to the Palace. His fears were calmed when the Queen informed him she had granted the delay on the advice of Dr Feckenham, the Dean of St Paul's. Mary had sent the prelate as solace for Jane during her last hours, and the good doctor had asked for three days in which to accomplish the conversion of the young prisoner from her heretical beliefs. His dedication was sincere, and he was certain of his powers of persuasion, which were notable. What he did not realise was that a conviction as deep and powerful, as wholly sincere as his own, also dwelt in the mind and heart of the doomed girl. These next three days were to prove enlightening to the prelate as well as to the prisoner.

The news that she must prepare for execution was no surprise to Lady Jane Grey. For the past three months, she had lived surrounded by death and all its miserable accompaniments: imprisonment, torture, and deprivation. Though she herself had been well treated and suffered only physical restraint, the death sentence rendered at the Guildhall hung over her 'woeful days' constantly. Only the Queen could remove such a threat. The news of Wyatt's march on London, the preparation in the Tower for any assault, the sound and fury of the fighting in the streets culminating in the arrival of the weary and broken prisoners into the Tower precincts—all spoke of an impending doom which anyone as intelligent as Jane could hardly overlook. She wept when she heard of her father's arrest and, when told her own execution would take place the following day, it was almost a relief. With great resignation, she told Dr Feckenham that death would be welcome. Her whole life had been a living death, she said, and she was ready to pay the penalty 'in whatever manner it may please the Queen to appoint . . .'. She said she was human enough to shudder 'at what I have to go through, but I fervently hope the spirit will spring rejoicingly into the presence of the Eternal God, Who will receive it'. When Feckenham offered to instruct her in the tenets of the old faith, Jane was curt and told him 'her time was too short for controversy'. Mistaking her abrupt remark for a latent interest which a prompt execution prohibited furthering, Feckenham had hurried to the Queen, asking a weekend reprieve that he might deal with Jane and save her soul from what he considered an irrevocable agony in hell.

When told she had three more days on earth in which to review her spiritual beliefs, Jane shook her head sadly and said, 'Alas, sir! It was not my desire to prolong my days. I did not intend what I said to be reported to the Queen, nor would I have had you think me covetous for a moment's longer life, for I am solicitous for a better life in

Eternity. . . .'¹⁵ When Feckenham suggested they arrange a disputation—a procedure for which he was notably and justifiably famous—by which she might be persuaded to die a Catholic convert, Jane only replied that 'disputation may be fit for the living, but not for the dying. Leave me to make my peace with God!' She was firm. 'You are much disappointed if you think I have any desire of a longer life. . . .' she said. Feckenham persisted that since he had been sent by the Queen 'to instruct you in the true doctrine of the right faith', he must continue and told Jane he hoped there would be 'little need to travail with you much herein'. And so Jane Grey's last hours on earth were spent in a verbal tilting, a challenging discussion on the merits of her doctrine as opposed to the Queen's. After several hours, Feckenham realised further discussion was futile, and he said to Jane, 'I am sorry for you, for I am certain that we two shall never meet [in the next world] . . .'. The strength of Jane's own convictions is evident in her next words, spoken almost saucily, that it was true they would never meet, 'except God turn your heart—for I am assured, unless you repent and turn to God, you are in evil case!' She ended, however, by paying tribute to the 'great gift of utterance' that God had given Feckenham, but told the good doctor she wished it had pleased Him 'to open the eyes of your heart!'¹⁶

Once the prelate had left, Jane Grey prepared for death. There were letters to write and the precious remaining hours must be used for strengthening her soul. Her thoughts lingered on her family—that family which had made her life so miserable 'that I think myself in hell'. For her father who, since his imprisonment in the Tower, had sent her remorseful messages—as much for his own sad plight as for hers—Jane had a farewell word. In his prayer book which she had in her possession, the condemned girl wrote:

The Lord comfort your Grace, and that in His word, wherein all creatures only are to be comforted. And though it hath pleased God to take away two of your children [referring also to Guildford Dudley] yet think not, I most humbly beseech your Grace, that you have lost them, but tried, that we, by losing this mortal life, have won an immortal life. And I, for my part, as I have honoured your Grace in this life, will pray for you in another life.

Your Grace's humble daughter,

Jane Dudley ¹⁷

[378]

Following the message, she concluded with a hopeful and prophetic sentence. 'If my fault deserved punishment, my youth, at least, and my imprudence were worthy of excuse. God and posterity will show me favour . . .'.[18]

Jane's younger sister, the fourteen-year-old Katherine Grey was residing not far from the Tower at Baynard's Castle. Some measure of affection which Jane felt for the girl—possibly the only one in her family for whom her feeling was genuine and not merely dutiful—may be seen in the exquisite letter written on the day of her death, on the blank pages of her favourite Greek Testament,* which she asked be sent to Katherine after the execution. Referring to the book, she says:

I have sent you, good sister Katherine, a book, which, though it be not outwardly trimmed with gold, yet inwardly it is of more worth than precious stones. It is the book, dear sister, of the laws of the Lord; it is His Testament and last Will, which He bequeathed to us poor wretches, which shall lead us to the path of eternal joy. . . .

Jane said if her sister would follow its teachings, it would bring immortal and everlasting life. 'It will teach you to live—it will teach you to die—it will win you more than you would have gained by the possession of your woeful father's lands. . . .' Urging that Katherine be 'steady in your faith . . . and follow the steps of your Master', Jane concluded the letter:

As touching my death, rejoice as I do, and adsist [i.e., consider] that I shall be delivered from corruption and put on incorruption, for I am assured that I shall, for losing a mortal life, find an immortal felicity. Pray God grant that ye live in His fear and die in His love . . . [here the words are blotted out by the tears of the writer] . . . neither for love of life nor fear of death. For if ye deny His truth to lengthen your life, God will deny you and shorten your days, and if ye will cleave to Him, He will prolong your days, to your comfort, and for His glory, to the which glory God bring mine and you hereafter, when it shall please Him to call you.

    Farewell dear sister; put your only trust in God, Who only must uphold you.

Your loving sister,

Jane Duddeley.[19]

For her mother, safe at Bradgate and unwilling to endanger her freedom by any attention to her doomed husband and daughter, there was no word at all.

* The book may be seen in the British Museum.

While Jane was writing her farewell words, workmen were busy erecting the scaffold on Tower Green—the same sad spot where Anne Boleyn and Katherine Howard had died. Guildford Dudley had requested a last meeting with Jane, and the Queen had granted permission. But Jane had declined; her thoughts were now on the ordeal facing her and on her eternal reward. Nothing of the material must intrude on her spiritual preparation. She sent word to the eighteen-year-old youth, whose last days were spent in tears, 'that he would do well to remit this interview till they met in a better world . . .'.[20]

On Monday, February 12, four days after Wyatt's capture, the execution of Lady Jane Grey and her husband took place. Guildford Dudley was beheaded first, on Tower Hill. At about ten o'clock, Jane had watched at a window as the youth was led in procession to the Bulwark Gate and handed over to the Sheriff of London. She was still at the window some half hour later when the straw-filled cart containing his body rudely flung upon the floor and his head wrapped in a bloody cloth, rumbled beneath her gaze. Breaking into tears of compassion, Jane cried, 'Oh Guildford! Guildford! The antepast that you have tasted and I shall soon taste, is not so bitter as to make my flesh tremble . . . for all this is nothing to the feast that you and I shall partake this day in Paradise!'[21]

Once the executioner had finished on Tower Hill and returned to Tower Green, everything was ready. It was almost noon and the sun was high as Jane left the 'Lieutenant's Lodgings' where she had existed for several months. The drums were beating as the small, sad procession wended its way to the scaffold near the White Tower. The bells of St Peter-ad-Vincula tolled as a company of 200 Yeomen of the Guard formed an escort for the diminutive figure of the condemned girl as she followed the Tower officials. She appeared composed, 'being nothing at all abashed' as she walked slowly, prayer book in hand, accompanied by Dr Feckenham, two other Tower chaplains, and her devoted ladies-in-waiting, Elizabeth Tilney and 'a Mistress Ellen', their eyes swollen with tears. Jane gave a visible start when she confronted the massive figure of the executioner, clad in a bright red wool garment, the black mask of his trade mercifully covering his features as, with arms crossed, he waited on the scaffold. Recovering her composure, the girl ascended the steps as a murmur appreciative of her youth, bearing, and courage swept through the assembled crowd. Dr Feckenham, crucifix in hand, began praying until Jane stopped him, saying, 'Go now, and God grant you all your desires, and accept my own warm thanks for your attentions to me, although indeed those attentions have tried me more than death can now terrify me!'[22] Feckenham, however, mindful of his spiritual duty to one whom he considered a heretic, refused to retreat. Ignoring him, Jane turned to the crowd clustered around the scaffold.

In an unshaken voice which rose clearly over the heads of the on-lookers, the prayer book still clutched in her hand, she said, 'Good people I am come hither to die, and by a law I am condemned to the same. The fact, in deed, against the Queen's Highness was unlawful, and the consenting thereunto by me, but touching the procurement and desire thereof by me or on my behalf, I do wash my hands thereof in innocence. . . .' Jane asked that all assembled bear witness that she died 'a true Christian woman, and that I look to be saved by none other means, but only by the mercy of God . . . and that I thank God of His goodness that He hath thus given me a time and respite to repent. And now, good people, while I am alive, I pray you to assist me with your prayers.' Turning to Dr Feckenham, who still stood nearby, she asked, 'Shall I say this Psalm?' pointing to the *Miserere mei, Deus* in English in her prayer book, and he nodded. Kneeling, Jane began the recitation, 'Have mercy upon me, Oh God . . .'.[23] As she finished, she spoke again to Feckenham, recognising his honest desire to assist her, saying, 'God I beseech Him abundantly reward you for your kindness towards me . . .'. For once, Feckenham was mute, either from depression at his failure to convert this doomed girl or from the horror she must face in a moment. Jane saw his distress. She took his hand and suddenly leaned over to kiss the cheek of the old prelate in farewell.

Turning to her ladies, now almost overcome with the intensity of their sorrow, she handed them her gloves and handkerchief, giving her prayer book to a Tower official in order that it might be conveyed to her father. Indicating she wanted no further ministrations, she untied the collar of her gown herself, and as she accepted a 'fair handkerchief' with which to bind her eyes, the executioner knelt before her to ask forgiveness. Jane nodded briefly, and as he led her to the straw sur-rounding the execution block, she said to him urgently, 'I pray you—dispatch me quickly . . .'. Turning to him, full face and suddenly trembling violently, she said fearfully, 'Will you take it off before I lay me down?' The executioner assured her he would wait until she had knelt and stretched her arms full length in signal.

Jane finished tying the handkerchief over her eyes. Thus, she could not see the block. As Dr Feckenham, the sobbing ladies-in-waiting, and the Tower officials watched in horror, the slight figure of Lady Jane Grey lurched blindly seeking the block, crying in a frightened voice, 'Where is it? What shall I do? *Where is it?*' She had lost her bearings in the darkness, and holding out her hands, she implored someone to guide her. All nearby were stunned with the poignancy of the moment, their horror paralysing them. At last, mercifully, someone from beneath the scaffold, perhaps not as moved as the others, quickly ascended and guided the shaking figure to the block. Jane knelt at once and—almost eagerly—stretched out her arms in signal. The axe crashed upon the fragile neck as her last words echoed clearly across Tower Green, 'Lord into Thy hands I commend my spirit . . .'.[24]

Half an hour later, the Traitor's Gate at the Tower of London opened to admit Edward Courtenay, the Earl of Devon. And at Ashridge, deep in the Hertfordshire countryside, commissioners from the Queen were dealing with the Princess Elizabeth.

Almost two weeks had passed since Elizabeth had taken to her bed at Mary's request that she return to court. During that time, nervous tension such as she had suffered from the Seymour affair returned, and the illness she had assumed as a protective pretence, became discomforting reality. The spectre of royal disapproval and its subsequent disgrace—which Mary's continued silence only emphasised—resulted in nausea and a shortness of breath. A few days later, a latent kidney infection developed which, combined with her chronic anaemia, caused her to be come very 'faint and feeble'. Elizabeth's face became swollen and 'dropsical'. She had little appetite, slept badly, and lost weight.

Upon hearing of her sister's condition, Mary sent her trusted Dr Wendy to Ashridge. He had known Elizabeth since her birth and liked the girl whose future he saw imperilled by the rumours of her complicity in the Wyatt rebellion. He calmed her fears, for Elizabeth believed she was being slowly and subtly poisoned. He told her she must make every effort to get well, so she might obey the Queen's instructions and depart for the court as quickly as possible. It was good advice but not what Elizabeth wanted to hear.

As London had waited for Wyatt's attack, Mary had listened to Simon Renard's continued admonitions that it would be impossible for Prince Philip ever to live safely in England unless both Elizabeth and Courtenay were imprisoned and tried for their parts in the rebellion. Impassionedly, the Spanish ambassador had denounced her sister and cousin as traitorous conspirators. The sooner Mary rid herself of both, the better for her own safety and the future of the commonwealth! The near-success of the insurrection and the severity of the punishment she was forced to mete out had badly shaken the Queen, and she recognised the merit of Renard's words. Men such as Suffolk, whose loyalty should have been unquestioned, had abandoned their sovereign instead. Courtenay was deeply implicated and, apparently from the evidence provided by the Wyatt notes and the intercepted French diplomatic mail packet, so was Elizabeth. There was no longer any excuse for tolerance. If her sister was guilty, the ambassador told the Queen, she must suffer as the others had suffered.

Therefore, on the Sunday before Jane Grey's death, Elizabeth's great-uncle, Lord William Howard, accompanied by Sir Edward Hastings and Sir Thomas Cornwallis, arrived at Ashridge with orders to bring the stricken Princess to court. It is indicative of Mary's kindness to her sister—even kindness tinged with suspicion—that the older Howard, a brother of Anne Boleyn's mother, was sent as escort, for Elizabeth's preference and fondness for the old Admiral was well known. Their late arrival, at ten o'clock at night, was a surprise to the household, but they were directed immediately to the Princess's chamber. Elizabeth was in bed, 'willing and conformable' but 'very feeble and faint of body'. When Howard revealed that she must accompany them to London in the morning, Elizabeth's distress showed plainly in her face. She said 'that she much feared her weakness to be so great' that she could never endure such a long journey 'without peril of life'. After some discussion with the doctors, it was agreed that 'without danger to her person, we might well proceed to require her ... to repair to your Highness with all convenient speed and diligence', Howard later wrote in report. Though Elizabeth protested the decision, in the face of such unanimity, she could do little but acquiesce. Pointedly she asked the doctors to request of the Queen 'that she may have a lodging, at her coming to court, somewhat further from the water than she had at her last being there ...'. With his letter to the Queen, Lord Howard enclosed a list of the resting places where Elizabeth might lodge overnight, so that she would travel no more than seven miles per day. Again the Princess's first inclination was to desist and delay, and here she was aided by the great-uncle whose own natural solicitude was awakened by the girl's plight. If the journey could be prolonged, there was a chance that Mary's anger might diminish and the fate of his great-niece not be decided in the heat of reprisal. If nothing else, Elizabeth would be spared the sight of the gruesome events taking place in the City of London.

On the day of Lady Jane's execution, Elizabeth Tudor left Ashridge, the faithful Ashley by her side. Still swollen in body and prostrate with the torture of a throbbing migraine, she lay in the litter until Redburn, where news of Courtenay's imprisonment and Jane's execution reached them. The impact of Jane's death was evident in the girl who was led, half fainting and nauseous, to the immediate comfort of her bed. The next morning, the journey commenced again, and so it went for the next five days—a nightmarish torment which the jolting of the litter over frozen roads did little to alleviate.

At Highgate, less than five miles from whatever fate awaited her, the appalling weather made further travel impossible. Elizabeth's condition had deteriorated, and the physicians advised a complete rest. Her respite lasted one week. When the weather then cleared, there was no logical excuse to delay longer. Therefore, by noon of the twenty-third, eleven days after her departure from Ashridge, the cavalcade bringing Elizabeth to court proceeded down Highgate Hill, northwest of London, in the direction of Whitehall. During her stay at Highgate, the Princess had learned of the rumour prevalent in the capital that she was pregnant—a scurrilous report that had commenced with the vivid imagination and vindictiveness of the Spanish ambassador, Simon Renard, upon being told of Elizabeth's swollen body. The invalid, therefore, had summoned every ounce of her strength—and courage—for the ordeal which lay ahead. She had clothed herself completely in white, a symbol of innocence. Ashley had dressed her hair with extreme care, to reveal the high brow and clear profile. And though her face was still swollen and the long fingers of which she was so proud were puffy with her disease, there was no distension of her figure indicative of pregnancy. As she entered the road leading directly to Whitehall, Elizabeth struggled to maintain a more regal pose and, in order to give the lie to the malicious rumour, disdainfully threw back the heavy rugs which protected her from the cold air. Better to endure the discomfort of biting cold so that the people who had rushed hurriedly along the route at the news of her approach might know that her poor sick body was devoid of such disgrace. There were many in the throng who were her friends. Elizabeth had never underestimated her own attraction, and she made her appeal now—without a smile, a gesture, or a direct glance. Instead, she sat upright in the litter, gazing straight ahead, her 'mien proud, lofty and disdainful ... an expression she assumed to disguise the mortification she felt!' Renard wrote to the Emperor the following day, mistaking Elizabeth's attitude and motive completely. As long as she was on view—through Smithfield, Fleet Street, and on to Whitehall—she kept herself uncovered, averting her eyes from the gibbets and the grinning corpses as they swung in the wind from the river. As she neared the Palace, 200 courtiers in bright red coats banded in black velvet joined her cavalcade by order of the Queen. They were meant as an escort of honour for a Princess; for Elizabeth, their arrival symbolised her loss of precious freedom and the beginning of an unwelcome restraint.

Upon arrival at Whitehall Palace, she was met by the Lord Chamberlain. Half frozen and depleted now of her little remaining strength, Elizabeth longed for the warmth of her bed and the welcome ministrations of Ashley. But first, she told the Chamberlain imperiously, she wanted to see her sister, the Queen. There was no reply. In silence, she was led to an obscure suite of rooms where she was told she might keep six ladies, two gentlemen, and four servants. The rest of her staff would be lodged in the City. As for any interview with the Queen, said the Chamberlain, that would be impossible until she had proved to the complete royal satisfaction that she was innocent of any covert activities against the Crown. She would be permitted no visitors, and there would be guards at the entrance to her chambers at all times. The Chamberlain then bowed out. And with that Elizabeth had to be satisfied.

But at least Ashley was left to her. And it was Ashley who brought her the news that on that very morning, the Duke of Suffolk, Lady Jane's father, 'who would have died more pitied for his weaknesses if his practices had not brought his daughter to her end', had been beheaded on Tower Hill.* The news did nothing to alleviate Elizabeth's anxiety. Other than Wyatt—whose fate as a traitor was foreseen—there now remained only Courtenay and herself to be dealt with at the royal pleasure.

---

* Two weeks later, his widow, the thirty-six-year-old Frances Brandon, Lady Jane's mother, promptly married a handsome red-headed groom, some fifteen years her junior. Despite her union with an inferior, Queen Mary remained loyal to her cousin who still took precedence over other ladies at court. Jane's sisters, Mary and Katherine Grey, were appointed Maids-of-Honour to the Queen, proving without doubt that Jane Grey's life was a political sacrifice and not one demanded for personal reasons.

Chapter Twenty-one

ELIZABETH remained at Whitehall for three weeks. With the careful ministrations of the doctors her condition improved so she was no longer confined to her bed. Time hung heavily. There were no diversions; visitors were still prohibited. Because of the severity of her illness and the rigour of the winter weather, she could not walk outdoors in the Palace courtyards. In the small suite of rooms where her servants strove to make her comfortable, Elizabeth tried to assess her future without yielding to panic. She had been in similar situations before, and her cunning, intelligence, and sheer good luck had saved her. She must not endanger her life and her position as heiress-presumptive now by any impulsive act.

The Queen still refused to see her. The estrangement from Mary, the enforced seclusion, and the painful awareness that somewhere in a nearby chamber her fate was being determined by others, all contributed to a sense of frustration and hopelessness the girl valiantly attempted to suppress. Daily, she mustered her courage and struggled out of bed, trying to give some semblance of normality to the endless hours. Little news was carried in by her servants, for they too were shunned. She had seen none of the Council. As the days passed and Mary remained silent, it was almost as if she, a Princess, were living in a vacuum or had ceased to exist.

Though Elizabeth recognised the seriousness of the charges against her and the problem her continued detention presented the Queen, it is doubtful if she realised the extent of the malice directed at her by Simon Renard and many on the Council. The Queen's ministers were of divided opinion regarding Elizabeth's alleged guilt; several persisted in putting as many obstacles as possible in the Spanish ambassador's path in bringing about the marriage with Philip. Renard's opinion of Mary's subjects was frankly revealed to the Emperor when he wrote: 'It is not only difficult, but well nigh impossible to foresee what the English may do, whose natural character is inconstant, faithless and treasonable; a character they have always exhibited and which the whole course of their actions and of their history has proved to be just.'[1] Even so the wily ambassador manipulated both Mary and her ministers with remarkable skill especially as his more adroit manœuvres were accomplished with the assistance of certain of the councillors themselves. While keeping Mary's doubts regarding Elizabeth at fever-heat, he shamelessly distributed pensions and massive gold chains to such as Arundel, Pembroke, and Derby to inspire enthusiasm for the Spanish marriage. The nature of his success was duly reported to the Emperor who had protested the huge amount of the bribery. 'The councillors,' wrote Renard, 'gave us such a good response, that if the result corresponds with their words, we have no doubt that safety will attend the coming of His Highness to this country.'[2]

In addition to her disillusionment with her sister's possible duplicity, Mary was also forced to look at her Council with realistic eyes. From the beginning, since their desertion at Edward's death, her ministers had done nothing in the interest of their sovereign without first considering their own advancement. In full possession of handsome ecclesiastical properties, they had thwarted the Queen's every endeavour to restore the lands to the Church. While Mary could exhibit great courage under pressure, she lacked the subtle dexterity needed to deal with as accomplished a group of scoundrels as had graced the English Council table in decades; her very lack of such experience was their greatest advantage. They shifted sides as expediency demanded, forming small factions which fought one another—and the Queen was in the middle. For one whose word was her bond, the deviousness of her ministers was a direct affront. She spared few of them her tongue—but to little avail. Painfully, their behaviour reminded Mary how completely alone and at their mercy she actually was. With the exception of Renard and one or two of her ministers, there was absolutely no one else of influence to rely on. It is ironical, then, that the very duplicity of her Council—the knowledge that many of her ministers secretly worked to avert the Spanish marriage—provided the catalyst that drove the Queen to see her marriage to Philip accomplished as quickly as possible. Once the realm possessed a King, even a sovereign in name only, her authority would not be so consistently or outrageously challenged.

Harassed by her Council, surrounded by recrimination from the subjects who deplored her choice of a husband, lectured by Simon Renard regarding the affairs of her kingdom, and condescended to by the French ambassadors, the brothers de Noailles,* Mary clearly revealed

---

* Antoine de Noailles's brother, François, arrived in London the day of Lady Jane Grey's execution to 'assist' the ambassador. With the bitter knowledge that Sir Peter Carew and dozens of other conspirators had fled to France, where they were being given sanctuary and urged to conspire against their mother country, Mary had now to contend with two extremely competent and experienced French ministers whose

her fears to the Spanish ambassador when she told him 'that she had neither rest nor sleep for the anxiety she took for the security of His Highness's coming . . .'. Her marriage treaty would be confirmed at the upcoming Parliament, and she was eager to do what she must to ensure Philip's early arrival. At which point Renard would throw up his hands in despair and chide the Queen to tears, criticising her hesitation regarding Courtenay and her sister Elizabeth. But that was not all. On the day before Elizabeth's arrival at Whitehall, the Queen ordered further executions to cease, the prisons to be cleared, and commanded the remaining rebels to assemble at Westminster Palace. There, 400 dirty, bedraggled wretches, with ropes around their necks, the foul prison odour still clinging to them, found the Queen at a gallery window. In the cold wet mud, they went down on their knees, crying for mercy and pardon. Mary raised her hand, her eyes wet with compassion, signifying they were free. In gratitude they thronged to Westminster Hall, threw off their halters, and tossed their caps at the great hammerbeam roof in exultant liberation. Such leniency horrified Renard who wrote to the Emperor: 'When I consider the state of things here, the condition of the Queen and this kingdom, the confusions in religion, the different parties among the Privy councillors, the intestine hatred between the nobility and the people, the character of the English—who are given so much to change, treason and infidelity—I feel the burden of this charge so heavy, its importance so great, and my mind so troubled, that I know not in what way to satisfy or be conformable to the commands of Your Majesty. . . .'[3]

As deeply as affairs in England distressed Renard, they delighted his French counterpart, Antoine de Noailles, who was jubilant over the outcome of the treasonous events he had done so much to encourage. He wrote to the French ambassador to Scotland of the 'great murmuring among the people regarding the marriage of this Queen with the Prince of Spain'. De Noailles thought Mary would have difficulty in ever bringing about the union. He exulted over the executions. 'You may be assured, my dear colleague, that the most beautiful sights which can be seen in this town, and indeed, all over the country, are the gibbets on which hang some of the bravest and most gallant men that she had in her kingdom. The prisons also are full of the nobility and some of the most prominent people . . . who are brought in daily . . . in order that she may more surely bring about her design in favour of the said Prince. . . .' De Noailles's final words were prophetic. 'I foresee by all these events . . . that matters are in a bad way for this Queen and are in a fair way to ruin this kingdom.'[4]

duplicity at times infuriated her. At one point, she cast diplomatic sophistry aside and snubbed de Noailles 'with such a wrathful countenance that there was no womanly gentleness to be seen in it!'

In early March, Count Egmont returned from Spain with the necessary Papal dispensations for the Queen's marriage and the gold crowns and chains for the councillors that had purchased their approval. On March 6, at three o'clock in the afternoon in the Queen's Oratory at Whitehall, Mary of England was wed to Philip of Spain in a proxy marriage ceremony attended by the whole Council, the French and Spanish ambassadors, and those closest of her ladies. The Queen knelt before the Sacrament and, in a voice thick with emotion, called all to witness that 'the marriage she had agreed to had not been prompted by any carnal affection, by cupidity, or any other reason than the honour, welfare and profit of her realm, the repose and tranquillity of her subjects . . .'. There was no doubting the fervid humility in the Queen's voice, 'saying all this with such grace' that for once even the hard-bitten councillors were touched and 'all the spectators were moved to tears'.[5] Count Egmont stood proxy for the absent bridegroom, placing the ring on Mary's finger, after which the marriage blessing was given by Lord Chancellor Gardiner.

Now that she was the wife of the Prince of Spain, Renard insisted the Queen must make some final decision about Elizabeth and Courtenay. Mary replied 'that she and her Council were labouring as much as possible to discover the truth . . . that as to Courtenay, it was certain he was accused by many of the prisoners of consenting and assisting in the plot . . .'.[6] With the aid of a cipher cut upon his guitar, the earl had corresponded with the ringleaders, such as Sir Peter Carew and 'had intrigued with the French . . . that a match had been projected between him and Elizabeth'. The Queen's sister, however, was another matter. Mary's attitude to Elizabeth drove Renard to distraction. She told the ambassador, 'The law of England condemns to death only those who have committed overt acts of treason; those who have merely implied consent by silence are punished by imprisonment . . .'.[7] This law, passed during Mary's brief time as sovereign and at her request, repealed the tyrannical treason laws extant during her father's and brother's reigns when execution had been justified on the flimsiest bits of circumstantial evidence. Mary had seen the vengeance of the law fall on the neck of a beloved governess. She had insisted on its repeal and an element of mercy for those victims whose guilt was in doubt.

And there was nothing against Elizabeth that could be proved. Letters had been sent to her by Wyatt; she had written none in reply. Copies of her correspondence had been found in the French mail packet, but it was common knowledge that spies placed in her household at Ashridge might easily have made them.* When, a week after

* Indeed, de Noailles had at this time been married to one of Elizabeth's Maids-of-Honour, leading one to wonder how much his heart was genuinely involved or the wedding motivated by the ease of his wife's access to Elizabeth's papers.

the Queen's marriage, Wyatt was tried and condemned, he implicated Elizabeth to the extent that he had written to the girl advising her removal to Donnington Castle, receiving her verbal thanks in reply. Upon hearing his execution would be delayed a month and declaring he was actually only the fourth or fifth in rank of the conspirators, Wyatt regretted 'the miserable, mischievous, brutish and beastly furious imagination' which had brought him to such an end and protested he 'had never meant hurt against her Highness's person'. Though disappointed that Wyatt had not implicated Elizabeth more deeply, the Council itself resolved to interrogate the Princess. On the day following Wyatt's sentencing, Gardiner and nine councillors informed Elizabeth of his testimony and accused her of equal guilt with the traitor. Gardiner advised her to seek the Queen's pardon. Elizabeth heatedly replied that to 'throw herself on the Queen would be the confession of a crime, and that pardon was for the guilty'. She challenged Gardiner to prove his case. Only then, she finished boldly, would she follow his advice.

Renard advised the Tower for the disgraced Princess, and when baulked by Elizabeth's spirited defence at her interrogation, Lord Chancellor Gardiner agreed. 'The Queen is advised to send her to the Tower,' wrote Renard elatedly to the Emperor, 'and assuredly, Sire, if now that the occasion offers, they do not punish her and Courtenay, the Queen will never be secure. . . .'[8] Mary had hoped to leave the burdens of her capital for the tranquillity of Windsor during the Easter festival, but the problem of Elizabeth's detention had first to be solved. She could not remain at Whitehall where she might be carried off during the Queen's absence.

The matter being brought to the Council's attention the few who were Elizabeth's partisans objected furiously to the Tower imprisonment, declaring there was 'no evidence to justify so violent a measure!' and all it implied. A bitter debate ensued until Gardiner arose and in carpingly sarcastic tones asked, 'if any of them would take charge of the Lady?' Immediately there was silence. To a man they shrank from the responsibility of caring for a Queen's sister and her household. Not even her staunchest advocate would diminish his purse and endanger his position by undertaking the safekeeping of Elizabeth Tudor.

And so Mary gave her consent. Now that she was Philip's wife she wanted him in England, and as Renard repeatedly cautioned, the Emperor refused to allow his son to leave Spain while Elizabeth was free, to serve as a figurehead—even an unwilling one—for the enemies of the Church and Spain. Mary knew the depth of Charles's hatred of Elizabeth; the girl was a living symbol of the social, religious, and political destruction Anne Boleyn had wrought in England, to the incalculable misery of her *own* mother, the valiant Catherine of Aragon. Charles was lusting for the blood of Elizabeth Tudor, as well as of

Courtenay, and the pressure upon the Queen—from councillors, ambassadors, and subjects—had become almost intolerable. For the time being, until she could face the problem of Elizabeth's future with some objectivity, Mary concluded the girl would be better off in the Tower.

It was Stephen Gardiner who visited Elizabeth with the news that she would be removed the next morning to the fortress-prison down the river. The effect on the girl was instantaneous. She paled visibly. Vehemently, she protested her innocence. 'I trust that her Majesty will be far more gracious than to commit to that place a true and innocent woman, who has never offended her in thought, word or deed!' Several of Gardiner's companions appeared moved, and to them she addressed a further appeal, asking them to intercede with the Queen. But when, four hours later, her attendants were reduced, an extra guard ordered outside her chamber, and 100 soldiers placed in the garden under her window, she knew her plea had failed. Thoroughly frightened, Elizabeth could only gaze at Ashley, whose pinched features reflected her own concern.

To deny Elizabeth's appeal had cost Mary some anguish. By nature, the Queen was kindly and forgiving; the larger decisions of royalty involving the life, fortunes, and, at times, the freedom of others never came easily to Mary. The constant pressure on her temperament and conscience accounts, in some measure, for her reluctance to see Elizabeth. Mary knew the extent of the hidden affection which—come what may—she still felt for her sister. From childhood, in one way or another, Elizabeth had always been able to beguile the older, more forthright Mary. A confrontation would only reawaken those feelings, and in her own nervous state, already depleted by the demands of the past several weeks, she might commit some blunder which would enrage Renard, engulf her Council in more pointless wrangling and ultimately imperil an early arrival of her husband. Until the Prince arrived in England, Elizabeth must remain in confinement.

The following morning, therefore, the Earl of Sussex and the Marquis of Winchester arrived to tell the Princess 'that a barge was in readiness to convey her to the Tower and she must prepare to go, as the tide served, which would tarry for no one'.[9] Again Elizabeth begged to see her sister. Being told the Queen had denied all requests for an interview, the girl asked permission to write a letter instead. Winchester hurriedly interrupted. There was no time, he said coldly, the barge was waiting. But Sussex was moved by the girl's obvious fear and, to Winchester's surprise, knelt on one knee before Elizabeth, promising to take any letter she might write and place it in the Queen's hands himself.

As they withdrew to await her letter, Elizabeth sat at her desk, attempting forcibly to restrain the trembling of her fingers by smoothing the paper in front of her. Aware of the lack of time, there was no opening salutation. She began with the first inspiration, and, as she proceeded, a composure so at odds with her near-panic of the previous moment settled upon the thin figure. Elizabeth was always at home with a pen in her hand, and it was never more evident than when—at a moment when her whole future and possibly her very life hung in the balance—she set words to paper in one of history's more famous letters:

If any ever did try this old saying 'that a King's word was more than another man's oath',* I most humbly beseech your Majesty to verify it in me and to remember your last promise and my last demand that I be not condemned without answer and due proof which it seems that now I am. For that without cause proved, I am by your Council from you commanded to go unto the Tower, a place more wonted for a false traitor, than a true subject which, though I know I deserve it not, yet in the face of all this realm appears that it is proved, which I pray God I may die the shamefullest death that ever any died, afore I may mean any such thing. And to this present hour, I protest afore God (Who shall know my truth) whatsoever malice may devise, that I never practised, concealed nor consented to anything that might be prejudicial to your person any way or dangerous to the State by any means.

And, therefore, I humbly beseech your Majesty to let me answer afore yourself and not suffer me to trust your Councillors—yea, and that afore I go to the Tower (if it be possible) if not afore I be further condemned; howbeit, I trust assuredly your Highness will give me leave to do it afore I go for that thus shamefully, I may not be cried out on as now I shall be—yea, and without cause!

In this one sentence, in which Elizabeth acknowledges her concern for the opinion of Mary's subjects, the Princess revealed an awareness at which her father would have laughed, and which only puzzled and angered Mary. In his youth, Henry had relied on a compelling personal magnetism and the loving forbearance of his subjects; later he had governed by terror. His daughter, Mary, while concerned with her people's welfare, was a firm believer in the divine right to rule and paid little attention to public opinion unless it endangered her throne, her religion, or dishonoured her name. In the teeth of her subjects' ill-concealed hatred for her choice of husband, the Queen had obstinately insisted that she and she alone should be the arbiter—that her marriage was right and just. Of all the Tudors, only Elizabeth intuitively recognised the power of the masses,[10] and while appealing for clemency, she

---

* A quotation from a speech given by King John of France when he voluntarily returned to a captivity in England.

decried the shame being cast upon her name which might deprive her of the popularity she enjoyed with Mary's subjects. The letter continues:

Let conscience move your Highness to take some better way with me than to make me to be condemned in all men's sight afore my desert known. Also, I most humbly beseech your Highness to pardon this my boldness which innocency procures me to do together with hope of your natural kindness which I trust will not see me cast away without desert, which, what it is I would desire no more of God but that you truly knew. Which thing I think and believe you shall never by report know unless by yourself you hear. I have heard in my time of many cast away for want of coming to the presence of their Prince and in late days I heard my Lord of Somerset say that if his brother [Thomas Seymour] had been suffered to speak with him, he had never suffered, but the persuasions were made to him so great that he was brought in belief that he could not live safely if the Admiral lived and that made him give his consent to his death.

Though these persuasions are not to be compared to your Majesty, yet I pray God as evil persuasions persuade not one sister against the other, and all for that they have heard false report and not harken to the truth known.

The painful allusion to Thomas Seymour past, the taut courage which she had manifested during the previous moments began to desert Elizabeth. She turned the page over and realising these final sentences constituted her last recourse, her lessening confidence is revealed* in the wavering letters, in the crossed-out words and insertions as she neared the end:

Therefore, once again kneeling with humbleness of my heart, because I am not suffered to bow the knees of my body, I humbly crave to speak with your Highness which I would not be so bold to desire if I knew not myself most clear, as I know myself most true. And, as for the traitor Wyatt, he might peradventure, write me a letter, but on my faith, I never received any from him. And as for the copy of my letter to the French King, I pray God confound me eternally if ever I sent word, message, token or letter by any means, and to this my truth, I will stand in to my death.

Elizabeth stared at the last ominous phrase; and suddenly her mind was blank and her spirit depleted. It had been a massive effort, and yet almost two-thirds of the second side of the notepaper remained vacant.

* Elizabeth's letter is still extant at the Public Record Office in London.

In that space, someone might attempt to forge some incriminating remarks. With her pen, the girl drew broad slanting lines down to the very edge of the paper, leaving only space to sign herself, 'Your Highness's most faithful subject, that hath been from the beginning, and will be to the end'. Signing her name with its usual flourishes, she noticed a small space to the left still unfilled. Hurriedly, she wrote her final words, and ones which undoubtedly came straight from her heart:

'I humbly crave but one word of answer from yourself. . . .'[11]

The last poignant request complete, she silently handed the letter to Sussex, and the nobles departed to dismiss the waiting barge. The tide had turned; any journey to the Tower by water was impossible. Once again Elizabeth's natural tendency to delay had won her a small reprieve.

Mary, however, was not touched. Her anger with Sussex and Winchester—who had failed to carry out her orders—effectively undermined the plea in Elizabeth's letter and only hardened the Queen's resistance. Apparently even her councillors were not proof against Elizabeth's artifices! Mary indulged in a display of royal temper, telling her ministers they 'were not travelling on the right path. They dared not have done such a thing in her father's lifetime—and she wished he were alive again, were it but for a month!'[12]

At ten o'clock the next morning, the chastened Sussex and Winchester returned to Whitehall and, by the expression on their faces, Elizabeth knew her plea had failed. 'Very well, then,' she said resignedly, 'if there be no remedy, I must be contented.' It was Palm Sunday, 1554— ironically, the very day the conspirators had originally determined for their uprising, before Courtenay had carelessly revealed the plot's details. Londoners were receiving their palms at church, unaware of the drama taking place in the Palace. As Elizabeth crossed the garden to the river, she glanced up to the Queen's windows, hoping to see her sister. But Mary, too, was at her devotions. The girl could not hide her disappointment, saying, 'I marvel that the nobles mean by suffering me, a Princess, to be led into captivity; the Lord knoweth wherefore, for myself, I do not!'[13]

The eagerness of her escorts to rid themselves of their unwelcome task had caused their departure to be precipitate, and the boatmen in the waiting barge indicated the tide had risen sufficiently to allow a safe passage to the Tower. But Sussex and Winchester would delay no longer. A fine rain had begun, and coupled with their own distaste for their commission, they ordered the boatman to leave at once. As they slipped away from the water-stairs and started down the Thames, the silence was broken only by the rhythmic dipping of the oars in the grey waters as, from the City, the sound of church bells

[394]

carried to the occupants huddled in the barge. On rounding the bend of the Thames as it curved towards London Bridge, the boatman attempted to check the pace of the craft, for the water eddied and boiled furiously against the bridge arches. As the Tower loomed ever larger in sight, suddenly the barge was caught in a whirlpool and only the boatmen's skill prevented the occupants from being tossed into the rushing water, as it struck repeatedly against the supports. The momentary emergency distracted everyone, and mercifully, Elizabeth did not see the traitors' rotting heads atop their pikes on London Bridge. Within minutes they were at the Traitor's Gate. The sight of the shameful portal struck Elizabeth forcefully; it seemed to symbolise her own peril. As the barge bumped against the water-stairs and everyone stood aside for her to disembark, terror engulfed the girl. She drew back and, contemplating the stairs, refused to land. In a loud voice she cried out that she was no traitor! One of the nobles replied, not unkindly, 'it was not for her to choose'. The rain had increased and the stairs were running with rivulets of water. Belatedly, Winchester offered the Princess his cloak. She waved it aside 'with a good dash' and, setting her foot on the stairs so the water 'drew well over her shoe', spoke despairingly, 'Here lands as true a subject, being prisoner, as ever landed at these stairs. Before Thee, oh God I speak it, having no other friend but Thee alone!' She was close to tears and did not hear Winchester's sparse remark, 'If that is so, it is better for you'.[14]

At the Gate, warders of the Tower were drawn up in formation; and beyond knelt the other minor officials and servants who had come to see the Princess's entrance. As she passed, many said quietly 'God preserve your Grace', causing Elizabeth to address them, saying, 'Oh Lord, I never thought to have come in here as prisoner; and I pray you all, good friends and fellows, bear me witness, that I come in no traitor, but as true a woman to the Queen's Majesty as any is now living, and thereon will I take my death!'[15] Gazing scornfully at the guard, clad in armour, she asked 'What! Are all these harnessed men here for me?' to which Sir John Gage, the Constable of the Tower, permitted himself a small perjury. 'No, Madam. . . .' Elizabeth's reply was bitter. 'Yes,' she said grimly, 'I know it is so. It is needed not for me, being, alas but a weak woman. . . .'[16]

As she approached the spot where her own mother had died, panic assailed her, and almost overwhelmed, she sat suddenly on the stone step of her prison and declared she would go no farther. 'Madam,' said Sir John Bridges, the lieutenant who had been awaiting her arrival, 'you had best come out of the rain, for you sit unwholesomely.' Pulling her cloak closer around her trembling form, Elizabeth replied in a voice in which anger mixed with fear, 'Better sit here than in a worse place, for God knoweth, not I, whither you will bring me!' At this one of her young male servants burst into tears—the Princess whirled around and rebuked the boy for giving way to his weakness. Rather he support and comfort her, she said; there was no need to weep, for she had committed no crime!

Then, as she realised that further resistance was futile, a forgotten pride rose in Elizabeth, the pride of a grandfather who had wrested a King's crown at Bosworth Field, the pride of a mother who had died defending her honour against a King's accusation. Elizabeth entered the Bell Tower, and slowly climbed the stairs. At last, having placed her safely inside the rooms which had been designated for her use, the nobles and Sir John Gage made ready to depart. Elizabeth had no final word for them; instead she stared dejectedly out of one window towards the river, now only a blur through the sheets of rain slashing the ancient stones of the Tower sill with dismal regularity. As the bolts were shot sharply into place and Gage issued orders to the waiting guard, Sussex spoke. The scene had grated on the earl's sensibilities, and he turned on his companions, crying, 'What mean ye, my Lords? What will ye do?' Pointing to the heavily barred and bolted door, 'Let us take heed, my lords, that we go not beyond our commission, for she was our King's daughter, and is, we know, the Prince next in blood; wherefore, let us so deal with her now, that we have not, if it so happen, to answer for our dealings hereafter.'[17]

The answer might have caused the Princess Elizabeth a wry comfort. As it was, numb with exhaustion and despair, she did not hear Sussex's warning remark but remained instead at the window wearily gazing at the grey river below.

Elizabeth remained in the Bell Tower for two months. Her servants were quartered elsewhere in the fortress precincts, and new attendants appeared to serve her. To the dismay of her cook, all meals were brought by the common guard. A few hundred feet away, under the cold stones in the church, lay the bones of her mother—that mother she could barely remember. There, too, was poor dear Thomas Seymour whom she could remember very well indeed. The stones that had been disturbed for the small form of Lady Jane Grey had barely settled. Elizabeth tried to drive such thoughts from her mind—certainly Mary would never condemn her only sister to such an ignominious death! The constant anxiety, the rigour of her confinement, the lack of companionship, of books and writing materials—all caused a deep depression in the young woman, so recently recovered from a similar serious illness. Daily, she was compelled to hear Mass in her chamber, to which she submitted with a stoical indifference. Years later Queen Elizabeth

[396]

was to tell the French ambassador, Michael Castelnau, that the week following Palm Sunday, 1554, was the one time in her life when she had felt herself 'utterly doomed and lost'. She had decided to request the Queen to let her be beheaded with a sword instead of an axe and that a Frenchman, notably more skilful with that weapon than an Englishman, might be summoned for that purpose. The request is significant, revealing that during her adolescence, someone had told the young Elizabeth of the identical request her mother, Anne Boleyn, had made of Henry Tudor.

After one week of isolation, the Princess had visitors. Bishop Gardiner and several of the Council arrived with the prime purpose of securing evidence to prove her guilt. Their arrival—unannounced and sudden— put Elizabeth immediately on the defensive. There were few formalities, and Gardiner immediately launched into the subject, questioning the proposal made by Wyatt that she move to Donnington Castle. Elizabeth sought safety in evasion and maintained she knew nothing of Donnington Castle, for she had never visited there. A fellow prisoner, Sir James Croft, was brought to face the Princess. The presence of a man so obviously implicated in the rebellion shook Elizabeth's small confidence and caused a hasty recollection. She said, 'Indeed I do now remember that I have such a place, but I never lay in it in all my life. And, as for any that hath moved me thereunto, I do not remember.' The tense scene, with the powerful Lord Chancellor and his companions all arraigned against one lone young woman, angered Croft. Suddenly, he knelt in front of the girl and said, 'But I assure your Grace, I have been marvellously tossed and examined touching your Highness, which, the Lord knoweth, is very strange to me; for, I take God to record, before all your honours, I do not know anything of that crime which you have laid to my charge, and will thereupon take my death, if I should be driven to so straight a trial!'[18] Croft's bravely impassioned outburst seemed to give Elizabeth courage. She turned to face her interrogators angrily, 'My Lords, methinks you do me wrong to examine every mean prisoner against me; if they have done evil, let them answer for it. I pray you join me not in such offenders! Touching my removal from Ashridge to Donnington, I do remember that Mr Hoby, mine officers and you, Sir James Croft, had some talk about it. But what is that to the purpose? Might I not, my lords, go to mine own houses at all times?'[19]

The councillors glanced uneasily at one another and then at Gardiner. The Chancellor remained silent as Elizabeth continued, her voice rising. For the moment, she had the advantage and she intended to use it. 'Well, my Lords,' she finished, 'you sift me narrowly, but you can do no more than God hath appointed—and so God forgive you all!'[20]

Croft's statement of Elizabeth's innocence and the plight of the Princess defending herself so fervently touched several of the councillors,

[397]

but only one had the audacity—and courage—to reveal his feelings. In an instinctive reaction which possibly surprised even himself, the Earl of Arundel went down on his knees to Elizabeth. 'Your Grace sayeth true,' he stated devoutly, 'and certainly we are very sorry that we have troubled you about so vain matters!' [21] Arundel's defection stunned the observers; even the indomitable Gardiner was effectively silenced for the moment.* The earl's efforts, combined with the influence of Elizabeth's great-uncle, Lord William Howard, resulted in the Princess being allowed to walk in the Queen's own apartments. When she complained of the lack of fresh air and outdoor exercise, Sir John Bridges, lieutenant of the Tower, expressed 'his regret at being compelled to refuse her, as it was contrary to his orders'. But he did carry her complaint to the Council. By the middle of April, the councillors relented, allowing her to walk in a small enclosed garden. All prisoners, whose cells abutted upon the area were warned 'not so much as to look in that direction while her Grace remained therein'. The two most distinguished prisoners were Robert Dudley, son of the executed Duke of Northumberland, and Courtenay, the Earl of Devon, and the Tower officials were wary of any communication between them and Elizabeth.

Their strict surveillance did not overlook even the children who lived within the Tower precincts. On her daily walks in the restricted garden, Elizabeth had met a little boy, the son of the keeper of the Queen's robes, and a small girl named Susanna. Daily Elizabeth delighted in the childish talk that provided a welcome respite from the tedium of her imprisonment. Her experience with children had been limited, but she found a genuine enjoyment in their attention. Often they brought her a handful of flowers, bestowing the blooms with grubby hands, blushes, and laughter. On one occasion, Susanna handed Elizabeth a ring containing some keys which had been carelessly dropped by a warder, saying, 'she had brought her the keys now, so she need not always stay there, but might unlock the gates and go abroad'. Elizabeth did not enlighten the child further. Instead she accepted the gifts with grave seriousness before returning to her chamber. The conversations between the children and the Princess, the exchange of flowers and keys, were all duly reported to the Council which saw in the innocent children means by which messages might be conveyed. The boy was duly brought before the commissioners and harshly questioned, but not even the stern faces and the loud voices of his interrogators could budge him. He had carried nothing, he said, nothing except flowers for the lady.

* From this point on, the Earl of Arundel seems to have had more than a surface interest in Elizabeth which she, recognising the merit and worth of his advocacy, did nothing to discourage. Both Arundel and his son were contenders for Elizabeth's hand in later life when the old earl did little to hide his outright jealousy at her preference for Robert Dudley.

His father was reprimanded and told to keep his 'crafty knave' at home, away from the Princess Elizabeth. For several days, the boy obeyed. But later, when he saw the Princess walking in the enclosure, obviously looking for her young friends, he forgot the warnings. Quickly, as she approached, he sped to the garden gate and waited. With the air of a conspirator, Elizabeth leaned down to talk to her young friend. Mindful of his father's wrath, however, the child was brief. 'Mistress,' he said hurriedly, 'Mistress—I can bring you no more flowers now.' And then, his courage failing, he darted off. Elizabeth's face showed her disappointment; she could guess what had happened.

On Wednesday, April 11, Thomas Wyatt was brought to the scaffold on Tower Hill where, before his beheading, he exonerated Courtenay and Elizabeth of active complicity in the rebellion, saying, '. . . it is not so, good people for I assure you neither they nor any other . . . was privy to my rising or commotion *before I began* . . . and this is most true'.[22] The fine distinction 'before I began' was lost upon the mob thronging about the scaffold and for days afterwards, as Wyatt's head was impaled 'on a stake beyond the gallows beyond St James' and the quarters of his body exhibited on Hay Hill beside Hyde Park, London rang with his words. Wyatt's recantation implied either a belated attack of conscience or a quixotic gamble to save the prisoners from his own fate. The indignation aroused in the citizens at his words—and at the continued imprisonment of the Queen's sister and Courtenay—contributed to a decline in feeling for the Queen and to a greater antagonism for her marriage.

When Wyatt was executed, Elizabeth had been in the Tower nearly three weeks, depressed and deeply apprehensive. She might well be next. If Wyatt had exonerated her of active complicity, why must she remain imprisoned like a common criminal?

The same question echoed frequently in Mary's Council chamber, as well as her private apartments, where Simon Renard constantly harangued the Queen to settle the matter of Courtenay and Elizabeth once and for all. But Mary would not agree to execution. The ambassador wrote to Charles, 'The Queen is irresolute about what should be done with her and Courtenay. . . . For Elizabeth, the lawyers can find no matter for her condemnation. . . .'[23] Even his explicit suggestion 'that it was of the utmost consequence that the trials and executions of the criminals . . . should take place before the arrival of His Highness' could not budge Mary—although it could and often did reduce the Queen to tears.

In the challenge Elizabeth presented to Mary's conscience, the Spanish ambassador was also ranged against the formidable influence and power of the Lord Chancellor, Stephen Gardiner. Brilliant and tough, with the authority of a vast experience which even a long imprisonment had not impaired, Gardiner was the natural enemy of both the Spanish and French ambassadors. Shamelessly patriotic, with great 'attachment to the ancient laws of England', he had no illusions about either Renard or the de Noailles brothers, extending them the barest of civilities. Without doubt the most surprisingly honest member of a larcenous Council, he was immune to the ambassadors' bribery, their flattery, and even—when all else failed—their candour. He had hoped Mary would wed Courtenay but, in face of the Queen's insistence upon Philip, realised he must give way. He was, however, determined that his friend of past prison days, Courtenay, would not be sacrificed—a victim of Renard's merciless intimidation of the Queen.

With the Chancellor's strong championing of the earl, amply buttressed by the revised treason law, there was also a tacit defence of Elizabeth,[24] since the two were accused together. If one was guiltless, so was the other. He argued that 'there was no proof of a treasonable correspondence between them during the late insurrection' and, indeed, there was not. Gardiner's defence of Courtenay even extended to a deliberate loss or misplacement of parts of the incriminating French correspondence. When de Noailles demanded the intercepted French papers be returned, Gardiner's glib excuse was that they had been lost when Wyatt's troops had plundered his Southwark library, leading to Renard's rueful comment that '. . it would have been very convenient if the original could have been found to serve as the ground of accusation against Elizabeth and Courtenay'.[25]

While he never ceased 'to admonish her Majesty as to the necessity of a prompt punishment of the prisoners', Renard was beginning to despair of combating Gardiner. 'The Chancellor manages the whole matter,' the ambassador wrote to the Emperor, and his discouragement shows in his letter. 'Things are in such disorder, that we know not who is well-disposed or ill-disposed, constant or inconstant, loyal or traitorous. One thing is certain, that the Chancellor has been extremely remiss in proceeding against the criminals and most ardent and hot-headed in the affairs of religion, being so hated in this kingdom that I have doubts whether the detestation against him will not recoil on the Queen.'[26] As for the councillors, Renard was contemptuous. 'Since my last letters, the party squabbles, jealousies and ill-feeling of the Councillors have so increased and become public that, at this moment some, from animosity against others, will not attend the Council. What one does, another undoes. What one counsels, another contradicts. One advises to save Courtenay—another Elizabeth. And all at last have got into such confusion that we only wait to see the quarrel end in arms and tumult. Thus is the Queen of England treated by those who ought to be her most intimate and devoted servants!'[27] That Mary reflected his anger is apparent in his remark that she 'spends her days in shouting at the Council, but with no results . . .'.

The Queen's disposition was not improved by the popular prejudice aroused in the City by religious agitators and troublemakers. Scurrilous handbills stating, among other charges, that Mary was pregnant were left in the stores, churches, and taverns. The anonymous slander shocked and horrified the Queen, who said 'she had always lived a chaste and honest life and would not bear imputations to the contrary!'[28] Even the effective device of ridicule and trickery was not overlooked. In a shabby house in Aldersgate Street a sepulchral voice was suddenly heard issuing from the walls. A mob of over 17,000 citizens crowded to hear 'the voice of an angel'. When they shouted 'God save Queen Mary!' there was no answer from the entombed supernatural being. Then someone shouted 'God save the Lady Elizabeth!' and the voice answered, 'So be it'. When asked, 'What is the Mass?' the voice mockingly replied, 'Idolatry . . .'.[29] Lord Paget was sent to investigate the incident and found a young woman within the walls, placed there by unfriendly factions intent upon defaming Mary. The girl was set in the pillory for 'exciting the people against the Queen, raising the heretics and troubling the Kingdom . . .'.

As the flood of hostile literature continued and the Council continued their time-wasting harangues, the distracted Mary longed for escape. When a dead cat, 'having a cloth like a vestment of the priest at Mass . . . the crown of the cat shorn . . .' was hanged on the gallows in Cheapside in a further attempt to discredit the Queen, it caused a sensation in the City. Similar episodes occurred within the Palace itself, with some of the embarrassing handbills being found in the Queen's own chambers. The pressure told on Mary. Her nerves were shattered, and she was unusually curt with those around her. One lady-in-waiting, near tears, stated that the Queen 'could not speak to no one without impatience and believed the whole world was in league to keep her husband from her'.

Mary was touchingly eager for Philip's arrival. There had been no contact between them; the marriage treaty and the proxy ceremony had all been accomplished through diplomatic channels. Yet her Council could not agree on the necessary provisions for Philip's entry into England, and Renard continued to emphasise the danger confronting his Prince in such a tumultuous realm. The lack of contact or interest on Philip's part was also noted by the councillors who 'expressed their astonishment that he has never written to the Queen, or sent any person to pay her a visit'. Renard had no legitimate explanation for Philip's silence. He wrote to Charles, 'I excuse as well as I can'. Mary told the ambassador that 'as his Highness had not yet written to her, she deferred writing to him till he began the correspondence'.

In the midst of the climactic events of the past several weeks, Mary still clung to the vision of her marriage and what it would mean, not only to herself, but to her country. Let her countrymen mock and defame! Let the councillors squabble and Elizabeth, Courtenay, and all their kind plot and intrigue! Once her husband—strong, handsome, and gallant—was in England, she might lay her burdens aside. Then the elegant form of a Prince of Spain, now a King of England, would stand between her and the many challenges facing a Queen. Her husband would be her adviser, confidante, and *protector*. The desire for a strong champion, coupled with the longings of an unawakened and frustrated woman deliciously anticipating the solace of love and affection had brought Mary's emotional resources almost to an end, and she teetered on the brink of a complete breakdown. She had given much of herself during several nerve-wracking months in her capital. Now she must hoard her physical and emotional resources for the arrival of her husband which only the dilatory behaviour of her Council—and the winter storms sweeping the Channel—had so long delayed.

As she prepared to close the Parliament at which her marriage articles had been confirmed, Mary wrote her first letter to her husband. Between the somewhat apologetically humble lines, in which she justifies her reasons for writing, may be discerned a tenuous desire for some evidence of Philip's interest:

Sir, my good and constant Ally,

Knowing that the Ambassador of the Emperor, my Lord and good father, resident at my court [*Simon Renard*], was despatching the bearer hereof to Your Highness; although you have not privately written to me since our alliance has been negotiated, so it is that, feeling myself so much obliged by the sincere and true affection which you bear me, which you have as much confirmed by deeds, as by the letters written to the said Ambassador and by the negotiation which the Sieur de'Egmont and others, and the Ambassador of my said Lord have managed, I could not omit signifying to you my good wishes and duty which I have ever to communicate with you; and I thank you very humbly for so many good offices, and apprise you at the same time that the Parliament, which represents the estates of my Kingdom, has heard the articles of our marriage without opposition, inasmuch as they find the conditions thereof honourable, advantageous, and more than reasonable, which puts me in entire confidence, that your coming hither will be certain and agreeable.

And, hoping shortly to supply the remainder verbally, I will make an end at present, praying the Creator to grant you, my good and constant

Ally, to make your journey hither in prosperity and health, commending myself very affectionately and humbly to Your Highness.

At London, 20th April,

Your entire assured and most obliged Ally,

Mary[30]

By May 3, the unrest in the City had subsided so it was thought safe for the Queen to participate in the Rogation Week ceremonies, walking 'to all her chapels in the Fields—to St Giles-in-the-Fields, to St Martin's-in-the-Fields, and to Westminster, and there they had a sermon and song-Mass and made good cheer'.[31] It was the first time Mary had ventured abroad since the outburst of seditious pamphlets had swamped the capital. Heartening cheers were heard from those who watched as the Queen walked in procession, accompanied by four mitred bishops. A similar change of attitude was evident when Parliament dissolved two days later. It had been a stormy session with the Queen, her councillors, the Chancellor, and the Commons often in heated disagreement. But little animosity was to be seen as Mary closed the sittings with a final speech. 'She was interrupted five or six times by cries of "God save the Queen!"' wrote Renard to the Emperor, 'and most wept at the eloquence and goodness of Her Highness . . .'—which caused the ambassador's irascible comment to Charles, 'The inconstancy of the people here is incredible, and equally so their power of inspiring confidence when they wish to deceive you . . .'. The ambassador also informed the Emperor that Edward Courtenay would soon be removed to Fotheringhay Castle in Northamptonshire and Elizabeth would be sent deeper into the countryside for safekeeping. All of which caused Renard to end, despairingly, 'Your Majesty may well believe in what danger the Queen is—so long as both are alive!'[32]

Chapter Twenty-two

THE royal manor house of Woodstock[1] in the pleasant Oxfordshire countryside had been in disrepair for several years. Once a majestic and comfortable country dwelling for a travelling sovereign, it had been little used by Edward or his nobles. The decaying wood, broken windows, and crumbling stone ornamentation presented a dismal sight to the company that approached from the east, along a road bordering on the choked and dying Privy gardens, past trees that had been uprooted by winter's violence. At the gates, the foresters and keepers of the park had assembled to watch the small band. All around them the landscape flaunted the green glory of an annual rebirth, and in the great dark forest behind, the sun shone on the young new growth of the massive trees. If, that late May afternoon of 1554, anyone noticed the extraordinary beauty of the day, they gave no sign. From the stocky, upright form of Sir Henry Bedingfield* who rode at the procession's head, to the carts bringing up the rear, there had been nothing but silence. And from the occupant of the litter that accompanied the travellers, its curtains drawn, silence as well.

During the several days' journey to Woodstock, a frightened Princess Elizabeth had anticipated not only confinement but possible assassination. Her ordeal had begun on May 5—as Mary was receiving the cheers of a refractory Parliament—when Sir Henry Bedingfield arrived at the Tower with a band of 100 men as further security for the imprisoned heiress-presumptive. After her seven weeks of anxious seclusion his arrival caused a near-panic in Elizabeth, and she quickly asked an attendant 'if the Lady Jane's scaffold had been removed'. It had been standing when the Princess entered the Tower, and in her isolated walks in the Privy garden, she could not see whether it still remained. When an official attempted to calm her, saying 'that she had no cause for alarm, but that his orders were to consign her into the charge of Sir

* Sir Henry Bedingfield was the son of the Norfolk knight of the same name who served as custodian of Catherine of Aragon at Kimbolton Castle until her death in January, 1536.

[404]

Henry Bedingfield to be conveyed . . . to Woodstock', Elizabeth was not consoled. Her inner fear was revealed when she hurriedly asked whether 'Bedingfield were a person who made conscience of murder, if such an order were entrusted to him'. Royal captives had 'disappeared' before. It was a mere seventy years since Elizabeth's small great-uncles, the 'little Princes in the Tower', had been murdered. She and Jane Grey, during that magic summer at Chelsea, had often whispered of the fate of their little relatives. Her anxieties were slightly alleviated when she was informed that Sir Henry was, indeed, an honest, conscientious, and courageous noble who would do her no harm.

As the days passed, she became more calm. Had Mary or the Council wished to dispose of her, Elizabeth reasoned, there had been ample opportunity during the past few weeks as, all around her, political prisoners had been dragged from their cells to the gallows or the block. Mary's conscience would not allow her sister to be surreptitiously executed. Elizabeth's great fear was that someone else, wishing her out of the way and willing to gamble on a whim of chance, might not be so scrupulous.

In the middle of May, Sir Henry received his orders. The Princess Elizabeth would proceed to Woodstock to remain there at the Queen's pleasure until her innocence of any traitorous action against the Crown was proved—or admitted. At one o'clock in the afternoon on a day in which Londoners revelled in a welcome warmth after the icy, grey winter which had seen armed mobs fighting in the street, Elizabeth left the Tower for Richmond. News of her release had filtered into the City, and crowds thronged the Thames's bank in the bright sunlight, awaiting her appearance. As she stepped into the first of many barges, there were hearty cheers from the onlookers who assumed that Elizabeth was honourably released and returning either to Ashridge or Hatfield. The news quickly carried into the City, and as the barges proceeded upstream, a church bell began to ring loudly. Suddenly, the bells of other City churches all rang simultaneously as people ran into the streets to hear the news. The clamour of the bells provided a melodious accompaniment to the three salvoes which were fired from the Steelyard, the riverside factories of the Hanseatic League—all notably Protestant— as Elizabeth's barge continued upstream. It swept past Whitehall and Westminster Palaces as the girl gazed at the many windows reflecting the light of the high midday sun. Behind one of these windows sat the Queen who had ordered her to further dreary captivity, and who had, apparently, little interest in the plight of the prisoner there on the river.*

* Mary was at Whitehall as Elizabeth's barge passed and inquired about the church bells and the noise of the cannon from the Steelyard. She revealed great displeasure ('as she considered this a demonstration') when told it was in honour of her sister.

[405]

At the massive red-brick Palace of Richmond, Elizabeth's servants were peremptorily dismissed, distressing the girl who felt safer with her own people. In great agitation, she told Cornwallis—the same young gentleman-usher who had wept at her arrival at the Tower—that 'this night, I think I must die . . .'. Then, in a startling departure from her usual composure, she burst into tears. The unnerved fellow rushed to Bedingfield's companion, Lord William of Thame, and asked whether the Princess was in danger of death that night, saying further that he and his companions 'wished to die with her'. Lord William assured him. 'Marry! God forbid!' he exclaimed, 'that any such wickedness should be intended. Rather than it would be wrought, I and my men will die at her feet.'[2] When the young man hastened to reassure his mistress, Elizabeth could only mutter, 'God grant it to be so . . .'.

The following day, as she entered her barge, the dismissed servants all waited in silent farewell on a nearby bank. Many of the women were in tears. Despite Bedingfield's comment that there was no time for lingering, Elizabeth summoned one of the guard to her and, in a bitter voice, said, 'Go to them and tell them for me "*Tanquem ovis*"—like a sheep to the slaughter—for so am I led!'

After a night's rest at the Dean of Windsor's lodgings at Windsor, Elizabeth set out on the final portion of her journey, a journey which —begun in fear and ignominy—was destined to assume the majestic proportions of a triumphant royal progress. As the travellers assembled in line to leave the town, Elizabeth was heartened by the sight of the Queen's own litter 'with 16 servants in tawney coats' to attend her. As the small cavalcade rumbled out of Windsor for the open road, the townspeople and students from Eton College all crowded around the conveyance, shouting their good wishes and waving a joyous farewell. The demonstration startled the Princess as much as it puzzled and irritated her guard. But the people would not be restrained. Alerted to the presence of the Queen's only sister, now released from her long detention, they thronged to the roadside and, amid cheers and cap waving, followed the litter to the very outskirts of the town. And as it journeyed onwards, passing through the small villages and hamlets towards West Wykeham, other citizens rushed to the road as church bells rang out, joyously proclaiming that the Princess Elizabeth was passing through. The people thrust 'cakes and wafers' into the lap of the astonished young woman; others lovingly piled flowers and sweet herbs at her feet. The spontaneous display of such favour so disconcerted Bedingfield that at Aston he ordered the gaoling of two men who rang the church bells. Though she was heartened by the people's obvious affection, Elizabeth was also intensely aware of her guardian's displeasure and, gesturing to the already overflowing litter, she 'desired the people to cease' in their loving homage.

And so it continued for the rest of the journey. At the Buckingham-shire home of Sir William Dormer, where Elizabeth received 'very good entertainment both in her diet and in her lodgings', she made the reacquaintance of a childhood playmate, the beautiful seventeen-year-old, Jane Dormer,[3] whom her brother had called 'my Jane'. Though Elizabeth took every opportunity throughout the festivities to gain much-needed exercise in her hosts' gardens, the presence of Sir Henry Bedingfield, never far off, was a potent reminder that however much honour was tendered her, she was still a captive.

At Woodstock, Elizabeth was lodged in the Gatehouse, a shabby building of four rooms. It was a dark, dilapidated and badly ventilated dwelling near the gates, which had been hastily improvised as a royal residence with worn, dusty hangings and a paltry assortment of furnish-ings some of which was 'the Queen's stuff and her Grace's own ...'. Even Bedingfield could barely conceal his dismay at the disreputable chambers, and a hasty tour of the small house did not allay his dis-comfort. He wrote to the Queen that 'there were but three doors only that were able to be locked and barred, to the great disquiet and trouble of mind of the persons committed to attend upon her Grace ...'.[4] Elizabeth seemed not to notice her surroundings. During the final portion of the journey, a broken mechanism on her litter had caused a constant and painful jolting, and in Bedingfield's words, the Princess 'seemed right weary in my judgment'.

For the next seven months, Elizabeth Tudor remained in the Gate-house at Woodstock in a sombre imprisonment that surpassed even her strict detention in the Tower. Sixty soldiers guarded the dwelling by day to be relieved by forty others at night. Only three women and two men-servants waited on the Princess. Immediately upon arrival at Woodstock, Thomas Parry, her cofferer, was dismissed 'as a suspicious person'. Belligerently, he went to the nearby village and lodged at the Bull Inn. Bedingfield was indignant at Parry's defiance, but since Elizabeth's revenues were expected to provide for all those lodged at Woodstock Gatehouse, the Council permitted the cofferer to remain nearby.

Within several days a series of small crises—a leaking roof, a fire in one of the rooms, suspicious visitors bringing equally suspicious gifts of 'fresh-water fish and two dead pheasant cocks'—presented themselves daily, causing Sir Henry to despair. Dutiful by temperament and upbringing, Bedingfield made up in conscientiousness what he lacked in imagination and initiative. He wished only to abide strictly by the orders entrusted him, but he was fearful of Elizabeth, of the Council, of the Queen, and of the entire burden thrust upon him so suddenly. Indecisive and dreading failure, he had little heart for his task, being by nature a kindly and unassuming old gentleman. It was completely outside his experience—or desire—to be entirely responsible for one of royal blood, but his obligation to the Queen, his own inborn sense of duty, caused him to 'trust only in God to make me able to do and accomplish the same'. As he wrote to the Council, 'I travail and shall do the best of my power until God and Her Highness shall dispose of me ...'. His scrupulousness soon exhausted and irritated those under his command at Woodstock. Elizabeth, with her superb ability to assess character, early discerned Sir Henry's insecurity, and for the next seven months he met the same devious harassment and steely determination that had plagued Sir Robert Tyrwhitt on a similar commission many years ago. It was to prove a mutually enlightening experience for captive and guardian, two extremely diverse personalities which—to both their credits—ended in a mutual respect bordering almost on admiration.*

But Sir Henry's immediate problem was the daily care and protection of the Princess Elizabeth, and two days after the arrival at Woodstock, he wrote to the Queen that he was 'marvellously perplexed' as to how rigid the Princess's confinement should be. 'Wherefore,' he begged, 'I most lowly and heartily do desire your Majesty or your Council how to demean myself in this your Highness's service, whereby I shall be the more able to do the same and also receive comfort and heart's ease. . . .' By fast courier, Mary's reply detailed Sir Henry's obligation. Noting her sister was confined on charges of which 'she be not at present thoroughly cleared', the Queen however wished Elizabeth to be 'honourably used . . . until such time as certain matters touching her case . . . may be thoroughly tried and examined'. She was explicit as to how this should be accomplished. 'Item: The said Sir Henry Bedingfield shall cause my said Sister to be safely watched for the safeguard of her person. . . . Item: He shall, at convenient times, suffer our said sister, for her recreation, to walk abroad and take the air in the garden . . . *as he himself shall be present in her company.* Item: He shall cause good heed to be given to our said Sister's behaviour, seeing that she be suffered neither to have conference with any suspected person out of his hearing, nor that she does, by any means, either receive or send any messages, letters or tokens to or from any manner of person. Item: He shall generally have good regard, not only to the Princess, according to the trust reposed in him, but shall also do his best to cause the country thereabouts to continue in good and quiet order. . . .'

Each line from the Queen was subjected to Bedingfield's deepest scrutiny and adjudged in the light of his ability to comply. Then he wrote to the Queen 'regarding conference with suspected persons. . . . I

* Years later Queen Elizabeth conferred various evidences of her esteem upon Sir Henry Bedingfield, and is said to have told him that should the necessity ever arise that she must confine any political prisoner, *he* would be her choice of gaoler.

dare not take it upon me that to do'. Elizabeth might receive messages from any of the 'three women in her private chamber, or her two grooms . . .'; he could hardly be in her presence at *all* times. But, said Sir Henry, 'according to my poor wit and endeavour . . . I trust only in God to make me able to do and accomplish the same . . .'. As for the other restrictions, 'that she not receive or send any messages', in this instance Bedingfield felt on surer ground. Paper, pen, and ink were prohibited; books were suspect. When Elizabeth asked for Cicero's *De Officiis* and a book of David's *Psalms*, it entailed the exchange of many communications between Queen, Council, and guardian to be certain the books contained no messages or cipher, that they did not 'serve to cloak matters of greater importance'.

Elizabeth had told Bedingfield that before departing for Woodstock, the Marquess of Winchester had told her she would have liberty to walk in Woodstock Park. Again the matter had to be debated earnestly and long by everyone. Even such a routine matter as 'putting up the cloth of state' for the Princess was prohibited until the Queen's pleasure was known. When one of the captive's ladies-in-waiting, Elizabeth Sands, was dismissed and replaced by another not to the Princess's liking, Elizabeth was annoyed. She 'refused to have any of these placed there', wrote Bedingfield to the Council, only to be admonished in return 'to persuade the Lady Elizabeth to be contented with this, Her Majesty's pleasure and determination'. The dismissed Mistress Sands did not go meekly, and Elizabeth was not contented. As Sir Henry noted, 'the same was done this day about two o'clock in the afternoon, not without great mourning by both my Lady's Grace and Sands'. That the guardian was glad to be rid of Sands's presence is apparent in his comment, 'I think her a woman who should be watched because of her obstinate disposition'.[5]

By the middle of June, Elizabeth's fear of assassination had subsided, but the enforced solitude of Woodstock contributed to a general melancholy which told on her health, and Bedingfield noted 'a swelling in her visage at certain times'. Edgy and curt, she badgered her guardian with small requests, each of which was quickly relayed to the Council. Elizabeth often appeared amused at Bedingfield's meticulous observance of his duty. One day, while walking in the garden, she turned and asked Bedingfield—who kept the proper few paces behind her—whether he had an English Bible? Possibly the sheer implausibility of the loyally Catholic Bedingfield possessing a volume which now savoured of heresy, provided the Princess with a small satisfaction. Shocked, Sir Henry quickly denied any possession of an English Bible and devoutly hoped the matter might be dropped there. But Elizabeth persisted.

Three days later, she again accosted him and asked sullenly, 'why I had not provided her the book of the Bible in English . . .?' But on this occasion Bedingfield was ready for her. Levelly he replied that while he did not have the English Bible, he did have the two books in Latin which she had formerly requested and, 'if it pleased her to have them . . . she should have *more* delight, seeing she understood the same [the Latin language] so well . . .' and would therefore have no need of the English Bible. 'An answer,' he noted, 'I perceived she took not in good part.'

For half an hour they walked in the garden in silence until 'suddenly, in the most unpleasant fashion that ever I saw her since coming from the Tower', Elizabeth spoke again. This time she was blunt. 'I think,' she said angrily, 'you make none of my Lords privy to my suit. . . .' When Bedingfield indignantly replied he had written to the Lord Chamberlain of her predicament, Elizabeth laughed scornfully, saying, 'although I know him to be a good gentleman, yet by his age. . . . I know he has occasion to forget many things'. Elizabeth then insisted that Bedingfield write requesting a Bible, and further ask the Council's permission to write to the Queen. Bedingfield was not to be backed into a corner and merely answered, 'I shall do for Your Grace what I am able to do'. He would inform the lords, he said, but 'then it must needs rest in their honourable consideration whether I shall have answer or no'. Realising Bedingfield would not be bullied, Elizabeth turned abruptly and left. 'Since which time Her Grace has never spoken to me,' he wrote to the Council ruefully.

Problems at Woodstock continued to mount. Money was in low supply, and Thomas Parry exhibited 'great doubts' as to the strain on her funds, even as he complained of the fare provided for his mistress. Parry had been joined by several others at the Bull Inn; many were known friends of those who had been executed after the Wyatt rebellion. 'I pray God it has been all for the good,' Bedingfield wrote gloomily. It was his constant fear that somehow communication between them and the Princess would be established via Parry, 'who is wondrously fit to do these enterprises if he be disposed thereto'.* Bedingfield summoned his brothers Humphrey, Edmund, and Anthony to Woodstock to assist him in observing the suspected treasonous activities at the Bull Inn, and— more probably—to bolster his own sagging confidence.

Surprisingly, the Council allowed Elizabeth to have an English Bible. She showed her disappointment when Bedingfield informed her that permission to write to the Queen had been refused and the Council advised 'that she be satisfied with some general good words' instead. The strain of waiting for such permission only further aggravated Elizabeth's

* That Parry was successful in this and other instances is fairly well proved by Elizabeth's remark later when, as Queen, she said that during her confinement in the Tower and at Woodstock, she learned all the means by which prisoners might communicate with one another and how intelligence from the outside might be received.

poor health, but pride prevented her asking for further indulgence. By the middle of June her symptoms were more pronounced, and she asked that the Queen's physicians be sent to 'devise remedy for the swelling in her face and other parts of her body, which I do see Her Grace often vexed withal', her guardian noted. The Council recommended, instead, that Elizabeth be attended by two 'honest learned men . . . at Oxford', some eight miles away. Indignantly, the young woman refused, saying, 'I am not minded to make any strangers privy to the state of my body. . . . [instead] I commit it to God!' Her condition deteriorated, and Bedingfield became distracted. At last permission to write to her sister arrived. Elizabeth spent many hours composing her letter which accompanied one of her ladies who left, at Mary's request, to attend the Queen at her wedding.

Twelve days later, from Farnham Castle, came the Queen's reply. Though its contents were obviously meant for Elizabeth, it was addressed to Sir Henry, and the Princess did not overlook the implied slight. Addressing Sir Henry as her 'trusty and well-beloved', the Queen referred to Elizabeth's letter 'which contains only certain arguments . . . in which arguments she would seem to persuade us that the testimony of those which have opened matters against her were not such as they are, or, being such, should have no credit'. Mary then detailed the charges against Elizabeth. Against this 'unnatural conspiracy', she said, 'we have for our part . . . used more clemency and favour towards her than it has been customary in like matters, yet these fair words cannot abuse us, but we do well understand how things have been wrought'.

Mary's letter emphasised her distrust of her sister. 'By the arguments and circumstances of her said letter, and with the other articles declared . . . to our Privy Council, it may well appear that her meaning and purpose is far other than her letters purport. Wherefore, our pleasure is that we shall not be hereafter molested any more with her disguised and colourable letters, but wish for her that it may please our Lord to grant her His grace that she may be towards Him as she ought to be, then shall she be the sooner towards us as it becomes her to be.' Mary's anger with Elizabeth had not softened her attitude, and, heartsick, Bedingfield put the letter away, unable to bring himself to reveal its contents to his languishing prisoner.

A week later, still refusing to accept any but the Queen's own physicians and, in addition to her physical discomfort, subject to bouts of depression, Elizabeth remained ill and apprehensive in her chamber, still hopeful of Mary's forgiveness. When Bedingfield arrived in the sick woman's room for Mass, he wondered how best to let the Princess know the Queen's response. His anxious expression may have made Elizabeth suspicious, for, after the service, she asked him urgently 'if there were any answer to her late letter to the Queen'. Bedingfield nodded and said he would give the answer at her convenience. 'Let it be even now,' said the sick woman eagerly. Bedingfield did not have the letter with him and requested Elizabeth 'to give me leave to fetch it.' He was astounded, therefore, upon hurriedly returning to the Princess's chamber with the letter in hand, to be informed by a lady-in-waiting that, as it was time for the noonday meal, 'to stay until her Grace had dined . . .'. The incident is revealing. Knowing her answer was at hand, Elizabeth wished to diminish its importance as she lingered over a luncheon which, under the circumstances, she could scarcely have enjoyed.

Bedingfield then approached the Princess and, kneeling in front of her, read the Queen's message. Elizabeth changed colour as she listened and 'uttered certain words bewailing her own chance in that her letter had taken no better effect'. She then asked that Sir Henry read it again. At its conclusion, she replied bitterly, 'I note especially to my great discomfort . . . that the Queen's Majesty is not pleased that I should molest her Highness with any more of my colourable letters, yet though they be termed "colourable" . . . I must say for myself that it was the plain truth, even as I desired to be saved before God Almighty . . .! So let it pass!' Her anger increased as—with just the proper tone of bitter reproach—she requested Bedingfield, 'if you think you may do so much for me', to write to the Council of her predicament 'so to pass it to my Lords for my better comfort in this my adversity'. Hastily, Bedingfield asked to be excused from what he considered an improper request. Loudly, Elizabeth asked 'Is it not likely that I shall be offered more than any prisoner in the Tower?' There, she said, any prisoner might complain to the Lieutenant, and he, in turn, must advise the Council. 'And you refuse to do the like!' she berated the old gentleman. Bedingfield pointed out the difference—it was the office of the lieutenant to hear the prisoners' complaints. It was not any office of *his* to be *commanded* to write to the Council on her behalf. Counselling patience, he rose from his knees and departed.

The following morning, as he puffed along behind her in the garden, Elizabeth, a bit more subdued, taxed Bedingfield with his attitude, saying that unless he contacted the Council of her plight, 'I shall be in worse case than the worst prisoners in Newgate!' Even in that vile prison, she said, friends of the prisoner could fight to 'have their cause opened and sued for'. If someone did not champion her, she cautioned, 'I must needs continue this life without all worldly hope, wholly resting in the truth of my cause . . . arming myself against whatsoever shall happen, to remain the Queen's true subject, as I have done during my life'. A fine rain had begun to fall, spoiling the walk. As Bedingfield sought a proper reply, Elizabeth said, 'It waxeth wet and therefore I will depart to my lodging again. . . .' as she left the unhappy guardian to his thoughts.

The concern which the Princess's illness had caused in Bedingfield was now compounded by a more intimate and sympathetic understanding of her perilous position. It is a true measure of his solicitude that on the same afternoon, the naturally timid man dispatched a letter to the Council noting that Elizabeth 'had willed and required me to conceive a suit of hers unto the Queen's Highness, which I have done . . .'. Enclosed with Sir Henry's letter was 'My Lady's Elizabeth's Suit', in which Bedingfield noted that since the Princess had received 'no such comfort as she had hoped' from the Queen, that the lords would 'considering her long imprisonment and restraint . . . either charge her with special matters to be answered . . . or grant her liberty . . .'. It was clear that Elizabeth had impressed her guardian that her one remaining hope lay with the Council, and, in her words, there was a challenge which they could hardly overlook. If she could not be proved guilty, there was no justifiable reason for her to be kept prisoner.

Through her guardian, Elizabeth begged the lords to see the Queen, 'whereby she may take relief not to think herself utterly desolate of all refuge in this world'. And at the end, Bedingfield wrote:

Requiring me further to move chiefly as many of you, my Lords as were [of the] Council party and privy to the execution of the Will of the King's Majesty, her father, to further this her Grace's suit above said.[6]

The appeal to those older members who had been part of her father's Council and whom she knew to be her friends, was a subtly clever allusion by Elizabeth. It would not hurt to remind them that, in default of any issue by Mary, they might very likely one day have to deal with *her*.

Bedingfield, however, was not so optimistic, and he ended his letter: 'If it shall be determined by the Queen's Highness, and you, my Lords, that this great Lady shall remain in this house, then of necessity there must be reparation done both to the covering of the house in lead and slate, and especially in glass and casements, or else neither she, nor any that attend upon her, shall be able to abide for cold. . . .'[7]

There was no immediate answer from the Council. The entire court was at Winchester, where, five days previously, the wedding of Philip and Mary had finally taken place.

Prince Philip sailed for England on July 11, 1554, aboard the galleon *The Holy Ghost*. As old John Russell, the Duke of Bedford, wrote from

[413]

Corunna where he had been sent to escort the Prince to England, Philip was accompanied by 'one hundred tall ships well furnished with men and ordnance'. Despite the warning of Simon Renard that the Spanish heir travel as simply as possible, between 6,000 and 8,000 Spanish nobles, their retainers, musicians, servants, and livestock had crowded aboard the ships which also carried bullion worth 400,000 ducats for the relief of the empty English treasury. The belief that Spanish influence would predominate in England is indicated in the desire of many of the travellers to sell their estates and bring their families with them. The Emperor left little doubt of his opinion of such foolhardiness, and he admonished his son, 'They tell me that some married women are going with their husbands in your company. I think they will be more difficult to govern and keep friends with the English women, than even soldiers would be! You had better see whether it would not be wiser to send them here [the Netherlands] until affairs in England are more settled.'[8]

Philip similarly warned his nobles—particularly his good friends, Ruy Gomez de Silva and Gomez Suarez de Figueroa, the Count de Feria—about severing their ties with their homeland. He would do his best to win the goodwill of the English people, he said, 'but I do not order you either to sell or not sell your property. For know ye, I am not going to a marriage feast, but to a fight.'[9] For one who had been advised always to wear a coat of mail under his clothing and bring his own cook for fear of poisoning, the Prince's foreboding is understandable.

For Philip himself, his marriage to Mary Tudor was one more sacrifice he must make for Spain, his father the Emperor, and the Catholic Church. The twenty-seven-year-old heir to all the vast Hapsburg dominions in Germany, Italy, the Low Countries, and the Spanish claims in the New World, had agreed to his proxy marriage with a stolid acquiescence accompanied by a notable lack of enthusiasm. He had '. . . unreservedly placed himself in the Emperor's hands to do with . . . as he thought best in the interest of their great cause'.[10] The great cause was nothing less than the restoration of the Catholic faith in a country still under Papal interdict. Such a union would also block, with formidable might, any accession to the English throne by Mary Stuart, now betrothed to the Dauphin. Philip wrote to his father, 'you know already that as an entirely obedient son, I have no other will than yours and, above all, on an affair of this importance, I leave it to your Majesty to act as you deem best'.[11]

Such willingness to act the dutiful son had led to Philip's first marriage to Princess Maria of Portugal. She died eleven months later giving birth to a son. Now a widower for several years, the Prince had enjoyed a liaison with the beautiful Dona Isabella de Osoria which had produced not only a conspicuous happiness for both but several illegitimate children as well. Though negotiations had been under way for another Portuguese marriage, the accession of Mary Tudor had signalled an abrupt shift in Spain's marital policy. Union with the English Queen would bring far greater advantages to the Emperor, even if the English treasury must be bailed out with Spanish gold.

During the months Mary had outmanœuvred Northumberland, and later, as she risked the challenges of the Wyatt rebellion, the Spanish monarch and his son had done nothing to assist her materially, but the counsel of their emissary, Renard, more often than not determined her direction. Once the marriage treaty was signed, Charles saw a vindication of his aunt Catherine, Mary's mother. More practically there was the pleasing redistribution of the balance of power against France —both England and Spain's natural enemy—and a means of redressing the enormous affront of the Queen's father, Henry VIII. In announcing himself the Supreme Head of the Church, Henry had recklessly imperilled the souls of thousands of Englishmen—consigning them to an eternal purgatory as they were denied the solaces of the Catholic faith. Charles had given his blessing as Philip departed for 'our new realm of England for the exaltation of our holy faith and the good of Christendom', secure in the awareness that he could send no other whose aims were so entirely in accord with his own, whose loyalty was so unquestioned and whose ambition so dedicated.

In appearance, temperament, and purpose, Philip was, indeed, his father's son. Wary and conservative, he could wait long for his goal to be achieved, his conduct being dictated by the exigencies of the moment. Although he dressed as a Prince when occasion demanded, by nature and intent, he abhorred extravagance; the Emperor, too was well known for his simplicity. Philip was as moderate in his eating and drinking habits as he was in the pursuits of any pleasure. He loathed military exercises and the demands of warfare, and he avoided the questionable pleasure of hunting or the more rigorous sports—two things not likely to endear him to the English. His natural inclination was towards solitary activities unusual in one of his youth and reminiscent of his father's proclivity for tinkering with clocks and other mechanical devices. Appreciative of the arts, particularly painting and sculpture, he was also an excellent student of history and languages; his proficiency in mathematics was admirable.

Philip's cautious reserve was often interpreted as disdain or aloofness —a misconception which had resulted in unfortunate repercussions on an earlier sojourn in the Netherlands. Aware that his son's grave manner often created rancour—if not outright dislike—the Emperor had warned Philip to take more personal interest in the English people and his surroundings and to actively participate in court activities. He must assume affability, advised Charles, eat unstintingly of English food with little comment, and—a penance for one with a sensitive appreciation for good wine—even drink the English ale. He must be sociable and deferential in a country where so much hatred and suspicion of the foreigner existed; where outright rebellion had occurred because of his betrothal to the Queen. Neither the Emperor nor the Prince judged the task would be easy.

Once the marriage terms were settled, Philip had been dutiful. He had sent Mary 'a table diamond set as a rose, beautifully wrought and worth 50,000 ducats; a necklace of brilliant diamonds consisting of eighteen stones worth 30,000 ducats, a great diamond with a large pendant pearl, one of the most beautiful pieces ever seen in the world,* worth 25,000 ducats, besides many jewels, necklaces, pearls, diamonds, emeralds and rubies in inestimable value . . .'.[12]

On Thursday, July 19, Lord William Howard with an escort of Flemish vessels led the Spanish fleet into Southampton Water. During the previous weeks, while patrolling the Channel to keep the French from harassing the oncoming Spanish, Howard had not endeared himself to the visitors. He had 'spoken with great scorn of the Spanish ships, and irreverently compared them to mussel-shells!'[13] Renard also wrote to the Emperor that he had mocked and insulted the Flemish admiral, Chapelle. The English sailors had provoked many brawls in Flemish taverns while 'hustling and pushing' and making disparaging remarks about Philip. Howard had further distressed the punctilious Spanish commander of The Holy Ghost by firing a salvo of cannon across the ship's bow, ordering the visitors to lower their flag once they were in English waters.

The combined Spanish and English fleet, some 160 ships, their scarlet silk streamers, banners, and heraldic pennons taut in the breeze, lay overnight in Southampton harbour. An attack of mal de mer kept Philip in his cabin until the next day when, early in the morning, a magnificent gilded state barge sliced through the waters from the shore. Lords Arundel, Derby, Shrewsbury, and many of the Council and court, all clad in their most exquisite finery, crowded into the barge whose attendants were all newly attired in the Tudor colours of green and white. Philip, smiling and apparently recovered, stood cap in hand on the deck and, with great courtesy, introduced his Spanish companions. With the Duke of Alva, Ruy Gomez, and the Count de Feria, he entered the barge; no other courtier, however, was allowed to leave until the Prince's foot touched English soil. Others, especially the soldiers and sailors, were prohibited from landing at all—a restriction which

---

* This is the famous La Peregrina, a pear-shaped pearl of great size purchased several years ago by actor Richard Burton for his wife, Elizabeth Taylor. It may be seen worn by Mary in the Antonio Moro portrait from the Prado in the photograph section.

led to disgruntled murmuring among those lesser grandees whose attitude at embarkation had held more than a touch of the conqueror.

As the guns on the mole of Southampton fired forth a mighty salute, Philip greeted the deputation of English nobles on the shore. The Earl of Arundel had come directly from the Queen to invest Philip with the Order of the Garter, after which, Sir Anthony Browne, identifying himself as the Queen's Master of the Horse, presented another of Mary's gifts—a magnificent Andalusian jennet, its saddle-cloth of crimson velvet embroidered with gold and pearls. As Philip cordially greeted the nobles, one John Elder, the tutor of a small boy who would later become the ill-fated Lord Darnley, the husband of Mary, Queen of Scots, saw him thus:

Of visage, he is well-favoured, with a broad forehead. . . . straight-nosed and manly countenance. From the forehead to the point of his chin, his face groweth small. His pace is princely; and gait so straight and upright as he loseth no inch of his height; with a yellow head and a yellow beard; and thus to conclude, he is so well-proportioned of body, arm, leg and every other limb to the same, as nature cannot work a more perfect pattern. . . .[14]

After a visit to the Church of the Holy Rood, where he gave thanks for a safe voyage, Philip saw the sensibilities of his Spanish companions again affronted when they were requested to leave the Church first, so that he might emerge accompanied only by Englishmen. The Prince was then taken to a palatial private home which had been sequestered by the Queen. No expense had been spared to make it fit for royalty, and Philip's chambers had been prepared with great care. A canopied chair of State was placed in the middle of the room in which all the trappings of royalty were obvious, even to the white, crimson, and gold tapestry which had belonged to the Queen's father. It had been hurriedly dispatched from another royal dwelling—and, in such haste, that no one had remembered the motto *Defender of the Faith and Head of the Church* embroidered, with suitable religious ornament, on the border. Philip diplomatically chose to overlook the murmuring of his shocked attendants as they viewed the sacrilegious phrase. Instead, he thanked the English courtiers who, in spite of themselves, seemed pleasantly impressed with their new sovereign, an impression Philip took care to nurture. At supper, he joined in their conversation, graciously accepting their attentions while his own Spanish nobles stood on the sidelines seething with jealous impatience. In reply to a toast from one of the Council, Philip pledged himself 'to be to them a right good and loving Prince', and, to seal the promise, he called for a tankard of English ale, 'the wine of the country', which he drank with every sign of appreciation.

After a day of rest in which the remainder of his shipbound courtiers were allowed to join him, the English and Spanish entourages prepared to merge for the journey to Winchester, where the Queen waited. Philip dined in public, to the delight of the people of Southampton, even as it further enraged his own gentlemen-in-waiting, for no one except the Duke of Alva was allowed to participate in serving the Prince. Only the English assisted at the table, leading one Spaniard to sneer '... we are of no more use here and are simply vagabonds ... we should be better employed in serving in the war ...'. And then, having had some experience during the previous day at the hands of the Southampton citizens, he ended plaintively, 'they make us pay twenty times what a thing is worth!'

By two o'clock on Monday, July 23, as Philip was en route to Winchester where Mary waited, he experienced a discomforting example of the English climate. The journey had commenced in a misty rain which, some two miles from Southampton, gathered the force of a violent tempest, almost blinding the travellers whose cloaks, plumed hats, and other belongings were soon sodden. As they rode slowly, bucking the heavy sheets of rain, a lone rider approached, shouting his message and gesturing with his hand. Philip, who did not understand the language, mistakenly assumed the messenger was warning of danger ahead. As the Spaniards drew together for a consultation, an English noble, seeing their apprehension, spoke to them in French. 'Sire, our Queen lovingly greets your Highness,' he said, presenting a small ring as a token to Philip, 'and has merely sent to say that she hopes you will not commence your journey to Winchester in such dreadful weather.' But Philip, wishing the ordeal over, gestured they would proceed onward.

At St Cross Hospital, near England's ancient capital of Winchester, he changed his soaked clothing and, at six in the evening 'on a fair white horse, in a rich coat embroidered with gold', rode past the assembled mayor and aldermen and the gaping crowds who had braved the rain, going directly to the west door of the cathedral. There he was received by Mary's Lord Chancellor, Stephen Gardiner, the Bishop of Winchester. Five other bishops accompanied the Prince through the nave to the altar, where, with sober reverence, he knelt. Perhaps as he dutifully gave thanks and prayed for guidance that he might be an instrument to heal a country afflicted with the sore of heresy, he also gave some thought to the woman who waited a few hundred yards away, the one who would be the means by which Spain would work to restore the old faith and who, if Providence so willed, might provide yet another half-Spanish heir to occupy the throne of the English nation.

*

While Philip was lodged in the deanery adjacent to the Cathedral close, Mary occupied the bishop's Palace nearby. There she had waited in anxious anticipation the moment when she and Philip would at last meet. Messengers had come to her throughout the day, telling of the Prince's progress in the disastrous weather. The thought that he had not delayed during the downpour suggested an eagerness matching her own. As the hours passed, the Queen's excitement mounted and, finally, would not be contained. As he made ready to retire, Philip was informed the Queen would receive him and a few of his closest companions, if he would wait upon her at that moment. If the bridegroom entertained the thought that a meeting at ten o'clock at night after a day of uncomfortable travel was less than considerate, he gave no sign. Dutifully he dressed himself with care and, accompanied by a few of his nobles and several of the English Council, crossed the cathedral green in a darkness lit only by the torches of the guides. Through the garden, over a path muddied by the rain and the water which still dripped from the trees, he entered the Palace, climbing a small stairway leading directly to the Queen's apartments. And there, reflecting how much wiser it would have been for Mary to have delayed until the public reception the following day, he paused until informed what might next be expected of him.

Inside, Mary waited with Gardiner and several of her ministers. She had dressed with extreme care, her small figure handsomely clad in a black velvet gown from which a petticoat of frosted silver peeped. A black velvet headdress trimmed with gold and flashing with jewels covered her dark auburn hair. Mary had indulged her love of jewellery and wore Philip's stones around her neck and on her fingers. They blazed now in the candlelight which, mercifully, masked the lines of the plain face—now rendered almost beautiful by the glow of honest pleasure shining from her eyes and gracing her happy smile. When she saw the slim, neat form of the Prince himself framed in the doorway, the Philip of her imagination quickly became the Philip of reality. She walked impulsively towards him and, in the Spanish fashion, kissed her hand before grasping his in a warm welcome. No words were spoken, but the Prince, taking his cue, responded in the English manner and bent suddenly, kissing his bride lightly on her lips. Happily, still holding his hand, she directed him towards two chairs beneath a canopy at the far end of the room.

As everyone watched in silence, the Queen spoke excitedly in French, as Philip answered in Spanish. Mary's choice of language reveals an awareness on her part of the intensity of the moment. Suddenly the speech of her mother, as spoken now by Philip, made her fearfully shy of using it herself. She welcomed the interval as each Spanish noble came forward to be introduced, and as her own ladies-in-waiting entered

[419]

the chamber, the Prince 'in order not to violate the custom of the country, kissed each of them on the lips as they passed him'. At the conclusion, there was an awkward pause, and Philip tactfully suggested that perhaps everyone should depart and let the Queen retire. But Mary would not hear of it. Obviously delighted with the Prince and the way the meeting was proceeding, she led him back to the chairs again and, with great animation, spoke to him at length. At the moment of leave taking, Philip appeared puzzled and asked the Queen what he should say to her nobles. Slowly, Mary spoke an English phrase which Philip repeated several times. At the doorway, he bowed gracefully to those inside and said, 'Good night, my Lords all', as he departed. Behind him he left an unexpectedly gratified Chancellor, an impressed Council, and a satisfied and happy Queen, one apparently enchanted with her Prince and a woman, obviously, already very much in love.

Two days later on St James's Day, July 25, at eleven o'clock, Mary was wed to Philip in a ceremony of unrivalled splendour and magnificence. Hundreds of citizens from the surrounding countryside, as well as the English court and the remaining Spanish nobles, crowded into the vast and ancient Winchester Cathedral, which was entirely hung with arras and cloth of gold. Mary was garbed in white satin with a mantle of cloth of gold studded and fringed with diamonds. Before the ceremony, emissaries from the Emperor brought two orders by which Charles resigned his kingdoms of Naples and Milan in favour of Philip because, as Gardiner announced, '. . . it was thought the Queen's Majesty. . . . should marry with a King'. Thus Mary's bridegroom spoke his vows as one equal in rank. While gratifying to Philip, it is doubtful if Mary cared.

Deeply stirred by the significance of her marriage ceremony, the Queen did not glance away from the crucifix during the whole time she knelt at the altar. At the conclusion, there were tears in her eyes as Philip slipped the plain golden wedding band—which she had requested 'because maidens so married in old times'—on her trembling finger. After Mass, as the bride and groom prepared to leave the Cathedral, the trumpets blared, and in the great silence which followed, Garter King of Arms, surrounded by his heralds, proclaimed the newlyweds, 'Philip and Mary, by the grace of God, King and Queen of England, France, Naples, Jerusalem and Ireland, Defenders of the Faith, Princes of Spain and Sicily, Archdukes of Austria, Dukes of Milan, Burgundy and Brabant, Counts of Hapsburg, Flanders and Tyrol!' The wedding ceremony and the Mass had lasted four hours.

Amid great cheering from the spectators outside the Cathedral, the newlyweds finally emerged into the mid-afternoon sunlight to walk the short distance to the Great Hall of the bishop's Palace for the nuptial feast. Once more the subtle demands of protocol enraged the visitors. Everywhere Mary took precedence of her husband—an action which bordered on profane irreverence to the proud Spaniards. They noted that while Mary dined from gold plate, Philip was served on silver. Again the King and Queen were attended only by the English nobles, as one glowering Spaniard muttered '. . . they had far better turn us all out as vagabonds!' Slowly, the role they must play in a country, where the Prince of the world's mightiest nation must take second place to Mary Tudor, became more clear. Dutifully, however, they danced with the English women, later gossiping unflatteringly about the ladies' clumsiness and their outlandish clothing. They watched in embittered silence as the King and Queen ate from a great pasty of red deer while young boys from the Cathedral school recited poems in their honour. They kept that silence even when Lord William Howard, flushed with wine and goaded by his companions, felt bound to indulge in several jokes of questionable taste.

At last it was over and by nine o'clock, a radiant and tremulous Mary was led to join the man for whom she had risked the censure of her people and the wrath of her nobles. A bishop blessed the couple and the marriage bed, then bowed out. For the first time, Mary was alone with Philip. Deeply in love with her husband, despite their short acquaintance, and convinced of the righteousness of her marriage, there was little reserve or constraint in the Queen. On her wedding night, Mary brought to Philip an overflowing reservoir of affection and passion, the result of long years of repression and denial. To the Queen, now blinded by the force of her own desire and shaken by the magnitude of her love, it was not noticeable that Philip's response, while adept, savoured more of a passive compliance tempered by resignation and a high sense of duty.

For nearly two months, Elizabeth had waited at Woodstock for some relaxation of her imprisonment. In view of the Council's negligence in replying to her suit, she asked Bedingfield to allow 'one of her own servants to wait upon the Lords'. Seeing his hesitation, she said, 'It is not against the order. . . . appointed unto you'. But Sir Henry remained unconvinced, attempting to soothe Elizabeth's impatience by saying, 'I trust it shall not be long before my Lords of the Council will remember your suit and answer the same'. Privately, the guardian was not so sure. The Council had been lax in commanding repairs for the Gatehouse, and money was still scarce despite their previous promise that 'order shall be taken . . . for your satisfaction in that behalf . . .'.

By the middle of September, the fearful Bedingfield—forgotten by the Queen and Council, busy with wedding festivities and honeymoon progresses—could only view the winter's approach with dismay. Two Bedingfield brothers had gone to London to remind the Council in person that financially and physically, the detention of the Princess Elizabeth at Woodstock was assuming hazardous proportions. As the long summer days wore on, the Princess's patience and endurance neared an end, and she was not above taunting her gaoler, 'laying to my charge that because I will not assent that her Grace may write *herself* to you, my Lords . . . that was the only cause why she had no manner of answer to her suit'. It is abundantly clear that the unhappy Bedingfield agreed with his captive, for he wrote, somewhat naïvely, to the distant ministers, 'Her Grace says she is sure your Lordships will *smile in your sleeves* when you know this, my scrupulousness'.[15]

By mid-September Elizabeth was once more granted permission to write to the lords of the Council. She must give the letter to Sir Henry and he, in turn, must enclose it in one of his own for delivery by one of Elizabeth's servants. Happy to be in a position to give some joyous news to his prisoner, the elated Bedingfield hurried to inform her of the Queen's decision. That the Princess still had reserves which had long since departed from her custodian is evident when she 'did neither command me to prepare things for her to write with, nor named who should be her messenger'. Puzzled, Bedingfield says, 'So I departed. Her Grace never spoke of that matter more *till the Sunday* following in the time of her walk in that afternoon'.

The delay of nearly a week again reveals Elizabeth's perverse obstinacy. Now that the long-desired permission to communicate directly with the Council had arrived, they might await *her* pleasure. When the pens, ink, and paper were delivered, Elizabeth was requested not to use them except in the sight of her ladies-in-waiting. The Princess chose Francis Verney, one of Thomas Parry's companions at the Bull Inn, to carry her message, which caused Bedingfield to write disconsolately, 'where I perceive they use as much privy conference to where they do lie, and they so politic as they are, I can get no knowledge of their doings by an espial . . .'. After beginning the letter, said Bedingfield, Elizabeth stopped suddenly, saying 'she had such a pain in her head that she could write no more that day'. Still the maddening delay continued, for, says her guardian, on the next day 'she washed her head'. Later in the afternoon she summoned Bedingfield to her and, as he entered, noted that she had never written to the Council except with the aid of a secretary. 'And,' she said, 'as I am not suffered at this time to have one, therefore you must needs do it!' Bedingfield longed for escape. To obtain the Council's permission was one thing; to actually write Elizabeth's many complaints was another and he 'prayed her

Grace to pardon me for that I was not able.' But with that 'spirit of incantation' with which Renard had charged her, Elizabeth argued and bullied. Some measure of her success may be seen as her guardian hesitantly complied and 'at her Grace's *importunate command and desire*, 1 wrote as she read unto me . . .'. Once the letter was finished, Elizabeth added a postscript, 'but what, God knows!' Bedingfield noted. The letter sealed, the Princess—'being very cold in manner'—directed Sir Henry to deliver it to Francis Verney at the Bull Inn, and so to the Council. Her intent had been gained and she departed, satisfied. Not so Bedingfield. With the letter went a communication from Sir Henry tacitly admitting his defeat at the hands of his prisoner. 'God knows how it grieves me that I am thus unable to serve the Queen's Majesty and you, my Lords, by reason of this, my evil writing, trusting her Highness will pardon my rudeness and you, my Lords, also!'[16]

With Elizabeth's letter, Sir Henry again implored the Council to authorise repairs at Woodstock against the winter cold. A new crisis had arisen concerning the soldiers 'who have been unpaid for a whole month, and they owe to the poor folk of Woodstock for their board and victualling . . .'. In addition to their lack of pay, the garrison also viewed a winter at Woodstock as a calamity, and Bedingfield wrote to the Council, 'I trust your Lordships do consider that the nights that shall be. . . . are long and cold, and many of them wet; whereby the poor soldiers shall not be able to continue their watch about this house standing upon the hill; without they may be suffered to keep the same within the gate . . .'. Despite Sir Henry's pleas, the funds were still lacking nine weeks later, and, frantic, he dispatched his brother Anthony to London to receive the soldiers' wages, writing that unless the monies were forthcoming, 'I shall be in danger of a late bond . . . of four hundred pounds. . . . at London within ten days next . . . which I have enterprised to be avoided of the daily exclaiming of the poor victuallers in Woodstock . . .'. Having personally gone into debt to pay for the soldiers' keep, taunted by his prisoner that he was 'wanting in knowledge, experience and unskilled in other matters requisite for such service' (in which he was only too willing to concur), the mournful Bedingfield could not refrain from ending one communication, saying that 'to receive the discharge of this, my service, without offence to the Queen's Majesty, or you, my good Lords, would be the joyfullest tidings that ever came to me, as our Lord Almighty knows, to whom all secrets be hidden!'

Elizabeth's letter to the Council bore no fruit. The Queen herself wrote to Sir Henry stating that she marvelled that Elizabeth should 'have so ill an opinion of our Council that they might keep letters from the Queen'. The trouble lay with Elizabeth herself, said Mary, and she might well have been restored to favour 'if her former answers might so well have satisfied indifferent ears as it seems to satisfy her own opinion'. Sir Henry was to placate Elizabeth, saying the Queen was 'not unmindful of her cause, and, as good occasion shall proceed from herself [Elizabeth] in deeds, so will we have further reconsideration of her as may stand with her honour and the good order of our realm'.

And so the duel between the royal sisters continued throughout the summer and early months of the autumn. The unvarying routine of life at Woodstock told on Elizabeth's disposition as much as it depleted her energies and led Sir Henry to remark 'she was very evil at ease'. A great restlessness plagued the young woman, surrounded as she was by others who were relatively free to come and go. She grew to loathe the small mean rooms of her living quarters, the wearisome sameness of the view, the familiar faces of the soldiers at their posts, and always the ever-present Sir Henry Bedingfield. When Elizabeth—perhaps not expecting anything but the diversion of an argument—asked for materials to write to the Council again, her guardian refused, saying she had been granted permission to write once but not 'as often as it pleased her'. Elizabeth's resentment exploded, and she 'took in so ill part', wrote Bedingfield, 'that her Grace, of displeasure wherein, did utter me more words of reproach of this . . . than ever I hard her speak before . . . too long to write!' Near tears, she hurled the epithet 'Gaoler!' at him, causing the harried old gentleman to go down on his knees before the girl and beg her 'not to give him that harsh name, for he was one of her officers appointed to serve her and guard her from the dangers by which she was beset'. To which Elizabeth caustically replied, 'God bless the Queen and from such officers, good Lord, deliver me!'

Elizabeth's general despair alternated with rage at her sister, at the Council, and at her guardian, and resulted in fits of moodiness and sullen reproachfulness. Normally good-humoured, she could reflect bitterly as she watched a young girl bringing milk to the Gatehouse, exclaiming, 'A milkmaid's lot is better than mine—and her life merrier!' To lessen the monotony of each day, she and Ashley often sat together at their needlework as Elizabeth embroidered a cover for a small book, the *Epistles of St Paul*, attempting to make the work last as long as possible. Once the delicate task was complete, she must await further supplies from London, a procedure becoming increasingly difficult as the autumn storms began. After reading the *Epistles* she secured pen and ink to write on the flyleaf of the book as Sir Henry watched.

August: I walked many times into the pleasant fields of the Holy Scripture, where I plucked up the goodlisome herbs of sentences by pruning, eat them by reading, chew them by musing, and lay them up at length in the high seat of memory by gathering them together; that so, having tasted their sweetness, I may the less perceive the bitterness of this miserable life.[17]*

By a unanimous vote of Parliament in November it was enacted 'that all such Divine Service and administration of Sacraments as were most commonly used in the realm of England in the last year of the reign of our late Sovereign Lord King Henry the Eighth shall be, from and after the twentieth day of December. . . . used and frequented through the whole realm of England, all other of the Queen's Majesty's dominions, and that no other kind nor order of Divine Service nor administration of Sacraments be. . . . used or ministered in any other manner form or degree . . .'.[18] The reinstatement of the outward semblances of the Catholic faith was the first step in Mary's cherished dream of restoring England to the Papal fold. Previously Elizabeth had been careful to comply with the Queen's request to 'move my Lady Elizabeth no more to use the suffrages and Litany in English, but in Latin, after the ancient and laudable customs of the Church'. Dutifully she attended Mass and, said Sir Henry Bedingfield, 'after her confession, as her chaplain declared to me, in Catholic form, did receive the most comfortable Sacrament'. Elizabeth's outward submission impressed even the Queen. She asked that the Princess be questioned as to her belief in Transubstantiation, to which the girl enigmatically replied in verse:

'Christ was the word that spake it;
He took the bread and brake it;
And what his Word did make it,
That I believe and take it.'[19]

Before a grim winter closed in on the reluctant participants in the royal drama at Woodstock, the assaults of tension and tedium again caused a dangerous swelling in Elizabeth's body, combined with poor appetite and colour and an unusual lackadaisical air.

Hurriedly Bedingfield requested the Queen to send physicians 'to repair hither to minister unto her physic, bringing, of their own choice, one expert surgeon to let her Grace's blood . . .'. Doctor Wendy and his companions, Dr Owen and Dr Huicke, attended Elizabeth, Bedingfield reported she was immediately bled in the arm and in the afternoon 'I saw her foot struck and bled; since which time, thanks be to God, as far as I can see or hear, she does reasonably well . . .'. Elizabeth asked the physicians to carry a plea to the Queen and Council that 'she might be

* The book is in the Bodleian Library at Oxford.

appointed nearer to London or her own house, to remain at the Queen's pleasure ...'. Sir Henry lost little time in fervently adding his own appeal. If the Council or the Queen did not wish to gratify the Princess, he said, 'it may content you to do it upon pity of the poor men which are daily sore travailed with extreme long journeys this winter weather and days in making the carriage of provision to serve here, which also if great wet once fall, as in this time of the year it is accustomed for the most part to do, then shall no carts be able to come ...'.[20]

Sir Henry's appeal did not impress the Council or the Queen. Mary was now obsessed by passion for her husband and her zeal to restore England to the Papacy. Seemingly abandoned by the Queen and her ministers, Elizabeth received no reprieve. For the Queen's sister, there was nothing to anticipate but five more months of confinement, deprivation, and shame.

Chapter Twenty-three

THE four months following her marriage were the happiest of Mary Tudor's life. In these months she acquainted Philip with the summer glories of Windsor Castle, and later in the autumn she proudly showed him the still feudal splendour of Richmond Palace, impressive in the mists rising off the river. The magnificent state entry into London had been an inspiring triumph for the Queen. Philip rode at her side as the entire court, swelled by the Spaniards, vivid in red and orange, followed behind. The King noted with approval the ornate river mansions of the nobles that lined the Strand, but, farther in the City, his distaste at the 'disfiguring ruins of the multitude of churches and monasteries belonging heretofore to friars and nuns', was apparent. The citizens, primed with wine, a natural curiosity momentarily supplanting their hatred of the foreigners, tumultuously cheered Philip, especially as they glimpsed the ninety-seven chests of Spanish bullion destined for the Tower. For the lesser members of the King's retinue, however, they had nothing but loud jeering and contemptuous gestures. Tauntingly, they pointed to the carts carrying the traveller's belongings and shouted they would not be needed 'since you won't be here that long!'

During the ensuing weeks, the Spaniards' wretchedness increased. As one disgusted visitor wrote home, 'We are miserable here, much worse than in Castile and some say they would rather be in the barest stubble fields of Toledo than here in the groves of Amadis!'[1] The Spanish contingent ultimately diminished when eighty disillusioned grandees and their retainers departed. Those who were left bore their discontent as the price they must pay to remain with Philip—and they knew he needed their support. 'Kings in this country do not command more than if they were subjects,' one of the visitors noted, 'the real rulers are the Council. . . . they are all Lords, but they are more feared and reverenced than the sovereign. . . .' Confrontation between Englishman and Spaniard on the City streets was often bloody. 'The English cannot bear the sight of the Spaniards,' lamented one of their victims, 'they would rather see the Devil. They rob us, even in the towns and on the road none of us dare to stray for a couple of miles for fear of being robbed. . . . The King commands us to raise no questions, but whilst we are here to put up with everything and suffer all their spite . . . so of course they treat us badly and despise us!'[2]

Certainly Philip practised what he preached. His tact and courtesy had softened many on the English Council. 'His behaviour towards them is such that they themselves confess that they never had a King in England who so won the hearts of all men!' was the extravagant praise of Ruy Gomez, Philip's best friend. And where Mary was concerned, the King could do no wrong. 'The King entertains the Queen excellently,' wrote Gomez, 'and well knows how to pass over what is not attractive in her for the sensibility of the flesh. He keeps her so pleased that verily when they were together the other day alone, she almost made love to him and he answered in the same fashion.'[3]

A description of Mary by Giocomo Sorranzo, a representative of the Venetian court, just before she was married is sympathetic:

She is of low stature, with a red and white complexion and very thin; her eyes are light and large, and her hair reddish, her face is round, with a nose rather low and wide, and were not her age on the decline, she might be called handsome, rather than contrary. She is not of a strong constitution, and is often obliged to take medicine and also to be blooded. Her Majesty's countenance indicates great benignity and clemency which are not belied by her conduct, for although she has many enemies, and though so many of them were by law condemned to death, yet, had the executions depended solely on Her Majesty's will, not one of them, perhaps, would have been enforced. . . .

Sorranzo said Mary arrayed herself 'elegantly and magnificently'; she also "makes great use of jewels, wearing them both on her girdle and round her neck, and as trimming for her gowns; in which jewels she delights greatly, and though she has a great plenty of them left her by her predecessors, yet were she better supplied with money than she is, she would doubtless buy many more'.[4]

When the Duke of Norfolk, the elderly war horse of Henry VIII, died and the court went into mourning, Mary and Philip went to Hampton Court where—in contrast to the Queen's previous custom—the doors to their chambers remained closed for days on end. When walking hand in hand in the garden, they made it obvious they preferred no companions. That Mary basked in such loving attention is clear in the letter she wrote to the Emperor saying that her marriage 'renders me happier than I can say, as I daily discover in the King . . . so many virtues and

[428]

perfections that I constantly pray God to grant me grace to please him, and behave in all things as befits one who is so deeply bounden to him'. To which Charles, pleasantly gratified at the intensity of the Queen's words, could only comment dryly that his son, indeed, must have changed considerably.

Philip was, with his usual conscientious preciseness, making the best of the bargain. Even as he closed his eyes and ears to the grumbling of his countrymen, he kept uppermost in his mind the reasons why he had come to England: to effect a reconciliation with the See of Rome and to beget an heir. Another more pressing reason existed, one never advanced openly but tacitly understood by the Emperor, Philip, and Renard, which was nothing less than the use of English armies to supplement Spain's forces in the event of French aggrandisement. And, several weeks before his wedding, it was apparent to Philip that the moment was not far off. Correctly suspecting that Spain would attempt to draw England into their war, the French King had not waited. He sent one army into Italy to take the Spanish-held provinces of Piedmont and Tuscany and himself headed the force that swept into the Low Countries with Brussels as its objective. Only when the Emperor, rising from a sickbed and with 'a great courage and no less skilfulness', rode to lead his troops in person, were the French stopped at Namur. It was only a matter of time, however, before the French King moved again. Handicapped by his lack of men and money and discouraged by his own poor health, Charles hoped for English support or, at least for Philip's return to Spain. The English people, equally aware of Spain's predicament, dreaded any involvement, their fear expressing itself in the scorn they continued to vent on the homesick foreigners.

By the terms of the marriage treaty, English aid to Spain was expressly prohibited. But the sophisticated Renard, a seasoned diplomat, knew the many ways around treaty restrictions. If Philip could be crowned, his influence as an anointed sovereign would be greater with the people and the Council. The Queen's firm promise that her nation would remain apart from any foreign wars was one both Renard and Philip knew she meant to keep. But it would be difficult also for the Queen to deny a crowned monarch who was also the husband she so dearly loved and dreaded losing. So, as the magical summer passed, Philip devoted himself unsparingly to his Queen even as he appraised the separate strengths and weaknesses of the councillors, seeking the individual or faction which might prove amenable to him.

His ambassador, Renard, wrote to the troubled Emperor that the time was not yet ripe for Philip to assert himself. First the country's religion must be stabilised and the return to the Church effected, a process Mary Tudor, in all good conscience, had enthusiastically encouraged. Already former nuns and friars were returning from exile, awaiting only

[429]

formal Parliamentary action. That this step which the Queen undertook in the warm belief that it was best for her nation would result in an England further rent with dissension, and in her name being blackened and reviled for centuries to come, was, mercifully, an eventuality Mary Tudor could not envisage.

Before the Council would agree to the reconciliation procedure, it insisted on Papal recognition of secular ownership of former church lands. Many of the ministers had begun the foundation of an impressive family fortune on the spoils of church and monastery. To Mary, reconciliation with Rome meant the restitution of all lands and properties to their rightful owners. Her insistence 'on whether it were not expedient to restore the church lands to their original purposes' had, for months, been a bitter source of contention within the Council, where the ministers swore 'that they would never part with their abbey lands while they could wield a weapon'. When Mary retorted that she herself intended 'to devote the lands she found in possession of the Crown to the support of learning and the relief of the most destitute poor', she was severely admonished by her nobles. If she yielded such revenues she would be a poor Queen indeed, they said, to which Mary tartly replied that 'she preferred the peace of her conscience to ten such crowns . . .'. Her attitude made little difference to the councillors.

Their refusal to co-operate was brought home most forcibly to Mary at one session when old John Russell, the Earl of Bedford, weary of the royal arguments, broke into a tirade and, violently pulling his rosary from his waist, flung the beads into the fire, swearing loudly that 'he valued his sweet abbey of Woburn more than any fatherly council from Rome!' The incident coupled with her ministers' continued obstinacy forced the shocked Mary—with the advice of the wise Renard—to one of the few compromises of her life. In what became an outright bargain, the Council agreed to England's spiritual reconciliation with Rome— provided the stolen ecclesiastical properties remained in secular hands.

In early November, Mary suspected she was pregnant; her joy, however, was diminished by the crises challenging her happiness. It being the 'fall of the leaf' ever a bad time for the Queen's health—her physical discomfort was agravated by signs of restlessness in Philip, his anxiety over Spain's war with France and over his father's health. Her husband's obvious homesickness terrified the Queen. The Council had refused even to consider the question of a coronation for Philip. His frustration and disappointment in accepting that he was only a figurehead in England simply increased his desire to leave the country. That he had discussed the possibility with Renard is apparent in the ambassador's advice to the Emperor. 'Let Parliament meet,' he said 'and pass off quietly and in February His Highness may safely go. Irreparable injury may and will follow however, should he leave England before.

Religion will be overthrown, the Queen's person will be in danger, and Parliament will not meet. . . .' Philip's early departure, cautioned Renard, would result in the Council listening to the blandishments of France, now arrogant with its success. 'As things are now,' Renard advised, 'prudence and moderation are more than ever necessary and we must allow neither the King nor the Queen to be led astray by unwise impatient advisers. . . . ready to compromise the commonwealth!'[5]

Though Philip attempted to hide his unhappiness, Mary was beginning to comprehend the fact—even as it tortured her to accept it—that much of his consideration and affectionate display evolved more from duty and courtesy than honest emotion. Coupled with her poor health and the distressing symptoms of an early pregnancy, Mary was further anguished as the detractors of her husband and the opponents of her religion once more became active. Again the court was flooded with vicious lampoons of Philip, even as ribald sonnets found eager listeners in the City streets. Insulting songs were sung in taverns, while profane rhymes ridiculing the royal couple, the Mass, and the Queen's pregnancy were circulated. Once more those reformers with more than a touch of the professional revolutionary went to work. They encouraged hatred for those who supported a return to orthodoxy, setting Englishman against Englishman, against the Spaniard, not even hesitating at suggesting assassination of Philip. Even the Queen, herself, did not escape their contempt. A placard nailed to the Palace gate read, 'Will you be such fools, oh noble Englishmen, to believe that our Queen is pregnant; and of what should she be, but of a monkey or a dog?' Others stated they wished 'they might turn the heart of the Queen from idolatry —or shorten her days'. Many of these dissenters had supported Northumberland and Wyatt. Said one Italian visitor, 'they were still proud of their authority they had exercised under the former reign and decidedly hostile to the restablishment of the Roman Catholic Faith'.[6]

In a brave attempt to put the painful incidents behind her, Mary rode with Philip on 12 November, 1554, to open their first Parliament. A previous session had repealed all church legislation of the former reigns; it remained only to repeal the attainder against the Papal Legate, Cardinal Reginald Pole, to effect England's return to Catholicism. With the removal of his former attainder and the Pope's assurance to the Queen that there would be restitution of church properties, the Cardinal was at least free to return home.

Reginald Pole was the son of Mary's beloved governess, the Countess of Salisbury, who had been brutally executed in 1541. His exile had begun some ten years earlier after a passionate argument with Henry VIII, when, with the assurance of a near relative, he had reproached the King for assuming the title Supreme Head of the Church. He had

[431]

further enraged Henry by criticizing his outrageous treatment of Catherine of Aragon. The King had been seen to lay his hand threateningly on his knife but, containing himself, had merely replied in a tight voice, 'I will consider what you have said and you shall have my answer'. Pole had not waited. Prudently he left England to begin a long voluntary exile in Rome later vilifying Henry with his book, *De Unitate Ecclesia*, which preceded the execution of Pole's brother and mother.

The Cardinal had served the Church with distinction and devotion. Latimer once said of Reginald Pole, 'I remember him. . . . a witty man, a learned man . . . a man of a noble house. If he had tarried in the realm. . . . I believe he would have been Bishop of York.' Instead the tall, ascetic Pole with the haunted eyes of the visionary, his noble Plantagenet features enhanced by a flowing luxuriant beard, had led a dedicated life in Rome and at his countryside villa where he pursued his love for all growing things. Moderate in temperament, a devotee of the classics and learning, the Cardinal spent hours writing his long involved religious treatises while maintaining a formidable correspondence with the distinguished clergy and scholars of many countries. His years abroad had not been unhappy; his calling was sincere, his devotion honest. But always the plight of England—that spiritually outcast nation which was his homeland—was a painful reminder that needed resolving and remedying. With the Queen's accession, he had thought his return home would be imminent. Pole had been frank to tell his cousin, when she contemplated marriage and motherhood, that she was too old for both. He had recommended diligence in England's return to the old faith and firmness on the return of the appropriated church lands. The Emperor, knowing Pole's influence with the Queen, had 'detained' the Cardinal on his homeward journey, until Mary's wedding had taken place, requesting the Papal Legate to assist in the peace negotiations with the French. But the Cardinal was not fooled. He was being deliberately restrained from returning to England while its Queen pursued her disastrous course which privately he considered nonsensical. He had not spared Mary. With the authority of his high position and the privilege of a close relative, he wrote thunderous letters reproaching her for a lack of firmness and decrying his delay in reaching England. And Mary, torn between the demands of her Council that they retain possession of their church lands, of Philip who refused to have the Cardinal home until the Council had considered the possibility of a coronation, and of Renard who counselled patience with everything, had found it easier to plead that Pole's attainder must first be lifted. It was easier to enrage the Cardinal than cross her husband, the Council, the Emperor, and his ambassador. Mary had quickly learned the prerogatives of royalty did not often include the comfort of self-satisfaction.

Once the marriage had taken place, however, the attainder was obligingly lifted, and Pole was free to return to England. He had waited a year and his patience was almost at an end. When at last allowed to depart from the Low Countries with the degrading assurance from the Pope that he must authorise the retention by the English nobles of their ill-gotten church possessions, he accepted the stipulation as the price of his recall. His sensitivities might be bruised, his idealism outraged—but he was going home.

Sailing from Gravesend in the Queen's barge, Reginald Pole arrived at Whitehall Stairs in late November—a returning Prince of the Church—the emblems of his privileged position, a large Cross and two silver poleaxes, carried before him. He was met by Lord Paget, Lord Montague, several bishops, William Cecil,[7] and others of the Council. Philip hastily arose from a midday meal to greet the prelate and escorted him to the Palace where the Queen and court had assembled. Quickly, the Cardinal crossed to Mary and knelt at the feet of the woman who had been a mere girl when he had gone into exile. It was an emotional moment for both. Overjoyed, Mary kissed her cousin warmly. 'The day I ascended the throne, I did not feel such joy!' she told the visitor, her deep voice vibrant with emotion, Pole seemed visibly moved himself. Not only was his return a significant meeting between monarch and prelate, but also a happy reunion between two friends, two relatives, with many mutually warm memories, for their mothers had been the dearest of friends. It was to Reginald Pole's mother that Catherine of Aragon had entrusted Mary when she went, as a child of nine, to live in the grey dankness of Ludlow Castle. And in the gaunt figure of the scarlet-clothed Papal Legate, Mary saw the physical representation of the means by which her country might be absolved of sin.

After four days of celebrating, of jousts and tournaments in the Palace courtyards, of solemn thanksgiving services in all the City churches, the lords and Commons assembled in the Great Chamber of Whitehall with the King, Queen, and Cardinal in attendance. Stephen Gardiner arose and, with great eloquence, introduced Reginald Pole, who said the Chancellor came 'upon one of the weightiest causes that ever happened in this realm . . .'. Slowly, appearing older than his fifty-three years, Pole arose and addressed the assembly. He spoke of his exile—those many years away from England which 'could not pull me from affection'. There was a respectful silence as he continued, 'coming more near to the matter of my commission', he said, 'I signify unto you all, that my principal travail is for the restitution of this noble realm to the ancient nobility and to declare unto you that the See Apostolic, from whence I come, hath a special respect to this realm above all others . . .'. He noted the steps by which all the ensuing 'lamentable schism' had been reached, 'when all lights of true religion seemed extinct, the churches defaced, the altars overthrown, the ministers corrupted. . . . even so in a few remained that confession of Christ's faith, namely, in the breast of the Queen's Excellency . . .'. He spoke of the challenges Mary had met, remembering the time when '. . . on her Grace's part, there was nothing but despair; for numbers conspired against her, and policies devised to destroy her right . . .'. It was an uncomfortable moment for the majority of the audience, who had given Mary little assistance, and Pole did not dwell upon it. Commending the Queen for her earnestness which had been rewarded with such stunning victory, the Cardinal declared he came 'with the keys of Him that sent me . . .' to effect the Englishman's spiritual return to Rome. 'My commission is not of prejudice to any person,' he announced, 'I come not to destroy, but to build; I come to reconcile, not to condemn; I am not come to compel, but to call again . . . . my commission is of grace and clemency to such as will receive it, for, touching all matters that be past, they shall be as things cast into the sea of forgetfulness. . . .'[8]

Two days later, in Westminster Abbey, England formally returned to the Papal fold, as a triumphant Cardinal Pole announced, 'And we, by Apostolic authority given unto us by the most holy Lord, Julius III. . . . do absolve and deliver you, and every one of you, with the whole realm and dominions thereof, from all heresy and schism and from all and every judgment, censure and pain, for that cause incurred; and also we do restore you again unto the unity of our Mother, the Holy Church, as in our letter more plainly it shall appear in the name of the Father, of the Son, and of the Holy Ghost. . . .'[9]

As Mary and Philip walked in procession from the Abbey, the Queen's face was luminous with happiness. Everywhere, people were weeping openly, embracing one another in the spontaneous joy of the moment. With the dearest wish of her heart accomplished in these last emotion-filled days, an exultant Mary Tudor left to await the birth of her child. She could not know as she began her journey to Hampton Court in a cold so great the Thames threatened one of its rare freezes, that her happiness was illusory. She could not realise that it would take more than a Papal Legate's announcement to bind her nation together spiritually or a child to keep her husband at her side. Mary was certain she had accomplished one good for her country. Now, with God's help, she would give it an heir to continue that grace.

The New Year of 1555, that year that was to bring a unified religion and an heir to the Crown of England, began with the dissolving of the Parliament. Not only had the lords and Commons repealed the Church legislation of the past two reigns, they had also sought to

[434]

strengthen the succession as well as the nation's spiritual solidarity. Stephen Gardiner's Heresy Bill restored the authority of the Church to examine and persecute all heretics if they persisted in their beliefs. The succession of the Queen's sister, Elizabeth, was secured, in default of any issue by Mary. Should the Queen die in childbirth, King Philip was appointed as Regent until the heir attained is majority. But that was all; there would be no coronation. Six months after his arrival in England, therefore, a disappointed monarch realised the articles of his marriage treaty were, indeed, binding. He had brought wealth and the hope of an heir to England. But for himself he had nothing but an ageing bride and an empty title, with no responsibility except the continual necessity of ingratiating himself with a Council that refused to consider any aid for his country, a homeland Philip missed more each day. His companions were still yearning 'to get away from such barbarous folk'. They had begun to fight back in the streets and taverns; several on both sides had been killed. But Philip must wait until May when Mary's child was expected, advised the Emperor. Then with the Crown secured by another half-Spanish heir and the religious question settled, Philip might safely return to Spain. Neither the Emperor, the ambassador, nor the King mentioned what that departure would mean to the Queen.

While Mary waited at Hampton Court for the birth of her child, three noted prelates, the 'fathers of the Reformation' were sentenced by Convocation to a heretics' fate—death by burning. Thomas Cranmer, former Archbishop of Canterbury; Hugh Latimer, a former Bishop of Worcester; and Nicholas Ridley, once the Bishop of London, were denounced as traitors and heretics despite the fact that the religious practices they favoured had, in the former reign, been compulsory for the nation.

Religious persecution did not begin with Mary's reign. It has not ended in the twentieth century, though the persecution is more subtle and devious than the agony of the stake. Persecution had been the ultimate weapon of the Roman *Ecclesia*[10] for hundreds of years and would continue long after Mary had gone. Years later Protestants, and the numerous divisions of the reformed faith which evolved, would adopt the same zeal in their own merciless persecutions. Before Mary, Henry VIII had—often without trial and for reasons best known to himself— burned, hung, disembowelled, beheaded, and starved religious dissenters. The uprisings under the Protector and Northumberland had claimed many Catholics who vigorously opposed the defacement of their churches and altars. Cranmer himself had, to Edward's dismay, insisted on the burning of Joan Bocher, and Latimer had been pitiless at the death of Father Forrest when he harangued the aged chaplain of Catherine of Aragon to recant as the agonized victim was slowly roasted to death in a cage suspended over flames.

It was not an age of religious tolerance—a fact to be remembered if the events for which the unhappy Mary Tudor has been vilified for centuries are to be viewed dispassionately. Any indulgence towards political or religious prisoners was regarded as weakness, vacillation, or fear. Mary's leniency with the Northumberland rebels, when only three had suffered the extreme penalty, had been misunderstood, and had encouraged an arrogant contempt for authority in Wyatt and his followers. People did not understand tolerance; they clearly understood the significance of a dozen gibbets with their gruesome cargo.

Mary sincerely believed, as did many of her more thoughtful subjects, that defiance of Papal authority was the root of all unrest and misery among her people. Only rebellion—with its companion sin, treason—sprang from heresy. Mary could remember back to the peaceful years of her childhood before 'the troubles' which her father's passion for Anne Boleyn had foisted upon the realm. Then large-scale religious opposition was relatively unknown, and when it came to light, it was promptly dealt with. Heresy, therefore, must be extinguished if she were to have peace. If that meant the fire, then the fire must claim its victims.

The three condemned prelates had rendered years of service to the Crown and Church. Cranmer and Ridley had significantly aided Henry VIII in his divorce from Catherine of Aragon. Cranmer had been Edward's godfather, while Ridley and Latimer had been favourite preachers at his court. Mary had known them well for many years and, upon coming to the throne, had struggled for a difficult objectivity in dealing with them. She convinced herself that she had extinguished any bitterness for those who had long ago worked against her mother. The full force of the Queen's animosity was centred upon the prisoners for having used Edward and the years of his minority to effect those disastrous religious changes in the realm—changes that had so directly imperilled her own life and liberty. But because of her own inclination—and at the Emperor's advice to 'move cautiously in the matters of religion'—she had at first refrained from taking any adverse measures against any of the three. She had pardoned Cranmer for his participation in the Northumberland rebellion, depriving him of his archbishopric, hoping he would escape to the sanctuary of the Continent as hundreds of others had done before him. Cranmer, however, had chosen to remain. And when he challenged the Queen's orthodoxy by publication of his creed and offered to dispute her faith, encouraging others to do likewise, he sealed his doom. He was charged not only with heresy but with sedition and imprisoned at Oxford. There he was soon joined by Latimer and Ridley who had been equally staunch in their beliefs; all three refused to recant.

In challenging the Crown's religious policy, Cranmer and his companions recognised the danger they were courting. They had often and unhesitantly wielded the whip of authority. But when, by an act of Parliament, authority to prosecute heretics was transferred to the Church, the guiding force of the religious prosecutions was not the Queen, but the Church itself. The responsibility of dealing with the alleged traitors and heretics—whether proud churchman or simple yeoman—passed to the bishops. It was a decision that was to claim many lives, to be misinterpreted and misunderstood by Mary's enemies who took full advantage of the sickening aftermath to blacken the Queen with the title of 'bloody'. The fires of Smithfield were lit by permission of the Queen, certainly. But her Council and her bishops and her Parliament shared in the decision. Mary tried to see that the procedure was just. 'Touching the punishment of heretics,' she wrote, 'we thinketh it ought to be done without rashness, not leaving meanwhile to do justice to such as by learning would seek to deceive the simple.'[11] In other words, there was to be no hurried or illegal judgment and every prisoner must be given—indeed must be encouraged—to recant. Recantations had been made before; Mary was only too aware of how flexible one's religious beliefs might become at the first sign of pressure. She was positive that many—including Cranmer—would recant now. Failing that, there was to be no justice for those who, knowing better, sought to influence the unlearned, the emotionally unstable, or those with other grievances against the Crown.

It is doubtful if, at the commencement of the religious burnings in January, 1555, any involved in the decision realised the frightful toll which would ultimately be exacted. There was, at first, no great protest. On the whole, the people seemed inured to cruelty; it existed in so many forms around them. They often aided in the ghastly work—executions were a form of entertainment one did not disdain on squeamish grounds.

The Church began its reprisal against its own by burning John Rogers, a popular young canon of St. Paul's. In early 1555, Rogers went to his death 'as if he were on his way to a festival'. He was followed shortly, on February 9 by John Hooper, the Bishop of Gloucester. Hooper, a former chaplain to the Protector, had enjoyed his days of power and influence. Now, facing death, he said, 'It was an easy thing to hold with Christ while the Prince and the world held with him; but now the world hateth Him, it is the true trial who will be His'.[12] Hooper did not have an easy death. He had begged the sheriffs for 'a quick fire, to make an end shortly', and they, in tears, had promised. It was the bishop's sad fate, however, to suffer on a wet and windy day, and as the old gentleman limped to the stake, there were many in the crowd of several thousand spectators who wondered whether the fire would stay lit or if the execution would be postponed. A pound of gunpowder was tied between Hooper's legs and more under each arm as others tied his body to the stake with an iron hoop. 'If you think I do amiss in anything, hold up your fingers . . .' he asked those around him and then thoughtfully, 'assisted with his own hands to arrange the faggots around him'. A torch was brought, but the green wood and wet straw did not kindle properly and merely smouldered. More faggots were brought and fresh flame applied, as the bishop cried, 'For God's love, good people, let me have more fire!' Still the flames were slow as the tormented man cried 'Lord Jesu, have mercy on me!' and beat his breast with his hands. It was forty-five minutes before the fire had done its work and Hooper was dead.[13]

The stake began to claim victims of lesser distinction: a butcher, a barber, a weaver, 'an apprentice boy of nineteen', and an 'aged fisherman from Cardiff'. When William Flower, a monk of Ely, interrupted the Easter services at St Margaret's Church in Westminster and stabbed the officiating priest, he was burned in the Palace yard adjacent to the abbey. Though there was genuine horror at the violence of Flower's action, for the most part, the victims' gentle nature and the meek, but unrelenting manner in which they met their tormented deaths began to turn the emotions of the people. There were increased mutterings and resentment against the Church and the Queen, and this was noted by Renard, who wrote Philip '. . . above all, there must be no more of this barbarous precipitancy in putting heretics to death. The people must be won from their errors by gentleness and by better instruction. Except in cases of especial scandal, the Bishops must not be permitted to irritate them by cruelty and the Legate (Pole) must see that a better example is set by the clergy themselves!'[14] The King possessed little feeling for the heretics—except possibly scorn. As his later life shows, persecution was not abhorrent to him. But Philip was a realist, and he knew the onus of the blame for the burnings might fall upon him and his country. Dutifully he recommended moderation to the bishops, and dutifully, they acquiesced—temporarily.

But the King's solicitude did not spare Latimer and Ridley. At Oxford the two old gentlemen were led to the execution site near Balliol College, and here they embraced each other. 'Be of good heart, brother,' said Ridley, 'God will either assuage the flame or else strengthen us to abide it.' As they knelt in prayer, they were given a chance to recant. Ridley answered for both. 'So long as breath is in my body,' he said, 'I will never deny my Lord Christ and His known truth. . . .' There was was only one stake, and as they were chained together, a bag of gunpowder was tied around Ridley's neck. Solicitously, he asked, 'I will take it to be sent to God. . . . have you more for my brother?' As the bag of powder was tied around his companion's neck and the flames began to approach their chained bodies, Latimer cried in the rising

[438]

smoke, 'Be of good comfort, Master Ridley. . . . play the man! We shall this day light such a candle, by God's grace, in England, as I trust shall never be put out!' Ridley was praying, '*Domine, recipe spiritum meum!*' as Latimer, bathing his hands in the flame, seemed to wash his face in the searing heat. Then the gunpowder exploded and he was dead. On Ridley's side of the stake, however, the gorse and sticks had been piled too thickly. He cried to the executioners, 'I cannot burn—Lord have mercy upon me! Let the fire come to me! *I cannot burn!*' Clumsily, someone threw additional wood on the pile. It merely subdued what small flame there was until, compassionately, another spectator 'lifted the pile with a bill and let in the air'. Tongues of bright red flame shot up, and Ridley 'wrested himself into the middle of them and the pow- der did its work'.[15]

A stone's throw away, on the leads of Bocardo Prison, Thomas Cran- mer had been brought to watch the suffering of his friends. His own time had not yet arrived.

By late spring, as Mary approached the final term of her pregnancy, her health was giving great concern. The distressing physical symptoms considered an aspect of pregnancy had continued, and the Queen's general tendency towards dropsy became more pronounced. The 'salu- brius air' of Hampton Court had not improved her condition. Com- bined with an acute physical discomfort, it seemed as though all the resulting tensions and anxieties that had faced Mary since her fight for her throne now merged in a massive assault upon her weakened body. Her emotional energies were further depleted by the constant fear that Philip would cease to show her the affection she so desperately needed. Searing headaches which reduced her to tears and near-hysteria spoke of aggravated nerves—a result of the Queen's nightmare fear that Philip would return to Spain, Abandoned once again to that life she had led before her marriage—a solitary, unloved, bereft woman—she knew she would be unhappier than many of the lowest of her subjects who had loving husbands and healthy bodies capable of bearing children. As the weeks passed, Mary took refuge in almost complete seclusion, a seclu- sion Philip found iritating, and he absented himself from their chambers as much as possible. As he walked in the St George's day procession on April 23, the Queen came to the window to watch, 'so that hundreds did see Her Grace . . .'. Her appearance helped alleviate the rumour that she had secretly died and the King merely waited the arrival of the Spanish legions to announce her death. An equally erroneous report swept the capital at the end of April when 'tidings came that the Queen's Grace was delivered of a prince . . .'. In the resulting frenzy of public celebration, the Tower guns boomed and the great bell of St Paul's preceded 'a ringing throughout the City and other places of *Te Deum* . . .'. Quickly, the news crossed the Channel, and at Antwerp startled English mariners were given 'a hundred crowns for drink' by the Regent. Only with the astonishing declaration that the announcement was false did the preparations for further rejoicing halt. Bonfires remained unlit and puzzled citizens shouted their disappointment. Almost immediately, London erupted with vituperative rumours that the Queen was dead, that the child had been stillborn, and that another infant would be secured and foisted upon them as the true heir! Once more, ridicule, derision, and scandal greeted any mention of the Queen, her husband, or her future child.

The sad episode so shocked and shamed Mary that she remained in her chamber for days. In a nearby room prepared for the nursery, the great gilded cradle waited, appropriately inscribed:

'The child which through Mary, Oh Lord of Might, has send,
To England's joy, in health preserve, keep and defend.'

Often Mary went to the room and gazed at the cradle, her longing visible on her stricken face, while her hands pressed at the swollen body. Seeing her distress, her ladies-in-waiting, 'to comfort the Queen and give her heart and courage', brought three newborn children to her chambers. The triplets had been born to a woman in the adjacent village 'a woman of great age like the Queen and who, after the delivery, found herself strong and out of all danger; and the sight of this woman and her infants greatly rejoiced her Majesty'.[16] The priests and bishops at Hampton Court also sought to comfort the Queen; they walked in procession through the Palace courtyards chanting and fingering their rosaries. Often their parading was interrupted by the clattering arrival of noble families from all over the kingdom to be present at the birth of the heir. In the City of London bishops walked by the light of flaring torches along Cheapside, supplicating divine favour for the Queen, and extra troops were quartered in the Tower and near the City gates 'on account of the many idle rogues there, to whom in case any misfortune at the time of the delivery, the slightest cause would become the greatest possible [reason] for enabling them to sack the houses of the citizens . . . .'.[17] Throughout England, court, subjects, King, and Queen waited.

By the third week in May, the Venetian ambassador wrote to his home court: 'Everything is in suspense and dependent on the result of this delivery, which, according to the opinion of the physicians, unless it takes place at this new phase of the moon two days hence, may be protracted beyond the full moon. . . . on the 4th or 5th of next month, Her

Majesty's belly having greatly declined, which is said yet more to indicate the approaching term'.[18] Every encouraging sign sent Mary's hopes soaring that the birth was imminent; she clung obstinately to her hope of a living child. Philip counted the days until the birth should take place—the birth which meant his release from bondage and his longed-for return to Spain.

Even as they waited, the problem of what to do with that royal nuisance, Elizabeth Tudor, confronted the King and Queen. Continued imprisonment at Pomfret Castle, exile at the court of Philip's aunt, the Queen of Hungary—all had been discussed and discarded, for Mary knew the people would be aroused if the heir-presumptive should be sent from England. Renard was explicit in his advice to Philip. 'Should the Queen's pregnancy prove a mistake, the heretics will place their hopes in Elizabeth, and here you are in a difficulty whatever be done, for if Elizabeth be set aside, the Crown will go to the Queen of Scots,' he wrote from Spain where he had been recalled temporarily. He cautioned that if Elizabeth ever attained the throne, 'she will restore heresy and naturally attach herself to France. Some step must be taken about this before you leave the country . . .'. Perhaps the danger of heresy and Elizabeth's succession could be averted if the girl were married, for 'to recognize her as heir-presumptive without providing her with a husband who can control her, will be perilous to the Queen . . .'. Renard stressed. Above all, he advised, 'the thing should be done without delay. Before you leave the country you should see the Princess yourself, give her your advice to be faithful to her sister and, on your part, promise that you will be her friend, and assist her where you can find opportunity.'* Renard did not put his thoughts as bluntly as the Venetian ambassador who said, '. . . in case of Her Majesty's demise. . . . the King's safety and security would depend more on her [Elizabeth] than on any other person . . .'. And, to further cement the union with England, Philip might 'make a second marriage with her, it not being improbable that she also might . . . incline that way. . .'.[19]

Mary, therefore, was compelled at last to deal with those two challenges to her crown, Edward Courtenay and Elizabeth. Courtenay was released from his Tower imprisonment and advised by his friend and patron, Stephen Gardiner, to leave England immediately. 'Provided he departed, he might return at his pleasure without further leave from Her Majesty, his absence at the moment of the delivery sufficing them. . . .'[20] With one potential troublemaker gone, the orders then went forth summoning the Queen's sister to come to court to be present,

* These words have a ring of irony, for in one of history's more magnificent coincidences, it was this same Philip and Elizabeth who would be the protagonists some thirty-three years later in the great conflict which resulted in the Spanish Armada attempting an invasion of England.

as heir-presumptive, at the birth of the Queen's child. Deep in the Oxfordshire countryside, an overjoyed Sir Henry Bedingfield gazed unbelievingly at the message from the Queen ". . . and as we have resolved to have the Lady Elizabeth repair near unto us, we do therefore pray and require you do declare unto her that our pleasure is that she shall come to us at Hampton Court in your company with as much speed as you can have things in order for that purpose . . .'.[21]

Sir Henry put the summons away with satisfaction. At long last, he might look forward to the morrow with anticipation. His prisoner, too, might once more re-enter that world which was hers by birth, from which she had been excluded for more than a year and a half. Elizabeth received the announcement in silence, but relief was visible on her face. As her ladies began the preparations for her journey, she viewed the hateful surroundings at Woodstock with little regret. She was leaving—and she was still safe. On the day of departure, with a small diamond from her meagre collection of jewellery, she wrote upon a windowpane:

'Much suspected by me,
Nothing proved can be.
Quoth Elizabeth, prisoner.'[22]

It was her farewell to Woodstock.

Elizabeth arrived at Hampton Court shortly after the disastrously false birth announcement. Courtenay had left for the Continent the day before. She entered by a back courtyard entrance without any formal reception, and immediately guards were placed at her chamber door and visitors were prohibited until further notice. Elizabeth had expected an immediate audience with the Queen, but it was soon obvious she had merely exchanged one confinement for another. Any hope of royal clemency or a reconciliation disappeared. Once more, doubt and fear returned to haunt her days; only now it was accompanied by baffling anxiety. Had Mary recalled her merely to observe the formalities—so that she, Elizabeth, might be present at the birth of the child who would rob her of every hope of achieving the throne? And why did the birth not take place? Why was everyone so cautious and concerned instead of expressing the joy that should accompany a royal child's birth? Elizabeth attempted to rationalize Mary's attitude, to find some justification for her own continued detention.

A marriage with Emmanuel Philibert, the Duke of Savoy and Prince of Piedmont, had been seriously considered by the King, Queen, and

Council. The handsome duke even journeyed to England to meet Elizabeth, but the Princess, realising she risked further imprisonment or exile, had nevertheless strongly resisted the proposal. De Noailles, the French ambassador, had found the means of advising her to renounce the duke, confirming her own belief that she should live abroad as the wife of a penniless Italian Prince, she would virtually abandon her claim to the throne. Mary had not pursued the issue, only too aware of the resentment that would be aroused should she force Elizabeth into an unwanted foreign marriage. Philibert had, therefore, left England without even glimpsing his intended bride, and Elizabeth attributed Mary's silence to royal pique. She had no way of knowing how ill the Queen had been, of the physical distress and emotional havoc Mary's shattered nerves had wrought.

For two weeks Elizabeth waited, two soft, lovely May weeks when the Privy gardens at Hampton Court came alive with bloom and the intense green of the huge trees in the park seemed almost unbelievable. The Princess had forgotten the astonishing magic of an English spring; the cold grey remoteness of Woodstock seemed more like a bad dream which must be quickly forgotten. At the waterstairs, which she could barely glimpse from her chamber, she could see the bright colours of the river barges and hear the cries of the boatmen. Elizabeth watched the great gilded barges of the nobles dexterously avoiding the smaller craft on the river, and the arrival of the noisy, laughing groups accompanied by their retainers as they passed beneath her window or walked leisurely through the gardens. She longed to be out on the river, in the garden, in the courtyards—*anywhere* so long as she was free. For almost two years she had been restrained; during that long period, there had been a guard at her door. How much longer must such shameful captivity be borne?

As each day passed, her misgivings grew. Was there something wrong with Mary that was being kept from her? When her uncle, Lord William Howard, whose affection and favour had never failed her, was allowed a brief visit, Elizabeth asked that—since the Queen would not see her—perhaps she might see some lords of the Council? Within, several days, Lord Chancellor Gardiner, accompanied by Arundel Shrewsbury, and Secretary Petre, waited upon the Princess in her small suite of rooms. Besides her uncle and those who had attended her, they were the first visitors the young woman had seen in almost two years. Her enthusiasm in greeting even those whom she knew to be her enemies is evident in her remark: 'My Lords, I am glad to see you, for methinks I have been kept a great while from you, desolately alone?' Before they could reply, Elizabeth solicited their goodwill and begged them to 'be a means to the King and Queen's Majesty that I may be delivered from my imprisonment, in which I have been kept a long time, as to you, my Lords, is not unknown!'

[443]

Gardiner parried Elizabeth's plea, sternly reminding her that 'she must then confess her fault and put herself on the Queen's mercy'. But the Princess had not suffered her long imprisonment to be confronted now with a possible submission. Instead she said, 'she would lie in prison all the days of her life . . .'. She noted that 'she craved no mercy at her Majesty's hand'. Rather, said Elizabeth, with no note of apology in her voice, the law should decide 'if ever she did offend her Majesty in thought, word or deed.' Elizabeth was well aware that previous attempts to find evidence of her complicity in the Wyatt plot had been fruitless. Her plea to the councillors, therefore, was little less than an outright challenge. But the young woman was convincing, and a measure of her success is evident in Stephen Gardiner's efforts on her behalf. Never any friend of the Princess, he nevertheless sought an audience with the Queen as Elizabeth had requested.

He was back the following day with the disappointing message 'that the Queen marvelled at her [Elizabeth]'s boldness in refusing to confess her offence, so that it might seem as if her Majesty had wrongfully imprisoned her Grace'. The artful suggestion, put so innocently, did not tempt Elizabeth to argument, and her intense obstinacy showed plainly on her face when she replied that if Mary still thought her guilty, then she might punish her 'as she thinketh good'. There would be no punishment, Gardiner replied, except that her freedom would be under continued restraint. 'Her Majesty willeth me to tell you,' he said, 'that you must tell another tale ere that you are set at liberty.' To which Elizabeth struggling to hide a hot anger at Mary's determination to humble her, only answered scornfully 'that she had as lief be in prison with honesty as to be abroad suspected of her Majesty'. Then, looking Gardiner in the eye, she said, 'And this that I have said, I will stand unto; for I will never belie myself!'

The prisoner's resoluteness impressed even the cynical Gardiner, and for a moment, he seemed nonplussed. Then he replied, 'Then your Grace has the vantage of me, and these Lords, for your wrong and long imprisonment . . .'. It was an acknowledgment of injustice of sorts and from one of the highest officials of her sister's government. Yet, Elizabeth wearily understood, it would not suffice to set her free. She refrained, nevertheless, from venting her anger on Gardiner and his companions. 'What advantage I have, you know,' she replied in a small voice, gesturing around the confines of her chamber. 'I see no advantage at your hands for so dealing with me—but God forgive you and me also!'[23] Surprisingly, the Chancellor and the lords knelt at Elizabeth's feet, and 'desiring her Grace that all might be forgotten,' they departed. The sound of the key being turned in the lock informed Elizabeth her visits were over for the day.

Within the next week, the King himself visited the prisoner. Curiosity had triumphed over caution, and with the Queen's consent, Philip appeared in Elizabeth's chamber. She had been warned of his coming, for Mary had sent an especially beautiful gown, suitable for such an important occasion, for Elizabeth to wear. It was the first piece of new clothing the Princess had seen in almost two years, and forgetting her former austere preferences, she donned it happily, hoping the Queen's husband would bring her some news that her long imprisonment was at an end. She was pleasantly surprised by Philip's own elegance and did not miss the flicker of appreciation in the aloof features of her royal brother-in-law. He had been announced at the door of her chamber as 'the King', and Elizabeth felt a twinge of irritation and annoyance as she watched Philip's head bent over her hand. The memory of that great figure who had been 'the King' for so many years came unbidden to her mind—England's great Henry—her own father. King, indeed! No sleek, trim sophisticate of a Spaniard could ever be King of England! She kept her aversion well hidden and the meeting proceeded pleasantly, but it had produced nothing other than the satisfaction of a mutual curiosity. Only the most commonplace subjects had been discussed; both Philip and Elizabeth deliberately avoiding any mention of the Queen. After he had gone, she wondered what the King would say to her sister. Surely the visit would be discussed. She had seen the Queen's Chancellor and now the Queen's husband. Surely some result must follow!

For another ten days Elizabeth waited, each passing hour diminishing the hope that her visitors' appearances had sent soaring. Whatever they told Mary, it had not changed the Queen's opinion. For Elizabeth the suspense became almost unbearable. She knew little of what was happening in other parts of the vast river Palace. Had the royal child been born? Had any decision been made concerning her own future? Must she spend the remainder of her life in a tedium that sapped her physical strength as it battered her frayed nerves? When Elizabeth had about given up hope of any leniency, suddenly, and incredibly a message arrived. While preparing for bed at ten o'clock, the startled Princess heard the Queen's summons with a relief mixed with dread. She had no idea what to expect. If the news were good, would the Queen have waited three weeks to see her? Had Philip perhaps prevailed upon his wife to show some clemency towards her sister? Elizabeth's tired mind revolved endlessly on her predicament while her ladies, visibly excited, helped her to dress. Whatever the Queen's decision, it would be final. She might be set free or she might be imprisoned for life—or worse. Suddenly, her young face drawn and white with fear, Elizabeth acknowledged that the Queen's decision might be very final indeed.

As she left her apartment to join the waiting guard, she turned to her companions whose faces now reflected her own inner foreboding and 'desired her gentlemen and gentlewomen to pray for her, for that she could not tell whether ever she should see them again or not'.[24] Dutifully, she then followed the guard and her sister's Mistress of the Robes, Susan Clarencieux, who smiled encouragingly at Elizabeth. Faithful old Sir Henry Bedingfield, whose plain, honest features vividly reflected his apprehension, joined them in the corridor. He had been hurriedly summoned from his nearby quarters and walked with the others, his spurs clicking on the Palace floors, creating the only sound in the ominous silence. The small procession left the corridor behind and walked out into the fresh damp smell of the river air where the guard's torch flared in the evening wind. Elizabeth was suddenly grateful for the presence of the familiar Bedingfield. Those damp black shadows near the Palace walls could easily harbour an assassin. With relief, she entered the well-lit entrance to the Queen's apartments. There, the guard told her, Sir Henry must wait. For a moment the eyes of the knight met those of his prisoner. Elizabeth's glance remained inscrutable, though the concern he felt still showed plainly in his.

The Princess entered the apartment and the door closed behind her. Quickly she crossed to the great bed where the Queen lay. She had last seen her sister in the months after Mary had triumphed over Northumberland. Then the joy of her victory had lent a shining radiance to the Queen's simple features. Now Elizabeth struggled to maintain the impassive look which had so impressed Bedingfield, for Mary must not see the painful shock her appearance caused. The Queen looked tired and ill; her worn features were tense. The eyes, ringed with exhaustion, seemed larger and more deeply set than usual. Her hands were folded on the bed linen; Elizabeth could see the distention of her figure under the coverings. Quickly she advanced to the bed and, falling on her knees, the tears in her eyes reflected in her shaking voice, she protested her truth and loyalty to her sovereign Majesty, 'let whosoever assert the contrary!'

Mary hunched herself forward, the deep eyes searching Elizabeth's tearful face. 'You will not confess your offence, I see, but rather stand stoutly on your truth. I pray God, your truth may become manifest!' Elizabeth bowed her head to escape the burning gaze; the harsh tone in her sister's voice did not bode well. She answered meekly, 'If it is not, I will look for neither favour nor pardon at your Majesty's hands . . .'. Mary's tone was scornful and held more than a trace of sarcasm as she replied, 'Well then, you stand so stiffly on your truth—perhaps you have been wrongfully punished?'

It was not meant as a snare. Elizabeth knew that deviousness was not any part of her sister's temperament; the remark was merely an invitation to further argument. But still she would not allow herself to be trapped. So, with almost a trace of the childish impudence which had once so captivated the more proper Mary, she answered, 'If so, I must not

[446]

say so to Your Majesty . . .'. She ventured a glance directly at the Queen and was heartened to see almost a glint of mirthful appreciation in the tired eyes. *Thank God, the worst is over*, she thought, and the taut shoulder slumped in what she hoped appeared as an overwhelming despair. Mary lay back on the pillows, a long sigh escaping her, as she continued, 'But you will report so to others it seemeth . . .'. Elizabeth raised her chin and, looking directly at Mary, fervidly and with hands clasped, cried, 'No, and if it please your Majesty, I have borne and must bear the burden thereof. But I humbly beseech your Grace's good opinion of me, as I am, and ever have been, your Majesty's true subject?'[25]

For a long moment the glances of the two sisters remained locked: Elizabeth's inscrutable and unyielding, Mary's doubtful—and tired. It was this exhaustion which caused the Queen to raise a thin hand to her brow as if to erase from her consciousness the implacability of her younger sister's gaze. 'God knoweth . . .' was all she muttered and then, lapsing into Spanish, '*Sabe Dios*'. After a moment, she signalled that Elizabeth might leave. Weak from the tension of the moment and with tears of relief still in her eyes, the Princess arose and looked with pity at her sister's haggard face. She wanted to say so much—to soothe—to comfort this wretched woman so soon to endure the ordeal of childbirth. But Mary's eyes were closed; the scene with Elizabeth had exhausted her. Silently, the Princess backed away from the bed to the door, already thinking of her ladies' joy and Bedingfield's relief when she told them all was well. Although Mary had not said so, Elizabeth knew the Queen had capitulated and she would now be free. What had caused her to change her mind? As Elizabeth opened the chamber door, a small gust of wind caused the tapestry hanging near the Queen's bed to move slightly. The movement revealed the slim, tapering feet of a man hidden behind the hanging. An elegant man, judging from the soft, supple leather of the slippers he wore.

Elizabeth quickly closed the door. Philip! It had been Philip behind the hanging. The King of England eavesdropping on the conversation between the Queen and her disgraced sister. And, apparently, all with Mary's knowledge and permission! A wide smile appeared on the Princess's face, enchanting old Bedingfield who was sure it was for him. He could not know the inner mirth replacing the tension in his prisoner, a mirth she successfully repressed until back in her own quarters. He could not know, either, as Elizabeth now did, exactly who they must thank for her new and precious freedom.

During the following week, Elizabeth moved freely about the court. Old friends, now that she was no longer in disgrace, flocked to her side.

Then, abruptly, she was given permission to leave for Ashridge. Her departure puzzled those who stayed in the hot and odorous rooms of Hampton Court that had housed too many for too long. By tradition they must remain to await the birth of the Queen's child—yet the heiress presumptive was allowed to depart! Elizabeth did not question the good fortune which, after two years, would return her to the familiar comfort of her own household. There was no formal farewell with her sister; she was told the Queen was unwell. Again, Elizabeth suspected Philip was responsible for her blessed release. With her confinement so imminent, Mary's thoughts would be elsewhere.

Elizabeth's suppositions were not far wrong. The Queen could think of little else but the child whose coming was so delayed—and the fact that her husband would leave her once it was born. Philip's grandmother, the 'mad Juana', a sister of Catherine of Aragon, had at last ended her tortured existence at the Palace of Tordesillas in Spain. Now that the crazed woman who, though a Queen of Spain, had spent decades in a brutal and degrading captivity was dead, her son, the Emperor, wished to abdicate, to relinquish his burdens to his son Philip. Charles's deteriorating health and the years of dedicated sovereignty he had rendered the Empire bore heavily upon him; he yearned for the solitude of a monastery and the peace an honourable retirement would bring him. Faced with such an urgent situation, Mary had to accept the bitter knowledge that soon she would lose her husband to the demands of Spain and its Emperor.

As the hot June weeks passed with no change in her condition, Mary convinced herself she had miscalculated. She was aided in the pitiful delusion by her doctors and a midwife who, said de Noailles, 'more to comfort her with words than anything, tells her from day to day that she has miscalculated her pregnancy by two months'. The Spanish ambassador, Renard, was also concerned about conditions as the nation awaited the child's birth. 'The entire future turns on the accouchement of the Queen; of which however, there are no signs,' he wrote to Charles. 'If all goes well, the state of feeling in this country will improve. If she is in error, I foresee convulsions and disturbances such as no pen can describe. . . . The looks of men are grown strange and impenetrable; those in whose loyalty I had much dependence, I have now most reason to doubt. Nothing is certain and I am more bewildered than ever at the things which I see going on around me. . . .' Renard finished ominously, 'I know not whether the King's person is safe; and the scandals and calumnies which the heretics are spreading about the Queen are beyond conception . . .'.[26]

By the end of June, when the people had not seen their sovereign for weeks, rumours were once more rampant that the Queen was dead. Instead, Mary—dreading the questioning probing eyes of court officials, servants, and friends—remained in her darkened chamber. Her ladies tiptoed in to whisper encouraging words while the physicians deliberated in the next room. Philip remained away as long as possible from the stuffy chamber and the disconcerting sight of the swollen figure of the Queen of England sunk in despondency on her cushions on the floor. Already many of his companions had left for Spain; others had packed their belongings and were only waiting the signal to depart.

Outside, chanting processions paraded through the courtyard, and in the chapel prayers were offered for the Queen's safe delivery. No one had any information, or if they did, they kept it to themselves. De Noailles was brutally frank when he wrote to his home court, 'The Queen would never bring any child into the world. Her own doctor had said she did not eat enough to keep the child alive'.

Still Mary's confidence remained unshaken. The humiliation of the false birth announcement in late April, which had made her so miserably self-conscious, only strengthened the stubborn belief that the Catholic heir to the throne of England was about to be born. To relinquish that hope was to admit failure—the failure of her marriage, the failure of the union with Spain—what did it all mean if there was to be no child to guarantee its permanence? There, as evidence, was her swollen body, the absence of her period, the nausea and discomfort of the past months. It was outside of Mary's experience, or her desire, to realise that all her symptoms might be attributable to other maladies—several of which she had suffered before.* Her doctors and ladies-in-waiting continued to assure her a child was about to be born. And so the pitiful illusion continued as she remained on the chamber floor, the one place where she felt comfortable. And, in the world outside, her enemies mocked the priestly processions, while others laughed at the Queen's fertility and made ribald remarks about Philip's sexual capacity and heartily wished the Spaniards would go home.

It took several more hot uncomfortable weeks, almost to the end of July, to convince the heartsick Mary that she was not about to become a mother. Philip, fretful, irritable, and longing to be gone, had made final preparations, even as the doctors maintained the Queen *was* pregnant and the birth might be delayed until August or even September. The brutal finality of her husband's eagerness to depart helped strip the pitiful delusion from Mary's eyes. Finally, one early August morning a haggard and stricken Queen rose from her floor cushions and faced the

* Amenorrhea, the cessation of the menses, which Mary called 'her old guest' had plagued her for years. She was also subject—as was Elizabeth—to the swelling discomfort of dropsy. But her condition at the time of her supposed pregnancy would be diagnosed by a modern physician as pseudocyesis, a false pregnancy. In pseudocyesis, all physical manifestations of pregnancy are present. It occurs primarily with older women who desperately want children and have passed their most fertile stage.

[449]

truth. She was not about to give birth; she probably would never be able to have a child. She was also about to lose her husband and with him went every hope of happiness, any semblance of a loving reality which had lent some meaning to her days. She still possessed the Crown. But was it enough? Could it compensate for the lack of children, the love of a man—comforts her subjects took for granted? Mary did not know. For the first time in years, the thirty-nine-year-old Queen dreaded the thought of the morrow and all the tomorrows yet to come when she would be old, perhaps ill—and alone.

Philip and the Queen left Hampton Court on August 3 for Oatlands. As Renard said, the move was made 'in order no longer to keep the people of England in suspense about this delivery . . .'. Also the 'gentlewomen and chief female nobility who had flocked to the court from all parts of the Kingdom in such very great numbers, all living at the cost of her Majesty . . . at Hampton Court, although one of the largest palaces . . . [cannot] contain them'. Mary was heartened on her journey to meet a crippled old man on crutches near the river barge and 'when he saw her . . . for joy he threw the staves away, and ran after her Grace, and she commanded that one should give him a reward'. His joy was mirrored in the behaviour of the more compassionate London citizens, for when the Queen rode through the City on her way to Greenwich on August 26, the people 'all ran from one place to another, as to an unexpected sight, and one that was well-nigh new, as if they were crazy, to ascertain thoroughly if it were she, and on recognising and seeing her . . . they, by shouts and salutations . . . gave yet greater signs of their joy . . .'.[27] Though Mary was gladdened by the reception of her subjects who had secretly thought her dead, still the spectre of Philip's leavetaking faced her. The Venetian ambassador wrote of her dread, 'As may be imagined with regard to a person extraordinarily in love, the Queen remains disconsolate, though she conceals it as much as she can, and from what I hear, mourns the more when alone and supposing herself invisible to any of her attendants . . .'. Mary had three days with Philip at Greenwich before his departure— days in which she prayed for a strength she knew she lacked to face the ordeal of farewell. Apparently her Saviour heard the plea of one who depended upon Him so utterly, for as one who accompanied the King and Queen on the day of Philip's leavetaking wrote: 'She really expressed very well the sorrow becoming a wife, and a wife such as she is, invested with the regal habit and dignity; for, without displaying much intrinsic disquietude, though evidently deeply grieved internally, she chose to come with him through all the chambers and galleries to the head of the stairs, constraining herself the whole way to avoid, in sight of such a crowd, any demonstration unbecoming her gravity, though she could not but be moved when the Spanish noblemen kissed her hand, and yet more, when she saw her ladies, in tears, take leave of the King. . . .'

It was not until Mary, accompanied by her tearful companions, had walked again through all the numerous chambers, past all the staring eyes, and returned to her own chambers that she allowed herself the luxury of tears. There, said the Venetian ambassador, 'placing herself at a window which looks on the river, not supposing herself any longer seen or observed by anyone, it was perceived that she gave free vent to her grief by a flood of tears, nor did she once quit the window until she had not only seen the King embark and depart, but remained looking after him as long as he was in sight; and the King, on his part, mounted aloft on the barge in the open air, in order to be better seen when the barge approached in sight of the window and, moreover, waved his bonnet from the distance to salute her, demonstrating great affection'.[28]

Philip had promised to return in a month or as soon as the affairs of the Empire were settled. It was, however, to be nearly two years before the Queen saw the man who, next to her duty to the Crown, was her only reason for living.

Chapter Twenty-four

THE immediate sadness of Philip's departure was soon replaced by the familiar loneliness Mary had hoped might be gone forever from her life. She kept before her the memory of a year of happiness and sought to fill her days with sufficiently exhausting activity to guarantee her rest at night. Mary had always experienced difficulty in sleeping, rarely retiring before midnight, to be up and abroad by five or six o'clock in the morning. Now the solace of sleep was almost impossible. In the early hours of the predawn, the Queen reluctantly faced the question that she sought to evade during the day by a vigorous pursuit of duty—would her husband return soon? Would he remain in England at her side to help in God's work of reclaiming those English souls so nearly lost in a false faith? And most important—*when* would he return?

To maintain some pretence of normality in their relationship, Mary busied herself in devising ways by which a close contact with Philip might be maintained. Couriers, booted and spurred, waited in the adjacent courtyards ready to ride to him with a letter, a ring, or a batch of meat pasties which he fancied. Any excuse sufficed. Before his departure, Philip had assembled the Council, 'and, in a very suitable language, recommended the government of the kingdom to them during his absence . . . leaving a writing in which . . . were noted all such warnings as he deemed most important and necessary, with a detailed list of such persons as could be trusted and employed . . .'.¹ But, well aware of the jealous, ambitious, and corrupt factions within the Council, Philip had prudently requested Cardinal Pole to assume charge, asking Mary's Council 'to defer to him in everything'. Thus the minutes of every Privy Council meeting were sent to the absent King, and no resolution could be enacted without his consent. While such restraint irked a good many of her ministers, they were aware that, as far as the Queen was concerned, it was one more tie with her husband, one more responsibility which might yet convince him that an early return to England was advisable.

Upon returning home, the Queen's couriers—with rare diplomacy and sympathy—refrained from detailing what they had seen and heard of Philip's activities in Brussels. In one of the rare such episodes in his life, the King of England was indulging in a protracted bout of dissipation which was all the more sharply enjoyable after an austere year in a foreign land with an ageing wife. Philip appeared at endless weddings, masques, and hunting expeditions—all of which ended in night-long sessions of drinking and dancing—all pleasantly attended by ladies of dubious reputation. The Venetian ambassador, Badoer, wrote from Brussels of Philip's many evenings at the home of Madame d'Aler, 'who is considered very handsome and of whom he seemed much enamoured'. Such unusual merrymaking, late hours, and the generous portions of hearty food and rich wines soon took their toll, and Philip spent several days in bed, leading Carindal Pole to observe the Queen's indulgent reaction to news of his illness: 'considering his habitual abstemiousness and sound constitution, she hoped the malady would neither be serious nor protracted'. The Queen also hastened to send him loving messages of sympathy and a prayer for his quick recovery in which she thanked her Saviour for the husband whom He had chosen for her, 'who more than all others, in his own acts and in his guidance of mine, reproduced Thy image . . .'.

Philip, careful in his handling of the woman he knew so well, returned her message with 'thanks for her loving office and protestations' and announced 'his firm intention of performing without fail the promise given her repeatedly, as soon as possible . . .'. The promise to return—that was all the Queen really wished to hear. Such promise guaranteed Mary a relatively happy day as she planned and anticipated her husband's arrival, and the couriers did not quench her enthusiasm. Instead they repeated Philip's admonitions 'but did not give account of His Majesty's having twice gone abroad on this wretched weather, and of his dancing . . . fearing the Queen, who is easily agitated, might take it too much to heart'.[2]

Throughout the months following the hot summer, inclement weather blighted the harvest, and England was dotted with rotting fields, 'which much discomforted the people'. In these months in which Mary sought to pick up the thread of a lonely life, she had the spiritual solace of Cardinal Pole and the sisterly companionship of Elizabeth. The Princess was unquestionably back in Mary's good graces and determined to remain so. Upon returning to Hampton Court to accompany Philip to his departure at Greenwich, Elizabeth had meekly accepted her sister's suggestion that she travel by ordinary barge with few attendants while Philip and Mary rode in state through the City. The intent was plain. Elizabeth, so recently absolved of disgrace, was to be dispatched with little ceremony and be given no opportunity to evoke the people's sympathy, either for her anomalous position or as a symbol of her former professed religion.

Now, at Greenwich, no one was more Catholic in her observances than Elizabeth. She attended Mass daily with the Queen and was fervent in her devotions. She was constantly at Mary's beck and call, often remaining far into the evening when Mary found it difficult to sleep. In those late hours, as they talked quietly together or played the card games Mary so loved, each sister regained a measure of her former affection—an affection resulting from their own unique relationship and the knowledge of the frightening risks they had endured because of their proximity to the Crown. If their affection was tempered with caution and perhaps lacking in an ultimate respect, it did not diminish the feeling itself. It was Elizabeth rather than Mary who profited the most from this late evening companionship. As she viewed her still grieving sister, the possessor of England's Crown, she saw only an inconsolable woman who had—though perhaps only momentarily—forgotten her heritage. Mary was sadly lacking in any real authority, badgered by a venal Council, obsessed by love and longing for her absent husband, a foreigner whose decisions for England could not help but be tempered by reactions in his own country. To be so defenceless a Queen was not Elizabeth Tudor's conception of sovereignty. Elizabeth pitied her sister as she sought to understand Mary's vulnerability. It was a lesson she absorbed with a well-concealed vexation and impatience. That honourable Englishmen—as boisterous, lusty, quarrelsome, and defiant as they might be—should be governed by a Queen who could think of little but her husband, stirred Elizabeth. If Mary's plight was the fate of a wedded Queen, better to remain unwed!

For Mary, reconciliation with Elizabeth was more puzzling. Often while her sister studied the next play of the cards, as she watched the Princess's narrowed eyes and intent absorption, Mary would wonder—for the hundredth time—about the integrity of this young woman who was the logical prey of every plotter in the realm, of every nation with a marriageable Prince. Had Elizabeth been as innocent in the Wyatt rebellion as she protested? Did she really wish to remain unmarried? Or was she merely biding her time until the Crown was hers and she might choose for herself or, before that, lend her support to Mary's enemies who might wrest it from her by force? It was an enigma the tired Queen chose not to dwell on at length; Elizabeth was there and devoting herself to regaining the faith and trust she'd so nearly lost. As subsequent events were to prove, she succeeded admirably.

In October, having consoled Mary through the immediate misery of Philip's absence, she obtained the Queen's permission to retire to Hatfield. After an affectionate farewell, as a token of esteem and a pledge of their reconciliation, Mary placed a ring on the delighted Elizabeth's

[454]

finger. De Noailles saw Mary's willingness to let Elizabeth depart as calculated: 'Everyone believes that the Queen has purposely sent her away so that she may not assist at the opening of Parliament and also to deaden the people's affection for her . . .'. Elizabeth was happy to leave; it would be wiser to be apart from the ceremonies in which she would have to participate if she remained in London. That the people's love, however, had not diminished, is shown in the French ambassador's comment, describing Elizabeth's journey toward Hatfield: 'Everyone in London . . . both great and small, made great demonstrations . . . making many signs of joy and all other customary salutations, and followed her out of town. For this cause, the Princess was obliged to order several of her gentlemen and officers to remain behind in order to keep the people in check . . .'.[3] For herself, Elizabeth refrained from gesturing, smiling or encouraging 'salutations or exclamations'. Nothing, not even the exhibition of public favour, was going to jeopardize her precious new freedom.

At Hatfield Elizabeth returned to the familiar and well-loved Palace, surrounded by the great oak forests and sunny gardens, to reunion with Ashley and her husband, to the comforting presence of Thomas Parry who, despite his ineptness with the account books, still remained her cofferer. And there was Roger Ascham, Elizabeth's old tutor, sent as a surprise from the Queen, so the Princess might resume her studies that had been interrupted two years before. Overjoyed, a grateful Elizabeth once more settled into the solitude of Hatfield, happy the poor roads and approaching winter weather would discourage outsiders. With Ascham she enthusiastically returned to her Greek, Italian, Latin, and French. That keen memory and diligence for work had not deserted her is revealed by Ascham's letter to a friend, describing the visit to Metullus, 'a learned foreigner', to Hatfield. The visitor, so impressed with Elizabeth's fluency and also her 'knowledge of things in general and with what a wise and accurate judgment she is endowed', had said that 'he thought it more to have seen Elizabeth than to have seen England . . .'.

On November 12, 1555, Stephen Gardiner died. He had rendered one last tremendous service for his sovereign by obtaining a subsidy from a grudging Parliament to relieve the Queen's chronic poverty. Mary had inherited her father's and brother's debts, but for the 'sake of not burdening anyone', she had remitted the taxes Parliament had given to Edward. 'Neither did she choose . . . to avail herself of the revenues and estates of many of her rebels, amounting to a very considerable sum, but to demonstrate her benignity and clemency, she made a free gift of both their lives and their lands . . .'. Gardiner explained in his opening speech. Though the Queen had been far from extravagant and Philip had brought more Spanish gold into the realm than Mary had spent since her accession, the expenses of the Wyatt rebellion and her wedding, in addition to the normal expenditures, had drained the treasury. Therefore, said the Chancellor, Parliament was to 'devise means for relief . . .'.

Instead Parliament was suspicious. If the Queen were so poor, why must she return valuable monastic holdings to the Church when the rents amounting to some £6,000 a year would help fill the exchequer? But Mary was adamant on the lands' return. She told the Parliament, 'You have shown that you care for my person; but that is no good if you care nothing for my soul.' The new Parliament, which had gained many young and outspoken members, suspected the money might be spent on a future coronation for Philip or to pay Spanish armies in his fight with France. Peace was imperative for England in view of its precarious financial condition and the internal stress promoted by 'the Queen's proceedings', as many called the restoration of the Catholic faith. At Gardiner's urging they had, however, reluctantly voted the required subsidy. Exhausted by this last struggle the Chancellor—the only one of that office fitted by temperament and ambition to wear the mantle of Henry's great Cardinal Wolsey—was too ill to reach his own Southwark residence. He went to the Palace, where he died several days later. Never had the Queen needed him more.

Parliament had additionally been aggravated by the Queen's desire to dispose of the Crown by will. The members feared that Mary might, if such were her privilege, give the Crown to Philip. Opposition to the measure had been such that Gardiner had felt compelled to announce 'that nothing would be said about the King's authority or His Majesty's person'. For Philip who was now blunt in stating he could not return 'unless he has a certain promise from the Queen that she will crown him . . .' the disappointment was as intense as his wife's. Paget on a mission to the King, noted that even Philip's relatives were urging coronation: 'Queen Maria of Hungary [Philip's aunt] is the person who well-nigh daily writes letters on this subject . . . exhorting her [Mary] to put aside every consideration . . . and crown her husband . . .'. Mary lamely suggested she might have sufficient influence with several of the more powerful lords to effect a coronation without Parliament's authority. That she was willing even to conceive such a possibility in direct opposition to her marriage contract and her subject's wishes, vividly illustrates the pathetic extent to which the Queen was willing to go— anything that might bring Philip back to her.

Weekly, one or another of the remaining Spaniards packed their possessions and left the court; each departure was a fresh wrench for the Queen. De Noailles wrote, 'No one is left but his [Philip's] confessor and

[456]

nothing seems to remain for her. See now what a reward this Queen is getting for having, against the wishes of her people ... sought at a great expense a foreign husband. ... It is clear enough to anyone that ambition and lust alone prompted this marriage!'[4]

In her loneliness, Mary turned, as she often had before, to her faith. She spent hours in her Chapel, and on Maundy Thursday, 1556, in the Great Hall at Greenwich, she washed the feet of forty-one elderly poor and ragged women, one for each year of her life. With a long linen apron over her purple, marten-trimmed gown and a towel around her neck, Mary moved along the rows, washing, drying, and then kissing the cleansed feet of each of the women. Then salted fish, bread, wine, and alms were dispensed, after which shoes, stockings, and forty-one pennies were distributed. Finally, the purple gown itself was given to one of the women.

On Good Friday, Mary participated in the ancient ceremony of the cramp-rings, or 'touching for the King's evil', in which ill or infirm persons might approach their Queen to have a ring of their own and one of hers blessed by Mary and Cardinal Pole. Then, with prayers and invocation, Mary presented each sick person a 'golden coin called an angel'. With the coin, the Queen touched the spot where illness was evident, then passed a ribbon through the coin's centre, and asking each petitioner never to part with hallowed object, tied it around their necks. The ceremony was often long and taxing and one observer was deeply affected by Mary's 'great and rare example of goodness'. He said the Queen performed 'all those acts with such humility and love ... offering up her prayers to God with so great devotion and affection and enduring for so long awhile and so patiently so much fatigue ... that ... I dare assert that never was a Queen in Christendom of greater goodness than this one ...'.[5]

While Mary's relationship with several of her Council or nobles was often one of barely concealed impatience or antagonism, in her association with her subjects, she was at her best. Many of her people came to know and depend upon 'the Queen's goodness'. Unlike previous monarchs, they knew, she would organise no progress or hunting expedition when the harvest or haymaking was at hand, for in her years of country living, she had observed that every person, wagon, and horse was needed in the fields and could not be pressed into the royal service. Apparently, a few of her household officers were not so scrupulous. While spending several weeks at Croydon, at one of her mother's dower-houses, she visited the home of a collier and, while he ate his supper, heard that one of her household had 'pressed his cart from London and had not paid him'. He had asked for his money, 'but they had given him neither his money nor good answer'. Mary was incensed that anyone would use his position to deprive a poorer subject. 'Friend, is this true what you tell me?' she asked. Upon being assured it was, she returned to the dower-house, after telling the man to call for his money the next morning. At her residence, the Queen 'called the Comptroller and gave him such a reproof for not satisfying poor men . . .!' wrote Jane Dormer in her *Memoirs*. 'The Queen said that he had ill officers who gave neither money nor goods to poor men and that hereafter he should see it amended, for if she understood it again, he should hear it to his dis-pleasure . . .'.[6]

Imitating her mother, whom she had accompanied incognito so many years ago on similar occasions, Mary visited in the villagers' houses. Dressed simply, with one or two of her ladies, the Queen harked back to the pleasures of her childhood and dandled a baby on her knee as she spoke to her people directly. She listened to their opinions, their complaints, and their hopes. Days later, several of them might be mysti-fied by the arrival of a bundle of clean clothing, a small purse of coins, or the gift of a beast of labour for their fields.

Not only the poor, but also those who spent their lives in her service were recipients of the Queen's kindness. When one of her retainers, a keeper of Enfield Chase and Marylebone Forest suddenly died, Mary arrived at the window's home within the hour. Finding the bereaved woman weeping bitterly, the Queen 'took her by the hand and lifted her up and bade her be of good cheer for her children should be well provided for'. And Mary kept her promise. In later life, one of the child-ren wrote, 'Afterward my brother Richard and I, being the two eldest, were sent to Harrow school and were there till we were almost men'.[7]

Mary's closest confidant, now that Philip was gone, was Reginald Pole, and with him, her most serene hours were spent planning the physical restoration of the ruined abbeys and monasteries. With no attempt to hide her tears of joy and excitement, she greeted the Grey-friars when they returned to Greenwich. The Benedictine monks were now established at Westminster Abbey, and the Blackfrairs had re-claimed St Bartholomew's Hospital near the martyrs' flaming pyre in Smithfield. The Carthusians returned to Richmond, and Northumber-land's old Syon House was re-established as a Brigittine nunnery. In all these accomplishments, Reginald Pole was Mary's mainstay, for, as with the Queen, religion was the heart, soul, and fabric of his life. He lived in the Palace and was constantly accessible to his lonely cousin who, because they were so much alike, found solace in the Legate's companionship.

This very similarity, however, worked considerably to Mary's dis-advantage. Pole obediently wrote to Philip of the Queen's activities, her health, and the advice he gave her—advice which was not always to England's or Mary's benefit. Pole was no realist. An impractical drea-mer, with little regard for politics, he had, within weeks, abandoned the role of chief councillor conveyed to him by Philip. He did not attend

Council meetings and was consulted only when the ministers differed on a matter to be referred to the King. He interfered little with the burnings—'briars and brambles . . . cast into the fire', he called the executions. He had full faith in his bishops' ability to dispense justice. Instead, he urged the people to rebuild their despoiled and ruined parish churches and to be more generous in their almsgiving. Any discussion of Mary's poverty, of England's relations with Spain or France, of the people's growing resentment of the burnings, merely bored him.

And there was, surprisingly, more dissatisfaction with the martyrs' fate than either Queen or Council had anticipated. Mary had naïvely assumed the majority of her people would welcome a return to the Catholic faith. In this she was upheld by many of her older subjects who argued that God had not prospered the reformers, while those of the old faith, 'which our Queen and old Bishops have professed . . . how hath God prospered and kept them!' When England returned to Catholicism, it was, for many, a happy formality, an acknowledged restitution of the belief they had always practised in their hearts, even as they had, for safety's sake, adopted the outward observances of the reformed religion. The vast majority of gentlefolk, yeomen, farmers, and peasants were still devout Catholics, and Mary, who had felt their strength during her fight for the throne, had great confidence in them. For the others who had changed for reasons of expediency or security, she had only scorn—which she took small care to hide—knowing they would now also shift with the prevailing wind.

The Queen, Council, and bishops were genuinely misled in their collective appraisal of the temper of a large number of Englishmen. Since the days of Mary's youth, a whole generation had grown to adulthood hating and reviling the Pope, abjuring his authority, even though the split with Rome had occurred long before their birth. They were the inheritors of their parents' honest desire to seek and worship their God without the mandatory rituals and obligations of Catholicism. They were the 'graduates' of a Church which proclaimed a King and not a Pope as its Supreme Head. Growing up in a 'reformed' England, they were joined in their zeal by the intellectuals and the religious fanatics found in any social movement, as well as those Continental reformers who had swarmed to England during Edward's reign. In both strength and a genuine belief in their ideology, their numbers were formidable.

These were now the victims of the stake, the victims of a relentless and terrible persecution by which the Church sought to regain its lost authority. Though Philip had cautioned against too indiscriminate burnings, realizing Spain would bear the burden of hatred once he left England, the Council and bishops resumed the persecutions with vigour. There was no hurried or wanton destruction. Instead, a methodical system of interrogation, and an opportunity to recant, gave the prisoner ample time to reflect and save his skin if he desired. But few availed themselves of the opportunity. They seemed instead eagerly to commit themselves to flames, as though they might expunge by immolation any last mortal waverings of doubt or physical weakness.

In the spring of 1556, while Mary pursued her religious duties and visited the humbler of her subjects, Thomas Cranmer suffered at Oxford. The Church dearly wanted Cranmer's recantation. Such a denial would be a tremendous victory to offset the appeal to popular sympathy the burnings had aroused. What a supreme vindication of the heretics' agonising sufferings, what a triumphant success for the Mother Church to have the father of the *Book of Common Prayer* deny his own false creed!

Mary Tudor had prophesied that the man who had twisted and turned ecclesiastical and secular law to suit the needs of her father's marriages and divorces, to accommodate the demands of Somerset and Northumberland, would not prove staunch when threatened by the stake. The Queen had been right. A ceremony of public degradation in the quadrangle of Christ Church at Oxford had commenced Cranmer's final weeks. His robes were stripped from his worn body, his ageing head clipped of hair, his nails sheared—symbolising the removal of the holy oil which gave power to bless and sanctify. As several bishops stood nearby in tears, he was given a shabby garment and an old cap. Being led back to his prison cell, he told them sadly, 'All this needed not—I had myself done with this gear long ago.'

In an effort to convince Cranmer of his errors, Cardinal Pole sent him a long letter. Telling the prisoner he had 'corrupted Scripture and broken through the communion of saints . . . destroyed your King, the realm and the Church and have brought to perdition thousands of human souls', Pole urged Cranmer's repentance. 'See yourself as you are!' he advised. 'Are you so vain, are you so foolish, as to suppose that it has been left to *you* to find the meaning of these Scriptures which have been in the hands of the fathers of the Church for so many ages?' Pole was scornful of Cranmer's continued resistance, 'God have mercy on you!' he ended the letter, 'May you now see your crimes. . . !'[8]

It was this letter perhaps, combined with the visit of two noted Spanish theologians, De Soto and Friar Gardia, in which a mirror image held up for Cranmer's pitiful gaze, made him give way to honest doubts. Possibly his whole life—that life of compromise and vacillation —had been a travesty of firm and enduring faith; perhaps he had made an enormous mistake. In his unending hours of solitude, he lost the dedicated belief that had been his, and these doubts, combined with an understandable fear of an agonising death, unnerved him. His flexible mind sought some release, and within weeks, he had convinced himself he could submit. He wrote several recantations, renouncing the 'heresies' of Luther and Zwingli, styling himself 'the most wicked wretch that earth has ever borne', because in his handling of the divorce of Henry and Catherine of Aragon, he was 'the cause and author . . . of the calamities of the realm'. When that did not seem to suffice, he accepted that, since the King and Queen by consent of Parliament had received the Pope's authority, he, too, could now accept the Pope 'for chief head of this Church of England'.

But it was too late. Not only had he neglected to escape to the Continent when escape was still possible, but he had chosen to challenge the Queen, and during his subsequent imprisonment, had disdained the 'period of grace' given to all prisoners to reflect and recant. His prolonged resistance 'even to the last hour', the 'enormity of his sins, for one in his high place of trust', accurately forecast little compassion from Council or Church.

On March 21, 1556, Cranmer was brought from the Bocardo Prison to St Mary's church. As a special concession, the doomed man had received permission to address the parishioners—the citizens and students of Oxford—as well as those doctors, priests, and peers who had journeyed from London for the spectacle. Public admission of his recent recantation was expected, and all eyes were on the haggard old gentleman in the shabby gown and tattered square cap who listened patiently as Dr Cole, Provost of Eton, preached the funeral sermon. It was a moving moment for Cole who bore great affection for Cranmer, and he called gently to the disgraced prelate to address the congregation. 'I pray you, Mr Cranmer, to perform that now which you promised long ago— namely, that you would openly express the true and undoubted profession of your faith . . . that men may understand that you are a Catholic indeed.'

Thomas Cranmer rose and asked the people to pray for him, 'a most wretched caitiff and miserable sinner'. He said he had offended 'both against Heaven and earth more than my tongue can express'. By their prayers, he hoped he might find a place of refuge or succour. 'To Thee, oh Lord, do I run; to Thee do I humble myself', he finished his own petition.

And then, rising from his knees, he faced the silent audience and, his voice growing stronger with each word, told them that, following custom, he wished 'to give some good exhortation, that others may remember the same before their death, and be the better thereby . . .'. As he now approached the end of his life Cranmer said, 'it is no time to dissemble, whatsoever I have said or written in time past'. Instead, he wished them to know of 'the great thing which so much troubleth my conscience . . . and that is the setting abroad of a writing contrary to the truth, *which now I here renounce and refuse*, as things written with my hand contrary to the truth which I thought in my heart, and written for fear of death and to save my life . . .'.

Those in the church had come expecting to witness the further humiliation of the man more than anyone else responsible for the destruction of their spiritual past. In some measure, his degradation would compensate for their despoiled churches and their ruined monasteries. But the former Archbishop, once the highest prelate in the land, was not recanting. Instead, his voice was clear and seemingly imbued with a fervour belied by a wasted and tired body, as he disclaimed the 'bills and papers which I have written or signed with my hand . . . wherein I have written many things untrue. And, foreasmuch as my hand hath offended—writing contrary to my heart—therefore, shall my hand first be punished, for, when I come to the fire, it shall be first burned . . .'. He waved his offending hand high as he shouted, '*As for the Pope, I refuse him, as Christ's enemy and anti-Christ, with all his false doctrine! As for the Sacrament, I believe as I have taught in my Book—which my Book teacheth so true a doctrine of the Sacrament, that it shall stand at the last day before the judgment of God, where the Papistrical doctrine contrary thereto, shall be ashamed to show her face!*' [9]

At Cranmer's words, the congregation rose to their feet, their astonishment loud in their cries of protest, mingling with the voice of the now stern Dr Cole. 'Stop the heretic's mouth and take him away!' he shouted as Cranmer was roughly pushed from the church. As people ran to the stake, several implored Cranmer to reconsider, but the prisoner remained silent. As they neared the site of Latimer's and Ridley's execution, a friar shouted, 'Thou will drag with thee innumerable souls to Hell!' But as the doomed man was tied to the stake and the fire quickly kindled, he seemed not to hear. Instead, he was intent upon redeeming his promise. The man who for the greater part of his life had dissembled, compromised, or submitted, now boldly held his right hand over the searing flames, addressing it, 'This was the hand that wrote it . . . therefore, it shall suffer punishment first . . .'. Mercifully, the wood was dry and well laid, and as the flames rose around him, he prayed, 'Lord Jesu, receive my spirit, Lord Jesu, receive my spirit!'

The same day Thomas Cranmer was burned at Oxford, Cardinal Pole was ordained a priest at Lambeth Palace. The following day, a Sunday, he was consecrated Archbishop of Canterbury at the Friars Church at Greenwich.

Cranmer's death, the challenging reversal of his recantation, and the continued burnings, jolted a previously apathetic national consciousness into active revulsion. Mary had hoped the executions would prove a deterrent to heresy; instead they seemed almost to have the opposite effect. More than a hundred had suffered a barbarous death. The plight of many who awaited sentencing in miserable prisons, where they nearly froze or starved to death, enraged the people. Their anger was evident in one who wrote to the Bishop of London, 'As for the obtaining of your Popish purpose in suppressing of the truth, I put you out of doubt you shall not obtain it so long as you go this way to work . . . you have lost the hearts of twenty thousand that were rank Papists within this twelve months!'[10]

Again Mary seemed to have failed. Her apparent inability to manage her realm's affairs with any skill tore at her conscience day and night. The Queen was a disciplined woman, one who took pride in good organisation, in a minute attention to detail, and pleasure in the predictable results. Yet after her two and a half year reign, her subjects were still resistant to her husband and her religion—the two things dearest to her heart—and she could even question their loyalty to the Crown itself. Philip's continued absence only seemed to symbolise that failure.

In a moving ceremony in the Great Hall of the Duke of Brabant's Palace in Brussels, the Emperor Charles had abdicated his Empire to his son. Philip did not refrain from congratulating Mary on the many crowns his sovereignty bequeathed her. And the taunt was implicit that she was not sufficiently mistress in her own country to give him the desired Crown of England, too. Until that was possible, Philip seemed in little haste to return.

Shortly after Charles's abdication, the international scene had been further disturbed when the new Pope, Paul IV, a militant opportunist, took advantage of a temporary lull in the French-Spanish war to declare that he would drive the Spanish armies out of Italy. He refused to negotiate any peace with Philip's emissary, saying, 'We have already ordered that should he come, there will be a short halter for him!' Mary, therefore, was in the quixotic and distressing position of the piously Catholic sovereign whose husband was now at war with the Vicar of Christ on earth, the Pope himself.

And, finally, there was the irritating matter of Elizabeth. Realising the need for English support while fighting on both the French and Italian fronts, Philip desired one more prop in England, should anything happen to his Queen. Again he insisted that Elizabeth's marriage to Emmanuel Philibert, the Duke of Savoy, be concluded. Failing that, he offered his own son, the young Don Carlos. But, as the Venetian ambassador Michiel wrote, to his home court, 'It has been told me that the matter is urged and earnestly canvassed by the Queen . . . who conceived that by removing her [Elizabeth] bodily from hence, there will be a riddance of all the causes for scandal and disturbances'. But Elizabeth, apparently, would have none of it, for Michiel wrote, 'She (I understand) having said plainly that she will not marry, even were they to give her the King's son, or find any other greater prince . . .'.[11]

Mary had wished above all to placate Philip. But even overlooking Elizabeth's refusal, she was convinced in her heart the union could not be effected. The Queen remembered the opposition to her *own* marriage; she knew the hue and cry that would result if Elizabeth were forced to marry outside the realm. Elizabeth, as Mary was well aware, also knew that Parliamentary and public support were her greatest protection. So once again Mary was forced to deny her husband. It reduced her to tears of frustration and a gnawing anxiety that each incident only enlarged the void growing between them.

The departure of the last of the Spaniards in England had been particularly unpleasant, with citizens 'repeating a variety of foul language' as the foreigners rode towards Dover. 'The incident,' said Michiel, 'made for great rejoicing, well-nigh universally.' For Mary it only emphasised her blighted hopes. The affront hurt. The Wyatt rebellion had shaken her confidence. Now her people's apparent rejection, and Philip's absence which became more pronounced as his countrymen daily deserted her court, broke the Queen's heart. She had tried her best. She had endeavoured to bring her country back to the old ways, to make a marriage that might guard that heritage. After a childhood bright with promise, she had endured a young womanhood poisoned with persecution, cruel treatment, and neglect. Now with the Crown won at last, she must endure abandonment by her adored husband. She had accepted the spiritual domination of Pole and the Church, and in her name, dozens were burning at Smithfield and throughout the country every day. She had accepted the physical domination of the Spanish King who seemed more intent upon his own Empire's welfare than his wife's peace of mind, and a nation fearful of war and seething with resentment was the result. It all had its effect, and Michiel noted worriedly, 'As for many months, the Queen has passed from one sorrow to another . . . she is intent upon enduring her troubles as patiently as she can. To say the truth, her face has lost flesh greatly since I was last with her, the extreme need of her Consort's presence harassing her, as she told me, she also having within the last few days lost her sleep . . .'.[12]

Then, once more, Mary was confronted by an enormous challenge to her Crown. This time, however, those involved were not the simple Kentishmen of Wyatt's rebellion. Her opponents were men of quality and distinction, with connections near the throne. And once more in the middle, willingly or unwillingly, was Elizabeth.

The popular discontent was noted by Michiel as he wrote the Doge, 'For many days a comet has been visible and it still is, and with this opportunity, a gang of rogues, some twelve in number, who have been arrested, went about the City saying we should soon see the Day of Judgment when everything would be burned and consumed ...'. A few days later Michiel revealed disturbances 'of a far different root and origin ... which if carried into effect ... would have placed the Queen and the whole kingdom in great trouble ...'.

The plot, hatched by the 'traitors, heretics and outlaws'—the English expatriates at the French court—included such distinguished names as Dudley, Throckmorton, and Kingston. Previously Lord Clinton had visited the French King to demand the expulsion of the vocal English group. Assisted by their confederates in Switzerland and Germany, they had kept a tremendous wave of seditious literature pouring into England and worked constantly for the overthrow of Mary and the elevation of Elizabeth. Henri II had been reluctant to accommodate the Queen and understandably cautious in admitting the existence of the trouble-makers since they provided a powerful source of potential and organised resistance to England and Spain. Henri did not wish to endanger the truce with Philip—a truce he had every intention of ultimately breaking —for the time was not yet ripe. He urged Henry Dudley, a cousin of Northumberland, and his fellow conspirators to delay. Then, through his constable, he wrote to de Noailles in England, urging the same restraint. The treaty, whereby Henri was left in undisturbed possession of his conquests for five years 'is as honourable and as advantageous as we could desire ...' he said. Therefore, 'we must act cautiously, principally on your account, matters being as they are through this treaty. Above all, restrain Madame Elizabeth from stirring at all in the affair of which you have written to me; for that would be to ruin everything and lose the object of our plans. It is necessary to negotiate with great care and to await our opportunity'.[13]

The French King's delay unwittingly contributed to the uncovering of the plot. In England, those concerned in the conspiracy awaited word to begin the insurrection. Sir Anthony Kingston was to raise the West and march on London. Fire would be set in several places in the City to divert attention while the Crown treasure was taken from the Tower and the Mint. In France, meanwhile, Dudley would have organised the exiled English to return to secure Portsmouth where his associates would make sure 'the cannon was pegged'. Another malcontent, Richard Uvedale, would secure Yarmouth Castle and deliver the Isle of Wight to the French; John Throckmorton would enlist French aid and boats. With these points secured, the Queen deposed or dead, the English would be delivered from the abominable Spanish domination, Elizabeth would be elevated to the throne, and Courtenay might then return from his Italian exile to marry her.

The plot seemed foolproof, but the French king's hesitancy could not restrain the impatient revels chafing in England. The delay resulted in sufficient intelligence being given to Cardinal Pole and the quick arrest of all who could be found. The sheer audacity of the plot shocked the Queen and caused her to write despairingly to Philip, imploring him to return and noting that 'when she looks around and carefully considers the men about her, she scarcely sees one who has not done her an injury, or who would fail to do so again if he had the chance . . .'. She ended with the pathetic hope that she might 'in a short time comfort his Majesty with that which he seems to desire'. In other words, the Crown of England—a Crown which, even as it rested precariously on her own brow, was still one she hoped to bestow upon her husband.

Surrounded by enemies, men she had trusted, honoured in her court, pardoned for previous offences, and, in some instances, even paid their debts, Mary's courage almost broke. As the Tower opened to receive the prisoners, the Queen was further embittered that again her sister and Courtenay's cause had come between her and her people. It may well have been that painful and humilitating awareness which sent Mary into a retreat similar to that of her mistaken pregnancy. She remained in her chamber for weeks on end, sick in body, mind, and spirit, 'sleeping as little as three hours a night and guarded by harnessed [armoured] men'.

Her depression was not helped by the results of the surprise visit the Council ordered at Hatfield. There, the commissioners had discovered piles of seditious literature, anti-Catholic pamphlets, and scurrilous diatribes against Mary and Philip. Two of Elizabeth's chief household officers, the Italian teacher, Battista, her governess, Katherine Ashley, and three of her ladies-in-waiting went to the Tower as Elizabeth wept and wrung her hands in an astonished innocence. 'I am told that they have already confessed to having known about the conspiracy,' said Michiel, 'so not having revealed it, were there nothing else against them, they may probably not quit the Tower alive, this alone subjecting them to capital punishment.' The Venetian ambassador also noted that 'the governess was found in possession of those writings and scandalous books against the religion and against the King and Queen which were scattered about some months ago and published all over the Kingdom'.[14]

The details of the plot, the fate of the prisoners, and Elizabeth's possible complicity were all subjects of the Queen's anxious letters to Philip. 'it being creditable that nothing is done, nor does anything take place, without having the King's opinion about it, and hearing his will', said Michiel. Mary, indeed, seemed almost incapable of independent judgment; her illness had worsened, and her continued absence from court and the Council table only emphasised her failure to cope with the dangerous situation.

[466]

But Philip was pre-occupied with his own troubles. With the memory of the infamous Sack of Rome by the Emperor's troops some thirty years previously momentarily forgotten, the Pope at last persuaded the French King to break his truce with Spain. Paul IV offered Naples and Milan as sovereignties for Henri's two sons if the Spanish could be expelled from Italy. Fearing the double threat of French and Papal armies and confronted with his Empire's chronic shortage of men, money, and war *matériel*, Philip realized he could wage a successful war only with English help. Mary must be won to his cause, even if it meant that two Catholic Majesties must fight the Holy Father. And if anything should happen to his Queen—whom he understood to be in almost perpetual ill-health—Elizabeth's goodwill must be gained. She must be kept safe and in a position to support him, even if it meant his return to England to achieve.

Therefore, upon being informed of the latent treachery at Hatfield, Philip recommended leniency for Elizabeth. With a dissimulation worthy of the Princess's own, he requested his wife to extend mercy and understanding to her unfortunate sister. And to soften the advice, he again promised to return to England soon. On this occasion, however, it was a promise Philip meant to keep.

As the Queen, 'in transports of joy', awaited her husband's arrival, Elizabeth remained at Hatfield, a garrison of soldiers reminding her uncomfortably of her Woodstock detention. News was rare in her depleted household, and the fate of the conspirators weighed heavily on her. Dudley had escaped to France and Sir Anthony Kingston committed suicide en route to London; lesser victims were executed on Tower Hill. Katherine Ashley was freed from her Tower cell but deprived of her office of governess and 'forbidden ever again to go to her Ladyship'. Before her own anxiety had become acute, however, a surprising letter from the Queen relieved Elizabeth's apprehension over her own fate.

Philip had recommended mercy for Elizabeth, and, dutifully, the Queen had acquiesced. Though she harboured her own private thoughts as to the degree of Elizabeth's guilt, Mary would not disobey the King. There was also a bitter awareness that she could do little else. Any move she made against the Princess would bring a stinging reprisal from her enemies, from Elizabeth's friends on the Council, and from her own husband as well. Each had his reasons for favouring her sister.

Mary played her part well. She sent Sir Edward Hastings and several councillors to Hatfield to present a ring to the Princess 'as a token of loving salutation and a message of goodwill', which, noted one, 'is considered most gracious'. The messengers were to acquaint Elizabeth

[467]

with the reasons for 'the removal from about her person of folks . . . of evil suspicion . . . to warn her of the licentious life led, especially in matters of religion by her household". They were to inform her she was neither neglected nor hated, but loved and esteemed, and 'provided she continues to live becomingly to Her Majesty's liking', all would be well.

In order that Elizabeth might 'live becomingly', the Queen appointed Sir Thomas Pope, 'a rich and grave gentleman of good name', to supervise her sister's household. The Princess, whose previous experience pointed only too well to the danger from which she had again escaped, said she 'bewailed such things, though my name had not been in them, yet it vexeth me so much that the Devil owes me such a hate, as to put me in any part of his mischievous instigations . . .'. Elizabeth declined an invitation to come to court and contented herself instead with a letter to Mary which contained profuse protestation of fidelity:

. . . and like as I have been your faithful subject from the beginning of your reign, so shall no wicked persons cause me to change to the end of my life. And thus I commit Your Majesty to God's tuition, Who I beseech long time to preserve, ending with the new remembrance of my old suit, more than for that I should not be forgotten, than for I think it not remembered. . . .[15]

Elizabeth was not, however, likely to be forgotten. Within weeks Philip would arrive determined to effect a marriage between the Princess and the Duke of Savoy. But shortly before his arrival a small tragedy at Venice in 'a place called Lio [Lido]' occurred which would emphasise the importance of her marriage even more. There, Edward Courtenay 'for his honest recreation . . . to see his hawks fly upon a wasted ground, without any houses' was caught in a 'great tempest of wind and rain'. Disdaining to leave, he further refused to change his wet clothing upon returning home and, within several days, had 'entered into a continued hot ague, sometimes more vehement than at another . . . so that his tongue had so stopped his mouth, and his teeth so clove together . . .'[16] that he could not take the Sacrament at the end. Within hours, the Earl of Devon was dead. With the death of the last descendant of the White Rose, one powerful support for Elizabeth and a great threat to the Queen was removed.

Chapter Twenty-five

'NOTHING is thought of, nothing expected save this blessed return of the King,' aptly described Mary Tudor's anticipation in the following months. Philip's arrival was the one joyous augury in an existence otherwise beset by seemingly insurmountable problems. During the previous summer, the countryside had experienced a severe drought with the resultant scarcity of goods, inflated prices, and the predictable number of starving citizens. The people still muttered at the burnings, and everywhere an open resentment was expressed at the possibility of war. Many denounced Philip's expected return as a mere excuse to drag England into his conflicts. The French ambassador, de Noailles, had been replaced by his brother, François, who continued the policy of fostering English dislike of Philip—anything that might undermine Queen Mary's influence. Though Mary herself had countenanced no hostility toward the French King, his ministers scarcely concealed their passionate dislike of both the King and Queen. Henri took good advantage of the opportunity offered by 'two strings to his bow'—a blow at Philip was also a blow at Mary. The Queen might logically have assumed her marriage gave her protection from aggression. Instead it was now disastrously apparent she had submitted her country to all the dangers besetting Spain.

French prowlings around Calais—that small remnant of England in France, so cherished by the English and resented by the French—had increased and were worriedly noted in the Council. As they did in London, the French were anxious to foment trouble for Mary on the Continent as well. They preferred the English Queen as forgetful of her English heritage, as gloating over the martyrs' agonies and lusting after a younger husband. Lampoons and pamphlets from the English refugees in France, stripping Mary of every dignity, reached a hateful zenith; even threats of assassination were common. The expatriates said that if France attacked England, the French King 'would find plenty of hands ... to help him ashore, providing it was under the screen of the Lady Elizabeth'. De Noailles observed that if Mary assisted Philip, who

[469]

might conceivably be beaten, 'the Crown would be sure to fall from her head, and would roll so far that someone else might pick it up before she had done crying for her mistake'.

There was little doubt that by 'someone else', the ambassador meant Elizabeth. When the Princess had not spontaneously come to court following the Dudley conspiracy, Mary summoned her to Whitehall, supposedly for the Christmas festivities. Philip had written, making it abundantly clear he expected his wife's help in urging the marriage of her sister to Emmanuel Philibert, the Duke of Savoy, stressing the importance of Savoy's support of England as well as Spain. Though Mary had honest doubts that Parliament would agree to such a marriage, her loyalty to Philip demanded that she pursue the subject with Elizabeth.

Accordingly, in late November 'with a handsome retinue . . . including lords and gentlemen, upwards of two hundred horsemen clad in her own livery' Elizabeth arrived at Somerset House prepared to spend several months at court. Three days later she visited the Queen and 'was received very graciously and familiarly'. The visit, however, was not a success. Neither sister ever committed to paper what transpired, but the Venetian ambassador, from the words of one who was present, wrote that all went well until Elizabeth's marriage was proposed. Mary was fearful that, should Elizabeth's marriage not comply, Philip's return might be delayed, and when the Princess refused to consider marriage, the Queen 'quite lost her usual self-control and [is said] to have given the Princess a scolding . . .'. Mary's Spanish temper was rarely exercised; once unleashed, it could be awesome. The Queen remembered the unusual clemency she had extended the sister who seemed to be in the middle of every plot to dethrone her. She knew of Elizabeth's popularity with the people and with several on her Council. All her pent-up anger was suddenly unleashed, and enraged, she promised Elizabeth she would eliminate her from the succession and name Mary, Queen of Scots, as heir. The parting between the sisters was rancorous, and Elizabeth abruptly left for Hatfield the following day, with nothing resolved.

Meanwhile, Philip's letters stressed the importance of the marriage; he frankly told the Queen he would hold her responsible for any failure. Faced with an insistent husband and a stubborn sister, Mary was in the middle. She dreaded her husband's displeasure, yet the marriage could not be effected simply through the King's desire. At last, in a tear-stained letter, its crossed-out words and many erasures poignantly revealing her emotional plight, Mary discussed the issue:

. . . In my last letter to Your Highness, I made an offer to agree to the marriage, *provided I have the consent of the realm,* and so I will; but without such consent, I fear that neither Your Highness nor the realm will be well served. . . .

Meantime, Your Highness, has written in the said letters, that, if a Parliament shall go contrary, Your Highness will impute the fault to me.

I beg, in all humility, that Your Highness will defer this matter till your return, and then it will be manifest whether I am culpable or not. Otherwise, I shall live in apprehension of Your Majesty's displeasure, which would be worse to me than death; for I have already begun to taste it too much, to my regret. . . .

Truth to say, in my simple judgment (and under correction of Your Highness) and seeing that the Duke of Savoy will be at this hour entered on the campaign, *unless a member of the Council, the nobility, and kingdom are with Your Highness, I cannot find by what means the matter can be properly treated.* . . .[1]

The Queen's logic was undeniable, a logic Philip—far removed from the circumstances—would find difficult to accept. Mary would not and indeed, could not, marry her sister out of the realm if her Parliament and subjects found another foreign marriage distasteful. The Queen longed for her husband's understanding, even as she pondered her own attitude towards the sister who was the centre of contention. She was troubled over Elizabeth's growing popularity, a popularity reflected in the statement of Lord Braye, whose wife was one of Mary's closest friends. 'If my neighbour at Hatfield should come to the crown,' said the optimistic gentleman, 'I might hope to pay my debts and be my own man again.' For this and other unwise actions, the foolish noble was briefly lodged in the Tower while his tearful wife came to plead his cause with the Queen. Mary was gentle with her friend and impressed by the woman's devotion. After giving orders for Braye's release, the Queen sighed and told her lady-in-waiting Susan Clarencieux, 'God oft-times sends to good women evil husbands . . . !'

Mary's jealousy of her sister was plainly evident to the Venetian who commented, 'what disquiets her [Mary] most of all is to see the eyes and hearts of the nation already fixed on this Lady as successor to the Crown from despair of descent by the Queen', One reason for Mary's attitude, he said, 'was . . . it would be most grievous, not only to her but to anyone to see the illegitimate child of a criminal who was punished as a public strumpet on the point of inheriting the throne . . .'.

That Elizabeth had ceased to display the meek and agreeable disposition she had affected in the past is shown by the ambassador's description of the Queen's sister who, at twenty-four, had recognized her appeal to the people. 'Her face is comely, rather than handsome,' he wrote, 'but she has fine eyes, and above all a beautiful hand of which she makes a display.' After extolling Elizabeth's education, he provides a

[471]

rare glimpse of the young woman who could see the sun of public approval setting behind an ageing sister's head, a Queen who undoubtedly would leave no heir:

She [Elizabeth] is proud and haughty and although she knows she was born of such a mother, she nevertheless does not consider herself of inferior degree to the Queen. She prides herself on her father and glories in him—everybody saying that she also resembles him more than the Queen does and he, therefore, always liked her and had her brought up in the same way as the Queen . . .[2]*

Despite her brave departure from London, Elizabeth was shaken by the intensity of Mary's attack. The Tower and Woodstock were not far from her memory; with Philip's return, she might be physically forced into an unwelcome marriage. Once the security of Hatfield was attained —and an ominous silence continued from London—the Princess 'experienced an attack of jaundice and the "green sickness"'. Severe heart palpitations and a shortness of breath frightened her as much as it panicked her servants. One of her ladies-in-waiting, perhaps at Elizabeth's instigation, was sufficiently anxious that she sent a trusted friend, the Countess of Sussex, to de Noailles for advice, even asking asylum in France for Elizabeth. On this occasion, however, remembering their support of Northumberland, the French were not about to duplicate their error by aiding the wrong party. De Noailles sent a soothing message to Elizabeth, reminding her of Mary's behaviour during the Northumberland conspiracy. It was a lesson for Elizabeth, he said, and he advised her—if she wished ever to wear England's Crown—to emulate her sister and remain in England.†

At five o'clock in the afternoon of March 20, 1557, Philip returned to Greenwich. As he stepped from his barge and walked to a reunion with the wife he had not seen in nineteen months, sixteen pieces of ordnance 'shot off twice'. For two days the King and Queen remained in seclusion and, on the twenty-third, rode with 'all the nobles of the realm' across London Bridge where the Lord Mayor, aldermen, sheriffs, and representatives of the Guilds dressed in their finest liveries 'and with trumpets

* As her later life proved, Elizabeth could be—especially where her ego was involved —a mistress of delusion. This is one of the first instances of blatant self-deception. Henry was never close enough to Elizabeth to show any great feeling for her; neither did she enjoy the close family relationship and affection which Mary had had for the first ten years of her life, until Anne Boleyn came upon the scene.

† Later, as Bishop D'Acqs, de Noailles was not too modest to say that because of his advice, Queen Elizabeth really owed her Crown to him.

blowing with great joy' welcomed the returning King. Not the least happy to see the sovereign was the Council 'owing the great rewards they have had from him' of revenues from Spain and Flanders. One ambassador noted that 'he found by experience what my father used to say of this kingdom is perfectly true—that all, first to last, are venal and do anything for money'.[3]

Though Mary never doubted the righteousness of her husband's quarrel with France, it had deeply grieved her that war must also be waged with her spiritual father, the Pope. It is a measure of Philip's influence, however, that within a few days, his wife was haranguing the Council to observe the ancient treaties between Spain and England and support him with troops. The Council demurred. They stressed her marriage treaty which expressly forbade involving England in Spain's conflicts. At home, it pointed to the lack of food and the empty treasury, important hindrances in equipping an army. Troops were one thing; money was another. The Queen quietly sold Crown property equal to an annual rental of 100,000 crowns and placed the entire sum at Philip's disposal.

In the midst of the clamour caused by the scarcity of food, the levy of a subsidy to raise future funds and, above all, the hatred of the Spaniard which was so great 'that neither His Majesty nor the Queen are well looked on by the multitude', the antagonism toward the Crown became more bold. It showed itself in a brazen attempt to outwit the 'devilish devices of Mary, right and unworthy Queen . . . who, by both will of her father . . . and by the laws of this noble realm of England hath forfeit the Crown for a marriage with a stranger'. The treasonous words were uttered by Thomas Stafford, a member of the near-royal line of Buckingham. With some 100 other malcontents, Stafford sailed from France on April 24, 1557 landing on the Yorkshire Coast. Seizing Scarborough Castle, he insolently issued a proclamation in which he assumed the title, 'Protector and Governor of the Realm'. While there were those who predicted an instantaneous uprising or that the 'Lady Elizabeth would send her forces to fetch him or come to him herself, nothing happened. Grumble though they might of the Spanish marriage, and the possibility of war, not one of Mary Tudor's subjects was willing to gamble on another Protector. The Queen, too, had learned a lesson. She sent the Earl of Westmorland to take the castle and bring its foolhardy occupants to London where they were swiftly executed. Again Elizabeth was suspect, leading the Venetian ambassador to write to his home court, 'the relics of this crime remained upon the Lady Elizabeth. It was her luck that King Philip had returned from Flanders into England, by whose singular favour she again escaped this plunge'.[4]

The abortive Stafford conspiracy emphasized to the reluctant councillors the adroit manoeuvring of the English expatriates in France, as

[473]

well as the French King's merciless methods to overthrow Mary. Suddenly Philip's demands—helped along by a bit of outright bribery—did not seem so outrageous. Indeed, alarm was widespread following the Stafford débâcle. The fear of invasion burned in the beacons lit all across England. Poole, Southampton, and the Isle of Wight received extra contingents of soldiers. The worried councillors ultimately compromised and, at the end of May, 'by virtue of the old treaty between England and Flanders', 5,000 soldiers and 1,000 horses were made available for five months.

There was, surprisingly, little dissent from the people who preferred warfare to invasion. The many volunteers for Philip's army reasoned it better to fight on the Continent than on their native soil or on their leaky ships in the Channel. Maintenance of the Navy—the pride of Henry VIII—had suffered during Edward's reign, and Mary had been too impoverished to effect any great remedy. The Venetian ambassador expressed surprise at the willingness of those who came 'some from a longing for novelty . . . some from rivalry and desire of glory . . . some to obtain grace and favour with his Majesty and the Queen . . .'. The one major difficulty in equipping the troops reflected the poor food supply. The same ambassador said the departure date was delayed, 'from want of victuals which is so great as to be almost incredible'.[5]

On June 5, 1557, a formal Declaration of War was sent to Henri II for the injuries offered to the English Queen in his support of the Northumberland conspiracy, the Wyatt rebellion, and the attempt of young Stafford and similar rebels whom the French King had 'entertained in his realm'. The declaration emphasised England was fighting her own war; she was not merely allying herself in Spain's quarrels. Henri did not accept the fine distinction and said sourly, 'I foresaw this war; it is the pledge of the Queen of England's submission to the will of her husband!'

With his aim accomplished, Philip hoped to leave England, but tactfully, he spent one more month with his Queen, exhibiting an understanding and tolerance that caused Michiel, the Venetian ambassador, to say the King was 'above all, a person who had such good companionship and good treatment as she [Mary] enjoyed with him. . . . In truth, no one could have been a better husband to her'. Perhaps Philip could see in the Queen's tired features, that once they were apart, they would not meet again. A compassionate and sympathetic portrait of Mary, valuable since it does much to refute the unattractive and false impression of the Queen so deliberately fostered during the next reign was drawn by Michiel. Calling Mary 'a very great and rare example of virtue and magnanimity, a real portrait of patience and humility and of the true fear of God', he details the sorrows of her past trials 'against which it seems impossible for her to have been able to struggle had she not been assisted by some favour from God, and by some especial care which He has of her innocence'. His description continues:

She is of low, rather than of middling stature, but although short, she has no personal defects in her limbs, nor is any part of her body deformed.* She is of spare and delicate frame, quite unlike her father who was tall and stout; nor does she resemble her mother, who, if not tall, was nevertheless massive. Her face is well-formed, as shown by her features and lineaments, and as seen by her portraits. When younger, she was considered not merely tolerably handsome, but of beauty exceeding mediocrity. At present, with the exception of some wrinkles caused more by anxieties than by age, which make her appear some years older, her aspect, for the rest, is very grave.[6]

Michiel spoke of the Queen's 'facility and quickness' in mind, and his praise of her courage and morale was unstinted:

. . . in certain things she is singular and without an equal, for, not only is she brave and valiant, unlike other timid and spiritless women, but so courageous and resolute, that neither in adversity nor peril, did she ever display or commit any act of cowardice. . . . maintaining always, on the contrary, a wonderful grandeur and dignity. . . .[7]

The summer of 'good companionship and good treatment', of tilts and jousts at Greenwich and Whitehall, of hunting 'the great hart' at Hampton Court, of walking in procession on Corpus Christi Day through the Great Hall and the courtyard 'attended with as goodly singing as ever was heard', was soon to end. Perhaps to have some remembrance of those blessed months with her husband, Mary caused their portrait to be painted. The King and Queen assembled for sittings in a State-chamber at Whitehall Palace, beneath an open casement window through which St Paul's and other City churches could be seen and the cries of the boatmen from the river wherries and eel boats could be heard. Two 'little hounds' lay docilely at their Majesties' feet. Philip stood near his wife who was seated under a canopied cloth of estate. Mary had dressed 'with royal magnificence, in a gold-cloth brocaded kirtle, hanging *rebras* sleeves and a jewelled hood'. Philip's plain gold band was on her marriage finger, her beautiful pearl on her breast.

The artist did not linger at his work, for the King's presence on the

* What may seem an odd statement is more understandable when it is known that there were several near-deformities in the Tudor line. Margaret Beaufort, Mary Tudor's great-grandmother, was an exceedingly small person and Mary, apparently, had inherited her build. A sister of Lady Jane Grey, Mary Grey, was so small as to be called a dwarf.

Continent was urgent. On July 1, all was ready. Though she was far from well and had to travel in a litter. Mary disdained an easy farewell at Greenwich. Instead, in her jolting conveyance, she rode the full distance from Gravesend through Canterbury to Dover, where the fleet that would take her husband to the Continent and to war, awaited him. They remained at Dover for two days and, on the fifth, a weakened Queen, clinging to her husband's arm, walked to the very edge of the sea and there, in the sand, embraced him for the last time. She watched the barge carrying him to the waiting galleon and then, unable to bear the sight of the actual departure, rejoined her ladies who waited at a respectful distance. Closing the curtains of her litter, Mary gave way to a wife's private tears. Immediately, the procession turned westwards towards Greenwich, back to royal duties, loneliness—and war.

Fortune at once favoured Philip as, at the same time, it abandoned the Queen. With Mary's troops and monies—and the knowledge these would indisputably be augmented if the necessity arose—the King's forces, under the Duke of Savoy, sustained a great victory at the battle of St Quentin on August 10. 'The town was . . . set on fire and a great piece of it burnt. Many were burnt in cellars and were killed immediately. Women and children gave such pitiful cries that it would grieve any Christian heart', the Lord Privy Seal wrote to William Cecil. On the twenty-eighth, Cambray fell and the way to Paris lay open to the English and Spanish troops. Stunned at their enemies' brilliant success, the French recalled the Duke of Guise's forces from Italy, leaving the Pope, who had been 'content to be the soul of the enterprise with France the body' with little alternative other than to make an uneasy peace.

In London, the celebrations of Thanksgiving commencing with the victory of St Quentin exploded with the news of the triumph at Cambray. The City was illuminated from dusk to dawn by bonfires. Church bells pealed, their high clamour mixed with the *Te Deums* and singing processions which wound rejoicing through the streets, and great throngs, dipping frequently into conduits running with free wine, banqueted throughout the night.

In the midst of the celebration, the Queen, too, had cause for thanksgiving, for again she experienced all the symptoms of pregnancy. The joyous news was carried to Philip who, whatever his private thoughts, proclaimed his happiness. And with the message went a warning to the Queen and Council that now that French forces had been recalled from Italy, England should look to that 'trophy of their ancient wars', the Pale of Calais. This low-lying, marshy, generally unwholesome area of nearly 120 square miles was all that remained of English conquests in

[476]

France, and was considered 'the brightest jewel in the English crown'. In 1541, Henry VIII had strengthened the defences of Calais by enlarging and clearing the dikes, shoring up the embankments, and repairing the fortress-castle. The Protector, too concerned with affairs at home, had shamefully neglected maintaining the Pale's defences, and Mary, with no money and preoccupied with gratifying the Church and her husband, had done nothing. Subsequently, as the fortifications drastically decayed, the morale within the town disintegrated; Calais was as badly in need of physical reinforcements as it was of rebuilding.

Philip's warning was not the first the King had given. However, with its magnificent tendency to procrastinate—and the prevalently gloomy reality of an empty exchequer—the obtuse English Council had done nothing. Therefore, when vast numbers of the French appeared seemingly out of nowhere and took the opposite town of Rysbank, Calais was suddenly—for the first time within living memory—in the incredible position of defending its very existence.

On January 4, 1558, at seven o'clock in the evening, a frantic Lord Grey de Wilton, the Governor of Guisnes, a nearby English fortress within the Pale, wrote to the Queen informing her the French were in the marshes between that town and Calais, that they had placed their cannon to threaten the town 'and are encamped upon St Peter's heath before it!' Grey implored the Queen's aid in the form of men, ordnance, and food, writing bitterly, '. . . now I am clean cut off from all relief and aid, which I looked to have, both out of England and from Calais, and know not how to have help by any means, either of man or victuals'. Prophetically, he ended, 'There resteth now none other way for the succour of Calais, and for the rest of your Highness's places on this side. . . .' The letter was endorsed, 'Haste! Haste! Haste! Post Haste for thy life! For thy life!'[8] It was the last communication received before Calais was lost.

Similarly frantic appeals had gone to Philip who quickly commissioned the Duke of Savoy to levy troops for the defence of Calais. But it was too late. The English had thrown up earthworks and barricades and fortified the road between the castle and the town—but opposed as they were by some 30,000 French constantly reinforced by supplies from Boulogne, there was never any real contest. Gale winds and bitter cold which had frozen the dikes hampered both sides. On the eighth, after two days of bombardment, the guarding wall was breached by gunfire, and it was only a matter of time before 'one of the inhabitants appeared on the ramparts with a flag of truce, praying the beseigers not to fire . . . as the townspeople were willing to surrender'. Enemy troops poured in and the inhabitants were roughly herded into the Churches of Our Lady and St Nicholas and made to place all their gold, silver, and jewellery upon the high altars while they listened to the

[477]

clamour of the French sacking their homes. All the long night and following day, the heartrending sounds echoed in their ears as they wondered at their own fate. Once the formal surrender had taken place, however, all were unceremoniously shipped—minus their possessions— to the homeland many had never before seen.

Across the Channel, the English forces had hastily deployed troops. supplies, and ordnance for a belated relief of their beseiged outpost. But heavy westerly gale winds caused the vessels to slip their moorings and make their way instead into the Thames with dismantled spar and rigging; others were dashed upon the Dover sands, mute evidence of nature's fury. When the ships Philip had sent from Antwerp and Dunkirk to escort the English fleet across the Channel arrived, the weather had already done its worst.

It took two days for the calamitous news to reach Dover. It took longer to accept that the great Pale—all that remained of Plantagenet conquests in France—was now irretrievably lost. 'On the 10th day of January, heavy news came to England', wrote Henry Machyn, a London undertaker, 'that the French had won Calais, the which was the heaviest tidings . . . that ever was heard of, for like a traitor, it was sold and delivered unto them'.[9] Though the citizens of Calais had fought nobly, it was suspected that many of the same disgruntled English expatriates who had sought to undermine the Queen for years had infiltrated the whole Pale. The suspicions were confirmed when Savoy, asking how Calais could have been lost so easily, was told that 'the cause was not only by the weakness of the castle and lack of men'. Many supposedly loyal English had left, he was informed, 'and the French had intelligence of all our estate . . .'. Those within the town with the most to gain by non-resistance had been the first to urge a quick surrender. And sharing equal blame was the 'Council at home and conspiracy of traitors elsewhere . . .' helped by the 'most terrible tempests of contrary winds and weather'.

The loss of Calais was an overwhelming personal calamity for Mary Tudor. Once more the galling spectre of failure ate at her conscience and heart. Ten days later the news of the fall of Guisnes—though stoutly and honourably defended by Lord Grey—constituted a national disaster. Mary was bitterly aware of the blow to British pride and morale and her own subsequent loss of prestige. People said she had enriched the Church at the expense of national security and raised money on Philip's behalf while endangering English possessions abroad. The grinding humiliation of her country's defeat in France was such that, ailing and miserable, Mary said that when she died and her body was opened, the word 'Calais' would be found written on her heart.

Philip sent his trusted friend, the Count de Feria, to England in late January to assess English tempers and examine the possibility of raising

[478]

additional funds and troops. Feria's first encounter with English re-action to war came at Dover. Incensed by the loss of Calais, recruits swarmed the entry port anxious to redeem the national honour. But their enthusiasm was not reflected in either Council or Parliament which, though stung by the defeat, pleaded poverty to Feria's requests for more help. Through his minister, Philip counselled the Queen to 'apply all her money to defending the English coast'—a subtlety not lost on the Council. Such forces might also conceivably be used on the Continent should the need arise. Mary's loss of power within her government ment was obvious to Feria. The stubborn ministers procrastinated and evaded the Count, and relations between them became strained, caus-ing Feria to write despairingly to Philip, 'Before God I can do no more, Sire! I do not know what to make of these people . . . from morning to night and from night to morning, they are changing their minds about everything. . . . If it were only for their sakes, I should like to leave them to the mercy of those who would treat them as they deserve! The Queen does and says all she can and she really has spirit and goodwill, but in all else there is trouble', Feria noted, as his ill-contained scorn for the Coun-cil again erupted. 'I really do not know which is the worst disposed to your interest. But I know that those whom you favoured most serve you the least. . . .'[10] Feria also said that Mary was much thinner, prone to more frequent despondency, and yearned only for her husband's return.

The Queen's health was indeed a source of deep concern for those who again hoped for a living heir. Mary's personality seemed rapidly deteriorating in the aftermath of sleepless nights during which, taut, her hands clutching her distended stomach, she nervously roamed the Palace galleries. Perhaps those solitary walks in the early morning hours revealed much that hurt—her own inadequacy, the solitary existence she must face if her child did not live, and her possible abandonment by the husband. From her people, she had nothing but a scornful pity and a deepening unpopularity. Perhaps in those pale hours, the Queen also faced the overwhelming reason for her subjects' lost favour—her mar-riage. All the mischief ensuing from that union, she must, apparently, bear alone. Tears were an easy release and Mary became prone to odd quirks of behaviour. As her self-control became more erratic, her ladies found her, on one occasion, attempting to put together a picture of Philip which, in a moment of pique, she had cut into many pieces.

Mary's edginess erupted in other ways. In April Gustavus Adolphus, the King of Sweden, requested the hand of Elizabeth for his son Eric. He flouted protocol and tradition by sending a secret mission to the young lady herself instead of the Queen, saying he 'thought it most proper to make the first application to herself [Elizabeth] in order to ascertain whether it would be agreeable to her . . .'. Prudently, the Prin-cess replied that 'she could not listen to any proposals . . . that were not conveyed to her through the Queen's authority' and insisted that, left to her own choice, she preferred and would *always* prefer the single life. Hearing of the situation through Elizabeth's custodian, Sir Thomas Pope, Mary commended her sister for her behaviour. For the Swedish King, she had nothing but anger and 'thought he had committed a gross breach of propriety in going to Hatfield . . .'. The Queen's reaction was more than personal affront. She confessed her anxiety to Feria. If Philip heard of the proposal, 'she was in great trouble, fearing that your Majesty would blame her for not having carried through that affair last year [with Savoy]', Feria wrote to the King. Though Elizabeth's sensible reaction had calmed Mary a little, 'she is still in a terrible taking about it', he said.

At the Swedish proposal, Elizabeth begged the Queen 'to give me leave to remain in that estate . . . which, of all others, best liked me or pleased me'. She asked for Mary's continued indulgence for, 'I persuade myself there is not any kind of life comparable to it'. Sir Thomas Pope, with the confidence of long friendship, chided Elizabeth that 'few or none would believe but her Grace would not be right well contented to marry, if there were some honourable marriage offered her by the Queen's Highness . . .'. To which, Elizabeth answered almost belligerently, 'What I shall do hereafter I know not; but I assure you, upon my truth and fidelity, and as God be merciful unto me, I am not at this time otherwise minded than I have declared unto you, no, though I were offered the greatest prince in all Europe!'[11]

Though it was beyond either the Queen's or Pope's discernment, Elizabeth's attitude towards marriage was the visible product of her shrewdness. She had observed Mary's loss of power and the demoralising lack of respect for the Crown while the English nation chafed at the Spanish domination. Its chronic poverty and poor defences could be laid to Mary's preoccupation with her husband, marriage, and Church. Elizabeth could remember the bright hopes with which Mary had ascended the throne. Then the whole country had been at her feet, their love and respect unquestioned. Now, five years later, there seemed little but rancour remaining. At her marriage, the Queen ceased maintaining the balance of power behind France, England, and Spain—a practice her father and old Cardinal Wolsey had honed to perfection. Now England must be perpetually watchful that it did not become a Spanish dependency. Poor Mary! The lessons of the last five years had been well observed—and were never to be forgotten—by the Queen's sister.

By the end of April Mary had to admit her pregnancy was once again an illusion. Amid her collapsing hopes, she persuaded herself that Philip might yet come to her. Horses and couriers were sent to Dover and ships ordered to await him. But all in vain. Again Feria recounted the pressure of the summer campaign, the 'one thousand other things' which kept the King abroad and intimated that, despite her ill-health and pregnancy disappointment, it was unreasonable for the Queen to expect him. Mary was left to face the brutal fact that, without a child, her husband might never return to England. She was getting older and she was sick; any future visits would be necessitated more by expediency than a desire for her company.

When Philip's city of Dunkirk was lost to the French, the Queen emerged temporarily from her seclusion. She proposed to send the English fleet to the King's aid, but the Council, weary of the demanding Feria and fearful of the nation's defence, vetoed it. For once the Council was firm. Feria wrote, 'To tell your Majesty the truth, I did not dare to contradict them, for I saw that if but four French ships were to land their companies in England, they would overturn everything'. With nothing to be gained, Feria's recall was immediate, and before his departure, his betrothal to the beautiful, twenty-one-year-old Jane Dormer, the Queen's beloved lady-in-waiting, was announced. Feria left with the opinion that not only was Mary mortally ill, but the religious and political system under which the Queen had existed was also dying. The eyes of the nation—and the Council—were now fixed firmly on the Princess Elizabeth.

The summer and autumn of 1558 were a wretched time for the English people, 'for there were many strange accidents at home that struck terror in them. In July, thunder broke near Nottingham with such violence that it beat down two little towns, with all the houses and churches in them. . . . The river Trent . . . broke out with extraordinary violence; many trees were plucked up by the roots, and with it there was such a wind that carried man and children a good way and dashed them against trees or houses. Hailstones fell that were 15 inches in other places . . .'.[12] An epidemic of quartan fever contributed to many deaths and, compounding the national food emergency, the cold wet weather promised little relief for the following months.

The challenges in pursuing war with France, or directing a rebellious Council seeking to deal with the country's internal problems, often escaped the ill Queen. Certainly the vicious enormities of injustice daily committed in her name at the stake were beyond her enterprise. Mary's eyes were fixed as always on the spiritual. Before her dream of bearing an heir had vanished forever, 'thinking myself to be with child in lawful marriage', she had made her will. Should she die in the 'perils of childbirth which by God's ordinance remain to all women . . .' she consigned her body to her executors, asking for 'daily Masses, Suffrages, and

Prayers'. She requested that the body of her mother, Catherine of Aragon, be brought from its lonely resting place at Peterborough Cathedral and 'laid nigh the place of my sepulchre ...'. The Queen's will was a trusting document, pitiful in its naïve conviction that her wishes would be honoured. A long list of bequests was a testament to her faith and generosity and a desire to guarantee her country's religious future, even from the grave. The monies to the religious houses at Sheen, Syon, and St Bartholomew's, to the Carthusians, the Observant Friars, and the 'poor nuns at Langley', reflected Mary's concern for those who had suffered so greatly during Edward's reign. Destitute scholars at Oxford and Cambridge were left £500 and 'for the relief and help of the poor and old soldiers'. Mary asked that some house—the first of its kind in England—be founded for them and left 400 marks yearly for its support. The Queen asked that her debts be paid and, fearful that her servants 'would have no certainty of living ... after my decease', left £2,000 to be distributed among them, and the executors were asked 'to have special regard unto such as have served me longest ...'.

At the end of the will, Mary remembered her husband. 'And I do humbly beseech my said most dearest lord and husband to accept of my bequest, and to keep for a memory of me, one jewel, being a table diamond which the Emperor's Majesty ... sent unto me ...'. She left the Crown of England to 'any issue and fruit of my body according to the laws of this realm'. For the 'order, government and rule of my said issue, and of my said Imperial Crown ... I especially recommend ... my said most dear and well-beloved husband'. She asked her subjects 'to bear and owe unto His Highness, the same duty and love that they naturally ... owe unto me ... which, I trust, he shall enjoy ...'.[13]

At the bottom of each page, she signed her name, 'Marye, The Quene'. The paragraph relating to Philip was written in the Queen's own hand.

In late October, Surian, the new Venetian ambassador, at Philip's court, wrote: 'A few days ago His Majesty received news from England that the Queen was grievously ill and her life in danger.... It was immediately determined to send the Count de Feria to visit the Queen ... and to treat another affair which ... is the marriage of my Lady Elizabeth, to keep that kingdom in any event in the hands of a person in Her Majesty's confidence'. Feria was to 'revive this project', said Surian, 'and dispose the Queen to consent to the Lady Elizabeth being married ... with the hope of succeeding to the Crown ...'. The ambassador stressed the importance of secrecy, for 'were the French to come to know it, they would easily find means to thwart the project, as the greater part of England is opposed to the Queen and most hostile to King Philip ...

and much inclined towards my Lady Elizabeth who has always shown a greater liking for the French faction . . .'.[14]

In England, Mary had taken to her bed, a victim of the fever that was decimating her subjects. Her lady-in-waiting, Jane Dormer, had also been ill, much to Mary's distress. 'It is strange the care and regard Her Majesty had of her—more like a mother or sister—than her Queen and mistress', said an observer. When Mary moved from Hampton Court to her father's 'house in the fields', St James's Palace, she thoughtfully sent Jane ahead in the royal litter. Later, upon arrival at the Palace, 'the first she asked for was Jane Dormer, who met her at the stairfoot and told her she was reasonably well. The Queen answered weakly, 'So am not I . . .' and took to her chamber and never came abroad again'. Mary's physicians worriedly noted the 'superfluity of black bile' as the fever grew stronger. Her discomfort was heightened by a return of her 'old guest' and the usual stress occasioned whenever it was 'the fall of the leaf'. Outside the Palace, groups of anxious citizens gathered, having walked from the City to await news of their sovereign. Across the fields, in the direction of the abbey, down 'the Streete', and on through the Strand towards Smithfield, the air was hazy with the smoke of the martyrs' burnings and odorous with the smell of charred flesh.

On October 18, as she reluctantly faced the issue of the succession, the mortally ill Queen added a codicil to her will. There was no child to inherit the Crown, no one other than Anne Boleyn's daughter whose birth twenty-five years ago had climaxed all 'the troubles' which had been unleashed upon the realm. Mary had no choice; the Crown must go as her father's will and Parliament ruled. It was no solace to the dying Queen to know the people would rejoice at Elizabeth's accession, but with the practical common sense so natural to her, Mary did not evade reality. Therefore, 'feeling my self weak in body (and yet of whole and perfect remembrance, our Lord be thanked), she required her executors to 'appoint . . . such portion of treasure, as would be needed to execute her previous bequests. As to the succession, she did not pay Elizabeth the compliment of using her name or designating her as sister, merely referring to 'my next heir and successor, by the laws and statutes of this realm . . . . As such, the new Queen was to be mindful of the advice and care of Mary's husband, Philip, whom she should regard "as a father in his care, as a brother or member of this realm in his love and fervour and as a most assured and undoubted friend in his power and strength . . .'.[15]

Feria arrived in England on November 9 and went immediately to the Queen's bedside. Mary was too weak to read the letter the Count carried from Philip. She smiled wanly at his glib excuses for the King's continued absence and declared herself 'well content'. Alarmed, Feria left for a meeting with the Privy Council. He declared Philip's approval of Elizabeth and emphasized he was there 'to serve her and to give her all the assistance in his power, to help her in entering into possession of the Crown . . .'. Then, mindful of the order that Elizabeth must be won to Philip's cause, he visited the Princess herself.

The meeting took place at the home of Lord Clinton some thirteen miles from London. Elizabeth greeted him warmly, but to Feria's discerning eye, 'not so cordially as on former occasions'. The Count, Lady Clinton, and Elizabeth dined together, afterwards joining several ladies-in-waiting where Feria, conversing in Spanish, was requested by Elizabeth to speak in English so her companions might understand. Feria heartily replied, 'he would be happy for the whole world to hear what he had to say', and launched into a profuse account of Philip's admiration for the Princess and his warm interest in her future. If anyone present thought such obsequious flattery of the dying sovereign's sister in questionable taste, they gave no sign. Elizabeth seemed pleased by Feria's attention. She was frank to say she was greatly beholden to the King because of his intervention with the Queen at the time of her Woodstock detention; he had since given her every evidence of friendship. Encouraged by the young woman's cordiality, Feria stressed Philip's preference for her, inferring her right in the succession was due as much to the King's pleasure as to any desire of the Parliament or the authority of her father's will. To which Elizabeth only looked incredulous. In one moment, he realised his mistake, for the Princess—caution momentarily forgotten—appeared highly indignant 'at the things that have been done against her during her sister's reign'. In a rare outburst, she addressed Feria at length, telling him she had lived on only £3,000 yearly, 'while the King has received large sums of money!' She told of the pressures upon her to marry and was frank to say that she knew the Queen had lost the love and favour of the people 'by marrying a foreigner'. Ignoring Feria's pained reaction, she proclaimed herself much attached to the English people, declaring that it was *they* 'that have placed her in the position she now holds as the declared successor to the Crown'. The people 'were all on her side', Elizabeth boasted, and Feria was forced to admit that such was 'indeed true'.

Elizabeth firmly refused to acknowledge that she owed Philip anything but gratitude. She owed nothing to the Council or the other nobles either, she said, though she could not refrain from stating, 'that they had all pledged themselves to remain faithful . . . to her'—further evidence of the fickle nature of those who now flocked to the heiress-presumptive's side, even before their dying Queen had drawn her last breath.

Shaken Feria returned to London, not as condescendingly confident as when he had left to bestow the right to England's Crown upon

Elizabeth. Neither was he optimistic about the religious future of the country, for he had assessed those who now surrounded the Princess. He wrote to Philip of the interview, giving his opinion of Elizabeth. 'It appears to me,' he noted, 'that she is a woman of extreme vanity, but acute. She seems greatly to admire her father's system of government. I fear much that in religions she will not go right, as she seemed inclined to favour men who are supposed to be heretics, and they tell me the ladies who are about her are also. . . . Indeed there is not a heretic or traitor in all the country who has not started—as if from the grave—to seek her with expressions of the greatest pleasure . . .'[16] was Feria's prophetic appraisal.

He sought out a councillor, William Paget, and asked his support in furthering Savoy as a husband for the Princess. Surprisingly, Paget would have no part of the scheme. He informed Feria that he 'did not intend to meddle'. He had urged the match between Philip and Mary, he said, and 'it turned out ill . . .'. In the curt words of his old friend, even one as dedicated as Feria undoubtedly could see the final turning of the tide.

The Queen of England lingered on as the nation held its breath. 'Every man's mind was travailed with strange confusions', said one citizen, 'every report was greedily inquired and received, all truths suspected, diverse tales believed, and improbable conjectures hatched and nourished. Invasion of strangers, civil dissensions, the doubtful disposition of the succeeding Prince, were cast in every man's conceit as present perils—but no man did busy his wits in contriving remedies.' All activity seemed to come to a standstill as the spirit of Mary Tudor sought release from a life which no longer offered solace of any kind.

To share in the good fortune of the English Crown being bestowed on the Queen of Scots, should Elizabeth not succeed, the French Dauphin wed the sixteen-year-old Mary Stuart. The move was not lost on Philip who requested Mary to give some official designation of Elizabeth as her successor. Dutifully—for it was not in her nature even on her deathbed to refuse Philip anything—the dying Queen complied. She sent Jane Dormer, now the Countess de Feria, to Elizabeth at Hatfield with a 'precious casket of gems . . . which he [Philip] particularly knew Elizabeth admired'. In addition to the jewellery, Jane was to extract from Elizabeth the promise that Mary's debts would be paid, her servants cared for, and that the Princess would 'keep religion as she found it'. Elizabeth answered, 'If it be God's Will that I come to this dignity, my will is none other than to keep the good Faith of my sister. . . .' She said she 'did hear two Masses daily, one for the living and another for the

[485]

dead ...'. Jane thought she seemed 'extraordinarily devout to our Blessed Lady ... and prayed God that the earth might open and swallow her up alive, if she were not a Roman Catholic!'[17]

At St James's Mary rapidly neared death. She endured periods of unconsciousness and then, with that notable lack of fuss which so characterized her, returned to a lucid consciousness. Then 'she comforted those of them that grieved about her. She told them what good dreams she had, seeing many little children like angels play before her, singing pleasing notes, giving her more than earthly comfort ...'. Mary's pleasant view of her afterlife seemed to give her a cheerfulness which she attempted to communicate to the sorrowing few who remained with her. The Queen's compassionate attitude led Jane Dormer —so happy now in her marriage—to say bitterly, 'From the time of her mother's trouble, this Queen had daily use of patience and few days of comfort ...'.[18]

But all 'the troubles' were now over for Mary Tudor. At daybreak on November 17, after a period of unconsciousness lasting for several hours, she awakened obviously in control of herself and seemed 'composed ... even cheerful'. The vast bedchamber in St James's Palace was nearly deserted, and outside in the fields, a few stragglers bent against the wind sweeping across the marshy ground as they made their way to their daily vigil at the Palace gates. Inside the sickroom, the faithful few—old Susan Clarencieux and Jane Dormer—their eyes swollen and reddened with tears, gazed sadly at the wasted form of the Queen of England, whose breathing seemed difficult but whose features, nevertheless, mirrored a peaceful calm. With native simplicity, Mary Tudor embraced death. She had received Extreme Unction and now followed the Mass, her pale lips silently mouthing the beloved words and following the service with devoted attention. 'At the levitation of the Sacrament, the strength of her body and use of her tongue being taken away, yet nevertheless she, at the instant, lifted up her eyes ... and in the benediction of the Church, she bowed down her head and withal yielded a mild and glorious spirit into the hands of her Maker.'[19] At the very end, she spoke faintly but clearly, 'Misere nobis, Misere nobis, Dona nobis pacem' gazing on the elevated Host as her eyes filled with tears.

With her last words a request for mercy and peace, she—who was to endure the iniquity of the centuries—turned her head serenely on her pillow, sighed deeply, and as her ladies said, 'seemed only to go to sleep'. The benign moment, one of the few of her life, had been one of deep peace.

Twelve hours later in Lambeth Palace, Reginald Pole, the Archbishop of Canterbury, died of the same fever. When informed of Mary's passing, he alluded to 'the similarity of their dispositions' and said 'that in the course of the Queen's life, and of his own, he had ever remarked a great conformity as she, like himself, had been harassed during many years, for one and the same cause . . .'. At death, the Cardinal, too, had 'just drifted off to sleep . . .'. Whatever their faults—and they were many —the God who received such loving attention from the Queen and the Cardinal, at the end bestowed upon his devoted subjects a peaceful departure from their earthly life.

A Queen

Chapter Twenty-six

AT Hatfield the scene was very different. The Great North Road swarmed with place-seekers, with nobles and their retainers, with defecting members of the Privy Council and foreign emissaries. They, along with plain and simple Englishmen, hurried anxiously to swear fealty to the new monarch. Outside, in the grounds of the old Palace where the curious lingered—and waited—the atmosphere was that of a holiday celebration.

News of the Queen's imminent death had been abroad for weeks. But Elizabeth Tudor was, outwardly at least, completely unaffected. Though anxiety, that daily companion of her last several years, had gnawed at her stomach, playing havoc with her digestion and sleep, she remained every inch the Queen's faithful subject. Not one word of Mary's condition—and its resultant tremendous effect upon her—had crossed Elizabeth's lips. No premature assumption of royal authority would now ensnare or imperil her. Nicholas Throckmorton had promised Elizabeth to bring her a black enamelled ring, a cherished gift from Philip which Mary always wore, at the Queen's death. Only in that way, would Elizabeth trust her sister was actually gone.

But she did not need the ring. The clogged roads, the hubbub in the Palace park, the distracted air of everyone who served her—her ladies seemed all thumbs—everything denoted powerful news in the making. Several times the Princess had wondered about her sister, old before her time and broken by the demands of the Court, and her conscience, isolated in a deserted Palace with few friends present.* Her subjects would probably cheer when she was gone; it would mean not only the end of the religious persecutions but also the end of Spain in England. Elizabeth herself had attempted a disarming detachment which was belied by the churning of her stomach, the assault on her nerves, and

* Years later, when Queen Elizabeth lay dying, she refused to name her own successor. She said she remembered the shameful example of the people who had deserted her sister Mary on her deathbed and flocked to Hatfield. She would not risk a similar incident.

the constant challenge to her wits and intelligence. The lessons of the past year now served her admirably well.

Relief came sooner than expected. She had taken some books, and, longing for exercise, had walked alone a short distance from the Palace, hoping for a respite. There, in the clean bracing Hertfordshire air, she might sort out her streaming thoughts, might yet grasp the one elusive method by which—when the great news came—she would be sustained and secure. She had just settled herself at the base of a sturdy young oak tree when a noise in the distance disturbed her thoughts. Annoyed, she turned to see William Cecil running towards her, waving something in the air. *Cecil!* Nothing would have brought him personally to her side but momentous news, she thought. Perhaps something had gone wrong. Perhaps Philip had arrived and asserted a control she would find difficult to combat; perhaps Mary had rallied. . . .

But one look at Cecil's features and she wondered no longer. His face was transformed as, breathless, he knelt at her feet and in husky words said her sister was dead, that she was the Queen, and he offered her his homage. Elizabeth had often wondered at this moment and, in her reveries (mindful that she was committing a justifiable mental treason), had played out her role. Now all was forgotten. There would be no noble speech, no solemn thanksgiving, no great doubt as to what her years of secret longing and fear of reprisal had meant. There was payment—and full payment—rendered in William Cecil's magnificent words, 'Your Majesty . . .'. That was the reward of course. The Crown— the Crown of England—in whose service both her brother and sister had died.

But *she* would not die. The good Lord would not see her perish—not she who had undergone so many trials and perils, all in pursuit of that great dream, a sovereignty. Suddenly a reaction she had not anticipated overwhelmed her. She felt her eyes fill, her throat constrict, and, reminiscent of the emotion experienced at Mary's coronation, she fell to her knees. Caution went to the winds, and overcome, she lapsed into the Latin which was as familiar as her native tongue, crying the noble words of the Psalm, '*Domine factuum est istud, et est mirabile in oculis nostris*!'[1] 'It is the Lord's doing; it is marvellous in our eyes!' Emotionally, she clutched William Cecil's hand. Looking over his shoulder, she saw several councillors, gasping and puffing in their haste to greet her. 'It is the Lord's doing,' she whispered again to Cecil as her eyes met his and he nodded. In that fleeting moment before the responsibilities of the Crown descended upon her, she recalled her brother and sister. As the ministers crowded around her, many of the very same who had consented to her imprisonment and disregarded her pleas for justice, she remembered they were also the ones who had exploited Edward and thwarted Mary.

But, oddly, they did not frighten her now. She did not know how, but she *knew* they would be no threat to her. She would be a match for *them*, instead. She might, as she was later to say, have a woman's body—but there was a man's heart in it. She would judge a man by his ability and the depth of his devotion to her as Queen.

A Queen. Happily aware that this time there was no treason involved, Elizabeth Tudor smiled at her nobles as she becomingly wiped away her tears. This was no time for tears, she thought, as she surrendered her books to the obliging Cecil and walked, in the midst of the happy group, to the Palace.

She would be the first of her name to occupy the throne, someone reminded her. With all her native intelligence and vanity, even Elizabeth could not know then of another name she would acquire. She could not know the name would become symbolic of the time when native sons sailed the high seas of conquest and an Empire was born. It was the time of '*Gloriana*', as she liked to be called, and her coronation ushered in the greatest moment in the nation's history, which was to endure for forty-five years: the reign of Elizabeth I of England.

Addendum

On December 13, 1558, the body of Mary Tudor was removed from the Chapel of St James's Palace to Westminster Abbey, where Dr White, the Bishop of Winchester preached the funeral service:

She was a King's daughter, she was a King's sister, she was a King's wife. She was a Queen and by the same title a King also. She was sister to her that by the like title and right is both King and Queen at this present of this realm. What she suffered in each of these degrees before and since she came to the Crown, I will not chronicle—only this I say, howsoever it pleased God to will her patience to be exercised in the world, she had in all estates, the fear of God in her heart... ![1]

The body of Queen Mary I was interred on the north side of the Chapel of her grandfather, Henry VII.

There was no monument raised to her memory by her sister Elizabeth. Neither did the new Queen pay her sister's debts, nor honour the bequests made in her will.

In fact, the will was so completely disregarded that it was not discovered by historians until more than two hundred and fifty years after Mary's death.

It was not until Elizabeth's death forty-five years later that her successor, King James I—the son of Mary, Queen of Scots—had two small tablets erected to point out the site of the Tudor sisters' tomb. A translation of the Latin inscription reads:

'Partners in the war and in the kingdom of the
dead, we, Elizabeth and Mary, sisters in the
hope of Resurrection, sleep here.'

Bibliography

Beckingsale, B. W., *Elizabeth I*. London, 1963.
Bedingfield Papers. Norfolk & Norwich Archaeological Society, 1855.
Bindoff, S. T., *Tudor England*. London, 1950.

Carpenter, Edward, *The House of Kings: The Official History of Westminster Abbey*. New York, 1966.
Chamberlin, Frederick, *The Private Character of Henry VIII*. New York, 1931.
——, *The Private Character of Queen Elizabeth*. New York, 1922.
Chapman, Hester W., *The Last Tudor King*. New York, 1959.
——, *Lady Jane Grey*. London, 1962.
Chidsey, Donald Barr, *Elizabeth I*. New York, 1955.
Clifford, Henry, *Life of Jane Dormer, Duchess of Feria*. London, 1887.
Constant, G., *The Reformation in England*. Paris, 1929.
Creighton, Mandell, *Queen Elizabeth*. London, 1908.

Davey, Richard, *The Nine Days' Queen*. New York, 1909.
——, *The Sisters of Lady Jane Grey*. New York, 1912.
Dent, John, *The Quest for Nonsuch*. London, 1962.
Dickens, A. G., *Thomas Cromwell & The English Reformation*. London, 1959.
Dutton, Ralph, *English Court Life*. London, 1963.

Ellis, Sir Henry, *Original Letters*, Second Series. London, 1827.
Encyclopaedia Americana.

Fisher, H. A. L., *The Political History of England*, Vol. 5. London, 1913.
Froude, J. A., *History of England*, 12 vols. London, 1862.
——, *The Reign of Edward VI*. London, 1909.
——, *The Reign of Mary Tudor*. London, 1910.

Gairdner, James, *The History of the English Church in the Sixteenth Century*. London, 1904.

Hackett, Frances, *Henry VIII*. New York, 1929.
Halliwell-Phillipps, James O., *Letters of the Kings of England*, 2 vols. London, 1848.
Harrison, David, *Tudor England*. London, 1953.
Hume, Martin A. S., *The Wives of Henry VIII and the Parts They Played in History*. London, 1905.
——, *Two English Queens and Philip*. New York, 1908.
——, *Philip II of Spain*. New York, 1897.
Hughes, Paul L., and Fries, Robert F., *Crown & Parliament in Tudor–Stuart England*. New York, 1959.

Innes, Arthur D., *England Under the Tudors*. London, 1905.
Irwin, Margaret, *Young Bess*. New York, 1945.

Letters and Papers of the Reign of Henry VIII, J. S. Brewer and J. Gairdner, eds., London, 1864.
Lewis, D. Bevan Wyndham, *Charles of Europe*. New York, 1931.
Locke, A. Audrey, III, *The Seymour Family*. New York, 1914.

Madden, Frederick, *The Privy Purse Expenses of Princess Mary*. London, 1831.
Morris, Christopher, *The Tudors*. New York, Macmillan, 1957.
Morrison, N. Brysson, *Henry VIII*. New York, 1964.
Mumby, Frank A., *The Girlhood of Queen Elizabeth*. London, 1909.

Neale, J. E., *Queen Elizabeth*. London, 1934.
Nichols, John Gough, ed., *Chronicle of Queen Jane and Two Years of Queen Mary*. London, Camden Society, 1849.
——, *Literary Remains of Edward VI*, 2 vols. London, Roxburghe Club, 1908.

Pollard, A. F., *Henry VIII*. London, 1902.
Prescott, H. F. M., *Mary Tudor*. New York, 1953.

Sanders, Margaret, *Intimate Letters of England's Queens*. New York, 1957.
Saunders, Beatrice, *Henry VIII*. London, 1963.
——, *The Age of Candlelight*. Chester Springs, Pa., 1961.
Sitwell, Edith, *Fanfare for Elizabeth*. New York, 1946.
Smith, Lacey Baldwin, *A Tudor Tragedy*. London, 1961.
——, 'Last Will & Testament of Henry VIII', *Journal of British Studies* (November, 1962). Reprint.
——, 'Henry VIII & the Protestant Triumph', *American Historical Review* (July, 1966). Reprint.
Spanish Calendar of State Papers, 1533–1558.
St Maur, H., *Annals of the Seymours*. London, 1902.
Stone, J. M., *Mary I, Queen of England*. London, 1901.
Strickland, Agnes, *Lives of the Bachelor Kings of England*. London, 1891.
——, *Lives of the Queens of England*, 16 vols. Philadelphia, 1902.
——, *Lives of the Tudor & Stuart Princesses*. London, 1888.

Taylor, I. A., *Lady Jane Grey and Her Times*. New York, 1908.
Thane, Elswyth, *The Tudor Wench*. New York, 1932.
Thirsk, Joan, *Tudor Enclosures*. London, Historical Association, 1959.
Tytler, Patrick Fraser, *England Under the Reign of Edward & Mary*, 2 vols. London, 1839.

Venetian Calendar of State Papers, 1533–1558.

Wiesner, Louis, *The Youth of Queen Elizabeth*, 2 vols. London, 1879.
Williams, Penry, *Life in Tudor England*. New York, 1964.
White, Beatrice, *Mary Tudor*. London, 1936.

Reference, Notes and Comments

CHAPTER 1

1. Madden, p. 40.
2. Strickland, *Lives of the Queens of England*, Vol. VI, p. 12.
3. *Ibid.*, p. 11.

Pollino, an Italian contemporary, says, 'She was declared rightful heir of the realm by the King, her father, and Princess of Wales which was the usual title of the King of England's eldest son. She likewise governed that province according to the custom of the male heir.'

4. *Ibid.*, p. 13.
5. *Ibid.*, p. 16.
6. Strickland, *Lives of the Tudor and Stuart Princesses*, p. 48.

Mary Tudor, Henry VIII's sister, had been wed very young to the ageing King of France, Louis XII. Upon his death, she eloped with a commoner, Charles Brandon, whom Henry created Duke of Suffolk. Mary, the Duchess of Suffolk, was always referred to as the French Queen, and when her first daughter was born at Hatfield, she named her Frances for her connection with that nation and because the child was born on July 16, 1517, St Francis's Day. It is the first instance of a woman with a masculine name of Francis appearing in England.

7. Henry's premise that his marriage was false was founded upon Catherine of Aragon's first marriage to his older brother, the fifteen-year-old Arthur. The boy had died three months after the marriage, and Catherine maintained to her dying day the marriage had never been consummated owing to their extreme youth. The Levitical prophesy, 'They shall be childless'—the penalty of marrying a brother's widow—was held by the King to account for so many of his Queen's unfortunate pregnancies. With the advent of Anne Boleyn and Henry's need for an heir, he was easily persuaded his marriage had been illegal—and cursed—from the beginning.

8. Stone, p. 47.
9. Mumby, p. 13.
10. Venetian Calendar, Vol. 4, p. 682.
11. The site of St James's Palace was formerly a hospital for leper nuns and other 'leper maydens'. It was known as The House in the Fields. Holbein designed the entrance consisting of a Gatehouse, tower, and twin turrets, all of which present the familiar façade in modern metropolitan London. Henry used it as a 'palace of ease' away from the pomp and ritual of Whitehall or Westminster. After Anne's death he rarely occupied it, but enclosed the park and laid out the gardens.
12. Strickland, *Lives of the Queens of England*, Vol. 6, p. 27.
13. Spanish Calendar, May 29, 1533, Vol. 6, Part 2.
14. Hume, *Wives of Henry VIII*, p. 214.

CHAPTER 2

1. Strickland, *Lives of the Queens of England*, Vol. 6, pp. 32–33.
2. *Ibid.*, p. 31.
3. Mumby, p. 9.

[497]

4. The Old Palace of Hatfield was rebuilt by Cardinal Morton in 1497 as a residence for the bishops of Ely. It was a plain, four-sided structure of glowing red brick around an inner courtyard, with a Great Hall and many chambers for living quarters and royal functions. It was used chiefly as a royal residence for the children of Henry VIII during his reign. It is not to be confused with the more ornate Hatfield House which stands just a few hundred yards away. Hatfield House was built by Robert Cecil, the son of William Cecil, Lord Burghley, Elizabeth's great minister. Unfortunately, he pulled down all but one wing of the Old Palace and used the brick for his new home. But it is still possible to walk the grounds of the Old Palace and visit the Great Hall which still remains. Visitors are served tea in the huge, cathedral-like room with the hammerbeam roof where the young Tudors lived a good deal of their childhood.

5. Mumby, p. 11.
6. Spanish Calendar, Vol. 4, Part 1, p. 4.
7. Fisher, p. 327.
8. Mumby, p. 12.
9. *Ibid.*, p. 13.
10. Spanish Calendar, Vol. 5, Part 1, p. 86.
11. Stone, p. 69.
12. Hume, *Wives of Henry VIII*, p. 202.
13. Spanish Calendar, Vol. 5, Part 1, p. 57.
14. Strickland, *Lives of the Queens of England*, Vol. IV, pp. 292–93.
15. Stone, p. 80.
16. Mumby, p. 220.

CHAPTER 3

1. Madden, pp. 68–69.
2. Stone, p. 99.
3. *Ibid.*, p. 87.
4. White, p. 61.
5. Lewis, p. 166.
6. Hume, *Wives of Henry VIII*, p. 263.
7. Froude, *History of England*, Vol. 2, p. 385.
8. *Ibid.*
9. *Ibid.*, p. 415.

10. Strickland, *Lives of the Queens of England*, Vol. 4, p. 307.

Lady Worcester ill-paid Anne Boleyn for her remarks. Several months previous to her arrest, Anne had lent Lady Worcester £100, apparently without Lord Worcester's knowledge. Lady Worcester was fearful her husband would be angry at her debt and, after Anne was dead, she wrote to Cromwell that she felt Anne would have forgiven her the debt and asked Cromwell to do likewise, saying, '... in that matter, I most heartily thank you for I am very loathe it should come to my husband's knowledge ... if he should have knowledge thereof, I am in doubt how he will take it!'

11. Strickland, *Lives of the Queens of England*, Vol. 4, p. 311.
12. *Ibid.*, p. 323.

Many years previously, before Henry had desired Anne, the young Henry Percy and Anne Boleyn had been very much in love and hoped to wed. Cardinal Wolsey had broken up the affair, and at the King's command, Percy had married elsewhere when threatened with the loss of his title and estates if he married Anne. As a peer of England, he was now required to listen to the sordid charges against his former love, but he became so agitated during the trial, he had to leave. He died a few months later.

13. Spanish Calendar, Vol. 4, Part 2, p. 54.
14. Strickland, *Lives of the Queens of England*, Vol. 4, p. 313.
15. *Ibid.*
16. Saunders, p. 165.
17. Strickland, *Lives of the Queens of England*, Vol. 4, p. 326.
18. *Ibid.*, p. 332.
19. *Ibid.*, pp. 333–34.
20. Locke, p. 13.
21. Strickland, *Lives of the Queens of England*, Vol. 5, p. 5.
22. *Ibid.*, p. 8.
23. Locke, p. 16.
24. *Ibid.*
25. Strickland, *Lives of the Queens of England*, Vol. 6, p. 41.
26. *Ibid.*, p. 42.
27. Stone, p. 105.

28. Strickland, *Lives of the Queens of England*, Vol. 6, p. 43.
29. Stone, p. 119.
30. Prescott, p. 80.
31. Strickland, *Lives of the Queens of England*, Vol. 6, p. 48.
32. Stone, p. 120.
33. *Ibid.*, pp. 126–27.

CHAPTER 4

1. Wiesner, Vol. 1, p. 8.
2. Stone, p. 134.
3. Madden, p. 74.
4. Stone, p. 140.
5. Strickland, *Lives of the Queens of England*, Vol. 6, p. 52.
6. *Ibid.*
7. Fisher, p. 403.
8. *Ibid.*, p. 416.
9. White, p. 86.
10. Strickland, *Lives of the Bachelor Kings of England*, p. 197.

CHAPTER 5

1. Nichols, *Literary Remains of Edward VI*, Vol. 1, p. 27.
2. Chapman, *The Last Tudor King*, p. 25.
3. Strickland, *Lives of the Queens of England*, Vol. 7, p. 11.
4. Nichols, *Literary Remains of Edward VI*, Vol. 1, p. 37.
5. White, p. 91.
6. Madden, p. 241.
7. *Ibid.*, p. 45.
8. Stone, p. 163.
9. Chapman, *The Last Tudor King*, p. 41.
10. Froude, *History of England*, Vol. 3, p. 326.
11. *Ibid.*, p. 327.
12. Fisher, p. 425.
13. Lewis, p. 166.
14. Froude, *History of England*, Vol. 3, p. 358.
15. *Ibid.*, p. 359.
16. Strickland, *Lives of the Queens of England*, Vol. 5, p. 36.
17. Hume, *Wives of Henry VIII*, p. 332.
18. Strickland, *Lives of the Queens of England*, Vol. 6, p. 58.

19. *Ibid.*
20. *Ibid.*
21. Froude, *History of England*, Vol. 3, p. 426.
22. *Ibid.*, p. 443.
23. Strickland, *Lives of the Queens of England*, Vol. 6, p. 72.
24. *Ibid.*, Vol. 5, p. 61.
25. Mumby, p. 21.
26. Strickland, *Lives of the Queens of England*, Vol. 5, p. 73.
27. *Ibid.*
28. Saunders, p. 143.
29. Gairdner, p. 211.
30. Morris, p. 93.
31. Fisher, p. 429.
32. Ellis, Second Series, Vol. 2, p. 114.
33. Strickland, *Lives of the Queens of England*, Vol. 5, p. 133.

CHAPTER 6

1. Brewer and Gairdner (eds.), Letters and Papers of the Reign of Henry VIII, Vol. 16, p. 1253.
2. Strickland, *Lives of the Queens of England*, Vol. 6, p. 79.
3. Prescott, p. 97.
4. Brewer and Gairdner (eds.), Letters and Papers, Vol. 17, p. 371.
5. Nichols, *Literary Remains of Edward VI*, Vol. 1, p. 38.
6. Hackett, p. 359.
7. Madden, p. 82.
8. Froude, *History of England*, p. 454.
9. Brewer and Gairdner (eds.), Letters and Papers, Vol. 15, p. 823.
10. Saunders, p. 208.
11. Strickland, *Lives of the Queens of England*, Vol. 5, p. 92.
12. Chapman, *The Last Tudor King*, p. 52.
13. Strickland, *Lives of the Queens of England*, Vol. 5, p. 138.
14. *Ibid.*
15. *Ibid.*, p. 139.
16. *Ibid.*
17. Hume, *Wives of Henry VIII*, p. 378.
18. *Ibid.*, p. 382.
19. Pollard, p. 271.
20. Hume, *Wives of Henry VIII*, p. 387.
21. *Ibid.*, p. 384.
22. Smith, p. 171.

23. Strickland, *Lives of the Queens of England*, Vol. 5, p. 174.

24. Pollard, p. 272.

25. Hume, *Wives of Henry VIII*, p. 393.

CHAPTER 7

1. For readers whose interest might lead them to retrace the footsteps of the Tudors, the Cockpit Gate of Whitehall Palace was situated roughly about where the Haig Statue stands today. The King Street Gate was at the site of the Cenotaph in modern Whitehall. The Cockpit Gate abutted on the present garden of No. 10 Downing Street while the Tiltyard was on the site of the present Horse Guards. The Tennis Court was near the façade of the Treasury Office Buildings. The Banqueting Hall, which dates from a later period, is on the site of the Tudor Banqueting Hall. In Horse Guards Avenue were Henry's Chapel, Great Hall, the entrance to the Waterstairs and the Wine Cellar. This last is still in existence and is open at specified times to the public, courtesy of the Ministry of Works.

2. Hume, *Wives of Henry VIII*, p. 407. A contemporary said of Katherine Parr, 'She was much quieter than any of the young wives of the King and, as she knew more of the world, she always got on pleasantly with the King and had no caprices. She had much honour to the Lady Mary and the wives of the nobles, but she kept her ladies very strictly. . . . the King was very well satisfied with her.'

3. Strickland, *Lives of the Queens of England*, Vol. 6, p. 83.

4. Strickland, *Lives of the Bachelor Kings of England*, p. 210.

5. Strickland, *Lives of the Queens of England*, Vol. 7, p. 15.

CHAPTER 8

1. Hume, *Wives of Henry VIII*, p. 391.

2. Fisher, p. 458.

3. Morris, p. 101.

4. Hume, *Wives of Henry VIII*, pp. 421–22.

5. Strickland, *Lives of the Queens of England*, Vol. 6, p. 86.

6. White, p. 116.

7. Strickland, *Lives of the Queens of England*, Vol. 6, p. 91.

8. Strickland, *Lives of the Bachelor Kings of England*, p. 211.

9. Strickland, *Lives of the Queens of England*, Vol. 7, p. 17.

10. *Ibid.*, Vol. 5, p. 221.

11. *Ibid.*

12. The Lady Margaret Douglas was a daughter of Henry's sister, Margaret, a former Queen of Scotland by her second marriage. Margaret Douglas later married the Earl of Lennox. Their child, Henry, became Lord Darnley. He married Mary Stuart, the widowed Queen of Scots, and later died in the murderous explosion at Kirk o' Fields in 1567. Mary Stuart's own close relationship with the Tudor line rendered her a threat to Elizabeth and resulted in her execution in 1587 after a long imprisonment for allegedly conspiring for Elizabeth's throne. The child of Darnley and Mary Stuart later became James I, the first of the Stuart kings of England.

13. Halliwell-Phillipps, *Letters of the Kings of England*, Vol. 1, p. 394.

14. Mumby, pp. 25–26.

15. Spanish Calendar, Vol. 8, p. 51.

16. White, p. 119.

17. Froude, *History of England*, Vol. 4, p. 451.

18. Fisher, p. 475.

19. Gairdner, p. 233.

20. Strickland, *Lives of the Queens of England*, Vol. 5, p. 245.

21. *Ibid.*, p. 248.

22. *Ibid.*, p. 250.

23. *Ibid.*, p. 251.

24. Fisher, p. 469.

25. *Ibid.*, p. 479.

26. *Ibid.*, p. 480.

27. Smith, p. 20.

28. J. J. Scarisbrick in his noted *Henry VIII* conjectures that Henry's affliction was probably acquired while jousting in 1528. He maintains the ulcer resulted from varicose veins or osteomyelitis, a chronic septic infection. The condition further aggravated with 'inadequate and often savage treatment, together with a lack of sufficient rest, would have caused

the veins to have become thrombosed, the leg to swell and extremely painful chronic ulcer to develop. . . .'

This would bear out both Professor Frederick Chamberlin's and Scarisbrick's contention that Henry VIII did *not* die of syphilis. 'There is no sign of his ever having received the established treatment for this well-known secondary symptom of the disease,' says Scarisbrick. Syphilis, which acts chiefly on bones, blood vessels, and the nervous system, can affect the brain or spinal cord with general paralysis or defects of vision in addition to other distressing symptoms. Chamberlin maintains, 'It is difficult to believe that a man who became infected with syphilis at or before the age of 18 years in a century when syphilis was such a grave and crippling complaint and its treatment so inadequate, could flourish for so many years as a consistently remarkable athlete.'

29. Madden, p. 186.
30. Strickland, *Lives of the Bachelor Kings of England*, p. 221.
31. *Ibid.*, p. 222.
32. *Ibid.*, p. 223.
33. Hume, *Wives of Henry VIII*, p. 445.
34. The exact date of affixing the dry stamp, by which Henry's will was signed, is one of history's royal enigmas. William Clerc, the custodian of the stamp, refers to it as 'His Majesty's Last Will and Testament, bearing date at Westminster the thirty day of December last past, written in a book of paper, signed above in the beginning and beneath in the end' and 'delivered then in our own sights with our own hand' to the Earl of Hertford. However, Clerc lists the will among the documents he dry-stamped 'at divers times and places in the month of January, 1547'. From these rather ordinary details, Lacey Baldwin Smith in an article on Henry's death, deduced that if the will had to be signed with a dry stamp—a device impressing his signature to paper which was later filled in with ink—on December 30, 1546, it shows the King's feebleness almost four weeks before death actually occurred and his continued reluctance to actually sign the will. If on the other hand, it was not in fact stamped (as Clerc's statement seems to indicate) until the late evening of January 27, 1547, almost four weeks after it was drawn and dated, it demonstrates even more emphatically how Henry kept all his Council 'in a dither of apprehension' for all those weeks.

Almost every historian has his own version of this intriguing situation. The truth probably lies somewhere in between. It is consistent with Henry VIII's character to have reviewed and changed the will somewhat in late December but, still in possession of his faculties, to refrain from actually signing it. And in this instance—as in the final deathbed confrontation with Cranmer—he waited just a little too long.

35. White, p. 123.

CHAPTER 9

1. Nichols, *Literary Remains of Edward VI*, Vol. 1, p. 57.
2. *Ibid.*, p. 5.
3. Strickland, *Lives of the Bachelor Kings of England*, p. 218.
4. Nichols, *Literary Remains of Edward VI*, Vol. 1, p. 31.
5. *Ibid.*, p. 32.
6. Froude, *The Reign of Edward VI*, p. 3.
7. Strickland, *Lives of the Queens of England*, Vol. 7, p. 20.
8. Nichols, *Literary Remains of Edward VI*, pp. 48–50.
9. Old Thomas Howard, the Duke of Norfolk, the premier noble in England, had providentially been saved from the block by the death of Henry VIII. His son, the Earl of Surrey, accused of treason, had been executed several weeks previously and Norfolk's own execution was scheduled for the morning of January 28. Henry died in the early hours of that day and only quick action by the Council, who thought the old Duke might still prove useful to them, prevented the sentence from being carried out. That Howard, a staunch pro-Catholic, was still regarded as undependable by the

Council of 'new men', however, is shown by the fact that he was exempt from the general pardon of prisoners at the beginning of the new reign.

10. Strickland, *Lives of the Queens of England*, Vol. 5, p. 263.

11. Davey, in *The Nine Days' Queen*, says, 'It was not the custom for women to attend the funeral of a male, except as an act of devotion'. In addition to his daughters, there were many female members of Henry's family who could qualify in this instance. However, the confusion attendant upon establishing proper rank and precedence on such short notice probably only served to emphasise the difficulty of allowing female attendance. The youth of Edward—plus the rigour of his coronation set for the next day—undoubtedly prohibited his attendance. Regarding the coronation, Miss Strickland, in her *Lives of the Bachelor Kings of England*, mentions the absence of any female relatives at the ceremony. With two living Queens (Anne of Cleves and Katherine Parr), the King's two daughters, the Protector's wife and all the lesser females of Henry's family, 'the Protector and Privy Council were baffled'. Since, apparently, the claims of precedence could not be settled amicably, 'it was considered most prudent to dispense with their presence altogether'.

12. Nichols, *Literary Remains of Edward VI*, Vol. 1, p. 238.

13. Strickland, *Lives of the Bachelor Kings of England*, p. 243.

14. This was Henry Brandon, seven years senior to Edward and one of his classmates. He was the son of Henry VIII's brother-in-law and close friend, Charles Brandon. The boy's mother was Katherine Willoughby, the young and beautiful daughter of Maria de Salinas, the intimate companion of Catherine of Aragon, in whose arms the rejected Queen had died. Katherine Willoughby was the ward of Charles Brandon and his wife, Henry's sister, Mary, 'the Tudor Rose'. Upon her death in 1533, he married the fourteen-year-old child disgracefully soon, and Henry Brandon and a younger brother Charles were sons of

this marriage. They died of the plague at Buckden Palace in 1551.

15. This is not to be confused with the present crown of that name. The crown used in the coronation ceremony of Edward VI was the actual crown of Edward the Confessor. This beautiful relic, as well as the small one made for Edward, was later brutally broken apart by the Puritan government and sold for the price of the gold.

16. Chapman, *The Last Tudor King*, p. 96.

CHAPTER 10

1. Strickland, *Lives of the Queens of England*, Vol. 6, p. 95.

2. *Ibid.*

3. *Ibid.*, pp. 96–97.

4. Mumby, pp. 30–31.

5. Thane, p. 349.

6. Strickland, *Lives of the Queens of England*, Vol. 5, p. 265.

7. The exact date of their marriage is unknown, but one of the later charges against Thomas Seymour was that he married the Queen so soon after the King's death that had Katherine become pregnant immediately, there would have been no way of knowing whether the child was Henry's or Seymour's 'to the great danger of the realm'.

8. Nichols, *Literary Remains of Edward VI*, Vol. 1, pp. 46–47.

9. Ellis, First Series, Vol. 7, p. 149.

10. Mumby, pp. 32–33.

11. Davey, *The Nine Days' Queen*, pp. 172–73.

12. *Ibid.*, p. 152.

CHAPTER 11

1. Froude, *History of England*, Vol. 5, p. 53.

2. *Ibid.*, p. 56.

3. *Ibid.*, p. 46.

4. Strickland, *Lives of the Bachelor Kings of England*, p. 76.

5. Locke, p. 55.

6. Strickland, *Lives of the Bachelor Kings of England*, p. 281.

7. St Maur, *Annals of the Seymours*, p. 49.

8. Strickland, *Lives of the Queens of England*, Vol. 7, p. 24.

9. Davey, *The Nine Days' Queen*, p. 138.

10. *Ibid.*

11. Tytler, Vol. 1, p. 70.

12. *Ibid.*, p. 149.

13. Davey, *The Nine Days' Queen*, pp. 166–67.

The fate af Mary Seymour is one of history's more intriguing puzzles. After her mother's death, she was conveyed to the home of Katherine Willoughby, the young Duchess of Suffolk, the widow of Charles Brandon. The Duchess received the child willingly enough, but when the Protector retained all the nursery plate, furniture, and no pension was ever paid for her support, her enthusiasm cooled. Thomas Seymour's estates were confiscated and Katherine's vast fortune somehow diverted, and the child was left penniless. Neither William Parr nor Seymour's brother, the Protector, would support the child and she seems to have lived in near neglect at the Duchess's grudging charity.

Accounts of her life after childhood vary. One historian states she died very young. However, at the end of the seventeenth century, many papers belonging to the Lawson family of Suffolk were found, in addition to many Tudor relics that had belonged to Katherine Parr. A family history showed that one Mary Seymour, allegedly the daughter of Katherine and Thomas Seymour, had married a Sir Edward Bushel, whose only grandchild had married into the Lawson family.

14. Strickland, *Lives of the Queens of England*, Vol. 5, p. 282.

15. *Ibid.*, p. 286.

16. Sudeley Castle and Church still stand near Cheltenham in Gloucestershire. The tomb of Katherine Parr has been beautifully restored after several riflings in the later 'religious troubles'. The lying-in chamber may be visited, and several mementoes of the Seymour family and of Katherine herself are displayed. Among these items are a tiny tooth and a lock of extremely fair hair taken from the coffin the first time the tomb was desecrated.

17. Strickland, *Lives of the Tudor and Stuart Princesses*, p. 64.

18. Froude, *The Reign of Edward VI*, p. 89.

19. Davey, *The Nine Days' Queen*, pp. 158–59.

20. Chapman, *Lady Jane Grey*, p. 114.

21. Chapman, *The Last Tudor King*, p. 132.

22. Nichols, *Literary Remains of Edward VI*, Vol. 1, p. 62.

23. Froude, *The Reign of Edward VI*, p. 94.

CHAPTER 12

1. Mumby, pp. 40–41.

2. Chamberlin, p. 5.

3. Mumby, p. 42.

4. Chamberlin, p. 6.

5. Mumby, p. 46.

6. *Ibid.*, p. 48.

7. *Ibid.*, p. 52.

8. *Ibid.*, p. 51.

9. *Ibid.*, p. 54.

10. *Ibid.*, p. 55.

11. *Ibid.*, pp. 55–57.

12. Katherine Ashley's husband was a minor relative of Elizabeth's mother, Anne Boleyn. Both Ashleys and Thomas Parry were released from the Tower following Seymour's execution, though they were not immediately returned to the Princess's household. Later, all three were permanently reinstated in her service. Katherine Ashley remained with Elizabeth until her death in 1565 at which Elizabeth was 'greatly grieved'. Thomas Parry, for all his inefficiency with the office, was named Comptroller of the Queen's Household. His daughter, Blanche Parry, became one of Elizabeth's ladies-in-waiting and one of her closest friends, with responsibility for the royal jewels and library. She became blind in 1587 and died in 1589. Elizabeth was with her at the end, paid for her funeral, and buried her with the rank of Baroness. Her heart is in St Margaret's Westminster; her body is buried at Bacton, Herefordshire, where a memorial shows

her kneeling before the Queen, with the inscription, 'Allways wythe Maeden Queene a Maede did ende my liffe'.

13. Mumby, pp. 57–60.

CHAPTER 13

1. Nichols, *Literary Remains of Edward VI*, Vol. 1, p. 62.
2. White, p. 137.
3. Davey, *The Nine Days' Queen*, pp. 195–96.
4. Froude, *The Reign of Edward VI*, p. 37.
5. The English Prayer Book now in use, the chief expression of the established religion of England for nearly four hundred years, is not the *Book of Common Prayer* issued during Edward's reign, but a later one, issued in 1552. It was revised in 1662 and as recently as 1928.
6. Tytler, Vol. 1, p. 329.
7. Nichols, *Literary Remains of Edward VI*, Vol. 1, p. 53.
8. Clifford, *Life of Jane Dormer*, pp. 61–62.
9. White, p. 134.
10. Strickland, *Lives of the Queens of England*, Vol. 6, p. 109.
11. Nichols, *Literary Remains of Edward VI*, Vol. 1, p. 43.
12. White, p. 150.
13. Taylor, p. 131.
14. Froude, *History of England*, Vol. 5, pp. 219–20.
15. Strickland, *Lives of the Bachelor Kings of England*, p. 310.
16. Tytler, Vol. 1, pp. 221–22.
17. *Ibid.*, pp. 222–27.
18. The absence of William Cecil's name in any of these discussions is an omission as remarkable as it was undoubtedly deliberate. As the Protector's secretary, he had Somerset's great confidence, but in this instance, while tilting with the Council, he had by some means managed to keep apart and, with shrewd wariness, did not implicate himself in Somerset's dilemma, thus ensuring himself a clear field should the Protector fail.
19. Tytler, Vol. 1, p. 223.
20. Chapman, *The Last Tudor King*, p. 169.

CHAPTER 14

1. Mumby, p. 64.
2. Strickland, *Lives of the Queens of England*, Vol. 7, p. 52.
3. Nichols, *Literary Remains of Edward VI*, Vol. 1, p. 141.
4. *Ibid.*, p. 278.
5. *Ibid.*, p. 279.
6. Strickland, *Lives of the Bachelor Kings of England*, p. 322.
7. Chapman, *The Last Tudor King*, p. 216.
8. Strickland, *Lives of the Bachelor Kings of England*, p. 323.
9. Nichols, *Literary Remains of Edward VI*, p. 147.
10. Robert Dudley was later to become celebrated as the Earl of Leicester, a great favourite of Elizabeth when she came to the throne. Amy Robsart, the ill-fated bride, was by then his wife of eight years. She died in a supposedly accidental fall at her home which resulted in scandalous rumours that her death had been deliberate.
11. Nichols, *Literary Remains of Edward VI*, p. 274.
12. Strickland, *Lives of the Bachelor Kings of England*, p. 263.
13. Stone, p. 198.
14. Chapman, *The Last Tudor King*, p. 160.
15. Nichols, *Literary Remains of Edward VI*, Vol. 2, pp. 475–86.
16. Spanish Calendar, Vol. 10, p. 98.
17. *Ibid.*, Vol. 10, pp. 204–5.
18. *Ibid.*, pp. 205–9.
19. *Ibid.*, pp. 204–5.
20. *Ibid.*, pp. 209–12.
21. *Ibid.*, pp. 212–13.
22. Strickland, *Lives of the Bachelor Kings of England*, p. 332.
23. Mumby, pp. 72–73.
24. Strickland, *Lives of the Queens of England*, Vol. 7, p. 54.
25. Mumby, pp. 65–66.

CHAPTER 15

1. White, p. 166.
2. Froude, *History of England*, Vol. 5, pp. 31–32.

3. *Ibid.*, p. 310.

4. *Ibid.*, p. 311.

5. Chapman, *The Last Tudor King*, p. 207.

6. Strickland, *Lives of the Queens of England*, Vol. 6, p. 116.

7. The choice of Richard Rich on this mission is ironic and a potent example of the manner in which Council members switched sides as religious and political expediency demanded. This is the same Richard Rich who perjured himself at the trial of Sir Thomas More for a Wardenship of Wales. ('But Richard,' said Sir Thomas, *'for Wales?'*) After More's conviction, he zealously pursued the so-called heretics during Henry VIII's reign for professing the identical religious beliefs he was now persecuting Mary Tudor into adopting.

8. *Ibid.*, p. 117.

9. Spanish Calendar, Vol. 10, pp. 356–64.

10. Strickland, *Lives of the Bachelor Kings of England*, p. 347.

11. Chapman, *The Last Tudor King*, p. 220.

12. Readers of the author's *Catherine, The Queen* will remember Henry Percy, the heir to the Northumberland title, who (under family pressure) renounced the youthful Anne Boleyn, rather than disgrace and lose the Northumberland title and estates. He died in 1537 shortly after her execution and the title remained extinct until 1551 when it was given to the Earl of Warwick.

13. Froude, *Reign of Edward VI*, p. 227.

14. Chapman, *The Last Tudor King*, p. 232.

15. Froude, *Reign of Edward VI*, p. 229.

16. Tytler, Vol. 1, p. 57.

17. Unfortunately, many of the depositions of witnesses and, particularly, Somerset's own alleged 'confession' acquired while a prisoner in the Tower, have disappeared. During Elizabeth's reign, her great Prime Minister, William Cecil, removed from the archives many papers relating to the former reigns. Possibly the Somerset papers were removed at this time.

18. The penalty for violating this Act which deemed 'any persons to the number of twelve . . . being assembled together, shall practise with force of arms . . . to murder, kill, slay, take or imprison any of the King's most honourable Privy Council. . . .' also carried the death penalty.

19. Froude, *Reign of Edward VI*, p. 231.

20. The only evidence of Somerset's alleged 'confession' lies in a letter which Edward wrote to his friend Barnaby Fitzpatrick in which he mentions the trial of the duke. 'The Lords . . . acquitted him of high treason and condemned him of felony, which he *seems* to have confessed.' No other official witnesses at the trial or any of the peers ever mentioned any confession by Somerset, indicating Northumberland deceived the boy in order to win the King's final condemnation and to justify the execution of the doomed man.

21. Chapman, *The Last Tudor King*, p. 237.

22. Tytler, Vol. 1, p. 71.

23. Thane, p. 360.

24. Strickland, *Lives of the Bachelor Kings of England*, p. 367.

CHAPTER 16

1. Nichols, *Literary Remains of Edward VI*, Vol. 1, p. 108.

2. Spanish Calendar, Vol. 10, p. 517.

3. Nichols, *Literary Remains of Edward VI*, Vol. 1, p. 209.

4. Strickland, *Lives of the Bachelor Kings of England*, p. 359.

5. Strickland, *Lives of the Queens of England*, Vol. 7, p. 55.

6. Despite his long association with Somerset, William Cecil emerged unscathed from the duke's tragedy. After the execution, one friend wrote to him congratulating him on his 'good fortune to be found undefiled with the folly' of Somerset and commending him for taking 'the King's part. . . . which leadeth to that life that is most laudable'.

7. Strickland, *Lives of the Queens of England*, Vol. 7, p. 58.

8. Mumby, p. 67.

9. Nichols, *Literary Remains of Edward VI*, Vol. 2, p. 408.

10. Mumby, pp. 66–67.

11. Nichols, *Literary Remains of Edward VI*, Vol. 1, p. 159.

12. *Ibid.*, Vol. 2, p. 448.

13. *Ibid.*, Vol. 1, p. 182.

14. Stone, pp. 212–13.

15. The Greys, formerly the Marquis and Marchioness of Dorset, were elevated in rank at the same time as Warwick became Earl of Northumberland. The Suffolk title, which normally would have been bestowed on Charles Brandon's oldest son, Henry, became vacant when the boy died of the plague at Buckden Palace. Henry Grey then inherited the title through the right of his wife, Frances, Charles Brandon's daughter, whose mother had been Mary Tudor, the younger sister of Henry VIII.

16. Chapman, *Lady Jane Grey*, p. 55.

17. White, p. 179.

18. Strickland, *Lives of the Bachelor Kings of England*, p. 404.

19. *Ibid.*, p. 405.

20. Nichols, *Literary Remains of Edward VI*, Vol. 1, p. 210.

21. Chapman, *The Last Tudor King*, pp. 258–61.

22. Strickland, *Lives of the Bachelor Kings of England*, p. 412.

23. Strickland, *Lives of the Queens of England*, Vol. 6, pp. 125–26.

24. Nichols, *Literary Remains of Edward VI*, Vol. 2, p. 165.

25. Davey, *The Nine Days' Queen*, p. 236.

26. Nichols, *Literary Remains of Edward VI*, Vol. 2, p. 566.

27. *Ibid.*, p. 568.

28. Venetian Calendar, Vol. 5, p. 537.

29. Mumby, pp. 78–79.

30. Chapman, *The Last Tudor King*, p. 285.

31. Mary was very friendly with the Throckmorton family and held the eldest son, Sir Robert Throckmorton, in great respect. At the time of Edward's death she said, 'If Robert had been at Greenwich, she would have hazarded all things and gauged her life on the leap', going straight to claim the Crown instead of fleeing into Norfolk. She later ably repaid her benefactor with many acts of kindness and preferment. An ornate robe belonging to her mother, Catherine of Aragon, was shown to the author during a stay at Coughton Court, where the present-day Sir Robert Throckmorton lives. The robe was probably a gift from the grateful Mary after her accession to the throne.

CHAPTER 17

1. Historians have long puzzled over the probable cause of Edward's death. Whenever a royal life came to an unexpected end, poisoning was always suspect. Had Edward's death been necessary, Northumberland was not the type to have hesitated. He had more to gain, however, if Edward lived. It was only when faced with the probable death of the King, that the duke devised the accession of the Lady Jane Grey, his daughter-in-law. Edward's original illness seems to have been consumption, and the woman to whose exclusive care he was committed, administered overdoses of her medicines—some of which contained arsenic—so that Edward was in fact poisoned, though not deliberately.

2. Stone, p. 218.

3. *Ibid.*, p. 221.

4. Strickland, *Lives of the Tudor and Stuart Princesses*, p. 91.

5. Davey, *The Nine Days' Queen*, pp. 276–77.

6. Strickland, *Lives of the Queens of England*, Vol. 6, p. 140.

7. Strickland, *Lives of the Tudor and Stuart Princesses*, pp. 94–95.

8. Nichols, *Chronicle of Queen Jane and Queen Mary*, pp. 6–7.

9. Tytler, Vol. 2, pp. 200–1.

10. Baynard's Castle, built by one Baynard, the Norman, was situated about three-quarters of a mile above London Bridge, between Paul's Wharf and the Blackfriars. When the Norman castle fell into ruins, Henry VII built an edifice with high-pitched turrets which soared over the surrounding area. The front of the building was set out into the river which washed the walls; the rear had extensive gardens which stretched to where the Bank of England stands today.

A large part was destroyed in the Great Fire of 1666, but the towers were standing as late as 1809. The Mermaid Theatre and Restaurant now occupy the site of the old castle.

11. One more personal grudge Arundel did not mention, but of which each councillor was surely aware, was Arundel's aversion to the Greys. Prior to his marriage with Frances Brandon, Henry Grey, Lady Jane's father had been wed to Arundel's sister, whom he had hastened to put aside as soon as a wedding with the niece of Henry VIII was possible.

12. Nichols, *Chronicle of Queen Jane and Queen Mary*, pp. 11–12.

13. *Ibid.*, p. 10.

14. Wiesner, Vol. 1, pp. 140–41.

15. Mumby, p. 74.

16. Historians often note a letter Elizabeth allegedly wrote to the Duke of Northumberland in which she scathingly denounced his proclamation of Jane Grey. This has been omitted. The letter, which is so unlike Elizabeth in phraseology as to be an undoubted forgery, is also completely out of character for her to have written at a critical period when she would have only endangered her own position and safety by such an outburst.

17. Edward Tudor was laid to rest near the altar in the Chapel of Henry VII, his grandfather. Thus the first and last Tudor Kings appropriately reposed together. The splendid monument of gilt brass which marked Edward's burial spot was pulled down by Oliver Cromwell in later years for the worth of the metal. It has never been replaced.

18. Chapman, *Lady Jane Grey*, p. 157.

19. Tytler, Vol. 2, p. 224.

20. *Ibid.*

21. *Ibid.*, pp. 225–26.

22. Nichols, *Chronicle of Queen Jane and Queen Mary*, pp. 17–18.

23. This dwelling is still in existence. Called the Queen's House, it is the home of the resident-governor of the Tower, Colonel Sir Thomas Pierce Butler, whose kindness permitted the author to view the many historic rooms not generally shown to the public. Among these were the rooms in which Lady Jane Grey lived

during her imprisonment, as well as the chamber in which Sir Thomas More languished during his confinement.

24. Davey, *The Nine Days' Queen*, p. 311.

25. Nichols, *Chronicle of Queen Jane and Queen Mary*, pp. 23–24.

CHAPTER 18

1. Spanish Calendar, Vol. 11, p. 110.
2. Stone, pp. 207–8.
3. *Ibid.*, pp. 241–42.
4. Froude, *History of England*, p. 86.
5. Mumby, p. 96.
6. *Ibid.*, p. 82.
7. White, p. 217.
8. *Ibid.*, p. 204.
9. Hume, *Two English Queens & Philip*, p. 20.
10. Froude, *Reign of Queen Mary*, p. 61.
11. Strickland, *Lives of the Queens of England*, Vol. 6, p. 167.
12. Froude, *Reign of Queen Mary*, p. 61.
13. *Ibid.*, p. 66.
14. *Ibid.*, p. 64.
15. *Ibid.*
16. Spanish Calendar, Vol. 11, p. 366.
17. *Ibid.*, p. 319.
18. Froude, *Reign of Mary Tudor*, p. 75.

CHAPTER 19

1. Prescott, p. 232.
2. Spanish Calendar, Vol. 11, p. 363.
3. Strickland, *Lives of the Queens of England*, Vol. 7, p. 69.
4. Morris, p. 130.
5. Froude, *Reign of Mary Tudor*, p. 86.
6. Nichols, *Chronicle of Queen Jane and Queen Mary*, p. 38.
7. *Ibid.*, p. 39.
8. White, p. 245.
9. Though the actual building in which Elizabeth lived is gone, the forests, the great Tithe Barn, and the Old Monks' Garden are still to be seen at Ashridge. The ornate structure which bears that name was modelled upon remains of the old building in 1815.

Today it is the home of Ashridge College.

10. Strickland, *Lives of the Queens of England*, Vol. 7, pp. 72–73.

11. Wiesner, Vol. 1, p. 274.

12. *Ibid.*, p. 255.

13. Nichols, *Chronicle of Queen Jane and Queen Mary*, pp. 41–42.

14. *Ibid.*, p. 43.

15. White, pp. 249–50.

CHAPTER 20

1. Nichols, *Chronicle of Queen Jane and Queen Mary*, p. 43.

2. White, p. 252.

3. Nichols, *Chronicle of Queen Jane and Queen Mary*, p. 46.

4. Strickland, *Lives of the Queens of England*, Vol. 6, p. 190.

5. Nichols, *Chronicle of Queen Jane and Queen Mary*, p. 48.

6. Strickland, *Lives of the Queens of England*, Vol. 6, p. 190.

7. *Ibid.*

8. Thane, p. 371.

9. Strickland, *Lives of the Queens of England*, Vol. 6, p. 195.

10. Nichols, *Chronicle of Queen Jane and Queen Mary*, p. 50.

11. *Ibid.*, p. 52.

12. Strickland, *Lives of the Queens of England*, Vol. 6, p. 198.

13. *Ibid.*

14. Froude, *Reign of Mary Tudor*, p. 109.

15. Davey, *The Nine Days' Queen*, pp. 330–31.

16. Chapman, *Lady Jane Grey*, p. 198.

17. Strickland, *Lives of the Tudor and Stuart Princesses*, p. 112.

18. *Ibid.*

19. Davey, *The Sisters of Lady Jane Grey*, pp. 99–101.

20. Davey, *The Nine Days' Queen*, p. 337.

21. *Ibid.*, p. 339.

22. Froude, *Reign of Mary Tudor*, p. 113.

23. Nichols, *Chronicle of Queen Jane and Queen Mary*, pp. 56–57.

24. *Ibid.*

CHAPTER 21

1. Tytler, Vol. 2, p. 329.

2. Hume, *Two English Queens and Philip*, p. 51.

3. Mumby, p. 111.

4. *Ibid.*

5. Hume, *Two English Queens and Philip*, p. 51.

6. Strickland, *Lives of the Queens of England*, Vol. 6, p. 200.

7. *Ibid.*

8. Mumby, p. 109.

9. Strickland, *Lives of the Queens of England*, Vol. 7, p. 84.

10. In her later years, this recognition of the power of popular acclaim was evident in Queen Elizabeth's attitude towards her subjects. Whereas, in her dealing with Parliament, she harassed, badgered, and gave her nobles little quarter, she handled the Commons more gingerly, more tolerantly, and more respectfully. Consequently, during her great forty-five-year reign, they gave her little trouble. This shrewd policy, combined with a knowing personal appeal, accounts in no little way for the tremendous personal popularity she enjoyed.

11. Mumby, pp. 115–17.

12. Tytler, Vol. 2, p. 343.

13. Wiesner, Vol. 2, p. 25.

14. *Ibid.*, p. 37.

15. Froude, *Reign of Mary Tudor*, p. 126.

16. *Ibid.*

17. Strickland, *Lives of the Queens of England*, Vol. 7, p. 88.

18. White, p. 272.

19. Strickland, *Lives of the Queens of England*, Vol. 7, p. 90.

20. Wiesner, Vol. 2, p. 46.

21. *Ibid.*

22. Nichols, *Chronicle of Queen Jane and Queen Mary*, p. 74.

23. Strickland, *Lives of the Queens of England*, Vol. 7, p. 97.

24. An uncorroborated report in Heywood's *England's Elizabeth* asserts that a warrant for Elizabeth's execution was delivered to Sir John Bridges at the Tower. The warrant bore the Queen's Seal, but lacked her signature and the Lieutenant

refused to carry out the order. He went immediately to the Queen who denied all knowledge of it. Mary allegedly 'called Gardiner and others whom she suspected . . . and blamed them for their inhuman usage of her sister and took measures for her better security'. Whether true or not, the story is tantalising. Gardiner had attempted a similar action with Queen Katherine Parr and Mary later *did* provide Elizabeth with a greater security guard.

25. Wiesner, Vol. 2, p. 77.
26. Tytler, Vol. 2, p. 346.
27. *Ibid.*, p. 372.
28. Strickland, *Lives of the Queens of England*, Vol. 6, p. 204.
29. *Ibid.*, p. 202.
30. Sanders, *Intimate Letters of England's Queens*, p. 55.
31. Strickland, *Lives of the Queens of England*, Vol. 6, p. 216.
32. Tytler, Vol. 2, p. 400.

CHAPTER 22

1. The site of the old Woodstock manor house is a few miles from the home of the Duke of Marlborough, Blenheim Castle, which was also the birthplace of Sir Winston Churchill.
2. Strickland, *Lives of the Queens of England*, Vol. 7, p. 100.
3. Jane Dormer later married the powerful Count de Feria who accompanied Prince Philip to England. She left England during Elizabeth's reign to escape religious harassment and lived the remainder of her life in Spain.
4. Wiesner, Vol. 2, p. 91.
5. The Bedingfield Papers.
6. *Ibid.*
7. *Ibid.*
8. Hume, *Two English Queens and Philip*, p. 65.
9. *Ibid.*
10. *Ibid.*, p. 27.
11. *Ibid.*
12. Hume, *Philip II of Spain*, p. 75.
13. Tytler, Vol. 2, p. 414.
14. Nichols, *Chronicle of Queen Jane and Queen Mary*, Appendix, p. 136.
15. The Bedingfield Papers.
16. *Ibid.*
17. Strickland, *Lives of the Queens of England*, Vol. 7, p. 106.
18. Hughes and Fries, *Crown and Parliament in Tudor-Stuart England*, p. 90.
19. Strickland, *Lives of the Queens of England*, Vol. 7, p. 108.
20. The Bedingfield Papers.

CHAPTER 23

1. Hume, *Two English Queens and Philip*, p. 84.
2. *Ibid.*, p. 89.
3. *Ibid.*, p. 92.
4. Stone, pp. 318–19.
5. Froude, *Reign of Mary Tudor*, p. 157.
6. Tytler, Vol. 2, p. 238.
7. It is indicative of William Cecil's religious flexibility to find him active in the Catholic court of Queen Mary. As fervid a Protestant as his former sponsor, the Protector, he emerged from semi-retirement on Mary's accession and adopted an outward compliance to the Catholic faith. Though he earned the Queen's pardon, she never trusted him sufficiently to give him any high office. Or as some historians have stated, Cecil was also wise enough not to seek or accept any responsibilities.
8. Froude, *Reign of Mary Tudor*, pp. 167–69.
9. *Ibid.*, p. 173.
10. *Encyclopaedia Americana*, Vol. 15, *see* 'Inquisition'.
The *Ecclesia Romana*:—the Roman Church claimed from its early beginning, and has never since renounced, the philosophical title of *Societas Perfecta*, a state in its own right, with power of legislation over all its subjects and even the extreme sanction of punishment over the disobedient, even to the extreme penalty of death.
11. Stone, Appendix, p. 503.
12. Froude, *Reign of Mary Tudor*, p. 194.
13. *Ibid.*
14. Mumby, p. 190.
15. Froude, *History of England*, Vol. 6, p. 364.

16. Venetian Calendar, Vol. 6, Part 1, p. 42.

17. Mumby, p. 192.

18. Venetian Calendar, Vol. 6, Part 1, p. 67.

19. Froude, *Reign of Mary Tudor*, p. 199.

20. Mumby, p. 192.

21. *Ibid.*, p. 187.

22. Wiesner, Vol. 2, p. 158.

23. Stone, p. 348.

24. *Ibid.*

25. *Ibid.*, p. 349.

26. Mumby, pp. 197–98.

27. Venetian Calendar, Vol. 6, Part 1, p. 200.

28. *Ibid.*, p. 204.

CHAPTER 24

1. Venetian Calendar, Vol. 6, Part 1, p. 204.

2. *Ibid.*, p. 315.

3. Mumby, p. 201.

4. White, p. 360.

5. Venetian Calendar, Vol. 6, Part 1, p. 473.

6. Clifford, *Life of Jane Dormer*, p. 64.

7. Stone, p. 354.

8. Froude, *Reign of Mary Tudor*, p. 249.

9. *Ibid.*, pp. 257–59.

10. *Ibid.*, p. 235.

11. Strickland, *Lives of the Queens of England*, Vol. 7, p. 131.

12. Stone, p. 422.

13. Mumby, p. 203.

14. *Ibid.*, p. 209.

15. *Ibid.*, pp. 214–15.

16. *Ibid.*, pp. 221–23.

CHAPTER 25

1. Sanders, *Intimate Letters of England's Queens*, p. 56.

2. Venetian Calendar, Vol. 6, Part 2, p. 884.

3. Stone, p. 437.

4. Clifford, *Life of Jane Dormer*, p. 89.

5. Stone, p. 441.

6. Venetian Calendar, Vol. 6, Part 2, p. 884.

7. *Ibid.*

8. Froude, *Reign of Mary Tudor*, p. 360.

9. Stone, p. 451.

10. Hume, *Two English Queens and Philip*, p. 161.

11. Strickland, *Lives of the Queens of England*, Vol. 7, p. 131.

12. Thane, p. 378.

13. Madden, *Privy Purse Expenses*, Appendix, pp. 85–87.

14. Mumby, p. 242.

15. Stone, Appendix, p. 520.

16. White, p. 425.

17. Clifford, *Life of Jane Dormer*, pp. 72–73.

18. *Ibid.*

19. Madden, *Privy Purse Expenses*, Introduction, p. 165.

CHAPTER 26

1. Strickland, *Lives of the English Queens*, Vol. 7, p. 137.

ADDENDUM:

1. Madden, *Privy Purse Expenses*, Introduction, p. 166.

Index

Agriculture, 218

Alva, Duke of, 416, 418

Anne (of Cleves), Queen, 94–8, 105, 110, 167, 338
  Katherine (Howard), Queen, and, 113

Anne (Boleyn), Queen, 34–6, 56–7, 64–5, 75, 121; *see also* Boleyn, Anne
  church separation from Rome, 45
  Cromwell and, 45, 50–1
  Elizabeth, birth of, 34–6
  flirtations, 58
  imprisonment and death, 58–63, 396–7
  Jane Seymour and, 57–8
  marriage, 32–4, 347; precariousness of, 50–2, 54 ff.
  Mary Tudor, Princess, and, 29, 34, 37, 38, 41 ff., 47–9, 54–5, 62, 66
  miscarriage, 55, 56–7
  unpopularity, 34 ff., 46, 56–7

Annebaut Claude d', 149

Arundel (Henry Fitzalan), Earl of, 308 ff., 317, 342, 387, 417
  Elizabeth and, 398, 443, 444

Arundel, Sir Thomas, 264, 267

Ascham, Roger, 129, 177–8, 184, 189–90, 235, 455

Ashley, Katherine, 189 ff., 197–8, 235, 274, 315, 324–5, 383–5, 391, 455
  conspiracy against Mary, 466, 467
  conspiracy against Protector, 202 ff., 213–14

Ashridge, 129 ff.

Attainder, Act of, 111, 120, 121

Audley, Thomas, 22, 65, 88, 100, 114
  Katherine (Howard), Queen, downfall of, 115 ff.

Aylmer, John, 178, 274

Barbaro, 261

Barton, Elizabeth, 46

Basset, Frances Roper, 338

Bath, Bishop of, 110

Bath, Earl of, 302

Baynham, Frances, 338

Baynton, Sir Edward, 61

Baynton, Margaret, 76

Beaulieu, 40 ff., 221 ff., 243 ff.

Becket, Thomas à, shrine of, 99

Bedford, Earl of, 360

Bedford, John Russell, Duke of *see* Russell, John

Bedingfield, Sir Henry, 302, 404 n.
  Elizabeth, imprisonment of, 404 ff., 421 ff., 442, 446, 447

Belmain, John, 156

Berkeley, Sir Maurice, 374

Bible, English, 93

Blount, Bessie, 79

Bocher, Joan, 240, 435

Boleyn, Anne, 27–9, 32–3; *see also* Anne (Boleyn), Queen
  created Marchioness of Pembroke, 32
  marriage to Henry VIII, 33–4

Boleyn, Thomas, 86

Book of Common Prayer, 219, 220–1, 225–6, 279, 329

Book of Homilies, 219

Borough, Thomas, 90

Boulogne, 141, 161–2, 181, 217, 227, 327

Bourne, Gilbert, 327

Brandon, Eleanor, 158

Brandon, Frances, Marchioness of Dorset, Duchess of Suffolk, 26, 39, 85, 108–9, 158, 177, 283 ff.

Brandon, Frances–*cont.*
　Jane Grey and, 288 ff., 304, 308, 319,
　　379
　Mary, Queen, and, 319, 385 n.
　remarriage, 385 n.
Braye, Lord, 471
Brereton, William, 58–61
Bridges, Sir John, 395, 398
Brown, Mary, 76
Browne, Sir Anthony, 116 ff., 148, 159,
　160, 321, 355, 417
Browne, Sir Edward, 168
Browne, Lady, 203
Brussels, 453, 463
Bryan, Lady Margaret, and:
　Edward, governess to, 87, 107, 130
　Elizabeth, governess to, 43, 73–4, 75–7,
　　96–7
　Mary, governess to, 26
Bucer, Martin, 245
Butts, Dr William, 89, 96, 115, 142, 156

Calais, 476–9
Canterbury, Abbey of, 99
Canterbury, Archbishop of, 45
Canterbury, Reginald Pole, Archbishop
　of *see* Pole, Reginald
Canterbury, Thomas Cranmer, Arch-
　bishop of *see* Cranmer, Thomas
Canterbury, Warham, Archbishop of, 32,
　81
Cardano, Giralomo, 285
Carew, Sir Peter, 357–8, 387 n., 389
Carlos, Don, 348, 463
Carthusian Order, 80, 109, 458, 482
Castelnau, Michael, 397
Catherine (of Aragon), Queen, 21, 22,
　64, 80, 102, 343, 432, 482
　Anne Boleyn's marriage to Henry
　　VIII, 33–4, 37, 38, 39
　birth of Mary, 25
　Charles V, Emperor, 28, 30, 41, 46
　death, 53, 54–5
　divorce proceedings against, 27–33,
　　45
　education, 26
　Mary, mutual attachment, 23, 24, 26,
　　37, 44, 52–3, 54–5
　popularity, 34, 53
　religion, 27, 54
　resistance to succession, 37 ff., 54, 67
Catholicism *see* Religion; Roman Catho-
　lic Church; individual names

Cecil, William, 228, 237, 255, 259, 263,
　326, 433, 476
　Mary, Queen, 313
　Elizabeth, 274, 293, 315, 482–3
　Seymour, Edward, treason charges
　　against, 264, 265, 268, 269
Chamberlain, Sir Thomas, 253
Chapuys, Eustace, 67, 78, 106, 118, 121,
　127, 134, 136–7
　Anne Boleyn, 35, 38, 43–4, 60
　Catherine, 39, 41, 52
　Jane Seymour, 51, 64
　Mary Tudor, Princess, 38, 41, 43–4,
　　47 ff., 51, 52, 54 ff., 64, 70, 76,
　　77, 142–3
Charles V, Holy Roman Emperor, 35, 41,
　79, 91, 142, 253 ff.
　abdication, 448, 463
　Catherine of Aragon, 28, 31, 41,
　　46
　Edward, succession to, 301, 306
　Elizabeth, hatred of, 390
　France, 92–3, 134, 141, 429
　French–English war, 137, 141
　Henry VIII and, 28, 30, 35, 41, 46, 56,
　　57
　Italy, 56, 79, 91, 429
　Mary, Princess *see also* Mary, Queen;
　　flight possible, 243; marriage to,
　　proposed, 22, 105–6; religious free-
　　dom, 243, 246–7, 253 ff.; succession,
　　301, 306
　Mary, Queen, 319; *see also* Mary,
　　Princess; marriage of, 333 ff., 343,
　　347–8, 414–15, 420, 428–9; religion,
　　327
Charles, Duke of Orleans, 105–6
Cheke, Dr John, 130, 155–6, 184, 220,
　237, 240, 278, 280
　illness, 277
　Katherine's jewel suit, 187–8
　knighted, 263
Chelsea, 189 ff.
Chichester, Bishop of, 68, 328
Christina of Denmark, 92–3
Christ's Church School, 280
Church of England *see also* Religion
　Mary, as head of, 336
　reform, 182–3, 217 ff.
　separation from Rome, 31, 45, 54
　Six Articles, Act of the, 93–4, 114, 143,
　　266, 326
　Ten Articles, 81–2

Clarencieux, Susan, 76, 338, 350, 446, 471, 486
Clement, Pope, 28, 30, 33, 45
Clere, Lady Alice, 43, 48
Cleves, Duke of, 94, 105, 110
Clinton, Lord, 238, 261, 364, 372, 484
Cole, Dr, 461–2
Commendone, Giovanni, 333–4
Constable, Robert, 114
Cooke, Sir Anthony, 156
Cornwallis, Sir Thomas, 364, 373, 383
Council, Henry's
    Anne Boleyn and, 58
    Catherine and, 29, 39
    Cromwell, downfall of, 109–10
    Katherine (Howard), downfall of, 116 ff.
    Mary, 40–1, 69 ff., 76–7
    theological supremacy, struggle for, 143 ff.
Council, Princess Mary's in Wales, 21
Council, Queen Mary's, 309 ff., 323, 387, 400–1, 457
    Elizabeth and, 386, 467; conspiracy against Mary, 369, 389, 443–4; imprisonment, 390 ff., 407 ff., 421–422; marriage, 334 ff., 341 ff., 347–348
    Philip, departure of, 452
    rebellion, 358–9, 360, 362, 364 ff., 371, 386, 389 ff., 397 ff.
    reconciliation, 336–7
    religion, 240 ff., 326; restoration of Catholic church, 430 ff.
    war with France, 473
Council, Regency, 148, 149–50, 151, 158 ff., 168, 239
    Dudley, John, downfall of, 310; Protector, 236 ff., 255 ff., 271; succession, 202 ff., 302 ff., 307 ff.
    Elizabeth, 189, 250 ff., 275; Seymour, Thomas, and, 202 ff.
    Jane (Grey), Queen, 307 ff., 315
    Mary, Princess, religious nonconformity of, 224–6, 235, 240 ff., 246 ff., 255 ff.
    Scotland, 182
    Seymour, Edward: conspiracies against, 227 ff., 262 ff., 322; dismissal, 236; opposition to, 277ff.; Protector and, 160 ff., 165 ff., 168, 173 ff., 194, 199 ff.
    Seymour, Thomas, 194, 200–1; succes-

sion to Edward VI, 292–3, 301 ff., 308 ff., 315
Court life, 21 ff., 26, 67, 88–91, 107–9, 123 ff., 183–4, 238 ff., 261, 272 ff., 284
Courtenay, Edward, 318, 351, 355
    conspiracy against Mary: first, 356 ff., 360, 373, 382, 383, 388 ff., 399 ff.; second, 466
    death, 468
    Devon, Earl of, 334
    Elizabeth and, 468; marriage to, proposed, 349, 389, 465
    imprisonment, 102, 318, 342, 346, 382, 398, 403, 442
    Mary, marriage to, proposed, 334, 336, 341
    release, 441, 442
    Wyatt, Thomas, and, 357, 371–2, 399–400
Courtenay, Henry, Marquis of Exeter, 102
Cox, Dr Richard, 130, 138–9, 155–6, 189, 220, 269
Cranmer, Thomas, 86, 114, 124, 166, 167 279 318
    Anne Boleyn and; marriage, 33, 58, 63; charges against, 59–60
    Anne of Cleves, marriage annulled, 98
    Archbishop of Canterbury, as, 33
    Catherine of Aragon, marriage annulled, 33
    Council of Regency, 148, 151, 160, 228
    Cromwell, downfall of, 110
    death, 435 ff., 460–2
    Henry VIII, death of, 150–1
    heresy, 144, 435 ff., 436–7, 460–2
    Katherine Howard, downfall of, 115 ff.
    Mary and: opposition to, 328–30, 339, 354; religious nonconformity of, 255
    rebellion and downfall, 328–30, 339, 354
    reform and heresy, 183, 218, 240, 435
    separation from Rome, 31
    succession to Edward VI, 292
Croft, Sir James, 356, 358, 397–8
Cromwell, Thomas, 45, 52, 56, 91, 107
    Anne Boleyn and, 44, 51, 55 ff.
    Anne of Cleves and, 94 ff., 97–8, 109–110
    Catherine of Aragon and, 30–1, 54
    downfall and death, 109–12

[513]

Cromwell, Thomas—*cont.*
  Elizabeth and, 73 ff.
  Lord Privy Seal, 77, 80
  Mary Tudor, Princess, and, 44, 66 ff.
  monasteries, suppression of, 80 ff., 98–100
  Six Articles, Act of the, 94
  Vicar-General, 50, 80
Culpeper, Thomas, 117–21

Darcy, Lord, 83–4
De Brion, Chabot, 51
De Chenault, M., 238
De Gante, Pedro, 137
De la Sa, Miguel, 52
De Marnix, Sieur de Thoulouse, 301
De Montmorency, Sieur de Couriers, Jean, 301, 355
Denny, Sir Anthony, 148, 150, 160
De Noailles, Antoine, 287, 310, 318, 337, 387, 387 n., 388, 388 n., 389 n., 400, 469
  Elizabeth and, 455; religious dissension, 330; succession conspiracies, 340–1, 465
  Mary, marriage of, 336, 341, 349, 354 ff., 448, 455–6
  succession conspiracies, 327, 340–1, 465
De Noailles, François, 387 n., 400, 469, 472
Derby, Lord, 261, 305, 416
Dereham, Francis, 116–17, 119, 120
De Salinas, Maria, 53
De Scheyve, Jean, 246, 247, 270, 271
De Theligney du Bois-Daulphin, 262
Devise for the Succession, 262, 320
Devon, Edward Courtenay, Earl of *see* Courtenay, Edward
Devon, Henry Courtenay, Earl of, 102
Dew, Old Good Wife, 279
Dodd, Randall, 76–7, 89
Dormer, Jane, 129–30, 322–3, 407, 458, 481, 483, 485–6
Dorrell, Christopher, 370
Dorset, Henry Grey, Marquess of *see* Grey, Henry
Dorset, Marchioness of *see* Brandon, Frances
Douglas, Lady Margaret, 128, 273, 350
Dudley, Lord, 22
Dudley, Ambrose, 239, 354
Dudley, Sir Andrew, 290

Dudley, Guildford, 289–90, 304, 308, 312, 354, 376, 380
Dudley, Henry, 354, 465 ff.
Dudley, John (Viscount Lisle, Earl of Warwick, Duke of Northumberland), 200
  conspiracies against Edward Seymour, 226 ff., 262 ff., 271–2, 322
  Council of Regency: Protector and, 236 ff., 255 ff., 271–2, 280, 285; rejection by, 308–9
  downfall and death, 312–13, 318–22
  Durham House, 275
  Edward and: illness, 280, 285 ff.; succession, 288 ff., 301 ff.
  Elizabeth and, 250–2, 274–5; succession, 288, 291 ff.
  Lord High Admiral, 161, 236
  Mary and: power struggle, 307; Queen, 312–13, 318 ff., 465 ff.; religion, 224, 241, 247 ff., 255; succession, 288, 291 ff., 301 ff.
  Northumberland, Duke of, created, 263 ff.
  religion, 244, 263, 321; rebellion, suppression of, 227; Mary, nonconformity of, 224, 241, 247 ff., 255 ff., 288
  Wales, Mary as Princess of, 236, 241
  Warwick, Earl of, created, 161, 236–237
Dudley, Robert, 156, 239, 301, 398
Durham, Cuthbert Tunstall, Bishop of, 110, 160, 339, 342
Durham House, 275
Dymoke, Sir Edward, 340
Dymoke, Sir John, 166

Economy, 217, 225, 245, 272, 279–80, 287
Edinburgh, 135
Education
  Edward, 129–30, 138–9, 155–6, 184, 237–8
  Elizabeth, 107–8, 129, 138–9, 189–90, 234–5, 274
  Grey, Jane, 177–8, 179–80
  Henry, 26, 30
  Mary, 24, 26–7
  monastries, 80
  Reformation and, 244 ff.
Edward VI, 141, 184 ff., 260 ff.
  betrothal, 261, 273

birth, 84–6
childhood, 87 ff., 91, 107, 115, 129 ff., 138–9, 184 ff.
coronation, 163–7
Council of Regency, 147, 150, 151, 158 ff., 168; Seymour, Edward, disaffection with, 228 ff.
court life, 238 ff., 261, 272 ff., 284
D'Annebaut, reception of, 149
death, 295–6, 314 ff., 318, 329
domestic policies, 245, 272, 279–80
Dudley John and: Edward's illness, 280, 285 ff.; Protector, 236 ff.; Seymour, Edward, treason, 266 ff., 271–272; succession, 288 ff., 301 ff.
education, 129–30, 138–9, 155–6, 184, 237–8
Elizabeth and, 167, 189, 276–7, 286; and childhood, 86, 87–8, 157 ff.; reconciliation, 250–2; succession, 292 ff.
Elizabeth, daughter of Henri II and; 261, 273
father and: funeral of, 163; relations with, 127, 148 ff., 155, 159
funeral, 314, 318, 325, 327
heritage, 147 ff., 158
household and daily life, 87 ff., 107 ff.
illness, 115, 276 ff., 284 ff.
illness, 115, 276 ff., 284 ff.
Katherine (Parr) Queen, and, 129 ff., 138, 144–5, 149, 156, 167, 196; jewel question, 186–7; marriage to Thomas Seymour, 173 ff.
King, 159–60
Mary and, 167, 168 ff., 189, 236, 276; and childhood, 107, 115, 129 ff., 150, 156–7, 158; Edward's illness, 286 ff.; religion, 235–6, 241 ff., 246 ff., 255 ff.; succession, 291 ff.
Mary Stuart, proposed marriage to, 181, 182, 217, 261, 273
money, 185 ff.
popularity, 291, 295
religion, 184, 220, 221 ff., 226, 240, 244–5; and Mary, nonconformity of, 235–6, 241 ff., 246 ff., 255 ff.
Seymour, Edward, and Council disaffection, 228 ff.; disillusionment with, 197; feud with brother, 186 ff., 197; Protector, 161 ff., 166 ff., 183 ff., treason, 267 ff., 271–2
Seymour, Thomas, and, 170, 183 ff.: and attempt to see Edward, 196–7;

death, 201; disillusionment of Edward, 197, 199; marriage to Queen-Dowager Katherine (Parr), 173 ff.
succession, 288 ff., 301 ff.
tour, 278–9
Egmont, Count, 355, 389
Elder, John, 417
Eleanor, Queen of France, 51
Elizabeth, Princess, 127, 130 ff., 141, 189 ff., 260, 274 ff., 471
adolescence, 175–6
Anne of Cleves and, 97
banishment from Henry's court, 132–3, 139–40
birth, 34–6
Cecil, William, and, 274, 293, 315, 492–3
Charles V, and, 390
childhood, 42–3, 48, 73 ff., 107–8, 113, 128 ff., 156 ff.
Courtenay, Edward, and, 468; and conspiracy against Mary, 383, 388, 399 ff.; marriage to, proposed, 334, 336, 341, 349, 389, 465
De Noailles, Antoine, and, 330, 340–1, 465
Dudley, John, and, 250–2, 274–5: and succession, 285, 291 ff., 465
Dudley, Robert, and, 156
education, 107–8, 129, 138–9, 189–90, 234–5, 274
Edward, and, 86, 87–8, 157 ff., 167, 189, 276–7, 286: and death, 314; funeral, 325, 330; reconciliation with, 250–2; succession, 292 ff.
father, relations with, 73, 75, 78, 87–8, 131 ff., 149 ff., 158, 472
Grey, Jane, and, 179, 190, 404: and death, 383–4; Queen, 315–16
households and daily life, 41, 73 ff., 107 ff., 189 ff., 234–5, 273 ff.
illegitimatization, 65, 88, 342, 347
illness, 215–16, 234, 274, 382 ff., 384, 411 ff., 425
imprisonment, 390–9, 403, 404–13, 442 ff.
Katherine (Howard), Queen, and, 112, 113
Katherine (Parr), Queen, and, 128 ff., 139–40, 141–2, 171–2, 194 ff.: and marriage to Thomas Seymour, 173–4
marriage and: attitude toward, 480; to Courtenay, proposed, 349, 389, 465;

[515]

Elizabeth, Princess—*cont.*
  to Eric of Sweden, proposed, 479; to
    Philibert, Prince of Piedmont, Duke
    of Savoy, proposed, 442–3, 463, 468,
    470, 485
  Mary, Princess, and, 223, 250, 252:
    and childhood, 42–3, 48, 75–8, 107–
    108
  Mary, Queen, and, 315 ff., 323 ff.: and
    appeal to, 391–4; conspiracy, first,
    against, 360 ff., 369, 382 ff., 396 ff.,
    442 ff.; conspiracy, second, against,
    465 ff.; conspiracy, third, against,
    473; coronation, 338 ff.; departure
    from court of, 351–3, 360; opposi-
    tion, focus of, 330, 332, 340–1,
    349 ff., 360 ff.; pregnancy, 442 ff.; re-
    conciliation, 454–5; release, 446–7;
    religion, 325 ff., 330–3, 350, 425–6;
    resentment of, 340–1; return to
    court of, 360, 354–5, 382–5, 441;
    succession, 347, 349, 435, 441–2,
    470, 482 ff., 491 ff.
  men, relationships with, 190 ff.
  Philip, and, 441, 445, 447, 454, 465 ff.,
    470, 482: and marriage, of Eliza-
    beth, 442–3, 463, 468, 470, 479, 482,
    485
  popularity, 405, 406, 455, 471, 483,
    484
  Protestant following, 252, 327, 330,
    349
  religion, 133, 221, 234–5, 276, 361–2,
    424–5, 454: and Mary, conflict with,
    325 ff., 330–3
  Renard, Simon, and, 330, 332, 341,
    349 ff., 360, 362–3, 382 ff.
  Seymour, Thomas, and, 177, 183, 188:
    and conspiracy, implication in, 202–
    216; Katherine (Parr), Queen,
    marriage to, 175 ff.; marriage pro-
    posal, 171–3; pursuit by, 190–4, 197–
    199, 205 ff.
  Somerset, treason charges against, 270
  succession, 46, 65, 158, 172, 288, 291 ff.,
    347, 349, 435, 441–2, 470, 482 ff.,
    491
  Wales, Princess of, 40–2
  Wyatt, Thomas, and, 360 ff., 382, 389,
    399
Elizabeth, daughter of Henri II, 261, 273
Enclosure, 82, 217–18
Excommunication, Bull of, 50

Exeter, Bishop of, 22, 328
Exeter, Marquis of *see* Courtenay,
  Edward
Exeter, Lady, 86

Featherstone, John, 22
Feckenham, Dr, 377–8, 380–1
Ferdinand, King, 254, 335
Feria, Count de, 414, 416, 478 ff., 483 ff.
Finances
  Edward, 185 ff.
  France, war with, 136, 141
  Henry, 80, 81, 91, 136, 141
  Mary, Queen, 337, 456, 473
  monasteries, seizure of, 80, 81
Finch, Mary, 89, 338
Fisher, Bishop John, 46, 50, 53, 98
Fitzpatrick, Barnaby, 156, 167, 272, 277,
  278
Fitzwilliam, Lord, 110, 116 ff.
Flanders, 46, 473, 474
  Anne of Cleves, marriage to Henry,
    94–8, 105
Flemish Protestants in England, 328
Flower, William, 438
Foreign Policy
  Henry VIII, 22, 24, 30, 33, 46, 56, 79,
    91 ff., 128, 134 ff.
  Mary and Philip II, 335, 341, 348–9,
    355 ff., 415, 429–30, 463, 473 ff.
  Seymour, Edward, 181–2
Forrest, Father, 53, 435
Fowler, Thomas, 171
Fowler, William, 185–6, 187, 188
Fox, Bishop, 41, 42
France, 22, 30, 32
  alliance with England, 105–6, 261–2,
    263, 266
  Boulogne, 141, 161–2, 181, 217, 227,
    327
  Calais, 476–9
  conspiracies against Mary: first, 363–4,
    387–8, 389–90, 399–400; second,
    464–5; third, 473–4
  Elizabeth and, 363–4, 400, 472
  Holy Roman Empire (Spain), 93, 128,
    134, 141, 254; Italy, 56, 79, 91, 429,
    467, 476
  invasion of England, 147
  Mary and Philip, marriage of, 335,
    341, 348–9, 355 ff., 415, 469–70
  Scotland, alliance with, 114, 134, 136,
    181–2, 217, 273, 327, 485

Spain, reconciliation with, 93
war with England, 136–7, 141, 472, 476
Francis I of France, 30, 32, 56, 79, 91, 134
Anne Boleyn and, 35, 51
Henry's search for wife, 92
invasion of England, 147
marriage of Mary to son, proposed, 105–6
war with England, 136–7, 141
Franciscans, 80
French Protestants in England, 328

Gage, Sir John, 120, 160, 395, 396
Gardiner, Stephen, Bishop of Winchester, 110, 117, 128, 262, 318
Courtenay, Edward, 441: and conspiracy charges, 400; marriage to Mary, proposed, 334, 336, 342
Cranmer, Thomas, alleged heresy of, 144
death, 455
Elizabeth and: conspiracy charges against, 390–1, 397–8, 400, 443–4
imprisonment, 218–19, 264, 318, 342, 346
Katherine (Parr), Queen, alleged heresy of, 144–5
Mary, Queen and: coronation, 339; Lord Chancellor, 326, 328; marriage, 389, 418 ff., 334, 336, 342 ff.; subsidy for, 455–6; uprising against, 357, 358, 366, 369 ff., 376, 389–90, 317
Protestant emigration, 328
reform of Church, 183, 218–19
Rome, reconciliation with, 433, 435
Scotland, 182
Gates, Sir John, 243, 309
downfall and death, 319 ff.
German Protestants in England, 328
Glastonbury, Abbey of, 99
Gloucester, John Hooper, Bishop of, 220, 234–5, 437–8
Gomez da Silver, Ruy, 414, 416, 428
Gontier, Palamedes, 51
Grey, Henry (Marquis of Dorset, Duke of Suffolk), 41, 85
conspiracy against Edward Seymour, 264, 267
death, 385
Dorset, Marquis of, 108–9, 165, 177 ff., 200

Dudley, John, and, 289
Jane Grey and, 378; and Seymour, Thomas, 178–9, 196; succession, 178–9, 289, 308, 310
Mary, Queen, 310, 319; and rebellion against, 357, 358, 375–6, 382
Seymour Thomas and Jane Grey, 178–179, 196
Suffolk, Duke of, 263 ff., 286
Grey, Jane, 85, 109, 137, 157, 167, 177 ff., 273, 354, 375–80
death sentence, 383–4
education, 177–8, 179–80
Elizabeth and, 179, 190, 315
imprisonment, 312, 319, 354
Katherine (Parr), Queen, and, 179–80, 195, 196
marriage, 289–90, 307–8
Mary, Queen, and, 283 ff., 319 ff.
mother, relations with, 177 ff., 289 ff., 303, 308, 319, 379
Queen, 303 ff., 307 ff.
religion, 283–4, 321, 377–8
Seymour, Thomas, and, 177, 178–9, 183, 188, 196, 199–200
succession, 178–9, 289 ff., 301
Grey, Lord John, 358
Grey, Katherine, 289, 379, 385 n.
Grey, Lord, 226
Grey, Mary, 289, 385 n., 475 n.
Grey, Lord Thomas, 358
Grey of Wilton (Grey de Wilton), Lord, 289, 477, 478
Grindal, William, 189
Guise, Duke of, 92
Guisnes, 477, 478
Gustavus Adolphus, King of Sweden, 479

Harrington, William, 179
Harvel, Edmund, 54
Hastings, Sir Edward, 305, 364, 383, 467
Hatfield, 41 ff., 202 ff., 274 ff., 455, 466 ff.
Havering-atte-Bower, 87 ff.
Hayes, John, 138
Heneage, John, 82
Henri II of France, 181, 227, 254
Edward VI and: Elizabeth, marriage to proposed, 261, 273; Mary Stuart, marriage to proposed, 261
Elizabeth and, 364, 400
Mary, conspiracies against, 364, 400, 465, 474
Henricians, 114

[517]

Henry VIII, 30, 32, 78–9, 108, 477
  Anne (Boleyn) and, 27–9, 32–6, 64–5, 96; imprisonment and death, 58 ff.; marriage to, 33–4, 347; miscarriage, 55, 56–6; rejection of, 55 ff.
  Anne (of Cleves) and, 94–8, 105
  Catherine of Aragon and, 24–7, 37, 342, 432; death, 53, 54–5; divorce proceedings against, 27–33, 45
  Charles V, Emperor, and, 28, 30, 35, 41, 46, 56, 57, 92–3
  Cromwell, Thomas and see Cromwell, Thomas
  death, 148–9, 155, 157 ff.
  education, 26, 30
  Edward and, 85–6, 87 ff., 115, 127, 148 ff., 155, 159
  Elizabeth and, 73, 75, 78, 87–8, 131 ff., 149 ff. 158, 472; and banishment from court, 132–3, 139–40
  excommunication, 45, 46, 50
  finances, 80, 81, 91, 136, 141
  foreign policy, 22, 24, 30, 33, 46, 56, 79, 91 ff., 128, 134 ff.
  France, war with, 136–7, 141
  funeral, 163
  illness, 142, 155, 157 ff.
  Jane (Seymour) and, 51, 57–8, 84–5, 87, 163; and Edward, birth of, 85–6; marriage, 63 ff., 161
  Katherine (Howard) and, 97, 112–13, 127; and indiscretions and death, 116–22
  Katherine (Parr) and, 126 ff., 139–40, 145; and death of Henry, 148 ff.; heresy, alleged, 145–7
  marriage alliance, search for, 92 ff.
  Mary, relations with, 24–5, 38, 42 ff., 88, 105 ff., 126, 141 ff.; betrothals, 22, 24, 94, 105–7; childhood, 21, 23–7; submission and reconciliation, 65 ff., 75 ff., 84–5; Wales, Princess of, 21, 23, 40–2, 44
  religion and: heresy, commission on, 144 ff.; monasteries, suppression of, 80 ff., 98–100; separation from Rome, 30–3, 45; Six Articles, Act of the, 93–4, 143; Supreme Head of the Church, 31, 431; Ten Articles, 81–82
  Richmond, Duke of, and, 79
  succession to, 25, 27–9, 43, 46, 55, 65, 79, 102

  tour of 'brute shires', 114 ff.
  will, 147 ff., 149–50, 158–9, 172, 249
Herbert, William (Earl of Pembroke), 160, 226, 261
  Jane Grey and, 289, 308
  Mary, Queen, and, 310–11; uprising against, 371 ff.
  Pembroke, Earl of, 263, 289
Heresy Bill, 435
Hertford, Edward Seymour, Earl of see Seymour, Edward
Hertford Castle, 88, 91
Hoby, Sir Philip, 231, 397
Holbein, Hans, 92, 94, 123, 221
Holy Roman Empire, 22, 30; see also Charles V, Spain
  English–French war, 472
  France and, 93, 128, 141, 254
  Italy and, 56, 79, 91, 429, 463, 467, 476
Hooper, John, Bishop of Gloucester, 220, 234–5, 347–8
Hopton, Dr, 224
Howard, Charles, 116
Howard, Edmund, 112
Howard, George, 116
Howard, Henry, Earl of Surrey, 60, 62, 112, 147, 162
Howard, Katherine 97–8; see also Katherine (Howard), Queen
Howard, Thomas see Norfolk, Thomas Howard, Duke of
Howard, Thomas (grandson), 305
Howard, Lord William, 356, 364, 374
  Elizabeth and, 383, 398, 443
  Philip, marriage to Mary, 416, 421
Huddlestone, John, 302
Huggons, Elizabeth, 271
Huicke, Dr, 425
Hull, 83, 114
Hunsdon, 43, 65 ff., 73 ff.

Inglefield, Sir Francis, 224, 257, 326, 344
Inquiry, Articles of, 80–1
Interim, 255
Italy and:
  Trent Council of, 255
  wars, 54, 80, 91, 429, 463, 468, 476

James V of Scotland, 22, 91, 134–5
  French alliance, 114, 134
Jane (Grey), Queen, 302 ff., 307 ff., 315–16; see also Grey, Jane

Jane (Seymour), Queen, 63–6, 88, 91, 161, 163
  Edward, birth of, 85–6
  Mary Tudor, Princess, and 64, 66–7, 76, 84
  monasteries, suppression of, 83
Jane the Fool, 90, 129
Jerningham, Sir Henry, 302, 306, 359

Katherine (Howard), Queen, 112–13, 127, 137
  indiscretions and death, 116–22
Katherine (Parr), Queen, 126 ff., 135, 139–40
  death, 196
  death of Henry VIII, 148 ff.
  Edward, 129 ff., 138, 144–5, 156, 167, 196; jewel question, 173 ff.
  Elizabeth and, 112 ff., 139–40, 141–2, 171–2, 194 ff.; Seymour's, Thomas, pursuit of, 190–4
  Grey, Jane, 179–80, 195, 196
  Mary, Princess, and 128–9, 137–8, 142, 169, 195, 196
  pregnancy, 188, 190, 195
  Queen-Dowager, 168, 170 ff., 186 ff.
  Queen-Regent, 137, 140
  religion, 137, 144–5
  Seymour, Thomas, and: Grey, Jane, and, 178–9; marriage to, 173–7, 186 ff.
  Stanhope, Anne, feud with, 186 ff.
Kent, rebellion in, 358 ff.
Kett rebellion, 226–7, 306
Kingston, Sir Anthony, 465 ff., 467
Kingston, Lady, 62, 66, 96
Kingston, Sir William, 59, 62
Knox, John, 279

Lady Shrines, 99
Lascelles, John, 117
Latimer, Hugh, Bishop of Worcester, 93, 339, 339 n., 432
  heresy and death, 435 ff., 438–9
Latimer, John Neville, Lord, 126, 127
Latimer, Lady (Katherine Parr), 126, 127
Layton, Dr Richard, 80–1
Legh, Dr Thomas, 80–1
Leith, 135
Lincolnshire, rebellion in, 82–3
Lisle, Lady, 88

Lisle, Lord (Viscount) see Dudley, John, Earl of Warwick
London, 123 ff.
  Anne Boleyn, hated by, 34–6
  Mary, Queen and: coronation, 337 ff.; loan, 337; uprising against, 358 ff., 363 ff., 369 ff.
London, Nicholas Ridley, Bishop of, 255, 279 ff., 339 n., 435 ff.
Louth, 82
Ludlow Castle, 21 ff.
Lutheranism, 34, 59, 96, 105, 110

Mallet, Dr Francis, 138
Manox, Henry, 116, 117, 119
Margaret (Tudor), Queen of Scotland, 22, 28, 134, 135, 158
Marillac, 118
Mary of Guise, 115, 135
Mary of Lorraine, 273
Mary, Princess, 37–8, 88 ff., 109, 137–8, 141, 221, 236, 274, 281 ff.; see also Mary I, Queen
  adolescence, 28–9
  Anne (Boleyn), Queen, and, 29, 34, 37, 38, 41 ff., 47–9, 54–5, 62, 66
  attempt on life, 168
  betrothals and marriage question, 22, 24, 94, 105–7, 169 ff.
  Charles V and, 243, 246–7, 253 ff.
  childhood, 21, 23–7
  Cromwell and, 68 ff., 77
  Dudley, John, and, 224, 236, 241, 247 ff.; succession, 288, 291 ff.
  education, 24, 26–7
  Edward and, 167, 168 ff., 189, 236, 276; childhood, 86, 88, 107, 115, 129 ff., 150, 156–7, 158; illness, 286 ff.; religion, 221 ff., 235–6, 241 ff., 246 ff., 255 ff.; succession, 291 ff.
  Elizabeth and, 223, 250, 252; birth, 34; childhood, 42–3, 48, 75–8, 107–8
  exile from court, 28–9, 37 ff.
  father, relations with, 24–5, 29, 38, 46 ff., 105 ff., 126, 141 ff.; meetings with, 38, 42 ff., 76, 84–5; submission and reconciliation, 65 ff., 75 ff., 84–5
  finances, 89 ff.
  flight considered, 55, 243
  Grey, Jane, and 283–4
  households and daily life, 21 ff., 38, 40, 42 ff., 67, 75–6, 88 ff., 107 ff.

Mary, Princess–*cont.*
illegitimatization, 43, 46, 126, 336
illnesses, 47, 49, 52–3, 75, 89, 96, 106,
    126, 128–9, 138, 156, 157, 223–4,
    235–6, 241
Jane (Seymour), Queen, and, 64, 66–7,
    76, 84
Katherine (Howard), Queen and, 113
Katherine (Parr), Queen and, 128–9,
    137–8, 142, 169, 195, 196; marriage
    to Thomas Seymour, 173–7
mother and: death, 53, 54–5; harass-
    ment by Henry, 37 ff., 46 ff.; mutual
    attachment, 23, 24, 26, 37, 44, 52–3,
    54–5
Pole, Margaret, and, 22, 23, 42, 101–4
popularity, 49, 53, 67, 77, 169
religion, 27, 38, 98, 108, 138, 171,
    221 ff., 227, 234 ff., 241 ff., 246 ff.,
    253 ff., 273, 282 ff.
Somerset, treason charges against, 262,
    266, 268–9
succession, 55, 79, 158, 288, 291 ff.
Wales, Princess of, 21–3, 40–1, 44, 236,
    241
Mary I, Queen, 296–7, 301 ff., 474–5;
    see also Mary, Princess
birth, 25
charity, 457–8
Charles V and, 301, 319, 327; marriage
    Mary's, 333 ff., 343, 347–8, 414–
    415, 420, 428–9
conspiracy, first against, 356 ff., 370 ff.,
    388 ff.; defeat of, and reprisals,
    374 ff., 387, 388; Elizabeth and, 360,
    369, 382 ff., 389 ff., 396 ff.
conspiracy, second against, 466 ff.
conspiracy, third against, 473
coronation, 337 ff.
Council and, 309, 318 ff., 323, 326–7,
    386–7, 400–1, 457, 466–7; concilia-
    tion of, 336–7; marriage, 334 ff.,
    341 ff., 347–8; Philip, departure of,
    452; restoration of Catholic Church,
    429–30, 459; uprising against Mary,
    358–9, 360, 362, 363 ff., 369, 386,
    388 ff., 397; war with France, 472,
    476 ff.
Courtenay, Edward, and, 334, 336,
    341; rebellion, 356 ff., 360, 373, 383,
    388; release, 441
Cranmer, Thomas, and, 328–30
death, 486–7, 491 ff.

De Noailles, Antoine, and, 327, 330,
    340–1; marriage, Mary's, 336, 341,
    349, 354 ff., 448, 455–6
domestic policies, 323 ff., 337
Dudley, John, and, 307 ff., 318 ff.
Edward and: death, 295–6; funeral,
    314, 318, 325, 327
Elizabeth and, 315 ff., 323 ff.; appeal
    by, 391–4; conspiracy, first, 360 ff.,
    368, 382 ff., 388 ff., 396 ff., 442 ff.;
    conspiracy, second, 465 ff.; conspir-
    acy, third, 473; departure from
    court, 351–3, 360; imprisonment,
    390 ff., 404 ff., 422 ff., 442 ff.; jea-
    lousy of, Mary's, 471; marriage
    proposed, 442–3, 463, 468, 470 ff.,
    480; pregnancy, Mary's, 442 ff.; re-
    conciliation, 454–5; release, 446–7;
    religion, 325 ff., 330–3, 350, 425–6;
    Renard, opposition to, 330, 332,
    341, 349 ff., 360, 362, 376–7, 382 ff.,
    386 ff.; resentment of Mary, 340–1;
    return to court, 354–5, 360, 382–5,
    441 ff.; succession, 347, 349, 435,
    441–2, 470, 482 ff., 491 ff.
finances, 337, 456, 473
foreign policy, 429–30, 473 ff.
Grey, Jane, and, 311, 319 ff., 321, 354,
    376 ff.
illness, 466, 479
legitimacy, 336, 342
leniency, 319, 352–3, 375 ff., 388, 436,
    467
marriage, 333 ff., 342 ff., 363 ff.; agree-
    ment with Philip, 347, 356, 429–
    430; attitude towards, 333 ff., 341,
    401–2; coronation of Philip, 430,
    456, 463; departure of Philip, first,
    450–1, 452 ff.; departure of Philip,
    second, 474, 475–6; deterioration of,
    431, 434, 439 ff., 447; meeting with
    Philip, 419–20; Philip and, 335–6,
    341 ff., 347 ff., 353 ff., 359, 375, 386,
    390, 401, 413 ff., 427; popular dis-
    like, 335–6, 341, 345 ff., 354 ff., 366–
    367, 388, 431, 469, 473, 479 ff.;
    pregnancy, 430–1, 434–5, 439–50;
    pregnancy, second, 476, 480; proxy
    wedding, 389, 401, 414; return of
    Philip, 466, 469, 472–5; wedding,
    420–1
Parliament and, 341 ff., 403, 431, 455–
    456

Mary I, Queen–*cont.*
Pole, Reginald, Cardinal, and, 453, 458; marriage to, proposed, 333; reconciliation to Rome, 432
popularity, 302, 310, 311, 312
proclamation, 311
religion, 314, 325 ff., 425; Church of England, Head of, 336; 429 ff., 457 ff.; heresy, persecution of, 435 ff., 458 ff.; Proclamation Concerning Religion, 328 ff.; restoration of old forms, 425
Renard, Simon, and, 301, 306, 319, 323, 326–7; Elizabeth, opposition to, 330, 332, 341, 349 ff., 360, 362, 376–377, 382 ff., 386 ff.; enemies, warning of, 341, 360; marriage, Mary's, 333 ff., 342 ff., 356, 375, 382, 386 ff., 401–2; uprising against Mary, 357–358, 363 ff., 371, 375, 382, 387 ff.
succession to, 336, 347, 349, 435, 441–442, 456
support, 304 ff., 309 ff.
unpopularity, 336, 341, 344 ff., 355 ff., 366–7, 388, 399 ff., 431, 438, 462 ff., 469, 473, 480
war with France, 472, 476
will, 482, 483, 494
Mary (Maria), Queen of Hungary, 246, 254, 268, 343, 456
Mary Stuart, Queen of Scots, 135, 158, 470
Edward, proposed marriage to, 181, 182, 217, 261, 273
French alliance, 136, 217, 273, 327, 485
Mary Tudor ('Tudor rose'), 26, 27, 38–9, 63, 75, 142, 158
Michiel, Venetian ambassador, 440, 450–451, 463, 466, 471, 473 ff.
Midlands, rebellion in, 226, 357
Milan, 56, 420, 467
Milan, Christina, Duchess of, 92–3
Monasteries and:
restoration of properties, 326, 430, 431, 458
secular control retained, 325, 342, 429–430, 431, 432
suppression, 80 ff., 98–100, 108 ff., 318, 435–6
Montague, Sir Edward, 292–3
Montague, Henry Pole, Lord, 102
Montague, Lord, 160, 433

Mordaunt, Sir John, 302
More, Sir Thomas, 30, 31, 61, 338
death, 46, 50, 53, 98, 111, 219, 295
resignation as Chancellor, 31
Morney, Lord, 41
Morrison, Sir Richard, 289
Morton, Margery, 118
Mountjoy, Lady, 27
My Devise for the Succession, 262, 320

Najera, Duke of, 136–7
Naples, 420, 467
Navy, 474
meeting in support of Mary, 306
New Learning, 61, 93, 137, 144, 178, 182, 220, 246; *see also* Religion
Nonsuch Palace, 108
Norfolk, Agnes, Dowager-Duchess of, 112, 116 ff.
Norfolk, rebellion in, 226
Norfolk, Thomas Howard, Duke of, 83, 86, 101, 110, 137, 342, 428
Anne Boleyn and, 35, 59, 60, 62
conservatism, 115–16
Council of Regency, 326
Katherine (Howard), Queen, indiscretions of, 118, 121
Mary and, 26–7, 41–2, 68, 320; uprising against, 359
Northumberland trial, 320
treason and imprisonment, 147, 219, 318
Norris, Sir Henry, 58–61
North, Sir Edward, 160
Northumberland, Henry Percy, Duke of, 60
Northumberland, John Dudley, Duke of *see* Dudley, John

Oath of Supremacy, 67–72, 80, 98
Observant Friars, 80
Orleans, Charles, Duke of, 105–6
Owen, Dr George, 87, 89, 128, 285, 291, 295–6, 425
Oxford, 244

Paget, William, Lord, 106, 433, 485
conspiracy against Edward Seymour, 228, 230–1, 264, 267
Council of Regency, 148, 160, 228, 237
Gardiner, Stephen, enmity for, 326, 346

Paget, William–*cont.*
  Henry's will, 158, 160
  Mary, Queen, and, 310, 312, 342, 456, 485
  Northumberland, Duke of, downfall of, 310, 312
  reform, Somerset's, 225 ff.
  Scotland and, 181
Palmer, Sir Thomas, 264, 267, 309
  downfall and death, 319 ff.
Parliament, 65, 124, 286–7, 320
  Mary I and, 341 ff., 403, 431
  monasteries, suppression of, 81
  'Reformation', 31, 45–6
  religious forms, reinstatement of old, 425
  separation from Rome, 31
Parr, Katherine *see* Katherine (Parr), Queen
Parr, William, 165, 197
Parry, Thomas, 193, 199, 235, 274, 407, 455
  conspiracy charges, 202 ff., 213
Partridge, Sir Miles, 264
Paul III, Pope, 50, 91, 93, 254
  Trent, Council of, 255
Paul IV, Pope, 463, 467, 476
Paulet, William, Marquis of Winchester, 40
  Council of Regency, 148, 266, 267, 310
  Winchester, Marquis of, 263, 266
Pembroke, Anne Boleyn, Marchioness of, 32
Pembroke, Earl of *see* Herbert, William
Penn, Sybilla, 87
Petre, Sir William, 258 ff., 342, 443, 444
Philibert, Emmanuel, Prince of Piedmont, Duke of Savoy, 335
  Elizabeth, marriage to, proposed, 442, 463, 468, 470, 485
  English–French war, 476 ff.
Philip, Duke of Bavaria, 96, 105
Philip II of Spain, 254, 413
  aims, 413 ff., 429
  attitudes toward English, 428
  attacks on, 431
  Elizabeth and, 441, 445, 447, 454, 465 ff., 470, 482; conspiracy against Mary, 467; marriage of, proposed, 442–3, 463, 468, 470, 480, 482, 485
  Emperor, 463–4
  English–French war, 473 ff.

  entourage in England, 413 ff., 427 ff., 449, 456, 464
  heresy, persecution of, 438, 459
  King of Naples and Milan, 420
  marriage to Mary, 335–6, 341 ff., 347 ff., 353 ff., 375, 382, 386 ff., 390, 414, 427 ff.; agreement, terms of, 347, 356; coronation, 430, 456, 463; departure, first, 450–1, 452 ff.; departure, second, 474, 475–6; disinterest, 401; dissatisfaction and departure, 431, 434, 439 ff., 447 ff., 450 ff.; meeting with Mary, 419–20; proxy wedding, 389, 401, 414; return to England, 466, 469, 472 ff.; wedding, 420–1
  Regent, 435
Piedmont, 429
Piedmont, Emmanuel Philibert, Prince of *see* Philibert, Emmanuel, Prince of Piedmont, Duke of Savoy
Pilgrimage of Grace, 82–4, 114, 134
Pinkie Cleugh, Battle of, 182, 217, 261
Piracy, 188, 197
Pole, Margaret, Countess of Salisbury, 22, 23–4, 42, 101–4, 111, 431, 433
Pole, Sir Geoffrey, 102
Pole, Henry, Lord Montague, 102
Pole, Reginald:
  Archbishop of Canterbury, 462
  Cardinal, 102 ff., 431 ff.
  death, 486–7
  heresy, persecution of, 438, 459
  Mary, Queen, and 453, 458, 466, 486; Council and, 453, 458–9; marriage to, proposed, 333; reconciliation to Rome, 333, 432 ff.
  reconciliation to Rome, 431–4
Pope, Sir Thomas, 468, 480
Poynings, Sir Nicholas, 370
Proclamation Concerning Religion, 328 ff.
Protector *see* Seymour, Edward
Protestantism *see also* Protestants; Religion; sects
  Smalcaldic League, 254
  Trent, Council of, 254–5
Protestants, 114
  Elizabeth, focus of, 252, 326, 330 ff.
  emigration, 328
  persecution of, 434 ff., 459

Randolph, Mr, 156

Rebellion and:
  'brute shires', Henry's tour of, 114 ff.
  against Mary, first, 356 ff., 388 ff.;
    defeat and reprisals, 374 ff., 387,
    388; France, 378 n., 388
  against Mary, second, 466 ff.
  against Mary, third, 473
  Pilgrimage of Grace, 82–4, 114,
    134
  religion and: reform, 226; suppression
    of monasteries, 82–4, 434 ff.
  Seymour, Thomas, and, 188, 197, 199–
    201; Elizabeth and, 202–16
Reformation, 31, 325; see also Church of
  England; Religion; Roman Catholic
  Church; individual names
Reformation Parliament, 31–2, 45–6
Religion see also Church of England;
  Roman Catholic Church; individual
  names
  Bible, English, 93
  Book of Common Prayer, 219, 220–1, 225–
    226, 279, 329
  Book of Homilies, 219
  dissension, 80 ff., 98–101, 108 ff., 114,
    143 ff., 226–7, 434 ff., 458 ff.
  monasteries, suppression of, 80 ff., 98–
    101, 108 ff.
  New Learning, 61, 93, 137, 144, 178,
    182, 220, 246
  Pilgrimage of Grace, 82–4, 114, 134
  Rome and: return to, 333, 425, 430 ff.;
    separation from, 30–3, 45
  Scotland, Catholicism, 134
  Six Articles, Act of the, 93–4, 114,
    143, 266, 326
  'strawberry preachers', 93
  Ten Articles, 81–2
  Terror, the, 46
  Trent, Council of, 254–5
Renard, Simon, 399, 414, 416
  Courtenay, opposition to, 382, 386 ff.,
    399
  Elizabeth, opposition to, 330, 332, 341,
    349 ff., 360, 362–3, 382 ff., 386 ff.,
    399 ff.; Philip II and, 441
  English aid to Spain, 429
  Grey, Jane, and, 376–7
  heresy, persecution of, 438
  Mary, Queen, and, 337, 375; accession
    of, 301, 306, 319, 323, 326–7; mar-
    riage, 333 ff., 342 ff., 356, 375, 382,
    386 ff., 401–2; pregnancy, 448 ff.;

uprising against, 357–8, 363 ff., 371,
    375, 382, 387 ff.
  Philip II and: departure from Eng-
    land, 431, 434; Elizabeth and, 441;
    marriage, 335–6, 341 ff., 356, 375,
    386 ff., 401
  restoration of Catholic Church, 430 ff.
Restraint of Appeals Act, 31–2
Rich, Richard, 111, 219, 258 ff.
Richmond, Duke of, 62, 79
Ridley, Nicholas, Bishop of London, 255,
  279 ff., 339 n.
  heresy and death, 435 ff.
Robsart, Amy, 239
Rochester, Sir Robert, 224, 258 ff., 326,
  342
Rochford, George Boleyn, Lord, 59–61,
  63, 118
Rochford, Lady, 60, 118, 121
Rogers, John, 437
Roke, Anthony, 77
Roman Catholic Church; see also indivi-
  dual names
  England and: monasteries, suppression
    of, 80 ff., 98–101, 108 ff., 434–5;
    persecution by, 434 ff., 458 ff.; per-
    secution of, 80 ff., 98–100, 108, 143,
    240, 435–6; recognition, 342; recon-
    ciliation, 333, 425, 430 ff.; restora-
    tion of properties, 326, 342, 430, 431,
    458; separation from Rome, 30–3,
    45, 54
  Henry, divorce proceedings against
    Catherine, 27–33, 45
  persecution by, 434
Roper, Margaret More, 338
Russell, John, Duke of Bedford, 22, 95,
  413
  Council of Regency and, 160, 310,
    430
  Cranmer, heresy charge, 144
  Jane (Seymour), Queen, and, 65
  Mary, Queen, and, 310, 430
  religion and: rebellion, suppression of,
    226; restoration of Catholic church,
    430 ff.
  Seymour, Thomas, pursuit of Eliza-
    beth, 198

St Andre, Marechal, 261–2
St John, Lord, 160
St Paul's, 244
St Thomas's Hospital, 280

Salisbury, Margaret Pole, Countess of, 22, 23–4, 42, 101–4, 111, 431, 433
Salmon, Christopher, 296
Sands, Elizabeth, 409
Savagnana, Mario, 29
Savoy, Duke of see Philibert, Emmanuel, Prince of Piedmont, Duke of Savoy
Scotland and:
 France, alliance with, 114, 134, 136, 181–2, 217, 273, 327, 485
 war with England, 134–6, 181–2, 273
Severance, Act of, 45
Seymour, Lady Anne, 239
Seymour, Edward, Duke of Somerset, Earl of Hertford, 63, 86, 114, 239
 Council of Regency, 147, 158 ff.; conspiracies against Seymour, 226, 262 ff.
 death, 267–70, 271–2, 322
 Dudley, John, and, 226 ff., 236, 262 ff., 322
 Earl Marshal of England, 161
 Elizabeth, conspiracy charges against, 204 ff.
 Hertford, Earl of, 135, 149
 Lord Treasurer, 161
 Katherine (Howard), Queen, downfall of, 115 ff.
 marriage of Thomas Seymour and Queen-Dowager Katherine (Parr), 173–4
 Paget, William, and, 181, 225 ff., 264, 267
 popularity with masses, 236, 268
 Protector, 168 ff., 173 ff., 194 ff., 477; arrest, 232–3, 234; Council opposition to, 226; dismissal as, 236; Edward and Council disaffection, 228 ff.; Edward's disillusionment with, 197; masses, concern for, 217, 225; religion, 182, 217 ff., 224; Thomas Seymour, treason of, 200–1, 217, 237
 Scotland and, 181–2, 217
 Somerset, Duke of, 161
 Thomas's envy of, 170 ff., 183, 185, 194, 197
 treason, charge of, 264, 322
 wife's feud with Queen-Dowager Katherine (Parr), 186 ff.
Seymour, Jane, 51, 57–8, 161; see also Jane (Seymour), Queen
Seymour, Sir John, 63

Seymour, Mary, 195
Seymour, Thomas, Lord Sudeley, 63, 127, 158, 165, 170 ff.
 downfall and death, 200–1, 202, 217, 237
 Edward VI and, 170, 173, 183 ff.; attempt to see, 196–7; death warrant, 201; disillusionment of, 197, 199
 Elizabeth and, 177, 183, 188; implication in conspiracy, 202–16; marriage proposal to, 171–3; pursuit of, 190–4, 197–9, 205 ff.
 envy of brother, 170 ff., 183, 185, 194, 197
 Grey, Jane, and, 177, 178–9, 183, 188, 196, 199–200
 Katherine (Parr), Queen and: death, 196; feud with Protector's wife, 186 ff.; marriage to, 173–7, 186 ff.
 Lord High Admiral, 161, 170 ff., 193, 197
 piracy, 188, 197
 rebellion, 188, 197, 199–201; Elizabeth and, 202–16
Sudeley, Lord, 161, 170
Shelton, Lady Anne, 43, 48, 54–5, 68
Shelton, Mr, 74
Sherington, Sir Thomas, 188, 200
Shrewsbury, Earl of, 310, 339, 342, 416, 443, 444
Sidney, Sir William, 87, 129
Six Articles, Act of the, 93–4, 114, 143, 266, 326
Smalcaldic League, 254
Smeaton, Mark, 58–61
Solway Moss, Battle of, 135
Somerset, Anne Stanhope, Duchess of see Stanhope, Anne, Duchess of Somerset
Somerset, Edward Seymour, Duke of see Seymour, Edward
Sorranzo, Giacomo, 293, 428
Southampton, Thomas Wriothesley, Earl of see Wriothesley, Thomas
Spain, 30, 46, 56, 142–3
 England and: aid, 429; religious conflict, 253; Spaniards in, treatment of, 414 ff., 427, 431, 464
 France and, 93, 467
 Philip, marriage to Mary, 335–6, 341 ff., 347 ff., 414 ff.
Stafford, Thomas, 473

Stanhope, Anne, Duchess of Somerset, 169, 200, 318
  Katherine (Parr), Queen, feud with, 186 ff.
Starkey, Ralph, 255
Starkey, Thomas, 54
Submission, Articles of, 70–2
Submission of the Clergy, Act for the, 45
Succession:
  to Edward VI, 218 ff., 301 ff.
  to Henry VIII, 25, 27–9, 43, 46, 55, 65, 79, 147, 158
  to Mary I, 336, 347, 349, 435, 441–2, 456, 470, 482 ff., 491
Succession Act(s) of, 45–6, 48, 65, 130
Sudeley, Thomas Seymour, Lord see Seymour, Thomas
Suffolk, Charles Brandon, Duke of, 47, 62, 86, 121, 123, 137, 142, 165
Suffolk, Duchess of see Brandon, Frances
Suffolk, Henry Grey, Duke of see Grey, Henry
Supremacy, Oath of, 67, 71, 80, 98
Surian, Venetian ambassador, 482
Surrey, Henry Howard, Earl of, 60, 62, 112, 147, 162
  treason, 147
Sussex, Countess of, 472
Sussex, Earl of, 68, 391

Ten Articles, 81–2
Terror, the, 46
Thirlby, Bishop of Westminster, 147
Throckmorton, John, 465
Throckmorton, Lady, 311
Throckmorton, Nicholas, 239–40, 296, 491
Tilney, Elizabeth, 380
Tower of London, 84, 317–18, 323 ff.
  imprisonment of: Anne (Boleyn), Queen, 59, 396–7; Courtney, Edward, 102, 318, 342, 346, 382, 398, 403, 442; Elizabeth, 394–9, 403; Gardiner, Stephen, 264, 318, 342, 346; Grey, Jane, 312, 375–80; Katherine (Howard), Queen, 120–1; Norfolk, Thomas Howard, Duke of, 147, 219, 318; Pole family, 102; Seymour, Edward, 238 ff.; Seymour, Thomas, 199 ff.; Wyatt, Thomas, 399
Trent, Council of, 254–5

Tunstal, Cuthbert, Bishop of Durham, 110, 160, 339, 342
Tuscany, 429
Tyrwhitt, Lady, 195, 198, 208 ff., 235
Tyrwhitt, Lord Robert, 198, 202 ff.

Udal, Nicholas, 138
Uniformity, Act of, 246, 257
Unlawful Assembly, Act of, 267
Uvedale, Richard, 465

Vane, Sir Ralph, 264
Van Wilder, Philip, 89
Verney, Francis, 442
Vives, Juan Luis, 26

Waldegrave, Mr, 257, 326, 344
Wales and:
  Elizabeth, Princess of, 40
  Mary, Princess of, 21–4, 40–1, 44, 236, 241
  rebellion in, 226
Warham, Archbishop of Canterbury, 32, 81
Warwick, Earl of see Dudley, John, Earl of Warwick
Wells, Bishop of, 328
Wendy, Dr Thomas, 146, 285, 291, 295, 382, 425
West Country, rebellion in, 225–6, 349, 357
Westminster, 123
Westminster, Thirlby, Bishop of, 147
Westmoreland, Earl of, 473
Weston, Dr, 369
Weston, Sir Francis, 58–61
Whalley, Richard, 263
Wharton, Sir Thomas, 135, 282
'Whip with the Six Strings', 94
Woburn Abbey, 98
White, Dr, 494
Whitehall, 123
Whiting, Abbot Richard, 99
William of Theme, Lord, 406
Winchester, Stephen Gardiner, Bishop of see Gardiner, Stephen, Bishop of Winchester
Winchester, William Paulet, Marquis of see Paulet, William
Wingfield, Sir Anthony, 258
Wolsey, Thomas Cardinal, 23, 26, 30, 31, 111
Woodstock, 404–13, 421, 442

Worcester, Hugh Latimer, Bishop of, 93,
    339, 339 n., 432, 435 ff.
Worcester, Lady, 58
Wotton, Dr Nicholas, 22, 94, 253
Wriothesley, Thomas, Earl of Southamp-
    ton, 88, 92, 96, 103, 219
  Council of Regency and, 148, 160
  Katherine (Howard), Queen, indis-
    cretions of, 116 ff.
  Katherine (Parr), Queen, alleged
    heresy of, 145
  Seymour, Thomas, pursuit of Eliza-
    beth, 198

Southampton, Earl of, 161
Wyatt, Mary, 62
Wyatt, Thomas, 121
Wyatt, Thomas (son) and:
  Courtenay, Edward, 357, 371–2, 399–
    400
  death, 390, 399
  Elizabeth and, 360 ff., 382, 389, 399
  rebellion, 356 ff., 369 ff., 436
  surrender, 374

York, 83, 114
Yorkshire, rebellion in, 82–3, 226